STERLING
Test Prep

GRE

Chemistry

Practice Questions

5th edition

www.Sterling-Prep.com

5   4   3   2   1

ISBN-13: 978-1-9475561-9-5

Sterling Test Prep products are available at special quantity discounts for sales, promotions, academic counseling offices, and other educational purposes.

For more information contact our Sales Department at:

Sterling Test Prep
6 Liberty Square #11
Boston, MA 02109

info@sterling-prep.com

Congratulations on choosing this book as part of your GRE Chemistry preparation!

Scoring well on the GRE Chemistry is important for admission to graduate school. To achieve a high score, you need to develop skills to properly apply the knowledge you have and quickly choose the correct answer. Understanding key science relationships and concepts is more valuable for the test than memorizing terms; therefore, you should solve numerous practice questions.

This book provides over 1,300 high-yield chemistry practice questions that test your knowledge of GRE Chemistry content. Detailed explanations provided in the book discuss why the answer is correct and include the foundations and details of important science topics needed to answer related questions on the test. By reading these explanations carefully and understanding how they apply to solve the question, you will learn important chemistry concepts and the relationships between them. This will prepare you for the GRE Chemistry and will significantly increase your score.

All the questions in this book are prepared by chemistry instructors with years of experience. This team of experts analyzed the content of the GRE Chemistry test and designed practice questions that will help you build knowledge and develop the skills necessary for your success on the test. The questions were reviewed for quality and effectiveness by our science editors who possess extensive credentials, are educated in top colleges and universities, and have years of teaching and editorial experience.

We wish you great success in your academic achievements and look forward to being an important part of your successful preparation for GRE Chemistry!

Sterling Test Prep Team

200320gdx

Our Commitment to the Environment

Sterling Test Prep is committed to protecting our planet's resources by supporting environmental organizations with proven track records of conservation, ecological research and education and preservation of vital natural resources. A portion of our profits is donated to help these organizations so they can continue their critical missions. These organizations include:

 Ocean Conservancy For over 40 years, Ocean Conservancy has been advocating for a healthy ocean by supporting sustainable solutions based on science and cleanup efforts. Among many environmental achievements, Ocean Conservancy laid the groundwork for an international moratorium on commercial whaling, played an instrumental role in protecting fur seals from overhunting and banning the international trade of sea turtles. The organization created national marine sanctuaries and served as the lead non-governmental organization in the designation of 10 of the 13 marine sanctuaries.

 For 25 years, Rainforest Trust has been saving critical lands for conservation through land purchases and protected area designations. Rainforest Trust has played a central role in the creation of 73 new protected areas in 17 countries, including the Falkland Islands, Costa Rica and Peru. Nearly 8 million acres have been saved thanks to Rainforest Trust's support of in-country partners across Latin America, with over 500,000 acres of critical lands purchased outright for reserves.

 Since 1980, Pacific Whale Foundation has been saving whales from extinction and protecting our oceans through science and advocacy. As an international organization, with ongoing research projects in Hawaii, Australia, and Ecuador, PWF is an active participant in global efforts to address threats to whales and other marine life. A pioneer in non-invasive whale research, PWF was an early leader in educating the public, from a scientific perspective, about whales and the need for ocean conservation.

With your purchase, you support environmental causes around the world.

Table of Contents

Table of Contents (*continued*)

GRE Chemistry: Exam Information

The GRE Chemistry Test contains approximately 130 multiple-choice questions drawn from the most common undergraduate-level courses within chemistry. Each question has five answer choices from which to select the best option. The test takes 2 hours and 50 minutes in total, with no separately-timed sections. A periodic table and a table of information showing physical constants and SI conversion factors are provided to test-takers. Some physical constants are printed in the question itself.

The exam covers four major areas: Analytical Chemistry, Inorganic Chemistry, Organic Chemistry, and Physical Chemistry. Some questions may have overlaps in different fields of chemistry. The knowledge to answer a question may be interpreted by one test-taker as belonging to one field but may have been covered in a different chemistry course in another field by a second test-taker. Therefore, the outline of the material given below is not definitive.

I. Analytical Chemistry — 15%

A. Data Acquisition and Use of Statistics — Errors, statistical considerations

B. Solutions and Standardization — Concentration terms, primary standards

C. Homogeneous Equilibria — Acid-base, oxidation-reduction, complexometry

D. Heterogeneous Equilibria — Gravimetric analysis, solubility, precipitation titrations, chemical separations

E. Instrumental Methods — Electrochemical methods, spectroscopic methods, chromatographic methods, thermal methods, calibration of instruments

F. Environmental Applications

G. Radiochemical Methods — Detectors, applications

II. Inorganic Chemistry — 25%

A. General Chemistry — Periodic trends, oxidation states, nuclear chemistry

B. Ionic Substances — Lattice geometries, lattice energies, ionic radii, and radius/ratio effects

C. Covalent Molecular Substances — Lewis diagrams, molecular point groups, VSEPR concept, valence bond description and hybridization, molecular orbital description, bond energies, covalent and van der Waals radii of the elements, intermolecular forces

D. Metals and Semiconductors — Structure, band theory, physical and chemical consequences of band theory

E. Concepts of Acids and Bases — Brønsted-Lowry approaches, Lewis theory, solvent system approaches

F. Chemistry of the Main Group Elements — Electronic structures, occurrences and recovery, physical and chemical properties of the elements and their compounds

G. Chemistry of the Transition Elements — Electronic structures, occurrences and recovery, physical and chemical properties of the elements and their compounds, coordination chemistry

H. Special Topics — Organometallic chemistry, catalysis, bioinorganic chemistry, applied solid-state chemistry, environmental chemistry

III. Organic Chemistry — 30%

A. Structure, Bonding and Nomenclature — Lewis structures, orbital hybridization, configuration and stereochemical notation, conformational analysis, systematic IUPAC nomenclature, spectroscopy (IR and ^{1}H and ^{13}C NMR)

B. Functional Groups — Preparation, reactions, and interconversions of alkanes, alkenes, alkynes, dienes, alkyl halides, alcohols, ethers, epoxides, sulfides, thiols, aromatic compounds, aldehydes, ketones, carboxylic acids, and their derivatives, amines

C. Reaction Mechanisms — Nucleophilic displacements and addition, nucleophilic aromatic substitution, electrophilic additions, electrophilic aromatic substitutions, eliminations, Diels-Alder, and other cycloadditions

D. Reactive Intermediates — Chemistry and nature of carbocations, carbanions, free radicals, carbenes, benzynes, enols

E. Organometallics — Preparation and reactions of Grignard and organolithium reagents, lithium organocuprates, and other modern main group and transition metal reagents and catalysts

F. Special Topics — Resonance, molecular orbital theory, catalysis, acid-base theory, carbon acidity, aromaticity, antiaromaticity, macromolecules, lipids, amino acids, peptides, carbohydrates, nucleic acids, terpenes, asymmetric synthesis, orbital symmetry, polymers

IV. Physical Chemistry — 30%

A. Thermodynamics — First, second, and third laws, thermochemistry, ideal and real gases, and solutions, Gibbs and Helmholtz energy, chemical potential, chemical equilibria, phase equilibria, colligative properties, statistical thermodynamics

B. Quantum Chemistry and Applications to Spectroscopy — Classical experiments, principles of quantum mechanics, atomic and molecular structure, molecular spectroscopy

C. Dynamics — Experimental and theoretical chemical kinetics, solution and liquid dynamics, photochemistry

What to Bring to the Exam

A number 2 pencil is required for marking answers on a separate machine-scorable sheet. Test questions are simplified to have mathematical calculations that do not require calculators, as calculators are not permitted during the exam. Multi-color markers and pencils are not allowed.

Scoring

The GRE Chemistry exam is graded electronically with points given for each correct answer provided. Your score is determined by the number of questions answered correctly. Missed questions and answers purposely left blank will be considered incorrect.

Incorrect answers are not subtracted from the final score, so it is better to guess an answer than not respond at all. At the end of the test, you may choose to cancel your scores if you feel your performance was not your best. The scores will not be made available for review online or be reported to score recipients.

GRE Chemistry Strategies

The GRE Chemistry exam is designed to challenge thinking. It is not enough to simply know the facts, however. Competent demonstration of higher-order thinking skills is needed to succeed. More than simple recall or recognition of fact abilities are required; critical thinking and the ability to link knowledge of a term or concept to other terms or concepts are also needed.

While preparation a few weeks or months in advance may help, the test is meant to assess knowledge and skills gained over a long period. Reviewing college course material is the best way to prepare for the exam.

- Read all questions carefully. Be sure to do this before looking over the answer choices. It is important to understand exactly what the question is asking for.

- After an answer is selected, quickly return to the question to ensure the selected choice does answer the question being asked. Make sure you marked the choice you intended to choose in the answer sheet.

- All answers are weighted equally, so it is best not to remain stuck on a difficult question or one you are not familiar with.

- Skip time-consuming questions and return to them later if possible. It may be beneficial to work through the test quickly by first answering questions you are confident in, and then returning later to those that require more thought.

- If the correct answer is not immediately clear, fall back as best as you can to the process of elimination. Be sure to look at all the possible answer choices before selecting one.

  Eliminate as many choices as possible. Usually, there is at least one answer choice that is easily identified as wrong. Eliminating even one choice will greatly increase your odds of selecting the correct one.

  After eliminating the most obvious incorrect choice(s), eliminate any answers that strike you as "almost right" or "half right." You should consider "half right" as synonymous with "wrong." These answer choices are purposely included to catch test takers off guard.

- Use guessing only as a last resort. Always remember that an unanswered question will be guaranteed to lower your score since the score is based only on the number of correct answers provided. Therefore, leave nothing unanswered and guess where no other strategies are useful.

- Record all answers on your answer sheet. If answers are recorded only in the test book, they will not count towards your final score.

- Do not wait until the last few minutes of the test to fill out the answer sheet.

9

Common Chemistry Equations

Throughout the test the following symbols have the definitions specified unless otherwise noted.

L, mL	=	liter(s), milliliter(s)	mm Hg	=	millimeters of mercury
g	=	gram(s)	J, kJ	=	joule(s), kilojoule(s)
nm	=	nanometer(s)	V	=	volt(s)
atm	=	atmosphere(s)	mol	=	mole(s)

ATOMIC STRUCTURE

$$E = h\nu$$
$$c = \lambda\nu$$

E = energy
ν = frequency
λ = wavelength

Planck's constant, $h = 6.626 \times 10^{-34}$ J s

Speed of light, $c = 2.998 \times 10^8$ m s^{-1}

Avogadro's number $= 6.022 \times 10^{23}$ mol^{-1}

Electron charge, $e = -1.602 \times 10^{-19}$ coulomb

EQUILIBRIUM

$$K_c = \frac{[C]^c[D]^d}{[A]^a[B]^b}, \text{ where } a\,A + b\,B \rightleftarrows c\,C + d\,D$$

$$K_p = \frac{(P_C)^c (P_D)^d}{(P_A)^a (P_B)^b}$$

$$K_a = \frac{[H^+][A^-]}{[HA]}$$

$$K_b = \frac{[OH^-][HB^+]}{[B]}$$

$$K_w = [H^+][OH^-] = 1.0 \times 10^{-14} \text{ at } 25°C$$
$$= K_a \times K_b$$

$$pH = -\log[H^+], \quad pOH = -\log[OH^-]$$

$$14 = pH + pOH$$

$$pH = pK_a + \log\frac{[A^-]}{[HA]}$$

$$pK_a = -\log K_a, \quad pK_b = -\log K_b$$

Equilibrium Constants

K_c (molar concentrations)
K_p (gas pressures)
K_a (weak acid)
K_b (weak base)
K_w (water)

KINETICS

$$\ln[A]_t - \ln[A]_0 = -kt$$

$$\frac{1}{[A]_t} - \frac{1}{[A]_0} = kt$$

$$t_{1/2} = \frac{0.693}{k}$$

k = rate constant
t = time
$t_{1/2}$ = half-life

GASES, LIQUIDS, AND SOLUTIONS

$$PV = nRT$$

$$P_A = P_{total} \times X_A, \text{ where } X_A = \frac{\text{moles A}}{\text{total moles}}$$

$$P_{total} = P_A + P_B + P_C + \ldots$$

$$n = \frac{m}{M}$$

$$K = {}^\circ C + 273$$

$$D = \frac{m}{V}$$

$$KE \text{ per molecule} = \frac{1}{2}mv^2$$

Molarity, M = moles of solute per liter of solution

$$A = abc$$

P = pressure
V = volume
T = temperature
n = number of moles
m = mass
M = molar mass
D = density
KE = kinetic energy
v = velocity
A = absorbance
a = molar absorptivity
b = path length
c = concentration

Gas constant, $R = 8.314 \text{ J mol}^{-1} \text{ K}^{-1}$
$= 0.08206 \text{ L atm mol}^{-1} \text{ K}^{-1}$
$= 62.36 \text{ L torr mol}^{-1} \text{ K}^{-1}$
1 atm = 760 mm Hg
$= 760$ torr

THERMOCHEMISTRY/ ELECTROCHEMISTRY

$$q = mc\Delta T$$

$$\Delta S^\circ = \sum S^\circ \text{ products} - \sum S^\circ \text{ reactants}$$

$$\Delta H^\circ = \sum \Delta H_f^\circ \text{ products} - \sum \Delta H_f^\circ \text{ reactants}$$

$$\Delta G^\circ = \sum \Delta G_f^\circ \text{ products} - \sum \Delta G_f^\circ \text{ reactants}$$

$$\Delta G^\circ = \Delta H^\circ - T\Delta S^\circ$$

$$= -RT \ln K$$

$$= -n F E^\circ$$

$$I = \frac{q}{t}$$

q = heat
m = mass
c = specific heat capacity
T = temperature
S° = standard entropy
H° = standard enthalpy
G° = standard free energy
n = number of moles
E° = standard reduction potential
I = current (amperes)
q = charge (coulombs)
t = time (seconds)

Faraday's constant, F = 96,485 coulombs per mole
of electrons
$$1 \text{ volt} = \frac{1 \text{ joule}}{1 \text{ coulomb}}$$

Periodic Table of the Elements

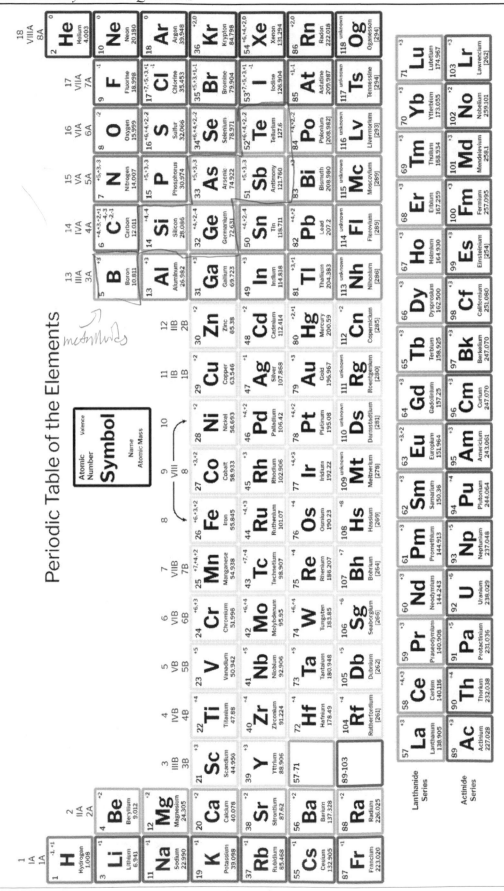

Practice

Questions

We want to hear from you

Your feedback is important to us because we strive to provide the highest quality prep materials. Email us if you have any questions, comments or suggestions, so we can incorporate your feedback into future editions.

Customer Satisfaction Guarantee

If you have any concerns about this book, including printing issues, contact us and we will resolve any issues to your satisfaction.

info@sterling-prep.com

We reply to all emails – please check your **spam** *folder*

Thank you for choosing our products to achieve your educational goals!

Chapter 1: Electronic and Atomic Structures; Periodic Table

1. The property defined as the energy required to remove one electron from an atom in the gaseous state is:

A. electronegativity   **C.** electron affinity

B. ionization energy   **D.** hyperconjugation   **E.** none of the above

2. Which of the following pairs has one metalloid element and one nonmetal element?

A. ^{82}Pb and ^{83}Bi **C.** ^{51}Sb and ^{20}Ca

B. ^{19}K and ^{9}F **D.** ^{33}As and ^{14}Si **E.** ^{32}Ge and ^{9}F

3. Periods on the periodic table represent elements:

A. in the same group   **C.** known as isotopes

B. with consecutive atomic numbers   **D.** with similar chemical properties

E. known as ions

4. Ignoring hydrogen and helium, which area(s) of the periodic table contain(s) both metals and nonmetals?

    I. s area   II. p area   III. d area

A. I only   **C.** III only

B. II only   **D.** I and II only   **E.** I, II and III

5. What is the number of known nonmetals relative to the number of metals?

A. About two times greater   **C.** About four times less

B. About fifty percent   **D.** About twenty-five percent greater

E. About three times greater

6. Which statement is true regarding the average mass of a naturally occurring isotope of iron that has an atomic mass equal to 55.91 amu?

A. 55.91 / 1.0078 times greater than a ^{1}H atom

B. 55.91 / 12.000 times greater than a ^{12}C atom

C. 55.91 times greater than a ^{12}C atom

D. 55.91 times greater than a ^{1}H atom

E. none of the above

7. Which is the principal quantum number?

A. n **B.** m **C.** l **D.** s **E.** $+\frac{1}{2}$

8. How many electrons can occupy the 4*s* subshell?

  A. 1   **B.** 2   **C.** 6   **D.** 8   **E.** 10

9. An excited hydrogen atom emits a light spectrum of specific, characteristic wavelengths. The light spectrum is a result of:

  A. energy released as H atoms form H_2 molecules
  B. the light wavelengths, which are not absorbed by valence electrons when white light passes through the sample
  C. particles being emitted as the hydrogen nuclei decay
  D. excited electrons being promoted to higher energy levels
  E. excited electrons dropping to lower energy levels

10. Which has the largest radius?

  A. Br^- **B.** K^+ **C.** Ar   **D.** Ca^{2+} **E.** Cl^-

11. In its ground state, how many unpaired electrons does a sulfur atom have?

  A. 0   **B.** 1   **C.** 2   **D.** 3   **E.** 4

12. Which of the elements would be in the same group as the element whose electronic configuration is $1s^22s^22p^63s^23p^64s^1$?

  A. ^{18}Ar   **B.** ^{34}Se   **C.** ^{12}Mg   **D.** ^{15}P   **E.** ^{3}Li

13. Which characteristic(s) is/are responsible for the changes seen in the first ionization energy when moving down a column?

  I. Increased shielding of electrons
  II. Larger atomic radii
  III. Increasing nuclear attraction for electrons

  A. I only   **B.** II only   **C.** III only   **D.** I and II only   **E.** I, II and III

14. What is the maximum number of electrons that can occupy the 4*f* subshell?

  A. 6   **B.** 8   **C.** 14   **D.** 16   **E.** 18

15. The attraction of the nucleus on the outermost electron in an atom tends to:

  A. decrease from right to left and bottom to top on the periodic table
  B. decrease from left to right and bottom to top on the periodic table
  C. decrease from left to right and top to bottom of the periodic table
  D. increase from right to left and top to bottom on the periodic table
  E. decrease from right to left and top to bottom on the periodic table

16. What must be the same if two atoms represent the same element?

    A. number of neutrons   **C.** number of electron shells

    B. atomic mass   **D.** atomic number

                                    E. number of valence electrons

17. Early investigators proposed that the ray of the cathode tube was a negatively charged particle because the ray was:

    A. not seen from the positively charged anode

    B. diverted by a magnetic field

    C. observed in the presence or absence of a gas

    D. able to change colors depending on which gas was within the tube

    E. attracted to positively charged electric plates

18. What is the value of quantum numbers n and l in the highest occupied orbital for the element carbon that has an atomic number of 6?

    A. $n = 1, l = 1$ **C.** $n = 1, l = 2$

    B. $n = 2, l = 1$ **D.** $n = 2, l = 2$ **E.** $n = 3, l = 3$

19. Which type of subshell is filled by the distinguishing electron in an alkaline earth metal?

    A. s **B.** p **C.** f **D.** d **E.** both s and p

20. If an element has an electron configuration ending in $3p^4$, which statements about the element's electron configuration is NOT correct?

    A. There are six electrons in the 3rd shell

    B. Five different subshells contain electrons

    C. There are eight electrons in the 2nd shell

    D. The 3rd shell needs two more electrons to be filled

    E. All are correct statements

21. Which of the following is the correct order of increasing atomic radius?

    A. Te < Sb < In < Sr < Rb   **C.** Te < Sb < In < Rb < Sr

    B. In < Sb < Te < Sr < Rb   **D.** Rb < Sr < In < Sb < Te

                                    E. In < Sb < Te < Rb < Sr

22. Which of the following electron configurations represents an excited state of an atom?

    A. $1s^2 2s^2 2p^6 3s^2 3p^3$ **C.** $1s^2 2s^2 2p^6 3d^1$

    B. $1s^2 2s^2 2p^6 3s^2 3p^6 4s^1$ **D.** $1s^2 2s^2 2p^6 3s^2 3p^6 4s^2 3d^1$

                                    E. $1s^2 2s^2 2p^6 3s^2 3p^6 4s^2 3d^{10} 4p^1$

23. An atom that contains 47 protons, 47 electrons and 60 neutrons is an isotope of:

A. Nd   **C.** Ag

B. Bh   **D.** Al   **E.** cannot be determined

24. What is the name for elements in the same column of the periodic table that have similar chemical properties?

A. congeners   **C.** diastereomers

B. stereoisomers   **D.** epimers   **E.** anomers

25. Which element would most likely be a metal with a low melting point?

A. K   **B.** B   **C.** N   **D.** C   **E.** Cl

26. Mg is an example of a(n):

A. transition metal   **C.** alkali metal

B. noble gas   **D.** halogen   **E.** alkaline earth metal

27. Metalloids:

    I. have some metallic and some nonmetallic properties

    II. may have low electrical conductivities

    III. contain elements in group IIIB

A. I and III only   **C.** II and III only   **E.** I, II and III

B. II only   **D.** I and II only

28. Silicon exists as three isotopes: ^{28}Si, ^{29}Si, and ^{30}Si with atomic masses of 27.98 amu, 28.98 amu and 29.97 amu, respectively. Which isotope is the most abundant in nature?

A. ^{28}Si   **C.** ^{30}Si

B. ^{29}Si   **D.** ^{28}Si and ^{30}Si are equally abundant

                    E. All are equally abundant

29. Which statement supports the reason why early investigators proposed that the ray of the cathode ray tube was due to the cathode?

A. The ray was diverted by a magnetic field

B. The ray was not seen from the positively charged anode

C. The ray was attracted to the electric plates that were positively charged

D. The ray changed color depending on the gas used within the tube

E. The ray was observed in the presence or absence of a gas

30. How many quantum numbers are needed to describe a single electron in an atom?

 A. 1   **B.** 2   **C.** 3   **D.** 4   **E.** 5

31. Which of the following is the electron configuration of a boron atom?

 A. $1s^2 2s^1 2p^2$ **B.** $1s^2 2p^3$ **C.** $1s^2 2s^2 2p^2$ **D.** $1s^2 2s^2 2p^1$ **E.** $1s^2 2s^1 2p^1$

32. Which element has the electron configuration $1s^2 2s^2 2p^6 3s^2 3p^6 4s^2 3d^{10} 4p^6 5s^2 4d^{10} 5p^2$?

 A. Sn   **B.** As   **C.** Pb   **D.** Sb   **E.** In

33. Which element has the lowest electronegativity?

 A. Mg   **B.** Al   **C.** Cl   **D.** Br   **E.** I

34. Refer to the periodic table and predict which of the following is a solid nonmetal under normal conditions.

 A. Cl   **B.** F   **C.** Se   **D.** As   **E.** Ar

35. Lines were observed in the spectrum of uranium ore (i.e., naturally occurring solid material) identical to those of helium in the spectrum of the Sun. Which of the following produced the lines in the helium spectrum?

 A. Excited protons jumping to a higher energy level
 B. Excited protons dropping to a lower energy level
 C. Excited electrons jumping to a higher energy level
 D. Excited electrons dropping to a lower energy level
 E. None of the above

36. Which set of quantum numbers is possible?

 A. $n = 1$; $l = 2$; $m_l = 3$; $m_s = -\frac{1}{2}$ **C.** $n = 2$; $l = 1$; $m_l = 2$; $m_s = -\frac{1}{2}$
 B. $n = 4$; $l = 2$; $m_l = 2$; $m_s = -\frac{1}{2}$ **D.** $n = 3$; $l = 3$; $m_l = 2$; $m_s = -\frac{1}{2}$
                 E. $n = 2$; $l = 3$; $m_l = 2$; $m_s = -\frac{1}{2}$

37. Which of the following elements is NOT correctly classified?

 A. Mo – transition element   **C.** K – representative element
 B. Sr – alkaline earth metal   **D.** Ar – noble gas
                 E. Po – halogen

38. Which of the following is the correct sequence of atomic radii from smallest to largest?

 A. $Al < S < Al^{3+} < S^{2-}$ **C.** $Al^{3+} < Al < S^{2-} < S$
 B. $S < S^{2-} < Al < Al^{3+}$ **D.** $Al^{3+} < S < S^{2-} < Al$ **E.** $Al < Al^{3+} < S^{2-} < S$

39. From the periodic table, which of the following elements is a semimetal?

    A. Ar   **B.** As   **C.** Al   **D.** Ac   **E.** Am

40. Which statement does NOT describe the noble gases?

    A. The more massive noble gases react with other elements
    B. They belong to group VIIIA (or 18)
    C. They contain at least one metalloid
    D. He, Ne, Ar, Kr, Xe, and Rn are included in the group
    E. They were once known as the inert gases

41. Which is a good experimental method to distinguish between ordinary hydrogen and deuterium, the rare isotope of hydrogen?

        I. Measure the density of the gas at STP
        II. Measure the rate at which the gas effuses
        III. Infrared spectroscopy

    A. I only   **C.** I and II only
    B. II only   **D.** I, II and III   **E.** II and III only

42. Which statement is true regarding the relative abundances of the ^{6}lithium or ^{7}lithium isotopes?

    A. The relative proportions change as neutrons move between the nuclei
    B. The isotopes are in roughly equal proportions
    C. The relative ratio depends on the temperature of the element
    D. ^{6}Lithium is much more abundant
    E. ^{7}Lithium is much more abundant

43. Which of the following statement(s) is/are true?

        I. The f subshell contains 7 orbitals
        II. The d subshell contains 5 orbitals
        III. The third energy shell ($n = 3$) has no f orbitals

    A. I only   **C.** I and II only
    B. II only   **D.** II and III only   **E.** I, II and III

44. Which element has the greatest ionization energy?

    A. Fr   **B.** Cl   **C.** Ga   **D.** I   **E.** Cs

45. Electrons fill up subshells in order of:

      I. decreasing distance from the nucleus
      II. increasing distance from the nucleus
      III. increasing energy

A. I only   **C.** I and II only
B. II only   **D.** II and III only   **E.** I, II and III

46. Which of the following produces the "atomic fingerprint" of an element?

A. Excited protons dropping to a lower energy level
B. Excited protons jumping to a higher energy level
C. Excited electrons dropping to a lower energy level
D. Excited electrons jumping to a higher energy level
E. None of the above

47. Which of the following is the electron configuration for manganese (Mn)?

A. $1s^2 2s^2 2p^6 3s^2 3p^6$ **C.** $1s^2 2s^2 2p^6 3s^2 3p^6 4s^2 3d^6$
B. $1s^2 2s^2 2p^6 3s^2 3p^6 4s^2 3d^{10} 4p^1$ **D.** $1s^2 2s^2 2p^6 3s^2 3p^6 4s^2 3d^8$
                               E. $1s^2 2s^2 2p^6 3s^2 3p^6 4s^2 3d^5$

48. Which element listed below has the greatest electronegativity?

A. I   **B.** Fr   **C.** H   **D.** He   **E.** F

49. Which of the following is NOT an alkali metal?

A. Fr   **B.** Cs   **C.** Ca   **D.** Na   **E.** Rb

50. What is the atomic number and the mass number of ^{79}Br, respectively?

A. 35; 44   **B.** 44; 35   **C.** 35; 79   **D.** 79; 35   **E.** 35; 114

51. Both ^{65}Cu and ^{65}Zn have the same:

A. mass number   **C.** number of ions
B. number of neutrons   **D.** number of electrons   **E.** number of protons

52. Which element(s) is/are alkali metal(s)?

    I. Na   II. Sr   III. Cs

A. I and II only   **C.** I only
B. I and III only   **D.** II only
                       E. I, II and III

53. Which of the following is/are a general characteristic of a nonmetallic element?

      I. reacts with metals   II. pliable   III. shiny luster

A. I only   **C.** III only

B. II only   **D.** I and II only   **E.** I, II and III

54. Which group of the periodic table has 3 nonmetals?

A. Group IIIA   **C.** Group VA

B. Group IVA   **D.** Group IA   **E.** Group VIA

55. The transition metals occur in which period(s) on the periodic table?

      I. 2   II. 3   III. 4

A. I only   **C.** III only   **E.** I, II and III

B. II only   **D.** I and III only

56. Which of Dalton's original proposals is/are still valid?

      I. Compounds contain atoms in small whole number ratios
      II. Atoms of different elements combine to form compounds
      III. An element is composed of tiny particles called atoms

A. I only   **C.** III only   **E.** I, II and III

B. II only   **D.** I and III only

57. Given that parent and daughter nuclei are isotopes of the same element, the ratio of α to β decay produced by the parent must be:

A. 1 to 1   **B.** 1 to 2   **C.** 2 to 1   **D.** 2 to 3   **E.** 3 to 2

58. ^{63}Cu isotope makes up 69% of the naturally occurring Cu. If only one other isotope is present for natural copper, what is it?

A. ^{59}Cu **B.** ^{65}Cu **C.** ^{61}Cu **D.** ^{62}Cu **E.** ^{60}Cu

59. Which does NOT contain cathode ray particles?

A. H_2O **C.** H

B. K   **D.** He   **E.** All contain cathode ray particles

60. Which principle or rule states that only two electrons can occupy an orbital?

      uli exclusion principle   **C.** Heisenberg uncertainty principle

      d's rule   **D.** Newton's principle

                                 E. None of the above

Chapter 2: Chemical Bonding

1. What is the number of valence electrons in tin (Sn)?

   A. 14   **B.** 8   **C.** 2   **D.** 4   **E.** 5

2. Unhybridized *p* orbitals participate in π bonds as double and triple bonds. How many distinct and degenerate *p* orbitals exist in the second electron shell, where n = 2?

   A. 3   **B.** 2   **C.** 1   **D.** 0   **E.** 4

3. What is the total number of valence electrons in a sulfite ion, SO_3^{2-}?

   A. 22   **B.** 24   **C.** 26   **D.** 34   **E.** none of the above

4. Which type of attractive forces occurs in all molecules regardless of the atoms they possess?

   A. Dipole–ion interactions   **C.** Dipole–dipole attractions
   B. Ion–ion interactions   **D.** Hydrogen bonding
                                E. London dispersion forces

5. Given the structure of glucose below, which statement explains the hydrogen bonding between glucose and water?

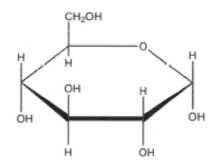

   A. Due to the cyclic structure of glucose, there is no H–bonding with water
   B. Each glucose molecule could H–bond with up to 17 water molecules
   C. H–bonds form, with water always being the H–bond donor
   D. H–bonds form, with glucose always being the H–bond donor
   E. Each glucose molecule could H–bond with up to 5 water molecules

6. How many valence electrons are in the Lewis dot structure of C_2H_6?

   A. 2   **B.** 14   **C.** 6   **D.** 8   **E.** 12

7. The term for a bond where the electrons are shared unequally is:

   A. ionic   **C.** coordinate covalent

   B. nonpolar covalent   **D.** nonpolar ionic   **E.** polar covalent

8. What is the name for the weak forces of attraction between nonpolar molecules due to temporary dipoles between adjacent nonpolar molecules?

   A. van der Waals forces   **C.** hydrogen bonding forces

   B. hydrophobic forces   **D.** nonpolar covalent forces   **E.** hydrophilic forces

9. Nitrogen has five valence electrons; which of the following types of bonding is/are possible?

      I. one single and one double bond
      II. three single bonds
      III. one triple bond

   A. I only   **C.** I and III only

   B. II only   **D.** I, II and III   **E.** none of the above

10. What is the number of valence electrons in antimony (Sb)?

   A. 1   **B.** 2   **C.** 3   **D.** 4   **E.** 5

11. How many total resonance structures, if any, can be drawn for a nitrite ion?

   A. 1   **B.** 2   **C.** 3   **D.** 4   **E.** 5

12. What is the formula of the ammonium ion?

   A. NH_4^- **B.** N_4H^+ **C.** NH_4^{2-} **D.** NH_4^{2+} **E.** NH_4^+

13. Which of the following series of elements are arranged in the order of increasing electronegativity?

   A. Fr, Mg, Si, O   **C.** F, B, O, Li

   B. Br, Cl, S, P   **D.** Cl, S, Se, Te   **E.** Br, Mg, Si, N

14. The attraction due to London dispersion forces between molecules depends on what two factors?

   A. Volatility and shape   **C.** Vapor pressure and size

   B. Molar mass and volatility   **D.** Molar mass and shape

                                      E. Molar mass and vapor pressure

15. Which of the substances below would have the largest dipole?

   A. CO_2 **C.** H_2O

   B. SO_2 **D.** CCl_4 **E.** CH_4

16. What is the name for the attraction between H_2O molecules?

   A. adhesion   **C.** cohesion

   B. polarity   **D.** van der Waals   **E.** hydrophilicity

17. Which compound contains only covalent bonds?

   A. $HC_2H_3O_2$ **C.** NH_4OH

   B. $NaCl$ **D.** $Ca_3(PO_4)_2$ **E.** LiF

18. The distance between two atomic nuclei in a chemical bond is determined by the:

   A. size of the valence electrons

   B. size of the nucleus

   C. size of the protons

   D. balance between the repulsion of the nuclei and the attraction of the nuclei for the bonding electrons

   E. size of the neutrons

19. Carbonic acid has the chemical formula of H_2CO_3. The carbonate ion has the molecular formula of CO_3^{2-}. From the Lewis structure for the CO_3^{2-} ion, what is the number of reasonable resonance structures for the anion?

   A. original structure only   **B.** 2   **C.** 3   **D.** 4   **E.** 5

20. Which of the following molecules would contain a dipole?

   A. F–F   **B.** H–H   **C.** Cl–Cl   **D.** H–F   **E.** *trans*-dichloroethene

21. Which is the correct formula for the ionic compound formed between Ca and I?

   A. Ca_3I_2 **B.** Ca_2I_3 **C.** CaI_2 **D.** Ca_2I **E.** Ca_3I_5

22. Which bonding is NOT possible for a carbon atom that has four valence electrons?

   A. 1 single and 1 triple bond   **C.** 4 single bonds

   B. 1 double and 1 triple bond   **D.** 2 single and 1 double bond

                                             E. 2 double bonds

23. During strenuous exercise, why does perspiration on a person's skin forms droplets?

A. Ability of H_2O to dissipate heat

B. High specific heat of H_2O

C. Adhesive properties of H_2O

D. Cohesive properties of H_2O

E. High NaCl content of perspiration

24. If an ionic bond is stronger than a dipole–dipole interaction, why does water dissolve an ionic compound?

A. Ions do not overcome their interatomic attraction and therefore are not soluble

B. Ion–dipole interaction causes the ions to heat up and vibrate free of the crystal

C. Ionic bond is weakened by the ion–dipole interactions and ionic repulsion ejects the ions from the crystal

D. Ion-dipole interactions of several water molecules aggregate with the ionic bond and dissociate it into the solution

E. None of the above

25. Which one of these molecules can act as a hydrogen bond acceptor, but not a donor?

A. CH_3NH_2

B. CH_3CO_2H

C. H_2O

D. C_2H_5OH

E. $CH_3–O–CH_3$

26. When NaCl dissolves in water, what is the force of attraction between Na^+ and H_2O?

A. ion–dipole

B. hydrogen bonding

C. ion–ion

D. dipole–dipole

E. van der Waals

27. Based on the Lewis structure, how many polar and nonpolar bonds are present in H_2CO?

A. 3 polar bonds and 0 nonpolar bonds

B. 2 polar bonds and 1 nonpolar bond

C. 1 polar bond and 2 nonpolar bonds

D. 0 polar bonds and 3 nonpolar bonds

E. 2 polar bonds and 2 nonpolar bonds

28. Which element likely forms a cation with a +2 charge?

A. Na B. S C. Si D. Mg E. Br

29. Which of the statements is an accurate description of the structure of the ionic compound NaCl?

A. Alternating rows of Na^+ and Cl^- ions are present

B. Six ions of opposite charge surround each ion present

C. Alternating layers of Na and Cl atoms are present

D. Alternating layers of Na^+ and Cl^- ions are present

E. Repeating layers of Na^+ and Cl^- ions are present

30. What is the name for the force holding two atoms together in a chemical bond?

- **A.** gravitational force
- **B.** strong nuclear force
- **C.** weak hydrophobic force
- **D.** weak nuclear force
- **E.** electrostatic force

31. Which of the following diatomic molecules contains the bond of greatest polarity?

- **A.** CH_4
- **B.** BrI
- **C.** Cl–F
- **D.** P_4
- **E.** Te–F

32. Why does H_2O have an unusually high boiling point compared to H_2S?

- **A.** Hydrogen bonding
- **B.** Van der Waals forces
- **C.** H_2O molecules pack more closely than H_2S
- **D.** Covalent bonds are stronger in H_2O
- **E.** This is a false statement because H_2O has a similar boiling point to H_2S

33. What is the shape of a molecule in which the central atom has 2 bonding electron pairs and 2 nonbonding electron pairs?

- **A.** trigonal planar
- **B.** trigonal pyramidal
- **C.** linear
- **D.** bent
- **E.** tetrahedral

34. Which of the following represents the breaking of a noncovalent interaction?

- **A.** Ionization of water
- **B.** Decomposition of hydrogen peroxide
- **C.** Hydrolysis of an ester
- **D.** Dissolving of salt crystals
- **E.** None of the above

35. Which pair of elements is most likely to form an ionic compound when reacted together?

- **A.** C and Cl
- **B.** K and I
- **C.** Ga and Si
- **D.** Fe and Mg
- **E.** H and O

36. Which of the following statements concerning coordinate covalent bonds is correct?

- **A.** Once formed, they are indistinguishable from any other covalent bond
- **B.** They are always single bonds
- **C.** One of the atoms involved must be a metal and the other a nonmetal
- **D.** Both atoms involved in the bond contribute an equal number of electrons to the bond
- **E.** The bond is formed between two Lewis bases

37. The greatest dipole moment within a bond is when:

A. both bonding elements have low electronegativity

B. one bonding element has high electronegativity, and the other has low electronegativity

C. both bonding elements have high electronegativity

D. one bonding element has high electronegativity, and the other has moderate electronegativity

E. both bonding elements have moderate electronegativity

38. Which of the following must occur for an atom to obtain the noble gas configuration?

A. lose, gain or share an electron

B. lose or gain an electron

C. lose an electron

D. share an electron

E. share or gain an electron

39. Based on the Lewis structure for hydrogen peroxide, H_2O_2, how many polar bonds and nonpolar bonds are present?

A. 3 polar and 0 nonpolar bonds

B. 2 polar and 2 nonpolar bonds

C. 1 polar and 2 nonpolar bonds

D. 0 polar and 3 nonpolar bonds

E. 2 polar and 1 nonpolar bond

40. Which compound is NOT correctly matched with the predominant intermolecular force associated with that compound in the liquid state?

Compound	Intermolecular force
A. CH_3OH	hydrogen bonding
B. HF	hydrogen bonding
C. Cl_2O	dipole–dipole interactions
D. HBr	van der Waals interactions
E. CH_4	van der Waals interactions

41. Which element forms an ion with the greatest positive charge?

A. Mg   **B.** Ca   **C.** Al   **D.** Na   **E.** Rb

42. What is the difference between a dipole–dipole and an ion–dipole interaction?

A. One interaction involves dipole attraction between neutral molecules, while the other involves dipole interactions with ions

B. One interaction involves ionic molecules interacting with other ionic molecules, while the other deals with polar molecules

C. One interaction involves salts and water, while the other does not involve water

D. One interaction involves hydrogen bonding, while others do not

E. None of the above

43. In the process of forming sodium nitride (Na_3N) from its elements, what happens to the electrons of each sodium and the electrons of each nitrogen, respectively?

A. one lost; three gained   **C.** three lost; one gained

B. three lost; three gained   **D.** one lost; two gained   **E.** two lost; three gained

44. Which species below has the least number of valence electrons in its Lewis symbol?

A. S^{2-} **B.** Ga^+ **C.** Ar^+ **D.** Mg^{2+} **E.** F^-

45. Which of the following occur(s) naturally as nonpolar diatomic molecules?

     I. sulfur   II. chlorine   III. argon

A. I only   **C.** I and III only

B. II only   **D.** I and II only   **E.** I, II and III

46. Which formula for an ionic compound is NOT correct?

A. $Al_2(CO_3)_3$ **B.** Li_2SO_4 **C.** Na_2S **D.** $MgHCO_3$ **E.** K_2O

47. What term best describes the smallest whole number repeating ratio of ions in an ionic compound?

A. lattice   **B.** unit cell   **C.** formula unit   **D.** covalent unit   **E.** ionic unit

48. In the nitrogen monoxide molecule, the dipole moment is 0.16 D, and the bond length is 115 pm. What is the sign and magnitude of the charge on the oxygen atom? (Use the conversion factor of $1 D = 3.34 \times 10^{30}$ C·m and the charge of 1 electron = 1.602×10^{-19} C)

A. $-0.098\ e$ **B.** $-0.71\ e$ **C.** $-1.3\ e$ **D.** $-0.029\ e$ **E.** $+1.3\ e$

49. From the electronegativity below, which single covalent bond is the most polar?

Element:	H	C	N	O
Electronegativity	2.1	2.5	3.0	3.5

A. O–C   **B.** O–N   **C.** N–C   **D.** C–H   **E.** C–C

50. Why are adjacent water molecules attracted to each other?

A. Ionic bonding between the hydrogens of H_2O

B. Covalent bonding between adjacent oxygens

C. Electrostatic attraction between the H of one H_2O and the O of another

D. Covalent bonding between the H of one H_2O and the O of another

E. Electrostatic attraction between the O of one H_2O and the O of another

51. What is the chemical formula for a compound that contains K^+ and CO_3^{2-} ions?

    A. $K(CO_3)_3$ **B.** $K_3(CO_3)_2$ **C.** $K_3(CO_3)_3$ **D.** KCO_3 **E.** K_2CO_3

52. Which of the following molecules is a Lewis acid?

    A. NO_3^- **B.** NH_3 **C.** NH_4^+ **D.** CH_3COOH **E.** BH_3

53. Which molecule(s) is/are most likely to show a dipole-dipole interaction?

    I. $H–C{\equiv}C–H$ II. CH_4 III. CH_3SH IV. CH_3CH_2OH

    A. I only   **B.** II only   **C.** III only   **D.** III and IV only   **E.** I and IV only

54. $C{=}C$, $C{=}O$, $C{=}N$, and $N{=}N$ bonds are observed in many organic compounds. However, $C{=}S$, $C{=}P$, $C{=}Si$, and other similar bonds are not often found. What is the most probable explanation for this observation?

    A. The comparative sizes of $3p$ atomic orbitals make effective overlap between them less likely than between two $2p$ orbitals
    B. S, P, and Si do not undergo hybridization of orbitals
    C. S, P, and Si do not form π bonds due to the lack of occupied p orbitals in their ground state electron configurations
    D. Carbon does not combine with elements found below the second row of the periodic table
    E. None of the above

55. Explain why chlorine, Cl_2, is a gas at room temperature, while bromine, Br_2, is a liquid.

    A. Bromine ions are held together by ionic bonds
    B. Chlorine molecules are smaller and, therefore, pack tighter in their physical orientation
    C. Bromine atoms are larger, which causes the formation of a stronger induced dipole–induced dipole attraction
    D. Chlorine atoms are larger, which causes the formation of a stronger induced dipole–induced dipole attraction
    E. Bromine molecules are smaller and therefore pack tighter in their physical orientation

56. What is the major intermolecular force in $(CH_3)_2NH$?

    A. hydrogen bonding   **C.** London dispersion forces
    B. dipole–dipole attractions   **D.** ion–dipole attractions
                                 E. van der Waals forces

57. Which of the following correctly describes the molecule potassium oxide and its bond?

    A. It is a weak electrolyte with an ionic bond

    B. It is a strong electrolyte with an ionic bond

    C. It is a non-electrolyte with a covalent bond

    D. It is a strong electrolyte with a covalent bond

    E. It is a non-electrolyte with a hydrogen bond

58. Based on the Lewis structure for $H_3C–NH_2$, the formal charge on N is:

    A. −1   **B.** 0   **C.** +2   **D.** +1   **E.** −2

59. The name of S^{2-} is:

    A. sulfite ion   **C.** sulfur

    B. sulfide ion   **D.** sulfate ion   **E.** sulfurous acid

60. Which of the following pairings of ions is NOT consistent with the formula?

    A. Co_2S_3 (Co^{3+} and S^{2-})   **C.** Na_3P (Na^+ and P^{3-})

    B. K_2O (K^+ and O^-)   **D.** BaF_2 (Ba^{2+} and F^-)   **E.** KCl (K^+ and Cl^-)

Notes

Chapter 3: Phases and Phase Equilibria

1. Which statement is NOT true regarding vapor pressure?

    I.   Solids do not have a vapor pressure

    II. Vapor pressure of a pure liquid does not depend on the amount of vapor present

    III. Vapor pressure of a pure liquid does not depend on the amount of liquid present

  A. I only   **B.** II only   **C.** III only   **D.** I and II only   **E.** I, II and III

2. How does the volume of a fixed sample of gas change if the temperature is doubled at constant pressure?

  A. Decreases by a factor of 2   **C.** Doubles

  B. Increases by a factor of 4   **D.** Remains the same   **E.** Requires more information

3. When a solute is added to a pure solvent, the boiling point [ ] and freezing point [ ]?

  A. decreases … decreases   **C.** increases … decreases

  B. decreases … increases   **D.** increases … increases

                               E. remains the same … remains the same

4. Consider the phase diagram for H_2O. The termination of the gas-liquid transition at which distinct gas or liquid phases do NOT exist is the:

  A. critical point   **C.** triple point

  B. endpoint   **D.** condensation point   **E.** inflection point

5. The van der Waals equation of state for a real gas is expressed as: $[P + n^2a / V^2] \cdot (V - nb) = nRT$. The van der Waals constant, *a*, represents a correction for:

  A. negative deviation in the measured value of P from that of an ideal gas due to the attractive forces between the molecules of a real gas

  B. positive deviation in the measured value of P from that of an ideal gas due to the attractive forces between the molecules of a real gas

  C. negative deviation in the measured value of P from that of an ideal gas due to the finite volume of space occupied by molecules of a real gas

  D. positive deviation in the measured value of P from that of an ideal gas due to the finite volume of space occupied by molecules of a real gas

  E. positive deviation in the measured value of P from that of an ideal gas due to the finite mass of the molecules of a real gas

6. What is the value of the ideal gas constant, expressed in units (torr × mL) / mole × K?

  A. 62.4   **C.** 0.0821

  B. 62,396   **D.** 1 / 0.0821   **E.** 8.21

7. If both the pressure and the temperature of a gas are halved, the volume is:

A. halved

B. the same

C. doubled

D. quadrupled

E. decreased by a factor of 4

8. If container X is occupied by 2.0 moles of O_2 gas, while container Y is occupied by 10.0 grams of N_2 gas, and both containers are maintained at 5.0 °C and 760 torr, then:

A. container X must have a volume of 22.4 L

B. the average kinetic energy of the molecules in X is equal to the average kinetic energy of the molecules in Y

C. container Y must be larger than container X

D. the average speed of the molecules in container X is greater than that of the molecules in container Y

E. the number of atoms in container Y is greater than the number of atoms in container X

9. Among the following choices, how tall should a properly designed Torricelli mercury barometer be?

A. 100 in

B. 380 mm

C. 76 mm

D. 400 mm

E. 800 mm

10. When volatile solvents X and Y are mixed in equal proportions, heat is released to the surroundings. If pure X has a higher boiling point than pure Y, which of the following statements is NOT true?

A. The vapor pressure of the mixture is lower than that of pure Y

B. The vapor pressure of the mixture is lower than that of pure X

C. The boiling point of the mixture is lower than that of pure X

D. The boiling point of the mixture is lower than that of pure Y

E. Not enough information is provided

11. How does a real gas deviate from an ideal gas?

    I. Molecules occupy a significant amount of space

    II. Intermolecular forces may exist

    III. Pressure is created from molecular collisions with the walls of the container

A. I only

B. II only

C. I and II only

D. II and III only

E. I, II and III

12. A 2.75 L sample of He gas has a pressure of 0.950 atm. What is the pressure of the gas if the volume is reduced to 0.450 L?

A. 5.80 atm

B. 0.520 atm

C. 0.230 atm

D. 0.960 atm

E. 3.40 atm

13. What is the relationship between the pressure and volume of a fixed amount of gas at constant temperature?

A. directly proportional   **C.** inversely proportional

B. equal   **D.** decreased by a factor of 2   **E.** none of the above

14. The combined gas law can NOT be written as:

A. $V_2 = V_1 \times P_1 / P_2 \times T_2 / T_1$ **C.** $T_2 = T_1 \times P_1 / P_2 \times V_2 / V_1$

B. $P_1 = P_2 \times V_2 / V_1 \times T_1 / T_2$ **D.** $V_1 = V_2 \times P_2 / P_1 \times T_1 / T_2$

        E. none of the above

15. Which singular molecule is most likely to show a dipole-dipole interaction?

A. CH_4 **B.** $H–C{\equiv}C–H$ **C.** SO_2 **D.** CO_2 **E.** CCl_4

16. What happens if the pressure of a gas above a liquid increases, such as by pressing a piston above a liquid?

A. Pressure goes down, and the gas moves out of the solvent

B. Pressure goes down, and the gas goes into the solvent

C. The gas is forced into the solution and the solubility increases

D. The solution is compressed, and the gas is forced out of the solvent

E. The amount of gas in the solution remains constant

17. Which of the following two variables are present in mathematical statements of Avogadro's law?

A. P and V   **B.** n and P   **C.** n and T   **D.** V and T   **E.** n and V

18. Which of the following acids has the lowest boiling point elevation?

Monoprotic Acids	Ka
Acid I	1.4×10^{-8}
Acid II	1.6×10^{-9}
Acid III	3.9×10^{-10}
Acid IV	2.1×10^{-8}

A. I   **C.** III

B. II   **D.** IV   **E.** Requires more information

19. An ideal gas differs from a real gas because the molecules of an ideal gas have:

A. no attraction to each other   **C.** molecular weight equal to zero

B. no kinetic energy   **D.** appreciable volumes

        E. none of the above

20. Which of the following is the definition of standard temperature and pressure?

A. 0 K and 1 atm   C. 298.15 K and 1 atm   E. 273.15 K and 10^5 Pa

B. 298.15 K and 760 mmHg   D. 273 °C and 760 torr

21. At constant volume, as the temperature of a sample of gas is decreased, the gas deviates from ideal behavior. Compared to the pressure predicted by the ideal gas law, actual pressure would be:

A. higher, because of the volume of the gas molecules

B. higher, because of intermolecular attractions between gas molecules

C. lower, because of the volume of the gas molecules

D. lower, because of intermolecular attractions among gas molecules

E. higher, because of intramolecular attractions between gas molecules

22. A flask contains a mixture of O_2, N_2 and CO_2. The pressure exerted by N_2 is 320 torr and by CO_2 is 240 torr. If the total pressure of the gas mixture is 740 torr, what is the percent pressure of O_2?

A. 14%   B. 18%   C. 21%   D. 24%   E. 29%

23. A balloon contains 40 grams of He with a pressure of 1,000 torr. When He is released from the balloon, the new pressure is 900 torr, and the volume is half of the original. If the temperature is the same, how many grams of He remains in the balloon?

A. 18 grams   B. 22 grams   C. 10 grams   D. 40 grams   E. 28 grams

24. Under which conditions does a real gas behave most nearly like an ideal gas?

A. High temperature and high pressure

B. High temperature and low pressure

C. Low temperature and low pressure

D. Low temperature and high pressure

E. If it remains in the gaseous state regardless of temperature or pressure

25. Which of the following compounds has the highest boiling point?

A. CH_3OH C. $CH_3OCH_2CH_2CH_2CH_3$

B. $CH_3CH_2CH_2CH_2CH_2OH$ D. $CH_3CH_2OCH_2CH_2CH_3$

E. $CH_3CH_2CH_2C(OH)HOH$

26. According to the kinetic theory of gases, which of the following is the average kinetic energy of the gas particles directly proportional to?

A. temperature   C. volume

B. molar mass   D. pressure   E. number of moles of gas

27. Under ideal conditions, which of the following gases is least likely to behave as an ideal gas?

    A. CF_4 **B.** CH_3OH **C.** N_2 **D.** O_3 **E.** CO_2

28. Which statement is true regarding gases when compared to liquids?

    A. Gases have lower compressibility and higher density
    B. Gases have lower compressibility and lower density
    C. Gases have higher compressibility and higher density
    D. Gases have higher compressibility and lower density
    E. None of the above

29. When nonvolatile solute molecules are added to a solution, the vapor pressure of the solution:

    A. stays the same
    B. increases
    C. decreases
    D. is directly proportional to the second power of the amount added
    E. is directly proportional to the square root of the amount added

30. Which of the following laws states that the pressure exerted by a mixture of gases is equal to the sum of the individual gas pressures?

    A. Gay-Lussac's law   **C.** Charles's law   **E.** Avogadro's law
    B. Dalton's law   **D.** Boyle's law

31. Which of the following statements is true, if three 2.0 L flasks are filled with H_2, O_2 and He, respectively, at STP?

    A. There are twice as many He atoms as H_2 or O_2 molecules
    B. There are four times as many H_2 or O_2 molecules as He atoms
    C. Each flask contains the same number of atoms
    D. There are twice as many H_2 or O_2 molecules as He atoms
    E. The number of H_2 or O_2 molecules is the same as the number of He atoms

32. Which of the following atoms could interact through a hydrogen bond?

    A. The hydrogen of an amine and the oxygen of an alcohol
    B. The hydrogen on an aromatic ring and the oxygen of carbon dioxide
    C. The oxygen of a ketone and the hydrogen of an aldehyde
    D. The oxygen of methanol and a hydrogen on the methyl carbon of methanol
    E. None of the above

33. Using the following unbalanced chemical reaction, what volume of H_2 gas at 780 mmHg and 23 °C is required to produce 12.5 L of NH_3 gas at the same temperature and pressure?

$$N_2(g) + H_2(g) \rightarrow NH_3(g)$$

A. 21.4 L   **B.** 15.0 L   **C.** 18.8 L   **D.** 13.0 L   **E.** 12.5 L

34. A mixture of gases containing 16 g of O_2, 14 g of N_2 and 88 g of CO_2 is collected above water at a temperature of 23 °C. The total pressure is 1 atm, and the vapor pressure of water is 38 torr. What is the partial pressure exerted by CO_2?

A. 283 torr   **B.** 367 torr   **C.** 481 torr   **D.** 549 torr   **E.** 583 torr

35. Which of the following demonstrate colligative properties?

       I. Freezing point   II. Boiling point   III. Vapor pressure

A. I only   **C.** III only
B. II only   **D.** I and II only   **E.** I, II and III

36. What is the proportionality relationship between the pressure of a gas and its volume?

A. directly   **C.** pressure is raised to the 2nd power
B. inversely   **D.** pressure raised to the $\sqrt{2}$ power   **E.** none of the above

37. Which of the following is NOT a unit used in measuring pressure?

A. kilometers Hg   **C.** atmosphere
B. millimeters Hg   **D.** Pascal   **E.** torr

38. Which of the following compounds has the highest boiling point?

A. CH_4 **B.** $CHCl_3$ **C.** CH_3COOH **D.** NH_3 **E.** CH_2Cl_2

39. A sample of N_2 gas occupies a volume of 190 mL at STP. What volume will it occupy at 660 mmHg and 295 K?

A. 1.15 L   **C.** 0.214 L
B. 0.760 L   **D.** 1.84 L   **E.** 0.197 L

40. A nonvolatile liquid would have:

A. a highly explosive propensity
B. strong attractive forces between molecules
C. weak attractive forces between molecules
D. a high vapor pressure at room temperature
E. weak attractive forces within molecules

41. A closed-end manometer was constructed from a U-shaped glass tube. It was loaded with mercury, so that the closed side was filled to the top, which was 820 mm above the neck, while the open end was 160 mm above the neck. The manometer was taken into a chamber used for training astronauts. What is the highest pressure that can be read with assurance on this manometer?

    A. 66.0 torr   **C.** 220 torr

    B. 660 torr   **D.** 760 torr   **E.** 5.13 torr

42. Vessels X and Y each contain 1.00 L of a gas at STP, but vessel X contains oxygen, while vessel Y contains nitrogen. Assuming the gases behave as ideal, they have the same:

    I. number of molecules   II. density   III. kinetic energy

    A. II only   **B.** III only   **C.** I and III only   **D.** I, II and III   **E.** I only

43. What condition must be satisfied for the noble gas Xe to exist in the liquid phase at 180 K, which is a temperature significantly greater than its normal boiling point?

    A. external pressure > vapor pressure of xenon

    B. external pressure < vapor pressure of xenon

    C. external pressure = partial pressure of water

    D. temperature is increased quickly

    E. temperature is increased slowly

44. Which transformation describes sublimation?

    A. solid → liquid   **C.** liquid → solid

    B. solid → gas   **D.** liquid → gas   **E.** gas → liquid

45. What is the ratio of the diffusion rate of O_2 molecules to the diffusion rate of H_2 molecules, if six moles of O_2 gas and six moles of H_2 gas are placed in a large vessel, and the gases and vessel are at the same temperature?

    A. 4:1   **B.** 1:4   **C.** 12:1   **D.** 1:1   **E.** 2:1

46. How many molecules of neon gas are present in 6 liters at 10 °C and 320 mmHg? (Use the ideal gas constant R = 0.0821 L·atm K^{-1} mol^{-1})

    A. (320 mmHg / 760 atm)·(0.821)·(6 L) / (6 × 10^{23})·(283 K)

    B. (320 mmHg / 760 atm)·(6 L)·(6 × 10^{23}) / (0.0821)·(283 K)

    C. (320 mmHg)·(6 L)·(283 K)·(6 × 10^{23})

    D. (320 mmHg / 760 atm)·(6 L)·(283 K)·(6 × 10^{23}) / (0.821)

    E. (320 mmHg / 283 K)·(6 L)·(6 × 10^{23}) / (0.0821)·(760 atm)

47. Which gas has the greatest density at STP:

A. CO_2 **B.** O_2 **C.** N_2 **D.** NO   **E.** more than one

48. A hydrogen bond is a special type of:

    A. dipole–dipole attraction involving hydrogen bonded to another hydrogen atom
    B. attraction involving any molecules that contain hydrogens
    C. dipole-dipole attraction involving hydrogen bonded to a highly electronegative atom
    D. dipole–dipole attraction involving hydrogen bonded to any other atom
    E. London dispersion force involving a hydrogen bonded to an electropositive atom

49. What is the mole fraction of H_2 in a gaseous mixture that consists of 9.50 g of H_2 and 14.0 g of Ne in a 4.50-liter container maintained at 37.5 °C?

A. 0.13   **B.** 0.43   **C.** 0.67   **D.** 0.87   **E.** 1.2

50. Which of the following is true about Liquid A, if the vapor pressure of Liquid A is greater than that of Liquid B?

    A. Liquid A has a higher heat of fusion
    B. Liquid A has a higher heat of vaporization
    C. Liquid A forms stronger bonds
    D. Liquid A boils at a higher temperature
    E. Liquid A boils at a lower temperature

51. When 25 g of non-ionizable compound X is dissolved in 1 kg of camphor, the freezing point of the camphor falls 2.0 K. What is the approximate molecular weight of compound X? (Use $K_{camphor} = 40$)

    A. 50 g/mol   **B.** 500 g/mol   **C.** 5,000 g/mol   **D.** 5,500 g/mol   **E.** 5,750 g/mol

52. The van der Waals equation $[(P + n^2a/v^2){\cdot}(V - nb) = nRT]$ is used to describe nonideal gases. The terms n^2a/v^2 and nb stand for, respectively:

    A. volume of gas molecules and intermolecular forces
    B. nonrandom movement and intermolecular forces between gas molecules
    C. nonelastic collisions and volume of gas molecules
    D. intermolecular forces and volume of gas molecules
    E. nonrandom movement and volume of gas molecules

53. What are the units of the gas constant R?

    A. atm·K/L·mol   **C.** mol·L/atm·K
    B. atm·K/mol   **D.** mol·K/L·atm   **E.** L·atm/mol·K

54. A sample of a gas occupying a volume of 120.0 mL at STP was placed in a different vessel with a volume of 155.0 mL, in which the pressure was measured at 0.80 atm. What was its temperature?

    A. 9.1 °C   **B.** 43.1 °C   **C.** 4.1 °C   **D.** 93.6 °C   **E.** 108.3 °C

55. Why does a beaker of water begin to boil at 22 °C when it is placed in a closed chamber, and a vacuum pump is used to evacuate the air from the chamber?

    A. The vapor pressure decreases   **C.** The atmospheric pressure decreases
    B. Air is released from the water   **D.** The vapor pressure increases
                                         E. The atmospheric pressure increases

56. A sample of SO_3 gas is decomposed to SO_2 and O_2.

$$2\ SO_3\,(g) \rightarrow 2\ SO_2\,(g) + O_2\,(g)$$

If the total pressure of SO_2 and O_2 is 1,250 torr, what is the partial pressure of O_2 in torr?

    A. 417 torr   **B.** 1,040 torr   **C.** 1,250 torr   **D.** 884 torr   **E.** 12.50 torr

57. According to Charles's law, what happens to gas as temperature increases?

    A. volume decreases   **C.** pressure decreases
    B. volume increases   **D.** pressure increases   **E.** mole fraction increases

58. How does the pressure of a sample of gas change, if the moles of gas remains constant while the volume is halved and the temperature is quadrupled?

    A. decrease by a factor of 8   **C.** decrease by a factor of 4
    B. quadruple   **D.** decrease by a factor of 2   **E.** increase by a factor of 8

59. The average speed at which a methane molecule effuses at 28.5 °C is 631 m/s. The average speed at which a krypton molecule effuses at the same temperature is:

    A. 123 m/s   **B.** 276 m/s   **C.** 312 m/s   **D.** 421 m/s   **E.** 633 m/s

60. A chemical reaction A (s) → B (s) + C (g) occurs when substance A is vigorously heated. The molecular mass of the gaseous product was determined from the following experimental data:

    Mass of A before reaction: 5.2 g

    Mass of A after reaction: 0 g

    Mass of residue B after cooling and weighing when no more gas evolved: 3.8 g

    When all of the gas C evolved, it was collected and stored in a 668.5 mL glass vessel at 32.0 °C, and the gas exerted a pressure of 745.5 torr. Use the ideal gas constant R equals 0.0821 L·atm K^{-1} mol^{-1}

From this data, determine the apparent molecular mass of *C*, assuming it behaves as an ideal gas:

    A. 6.46 g/mol   **B.** 46.3 g/mol   **C.** 53.9 g/mol   **D.** 72.2 g/mol   **E.** 142.7 g/mol

Notes

Chapter 4: Stoichiometry

1. What is the volume of three moles of O_2 at STP?

   A. 11.20 L   **B.** 22.71 L   **C.** 68.13 L   **D.** 32.00 L   **E.** 5.510 L

2. In the following reaction, which of the following describes H_2SO_4?

$$H_2SO_4 + HI \rightarrow I_2 + SO_2 + H_2O$$

   A. reducing agent and is reduced   **C.** oxidizing agent and is reduced
   B. reducing agent and is oxidized   **D.** oxidizing agent and is oxidized
                                         E. neither an oxidizing nor reducing agent

3. Select the balanced chemical equation for the reaction: $C_6H_{14} + O_2 \rightarrow CO_2 + H_2O$

   A. $3\ C_6H_{14} + O_2 \rightarrow 18\ CO_2 + 22\ H_2O$
   B. $2\ C_6H_{14} + 12\ O_2 \rightarrow 12\ CO_2 + 14\ H_2O$
   C. $2\ C_6H_{14} + 19\ O_2 \rightarrow 12\ CO_2 + 14\ H_2O$
   D. $2\ C_6H_{14} + 9\ O_2 \rightarrow 12\ CO_2 + 7\ H_2O$
   E. $C_6H_{14} + O_2 \rightarrow CO_2 + H_2O$

4. An oxidation number is the [ ] that an atom [ ] when the electrons in each bond are assigned to the [ ] electronegative of the two atoms involved in the bond.

   A. number of protons … definitely has … more
   B. charge … definitely has … less
   C. number of electrons … definitely has … more
   D. number of electrons … appears to have … less
   E. charge … appears to have … more

5. What is the empirical formula of acetic acid, CH_3COOH?

   A. CH_3COOH **B.** $C_2H_4O_2$ **C.** CH_2O **D.** CO_2H_2 **E.** CHO

6. In which of the following compounds does Cl have an oxidation number of +7?

   A. $NaClO_2$ **B.** $Al(ClO_4)_3$ **C.** $Ca(ClO_3)_2$ **D.** $LiClO_3$ **E.** none of the above

7. What is the formula mass of a molecule of CO_2?

   A. 44 amu   **C.** 56.5 amu
   B. 52 amu   **D.** 112 amu   **E.** None of the above

8. What is the product of heating cadmium metal and powdered sulfur?

    A. CdS_2 **C.** CdS

    B. Cd_2S_3 **D.** Cd_2S **E.** Cd_3S_2

9. Which substance listed below is the strongest reducing agent, given the following *spontaneous* redox reaction?

$$FeCl_3\ (aq) + NaI\ (aq) \rightarrow I_2\ (s) + FeCl_2\ (aq) + NaCl\ (aq)$$

    A. $FeCl_2$ **B.** I_2 **C.** NaI **D.** $FeCl_3$ **E.** $NaCl$

10. 14.5 moles of N_2 gas is mixed with 34 moles of H_2 gas in the following reaction:

$$N_2\ (g) + 3\ H_2\ (g) \rightarrow 2\ NH_3\ (g)$$

How many moles of N_2 gas remains, if the reaction produces 18 moles of NH_3 gas when performed at 600 K?

    A. 0.6 moles   **C.** 5.5 moles

    B. 1.4 moles   **D.** 7.4 moles   **E.** 9.6 moles

11. Which equation is NOT correctly classified by the type of chemical reaction?

    A. $AgNO_3 + NaCl \rightarrow AgCl + NaNO_3$ (double-replacement/non-redox)
    B. $Cl_2 + F_2 \rightarrow 2\ ClF$ (synthesis/redox)
    C. $H_2O + SO_2 \rightarrow H_2SO_3$ (synthesis/non-redox)
    D. $CaCO_3 \rightarrow CaO + CO_2$ (decomposition/redox)
    E. All are correctly classified

12. How many grams of H_2O can be formed from a reaction between 10 grams of oxygen and 1 gram of hydrogen?

    A. 11 grams of H_2O are formed since mass must be conserved
    B. 10 grams of H_2O are formed since the mass of water produced cannot be greater than the amount of oxygen reacting
    C. 9 grams of H_2O are formed because oxygen and hydrogen react in an 8:1 mass ratio
    D. No H_2O is formed because there is insufficient hydrogen to react with the oxygen
    E. Not enough information is provided

13. How many grams of Ba^{2+} ions are in an aqueous solution of $BaCl_2$ that contains 6.8×10^{22} Cl ions?

    A. 3.2×10^{48} g   **B.** 12 g   **C.** 14.5 g   **D.** 7.8 g   **E.** 9.8 g

14. What is the oxidation number of Br in $NaBrO_3$?

    A. −1   **B.** +1   **C.** +3   **D.** +5   **E.** none of the above

15. When aluminum metal reacts with ferric oxide (Fe_2O_3), a displacement reaction yields two products with one being metallic iron. What is the sum of the coefficients of the products of the balanced reaction?

   A. 4   **B.** 6   **C.** 2   **D.** 5   **E.** 3

16. Which of the following reactions is NOT correctly classified?

   A. $AgNO_3$ (*aq*) + KOH (*aq*) → KNO_3 (*aq*) + AgOH (*s*) : non-redox / double-replacement

   B. 2 H_2O_2 (*s*) → 2 H_2O (*l*) + O_2 (*g*) : non-redox / decomposition

   C. $Pb(NO_3)_2$ (*aq*) + 2 Na (*s*) → Pb (*s*) + 2 $NaNO_3$ (*aq*) : redox / single-replacement

   D. HNO_3 (*aq*) + LiOH (*aq*) → $LiNO_3$ (*aq*) + H_2O (*l*) : non-redox / double-replacement

   E. All are correctly classified

17. Calculate the number of O_2 molecules, if a 15.0 L cylinder was filled with O_2 gas at STP. (Use the conversion factor of 1 mole of $O_2 = 6.02 \times 10^{23}$ O_2 molecules)

   A. 443 molecules

   B. 6.59×10^{24} molecules

   C. 4.03×10^{23} molecules

   D. 2.77×10^{22} molecules

   E. 4,430 molecules

18. Which of the following is a guideline for balancing redox equations by the oxidation number method?

   A. Verify that the total number of atoms and the total ionic charge are the same for reactants and products

   B. In front of the substance reduced, place a coefficient that corresponds to the number of electrons lost by the substance oxidized

   C. In front of the substance oxidized, place a coefficient that corresponds to the number of electrons gained by the substance reduced

   D. Determine the electrons lost by the substance oxidized and gained by the substance reduced

   E. All of the above

19. How many moles of phosphorous trichloride is required to produce 365 grams of HCl when the reaction yields 75%?

     PCl_3 (*g*) + 3 NH_3 (*g*) → $P(NH_2)_3$ + 3 HCl (*g*)

   A. 1 mol   **B.** 2.5 mol   **C.** 3.5 mol   **D.** 4.5 mol   **E.** 5 mol

20. What is the oxidation number of liquid bromine in the elemental state?

   A. 0   **B.** –1   **C.** –2   **D.** –3   **E.** None of the above

21. Campers use propane burners for cooking. What volume of H_2O is produced by the complete combustion, as shown in the unbalanced equation, of 2.6 L of propane (C_3H_8) gas when measured at the same temperature and pressure?

$$C_3H_8\,(g) + O_2\,(g) \rightarrow CO_2\,(g) + H_2O\,(g)$$

A. 0.65 L　　**B.** 10.4 L　　**C.** 5.2 L　　**D.** 2.6 L　　**E.** 26.0 L

22. Which substance is reduced in the following redox reaction?

$$HgCl_2\,(aq) + Sn^{2+}\,(aq) \rightarrow Sn^{4+}\,(aq) + Hg_2Cl_2\,(s) + Cl^-\,(aq)$$

A. Sn^{4+}　　**B.** Hg_2Cl_2　　**C.** $HgCl_2$　　**D.** Sn^{2+}　　**E.** None of the above

23. What is the coefficient (n) of P for the balanced equation: $nP\,(s) + nO_2\,(g) \rightarrow nP_2O_5\,(s)$?

A. 1　　**B.** 2　　**C.** 4　　**D.** 5　　**E.** none of the above

24. How many formula units of lithium iodide (LiI) have a mass equal to 6.45 g? (Use the molecular mass of LiI = 133.85 g)

A. 3.45×10^{23} formula units
B. 6.43×10^{23} formula units

C. 1.65×10^{24} formula units
D. 7.74×10^{25} formula units
E. 2.90×10^{22} formula units

25. What is/are the product(s) of the reaction of N_2 and O_2 gases in a combustion engine?

I. NO　　　　II. NO_2　　　　III. N_2O

A. I only
B. II only

C. III only
D. I and II only　　**E.** I, II and III

26. Which substance is the weakest reducing agent given the spontaneous redox reaction?

$$Mg\,(s) + Sn^{2+}\,(aq) \rightarrow Mg^{2+}\,(aq) + Sn\,(s)$$

A. Sn　　**B.** Mg^{2+}　　**C.** Sn^{2+} **D.** Mg　　**E.** None of the above

27. Which substance contains the greatest number of moles in a 10 g sample?

A. SiO_2　　**B.** SO_2　　**C.** CBr_4　　**D.** CO_2　　**E.** CH_4

28. Which chemistry law is illustrated when ethyl alcohol always contains 52% carbon, 13% hydrogen, and 35% oxygen by mass?

A. law of constant composition
B. law of constant percentages

C. law of multiple proportions
D. law of conservation of mass
E. none of the above

29. Which could NOT be true for the following reaction: $N_2(g) + 3 H_2(g) \rightarrow 2 NH_3(g)$?

   A. 25 grams of N_2 gas reacts with 75 grams of H_2 gas to form 50 grams of NH_3 gas

   B. 28 grams of N_2 gas reacts with 6 grams of H_2 gas to form 34 grams of NH_3 gas

   C. 15 moles of N_2 gas reacts with 45 moles of H_2 gas to form 30 moles of NH_3 gas

   D. 5 molecules of N_2 gas reacts with 15 molecules of H_2 gas to form 10 molecules of NH_3 gas

   E. None of the above

30. From the following reaction, if 0.2 moles of Al is allowed to react with 0.4 moles of Fe_2O_3, how many grams of aluminum oxide is produced?

$$2 Al + Fe_2O_3 \rightarrow 2 Fe + Al_2O_3$$

   A. 2.8 g   **B.** 5.1 g   **C.** 10.2 g   **D.** 14.2 g   **E.** 18.6 g

31. In all of the following compounds, the oxidation number of hydrogen is +1, EXCEPT:

   A. NH_3 **B.** $HClO_2$ **C.** H_2SO_4 **D.** NaH   **E.** none of the above

32. Which equation is NOT correctly classified by the type of chemical reaction?

   A. $PbO + C \rightarrow Pb + CO$: single-replacement/non-redox

   B. $2 Na + 2 HCl \rightarrow 2 NaCl + H_2$: single-replacement/redox

   C. $NaHCO_3 + HCl \rightarrow NaCl + H_2O + CO_2$: double-replacement/non-redox

   D. $2 Na + H_2 \rightarrow 2 NaH$: synthesis/redox

   E. All are correctly classified

33. A latex balloon has a volume of 500 mL when filled with gas at a pressure of 780 torr, and a temperature of 320 K. How many moles of gas does the balloon contain? (Use the ideal gas constant $R = 0.08206$ L·atm K^{-1} mol^{-1})

   A. 0.0195   **B.** 0.822   **C.** 3.156   **D.** 18.87   **E.** 1.282

34. Which of the following is a method for balancing a redox equation in acidic solution by the half-reaction method?

   A. Multiply each half-reaction by a whole number, so that the number of electrons lost by the substance oxidized is equal to the electrons gained by the substance reduced

   B. Add the two half-reactions together and cancel identical species from each side of the equation

   C. Write a half-reaction for the substance oxidized and the substance reduced

   D. Balance the atoms in each half-reaction; balance oxygen with water and hydrogen with H^+

   E. All of the above

35. What is the formula mass of a molecule of $C_6H_{12}O_6$?

　A. 148 amu　　**B.** 27 amu　　**C.** 91 amu　　**D.** 180 amu　　**E.** None of the above

36. Is it possible to have a macroscopic sample of oxygen that has a mass of 12 atomic mass units?

　A. No, because oxygen is a gas at room temperature
　B. Yes, because it would have the same density as nitrogen
　C. No, because this is less than a macroscopic quantity
　D. Yes, but it would need to be made of isotopes of oxygen atoms
　E. No, because this is less than the mass of a single oxygen atom

37. Which element is reduced in the following redox reaction?

$$BaSO_4 + 4\,C \rightarrow BaS + 4\,CO$$

　A. O in CO　　　　　　　**C.** S in BaS
　B. Ba in BaS　　　　　　**D.** C in CO　　　　　**E.** S in $BaSO_4$

38. Ethanol (C_2H_5OH) is blended with gasoline as a fuel additive. If the combustion of ethanol produces carbon dioxide and water, what is the coefficient of oxygen in the balanced equation?

Spark

$$\_\,C_2H_5OH\ (g) + \_\,O_2\,(g) \rightarrow \_\,CO_2\,(g) + \_\,H_2O\,(g)$$

　A. 1　　　　**B.** 2　　　　**C.** 3　　　　**D.** 6　　　　**E.** None of the above

39. Upon combustion analysis, a 6.84 g sample of a hydrocarbon yielded 8.98 grams of carbon dioxide. The percent, by mass, of carbon in the hydrocarbon is:

　A. 18.6%　　　　　　　**C.** 35.8%
　B. 23.7%　　　　　　　**D.** 11.4%　　　　　　**E.** 52.8%

40. Select the balanced chemical equation:

　A. $2\,C_2H_5OH + 2\,Na_2Cr_2O_7 + 8\,H_2SO_4 \rightarrow 2\,HC_2H_3O_2 + 2\,Cr_2(SO_4)_3 + 4\,Na_2SO_4 + 11\,H_2O$
　B. $2\,C_2H_5OH + Na_2Cr_2O_7 + 8\,H_2SO_4 \rightarrow 3\,HC_2H_3O_2 + 2\,Cr_2(SO_4)_3 + 2\,Na_2SO_4 + 11\,H_2O$
　C. $C_2H_5OH + 2\,Na_2Cr_2O_7 + 8\,H_2SO_4 \rightarrow HC_2H_3O_2 + 2\,Cr_2(SO_4)_3 + 2\,Na_2SO_4 + 11\,H_2O$
　D. $C_2H_5OH + Na_2Cr_2O_7 + 2\,H_2SO_4 \rightarrow HC_2H_3O_2 + Cr_2(SO_4)_3 + 2\,Na_2SO_4 + 11\,H_2O$
　E. $3\,C_2H_5OH + 2\,Na_2Cr_2O_7 + 8\,H_2SO_4 \rightarrow 3\,HC_2H_3O_2 + 2\,Cr_2(SO_4)_3 + 2\,Na_2SO_4 + 11\,H_2O$

41. Assuming STP, if 49 g of H_2SO_4 are produced in the following reaction, what volume of O_2 must be used in the reaction?

$$4\,RuS\ (s) + O_2 + H_2O \rightarrow 2\,Ru_2O_3\ (s) + H_2SO_4$$

　A. 20.6 liters　　　　　**C.** 28.3 liters
　B. 31.2 liters　　　　　**D.** 29.1 liters　　　**E.** 25.2 liters

42. From the following reaction, if 0.20 mole of Al is allowed to react with 0.40 mole of Fe_2O_3, how many moles of iron are produced?

$$2\ Al + Fe_2O_3 \rightarrow 2\ Fe + Al_2O_3$$

A. 0.05 mole

B. 0.075 mole

C. 0.20 mole

D. 0.10 mole

E. 0.25 mole

43. What are the oxidation numbers for the elements in Na_2CrO_4?

A. +2 for Na, +5 for Cr and −6 for O

B. +2 for Na, +3 for Cr and −2 for O

C. +1 for Na, +4 for Cr and −6 for O

D. +1 for Na, +6 for Cr and −2 for O

E. +1 for Na, +5 for Cr and −2 for O

44. What is the oxidation state of sulfur in sulfuric acid?

A. +8　　　**B.** +6　　　**C.** −2　　　**D.** −6　　　**E.** +4

45. Which substance is oxidized in the following redox reaction?

$$HgCl_2\,(aq) + Sn^{2+}\,(aq) \rightarrow Sn^{4+}\,(aq) + Hg_2Cl_2\,(s) + Cl^-\,(aq)$$

A. Hg_2Cl_2

B. Sn^{4+}

C. Sn^{2+}

D. $HgCl_2$

E. None of the above

46. Which of the following represents 1 mol of phosphine gas (PH_3)?

　　I. 22.71 L phosphine gas at STP

　　II. 34.00 g phosphine gas

　　III. 6.02×10^{23} phosphine molecules

A. I only

B. II only

C. III only

D. I and II only

E. II and III only

47. Carbon tetrachloride (CCl_4) is a potent hepatotoxin (toxic to the liver) commonly used in the past in fire extinguishers and as a refrigerant. What is the percent by mass of Cl in carbon tetrachloride?

A. 25%　　　**B.** 66%　　　**C.** 78%　　　**D.** 92%　　　**E.** 33%

48. For a redox reaction to be balanced, which of the following is true?

　　I. Total ionic charge of reactants must equal total ionic charge of products

　　II. Atoms of each reactant must equal atoms of the product

　　III. Electron gain must equal electron loss

A. I only

B. II only

C. I and II only

D. I and III only

E. I, II and III

49. The mass percent of a compound is approximately 71.8% Cl, 24.2% C, and 4.0% H. If the molecular weight of the compound is 99 g/mol, what is the molecular formula of the compound?

A. $Cl_2C_3H_6$

B. $Cl_2C_2H_4$

C. $ClCH_3$

D. ClC_2H_2

E. Cl_3CH_3

50. In the early 1980s, benzene that had been used as a solvent for waxes and oils was listed as a carcinogen by the EPA. What is the molecular formula of benzene, if the empirical formula is C_1H_1 and the approximate molar mass is 78 g/mol?

A. CH_{12}　　　B. $C_{12}H_{12}$　　　C. CH　　　D. CH_6　　　E. C_6H_6

51. Which reaction represents the balanced reaction for the combustion of ethanol?

A. $4 C_2H_5OH + 13 O_2 \rightarrow 8 CO_2 + 10 H_2$

B. $C_2H_5OH + 3 O_2 \rightarrow 2 CO_2 + 3 H_2O$

C. $C_2H_5OH + 2 O_2 \rightarrow 2 CO_2 + 2 H_2O$

D. $C_2H_5OH + O_2 \rightarrow CO_2 + H_2O$

E. $C_2H_5OH + ½ O_2 \rightarrow 2 CO_2 + 3 H_2O$

52. What is the coefficient for O_2 when the following equation is balanced with the lowest whole number coefficients?

$\underline{1}\ C_3H_7OH + \underline{\frac{9}{2}}\ O_2 \rightarrow \underline{3}\ CO_2 + \underline{4}\ H_2O$

A. 3　　　B. 6　　　C. 9　　　D. 13/2　　　E. 12

53. In the following reaction performed at 500 K, 18.0 moles of N_2 gas is mixed with 24.0 moles of H_2 gas. What is the percent yield of NH_3, if the reaction produces 13.5 moles of NH_3?

$N_2 (g) + 3 H_2 (g) \rightarrow 2 NH_3 (g)$

A. 16%　　　B. 66%　　　C. 72%　　　D. 84%　　　E. 100%

54. How many grams of H_2O can be produced from the reaction of 25.0 grams of H_2 and 225 grams of O_2?　　2 H_2 + O_2 → 2 H_2O

A. 266 grams　　　B. 223 grams　　　C. 184 grams　　　D. 27 grams　　　E. 2.5 grams

55. What is the oxidation number of Cl in $LiClO_2$?

A. −1　　　B. +1　　　C. +3　　　D. +5　　　E. None of the above

$4 MnO_4^- + 4 C_3H_8O \rightarrow 4 Mn^{2+} + 4 C_3H_6O_2 + 8 H^+$

56. In acidic conditions, what is the sum of the coefficients in the products of the balanced reaction?

$MnO_4^- + C_3H_7OH \rightarrow Mn^{2+} + C_2H_5COOH$

A. 12　　　B. 16　　　C. 18　　　D. 20　　　E. 24

$MnO_4^- + 6 C_3H_8O \rightarrow Mn^{2+} + 8 C_3H_6O_2$

57. Which reaction is NOT correctly classified?

    A. PbO (*s*) + C (*s*) → Pb (*s*) + CO (*g*) : (double-replacement)

    B. CaO (*s*) + H_2O (*l*) → $Ca(OH)_2$ (*aq*) : (synthesis)

    C. $Pb(NO_3)_2$ (*aq*) + 2 $LiCl$ (*aq*) → 2 $LiNO_3$ (*aq*) + $PbCl_2$ (*s*) : (double-replacement)

    D. Mg (*s*) + 2 HCl (*aq*) → $MgCl_2$ (*aq*) + H_2 (*g*) : (single-replacement)

    E. All are classified correctly

58. The reactants for this chemical reaction are:

$$C_6H_{12}O_6 + 6\ H_2O + 6\ O_2 \rightarrow 6\ CO_2 + 12\ H_2O$$

    A. $C_6H_{12}O_6$, H_2O, O_2 and CO_2 **C.** $C_6H_{12}O_6$

    B. $C_6H_{12}O_6$ and H_2O **D.** $C_6H_{12}O_6$ and CO_2

                                      E. $C_6H_{12}O_6$, H_2O and O_2

59. What is the total charge of all the electrons in 4 grams of He? (Use Faraday constant F − 96,500 C/mol)

    A. 48,250 C   **C.** 193,000 C

    B. 96,500 C   **D.** 386,000 C   **E.** Cannot be determined

60. What is the oxidation number of iron in the compound $FeBr_3$?

    A. −2   **B.** +1   **C.** +2   **D.** +3   **E.** −1

Please, leave your Customer Review on Amazon

Notes

Chapter 5: Kinetics and Equilibrium

1. What is the general equilibrium constant (K_{eq}) expression for the following reversible reaction?

$$2 A + 3 B \leftrightarrow C$$

A. $K_{eq} = [C] / [A]^2 \cdot [B]^3$

B. $K_{eq} = [C] / [A] \cdot [B]$

C. $K_{eq} = [A] \cdot [B] / [C]$

D. $K_{eq} = [A]^2 \cdot [B]^3 / [C]$

E. none of the above

2. What are gases A and B likely to be, if in a mixture of these two gases gas A has twice the average velocity of gas B?

A. Ar and Kr   **B.** N and Fe   **C.** Ne and Ar   **D.** Mg and K   **E.** B and Ne

3. For a hypothetical reaction, A + B → C, predict which reaction occurs at the slowest rate from the following reaction conditions.

Reaction	Activation energy	Temperature
1	103 kJ/mol	15 °C
2	46 kJ/mol	22 °C
3	103 kJ/mol	24 °C
4	46 kJ/mol	30 °C

A. 1   **B.** 2   **C.** 3   **D.** 4   **E.** requires more information

4. From the data below, what is the order of the reaction with respect to reactant A?

Determining Rate Law from Experimental Data

A + B → Products

Exp.	Initial [A]	Initial [B]	Initial Rate M/s
1	0.015	0.022	0.125
2	0.030	0.044	0.500
3	0.060	0.044	0.500
4	0.060	0.066	1.125
5	0.085	0.088	?

A. Zero   **B.** First   **C.** Second   **D.** Third   **E.** Fourth

5. For the combustion of ethanol (C_2H_6O) to form carbon dioxide and water, what is the rate at which carbon dioxide is produced, if the ethanol is consumed at a rate of 4.0 M s^{-1}?

A. 1.5 M s^{-1}

B. 12.0 M s^{-1}

C. 8.0 M s^{-1}

D. 9.0 M s^{-1}

E. 10.0 M s^{-1}

6. The position of the equilibrium for a system where $K_{eq} = 6.3 \times 10^{-14}$ can be described as being favored for [   ] and the concentration of products is relatively [   ].

A. the left; large

B. the left; small

C. the right; large

D. the right; small

E. neither direction; large

Questions **7** through **11** are based on the following:

Energy profiles for four reactions (with the same scale).

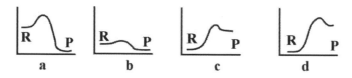

R = reactants   P = products

7. Which reaction requires the most energy?

A. a   B. b   C. c   D. d   E. None of the above

8. Which reaction has the highest activation energy?

A. a   B. b   C. c   D. d   E. c and d

9. Which reaction has the lowest activation energy?

A. a   B. b   C. c   D. d   E. a and b

10. Which reaction proceeds the slowest?

A. a   B. b   C. c   D. d   E. c and d

11. If the graphs are for the same reaction, which most likely has a catalyst?

A. a   B. b   C. c   D. d   E. All have a catalyst

12. What is an explanation for the observation that the reaction stops before all reactants are converted to products in the following reaction?

$$NH_3\,(aq) + HC_2H_3O_2\,(aq) \rightarrow NH_4^+\,(aq) + C_2H_3O_2^-\,(aq)$$

A. The catalyst is depleted

B. The reverse rate increases, while the forward rate decreases until they are equal

C. As [products] increases, the acetic acid begins to dissociate, stopping the reaction

D. As [reactants] decreases, NH_3 and $HC_2H_3O_2$ molecules stop colliding

E. As [products] increases, NH_3 and $HC_2H_3O_2$ molecules stop colliding

13. The system, $H_2(g) + X_2(g) \leftrightarrow 2\,HX(g)$ has a value of 24.4 for K_c. A catalyst was introduced into a reaction within a 4.0-liters reactor containing 0.20 moles of H_2, 0.20 moles of X_2 and 0.800 moles of HX. The reaction proceeds in which direction?

A. to the right, $Q > K_c$

B. to the left, $Q > K_c$

C. to the right, $Q < K_c$

D. to the left, $Q < K_c$

E. requires more information

14. Which of the following concentrations of CH_2Cl_2 should be used in the rate law for Step 2, if CH_2Cl_2 is a product of the fast (first) step and a reactant of the slow (second) step?

A. $[CH_2Cl_2]$ at equilibrium

B. $[CH_2Cl_2]$ in Step 2 cannot be predicted because Step 1 is the fast step

C. Zero moles per liter

D. $[CH_2Cl_2]$ after Step 1 is completed

E. None of the above

15. What is the rate law when rates were measured at different concentrations for the dissociation of hydrogen gas: $H_2(g) \rightarrow 2\,H(g)$?

$[H_2]$	Rate M/s s^{-1}
1.0	1.3×10^5
1.5	2.6×10^5
2.0	5.2×10^5

A. rate $= k^2[H] / [H_2]$

B. rate $= k[H]^2 / [H_2]$

C. rate $= k[H_2]^2$

D. rate $= k[H_2] / [H]^2$

E. requires more information

16. Which change to this reaction system causes the equilibrium to shift to the right?

$$N_2(g) + 3\,H_2(g) \leftrightarrow 2\,NH_3(g) + heat$$

A. Heating the system

B. Removal of $H_2(g)$

C. Addition of $NH_3(g)$

D. Lowering the temperature

E. Addition of a catalyst

17. Which statement is NOT correct for $aA + bB \rightarrow dD + eE$ whereby rate $= k[A]^q[B]^r$?

A. The overall order of the reaction is $q + r$

B. The exponents q and r are equal to the coefficients a and b, respectively

C. The exponents q and r must be determined experimentally

D. The exponents q and r are often integers

E. The symbol k represents the rate constant

Questions **18-21** are based on the following graph and net reaction:

The reaction proceeds in two consecutive steps.

$$XY + Z \leftrightarrow XYZ \leftrightarrow X + YZ$$

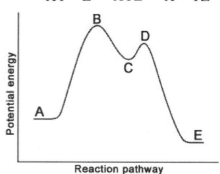

18. Where is the activated complex for this reaction?

A. A

B. A and C

C. C

D. E

E. B and D

19. The activation energy of the slow step for the forward reaction is given by:

A. A → B

B. A → C

C. B → C

D. C → E

E. A → E

20. The activation energy of the slow step for the reverse reaction is given by:

A. C → A

B. E → C

C. C → B

D. E → D

E. E → A

21. The change in energy (ΔE) of the overall reaction is given by the difference between:

A. A and B

B. A and E

C. A and C

D. B and D

E. B and C

22. A chemical system is considered to have reached dynamic equilibrium when the:

A. activation energy of the forward reaction equals the activation energy of the reverse reaction

B. rate of production of each of the products equals the rate of their consumption by the reverse reaction

C. frequency of collisions between the reactant molecules equals the frequency of collisions between the product molecules

D. sum of the concentrations of each of the reactant species equals the sum of the concentrations of each of the product species

E. none of the above

---

23. Chemical equilibrium is reached in a system when:

  A. complete conversion of reactants to products has occurred
  B. product molecules begin reacting with each other
  C. reactant concentrations steadily decrease
  D. reactant concentrations steadily increase
  E. product and reactant concentrations remain constant

24. At a given temperature, $K = 46.0$ for the reaction:

$$4 \, HCl \, (g) + O_2 \, (g) \leftrightarrow 2 \, H_2O \, (g) + 2 \, Cl_2 \, (g)$$

At equilibrium, $[HCl] = 0.150$, $[O_2] = 0.395$ and $[H_2O] = 0.625$. What is the concentration of Cl_2 at equilibrium?

  A. 0.153 M   **B.** 0.444 M   **C.** 1.14 M   **D.** 0.00547 M   **E.** 2.64 M

25. Hydrogen gas reacts with iron (III) oxide to form iron metal (which produces steel), as shown in the reaction below. Which statement is NOT correct concerning the equilibrium system?

$$Fe_2O_3 \, (s) + 3 \, H_2 \, (g) + heat \leftrightarrow 2 \, Fe \, (s) + 3 \, H_2O \, (g)$$

  A. Continually removing water from the reaction chamber increases the yield of iron
  B. Decreasing the volume of hydrogen gas reduces the yield of iron
  C. Lowering the reaction temperature increases the concentration of hydrogen gas
  D. Increasing the pressure on the reaction chamber increases the formation of products
  E. Decreasing the reaction temperature reduces the formation of iron

26. Carbonic acid equilibrium in blood:

$$CO_2 \, (g) + H_2O \, (l) \leftrightarrow H_2CO_3 \, (aq) \leftrightarrow H^+ \, (aq) + HCO_3^- \, (aq)$$

If a person hyperventilates, the rapid breathing expels carbon dioxide gas. Which of the following decreases when a person hyperventilates?

  I. $[HCO_3^-]$ II. $[H^+]$ III. $[H_2CO_3]$

  A. I only   **B.** II only   **C.** III only   **D.** I and II only   **E.** I, II and III

27. What is the overall order of the reaction if the units of the rate constant for a particular reaction are min^{-1}?

  A. Zero   **B.** First   **C.** Second   **D.** Third   **E.** Fourth

28. Predict which reaction occurs at a faster rate for a hypothetical reaction $X + Y \rightarrow W + Z$.

Reaction	Activation energy	Temperature
1	low	low
2	low	high
3	high	high
4	high	low

A. 1   **B.** 2   **C.** 3   **D.** 4   **E.** 1 and 4

29. For the reaction, $2\,XO + O_2 \rightarrow 2\,XO_2$, data obtained from measurement of the initial rate of reaction at varying concentrations are:

Experiment	[XO]	[O₂]	Rate (mmol L⁻¹ s⁻¹)
1	0.010	0.010	2.5
2	0.010	0.020	5.0
3	0.030	0.020	45.0

What is the expression for the rate law?

A. rate = $k[XO]\cdot[O_2]$ **C.** rate = $k[XO]^2\cdot[O_2]$

B. rate = $k[XO]^2\cdot[O_2]^2$ **D.** rate = $k[XO]\cdot[O_2]^2$ **E.** rate = $k[XO]^2/[O_2]^2$

30. If a reaction does not occur extensively and gives a low concentration of products at equilibrium, which of the following is true?

A. The rate of the forward reaction is greater than the reverse reaction

B. The rate of the reverse reaction is greater than the forward reaction

C. The equilibrium constant is greater than one; that is, K_{eq} is larger than 1

D. The equilibrium constant is less than one; that is, K_{eq} is smaller than 1

E. The equilibrium constant equals 1

31. Which of the following changes most likely decreases the rate of a reaction?

A. Increasing the reaction temperature

B. Increasing the concentration of a reactant

C. Increasing the activation energy for the reaction

D. Decreasing the activation energy for the reaction

E. Increasing the reaction pressure

32. Which factors would increase the rate of a reversible chemical reaction?

I. Increasing the temperature of the reaction
II. Removing products as they form
III. Adding a catalyst to the reaction vessel

A. I only   **B.** II only   **C.** I and II only   **D.** I and III only   **E.** I, II and III

33. What is the ionization equilibrium constant (K_i) expression for the following weak acid?

$H_2S\ (aq) \leftrightarrow H^+\ (aq) + HS^-\ (aq)$

A. $K_i = [H^+]^2 \cdot [S^{2-}] / [H_2S]$
B. $K_i = [H_2S] / [H^+] \cdot [HS^-]$
C. $K_i = [H^+] \cdot [HS^-] / [H_2S]$
D. $K_i = [H^+]^2 \cdot [HS^-] / [H_2S]$
E. $K_i = [H_2S] / [H^+]^2 \cdot [HS^-]$

34. Reaction rates are determined by all of the following factors, EXCEPT:

A. orientation of collisions between molecules
B. spontaneity of the reaction
C. force of collisions between molecules
D. number of collisions between molecules
E. the activation energy of the reaction

35. Coal burning plants release sulfur dioxide, into the atmosphere, while nitrogen monoxide is released into the atmosphere via industrial processes and from combustion engines. Sulfur dioxide can also be produced in the atmosphere by the following equilibrium reaction:

$SO_3\ (g) + NO\ (g) + heat \leftrightarrow SO_2\ (g) + NO_2\ (g)$

Which of the following does NOT shift the equilibrium to the right?

A. [NO_2] decrease
B. [NO] increase
C. Decrease the reaction chamber volume
D. Temperature increase
E. All of the above shift the equilibrium to the right

36. At equilibrium, increasing the temperature of an exothermic reaction likely:

A. increases the heat of reaction
B. decreases the heat of reaction
C. increases the forward reaction
D. decreases the forward reaction
E. increases the heat of reaction and increases the forward reaction

37. Which shifts the equilibrium to the left for the reversible reaction in an aqueous solution?

$HC_2H_3O_2\ (aq) \leftrightarrow H^+\ (aq) + C_2H_3O_2^-\ (aq)$

I. increase pH
II. increase [$HC_2H_3O_2$]
III. add solid $KC_2H_3O_2$

A. I only
B. I and III only
C. II only
D. II and III only
E. III only

38. Which of the following statements is true concerning the equilibrium system, whereby S combines with H_2 to form hydrogen sulfide, toxic gas from the decay of organic material? (Use the equilibrium constant, $K_{eq} = 2.8 \times 10^{-21}$)

$$S\ (g) + H_2\ (g) \leftrightarrow H_2S\ (g)$$

A. Almost all the starting molecules are converted to product
B. Decreasing $[H_2S]$ shifts the equilibrium to the left
C. Decreasing $[H_2]$ shifts the equilibrium to the right
D. Increasing the volume of the sealed reaction container shifts the equilibrium to the right
E. Very little hydrogen sulfide gas is present in the equilibrium

39. Which statement is NOT true regarding an equilibrium constant for a particular reaction?

A. It does not change as the product is removed
B. It does not change as an additional quantity of a reactant is added
C. It changes when a catalyst is added
D. It changes as the temperature increases
E. All are true statements

Questions **40** through **42** refer to the rate data
for the conversion of reactants W, X, and Y to product Z.

Trial Number	Concentration (moles/L)			Rate of Formation of Z (moles/l·s)
	W	X	Y	
1	0.01	0.05	0.04	0.04
2	0.015	0.07	0.06	0.08
3	0.01	0.15	0.04	0.36
4	0.03	0.07	0.06	0.08
5	0.01	0.05	0.16	0.08

40. From the above data, what is the overall order of the reaction?

A. 3½   B. 4   C. 3   D. 2   E. 2½

41. From the above data, the order with respect to W suggests that the rate of formation of Z is:

A. dependent on [W]   C. semi-dependent on [W]
B. independent of [W]   D. unable to be determined
                                        E. inversely proportional to [W]

42. From the above data, the magnitude of k for trial 1 is:

A. 20   B. 40   C. 60   D. 80   E. 90

43. For a collision between molecules to result in a reaction, the molecules must possess both a favorable orientation relative to each other and:

A. be in the gaseous state

B. have a certain minimum energy

C. adhere for at least 2 nanoseconds

D. exchange electrons

E. be in the liquid state

44. Find the reaction rate for $A + B \rightarrow C$:

Trial	$[A]_{t=0}$	$[B]_{t=0}$	Initial rate (M/s)
1	0.05 M	1.0 M	1.0×10^{-3}
2	0.05 M	4.0 M	16.0×10^{-3}
3	0.15 M	1.0 M	3.0×10^{-3}

A. rate $= k[A]^2 \cdot [B]^2$

B. rate $= k[A] \cdot [B]^2$

C. rate $= k[A]^2 \cdot [B]$

D. rate $= k[A] \cdot [B]$

E. rate $= k[A]^2 \cdot [B]^3$

45. Why does a glowing splint of wood burn only slowly in air, but rapidly in a burst of flames when placed in pure oxygen?

A. A glowing wood splint is extinguished within pure oxygen because oxygen inhibits the smoke

B. Pure oxygen is able to absorb carbon dioxide at a faster rate

C. Oxygen is a flammable gas

D. There is an increased number of collisions between the wood and oxygen molecules

E. There is a decreased number of collisions between the wood and oxygen

46. Which of the changes does not affect the equilibrium for the reversible reaction in an aqueous solution?

$$HC_2H_3O_2\,(aq) \leftrightarrow H^+\,(aq) + C_2H_3O_2^-\,(aq)$$

A. Adding solid $NaC_2H_3O_2$

B. Adding solid $NaNO_3$

C. Increasing $[HC_2H_3O_2]$

D. Increasing $[H^+]$

E. Adding solid NaOH

47. Consider the following reaction: $H_2\,(g) + I_2\,(g) \rightarrow 2\,HI\,(g)$

At 160 K, this reaction has an equilibrium constant of 35. If at 160 K, the concentration of hydrogen gas is 0.4 M, iodine gas is 0.6 M, and hydrogen iodide gas is 3 M:

A. system is at equilibrium

B. [iodine] decreases

C. [hydrogen iodide] increases

D. [hydrogen iodide] decreases

E. [hydrogen] decreases

48. For the following reaction where $\Delta H < 0$, which factor decreases the magnitude of the equilibrium constant K?

$$CO\ (g) + 2\ H_2O\ (g) \leftrightarrow CH_3OH\ (g)$$

A. Decreasing the temperature of this system
B. Decreasing volume
C. Decreasing the pressure of this system
D. All of the above
E. None of the above

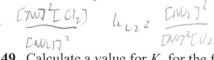

49. Calculate a value for K_c for the following reaction:

$$NOCl\ (g) + \tfrac{1}{2}\ O_2\ (g) \leftrightarrow NO_2\ (g) + \tfrac{1}{2}\ Cl_2\ (g)$$

Use the data:

$2\ NO\ (g) + Cl_2\ (g) \leftrightarrow 2\ NOCl\ (g)$ $\qquad K_c = 3.20 \times 10^{-3}$

$2\ NO_2\ (g) \leftrightarrow 2\ NO\ (g) + O_2\ (g)$ $\qquad K_c = 15.5$

A. 4.49
B. 0.343
C. 4.32×10^{-4}
D. 1.33×10^{-5}
E. 18.4

50. Assuming vessel a, b and c are drawn to relative proportions, which of the following reactions proceeds the fastest? (Assume equal temperatures)

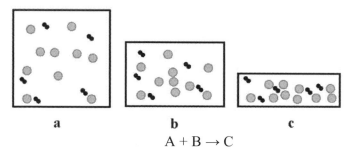

$$A + B \rightarrow C$$

A. a
B. b
C. c
D. All proceed at the same rate
E. Not enough information given

51. With respect to A, what is the order of the reaction, if the rate law $= k[A]^3[B]^6$?

A. 2 **B.** 3 **C.** 4 **D.** 5 **E.** 6

52. Nitrogen monoxide reacts with bromine at elevated temperatures according to the equation:

$$2\ NO\ (g) + Br_2\ (g) \rightarrow 2\ NOBr\ (g)$$

What is the rate of consumption of $Br_2\ (g)$ if, in a certain reaction mixture, the rate of formation of $NOBr\ (g)$ was 4.50×10^{-4} mol L^{-1} s^{-1}?

A. 3.12×10^{-4} mol L^{-1} s^{-1}
B. 8.00×10^{-4} mol L^{-1} s^{-1}
C. 2.25×10^{-4} mol L^{-1} s^{-1}
D. 4.50×10^{-4} mol L^{-1} s^{-1}
E. 4.00×10^{-3} mol L^{-1} s^{-1}

53. What is the effect on the equilibrium after adding H_2O to the equilibrium mixture if CO_2 and H_2 react until equilibrium is established?

$$CO_2\ (g) + H_2\ (g) \leftrightarrow H_2O\ (g) + CO\ (g)$$

A. $[H_2]$ decreases and $[H_2O]$ increases
B. $[CO]$ and $[CO_2]$ increase
C. $[H_2]$ decreases and $[CO_2]$ increases
D. Equilibrium shifts to the left
E. Equilibrium shifts to the right

54. For a reaction that has an equilibrium constant of 4.3×10^{-17} at 25 °C, the relative position of equilibrium is described as:

A. equal amounts of reactants and products
B. significant amounts of both reactants and products
C. mostly products
D. mostly reactants
E. amount of product is slightly greater than reactants

55. What is the equilibrium constant K_c value if, at equilibrium, the concentrations of $[NH_3] =$ 0.40 M, $[H_2] = 0.12$ M and $[N_2] = 0.040$ M?

$$2\ NH_3\ (g) \leftrightarrow N_2\ (g) + 3\ H_2\ (g)$$

A. 6.3×10^{12} **C.** 4.3×10^{-4}
B. 7.1×10^{-7} **D.** 3.9×10^{-3} **E.** 8.5×10^{-9}

56. For the following reaction with $\Delta H < 0$, which factor increases the equilibrium yield for methanol?

$$CO\ (g) + 2\ H_2O\ (g) \leftrightarrow CH_3OH\ (g)$$

  I. Decreasing the volume
  II. Decreasing the pressure
  III. Lowering the temperature of the system

A. I only   **B.** II only   **C.** I and II only   **D.** I and III only   **E.** I, II and III

57. If there is too much chlorine in the water, swimmers complain that their eyes burn. Consider the equilibrium found in swimming pools. Predict which increases the chlorine concentration.

$$Cl_2\ (g) + H_2O\ (l) \leftrightarrow HClO\ (aq) \leftrightarrow H^+\ (aq) + ClO^-\ (aq)$$

A. Decreasing the pH   **C.** Adding hypochlorous acid, $HClO$ (aq)
B. Adding hydrochloric acid, HCl (aq)   **D.** Adding sodium hypochlorite, $NaClO$
                                       E. All of the above

58. Which of the following increases the amount of product formed from a reaction?

      I. Using a UV light catalyst
      II. Adding an acid catalyst
      III. Adding a metal catalyst

A. I only   **B.** II only   **C.** III only   **D.** I and II only   **E.** None of the above

59. A mixture of 1.40 moles of A and 2.30 moles of B reacted. At equilibrium, 0.90 moles of A are present. How many moles of C is present at equilibrium?

$$3 \text{ A } (g) + 2 \text{ B } (g) \rightarrow 4 \text{ C } (g)$$

A. 2.7 moles   **B.** 1.3 moles   **C.** 0.09 moles   **D.** 1.8 moles   **E.** 0.67 moles

60. What is the equilibrium constant K_c for the following reaction?

$$PCl_5 (g) + 2 \text{ NO } (g) \leftrightarrow PCl_3 (g) + 2 \text{ NOCl } (g)$$

$$K_1 = PCl_3 (g) + Cl_2 (g) \leftrightarrow PCl_5 (g)$$

$$K_2 = 2 \text{ NO } (g) + Cl_2 (g) \leftrightarrow 2 \text{ NOCl } (g)$$

A. K_1 / K_2 **B.** $(K_1 K_2)^{-1}$ **C.** $K_1 \times K_2$ **D.** K_2 / K_1 **E.** $K_2 - K_1$

Chapter 6: Solution Chemistry

1. If the solubility of nitrogen in blood is 1.90 cc/100 cc at 1.00 atm, what is the solubility of nitrogen in a scuba diver's blood at a depth of 125 feet where the pressure is 4.5 atm?

 A. 1.90 cc/100 cc   **C.** 4.5 cc/100 cc

 B. 2.36 cc/100 cc   **D.** 0.236 cc/100 cc   **E.** 8.55 cc/100 cc

2. All of the statements about molarity are correct, **EXCEPT:**

 A. volume = moles/molarity

 B. moles = molarity × volume

 C. molarity of a diluted solution is less than the molarity of the original solution

 D. abbreviation is M

 E. molarity equals moles of solute per mole of solvent

3. Which of the following molecules is expected to be most soluble in water?

 A. NaCl   **C.** $CH_3CH_2CH_2 OH$

 B. $CH_3CH_2CH_2COOH$ **D.** $Al(OH)_3$

            E. CH_4

4. In commercially prepared soft drinks, carbon dioxide gas is injected into soda. Under what conditions are carbon dioxide gas most soluble?

 A. High temperature, high-pressure   **C.** Low temperature, low-pressure

 B. High temperature, low-pressure   **D.** Low temperature, high-pressure

                E. Solubility is the same for all conditions

5. How many ions are produced in solution by dissociation of one formula unit of $Co(NO_3)_2 \cdot 6H_2O$?

 A. 2   **B.** 3   **C.** 4   **D.** 6   **E.** 9

6. Which of the following is NOT soluble in H_2O?

 A. Iron (III) hydroxide   **C.** Potassium sulfate

 B. Iron (III) nitrate   **D.** Ammonium sulfate   **E.** Sodium chloride

7. What is the v/v% concentration of a solution made by adding 25 mL of acetone to 75 mL of water?

 A. 33% v/v   **C.** 25% v/v

 B. 0.33% v/v   **D.** 2.5% v/v   **E.** 3.3% v/v

8. What is the K_{sp} for slightly soluble copper (II) phosphate in an aqueous solution?

$$Cu_3(PO_4)_2 \, (s) \leftrightarrow 3 \, Cu^{2+} \, (aq) + 2 \, PO_4^{3-} \, (aq)$$

A. $K_{sp} = [Cu^{2+}]^3 \cdot [PO_4^{3-}]^2$

B. $K_{sp} = [Cu^{2+}] \cdot [PO_4^{3-}]^2$

C. $K_{sp} = [Cu^{2+}]^3 \cdot [PO_4^{3-}]$

D. $K_{sp} = [Cu^{2+}] \cdot [PO_4^{3-}]$

E. $K_{sp} = [Cu^{2+}]^2 \cdot [PO_4^{3-}]^3$

9. In which of the following pairs of substances would both species in the pair be written in the molecular form in a net ionic equation?

      I. CO_2 and H_2SO_4 II. $LiOH$ and H_2 III. HF and CO_2

A. I only   **B.** II only   **C.** III only   **D.** I, II and III   **E.** None of the above

10. What is the mass of a 7.50% urine sample that contains 122 g of dissolved solute?

A. 1,250 g   **B.** 935 g   **C.** 49.35 g   **D.** 155.4 g   **E.** 1,627 g

11. Calculate the molarity of a solution prepared by dissolving 15.0 g of NH_3 in 250 g of water with a final density of 0.974 g/mL.

A. 36.2 M   **C.** 0.0462 M

B. 3.23 M   **D.** 0.664 M   **E.** 6.80 M

12. Which of the following compounds has the highest boiling point?

A. 0.2 M $Al(NO_3)_3$ **C.** 0.2 M glucose ($C_6H_{12}O_6$)

B. 0.2 M $MgCl_2$ **D.** 0.2 M Na_2SO_4 **E.** Pure H_2O

13. Which compound produces four ions per formula unit by dissociation when dissolved in water?

A. Li_3PO_4 **B.** $Ca(NO_3)_2$ **C.** $MgSO_4$ **D.** $(NH_4)_2SO_4$ **E.** $(NH_4)_4Fe(CN)_6$

14. The ions Ca^{2+}, Mg^{2+}, Fe^{2+}, Fe^{3+}, which are present in all ground water, can be removed by pretreating the water with:

A. $PbSO_4$ **C.** KNO_3

B. $Na_2CO_3 \cdot 10H_2O$ **D.** $CaCl_2$ **E.** 0.05 M HCl

15. Choose the spectator ions: $Pb(NO_3)_2 \, (aq) + H_2SO_4 \, (aq) \rightarrow ?$

A. NO_3^- and H^+ **C.** Pb^{2+} and H^+

B. H^+ and SO_4^{2-} **D.** Pb^{2+} and NO_3^- **E.** Pb^{2+} and SO_4^{2-}

16. From the *like dissolves like* rule, predict which of the following vitamins is soluble in water:

A. α-tocopherol ($C_{29}H_{50}O_2$)   **C.** ascorbic acid ($C_6H_8O_6$)   **E.** none of the above
B. calciferol ($C_{27}H_{44}O$)   **D.** retinol ($C_{20}H_{30}O$)

17. How much water must be added when 125 mL of a 2.00 M solution of HCl is diluted to a final concentration of 0.400 M?

A. 150 mL   **B.** 850 mL   **C.** 625 mL   **D.** 750 mL   **E.** 500 mL

18. Which of the following is the sulfate ion?

A. SO_4^{2-} **B.** S^{2-} **C.** CO_3^{2-} **D.** PO_4^{3-} **E.** S^-

19. Which is a correctly balanced hydration equation for the hydration of Na_2SO_4?

A. $Na_2SO_4 (s) \xrightarrow{H_2O} Na^+ (aq) + 2SO_4^{2-} (aq)$

B. $Na_2SO_4 (s) \xrightarrow{H_2O} 2 Na^{2+} (aq) + S^{2-} (aq) + O_4^{2-} (aq)$

C. $Na_2SO_4 (s) \xrightarrow{H_2O} Na_2^{2+} (aq) + SO_4^{2-} (aq)$

D. $Na_2SO_4 (s) \xrightarrow{H_2O} 2 Na^+ (aq) + SO_4^{2-} (aq)$

E. $Na_2SO_4 (s) \xrightarrow{H_2O} 2 Na^{2+} (aq) + S^2 (aq) + SO_4^{2-} (aq) + O_4^{2-} (aq)$

20. Which type of compound is likely to dissolve in H_2O?

    I.   One with hydrogen bonds
    II. Highly polar compound
    III. Salt

A. I only   **B.** II only   **C.** III only   **D.** I and III only   **E.** I, II and III

21. Which of the following might have the best solubility in water?

A. CH_3CH_3 **B.** CH_3OH **C.** CCl_4 **D.** O_2 **E.** None of the above

22. What is the net ionic equation for the reaction shown?
    $CaCO_3 + 2 HNO_3 \rightarrow Ca(NO_3)_2 + CO_2 + H_2O$

A. $CO_3^{2-} + H^+ \rightarrow CO_2$
B. $CaCO_3 + 2 H^+ \rightarrow Ca^{2+} + CO_2 + H_2O$
C. $Ca^{2+} + 2 NO_3^- \rightarrow Ca(NO_3)_2$
D. $CaCO_3 + 2 NO_3^- \rightarrow Ca(NO_3)_2 + CO_3^{2-}$
E. None of the above

23. What is the volume of a 0.550 M $Fe(NO_3)_3$ solution needed to supply 0.950 moles of nitrate ions?

   A. 265 mL   **B.** 0.828 mL   **C.** 22.2 mL   **D.** 576 mL   **E.** 384 mL

24. If 36.0 g of LiOH is dissolved in water to make 975 mL of solution, what is the molarity of the LiOH solution? (Use molecular mass of LiOH = 24.0 g/mol)

   A. 1.54 M   **B.** 2.48 M   **C.** 0. 844 M   **D.** 0.268 M   **E.** 0.229 M

25. In an AgCl solution, if the K_{sp} for AgCl is A, and the concentration Cl^- in a container is B molar, what is the concentration of Ag (in moles/liter)?

   I. A moles/liter   II. B moles/liter   III. A/B moles/liter

   A. I only   **C.** III only
   B. II only   **D.** II and III only   **E.** I and III only

26. Which statement below is generally true?

   A. All bases are strong electrolytes and ionize completely when dissolved in water
   B. All salts are strong electrolytes and dissociate completely when dissolved in water
   C. All acids are strong electrolytes and ionize completely when dissolved in water
   D. All bases are weak electrolytes and ionize completely when dissolved in water
   E. All salts are weak electrolytes and ionize partially when dissolved in water

27. What is the concentration of I^- ions in a 0.40 M solution of magnesium iodide?

   A. 0.05 M   **C.** 0.60 M
   B. 0.80 M   **D.** 0.20 M   **E.** 0.40 M

28. Which of the following represents the symbol for the chlorite ion?

   A. ClO_2^- **B.** ClO^- **C.** ClO_4^- **D.** ClO_3^- **E.** ClO_2

29. Which of the following statements best describes what is happening in a water softening unit?

   A. Sodium is removed from the water, making the water interact less with the soap molecules
   B. Ions in the water softener are softened by chemically bonding with sodium
   C. Hard ions are all trapped in the softener, which filters out all the ions
   D. Hard ions in water are exchanged for ions that do not interact as strongly with soaps
   E. None of the above

30. The hydration number of an ion is the number of:

   A. water molecules bonded to an ion in an aqueous solution
   B. water molecules required to dissolve one mole of ions
   C. ions bonded to one mole of water molecules
   D. ions dissolved in one liter of an aqueous solution
   E. water molecules required to dissolve the compound

31. Which species is NOT written as its constituent ions when the equation is expanded into the ionic equation?

$$Mg(OH)_2 \ (s) + 2 \ HCl \ (aq) \rightarrow MgCl_2 \ (aq) + 2 \ H_2O \ (l)$$

   A. $Mg(OH)_2$ only   **C.** HCl
   B. H_2O and $Mg(OH)_2$ **D.** $MgCl_2$ **E.** HCl and $MgCl_2$

32. If x moles of $PbCl_2$ fully dissociate in 1 liter of H_2O, the K_{sp} is equivalent to:

   A. x^2 **B.** $2x^4$ **C.** $3x^2$ **D.** $2x^3$ **E.** $4x^3$

33. Which of the following are strong electrolytes?

   I. salts   II. strong bases   III. weak acids

   A. I only   **B.** I and II only   **C.** III only   **D.** I, II and III   **E.** I and III only

34. What volume of 14 M acid must be diluted with distilled water to prepare 6.0 L of 0.20 M acid?

   A. 86 mL   **B.** 62 mL   **C.** 0.94 mL   **D.** 6.8 mL   **E.** 120 mL

35. Which compound is most likely to be more soluble in the nonpolar solvent of benzene than in water?

   A. SO_2 **B.** CO_2 **C.** Silver chloride   **D.** H_2S **E.** CH_2Cl_2

36. Which of the following concentrations is dependent on temperature?

   A. Mole fraction   **C.** Mass percent
   B. Molarity   **D.** Molality   **E.** More than one of the above

37. Which of the following solutions is the most concentrated?

   A. One liter of water with 1 gram of sugar
   B. One liter of water with 2 grams of sugar
   C. One liter of water with 5 grams of sugar
   D. One liter of water with 10 grams of sugar
   E. All are the same

38. What mass of NaOH is contained in 75.0 mL of a 5.0% (w/v) NaOH solution?

A. 6.50 g   **B.** 15.0 g   **C.** 7.50 g   **D.** 0.65 g   **E.** 3.75 g

---

Questions **39** through **41** are based on the following data:

	K_{sp}
$PbCl_2$	1.0×10^{-5}
AgCl	1.0×10^{-10}
$PbCO_3$	1.0×10^{-15}

39. Consider a saturated solution of $PbCl_2$. The addition of NaCl would:

   I.   decrease $[Pb^{2+}]$
   II. increase the precipitation of $PbCl_2$
   III. have no effect on the precipitation of $PbCl_2$

A. I only   **B.** II only   **C.** III only   **D.** I and II only   **E.** I and III only

40. What occurs when $AgNO_3$ is added to a saturated solution of $PbCl_2$?

   I.   AgCl precipitates
   II. $Pb(NO_3)_2$ forms a white precipitate
   III. More $PbCl_2$ forms

A. I only   **B.** II only   **C.** III only   **D.** I, II and III   **E.** I and II only

41. Comparing equal volumes of saturated solutions for $PbCl_2$ and AgCl, which solution contains a greater concentration of Cl^-?

   I. $PbCl_2$
   II. AgCl
   III. Both have the same concentration of Cl^-

A. I only   **B.** II only   **C.** III only   **D.** I and II only   **E.** Cannot be determined

42. Which of the following is the reason why hexane is significantly soluble in octane?

   A. Entropy increases for the two substances as the dominant factor in the ΔG when mixed
   B. Hexane hydrogen bonds with octane
   C. Intermolecular bonds between hexane-octane are much stronger than either hexane-hexane or octane-octane molecular bonds
   D. ΔH for hexane-octane is greater than hexane-H_2O
   E. Hexane and octane have similar molecular weights

---

43. Which of the following are characteristics of an ideally dilute solution?

       I.   Solute molecules do not interact with each other
      II.   Solvent molecules do not interact with each other
      III. The mole fraction of the solvent approaches 1

    A. I only   **B.** II only   **C.** I and III only   **D.** I, II and III   **E.** I and II only

44. Which principle states that the solubility of a gas in a liquid is proportional to the partial pressure of the gas above the liquid?

    A. Solubility principle   **C.** Colloid principle
    B. Tyndall effect   **D.** Henry's law   **E.** None of the above

45. Which of the following solid compounds is insoluble in water?

      I. $BaSO_4$ II. Hg_2Cl_2 III. $PbCl_2$

    A. I only   **C.** III only
    B. II only   **D.** I and III only   **E.** I, II and III

46. The net ionic equation for the reaction between zinc and hydrochloric acid solution is:

    A. $Zn\ (s) + 2\ H^+\ (aq) + 2\ Cl^-\ (aq) \rightarrow Zn^{2+}\ (aq) + 2\ Cl^-\ (aq) + H_2\ (g)$
    B. $ZnCl_2\ (aq) + H_2\ (g) \rightarrow Zn\ (s) + 2\ HCl\ (aq)$
    C. $Zn\ (s) + 2\ H^+\ (aq) \rightarrow Zn^{2+}\ (aq) + H_2\ (g)$
    D. $Zn\ (s) + 2\ HCl\ (aq) \rightarrow ZnCl_2\ (aq) + H_2\ (g)$
    E. None of the above

47. A 4 M solution of H_3A is completely dissociated in water. How many equivalents of H^+ are found in 1/3 liter?

    A. ¼   **B.** 1   **C.** 1.5   **D.** 3   **E.** 4

48. Which of the following aqueous solutions is a poor conductor of electricity?

      I.   sucrose, $C_{12}H_{22}O_{11}$
      II. barium nitrate, $Ba(NO_3)_2$
      III. calcium bromide, $CaBr_2$

    A. I only   **C.** III only
    B. II only   **D.** I and II only   **E.** I, II and III

49. Which of the following solid compounds is insoluble in water?

    A. $BaSO_4$ **C.** $(NH_4)_2CO_3$
    B. Na_2S **D.** K_2CrO_4 **E.** $Sr(OH)_2$

50. Under which conditions is the expected solubility of oxygen gas in water the highest?

A. High temperature and high O_2 pressure above the solution
B. Low temperature and low O_2 pressure above the solution
C. Low temperature and high O_2 pressure above the solution
D. High temperature and low O_2 pressure above the solution
E. The O_2 solubility is independent of temperature and pressure

51. What is the molarity of an 8.60 molal solution of methanol (CH_3OH) with density 0.94 g/mL?

A. 0.155 M
C. 6.34 M
B. 23.5 M
D. 9.68 M
E. 2.35 M

52. Which of the following is NOT a unit factor related to a 15.0% aqueous solution of potassium iodide (KI)?

A. 100 g solution / 85.0 g water
C. 85.0 g water / 100 g solution
B. 85.0 g water / 15.0 g KI
D. 15.0 g KI / 85.0 g water
E. 15.0 g KI / 100 g water

53. If 25.0 mL of seawater has a mass of 25.88 g and contains 1.35 g of solute, what is the mass/mass percent concentration of solute in the seawater sample?

A. 1.14%
B. 12.84%
C. 2.62%
D. 5.22%
E. 9.45%

54. Which of the following statements describing solutions is NOT true?

A. Solutions are colorless
B. The particles in a solution are atomic or molecular
C. Making a solution involves a physical change
D. Solutions are homogeneous
E. Solutions are transparent

55. Calculate the solubility product of AgCl if the solubility of AgCl in H_2O is 1.3×10^{-4} mol/L?

A. 1.3×10^{-4}
C. 2.6×10^{-4}
B. 1.3×10^{-2}
D. 3.9×10^{-5}
E. 1.7×10^{-8}

56. Which of the following solutions is the most dilute?

A. 0.1 liters of H_2O with 1 gram of sugar
B. 0.2 liters of H_2O with 2 grams of sugar
C. 0.5 liters of H_2O with 5 grams of sugar
D. 1 liter of H_2O with 10 grams of sugar
E. All have the same concentration

57. When salt A is dissolved into water to form a 1 molar unsaturated solution, the temperature of the solution decreases. Under these conditions, which statement is accurate when salt A is dissolved in water?

    A. $\Delta H°$ and $\Delta G°$ are positive

    B. $\Delta H°$ is positive and $\Delta G°$ is negative

    C. $\Delta H°$ is negative and $\Delta G°$ is positive

    D. $\Delta H°$ and $\Delta G°$ are negative

    E. $\Delta H°$, $\Delta S°$ and $\Delta G°$ are positive

58. The heat of a solution measures the energy absorbed during:

    I.   the formation of solvent-solute bonds
    II. the breaking of solute-solute bonds
    III. the breaking of solvent-solvent bonds

    A. I only   **C.** I and II only

    B. II only   **D.** I and III only   **E.** II and III only

59. Why does the reaction proceed if, when solid potassium chloride is dissolved in H_2O, the energy of the bonds formed is less than the energy of the bonds broken?

    A. The electronegativity of the H_2O increases from interaction with potassium and chloride ions

    B. The reaction does not take place under standard conditions

    C. The decreased disorder due to mixing decreases entropy within the system

    D. Remaining potassium chloride which does not dissolve offsets the portion that dissolves

    E. The increased disorder due to mixing increases entropy within the system

60. What is the formula of the solid formed when aqueous barium chloride is mixed with aqueous potassium chromate?

    A. K_2CrO_4 **C.** KCl

    B. K_2Ba **D.** $BaCrO_4$ **E.** $BaCl_2$

Notes

Chapter 7: Acids and Bases

1. Which is the conjugate acid–base pair in the reaction?

$$CH_3NH_2 + HCl \leftrightarrow CH_3NH_3^+ + Cl^-$$

A. HCl and Cl^-

B. $CH_3NH_3^+$ and Cl^-

C. CH_3NH_2 and Cl^-

D. CH_3NH_2 and HCl

E. HCl and H_3O^+

2. Which reactant is a Brønsted-Lowry acid?

$$HCl\ (aq) + KHS\ (aq) \rightarrow KCl\ (aq) + H_2S\ (aq)$$

A. KCl **B.** H_2S **C.** HCl **D.** KHS **E.** None of the above

3. If a light bulb in a conductivity apparatus glows brightly when testing a solution, which of the following must be true about the solution?

A. It is highly reactive

B. It is slightly reactive

C. It is highly ionized

D. It is slightly ionized

E. It is not an electrolyte

4. What is the approximate pH of a solution of a strong acid where $[H_3O^+] = 8.30 \times 10^{-5}$?

A. 9 **B.** 11 **C.** 3 **D.** 5 **E.** 4

5. Which of the following reactions represents the ionization of H_2O?

A. $H_2O + H_2O \rightarrow 2\ H_2 + O_2$

B. $H_2O + H_2O \rightarrow H_3O^+ + {}^-OH$

C. $H_2O + H_3O^+ \rightarrow H_3O^+ + H_2O$

D. $H_3O^+ + {}^-OH \rightarrow H_2O + H_2O$

E. None of the above

6. Which set below contains only weak electrolytes?

A. $NH_4Cl\ (aq)$, $HClO_2\ (aq)$, $HCN\ (aq)$

B. $NH_3\ (aq)$, $HCO_3^-\ (aq)$, $HCN\ (aq)$

C. $KOH\ (aq)$, $H_3PO_4\ (aq)$, $NaClO_4\ (aq)$

D. $HNO_3\ (aq)$, $H_2SO_4\ (aq)$, $HCN\ (aq)$

E. $NaOH\ (aq)$, $H_2SO_4\ (aq)$, $HC_2H_3O_2\ (aq)$

7. Which of the following statements describes a neutral solution?

A. $[H_3O^+] / [{}^-OH] = 1 \times 10^{-14}$

B. $[H_3O^+] / [{}^-OH] = 1$

C. $[H_3O^+] < [{}^-OH]$

D. $[H_3O^+] > [{}^-OH]$

E. $[H_3O^+] \times [{}^-OH] \neq 1 \times 10^{-14}$

8. What is the pI for glutamic acid that contains two carboxylic acid groups and an amino group? (Use the carboxyl $pK_{a1} = 2.2$, carboxyl $pK_{a2} = 4.2$ and amino $pK_a = 9.7$)

A. 3.2 **B.** 1.0 **C.** 6.4 **D.** 5.4 **E.** 5.95

9. Which of the following compounds cannot act as an acid?

A. NH_3 **B.** H_2SO_4 **C.** HSO_4^{1-} **D.** SO_4^{2-} **E.** CH_3CO_2H

10. If $[H_3O^+]$ in an aqueous solution is 7.5×10^{-9} M, what is the $[^-OH]$?

A. 6.4×10^{-5} M   **C.** 7.5×10^{-23} M

B. $3.8 \times 10^{+8}$ M   **D.** 1.3×10^{-6} M   **E.** 9.0×10^{-9} M

11. Which species has a K_a of 5.7×10^{-10} if NH_3 has a K_b of 1.8×10^{-5}?

A. H^+ **B.** NH_2^- **C.** NH_4^+ **D.** H_2O **E.** $NaNH_2$

12. Which of the following are the conjugate bases of HSO_4^-, CH_3OH and H_3O^+, respectively:

A. SO_4^{2-}, CH_2OH^- and ^-OH **C.** SO_4^-, CH_3O^- and ^-OH

B. CH_3O^-, SO_4^{2-} and H_2O **D.** SO_4^-, CH_2OH^- and H_2O

     E. SO_4^{2-}, CH_3O^- and H_2O

13. If 30.0 mL of 0.10 M $Ca(OH)_2$ is titrated with 0.20 M HNO_3, what volume of nitric acid is required to neutralize the base according to the following expression?

$$2\ HNO_3\ (aq) + Ca(OH)_2\ (aq) \rightarrow 2\ Ca(NO_3)_2\ (aq) + 2\ H_2O\ (l)$$

A. 30.0 mL   **B.** 15.0 mL   **C.** 10.0 mL   **D.** 20.0 mL   **E.** 45.0 mL

14. Which of the following expressions describes an acidic solution?

A. $[H_3O^+]/[^-OH] = 1 \times 10^{-14}$ **C.** $[H_3O^+] < [^-OH]$

B. $[H_3O^+] \times [^-OH] \neq 1 \times 10^{-14}$ **D.** $[H_3O^+] > [^-OH]$ **E.** $[H_3O^+]/[^-OH] = 1$

15. Which is incorrectly classified as an acid, a base, or an amphoteric species?

A. LiOH / base   **C.** H_2S / acid

B. H_2O / amphoteric   **D.** NH_4^+ / base   **E.** None of the above

16. What are the products from the complete neutralization of phosphoric acid with aqueous lithium hydroxide?

A. $LiHPO_4$ (aq) and H_2O (l)   **C.** Li_2HPO4 (aq) and H_2O (l)

B. Li_3PO_4 (aq) and H_2O (l)   **D.** LiH_2PO_4 (aq) and H_2O (l)

     E. Li_2PO_4 (aq) and H_2O (l)

17. Which of the following compounds is NOT a strong base?

A. $Ca(OH)_2$ **B.** $Fe(OH)_3$ **C.** KOH   **D.** NaOH   **E.** $^-NH_2$

18. What is the $[H^+]$ in stomach acid that registers a pH of 2.0 on a strip of pH paper?

A. 0.2 M   **B.** 0.1 M   **C.** 0.02 M   **D.** 0.01 M   **E.** 2 M

19. Which of the following compound-classification pairs is incorrectly matched?

A. HF – weak acid   **C.** NH_3 – weak base
B. $LiC_2H_3O_2$ –salt   **D.** HI – strong acid   **E.** $Ca(OH)_2$ – weak base

20. Citric acid is a triprotic acid with three carboxylic acid groups having pK_a values of 3.2, 4.8, and 6.4. At a pH of 5.7, what is the predominant protonation state of citric acid?

A. All three carboxylic acid groups are deprotonated
B. All three carboxylic acid groups are protonated
C. One carboxylic acid group is deprotonated, while two are protonated
D. Two carboxylic acid groups are deprotonated, while one is protonated
E. The protonation state cannot be determined

21. When fully neutralized by treatment with barium hydroxide, a phosphoric acid yields $Ba_2P_2O_7$ as one of its products. The parent acid for the anion in this compound is:

A. monoprotic acid   **C.** triprotic acid
B. diprotic acid   **D.** hexaprotic acid   **E.** tetraprotic acid

22. Does a solution become more or less acidic when a weak acid solution is added to a concentrated solution of HCl?

A. Less acidic, because the concentration of OH^- increases
B. No change in acidity, because [HCl] is too high to be changed by the weak solution
C. Less acidic, because the solution becomes more dilute with a less concentrated solution of H_3O^+ being added
D. More acidic, because more H_3O^+ is being added to the solution
E. More acidic, because the solution becomes more dilute with a less concentrated solution of H_3O^+ being added

23. For which of the following pairs of substances do the two members of the pair NOT react?

A. Na_3PO_4 and HCl   **C.** HF and LiOH
B. KCl and NaI   **D.** $PbCl_2$ and H_2SO_4 **E.** All react to form products

24. Which of the following is the acidic anhydride of phosphoric acid (H_3PO_4)?

A. P_2O **B.** P_2O_3 **C.** PO_3 **D.** PO_2 **E.** P_4O_{10}

25. Why does boiler scale form on the walls of hot water pipes from groundwater?

A. Transformation of $H_2PO_4^-$ ions to PO_4^{3-} ions, which precipitate with the "hardness ions," Ca^{2+}, Mg^{2+}, Fe^{2+}/Fe^{3+}

B. Transformation of HSO_4^- ions to SO_4^{2-} ions, which precipitate with the "hardness ions," Ca^{2+}, Mg^{2+}, Fe^{2+}/Fe^{3+}

C. Transformation of HSO_3^- ions to SO_3^{2-} ions, which precipitate with the "hardness ions," Ca^{2+}, Mg^{2+}, Fe^{2+}/Fe^{3+}

D. Transformation of HCO_3^- ions to CO_3^{2-} ions, which precipitate with the "hardness ions," Ca^{2+}, Mg^{2+}, Fe^{2+}/Fe^{3+}

E. The reaction of the CO_3^{2-} ions present in all groundwater with the "hardness ions," Ca^{2+}, Mg^{2+}, Fe^{2+}/Fe^{3+}

26. Which of the following substances, when added to a solution of sulfoxylic acid (H_2SO_2), could be used to prepare a buffer solution?

A. H_2O **B.** $HC_2H_3O_2$ **C.** KCl   **D.** HCl   **E.** $NaHSO_2$

27. Which of the following statements is NOT correct?

A. Acidic salts are formed by partial neutralization of a diprotic acid by a diprotic base

B. Acidic salts are formed by partial neutralization of a triprotic acid by a diprotic base

C. Acidic salts are formed by partial neutralization of a monoprotic acid by a monoprotic base

D. Acidic salts are formed by partial neutralization of a diprotic acid by a monoprotic base

E. Acidic salts are formed by partial neutralization of a polyprotic acid by a monoprotic base

28. Identify the acid/base behavior of each substance for the reaction:

$$H_3O^+ + Cl^- \rightleftharpoons H_2O + HCl$$

A. H_3O^+ acts as an acid, Cl^- acts as a base, H_2O acts as a base and HCl acts as an acid

B. H_3O^+ acts as a base, Cl^- acts as an acid, H_2O acts as a base and HCl acts as an acid

C. H_3O^+ acts as an acid, Cl^- acts as a base, H_2O acts as an acid and HCl acts as a base

D. H_3O^+ acts as a base, Cl^- acts as an acid, H_2O acts as an acid and HCl acts as a base

E. H_3O^+ acts as an acid, Cl^- acts as a base, H_2O acts as a base and HCl acts as a base

29. Given the pK_a values for phosphoric acid of 2.15, 6.87, and 12.35, what is the ratio of $HPO_4^{2-} / H_2PO_4^-$ in a typical muscle cell when the pH is 7.35?

A. 6.32×10^{-6} **B.** 1.18×10^5 **C.** 0.46   **D.** 3.02   **E.** 3.31×10^3

30. If a light bulb in a conductivity apparatus glows dimly when testing a solution, which of the following must be true about the solution?

     I. It is slightly reactive   II. It is slightly ionized   III. It is highly ionized

A. I only   **B.** II only   **C.** III only   **D.** I and II only   **E.** II and III only

31. What is the term for a substance that releases hydroxide ions in water?

A. Brønsted-Lowry base   **C.** Arrhenius base

B. Brønsted-Lowry acid   **D.** Arrhenius acid   **E.** Lewis base

32. For the reaction below, which of the following is the conjugate acid of C_5H_5N?

$$C_5H_5N + H_2CO_3 \leftrightarrow C_5H_6N^+ + HCO_3^-$$

A. $C_5H_6N^+$ **B.** HCO_3^- **C.** C_5H_5N **D.** H_2CO_3 **E.** H_3O^+

33. Which of the following is the chemical species present in all acidic solutions?

A. $H_2O^+ (aq)$ **C.** $H_2O (aq)$

B. $H_3O^+ (l)$ **D.** $^-OH (aq)$ **E.** $H_3O^+ (aq)$

34. Which compound has a value of K_a that is approximately equal to 10^{-5}?

A. $CH_3CH_2CH_2CO_2H$ **C.** NaBr

B. KOH   **D.** HNO_3 **E.** NH_3

35. What is the pH of this buffer system if the concentration of undissociated weak acid is equal to the concentration of the conjugate base? (Use the K_a of the buffer $= 4.6 \times 10^{-4}$)

A. 1 and 2   **B.** 3 and 4   **C.** 5 and 6   **D.** 7 and 8   **E.** 9 and 10

36. What is the value of K_w at 25 °C?

A. 1.0   **C.** 1.0×10^{-14}

B. 1.0×10^{-7} **D.** 1.0×10^7 **E.** 1.0×10^{14}

37. The Brønsted-Lowry acid and base in the following reaction are, respectively:

$$NH_4^+ + CN^- \rightarrow NH_3 + HCN$$

A. NH_4^+ and ^-CN **C.** NH_4^+ and HCN

B. ^-CN and HCN   **D.** NH_3 and ^-CN **E.** NH_3 and NH_4^+

38. Which would NOT be used to make a buffer solution?

A. H_2SO_4 **C.** NH_4OH

B. H_2CO_3 **D.** CH_3COOH **E.** Tricene

39. If a buffer is made with the pH below the pK_a of the weak acid, the [base] / [acid] ratio is:

A. equal to 0   **C.** greater than 1

B. equal to 1   **D.** less than 1   **E.** undetermined

40. Complete neutralization of phosphoric acid with barium hydroxide, when separated and dried, yields $Ba_3(PO_4)_2$ as one of the products. Therefore, which term describes phosphoric acid?

A. Monoprotic acid

B. Diprotic acid

C. Hexaprotic acid

D. Tetraprotic acid

E. Triprotic acid

41. Which is the correct net ionic equation for the hydrolysis reaction of Na_2S?

A. $Na^+ (aq) + H_2O (l) \rightarrow NaOH (aq) + H_2 (g)$

B. $Na^+ (aq) + 2 H_2O (l) \rightarrow NaOH (aq) + H_2O^+ (aq)$

C. $S^{2-} (aq) + H_2O (l) \rightarrow 2 HS^- (aq) + OH^- (aq)$

D. $S^{2-} (aq) + 2 H_2O (l) \rightarrow HS^- (aq) + H_3O^+ (aq)$

E. $S^{2-} (aq) + 2 H_2O (l) \rightarrow HS^- (aq) + 2 OH^- (aq)$

42. Which reaction produces $NiCr_2O_7$ as a product?

A. Nickel (II) hydroxide and dichromic acid

B. Nickel (II) hydroxide and chromic acid

C. Nickelic acid and chromium (II) hydroxide

D. Nickel (II) hydroxide and chromate acid

E. Nickel (II) hydroxide and trichromic acid

Questions **43–47** are based on the following titration graph:

The unknown acid is completely titrated with NaOH as shown on the following titration curve:

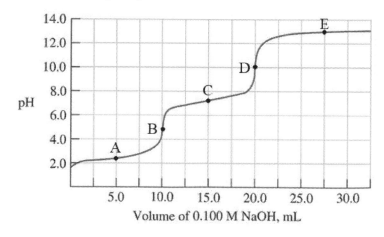

43. The unknown acid shown in the graph must be a(n):

A. monoprotic acid

B. diprotic acid

C. triprotic acid

D. weak acid

E. aprotic acid

44. The pK_{a2} for this acid is located at point:

A. A   **B.** B   **C.** C   **D.** D   **E.** E

---

45. At which point does the acid exist as 50% fully protonated and 50% singly deprotonated?

   A. A   **B.** B   **C.** C   **D.** D   **E.** E

46. At which point is the acid 100% singly deprotonated?

   A. A   **B.** B   **C.** C   **D.** D   **E.** E

47. Which points are the best buffer regions?

   A. A and B   **B.** A and C   **C.** B and D   **D.** C and B   **E.** C and D

48. Sodium hydroxide is a strong base. If a concentrated solution of NaOH spills on a latex glove, it feels like water. Why is it that if the solution were to splash directly on a person's skin, it feels very slippery?

   A. As a liquid, NaOH is slippery, but this cannot be detected through a latex glove because of the friction between the latex surfaces

   B. NaOH destroys skin cells on contact, and the remnants of skin cells feel slippery because the cells have been lysed

   C. NaOH lifts oil directly out of the skin cells, and the extruded oil causes the slippery sensation

   D. NaOH reacts with skin oils, transforming them into soap

   E. NaOH, as a liquid, causes the skin to feel slippery from low viscosity

49. Which of the following statements is/are always true for a neutralization reaction?

     I. Water is formed
     II. It is the reaction of an OH with an H^+
     III. One molecule of acid neutralizes one molecule of base

   A. I only   **C.** III. only

   B. II only   **D.** I and II only   **E.** I and III only

50. What is the salt to acid ratio needed to prepare a buffer solution with pH = 4.0 and an acid with a pK_a of 3.0?

   A. 1:1   **B.** 1:1000   **C.** 1:100   **D.** 1:5   **E.** 10:1

51. Which of the following must be true if an unknown solution is a poor conductor of electricity?

   A. The solution is slightly reactive   **C.** The solution is highly ionized

   B. The solution is highly corrosive   **D.** The solution is slightly ionized

                                          E. The solution is highly reactive

52. Since $pK_a = -\log K_a$, which of the following is a correct statement?

   A. Since the pK_a for the conversion of the ammonium ion to ammonia is 9.3, ammonia is a weaker base than the ammonium ion

   B. For carbonic acid with pK_a values of 6.3 and 10.3, the bicarbonate ion is a stronger base than the carbonate ion

   C. Acetic acid ($pK_a = 4.8$) is a weaker acid than lactic acid ($pK_a = 3.9$)

   D. Lactic acid ($pK_a = 3.9$) is weaker than all forms of phosphoric acid ($pK_a = 2.1$, 6.9 and 12.4)

   E. None of the above

53. A sample of $Mg(OH)_2$ salt is dissolved in water and reaches equilibrium with its dissociated ions. Addition of the strong base NaOH increases the concentration of:

   A. H_2O^+

   B. Mg^{2+}

   C. undissociated sodium hydroxide

   D. undissociated magnesium hydroxide

   E. H_2O^+ and undissociated sodium hydroxide

54. In which of the following pairs of acids are both chemical species weak acids?

   A. $HC_2H_3O_2$ and HI

   B. H_2CO_3 and HBr

   C. HCN and H_2S

   D. H_3PO_4 and H_2SO_4

   E. HCl and HBr

55. Which of the following indicators is/are yellow in an acidic solution and blue in a basic solution?

   I. methyl red   II. phenolphthalein   III. bromothymol blue

   A. I only

   B. II only

   C. I and III only

   D. III only

   E. I, II and III

56. What is the pK_a of an unknown acid if, in a solution at a pH of 7.0, 24% of the acid is in its deprotonated form?

   A. 6.0   **B.** 6.5   **C.** 7.5   **D.** 8.0   **E.** 10.0

57. Which of the following acids listed below is the strongest acid?

Monoprotic Acids	K_a
Acid I	1.0×10^{-8}
Acid II	1.8×10^{-9}
Acid III	3.7×10^{-10}
Acid IV	4.6×10^{-8}

   A. Acid I

   B. Acid II

   C. Acid III

   D. Acid IV

   E. Requires more information

58. In a basic solution, the pH is […] and the $[H_3O^+]$ is […].

A. < 7 and $> 1 \times 10^{-7}$ M

C. $= 7$ and 1×10^{-7} M

B. < 7 and $< 1 \times 10^{-7}$ M

D. < 7 and 1×10^{-7} M

E. > 7 and $< 1 \times 10^{-7}$ M

59. If a battery acid solution is a strong electrolyte, which of the following must be true of the battery acid?

A. It is highly ionized

C. It is highly reactive

B. It is slightly ionized

D. It is slightly reactive

E. It is slightly ionized and weakly reactive

60. Which statement concerning the Arrhenius acid–base theory is NOT correct?

A. Neutralization reactions produce H_2O, plus a salt

B. Acid–base reactions must take place in aqueous solution

C. Arrhenius acids produce H^+ in H_2O solution

D. Arrhenius bases produce OH^- in H_2O solution

E. All are correct

Notes

Chapter 8: Electrochemistry

1. Which is NOT true regarding the redox reaction occurring in a spontaneous electrochemical cell?

$$Cl_2 (g) + 2 Br^- (aq) \rightarrow Br_2 (l) + 2 Cl^- (aq)$$

A. Anions flow towards the anode
B. Electrons flow from the anode to the cathode
C. Cl_2 is reduced at the cathode
D. Br^- is oxidized at the cathode
E. Br^- is oxidized at the anode

2. How many electrons are needed to balance the following half reaction $H_2S \rightarrow S_8$ in acidic solution?

A. 14 electrons to the left side
B. 6 electrons to the right side

C. 12 electrons to the left side
D. 8 electrons to the right side
E. 16 electrons to the right side

3. Which is NOT true regarding the following redox reaction occurring in an electrolytic cell?

$$3\ C + 2\ Co_2O_3 \xrightarrow{\text{Electricity}} 4\ Co + 3\ CO_2$$

A. $CO_2 (g)$ is produced at the anode
B. Co metal is produced at the anode
C. Oxidation half-reaction: $C + 2\ O^{2-} \rightarrow CO_2 + 4\ e^-$
D. Reduction half-reaction: $Co^{3+} + 3\ e^- \rightarrow Co$
E. Co metal is produced at the cathode

4. The electrode with the standard reduction potential of 0 V is assigned as the standard reference electrode and uses the half-reaction:

A. $2\ NH_4^+ (aq) + 2\ e^- \leftrightarrow H_2 (g) + 2\ NH_3 (g)$
B. $Ag^+ (aq) + e^- \leftrightarrow Ag (s)$
C. $Cu^{2+} (aq) + 2\ e^- \leftrightarrow Cu (s)$
D. $Zn^{2+} (aq) + 2\ e^- \leftrightarrow Zn (s)$
E. $2\ H^+ (aq) + 2\ e^- \leftrightarrow H_2 (g)$

5. In the reaction for a discharging nickel–cadmium (NiCad) battery, which substance is being oxidized?

$$Cd (s) + NiO_2 (s) + 2\ H_2O (l) \rightarrow Cd(OH)_2 (s) + Ni(OH)_2 (s)$$

A. H_2O B. $Cd(OH)_2$ C. Cd   D. NiO_2 E. $Ni(OH)_2$

6. What happens at the anode if rust forms when Fe is in contact with H_2O?

$$4\ Fe + 3\ O_2 \rightarrow 2\ Fe_2O_3$$

A. Fe is reduced
C. Oxygen is oxidized
B. Oxygen is reduced
D. Fe is oxidized
E. None of the above

7. Which is true regarding the redox reaction occurring in the spontaneous electrochemical cell for $Cl_2\ (g) + 2\ Br^-\ (aq) \rightarrow Br_2\ (l) + 2\ Cl^-\ (aq)$?

A. Electrons flow from the cathode to the anode
B. Cl_2 is oxidized at the cathode
C. Br^- is reduced at the anode
D. Cations in the salt bridge flow from the Br_2 half-cell to the Cl_2 half-cell
E. Br^- is reduced at the anode, and Cl_2 is oxidized at the cathode

8. Using the following metal ion/metal reaction potentials,

$$Cu^{2+}\ (aq)|Cu\ (s) \quad Ag^+\ (aq)|Ag\ (s) \quad Co^{2+}\ (aq)|Co\ (s) \quad Zn^{2+}\ (aq)|Zn\ (s)$$

$$+0.34\ V \qquad\qquad +0.80\ V \qquad\qquad -0.28\ V \qquad\qquad -0.76\ V$$

calculate the standard cell potential for the cell whose reaction is:

$$Co\ (s) + Cu^{2+}\ (aq) \rightarrow Co^{2+}\ (aq) + Cu\ (s)$$

A. +0.62 V
C. +0.48 V
B. −0.62 V
D. −0.48 V
E. +0.68 V

9. How are photovoltaic cells different from many other forms of solar energy?

A. Light is reflected, and the coolness of the shade is used to provide a temperature differential
B. Light is passively converted into heat
C. Light is converted into heat and then into steam
D. Light is converted into heat and then into electricity
E. Light is converted directly to electricity

10. What is the term for an electrochemical cell that has a single electrode where oxidation or reduction can occur?

A. Half-cell
C. Dry cell
B. Voltaic cell
D. Electrolytic cell
E. None of the above

11. By which method could electrolysis be used to raise the hull of a sunken ship?

    A. Electrolysis could only be used to raise the hull if the ship is made of iron. If so, the electrolysis of the iron metal might produce sufficient gas to lift the ship

    B. The gaseous products of the electrolysis of H_2O are collected with bags attached to the hull of the ship and the inflated bags raise the ship

    C. The electrolysis of the H_2O beneath the hull of the ship boils H_2O and creates upward pressure to raise the ship

    D. An electric current passed through the hull of the ship produces electrolysis and the gases trapped in compartments of the vessel would push it upwards

    E. Electrolysis of the ship's hull decreases its mass, and the reduced weight causes the ship to rise

12. What are the products for the single-replacement reaction Zn (s) + $CuSO_4$ (aq) → ?

    A. CuO and $ZnSO_4$ **C.** Cu and $ZnSO_4$

    B. CuO and $ZnSO_3$ **D.** Cu and $ZnSO_3$ **E.** No reaction

13. Which of the following is a true statement about the electrochemical reaction for an electrochemical cell that has a cell potential of +0.36 V?

    A. The reaction favors the formation of reactants and would be considered a galvanic cell

    B. The reaction favors the formation of reactants and would be considered an electrolytic cell

    C. The reaction is at equilibrium and is a galvanic cell

    D. The reaction favors the formation of products and would be considered an electrolytic cell

    E. The reaction favors the formation of products and would be considered a galvanic cell

14. Which observation describes the solution near the cathode when an aqueous solution of sodium chloride is electrolyzed, and hydrogen gas is evolved at the cathode?

    A. Colored   **B.** Acidic   **C.** Basic   **D.** Frothy   **E.** Viscous

15. How many grams of Ag is deposited in the cathode of an electrolytic cell if a current of 3.50 A is applied to a solution of $AgNO_3$ for 12 minutes? (Use the molecular mass of Ag = 107.86 g/mol and the conversion of 1 mole e^- = 9.65×10^4 C)

    A. 0.32 g   **B.** 0.86 g   **C.** 2.82 g   **D.** 3.86 g   **E.** 4.38 g

16. In an electrochemical cell, which of the following statements is FALSE?

    A. The anode is the electrode where oxidation occurs

    B. A salt bridge provides electrical contact between the half-cells

    C. The cathode is the electrode where reduction occurs

    D. A spontaneous electrochemical cell is called a galvanic cell

    E. All of the above are true

17. What is the relationship between an element's ionization energy and its ability to function as an oxidizing and reducing agent? Elements with high ionization energy are:

A. strong oxidizing and weak reducing agents
B. weak oxidizing and weak reducing agents
C. strong oxidizing and strong reducing agents
D. weak oxidizing and strong reducing agents
E. weak oxidizing and neutral reducing agents

18. Which statement is true regarding the following redox reaction occurring in an electrolytic cell?

$$\overset{\text{Electricity}}{3 \; C \, (s) + 2 \; Co_2O_3 \, (l) \; \rightarrow \; 4 \; Co \, (l) + 3 \; CO_2 \, (g)}$$

A. CO_2 gas is produced at the anode
B. Co^{3+} is produced at the cathode
C. Oxidation half-reaction: $Co^{3+} + 3 \; e^- \rightarrow Co$
D. Reduction half-reaction: $C + 2 \; O^{2-} \rightarrow CO_2 + e^-$
E. None of the above

19. Which is true regarding the following redox reaction occurring in a spontaneous electrochemical cell?

$$Sn \, (s) + Cu^{2+} \, (aq) \rightarrow Cu \, (s) + Sn^{2+} \, (aq)$$

A. Anions in the salt bridge flow from the Cu half-cell to the Sn half-cell
B. Electrons flow from the Cu electrode to the Sn electrode
C. Cu^{2+} is oxidized at the cathode
D. Sn is reduced at the anode
E. None of the above

20. In galvanic cells, reduction occurs at the:

I. salt bridge   II. cathode   III. anode

A. I only   **B.** II only   **C.** III only   **D.** I and II only   **E.** I, II and III

21. For a battery, what is undergoing a reduction in the following oxidation-reduction reaction?

$$Mn_2O_3 + ZnO \rightarrow 2 \; MnO_2 + Zn$$

A. Mn_2O_3 **B.** MnO_2 **C.** ZnO   **D.** Zn   **E.** Mn_2O_3 and Zn

22. Given that the following redox reactions go essentially to completion, which of the metals listed below has the greatest tendency to undergo oxidation?

$$Ni\ (s) + Ag^+\ (aq) \rightarrow Ag\ (s) + Ni^{2+}\ (aq)$$

$$Al\ (s) + Cd^{2+}\ (aq) \rightarrow Cd\ (s) + Al^{3+}\ (aq)$$

$$Cd\ (s) + Ni^{2+}\ (aq) \rightarrow Ni\ (s) + Cd^{2+}\ (aq)$$

$$Ag\ (s) + H^+\ (aq) \rightarrow no\ reaction$$

A. (H)   **B.** Cd   **C.** Ni   **D.** Ag   **E.** Al

23. What is the purpose of the salt bridge in a voltaic cell?

A. Allows for a balance of charge between the two chambers
B. Allows the Fe^{2+} and the Cu^{2+} to flow freely between the two chambers
C. Allows for the buildup of positively charged ions in one container and negatively charged ions in the other container
D. Prevents any further migration of electrons through the wire
E. None of the above

24. If $\Delta G°$ for a cell is positive, the $E°$ is:

A. neutral   **C.** positive
B. negative   **D.** unable to be determined   **E.** greater than 1

25. In an electrochemical cell, which of the following statements is FALSE?

A. Oxidation occurs at the anode
B. Reduction occurs at the cathode
C. Electrons flow through the salt bridge to complete the cell
D. A spontaneous electrochemical cell is called a voltaic cell
E. All of the above are true

26. Which of the following statements about electrochemistry is NOT true?

A. The study of how protons are transferred from one chemical compound to another
B. The use of electrical current to produce an oxidation-reduction reaction
C. The use of a set of oxidation-reduction reactions to produce an electrical current
D. The study of how electrical energy and chemical reactions are related
E. The study of how electrons are transferred from one chemical compound to another

27. In an operating photovoltaic cell, electrons move through the external circuit to the negatively charged *p*-type silicon wafer. How can the electrons move to the negatively charged silicon wafer if electrons are negatively charged?

    A. The *p*-type silicon wafer is positively charged
    B. The energy of the sunlight moves electrons in a nonspontaneous direction
    C. Advancements in photovoltaic technology have solved this technological impediment
    D. An electric current occurs because the energy from the sun reverses the charge of the electrons
    E. The *p*-type silicon wafer is negatively charged

28. What is the term for the value assigned to an atom in a substance that indicates whether the atom is electron-poor or electron-rich compared to a free atom?

    A. Reduction number   **C.** Cathode number
    B. Oxidation number   **D.** Anode number   **E.** None of the above

29. What is the primary difference between a fuel cell and a battery?

    A. Fuel cells oxidize to supply electricity, while batteries reduce to supply electricity
    B. Batteries supply electricity, while fuel cells supply heat
    C. Batteries can be recharged, while fuel cells cannot
    D. Fuel cells do not run down because they can be refueled, while batteries run down and need to be recharged
    E. Fuel cells do not use metals as oxidants and reductants, while batteries have a static reservoir of oxidants and reductants

30. In balancing the equation for a disproportionation reaction, using the oxidation number method, the substance undergoing disproportionation is:

    A. initially written twice on the reactant side of the equation
    B. initially written twice on the product side of the equation
    C. initially written on both the reactant and product sides of the equation
    D. always assigned an oxidation number of zero
    E. always assigned an oxidation number of $+1$

31. What is the term for an electrochemical cell in which electrical energy is generated from a spontaneous redox reaction?

    A. Voltaic cell   **C.** Dry cell
    B. Photoelectric cell   **D.** Electrolytic cell   **E.** Wet cell

32. Which observation describes the solution near the anode when an aqueous solution of sodium sulfate is electrolyzed and gas is evolved at the anode?

    A. Colored   **B.** Acidic   **C.** Basic   **D.** Frothy   **E.** Viscous

33. Which of the statements listed below is true regarding the following redox reaction occurring in a nonspontaneous electrochemical cell?

$$Cd\ (s) + Zn(NO_3)_2\ (aq) + electricity \rightarrow Zn\ (s) + Cd(NO_3)_2\ (aq)$$

A. Oxidation half-reaction: $Zn^{2+} + 2\ e^- \rightarrow Zn$
B. Reduction half-reaction: $Cd \rightarrow Cd^{2+} + 2\ e^-$
C. Cd metal is produced at the anode
D. Zn metal is produced at the cathode
E. None of the above

34. Which statement is true for electrolysis?

A. A spontaneous redox reaction produces electricity
B. A nonspontaneous redox reaction is forced to occur by applying an electric current
C. Only pure, drinkable water is produced
D. There is a cell which reverses the flow of ions
E. None of the above

35. Which substance is undergoing reduction for a battery if the following two oxidation-reduction reactions take place?

Reaction I: $Zn + 2\ OH^- \rightarrow ZnO + H_2O + 2\ e^-$
Reaction II: $2\ MnO_2 + H_2O + 2\ e^- \rightarrow Mn_2O_3 + 2\ OH^-$

A. OH^- B. H_2O C. Zn   D. ZnO   E. MnO_2

36. Which of the statements is true regarding the following redox reaction occurring in a galvanic cell?

$$Cl_2\ (g) + 2\ Br^-\ (aq) \rightarrow Br_2\ (l) + 2\ Cl^-\ (aq)?$$

A. Cations in the salt bridge flow from the Cl_2 half-cell to the Br_2 half-cell
B. Electrons flow from the anode to the cathode
C. Cl_2 is reduced at the anode
D. Br^- is oxidized at the cathode
E. None of the above

37. Which of the statements listed below is true regarding the following redox reaction occurring in a nonspontaneous electrolytic cell?

$$3\ C\ (s) + 4\ AlCl_3\ (l) \xrightarrow{\text{Electricity}} 4\ Al\ (l) + 3\ CCl_4\ (g)$$

A. Cl^- is produced at the anode
B. Al metal is produced at the cathode
C. Oxidation half-reaction is $Al^{3+} + 3\ e^- \rightarrow Al$
D. Reduction half-reaction is $C + 4\ Cl^- \rightarrow CCl_4 + 4\ e^-$
E. None of the above

38. Which of the following materials is most likely to undergo oxidation?

      I. Cl^- II. Na   III. Na^+

  A. I only   **B.** II only   **C.** III only   **D.** I and II only   **E.** I, II and III

39. Which of the statements is NOT true regarding the redox reaction occurring in a spontaneous electrochemical cell?

$$Zn\ (s) + Cd^{2+}\ (aq) \rightarrow Cd\ (s) + Zn^{2+}\ (aq)$$

  A. Anions in the salt bridge flow from the Zn half-cell to the Cd half-cell
  B. Electrons flow from the Zn electrode to the Cd electrode
  C. Cd^{2+} is reduced at the cathode
  D. Zn is oxidized at the anode
  E. Anions in the salt bridge flow from the Cd half-cell to the Zn half-cell

40. Which is capable of oxidizing $Cu\ (s)$ to $Cu^{2+}\ (aq)$ when added to $Cu\ (s)$ in solution?

  A. $Al^{3+}\ (aq)$ **B.** $Ag^+\ (aq)$ **C.** $Ni\ (s)$ **D.** $I^-\ (aq)$ **E.** $Zn^{2+}\ (aq)$

41. Why is the anode of a battery indicated with a negative (–) sign?

  A. Electrons move to the anode to react with NH_4Cl in the battery
  B. It indicates the electrode where the chemicals are reduced
  C. Electrons are attracted to the negative electrode
  D. The cathode is the source of negatively charged electrons
  E. The electrode is the source of negatively charged electrons

42. What is the term for the conversion of chemical energy to electrical energy from redox reactions?

  A. Redox chemistry   **C.** Cell chemistry
  B. Electrochemistry   **D.** Battery chemistry   **E.** None of the above

43. In electrolysis, E° tends to be

  A. zero   **B.** neutral   **C.** positive   **D.** greater than 1   **E.** negative

44. A major source of chlorine gas is the electrolysis of concentrated saltwater, $NaCl\ (aq)$. What is the sign of the electrode where the chlorine gas is formed?

  A. Neither, since chlorine gas is a neutral molecule and there is no electrode attraction
  B. Negative, since the chlorine gas needs to deposit electrons to form chloride ions
  C. Positive, since the chloride ions lose electrons to form chlorine molecules
  D. Both, since the chloride ions from $NaCl\ (aq)$ are attracted to the positive electrode to form chlorine molecules, while the produced chlorine gas molecules move to deposit electrons at the negative electrode
  E. Positive, since the chloride ions gain electrons to form chlorine molecules

45. Which statement is correct for an electrolytic cell that has two electrodes?

    A. Oxidation occurs at the anode, which is negatively charged

    B. Oxidation occurs at the anode, which is positively charged

    C. Oxidation occurs at the cathode, which is positively charged

    D. Oxidation occurs at the cathode, which is negatively charged

    E. Oxidation occurs at the dynode, which is uncharged

46. Which battery system is based on half reactions involving zinc metal and manganese dioxide?

    A. Alkaline batteries

    B. Fuel cells

    C. Lead-acid storage batteries

    D. Dry-cell batteries

    E. None of the above

47. Which of the following equations is a disproportionation reaction?

    A. $2 H_2O \rightarrow 2 H_2 + O_2$

    B. $H_2SO_3 \rightarrow H_2O + SO_2$

    C. $HNO_2 \rightarrow NO + HNO_3$

    D. $Mg + H_2SO_4 \rightarrow MgSO_4 + H_2$

    E. None of the above

48. How is electrolysis different from the chemical process inside a battery?

    A. Pure compounds cannot be generated *via* electrolysis

    B. Electrolysis only uses electrons from a cathode

    C. Electrolysis does not use electrons

    D. They are the same process in reverse

    E. Chemical changes do not occur in electrolysis

49. Which fact about fuel cells is FALSE?

    A. Fuel cell automobiles are powered by water and only emit hydrogen

    B. Fuel cells are based on the tendency of some elements to gain electrons from other elements

    C. Fuel cell automobiles are quiet

    D. Fuel cell automobiles are environmentally friendly

    E. All of the above

50. Which process occurs when copper is refined using the electrolysis technique?

    A. Impure copper goes into solution at the anode, and pure copper plates out on the cathode

    B. Impure copper goes into solution at the cathode, and pure copper plates out on the anode

    C. Pure copper goes into solution from the anode and forms a precipitate at the bottom of the tank

    D. Pure copper goes into solution from the cathode and forms a precipitate at the bottom of the tank

    E. Pure copper on the bottom of the tank goes into solution and plates out on the cathode

51. Which of the following statements describes electrolysis?

A. A chemical reaction which results when electrical energy is passed through a metallic liquid
B. A chemical reaction resulting when electrical energy is passed through a liquid electrolyte
C. The splitting of atomic nuclei by electrical energy
D. The splitting of atoms by electrical energy
E. The passage of electrical energy through a split-field armature

52. In a battery, which of the following species in the two oxidation-reduction reactions is undergoing oxidation?

Reaction I: $Zn + 2\,OH^- \rightarrow ZnO + H_2O + 2\,e^-$

Reaction II: $2\,MnO_2 + H_2O + 2\,e^- \rightarrow Mn_2O_3 + 2\,OH^-$

A. H_2O **B.** MnO_2 **C.** ZnO **D.** Zn **E.** OH^-

53. How many electrons are needed to balance the charge for the following half-reaction in an acidic solution?

$C_2H_6O \rightarrow HC_2H_3O_2$

A. 6 electrons to the right side
B. 4 electrons to the right side
C. 3 electrons to the left side
D. 2 electrons to the left side
E. 8 electrons to the right side

54. Which of the statements is true regarding the following redox reaction occurring in an electrolytic cell?

$$3\,C\,(s) + 4\,AlCl_3\,(l) \xrightarrow{\text{Electricity}} 4\,Al\,(l) + 3\,CCl_4\,(g)$$

A. Al^{3+} is produced at the cathode
B. CCl_4 gas is produced at the anode
C. Reduction half-reaction: $C + 4\,Cl^- \rightarrow CCl_4 + 4\,e^-$
D. Oxidation half-reaction: $Al^{3+} + 3\,e^- \rightarrow Al$
E. None of the above

55. What is the term for an electrochemical cell that spontaneously produces electrical energy?

I. half-cell   II. electrolytic cell   III. dry cell

A. I and II only
B. II only
C. III only
D. II and III only
E. None of the above

56. The anode of a battery is indicated with a negative (–) sign because the anode is:

A. where electrons are adsorbed
B. positive
C. negative
D. where electrons are generated
E. determined by convention

57. Which is the strongest reducing agent for the following half-reaction potentials?

$$Sn^{4+} (aq) + 2\ e^- \rightarrow Sn^{2+} (aq) \qquad\qquad E° = -0.13\text{ V}$$
$$Ag^+ (aq) + e^- \rightarrow Ag\ (s) \qquad\qquad E° = +0.81\text{ V}$$
$$Cr^{3+} (aq) + 3\ e^- \rightarrow Cr\ (s) \qquad\qquad E° = -0.75\text{ V}$$
$$Fe^{2+} (aq) + 2\ e^- \rightarrow Fe\ (s) \qquad\qquad E° = -0.43\text{ V}$$

A. Cr (s)   **B.** Fe^{2+} (aq)   **C.** Sn^{2+} (aq)   **D.** Ag (s)   **E.** Sn^{2+} (aq) and Ag (s)

58. Which is true for the redox reaction occurring in a spontaneous electrochemical cell?

$$Zn\ (s) + Cd^{2+} (aq) \rightarrow Cd\ (s) + Zn^{2+} (aq)$$

A. Electrons flow from the Cd electrode to the Zn electrode

B. Anions in the salt bridge flow from the Cd half-cell to the Zn half-cell

C. Zn is reduced at the anode

D. Cd^{2+} is oxidized at the cathode

E. None of the above

59. Based upon the reduction potential: $Zn^{2+} + 2\ e^- \rightarrow Zn\ (s)$; $E° = -0.76$ V, does a reaction take place when Zinc (s) is added to aqueous HCl, under standard conditions?

A. Yes, because the reduction potential for H^+ is negative

B. Yes, because the reduction potential for H^+ is zero

C. No, because the oxidation potential for Cl^- is positive

D. No, because the reduction potential for Cl^- is negative

E. Yes, because the reduction potential for H^+ is positive

60. If 1 amp of current passes a cathode for 10 minutes, how much Zn (s) forms in the following reaction? (Use the molecular mass of Zn = 65 g/mole)

$$Zn^{2+} + 2\ e^- \rightarrow Zn\ (s)$$

A. 0.10 g   **B.** 10.0 g   **C.** 0.65 g   **D.** 2.20 g   **E.** 0.20 g

Notes

Chapter 9: Thermochemistry

1. Which of the following statement regarding the symbol ΔG is NOT true?

   A. Specifies the enthalpy of the reaction
   B. Refers to the free energy of the reaction
   C. Predicts the spontaneity of a reaction
   D. Describes the effect of both enthalpy and entropy on a reaction
   E. None of the above

2. What happens to the kinetic energy of a gas molecule when the gas is heated?

   A. Depends on the gas
   B. Kinetic energy increases

   C. Kinetic energy decreases
   D. Kinetic energy remains constant
   E. None of the above

3. How much heat energy (in Joules) is required to heat 21.0 g of copper from 21.0 °C to 68.5 °C? (Use the specific heat c of Cu = 0.382 J/g·°C)

   A. 462 J   B. 188 J   C. 522 J   D. 662 J   E. 381 J

4. For n moles of gas, which term expresses the kinetic energy?

   A. nPA, where n = number of moles of gas, P = total pressure and A = surface area of the container walls
   B. ½nPA, where n = number of moles of gas, P = total pressure and A = surface area of the container walls
   C. ½MV^2, where M – molar mass of the gas and V = volume of the container
   D. MV^2, where M = molar mass of the gas and V = volume of the container
   E. 3/2 nRT, where n = number of moles of gas, R = ideal gas constant, and T = absolute temperature

5. Which of the following is NOT an endothermic process?

   A. Condensation of water vapor
   B. Boiling liquid

   C. Water evaporating
   D. Ice melting

   E. All are endothermic

6. What is true of an endothermic reaction if it causes a decrease in the entropy (S) of the system?

   A. Only occurs at low temperatures when ΔS is insignificant
   B. Occurs if coupled to an endergonic reaction
   C. Never occurs because it decreases ΔS of the system
   D. Never occurs because ΔG is positive
   E. None of the above

7. Which of the following terms describe(s) energy contained in an object or transferred to an object?

       I. chemical   II. electrical   III. heat

  A. I only   **B.** II only   **C.** I and II only   **D.** I and III only   **E.** I, II and III

8. The greatest entropy is observed for which 10 g sample of CO_2?

  A. $CO_2 (g)$ **B.** $CO_2 (aq)$ **C.** $CO_2 (s)$ **D.** $CO_2 (l)$ **E.** All are equivalent

9. If a chemical reaction has $\Delta H = X$, $\Delta S = Y$, $\Delta G = X - RY$ and occurs at R K, the reaction is:

  A. spontaneous   **C.** nonspontaneous
  B. at equilibrium   **D.** irreversible   **E.** cannot be determined

10. The thermodynamic systems that have high stability tend to demonstrate:

  A. maximum ΔH and maximum ΔS **C.** minimum ΔH and maximum ΔS
  B. maximum ΔH and minimum ΔS **D.** minimum ΔH and minimum ΔS
                                       E. none of the above

11. Whether a reaction is endothermic or exothermic is determined by:

  A. an energy balance between bond breaking and bond forming, resulting in a net loss or gain of energy
  B. the presence of a catalyst
  C. the activation energy
  D. the physical state of the reaction system
  E. none of the above

12. What role does entropy play in chemical reactions?

  A. The entropy change determines whether the reaction occurs spontaneously
  B. The entropy change determines whether the chemical reaction is favorable
  C. The entropy determines how much product is produced
  D. The entropy change determines whether the reaction is exothermic or endothermic
  E. The entropy determines how much reactant remains

13. Calculate the value of $\Delta H°$ of reaction using provided bond energies.

       $H_2C=CH_2 (g) + H_2 (g) \rightarrow H_3C-CH_3 (g)$
       C–C: 348 KJ C≡C: 960 kJ
       C=C: 612 kJ C–H: 412 kJ   H–H: 436 kJ

  A. –348 kJ   **B.** +134 kJ   **C.** –546 kJ   **D.** –124 kJ   **E.** –238 kJ

14. The bond dissociation energy is:

    I. useful in estimating the enthalpy change in a reaction
    II. the energy required to break a bond between two gaseous atoms
    III. the energy released when a bond between two gaseous atoms is broken

A. I only
B. II only

C. I and II only
D. I and III only

E. I, II and III

15. Based on the following reaction, which statement is true?

$$N_2 + O_2 \rightarrow 2\ NO\ \text{(Use the value for enthalpy, } \Delta H = 43.3\ \text{kcal)}$$

A. 43.3 kcal are consumed when 2.0 mole of O_2 reacts
B. 43.3 kcal are consumed when 2.0 moles of NO are produced
C. 43.3 kcal are produced when 1.0 g of N_2 reacts
D. 43.3 kcal are consumed when 2.0 g of O_2 reacts
E. 43.3 kcal are produced when 2.0 g of NO are produced

16. Which of the following properties of a gas is/are a state function?

    I. temperature   II. heat   III. work

A. I only
B. I and II only

C. II and III only
D. I, II and III

E. II only

17. All of the following statements concerning temperature change as a substance is heated are correct, EXCEPT:

A. As a liquid is heated, its temperature rises until its boiling point is reached
B. During the time a liquid is changing to the gaseous state, the temperature gradually increases until all the liquid is changed
C. As a solid is heated, its temperature rises until its melting point is reached
D. During the time for a solid to melt to a liquid, the temperature remains constant
E. The temperature remains the same during the phase change

18. Calculate the value of $\Delta H°$ of reaction for:

$$O{=}C{=}O\ (g) + 3\ H_2\ (g) \rightarrow CH_3{-}O{-}H\ (g) + H{-}O{-}H\ (g)$$

Use the following bond energies, $\Delta H°$:

C–C: 348 kJ	C=C: 612 kJ	C≡C: 960 kJ	C–H: 412 kJ
C–O: 360 kJ	C=O: 743 kJ	H–H: 436 kJ	H–O: 463 kJ

A. –348 kJ
B. +612 kJ

C. –191 kJ
D. –769 kJ

E. +5,779 kJ

19. Which statement(s) is/are true for ΔS?

    I. ΔS of the universe is conserved
    II. ΔS of a system is conserved
    III. ΔS of the universe increases with each reaction

  A. I only   **B.** II only   **C.** III only   **D.** I and II only   **E.** I and III only

20. Which of the following reaction energies is the most endothermic?

  A. 360 kJ/mole   **B.** –360 kJ/mole   **C.** 88 kJ/mole   **D.** –88 kJ/mole   **E.** 0 kJ/mole

21. Which of the following is true for the ΔG of formation for N_2 (g) at 25 °C?

  A. 0 kJ/mol   **C.** negative
  B. positive   **D.** 1 kJ/mol   **E.** more information is needed

22. Which of the statements best describes the following reaction?

$$HC_2H_3O_2 \ (aq) + NaOH \ (aq) \rightarrow NaC_2H_3O_2 \ (aq) + H_2O \ (l)$$

  A. Acetic acid and NaOH solutions produce sodium acetate and H_2O
  B. Aqueous solutions of acetic acid and NaOH produce aqueous sodium acetate and H_2O
  C. Acetic acid and NaOH solutions produce sodium acetate solution and H_2O
  D. Acetic acid and NaOH produce sodium acetate and H_2O
  E. An acid plus a base produce H_2O and a salt

23. If a chemical reaction is spontaneous, which value must be negative?

  A. C_p **B.** ΔS **C.** ΔG **D.** ΔH **E.** K_{eq}

24. What is the purpose of the hollow walls in a closed hollow-walled container that is effective at maintaining the temperature inside?

  A. To trap air trying to escape from the container, which minimizes convection
  B. To act as an effective insulator, which minimizes convection
  C. To act as an effective insulator, which minimizes conduction
  D. To provide an additional source of heat for the container
  E. Reactions occur within the walls that maintain the temperature within the container

25. If the heat of reaction is exothermic, which of the following is always true?

  A. The energy of the reactants is greater than the products
  B. The energy of the reactants is less than the products
  C. The reaction rate is fast
  D. The reaction rate is slow
  E. The energy of the reactants is equal to that of the products

26. How much heat must be absorbed to evaporate 16 g of NH_3 to its condensation point at −33 °C? (Use heat of condensation for NH_3 = 1,380 J/g)

    A. 86.5 J   **B.** 2,846 J   **C.** 118 J   **D.** 22,080 J   **E.** 1,380 J

27. Which of the reactions is the most exothermic, if the following energy profiles have the same scale? (Use the notation of R = reactants and P = products)

           a   **b**   **c**   **d**

    A. a   **B.** b   **C.** c   **D.** d   **E.** Cannot be determined

28. What is the heat of formation of NH_3 (g) of the following reaction:

    $2\ NH_3\ (g) \rightarrow N_2\ (g) + 3\ H_2\ (g)$ (Use $\Delta H° = 92.4$ kJ/mol)

    A. −92.4 kJ/mol   **C.** 46.2 kJ/mol

    B. −184.4 kJ/mol   **D.** 92.4 kJ/mol   **E.** −46.2 kJ/mol

29. If a chemical reaction has a positive ΔH and a negative ΔS, the reaction tends to be:

    A. at equilibrium   **C.** spontaneous

    B. nonspontaneous   **D.** irreversible

                               E. unable to be determined

30. What happens to the entropy of a system as the components of the system are introduced to a larger number of possible arrangements, such as when liquid water transforms into water vapor?

    A. The entropy of a system is solely dependent upon the amount of material undergoing reaction

    B. The entropy of a system is independent of introducing the components of the system to a larger number of possible arrangements

    C. The entropy increases because there are more ways for the energy to disperse

    D. The entropy decreases because there are fewer ways in which the energy can disperse

    E. The entropy increases because there are fewer ways for the energy to disperse

31. Which of the following quantities is needed to calculate the amount of heat energy released as water turns to ice at 0 °C?

    A. The heat of condensation for water and the mass

    B. The heat of vaporization for water and the mass

    C. The heat of fusion for water and the mass

    D. The heat of solidification for water and the mass

    E. The heat of fusion for water only

32. A nuclear power plant uses ^{235}U to convert water to steam that drives a turbine which turns a generator to produce electricity. What are the initial and final forms of energy, respectively?

A. Heat energy and electrical energy
B. Nuclear energy and electrical energy
C. Chemical energy and mechanical energy
D. Chemical energy and heat energy
E. Nuclear energy and mechanical energy

33. Which statement(s) is/are correct for the entropy?

I. Higher for a sample of gas than for the same sample of liquid
II. A measure of the disorder in a system
III. Available energy for conversion into mechanical work

A. I only   B. II only   C. III only   D. I and II only   E. I, II and III

34. Given the following data, what is the heat of formation for ethanol?

$C_2H_5OH + 3 O_2 \rightarrow 2 CO_2 + 3 H_2O$: $\Delta H = 327.0$ kcal/mole

$H_2O \rightarrow H_2 + \frac{1}{2} O_2$: $\Delta H = +68.3$ kcal/mole

$C + O_2 \rightarrow CO_2$: $\Delta H = -94.1$ kcal/mole

A. −720.1 kcal   B. −327.0 kcal   C. +62.6 kcal   D. +720.1 kcal   E. +327.0 kcal

35. Based on the reaction shown, which statement is true?

$S + O_2 \rightarrow SO_2 + 69.8$ kcal

A. 69.8 kcal are consumed when 32.1 g of sulfur reacts
B. 69.8 kcal are produced when 32.1 g of sulfur reacts
C. 69.8 kcal are consumed when 1 g of sulfur reacts
D. 69.8 kcal are produced when 1 g of sulfur reacts
E. 69.8 kcal are produced when 1 g of sulfur dioxide is produced

36. In the reaction, $2 H_2 (g) + O_2 (g) \rightarrow 2 H_2O (g)$, entropy is:

A. increasing   C. inversely proportional
B. the same   D. decreasing   E. unable to be determined

37. For an isolated system, which of the following can NOT be exchanged between the system and its surroundings?

I. Temperature   II. Matter   III. Energy

A. I only   C. III only
B. II only   D. II and III only   E. I, II and III

38. Which is a state function?

    I. ΔG II. ΔH III. ΔS

  A. I only   **B.** II only   **C.** III only   **D.** I and II only   **E.** I, II and III

39. To simplify comparisons, the energy value of fuels is expressed in units of:

  A. kcal/g   **B.** kcal/L   **C.** J/kcal   **D.** kcal/mol   **E.** kcal

40. Which process is slowed down when an office worker places a lid on a hot cup of coffee?

    I. Radiation   II. Conduction   III. Convection

  A. I only   **B.** II only   **C.** III only   **D.** I and III only   **E.** I, II and III

41. Which statement below is always true for a spontaneous chemical reaction?

  A. $\Delta S_{sys} - \Delta S_{surr} = 0$ **C.** $\Delta S_{sys} + \Delta S_{surr} < 0$

  B. $\Delta S_{sys} + \Delta S_{surr} > 0$ **D.** $\Delta S_{sys} + \Delta S_{surr} = 0$

                                              E. $\Delta S_{sys} - \Delta S_{surr} < 0$

42. A fuel cell contains hydrogen and oxygen gas that react explosively, and the energy converts water to steam, which drives a turbine to turn a generator that produces electricity. What energy changes are employed in the process?

    I. Mechanical → electrical energy
    II. Heat → mechanical energy
    III. Chemical → heat energy

  A. I only   **C.** I and II only

  B. II only   **D.** I and III only   **E.** I, II and III

43. Determine the value of $\Delta E°_{rxn}$ for this reaction, whereby the standard enthalpy of reaction $(\Delta H_{rxn}°)$ is –311.5 kJ mol^{-1}:

    $C_2H_2\,(g) + 2\,H_2\,(g) \rightarrow C_2H_6\,(g)$

  A. –306.5 kJ mol^{-1} **C.** +346.0 kJ mol^{-1}

  B. –318.0 kJ mol^{-1} **D.** +306.5 kJ mol^{-1} **E.** +466 kJ mol^{-1}

44. Once an object enters a black hole, astronomers consider it to have left the universe which means the universe is:

  A. entropic   **C.** closed

  B. isolated   **D.** open   **E.** exergonic

45. Which reaction is accompanied by an *increase* in entropy?

    A. Na_2CO_3 (s) + CO_2 (g) + H_2O (g) → 2 $NaHCO_3$ (s)
    B. BaO (s) + CO_2 (g) → $BaCO_3$ (s)
    C. CH_4 (g) + H_2O (g) → CO (g) + 3 H_2 (g)
    D. ZnS (s) + 3/2 O_2 (g) → ZnO (s) + SO_2 (g)
    E. N_2 (g) + 3 H_2 (g) → 2 NH_3 (g)

46. Under standard conditions, which reaction has the largest difference between the energy of reaction and enthalpy?

    A. C (*graphite*) → C (*diamond*)
    B. C (*graphite*) + O_2 (g) → C (*diamond*)

    C. 2 C (*graphite*) + O_2 (g) → 2 CO (g)
    D. C (*graphite*) + O_2 (g) → CO_2 (g)
    E. CO (g) + NO_2 (g) → CO_2 (g) + NO (g)

47. Which is true for the thermodynamic functions *G*, *H* and *S* in $\Delta G = \Delta H - T\Delta S$?

    A. *G* refers to the universe, *H* to the surroundings and *S* to the system
    B. *G*, *H* and *S* refer to the system
    C. *G* and *H* refers to the surroundings and *S* to the system
    D. *G* and *H* refer to the system and *S* to the surroundings
    E. *G* and *S* refers to the system and *H* to the surroundings

48. Which of the following statements is true for the following reaction? (Use the change in enthalpy, $\Delta H° = -113.4$ kJ/mol and the change in entropy, $\Delta S° = -145.7$ J/K mol)

    2 NO (g) + O_2 (g) → 2 NO_2 (g)

    A. The reaction is at equilibrium at 25 °C under standard conditions
    B. The reaction is spontaneous at only high temperatures
    C. The reaction is spontaneous only at low temperatures
    D. The reaction is spontaneous at all temperatures
    E. $\Delta G°$ becomes more favorable as temperature increases

49. Which of the following expressions defines enthalpy? (Use the conventions: q = heat, U = internal energy, P = pressure and V = volume)

    A. $q - \Delta U$ **B.** $U + q$ **C.** q **D.** ΔU **E.** $U + PV$

50. Which statement is true regarding entropy?

    I. It is a state function
    II. It is an extensive property
    III. It has an absolute zero value

    A. I only   **B.** III only   **C.** I and II only   **D.** I and III only   **E.** I, II and III

51. Where does the energy released during an exothermic reaction originate from?

    A. The kinetic energy of the surrounding
    B. The kinetic energy of the reacting molecules
    C. The potential energy of the reacting molecules
    D. The thermal energy of the reactants
    E. The potential energy of the surrounding

52. The species in the reaction $KClO_3$ (*s*) → KCl (*s*) + $3/2O_2$ (*g*) have the values for standard enthalpies of formation at 25 °C. At constant physical states, assume that the values of $\Delta H°$ and $\Delta S°$ are constant throughout a broad temperature range. Which of the following conditions may apply for the reaction? (Use $KClO_3$ (*s*) with $\Delta H_f° = -391.2$ kJ mol^{-1} and KCl (*s*) with $\Delta H_f° = -436.8$ kJ mol^{-1})

    A. Nonspontaneous at low temperatures, but spontaneous at high temperatures
    B. Spontaneous at low temperatures, but nonspontaneous at high temperatures
    C. Nonspontaneous at all temperatures over a broad temperature range
    D. Spontaneous at all temperatures over a broad temperature range
    E. No conclusion can be drawn about spontaneity based on the information

53. What is the standard enthalpy change for the reaction?

$$P_4 \text{ (s)} + 6\ Cl_2 \text{ (g)} \rightarrow 4\ PCl_3 \text{ (l)} \quad \Delta H° = -1{,}289 \text{ kJ}$$

$$3\ P_4 \text{ (s)} + 18\ Cl_2 \text{ (g)} \rightarrow 12\ PCl_3 \text{ (l)}$$

    A. 426 kJ   **C.** −366 kJ
    B. −1,345 kJ   **D.** 1,289 kJ   **E.** −3,837 kJ

54. Which of the following reactions is endothermic?

    A. $PCl_3 + Cl_2 \rightarrow PCl_5 +$ *heat*   **C.** $CH_4 + NH_3 +$ *heat* $\rightarrow HCN + 3\ H_2$
    B. $2\ NO_2 \rightarrow N_2 + 2\ O_2 +$ *heat*   **D.** $NH_3 + HBr \rightarrow NH_4Br$
                                        E. $PCl_3 + Cl_2 \rightarrow PCl_5 +$ *heat*

55. When the system undergoes a spontaneous reaction, is it possible for the entropy of a system to decrease?

    A. No, because this violates the second law of thermodynamics
    B. No, because this violates the first law of thermodynamics
    C. Yes, but only if the reaction is endothermic
    D. Yes, but only if the entropy gain of the environment is greater than the entropy loss in the system
    E. Yes, but only if the entropy gain of the environment is smaller than the entropy loss in the system

56. A 500 ml beaker of distilled water is placed under a bell jar, which is then covered by a layer of opaque insulation. After several days, some of the water evaporated. The contents of the bell jar are what kind of system?

    A. endothermic   **C.** closed

    B. exergonic   **D.** open   **E.** isolated

57. If a stationary gas has a kinetic energy of 500 J at 25 °C, what is its kinetic energy at 50 °C?

    A. 125 J   **B.** 450 J   **C.** 540 J   **D.** 1,120 J   **E.** 270 J

58. Which is NOT true for entropy in a closed system according to the equation $\Delta S = Q/T$?

    A. Entropy is a measure of energy dispersal of the system

    B. The equation is only valid for a reversible process

    C. Changes due to heat transfer are greater at low temperatures

    D. Disorder of the system decreases as heat is transferred out of the system

    E. Increases as temperature decreases

59. In which of the following pairs of physical changes are both processes exothermic?

    A. Melting and condensation   **C.** Sublimation and evaporation

    B. Freezing and condensation   **D.** Freezing and sublimation

                                          E. None of the above

60. Which must be true concerning a solution that reached an equilibrium where chemicals are mixed in a redox reaction?

    A. $\Delta G° = \Delta G$ **B.** $E = 0$ **C.** $\Delta G° < 1$ **D.** $K = 1$ **E.** $K < 1$

Please, leave your Customer Review on Amazon

Chapter 10: Atomic and Nuclear Structure

1. The Bohr model of the atom was able to explain the Balmer series because:

   A. electrons could exist only in specific orbits and nowhere else
   B. differences between the energy levels of the orbits matched the differences between the energy levels of the line spectra
   C. smaller orbits require electrons to have more negative energy to match the angular momentum
   D. differences between the energy levels of the orbits were exactly half the differences between the energy levels of the line spectra
   E. none of the above

2. Which is the missing species in the nuclear equation: $^{100}_{44}\text{Ru} + ^{\,\,0}_{-1}\text{e}^- \rightarrow$ ___?

   A. $^{100}_{45}\text{Ru}$　　　 B. $^{100}_{43}\text{Ru}$　　　 C. $^{101}_{44}\text{Ru}$　　　 D. $^{100}_{43}\text{Tc}$　　　 E. $^{101}_{43}\text{Tc}$

3. An isolated ^9Be atom spontaneously decays into two alpha particles. What can be concluded about the mass of the ^9Be atom?

   A. The mass is less than twice the mass of the ^4He atom, but not equal to the mass of ^4He
   B. No conclusions can be made about the mass
   C. The mass is exactly twice the mass of the ^4He atom
   D. The mass is equal to the mass of the ^4He atom
   E. The mass is greater than twice the mass of the ^4He atom

4. Which of the following correctly balances this nuclear fission reaction?

   $$^1_0\text{n} + ^{235}_{92}\text{U} \rightarrow ^{131}_{53}\text{I} + \underline{\quad} + 3\,^1_0\text{n}$$

   A. $^{102}_{39}\text{Y}$　　　 B. $^{102}_{36}\text{Kr}$　　　 C. $^{104}_{39}\text{Y}$　　　 D. $^{105}_{36}\text{Kr}$　　　 E. $^{131}_{54}\text{I}$

5. Rubidium $^{87}_{37}\text{Rb}$ is a naturally-occurring nuclide which undergoes β^- decay. What is the resultant nuclide from this decay?

   A. $^{86}_{36}\text{Rb}$　　　 B. $^{87}_{38}\text{Kr}$　　　 C. $^{87}_{38}\text{Sr}$　　　 D. $^{87}_{36}\text{Kr}$　　　 E. $^{86}_{37}\text{Rb}$

6. Which of the following statements best describes the role of neutrons in the nucleus?

   A. The neutrons stabilize the nucleus by attracting protons
   B. The neutrons stabilize the nucleus by balancing charge
   C. The neutrons stabilize the nucleus by attracting other nucleons
   D. The neutrons stabilize the nucleus by repelling other nucleons
   E. The neutrons stabilize the nucleus by attracting electrons

7. An isolated ^{235}U atom spontaneously undergoes fission into two approximately equal-sized fragments. What is missing from the product side of the reaction: ^{235}U → ^{141}Ba + ^{92}Kr + ___ ?

    A. A neutron   **C.** Two protons and two neutrons

    B. Two neutrons   **D.** Two protons and a neutron

                               E. A proton and two neutrons

8. Which of the following nuclear equations correctly describes alpha emission?

    A. $^{238}_{92}$U → $^{242}_{94}$Pu + $^{4}_{2}$He   **C.** $^{238}_{92}$U → $^{234}_{90}$Th + $^{4}_{2}$He

    B. $^{238}_{92}$U → $^{4}_{2}$He   **D.** $^{238}_{92}$U → $^{235}_{90}$Th + $^{4}_{2}$He   **E.** None of the above

9. If ^{14}Carbon is a beta emitter, what is the likely product of radioactive decay?

    A. ^{22}Silicon   **C.** ^{14}Nitrogen

    B. ^{13}Boron   **D.** ^{12}Carbon   **E.** None of the above

10. Hydrogen atoms can emit four spectral lines with visible colors from red to violet. These four visible lines emitted by hydrogen atoms are produced by electrons that:

    A. end in the ground state   **C.** end in the n = 2 level

    B. end in the n = 3 level   **D.** start in the ground state   **E.** start in the n = 3 level

11. Why are some smaller nuclei such as ^{14}Carbon often radioactive?

        I. The attractive force of the nucleons has a limited range

        II. The neutron to proton ratio is too large or too small

        III. Most smaller nuclei are not stable

    A. I only   **B.** II only   **C.** III only   **D.** II and III only   **E.** I and III only

12. Scandium ^{44}Sc decays by emitting a positron. What is the resultant nuclide which is produced by this decay?

    A. $^{43}_{21}$Sc   **B.** $^{45}_{21}$Sc   **C.** $^{44}_{20}$Ca   **D.** $^{43}_{20}$Ca   **E.** $^{45}_{22}$Ti

13. According to the Pauli Exclusion Principle, how many electrons in an atom may have a particular set of quantum numbers?

    A. 1   **B.** 2   **C.** 3   **D.** 4   **E.** 5

14. The rest mass of a proton is 1.0072764669 amu and that of a neutron is 1.0086649156 amu. The ^{4}He nucleus weighs 4.002602 amu. What is the total binding energy of the nucleus? (Use the speed of light $c = 3 \times 10^8$ m/s and the conversion of 1 amu = 1.6606×10^{-27} kg)

A. 2.7×10^{-11} J

C. 1.6×10^{-7} J

B. 4.4×10^{-12} J

D. 2.6×10^{-12} J

E. 4.4×10^{-10} J

15. The material used in nuclear bombs is ^{239}Pu, with a half-life of about 20,000 years. What is the approximate amount of time that must elapse for a buried stockpile of this substance to decay to 3% of its original ^{239}Pu mass?

A. 0.8 thousand years

C. 90 thousand years

B. 65 thousand years

D. 101 thousand years

E. 184 thousand years

16. The radial distance between the nucleus and the orbital shell in a hydrogen atom:

A. varies randomly with increasing values of n

B. remains constant for all values of n

C. decreases with increasing values of n

D. increases with increasing values of n

E. increases with decreasing values of n

17. Which is the best description of an alpha particle?

A. Charge of –1; mass of 0 amu; low penetrating power

B. Charge of –2; mass of 4 amu; medium penetrating power

C. Charge of +2; mass of 4 amu; low penetrating power

D. Charge of +2; mass of 4 amu; high penetrating power

E. Charge of 0; mass of 4 amu; high penetrating power

18. Which isotope has the maximum binding energy per nucleon and therefore is represented as the maximum in the binding energy per nucleon curve?

A. ^{56}Fe   B. ^{1}H   C. ^{251}Cf   D. ^{197}Au   E. ^{4}He

19. If the nucleus $^{15}_{7}$N is bombarded with a proton, one or more products are formed. Which of the following represents a possible set of products from this reaction?

A. ^{16}N + γ B. ^{14}B + ^{2}Li   C. ^{15}O + γ D. ^{12}C + ^{4}He   E. ^{12}C + ^{2}He

20. How many 3d electron states can an atom have?

A. 0   B. 4   C. 6   D. 8   E. 10

21. Beyond which element in the periodic table (based on atomic number) are the successive elemental nuclei considered to be radioactive?

    A. Barium   **B.** Bismuth   **C.** Uranium   **D.** Radium   **E.** Lead

22. To which of the following values of n does the shortest wavelength in the Balmer series correspond? (Use the Balmer series constant $B = 3.645 \times 10^{-7}$ m)

    A. 1   **B.** 5   **C.** 3   **D.** 7   **E.** ∞

23. A common reaction in the Sun involves the encounter of two nuclei of light helium ($^3_2$He). If one ^{3}He nucleus encounters another, which products are possible?

    A. ^{2}H + ^{2}H + ^{2}H   **C.** ^{4}He + ^{1}H + ^{1}H

    B. ^{7}Li + ^{1}H   **D.** ^{4}He + ^{2}H   **E.** ^{4}He + ^{1}H

24. Suppose the half-life of some element is two days. 10 grams of this element is contained in a mixture produced by a laboratory three days ago. If the element is isolated from the mixture, how much of it would remain after three days from its separation from the mixture?

    A. 0.75 grams   **B.** 3.5 grams   **C.** 2.5 grams   **D.** 4.5 grams   **E.** 1.25 grams

25. Nuclear fusion:

    A. produces non-radioactive elements
    B. is the energy source of the Sun and stars
    C. releases a larger amount of heat than nuclear fission
    D. is the formation of heavier elements from lighter ones
    E. all of the above

26. Which of the following statements is true for the Bohr model of the atom?

    A. As the electron shells increase, the shells get further apart, but the difference in the energy between them gets smaller
    D. As electron shells increase, they get closer together, but the difference in energy between them gets greater
    C. The energy difference between all the electron shells is the same
    D. The spacing between all the electron shells is the same
    E. There is no general pattern in the spacing of the electron shells or their energy differences

27. The control rods of a nuclear reactor regulate the chain reaction because they:

    A. produce positrons   **C.** absorb the ^{235}U atoms
    B. absorb the neutrons   **D.** contain catalysts
                               E. absorb the protons

28. Which statement describes an atom that loses an alpha particle?

    A. The atomic number remains the same and the mass number decreases

    B. The mass number decreases by 2, but its atomic number remains the same

    C. The atomic number increases by 1, but its mass number remains the same

    D. The atomic number decreases by 2, and its mass number decreases by 4

    E. The mass number remains the same and atomic number decreases

29. In order for the atoms in a neon discharge tube to emit light characteristic of a brilliant red color, it is necessary that:

    A. the electrons gain energy to be promoted from their ground state to an excited state

    B. the atoms be continually replaced with fresh atoms

    C. each atom carries a net electric charge

    D. there be no unoccupied energy levels in each atom

    E. the current fluctuates to modulate the activity of the electrons

30. Neon has 10 electrons. What is the value for Z of the element with the next larger Z that has chemical properties very similar to those of neon?

    A. 10   **B.** 16   **C.** 18   **D.** 24   **E.** 32

31. Observing the emission spectrum of a hypothetical atom, a line corresponding to a wavelength 1.25×10^{-7} m is observed from the transition to the ground state. If the ground state has zero energy, what other energy level must exist in this atom? (Use Planck's constant $h = 6.63 \times 10^{-34}$ J·s and the speed of light $c = 3 \times 10^8$ m/s)

    A. -3.3×10^{-18} J   **C.** 1.6×10^{-18} J

    B. -1.6×10^{-18} J   **D.** 3.3×10^{-32} J   **E.** 3.3×10^{-18} J

32. In massive stars, three helium nuclei fuse, forming a carbon nucleus, and this reaction heats the core of the star. What is the net mass of the three helium nuclei?

    A. Same as the carbon nucleus because energy is always conserved

    B. Same as the carbon nucleus because mass is always conserved

    C. Less than that of the carbon nucleus

    D. Greater than the carbon nucleus

    E. Same as the carbon nucleus because mass and energy are always conserved

33. Why is the planetary model of an atom, with the nucleus playing the role of the Sun and the electrons playing the role of planets, flawed?

    A. The electrical attraction between a proton and an electron is too weak

    B. An electron is accelerating and loses energy

    C. The nuclear attraction between a proton and an electron is too strong

    D. An electron is accelerating and gains energy

    E. The planetary model is valid to describe the electrons around an atom

34. Natural line broadening can be understood in terms of the:

    A. Schrodinger wave equation   **C.** de Broglie wavelength

    B. Pauli exclusion principle   **D.** uncertainty principle   **E.** quantum numbers

35. Elements combine in fixed mass ratios to form compounds. This requires that those elements:

    A. have unambiguous atomic numbers

    B. are always chemically active

    C. are composed of continuous matter without subunits

    D. are composed of discrete subunits called atoms

    E. none of the above are required

Notes

Chapter 11: Quantum Chemistry

1. The work function of a certain metal is 1.90 eV. What is the longest wavelength of light that can cause photoelectron emission from this metal?

A. 64 nm

B. 98 nm

C. 247 nm

D. 449 nm

E. 653 nm

2. Which of the following statements is correct if the frequency of the light in a laser beam is doubled while the number of photons per second in the beam is fixed?

    I. The power in the beam does not change

    II. The intensity of the beam doubles

    III. The energy of individual photons does not change

A. I only

B. II only

C. III only

D. I and II only

E. I, II and III

3. A high energy photon collides with matter and creates an electron-positron pair. What is the minimum frequency of the photon? (Use the $m_{electron} = 9.11 \times 10^{-31}$ kg, the speed of light $c = 3.00 \times 10^{8}$ m/s, and Planck's constant $h = 6.626 \times 10^{-34}$ J·s)

A. greater than 1.24×10^{12} Hz

B. greater than 2.47×10^{16} Hz

C. greater than 2.47×10^{20} Hz

D. greater than 2.47×10^{22} Hz

E. greater than 1.24×10^{24} Hz

4. What is the longest wavelength of light that can cause photoelectron emission from a metal that has a work function of 2.20 eV?

A. 216 nm

B. 372 nm

C. 484 nm

D. 564 nm

E. 642 nm

5. What is the energy of an optical photon of frequency 6.43×10^{14} Hz (Use Planck's constant $h = 6.626 \times 10^{-34}$ J·s and the conversion of 1 eV $= 1.60 \times 10^{-19}$ J)

A. 1.04 eV

B. 1.86 eV

C. 2.66 eV

D. 3.43 eV

E. 5.37 eV

6. A photocathode has a work function of 2.4 eV. The photocathode is illuminated with monochromatic radiation whose photon energy is 3.4 eV. What is the maximum kinetic energy of the photoelectrons produced? (Use the conversion of 1 eV $= 1.60 \times 10^{-19}$ J)

A. 3.4×10^{-20} J

B. 1.6×10^{-19} J

C. 4.6×10^{-19} J

D. 5.8×10^{-19} J

E. 7.2×10^{-18} J

7. A photocathode whose work function is 2.9 eV is illuminated with a white light that has a continuous wavelength band from 400 nm to 700 nm. What is the range of the wavelength band in this white light illumination for which photoelectrons are NOT produced?

A. 360 to 440 nm   **C.** 430 to 500 nm

B. 400 to 480 nm   **D.** 430 to 700 nm   **E.** 460 to 760 nm

8. What is the energy of the photon emitted when an electron drops from the $n = 20$ state to the $n = 7$ state in a hydrogen atom?

A. 0.244 eV   **C.** 0.336 eV

B. 0.288 eV   **D.** 0.404 eV   **E.** 0.492 eV

9. Protons are being accelerated in a particle accelerator. What is the de Broglie wavelength when the energy of the protons is doubled if the protons are non-relativistic (i.e., their kinetic energy is much less than mc^2)?

A. increases by a factor of 2   **C.** decreases by a factor of 2

B. increases by a factor of 3   **D.** decreases by a factor of $\sqrt{2}$

                                           E. increases by a factor of $\sqrt{2}$

10. A certain photon, after being scattered from a free electron that was at rest, moves at an angle of 120° with respect to the incident direction. If the wavelength of the incident photon is 0.591 nm, what is the wavelength of the scattered photon? (Use $m_{electron} = 9.11 \times 10^{-31}$ kg, the speed of light $c = 3.00 \times 10^8$ m/s and Planck's constant $h = 6.626 \times 10^{-34}$ J·s)

A. 0.0 nm   **C.** 0.252 nm

B. 0.180 nm   **D.** 0.366 nm   **E.** 0.595 nm

11. What is the wavelength of the most intense light emitted by a giant star of surface temperature 5000 K? (Use the constant in Wien's law = 0.00290 m·K)

A. 366 nm   **C.** 490 nm

B. 448 nm   **D.** 540 nm   **E.** 580 nm

12. A laser produces a beam of 4000 nm light. A shutter allows a pulse of light, for 30.0 ps, to pass. What is the uncertainty in the energy of a photon in the pulse? (Use Planck's constant $h = 6.626 \times 10^{-34}$ J·s and the conversion of 1 eV $= 1.60 \times 10^{-19}$ J)

A. 2.6×10^{-2} eV   **C.** 6.8×10^{-4} eV

B. 4.2×10^{-3} eV   **D.** 2.2×10^{-5} eV   **E.** 2.4×10^{-6} e

13. A photocathode has a work function of 2.4 eV. The photocathode is illuminated with monochromatic radiation whose photon energy is 3.5 eV. What is the wavelength of the illuminating radiation?

   A. 280 nm   **C.** 350 nm

   B. 325 nm   **D.** 395 nm   **E.** 420 nm

14. If the wavelength of a photon is doubled, what happens to its energy?

   A. It is reduced to one-half of its original value

   B. It stays the same

   C. It is doubled

   D. It is increased to four times its original value

   E. It is reduced to one-fourth of its original value

15. A photocathode has a work function of 2.8 eV. The photocathode is illuminated with monochromatic radiation. What is the threshold frequency for the monochromatic radiation required to produce photoelectrons?

   A. 1.2×10^{14} Hz   **C.** 4.6×10^{14} Hz

   B. 2.8×10^{14} Hz   **D.** 6.8×10^{14} Hz   **E.** 8.4×10^{14} Hz

16. When the surface of a metal is exposed to blue light, electrons are emitted. Which of the following increases if the intensity of the blue light increases?

      I. the maximum kinetic energy of the ejected electrons

      II. the number of electrons ejected per second

      III. the time lag between the onset of the absorption of light and the ejection of electrons

   A. I only   **C.** III only

   B. II only   **D.** I and II only   **E.** I, II and III

17. In the spectrum of Hydrogen, the lines obtained by setting m = 1 in the Rydberg formula is referred to as the Lyman series. What is the wavelength of the spectral line of the 15th member of the Lyman series?

   A. 91.6 nm   **C.** 244.6 nm

   B. 126.2 nm   **D.** 368.2 nm   **E.** 462.8 nm

18. A photocathode whose work function is 2.5 eV is illuminated with a white light that has a continuous wavelength band from 360 nm to 700 nm. What is the stopping potential for this white light illumination?

   A. 0.95 V   **C.** 1.90 V

   B. 1.45 V   **D.** 2.6 V   **E.** 3.2 V

19. If the momentum of an electron is 1.95×10^{-27} kg·m/s, what is its de Broglie wavelength? (Use Planck's constant $h = 6.626 \times 10^{-34}$ J·s)

A. 86.2 nm

B. 130.6 nm

C. 240.8 nm

D. 340.0 nm

E. 640.5 nm

20. A Hydrogen atom is excited to the n = 9 level. Its decay to the n = 6 level is detected in a photographic plate. What is the frequency of the light photographed?

A. 3,810 Hz

B. 7,240 Hz

C. 5.08×10^{13} Hz

D. 3.28×10^{-9} Hz

E. 2.24×10^{6} Hz

21. How much energy is carried by a photon of light having frequency 110 GHz? (Use Planck's constant $h = 6.626 \times 10^{-34}$ J·s)

A. 7.3×10^{-23} J

B. 2.9×10^{-25} J

C. 1.7×10^{-26} J

D. 1.1×10^{-21} J

E. 4.4×10^{-22} J

22. How many of the infinite number of Balmer spectrum lines are in the visible spectrum range?

A. 0

B. 2

C. 4

D. 6

E. infinite

23. Each photon in a beam of light has an energy of 4.20 eV. What is the wavelength of this light? ($c = 3.00 \times 10^{8}$ m/s, Planck's constant $h = 6.626 \times 10^{-34}$ J·s and 1 eV = 1.60×10^{-19} J)

A. 118.0 nm

B. 296.0 nm

C. 365.0 nm

D. 462.0 nm

E. 520.0 nm

24. Electrons are emitted from a surface when the light of wavelength 500.0 nm is shone on the surface, but electrons are not emitted for longer wavelengths of light. What is the work function of the surface?

A. 0.5 eV

B. 1.6 eV

C. 2.5 eV

D. 3.8 eV

E. 5.6 eV

25. In the Bohr theory, the orbital radius depends upon the principal quantum number in what way?

A. n

B. 1/n

C. n^2

D. n^3

E. $1/n^2$

26. What is the wavelength of the light emitted by atomic Hydrogen according to the Balmer formula with m = 9 and n = 11?

A. 8,500 nm   **C.** 22,300 nm

B. 14,700 nm   **D.** 31,900 nm   **E.** 39,400 nm

27. Upon being struck by 240.0 nm photons, a material ejects electrons with a maximum kinetic energy of 2.58 eV. What is the work function of this material?

A. 1.20 eV   **C.** 2.60 eV

B. 2.82 eV   **D.** 3.46 eV   **E.** 4.60 eV

28. A beam of light falling on a metal surface is causing electrons to be ejected from the surface. If the frequency of the light now doubles, which of the following statements is always true?

A. The number of electrons ejected per second doubles
B. Twice as many photons hit the metal surface as before
C. The kinetic energy of the ejected electrons doubles
D. The speed of the ejected electrons doubles
E. None of the above statements is always true

29. What is the longest wavelength of a photon that can be emitted by a hydrogen atom, for which the initial state is n = 3?

A. 486 nm   **C.** 540 nm

B. 510 nm   **D.** 610 nm   **E.** 656 nm

30. Which of the following always increases if the brightness of a beam of light is increased without changing its color?

    I. the speed of the photons
    II. the average energy of each photon
    III. the number of photons

A. I only   **C.** III only

B. II only   **D.** I and II only   **E.** I, II and III

31. The radius of a typical nucleus is about 5.0×10^{-15} m. Assuming this to be the uncertainty in the position of a proton in the nucleus, what is the uncertainty in the proton's energy? (Use 1.67×10^{-27} kg as the proton mass)

A. 0.06 MeV   **C.** 0.4 MeV

B. 0.25 MeV   **D.** 0.8 MeV   **E.** 1.2 MeV

32. A photocathode has a work function of 2.4 eV. The photocathode is illuminated with monochromatic radiation, and electrons are emitted with a stopping potential of 1.1 volts. What is the wavelength of the illuminating radiation? (Use the speed of light $c = 3.00 \times 10^8$ m/s, Planck's constant $h = 6.626 \times 10^{-34}$ J·s and the conversion of 1 eV $= 1.60 \times 10^{-19}$ J)

A. 300 nm   **C.** 390 nm

B. 350 nm   **D.** 420 nm   **E.** 480 nm

33. The Compton effect directly demonstrated which property of electromagnetic radiation?

     I. energy content
     II. particle nature
     III. momenta

A. I only   **C.** I and II only

B. II only   **D.** II and III only   **E.** I, II and III

34. What is the wavelength of the matter wave associated with an electron moving with a speed of 2.5×10^7 m/s? (Use the $m_{electron} = 9.11 \times 10^{-31}$ kg and Planck's constant $h = 6.626 \times 10^{-34}$ J·s)

A. 17 pm   **C.** 39 pm

B. 29 pm   **D.** 51 pm   **E.** 76 pm

Notes

Chapter 12: Organic Chemistry Nomenclature

1. Name the structure:

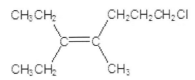

A. *cis*-7-chloro-3-ethyl-4-methyl-3-heptene   C. 1-chloro-5-ethyl-4-methyl-3-heptene

B. 1-chloro-3-pentenyl-2-pentene   D. 7-chloro-3-ethyl-4-methyl-3-heptene

                                    E. *trans*-7-chloro-3-ethyl-4-methyl-3-heptene

2. What is the IUPAC name for the following compound?

A. 1-methyl-4-cyclohexene   C. 4-methylcyclohexene

B. 1-methyl-3-cyclohexene   D. 5-methylcyclohexene

                                E. methylcyclohexene

3. Give the formula of the structure below:

A. C_8H_{14} B. C_8H_{12} C. C_8H_{10} D. C_8H_8 E. C_8H_{16}

4. Which structure is *para*-dibromobenzene?

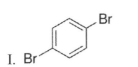

A. I only   B. II only   C. III only   D. I and II only   E. I, II and III

5. Ignoring geometric isomers, what is the IUPAC name for the following compound:

         $CH_3–CH=CH–CH_3$, is:

A. but-2-yne   C. butene-3

B. but-2-ene   D. butene-2   E. 2-butyl

6. What is the IUPAC name for the following structure:

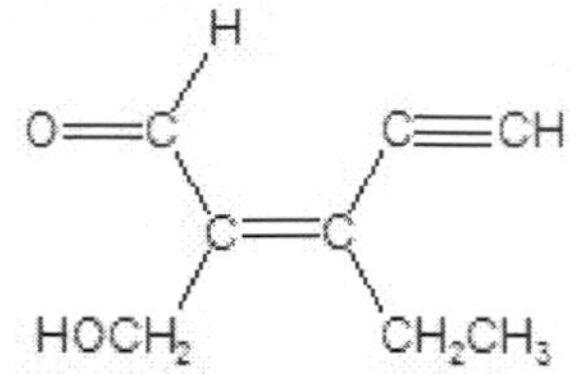

    A. (*Z*)-3-ethyl-5-hydroxymethyl-3-penten-1-ynal
    B. (*E*)-3-ethyl-5-hydroxymethyl-3-penten-1-ynal
    C. (*Z*)-3-ethyl-2-hydroxymethyl-2-penten-4-ynal
    D. (*E*)-3-ethyl-2-hydroxymethyl-2-penten-4-ynal
    E. 3-ethyl-5-hydroxymethyl-3-penten-1-ynal

7. Give the IUPAC name for the following structure:

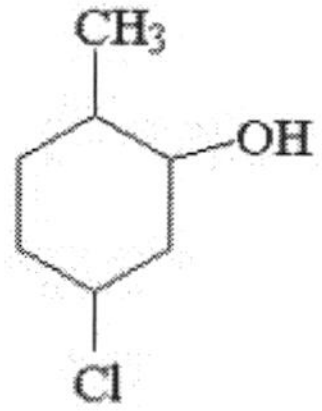

    A. 1-chloro-4-methylcyclohexanol   **C.** 3-chloro-2-methylcyclohexanol
    B. 5-chloro-2-methylcyclohexanol   **D.** 2-methyl-5-chlorocyclohexanol
                                   E. 2-methyl-3-chlorocyclohexanol

8. What is the name of the following compound?

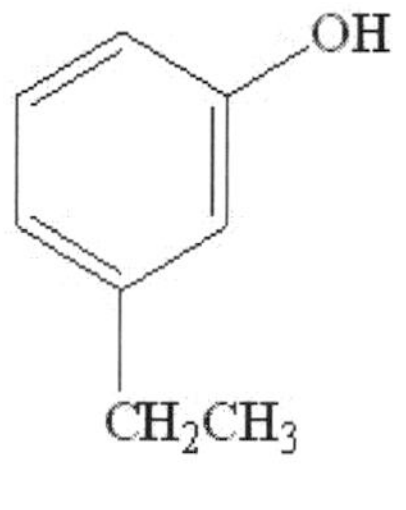

    A. *p*-ethylphenol   **C.** *o*-ethylphenol
    B. *m*-ethylbenzene   **D.** *m*-ethylphenol   **E.** none of the above

9. Provide the IUPAC name of the compound:

A. *N,N,*2-trimethyl-1-propanamine

B. *N,N,*2-trimethylpropanamine

C. *N,N,*1,1-tetramethylethanamine

D. *N,N*-dimethyl-2-butanamine

E. *N,N,*2-trimethyl-2-propanamine

10. Name the following structure:

A. *cis*-3,4-dimethyl-3-hepten-7-ol

B. *trans*-4,5-dimethyl-4-hepten-1-ol

C. *cis*-4,5-dimethyl-4-hepten-1-ol

D. *trans*-3,4-dimethyl-3-hepten-7-ol

E. *trans*-4,5-dimethyl-4-heptenol

11. What is the systematic name for the following compound?

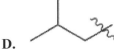

A. 3-methyl-2-pentanol

B. 4-methyl-3-pentanol

C. 2-methyl-3-pentenol

D. 2-methyl-3-pentanol

E. 3-methyl-3-pentanol

12. Which condensed structural formula is known as the isopropyl group?

A.

C.

B.

D.

E.

13. Which of the following compounds is named correctly?

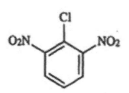

A. *meta*-fluorobenzoic acid

C. 2-iodo-1-bromobenzene

B. 2,5-dinitro-1-chlorobenzene

D. 1,3,dichloro-2-nitrobenzene

E. None of the above

14. Name the compound shown below.

A. *cis*-1,3-dichlorocyclohexane
B. *trans*-1,3-dichlorocyclohexane

C. *cis*-1,2-dichlorocyclohexane
D. *trans*-1,2-dichlorocyclohexane
E. *cis*-1,4-dichlorocyclohexane

15. What is the IUPAC name of the compound shown?

$$CH_3 - CH - CH_2 - CH - CH_3$$
$$\quad\quad | \quad\quad\quad\quad |$$
$$\quad\quad CH_3 \quad\quad\quad OH$$

A. 2, 2-dimethyl-4-butanol
B. 4, 4-dimethyl-2-butanol

C. 2-methyl-4-pentanol
D. 4-methyl-2-pentanol
E. 2-isohexanol

16. What is the IUPAC name of the compound shown below?

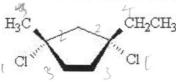

A. (1*R*,4*S*)-1,4-dichloro-1-ethyl-4-methylcyclopentane
B. (1*R*,3*S*)-1,3-dichloro-1-ethyl-3-methylcyclopentane
C. (1*S*,3*S*)-1,3-dichloro-1-ethyl-3-methylcyclopentane
D. (1*R*,3*S*)-1,3-dichloro-1-methyl-3-ethylcyclopentane
E. (1*S*,3*R*)-1,3-dichloro-3-ethyl-1-methylcyclopentane

17. The compound $CH_3(CH_2)_5CH_3$ is known as:

    A. heptane   **B.** hexene   **C.** hexane   **D.** pentane   **E.** octene

18. Name the following structure:

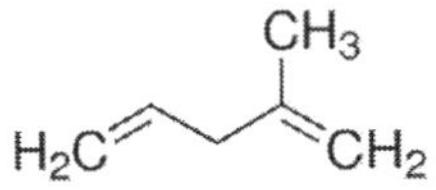

    A. 2-methylene-4-pentene   **C.** 2-methyl-2,4-pentadiene
    B. 4-methylene-2-pentene   **D.** 4-methyl-1,4-pentadiene
                                   E. 2-methyl-1,4-pentadiene

19. The name of the following alkyl group is $\sim CH_2CH_2CH_3$:

    A. ethyl   **C.** isopropyl
    B. propyl   **D.** *sec*-butyl   **E.** butyl

20. What is the complete systematic IUPAC name for the following compound?

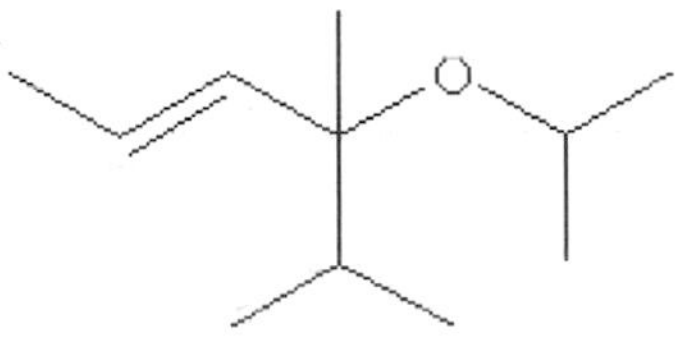

    A. isopropyl-(4-isopropyl-4-methylbut-2-enyl) ether
    B. (*E*)-4-isopropoxy-4,5-dimethylhex-2-ene
    C. 4-(1-methylethoxy)-4-isopropyl-4-methylpent-2-ene
    D. 4-isopropyl-2,4-dimethylhept-5-en-3-ol
    E. 4-isopropyl-4-methylbut-2-en-isopropyl ether

21. The IUPAC name for the compound $H_2C=CH–CH=CH_2$ is:

    A. 1,3-butadiene   **C.** butene-2
    B. butane-1,3   **D.** 1,3-dibutene   **E.** 2-butyne

22. What is the IUPAC name for salicylic acid shown below:

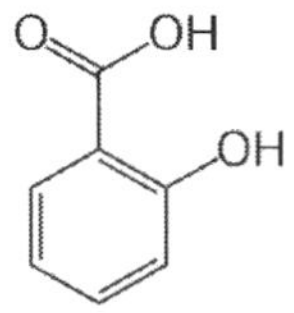

    A. 2-hydroxybenzoic acid   **C.** 1-hydroxybenzoic acid
    B. α-hydroxybenzoic acid   **D.** meta-hydroxybenzoic acid   **E.** 3-hydroxybenzoic acid

---

23. What is the common name for the simplest ketone, propanone?

    A. acetal   **C.** carbanone

    B. acetone   **D.** formalin   **E.** none of the above

24. The name of the compound shown below is:

    A. 3-ethyltoluene   **C.** 1-ethyl-4-methylbenzene

    B. 2-ethyltoluene   **D.** 1-ethyl-2-methylbenzene   **E.** 4-ethyltoluene

25. A compound with the molecular formula C_3H_6 is:

    A. butane   **C.** 2-methylpropane

    B. butyne   **D.** cyclopropane   **E.** propane

26. What is the correct IUPAC name for the following compound?

    A. 2-ethyl-4-methylhexane   **C.** 4-ethyl-2-methylhexane

    B. 2,4-dimethylhexane   **D.** 3,5-dimethylheptane   **E.** *sec*-butylpropane

27. Name the following structure according to IUPAC nomenclature:

    A. 3-ethyl-3-hexene   **C.** 2-propyl-1-butene

    B. 4-methylenehexane   **D.** 2-ethyl-1-pentene   **E.** ethyl-propylethene

28. What is the IUPAC name for the following structure?

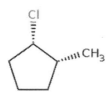

    A. *cis*-methylcyclohexane   **C.** *Z*-chloro-methylcyclohexane

    B. *cis*-1-chloro-2-methylcyclopentane   **D.** *cis*-2-chloro-2-methylcyclohexane

                                              E. *Z*-2-chloro-1-methylcyclohexane

29. The compound below is named:

A. pentanone

B. pentanal

C. butanaldehyde

D. pentaketone

E. pentanoic acid

30. Provide the common name of the compound:

A. neobutyldimethylamine

B. *sec*-butyldimethylamine

C. *tert*-butyldimethylamine

D. isobutyldimethylamine

E. *n*-butyldimethylamine

31. What is the correct IUPAC name for the following compound?

A. 2-oxocyclohex-3-ene-1-carboxylic acid

B. 5-formylcyclohex-2-enone-oic acid

C. 2-formylcyclohex-5-enone

D. 3-oxocyclohex-4-enoic acid

E. 2-oxocyclohex-3-ene carboate

32. What is the IUPAC name of the compound shown?

A. 3,4,6-trimethylheptane

B. 2,4,5-trimethylheptane

C. 3,5-dimethyl-2-ethylhexane

D. 2-ethyl-3,5-dimethylhexane

E. 5-ethyl-2,4-dimethylhexane

33. What is the IUPAC name for the following structure?

A. 5,6-dimethyl cyclohexane

B. *cis*-1,2-dimethyl cyclohexane

C. *trans*-1,2-dimethyl cyclohexane

D. 1,2-dimethyl cyclohexane

E. none of the above

34. Give the IUPAC name for the following structure:

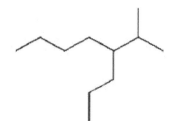

A. 4-isopropyloctane

B. 5-isopropyloctane

C. 3-ethyl-2-methylheptane

D. 2-methyl-3-ethylheptane

E. 2-methyl-3-propylheptane

35. Which name is NOT correct for IUPAC nomenclature?

A. 2,2-dimethylbutane

B. 2,3-dimethylpentane

C. 2,3,3-trimethylbutane

D. 2,3,4-trimethylpentane

E. All are correct names

36. Which compound has the common name *sec*-butylamine?

A. 1-butanamine

B. 2-butanamine

C. *N*-methyl-1-propanamine

D. *N*-methyl-2-propanamine

E. *N*-ethylethanamine

37. Which of the following is *cis*-2,3-dichloro-2-butene?

A.

C.

B.

D.

E. None of the above

38. Which of the following is the IUPAC name for this compound?

A. 3-ethylhexan-2-one

B. 4-ethylhexan-5-one

C. 3-propylpentan-2-one

D. 3-propylpentan-4-one

E. hexana-3-one

39. Name the structure shown below:

A. 1-chloro-3-cycloheptene
B. 4-chlorocycloheptane

C. 4-chlorocyclohexene
D. 1-chloro-3-cyclohexene   **E.** 4-chlorocycloheptene

40. Provide the IUPAC name of the compound:

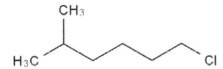

A. 1,1-dimethyl-5-chloropentane
B. 6-chloro-2-methylhexane

C. 1-chloro-5-methylhexane
D. 2-methyl-chloro-heptane
E. 1,1-dichloro-5-methylpentane

41. Ethyl propanoate is a(n):

A. ester   **B.** alcohol   **C.** aldehyde   **D.** carboxyl alcohol   **E.** amide

42. Provide the common name of the compound:

A. isoheptyl chloride
B. *tert*-heptyl chloride

C. neoheptyl chloride
D. *sec*-heptyl chloride   **E.** n-heptyl chloride

43. What is the IUPAC name of the molecule shown?

$$CH_2{=}CH{-}CH_2{-}CH_2{-}\underset{\underset{\displaystyle CH_3}{\overset{\displaystyle |}{CH_2}}}{\overset{\displaystyle |}{CH}}{-}CH_3$$

A. 2-ethyl-5-hexene
B. 5-ethyl-1-hexene

C. 5-methyl-1-heptene
D. 3-methyl-6-heptene   **E.** octane

44. Which of the following is NOT a proper condensed structural formula for an alkane?

A. $CH_3CHCH_3CH_2CH_3$

B. $CH_3CH_2CH_2CH_2CH_3$

C. $CH_3CH_3CH_3$

D. $CH_3CH_2CH_2CH_3$

E. CH_3CH_3

45. Which of the following is the IUPAC name for this compound?

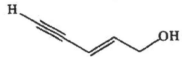

A. (*Z*)-pent-3-en-1-yn-5-ol

B. (*E*)-pent-3-en-1-yn-5-ol

C. (*Z*)-pent-2-en-4-yn-1-ol

D. (*E*)-pent-2-en-4-yn-1-ol

E. *Cis*-pent-2-en-4-yn-1-ol

46. What is the name of the following compound?

$H_3CCH_2CH_2CH_2CH_2CONH_2$

A. 1-hexanamide

B. hexanamide

C. hexanamine

D. hexamine

E. hexketoneamine

Notes

Chapter 13: Covalent Bond

1. Which of the following is a benzylic cation?

A.

C.

B. $\oplus CH_2$

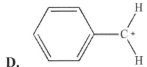

D.

E. CH_3

2. Which orbitals overlap to create the H–C bond in CH_3^+?

    A. s–p **B.** s–sp^2 **C.** sp^3–sp^3 **D.** sp^2–sp^3 **E.** s–sp^3

3. Which of the following structures, including formal charges, is correct for diazomethane, CH_2N_2?

    A. $H_2C=N^+=N^-$ **C.** $H2C=N^-=N^+$

    B. $H_2C=N^+\equiv N$ **D.** $^-CH_2-N\equiv N:$ **E.** $H_2C-N^{+3}\equiv N^{-3}$

4. What chemical reaction was used by German chemist Friedrich Wohler to synthesize urea for the first time?

    A. Heating ammonium cyanide

    B. Combining the elements carbon, hydrogen, oxygen and nitrogen

    C. Evaporating urine

    D. Heating ammonium cyanate

    E. None of the above

5. Which of the following is an allylic cation?

A.

C.

B.

D.

    E. $CH_3C^+HCH_3$

6. Which of the following best approximates the C–C–C bond angle of propene?

   A. 90°   **B.** 109°   **C.** 120°   **D.** 150°   **E.** 180°

7. What determines the polarity of a covalent bond?

   A. The difference in the total number of protons
   B. The difference in the total number of valence electrons
   C. The difference in the atomic size
   D. The difference in the electronegativity
   E. None of the above

8. What is the molecular geometry of an open-chain noncyclical hydrocarbon with the generic molecular formula C_nH_{2n-2}?

   A. trigonal pyramidal   **C.** tetrahedral
   B. trigonal planar   **D.** linear   **E.** none of the above

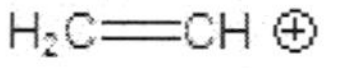

9. Identify the most stable carbocation:

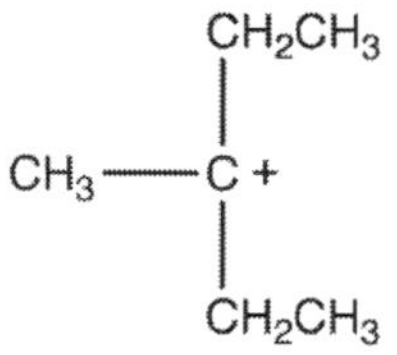

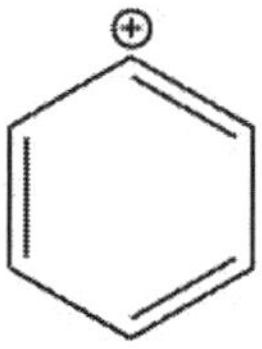

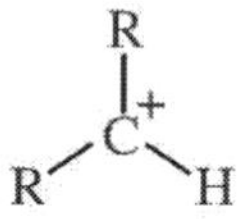

10. Consider the interaction of two hydrogen $1s$ atomic orbitals of the same phase. Which of the statements below is NOT a correct description of this interaction?

   A. The molecular orbital formed is cylindrically symmetric
   B. The molecular orbital formed has a node between the atoms
   C. The molecular orbital formed is lower in energy than a hydrogen $1s$ atomic orbital
   D. A *sigma* bonding molecular orbital is formed
   E. A maximum of two electrons may occupy the molecular orbital formed

11. In *trans*-hept-4-en-2-yne the shortest carbon-carbon bond is between carbons:

   A. 1 and 2   **C.** 3 and 4
   B. 2 and 3   **D.** 4 and 5   **E.** 5 and 6

12. What two atomic orbitals (or hybrid atomic orbitals) overlap to form the C=C π bond in ethylene?

A. C sp^2 + C p

B. C sp^2 + C sp^2

C. C sp^3 + C sp^2

D. C sp^3 + C sp^3

E. C p + C p

13. Which of the following is the most stable resonance contributor to acetic acid?

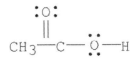

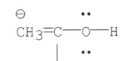

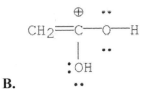   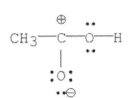

A.   **C.**

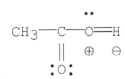

B.   **D.**   **E.**

14. The compound methylamine, CH_3NH_2, contains a C–N bond. In this bond, which of the following best describes the charge on the nitrogen atom?

A. uncharged

B. slightly negative

C. +1

D. slightly positive

E. −1

15. Which of the following molecules is the most polar?

A. acetaldehyde

B. acetic acid

C. ethane

D. ethylene

E. benzene

16. A molecule of acetylene (C_2H_2) has a [ ] geometry and a molecular dipole moment that is [ ].

A. bent, zero

B. linear, nonzero

C. tetrahedral, nonzero

D. bent, nonzero

E. linear, zero

17. Which of the following is NOT a resonance structure of the species shown?

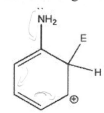

A.

B.

C.

D.

E. All are resonance forms

18. In an aqueous environment, which bond requires the most energy to break?

A. hydrogen

B. dipole-dipole

C. *sigma*

D. ionic

E. *pi*

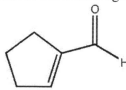

19. The nitrogen atom of trimethylamine is [   ] hybridized which is reflected in the C–N–C bond angle of [   ]:

A. *sp*, 180°

B. *sp²*, 120°

C. *sp²*, 108°

D. *sp³*, 120°

E. *sp³*, 108°

20. Which of the following statements concerning the cyclic molecule shown is NOT true?

A. It contains a π molecular orbital formed by the overlap of carbon *p* atomic orbitals

B. It contains a σ molecular orbital formed by the overlap of carbon *sp³* hybrid atomic orbitals

C. It contains a σ molecular orbital formed by the overlap of carbon *sp²* hybrid atomic orbitals

D. It contains a π molecular orbital formed by the overlap of a carbon *p* atomic orbital with an oxygen *p* atomic orbital

E. It contains a σ molecular orbital formed by the overlap of a carbon *p* atomic orbital with an oxygen *sp³* atomic orbital

21. Draw a structural formula for cyclohexane, a cyclic saturated hydrocarbon (C_6H_{12}). How many π bonds are in a cyclohexane molecule?

    A. 3   **B.** 4   **C.** 0   **D.** 2   **E.** 6

22. The N–H bond in the ammonium ion, NH_4^+, is formed by the overlap of which two orbitals?

    A. *sp²–s*   **B.** *sp²–sp²*   **C.** *sp³–sp²*   **D.** *sp³–sp³*   **E.** *sp³–s*

23. Among the hydrogen halides, the strongest bond is in [ ], and the longest bond is in [ ]?

    A. HI … HI   **C.** HF … HI

    B. HI … HF   **D.** HF … HF   **E.** HCl … HBr

24. Which of the following is the most stable carbocation?

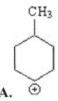

25. Which of the following is the least stable carbocation? (Use Ph = phenyl group)

    A. PhH_2C^+ **C.** Ph_3C^+

    B. $CH_3CH_2CH_2^+$ **D.** Ph_2HC^+ **E.** $CH_3CH_2C^+HCH_3$

26. The energy of an *sp³* hybridized orbital for a carbon atom is:

    A. lower in energy than both the 2*s* and the 2*p* atomic orbitals

    B. higher in energy than both the 2*s* and the 2*p* atomic orbitals

    C. higher in energy than the 2*p* atomic orbital, but lower in energy than the 2*s* atomic orbital

    D. higher in energy than the 2*s* atomic orbital, but lower in energy than the 2*p* atomic orbital

    E. equal in energy to the 2*p* atomic orbital

27. Which of the following pairs are resonance structures?

A. 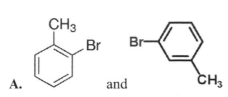 and

B. and

C. 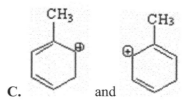 and

D. and

E. 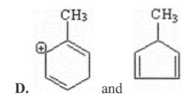 and

28. Due to electron delocalization, the carbon-oxygen bond in acetamide, CH_3CONH_2:

A. is longer than the carbon-oxygen bond of dimethyl ether, $(CH_3)_2O$
B. is longer than the carbon-oxygen bond of acetone, $(CH_3)_2CO$
C. is nonpolar
D. has more double bond character than the carbon-oxygen bond of acetone, $(CH_3)_2CO$
E. is formed by overlapping sp^3 orbitals

29. Which of the compounds listed below is linear?

A. 1,3,5-heptatriene
B. acetylene
C. 2-butyne
D. dichloromethane
E. 1,3-hexadiene

30. How many single and double bonds are in the benzene molecule (not including the C–H bonds)?

A. 6 single, 2 double
B. 5 single, 2 double
C. 6 single, 0 double
D. 5 single, 0 double
E. 6 single, 3 double

31. Determine the number of *pi* bonds in CH_3CN:

A. 0   **B.** 1   **C.** 2   **D.** 3   **E.** 4

32. Give the hybridization, shape, and bond angle for carbon in ethene:

A. sp^3, tetrahedral, 120°   C. sp^2, trigonal planar, 120°

B. sp^3, tetrahedral, 109.5°   D. sp^2, trigonal planar, 109.5°   E. none of the above

33. C=C, C=O, C=N, and N=N bonds are observed in many organic compounds. However, C=S, C=P, C=Si, and other similar bonds are not often found. What is the most probable explanation for this observation?

A. the comparative sizes of $3p$ atomic orbitals make effective overlap between them less likely than between two $2p$ orbitals

B. S, P, and Si do not undergo hybridization of orbitals

C. S, P and Si do not form π bonds due to the lack of occupied p orbitals in their ground state electron configurations

D. carbon does not combine with elements found below the second row of the periodic table

E. none of the above

34. How many σ bonds are in cyclohexane (C_6H_{12}), a saturated cyclic hydrocarbon?

A. 12   B. 14   C. 16   D. 18   E. 20

35. Triethylamine [$(CH_3CH_2)_3N$] is a molecule in which the nitrogen atom is [ ] hybridized, and the C–N–C bond angle is approximately [ ].

A. sp^3 ... < 107°   C. sp^2 ... > 109.5°

B. sp^3 ... 109.5°   D. sp^2 ... < 109.5°   E. sp ... 109.5°

36. How many distinct and degenerate p orbitals exist in the second electron shell, where n = 2?

A. 3   B. 2   C. 1   D. 0   E. 4

37. Which of the following compounds exhibits the greatest dipole moment?

A. (1S,2S)-1,2-dichloro-1,2-diphenylethane

B. 1,2-dichlorobutane

C. (1R,2S)-1,2-dichloro-1,2-diphenylethane

D. (E)-1,2-dichlorobutene

E. (Z)-1,2-dibromobutene

38. Draw a structural formula for benzene. How many σ bonds are in the molecule?

A. 14   B. 18   C. 6   D. 12   E. 20

39. Which is the formal charge of nitrogen in NH_4?

   A. −2   **B.** −1   **C.** 0   **D.** +1   **E.** +2

40. The nitrogen's lone pair in pyrrolidine is occupying which type of orbital?

   A. s **B.** sp^3 **C.** sp^2 **D.** sp **E.** p

41. Acetone is a common solvent used in organic chemistry laboratories. Which of the following statements is/are correct regarding acetone?

Acetone

   I. One atom is sp^3 hybridized and tetrahedral
   II. One atom is sp^2 hybridized and trigonal planar
   III. The carbonyl carbon contains an unshared pair of electrons

   A. I only   **B.** II only   **C.** I and II only   **D.** II and III only   **E.** I, II and III

42. Which of the following molecules represents the most stable carbocation?

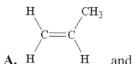

43. Which of the following pairs are resonance structures?

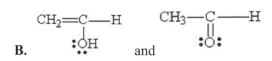

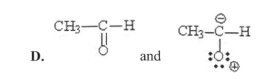

44. Which of the following is closest to the C–O–C bond angle in CH_3–O–CH_3?

A. 109.5° **B.** 90° **C.** 180° **D.** 120° **E.** 140°

45. Identify the number of carbon atoms for each hybridization in the molecule?

O=CH–CH_2–CH=C=C=CH_2

	sp	*sp*^{2}	*sp*^{3}
A.	1	4	1
B.	2	3	1
C.	0	3	3
D.	1	3	2
E.	2	3	2

46. Identify the correctly drawn arrows:

A. 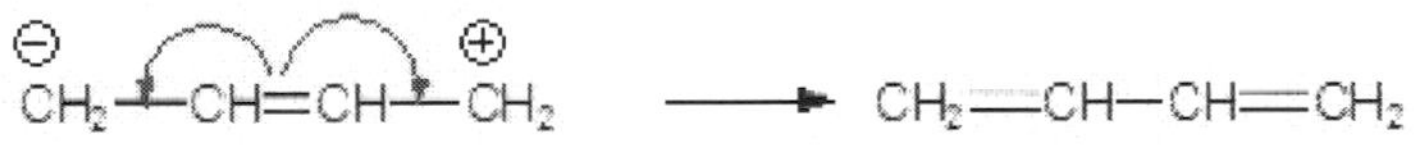

B. 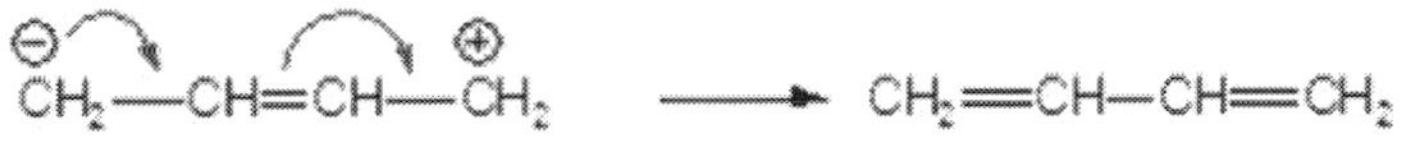

C. 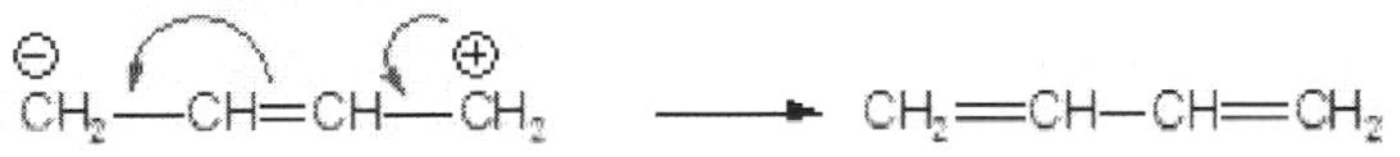

D. 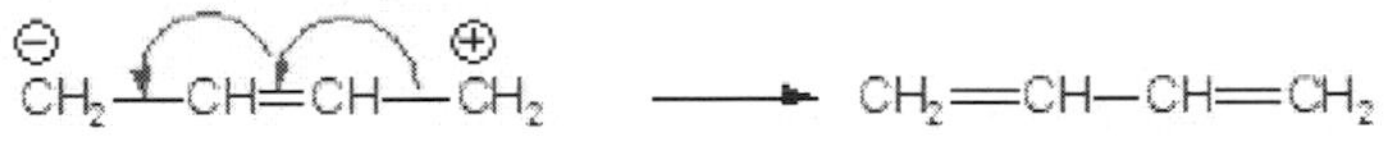

E. 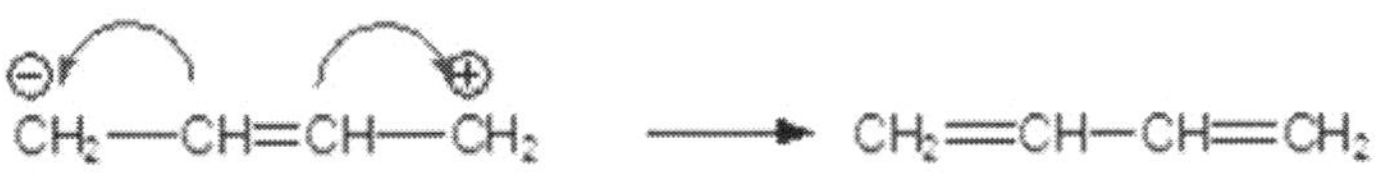

47. Triethylamine, $(CH_3CH_2)_3N$, is a molecule in which the nitrogen atom is [ ] hybridized and the molecular shape is [ ].

A. *sp*^{3} … trigonal pyramidal
B. *sp*^{3} … tetrahedral
C. *sp*^{2} … tetrahedral
D. *sp*^{2} … trigonal planar
E. *sp* … bent

48. Which of the following is the most stable cation?

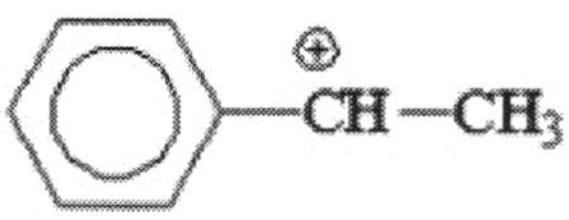

A. $CH_3\overset{\oplus}{C}{=}CH_2$

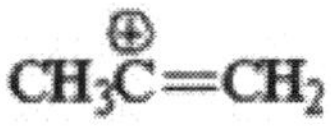

B. $CH_3CH{=}\overset{\oplus}{C}-$ ⬡

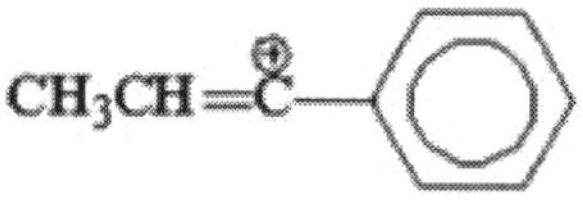

C. $CH_3-\underset{\overset{|}{\oplus}}{\overset{\overset{CH_3}{|}}{C}}$ ⬡

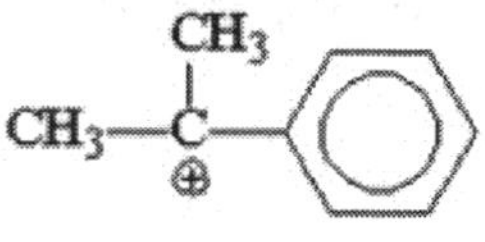

D. $H_3C-\underset{\oplus}{C}\overset{CH_3}{\underset{CH_3}{\diagdown}}$

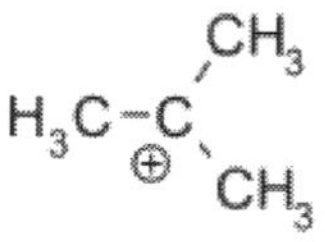

E. ⬡ $-\overset{\oplus}{CH}-CH_3$

Notes

Chapter 14: Stereochemistry

1. Butene, C_4H_8, is a hydrocarbon with one double bond. How many isomers are there of butene?

    A. two   **B.** three   **C.** four   **D.** five   **E.** no isomers

2. Which of the following compounds has an asymmetric center?

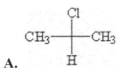

A.

C.

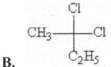

B.

D.

E.

3. How many stereoisomers are possible for the structure below?

    A. 2   **B.** 4   **C.** 8   **D.** 16   **E.** 32

4. *Cis-trans* isomerism occurs when:

    A. each carbon in an alkene double bond has two different substituent groups
    B. the carbons in the *para* position of an aromatic ring have the same substituent groups
    C. a branched alkane has a halogen added to two adjacent carbon atoms
    D. an alkene is hydrated according to Markovnikov's Rule
    E. hydrogen is added to both carbon atoms in a double bond

5. What is the relationship between the following molecules?

CH₃
CHCH₃   CH₂CH₃
CH₃CH₂—CH—CH—CH₂-CH—CH—CH₂CH₂CH₃
CH₃   CH₃

CH₂CH₃   CH₃
CH₂   CHCH₃
CH₃CH₂—CH—CH—CH₂-CH—CH—CH₃
CH₃   CH₂CH₃

A. different molecules   **C.** identical

B. enantiomers   **D.** isomers   **E.** diastereomers

6. What is the relationship between the structures shown below?

A. geometric isomers   **C.** constitutional isomers

B. conformational isomers   **D.** diastereomers   **E.** enantiomers

7. What is the relationship between the following compounds?

A. conformational isomers   **C.** superimposable without bond rotation

B. diastereomers   **D.** constitutional isomers

                                    E. enantiomers

8. Which of the following is NOT true of enantiomers?

A. Enantiomers have the same chemical reactivity with non-chiral reagents

B. Enantiomers have the same density

C. Enantiomers have the same melting point

D. Enantiomers have the same boiling point

E. Enantiomers have the same direction of specific rotation

9. When two compounds are made up of the same number and kind of atom but differ in their molecular structure, they are known as:

A. hydrocarbons

B. isomers

C. homologs

D. isotopes

E. allotropes

10. Identify the relationship between the compounds:

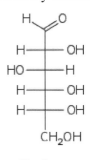

A. constitutional isomers

B. configurational isomers

C. identical

D. conformational isomers

E. none of the above

11. Which of the following carbons in the molecule below are chiral carbons?

$$\underset{1}{CH_2}-\underset{2}{\overset{O}{\overset{\|}{C}}}-\underset{3}{\overset{OH}{\overset{|}{CH}}}-\underset{4}{\overset{OH}{\overset{|}{CH}}}-\underset{5}{CH_2OH}$$

with OH on carbon 1

A. carbons 1 and 5

B. carbons 3 and 4

C. carbons 2, 3 and 4

D. all carbons are chiral

E. none of the carbon atoms are chiral

12. How many different stereoisomers can the following compound have?

D-glucose

A. 2   B. 4   C. 8   D. 16   E. 32

13. $CH_3–CH_2–O–H$ and $CH_3–O–CH_3$ are a pair of compounds that are:

A. isomers

B. epimers

C. anomers

D. allotropes

E. geometric isomers

---

14. What is the relationship between the two structures shown below?

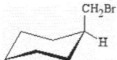 

and

A. conformational isomers

B. configurational isomers

C. enantiomers

D. constitutional isomers

E. not isomers

15. Among the butane conformers, which occur at energy minima on a graph of potential energy versus dihedral angle?

A. *anti*

B. eclipsed

C. *gauche*

D. eclipsed and *gauche*

E. *gauche* and *anti*

16. How many different isomers are there for dibromobenzene, $C_6H_4Br_2$?

A. 0   **B.** 1   **C.** 2   **D.** 3   **E.** 4

17. How many isomers are there of butane, C_4H_{10}?

A. 3   **B.** 4   **C.** 1 (no isomers)   **D.** 2   **E.** 5

18. What is the relationship between the following compounds?

 and

A. constitutional isomers

B. structural isomers

C. geometric isomers

D. conformational isomers

E. positional isomers

19. Which of the following compounds are isomers?

    I. $CH_3CH_2OCH_3$

    II. $CH_3CH_2CH_2OH$

    III. $CH_2COHCH_2CH_3$

    IV. $CH_3CH_2OCH_2CH_3$

A. I and II only

B. II and III only

C. III and IV only

D. I, II and III only

E. I, II, III and IV

20. The cause of *cis-trans* isomerism is:

A. short length of the double bond

B. strength of the double bond

C. lack of rotation of the double bond

D. stability of the double bond

E. vibration of the double bond

21. Which of the following compounds is an isomer of $CH_3CH_2CH_2CH_2OH$?

A. $CH_3CH_2CH_2OH$

B. $CH_3(OH)CHCH_3$

C. $CH_3CH_2CH_2CHO$

D. $CH_3CH_2(OH)CHCH_3$

E. CH_3OH

22. If two of the hydrogen atoms in ethylene, $H_2C=CH_2$, are replaced by one chlorine atom and one fluorine atom to form chlorofluoroethene, C_2H_2ClF, how many different chlorofluoro-ethene isomers are there?

A. 4 **B.** 3 **C.** 2 **D.** 1 **E.** 6

23. In the Fischer projection below, what are the configurations of the two asymmetric centers?

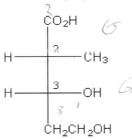

A. 2*S*, 3*S* **B.** 2*S*, 3*R* **C.** 2*R*, 3*S* **D.** 2*R*, 3*R* **E.** Cannot be determined

24. Which of the following terms best describes the pair of compounds shown?

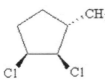

A. same molecule

B. conformational isomers

C. enantiomers

D. diastereomers

E. configurational isomers

25. If two of the hydrogen atoms in ethylene, $H_2C=CH_2$, are replaced by two chlorine atoms to form dichloroethylene, how many different dichloroethylene isomers are there?

A. 3 **B.** 4 **C.** 1 **D.** 2 **E.** 6

26. The enantiomer of the compound below is:

```
        CHO
         |
   H —— C —— OH
         |
   H —— C —— OH
         |
       CH₂OH
```

```
        CHO                          CHO
         |                            |
   H —— C —— OH              HO —— C —— H
         |                            |
  HO —— C —— H                 H —— C —— OH
         |                            |
       CH₂OH                        CH₂OH
A.                          C.
```

```
        CHO                          CHO
         |                            |
  HO —— C —— H                 H —— C —— OH
         |                            |
  HO —— C —— H                 H —— C —— OH
         |                            |
       CH₂OH                        CH₂OH
B.                          D.                    E. none of the above
```

27. Which of the statements correctly describes an achiral molecule?

A. The molecule has an enantiomer
B. The molecule may be a *meso* form
C. The molecule has a nonsuperimposable mirror image
D. The molecule exhibits optical activity when it interacts with plane-polarized light
E. None of the above

28. Which of the following statements does NOT correctly describe *cis*-1,2-dimethylcyclopentane?

A. Its diastereomer is *trans*-1,2-dimethylcyclopentane
B. It contains two asymmetric carbons
C. It is achiral
D. It is a *meso* compound
E. It has an enantiomer

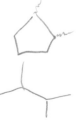

29. How many structural isomers of C₄H₈Cl₂ exhibit optical activity?

A. 0   B. 1   C. 2   D. 3   E. 4

30. How many chiral carbon atoms are in this structure?

$$CH_2-CH-CH-CHCH_3$$
$$\qquad|\qquad|\qquad|\qquad|$$
$$\;\;OH\quad OH\quad Br\quad Cl$$

A. 6 **B.** 5 **C.** 3 **D.** 4 **E.** 2

31. Which of the following is a true statement?

A. A mixture of achiral compounds is optically inactive

B. All molecules that possess a single chirality center of the *S* configuration are levorotatory

C. All achiral molecules are *meso*

D. All chiral molecules possess a plane of symmetry

E. All molecules that possess 2 or more chiral centers are chiral

32. Which of the following best describes the geometry about the carbon-carbon double bond in the alkene below?

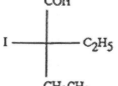

A. *E* **B.** *Z* **C.** *cis* **D.** *R* **E.** *S*

33. Which of the following compounds share the same absolute configuration?

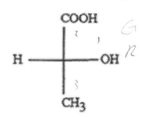

I.

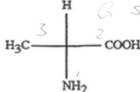

II.

III.

IV.

A. I and III only **C.** I and IV only

B. I and II only **D.** II, III and IV only **E.** II and IV only

34. What is the correct IUPAC name for the following structure?

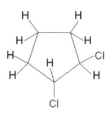

A. *trans*-1,2-dichlorocyclopentane
B. 1,2-dichlorocyclopentane

C. *cis*-1,2-dichlorocyclopentane
D. *trans*-dichlorocyclopentane
E. *Z*-dichlorocyclopentane

35. Which of the following compounds is NOT chiral?

A. 1,2-dichlorobutane
B. 1,4-dibromobutane

C. 2,3-dibromobutane
D. 1,3-dibromobutane

E. 1-bromo-2-chlorobutane

36. The specific rotation of a pure enantiomeric substance is –6.30°. What is the percentage of this enantiomer in a mixture with an observed specific rotation of –3.15°?

A. 75%   B. 80%   C. 25%   D. 50%   E. 0%

37. Which of the following is a result of the reaction below?

(S)-3-bromo-3-methylhexane + HCN

A. loss of optical activity
B. mutarotation

C. retention of optical activity
D. inversion of absolute configuration
E. epimerization

38. If two chlorine atoms replace two of the hydrogen atoms in butane, how many different dichlorobutane constitutional isomers can there be?

A. 4   B. 3   C. 2   D. 1   E. 6

39. How many asymmetric centers are present in the compound shown below?

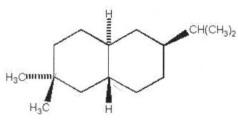

A. 1   B. 2   C. 3   D. 4   E. 5

40. What is the relationship between the structures shown below?

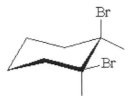

A. identical compounds   **C.** diastereomers

B. configurational isomers   **D.** enantiomers

                       E. constitutional isomers

41. Which of the following statement(s) for the compound *meso*-tartaric acid is/are true?

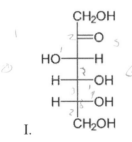

I. achiral

II. the polarimeter reads a zero deflection

III. racemic mixture

A. I only   **B.** II only   **C.** III only   **D.** I and II only   **E.** II and III only

42. Which of the following molecules are identical?

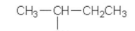

A. I and II   **C.** II and III

B. I and III   **D.** I, II and III   **E.** None of the above

43. Which of the following molecules contains a chiral carbon?

A. $CH_3-CH-CH_2CH_3$
             |
             CH_3

C. $CH_3-C-CH_2CH_3$ with $=O$

B. $CH_3-CH-CH_2CH_3$
             |
             OH

D. $CH_3-CH-CH_3$
             |
             OH

E. none of the above

44. What is the relationship between the following compounds?

and

A. conformational isomers
B. constitutional isomers
C. diastereomers
D. enantiomers
E. identical

45. Which of the following statements about *cis-* / *trans*-isomers is NOT correct?

A. Conversion between *cis–* and *trans*-isomers occurs by rotation around the double bond
B. In the *trans*-isomer, the groups of interest are on opposite sides across the double bond
C. In the *cis*-isomer, the reference groups are on the same side of the double bond
D. There are no *cis-* / *tran*-isomers in alkynes
E. There are no *cis* / *trans* isomers in alkanes

46. Which of the following best describes the geometry about the carbon-carbon double bond in the alkene below?

A. *E*
B. *Z*
C. *cis*

D. *S*
E. *R*

47. Which of the following is a structural isomer of 2-methylbutane?

A. *n*-propane
B. 2-methylpropane
C. *n*-butane
D. *n*-pentane
E. *n*-heptane

Notes

Chapter 15: Molecular Structure and Spectra

1. In the proton NMR, in what region of the spectrum does one typically observe hydrogens bound to the aromatic ring?

 A. 1.0-1.5 ppm   **C.** 4.5-5.5 ppm

 B. 2.0-3.0 ppm   **D.** 6.0-8.0 ppm   **E.** 8.0-9.0 ppm

2. ^1H nuclei located near electronegative atoms are [ ] relative to ^1H nuclei which are not near them.

 A. coupled   **C.** shielded

 B. split   **D.** deshielded   **E.** none of the above

3. Which compound is expected to show intense IR absorption at 1,715 cm^{-1}?

 A. $(CH_3)_2CHNH_2$ **C.** 2-methylhexane

 B. hex-1-yne   **D.** $(CH_3)_2CHCO_2H$ **E.** $CH_3CH_2CH_2COH_2CH_3$

4. Free-radical chlorination of propane gives two isomeric monochlorides: 1-chloropropane and 2-chloropropane. How many NMR signals does each of these compounds display, respectively?

 A. 3, 2   **B.** 3, 3   **C.** 2, 2   **D.** 2, 3   **E.** None of the above

5. Which of the following transitions is usually observed in the UV spectra of ketones?

 A. n to π^* **C.** σ to n

 B. n to π **D.** σ to σ^* **E.** n to σ^*

6. What is the relative area of each peak in a quartet spin-spin splitting pattern?

 A. 1:1:1:1   **C.** 1:2:1

 B. 1:4:4:1   **D.** 1:2:2:1   **E.** 1:3:3:1

7. Which NMR signal represents the most deshielded proton?

 A. δ 2.0   **B.** δ 3.8   **C.** δ 6.5   **D.** δ 7.3   **E.** δ 4.5

8. The mass spectrum of alcohols often fails to exhibit detectable M peaks, instead showing relatively large [ ] peaks.

 A. M+1   **B.** M+2   **C.** M−16   **D.** M−17   **E.** M−18

9. In ^{1}H NMR, protons on the α-carbon of amines typically resonate between:

A. 0.5 and 1.0 ppm C. 3.0 and 4.0 ppm
B. 2.0 and 3.0 ppm D. 6.0 and 7.0 ppm E. 9.0 and 10.0 ppm

10. A researcher recorded the NMR spectra of each of the following compounds. Disregarding chemical shifts, which possesses a spectrum significantly different from the others?

A. 1,1,2-tribromobutane C. 3,3-dibromoheptane
B. bromobutane D. dibutyl ether
  E. all of the spectra are similar

11. Which compound(s) show(s) intense IR absorption at 1680 cm^{-1}?

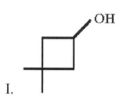

I.

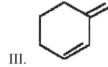

II.

III.

A. I only C. III only
B. II only D. II and III only E. I, II and III

12. What is the relationship between H$_a$ and H$_b$ in the following structure?

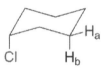

A. diastereotopic C. homotopic
B. enantiotopic D. isotopic
  E. conformers

13. Which of the following compounds gives the greatest number of proton NMR peaks?

A. 3,3-dichloropentane ✗ C. 1-chlorobutane
B. 4,4-dichloroheptane ✗ D. 1,4-dichlorobutane ✗
  E. dichloromethane

14. Where would one expect to find the ^{1}H NMR signal for the carboxyl group's hydrogen in propanoic acid?

A. δ 4.1-5.6 ppm C. δ 8-9 ppm
B. δ 10-13 ppm D. δ 6.1-7.8 ppm E. δ 9.5-10 ppm

15. While the carbonyl stretching frequency for simple aldehydes, ketones and carboxylic acids is about 1710 cm^{-1}, the carbonyl stretching frequency for acid chlorides is about:

    A. 1700 cm^{-1} **B.** 1735 cm^{-1} **C.** 1800 cm^{-1} **D.** 1660 cm^{-1} **E.** 2200 cm^{-1}

16. A clear liquid is subjected to infrared spectroscopy and produces a spectrum with a prominent, broad peak at approximately 3000 cm^{-1} and a sharp peak at 1710 cm^{-1}, as well as several smaller peaks between 1420 cm^{-1} and 940 cm^{-1}. This substance is most likely:

    A. ketone   **C.** alcohol
    B. carboxylic acid   **D.** aldehyde   **E.** anhydride

17. Which of the following laboratory techniques is used primarily as a compound identification procedure?

    A. extraction   **C.** crystallization
    B. NMR spectroscopy   **D.** distillation   **E.** none of the above

18. While the carbonyl stretching frequency for simple aldehydes, ketones, and carboxylic acids is about 1710 cm^{-1}, the carbonyl stretching frequency for esters is about:

    A. 1660 cm^{-1} **B.** 1700 cm^{-1} **C.** 1735 cm^{-1} **D.** 1800 cm^{-1} **E.** 2200 cm^{-1}

19. A compound with nine carbon atoms produces a single NMR signal. What is a possible structural formula for the compound?

    A. $(CH_3)_3CCCl_2C(CH_3)_3$ **C.** $(CH_3)_2CHCH_2(CH_2)_4CH_3$
    B. $(CH_3)_2CHCH_2CH_2CH(CH_3)CH_2CH_3$ **D.** $CH_3(CH_2)_7CH_3$
                                                  E. None of the above

20. In mass spectrometry plots, the relative abundance is the unit along the *y*-axis in a mass spectrum. What are the units on the *x*-axis?

    A. mass / charge (m/z)   **C.** molecular weight (amu)
    B. mass (m)   **D.** frequency (v)   **E.** wavelength (λ)

21. How many nuclear spin states are allowed for the ^1H nucleus?

    A. 1   **B.** 2   **C.** 3   **D.** 4   **E.** 10

22. Infrared spectroscopy provides a scientist with information about:

    A. molecular weight   **C.** functional group
    B. distribution of protons   **D.** conjugation   **E.** polarity

23. In the mass spectrum of 3,3-dimethyl-2-butanone, the base peak occurs at *m/z*:

    A. 43   **B.** 58   **C.** 84   **D.** 85   **E.** 100

24. The protons marked H_a and H_b in the molecule below are:

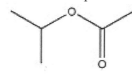

    A. diastereotopic   **B.** heterotopic   **C.** homotopic   **D.** enantiotopic   **E.** endotopic

25. Which of the following compounds is NOT IR active?

    A. Cl_2 **C.** $CH_3CH_2CH_2OH$

    B. CO **D.** CH_3Br **E.** HCN

26. Which sequence correctly ranks the regions of the electromagnetic spectrum in order of increasing energy?

    1) infrared   2) ultraviolet   3) radio wave

    A. $3 < 1 < 2$ **B.** $3 < 2 < 1$ **C.** $2 < 1 < 3$ **D.** $1 < 3 < 2$ **E.** $1 < 2 < 3$

27. In the UV-visible spectrum of (*E*)-1,3,5-hexatriene, the lowest energy absorption corresponds to a:

    A. π to σ^* transition   **C.** σ to π transition

    B. σ to σ^* transition   **D.** σ to π^* transition   **E.** π to π^* transition

28. What type of spectroscopy would be the LEAST useful in distinguishing dimethyl ether from bromoethane?

    A. UV spectroscopy   **C.** IR spectroscopy

    B. mass spectrometry   **D.** ^{1}H NMR spectroscopy

                                     E. ^{13}C NMR spectroscopy

29. What 1H NMR spectral data is expected for the compound shown?

    A. 4.9 (1H, sextet), 4.3 (3H, s), 3.0 (6H, d)

    B. 3.6 (3H, s), 2.8 (3H, septet), 1.2 (6H, d)

    C. 4.3 (1H, septet), 3.3 (3H, s), 1.2 (6H, d)

    D. 3.8 (1H, septet), 2.2 (3H, s), 1.0 (6H, d)

    E. 2.8 (1H, septet), 2.2 (3H, s), 1.0 (6H, d)

30. Which of the following compounds absorbs the longest wavelength of UV-visible light?

  A. (*Z*)-1,3-hexadiene   **C.** (*Z*)-but-2-ene

  B. hex-1-ene   **D.** (*E*)-but-2-ene   **E.** (*E*)-1,3,5-hexatriene

31. Which of the following compounds generates only one signal on its ^{1}H NMR spectrum?

  A. *tert*-butyl alcohol   **C.** toluene

  B. 1,2-dibromoethane   **D.** methanol   **E.** phenol

32. Both methyl salicylate and aspirin exhibit a strong absorption for IR at 1,735 cm^{-1}. This absorption indicates the presence of:

  A. ester   **C.** alcohol

  B. aromatic ring   **D.** phenol   **E.** amine

33. Absorption of what type of electromagnetic radiation results in electronic transitions?

  A. X-rays   **C.** microwaves

  B. radio waves   **D.** ultraviolet light   **E.** infrared light

34. Which of the following is NOT true?

  A. NMR spectroscopy utilizes magnetic fields

  B. IR spectroscopy utilizes light of wavelength 200-400 nm

  C. UV spectroscopy utilizes transitions in electron states

  D. Mass spectrometry utilizes fragmentation of the sample

  E. IR spectroscopy is useful in the absorption region of 1500 to 3500 cm^{-1}

35. The IR absorption at 1710 cm^{-1} most likely indicates the presence of which of the following functional groups?

  A. carbon-carbon double bond   **C.** alcohol

  B. ketone   **D.** ether   **E.** sulfide

36. A compound with a broad, deep IR absorption at 3300 cm^{-1} indicates the presence of:

  A. acyl halide   **C.** alkene

  B. alcohol   **D.** ketone   **E.** alkyne

Please, leave your Customer Review on Amazon

Notes

Chapter 16: Alkanes and Alkyl Halides

1. A nucleophile is:

    A. an oxidizing agent   **C.** a Lewis base

    B. electron deficient   **D.** a Lewis acid   **E.** none of the above

2. Identify the number of tertiary carbons in the following structure:

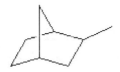

    A. 4   **B.** 5   **C.** 2   **D.** 3   **E.** 6

3. If the concentration of ¯OH doubles in a reaction with bromopropane, then the reaction rate:

    A. quadruples   **C.** remains the same

    B. doubles   **D.** is halved   **E.** none of the above

4. The rate of an S_N1 reaction depends on:

    A. the concentration of both the nucleophile and the electrophile

    B. neither the concentration of the nucleophile nor of the electrophile

    C. the concentration of the nucleophile only

    D. the concentration of the electrophile only

    E. none of the above

5. Which of the following properties is NOT characteristic of alkanes?

    A. They are tasteless and colorless

    B. They are nontoxic

    C. Their melting points increase with molecular weight

    D. They are generally less dense than water

    E. They have strong hydrogen bonds

6. Predict the most likely mechanism for the reaction shown below:

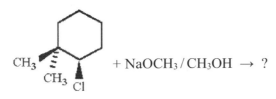

    A. E_2 **B.** E_1 **C.** S_N2 **D.** S_N1 **E.** Cannot be determined

7. An alkyl halide forms a carbocation that is more stable than the carbocation formed from isopropyl bromide. Which of the following alkyl halides forms the most stable carbocation?

A. *n*-propyl chloride

B. *tert*-butyl chloride

C. methyl chloride

D. ethyl chloride

E. propyl chloride

8. Which of the following reactions is most likely to proceed by an S$_N$2 mechanism?

A. *t*-butyl iodide with ethanol

B. 2-bromo-3-methyl pentane with methanol

C. 2-bromo-2-methyl pentane with HCl

D. 1-bromopropane with NaOH

E. None of the above

9. Which of the following molecules can rotate freely around its carbon-carbon bond?

A. acetylene

B. cyclopropane

C. ethane

D. ethylene

E. none of the above

10. The rate of an S$_N$2 reaction depends on:

A. neither the concentration of the nucleophile nor the substrate

B. the concentration of both the nucleophile and the substrate

C. the concentration of the substrate only

D. the concentration of the nucleophile only

E. none of the above

11. The heat of combustion of propane is –530 kcal/mol. A reasonable approximation for the heat of combustion for heptane is:

A. –432 kcal/mol

B. –682 kcal/mol

C. –865 kcal/mol

D. –1158 kcal/mol

E. None of the above

12. Which compound is least soluble in water?

A.

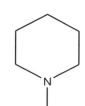

B.

C.

D.

E.

13. Which of the following statements best describes the mechanism of the unimolecular elimination of *tert*-butyl chloride with ethanol?

A. The reaction is a concerted single-step process

B. The reaction involves homolytic cleavage of the C–Cl bond

C. The rate-determining step is the formation of $(CH_3)_3C\cdot$

D. The rate-determining step is the formation of $(CH_3)_3C^+$

E. None of the above

14. Which of the following best describes the process of an S_N1 reaction in which the leaving group is on a chiral carbon atom?

A. inversion of stereochemistry

B. double inversion of stereochemistry

C. racemic mixture

D. retention of stereochemistry

E. none of the above

15. Which of the following is true regarding S_N1 and S_N2 reactions?

A. The rates of S_N1 reactions depend mostly on steric factors, while the rates of S_N2 reactions depend mostly on electronic factors

B. S_N1 reactions proceed more readily with a tertiary alkyl halide substrate, while S_N2 reactions proceed more readily with a primary alkyl halide substrate

C. Both S_N1 and S_N2 reactions produce rearrangement products

D. S_N1 reactions proceed via a carbocation intermediate, while S_N2 reactions proceed via a carbocation intermediate under certain conditions

E. S_N1 reactions proceed more readily with a polar aprotic solvent, while S_N2 reactions proceed more readily with a polar protic solvent

16. Which of the compounds listed below has the lowest boiling point?

A. 3-methylheptane

B. 2,4-dimethylhexane

C. octane

D. 2,2,4-trimethylpentane

E. decane

17. Which of the following is NOT a feature of S_N2 reactions?

A. single-step mechanism

B. pentacoordinate transition state

C. bimolecular kinetics

D. carbocation intermediate

E. nucleophilic substitution

18. Which conformer is at a local energy minimum on the potential energy diagram in the chair-chair interconversion of cyclohexane?

A. boat

B. twist-boat

C. half-chair

D. planar

E. fully eclipsed

19. If propane was reacted with Cl_2 in the presence of UV light, what products form, and what are their approximate percentages?

A. Propyl chloride yields 100%

B. Propyl chloride yields 42%, and isopropyl chloride yields 58%

C. Propyl chloride yields 75%, and isopropyl chloride yields 25%

D. Propyl chloride yields 90%, and isopropyl chloride yields 10%

E. None of the above

20. What is true about an S_N1 reaction?

    I. A carbocation intermediate is formed

    II. The rate determining step is bimolecular

    III. The mechanism has two steps

A. I only   B. II only   C. I and II only   D. I and III only   E. I, II and III

21. The most stable conformational isomer of 1,2-dibromoethane is:

A. eclipsed, *anti*   C. staggered, *anti*

B. staggered, *gauche*   D. eclipsed, *gauche*   E. staggered, eclipsed

22. What is the most likely mechanism for the reaction between 1-bromobutane and sodium cyanide?

A. E_1 B. E_2 C. S_N1 D. S_N2 E. S_N1 and S_N2

23. Which of the following alkyl halogens reacts the fastest with NaOH?

A. *t*-butyl bromide   C. *t*-butyl fluoride

B. *t*-butyl iodide   D. *t*-butyl chloride   E. *t*-butyl cyanide

24. Acetate can react with a tertiary alkyl chloride to form an ester. The reaction occurs more rapidly in water than in dimethylsulfoxide (DMSO) because water stabilizes the:

A. intermediate racemates   C. carbocation intermediate

B. configuration inversion   D. acetate   E. anion intermediate

25. Ethers can be formed from ethyl bromide in a reaction whereby the incoming ‾OR group represents a(n):

A. substrate   C. nucleophile

B. electrophile   D. leaving group   E. solvent

26. Which of the following compounds can most easily undergo both E_1 and S_N2 reactions?

A. $(CH_3CH_2CH_2)_2CHBr$

B. $(CH_3CH_2CH_2)_3CBr$

C. $(CH_3CH_2CH_2)_3CCH_2Cl$

D. $(CH_3CH_2CH_2)_2CHCN$

E. $CH_3CH_2CH_2CH_2Br$

27. Which of the following molecules has the lowest boiling point?

A. *cis*-2-pentene

B. 2-pentyne

C. pentane

D. neopentane

E. 3-pentanol

28. Which of the following is the most stable conformer of *trans*-1-isopropyl-3-methylcyclohexane?

A. methyl and isopropyl are axial

B. methyl and isopropyl are equatorial

C. methyl is axial, and isopropyl is equatorial

D. methyl is equatorial, and isopropyl is axial

E. none of the above

29. Which of the following compounds readily undergoes E_1, S_N1 and E_2 reactions, but not S_N2 reactions?

A. $(CH_3CH_2CH_2)_3CBr$

B. $CH_3CH_2CH_2CH_3$

C. $(CH_3CH_2)_3COH$

D. $CH_3CH_2CH_2CH_2Br$

E. none of the above

30. The complete combustion of one mole of nonane in oxygen would produce [   ] moles of CO_2 and [   ] moles of H_2O?

$C_9H_{20} + O_2 \rightarrow 9CO_2 + 10H_2O$

A. 9 … 10

B. 9 … 9

C. 9 … 4.5

D. 4.5 … 4.5

E. 4.5 … 9

31. Halogenation of alkanes proceeds by the mechanism shown below:

I. $Br_2 + h\nu \rightarrow 2\ Br\bullet$

II. $Br\bullet + RH \rightarrow HBr + R\bullet$

III. $R\bullet + Br_2 \rightarrow RBr + Br\bullet$

Which of these steps involve chain propagation?

A. I only

B. III only

C. I and II only

D. II and III only

E. I and III only

32. What statement(s) is/are true about an S_N2 reaction?

    I. A carbocation intermediate is formed
    II. The rate-determining step is bimolecular
    III. The mechanism has two steps

  A. I only   **C.** I and III only
  B. II only   **D.** II and III only   **E.** I, II and III

33. Which of the following compounds undergo(es) a substitution reaction?

    I. C_2H_6 II. C_2H_2 III. C_2H_4

  A. I only   **C.** I and II only
  B. II only   **D.** II and III only   **E.** I, II and III

34. Which of the following undergoes bimolecular nucleophilic substitution at the fastest rate?

  A. 1-chloro-2,2-diethylcyclopentane   **C.** 1-chlorocyclopentene
  B. 1-chlorocyclopentane   **D.** 1-chloro-1-ethylcyclopentane
                                       E. *tert*-butylchloride

35. Which of the following is the best leaving group?

  A. Cl^- **B.** NH_2^- **C.** ^-OH **D.** Br^- **E.** F^-

36. Which of the following is an example of the termination step for a free-radical chain reaction?

  A. $Cl–Cl + hv \rightarrow 2\ Cl\cdot$

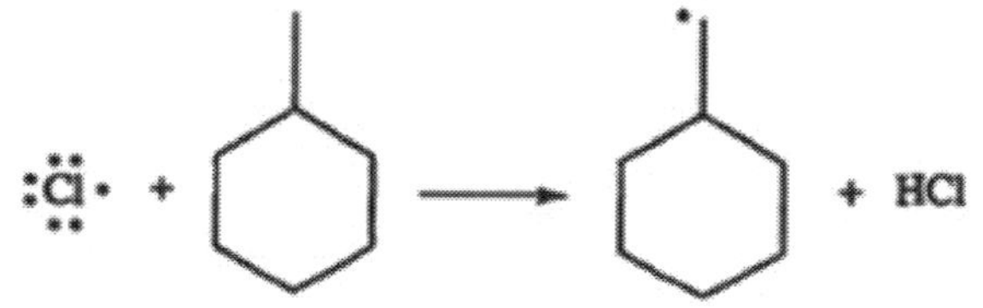

  B.

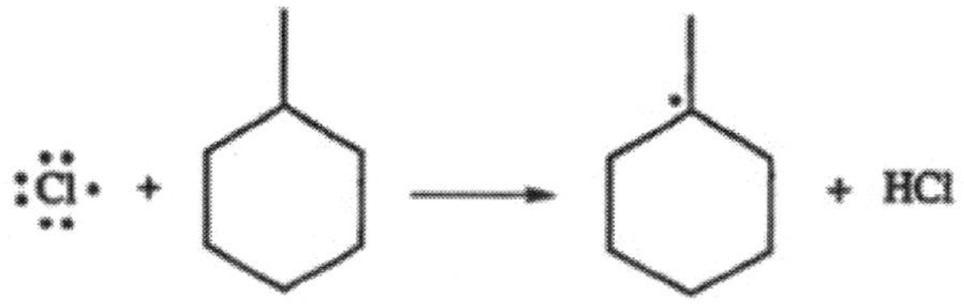

  C.

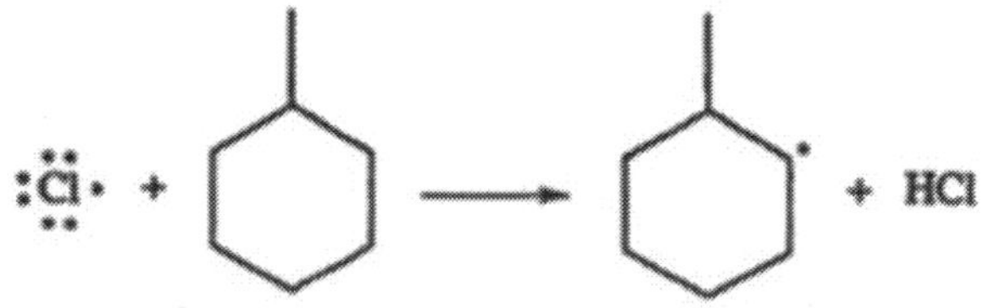

  D.

  E. $Cl\cdot + Cl\cdot \rightarrow Cl_2$

Chapter 17: Alkenes

1. Both (*E*)- and (*Z*)-hex-3-ene can be subjected to a hydroboration-oxidation sequence. How are the products from these two reactions related?

    A. The products of the two isomers are diastereomers

    B. The products of the two isomers are constitutional isomers

    C. The (*E*)- and (*Z*)-isomers generate the same products in the same amounts

    D. The (*E*)- and (*Z*)-isomers generate the same products but in differing amounts

    E. The products of the two isomers are not structurally related

2. What is the major product of this reaction?

$D_2/Pt \rightarrow$?

    A.   **B.**   **C.**   **D.**   **E.** None of the above

3. Give the best product for the following reaction:

H_2C ... CH_3 + 1) $Hg(O_2CCF_3)_2$, CH_3CH_2OH; 2) $NaBH_4 \rightarrow$?

    A. $CH_3-CH-C(CH_3)-CH_3$ with CH_3 OCH_2CH_3

    C. $CH_2-CH_2-C(CH_3)-CH_3$ with OCH_2CH_3 CH_3

    B. $CH_3-CH_2-C(CH_3)-CH_2OCH_2CH_3$

    D. $CH_3-CH-C(CH_3)-CH_3$ with CH_3CH_2O CH_3

    E. $CH_3-CH-C(CH_3)-CH_3$ with $HOCH_2CH_2$ CH_3

4. Which of the following correctly ranks the halides in order of increasing rate of addition to 3-hexene in a nonpolar aprotic solvent?

A. HI < HBr < HCl

B. HBr < HCl < HI

C. HCl < HI < HBr

D. HCl < HBr < HI

E. None of the above

5. The carbon–carbon single bond in 1,3-butadiene has a bond length that is shorter than a carbon–carbon single bond in an alkane. This is a result of the:

A. overlap of two sp^3 orbitals

B. overlap of one sp^2 and one sp^3 orbital

C. partial double-bond character due to the σ electrons

D. overlap of two sp^2 orbitals

E. none of the above

6. What is the name of the major organic product of the following reaction?

$$(CH_3)_2C=C(CH_3)_2 + H^+ / H_2O \rightarrow ?$$

A. 2,3-dimethyl-2-butanol

B. 2,3-dimethyl-1-butanol

C. 3,3-dimethyl-1-butanol

D. 3,3-dimethyl-2-butanol

E. 4-methyl-2-pentanol

7. The rate law for the addition of HBr to many simple alkenes may be approximated as rate = k[alkene]·[HBr]. This rate law indicates all of the following EXCEPT that the reaction:

A. occurs in a single step involving one HBr molecule and one alkene molecule

B. involves one HBr molecule and one alkene molecule in the rate-determining step, and may involve many steps

C. is first order in HBr

D. is second order overall

E. is first order in the alkene

8. Which reactant is used to convert propene to 1,2-dichloropropane?

A. HCl   B. NaCl   C. H_2 D. Cl_2 E. BrCl

9. Using Zaitsev's rule, choose the most stable alkene among the following:

A. 1-methylcyclohexene

B. 3-methylcyclohexene

C. 4-methylcyclohexene

D. 3,4-dimethylcyclohexene

E. they are all of equal stability

10. Which of the following has the lowest heat of hydrogenation per mole of H_2 absorbed?

A. 1,2-hexadiene

B. 1,3-hexadiene

C. 1,3,5-heptatriene

D. 1,5-hexadiene

E. 1,2,3-heptatriene

11. Which of the following is the best solvent for the addition of HCl to 3-hexene?

A. 3-hexene

B. CH_3CH_3

C. CH_3OH

D. H_2O

E. None of the above

12. What is the major product of the following reaction?

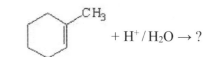

$+ H^+/H_2O \rightarrow$?

A. (cyclohexane with CH_2OH group)

C. (cyclohexane with CH_3 and OH)

B. (cyclohexane with OH and CH_3)

D. (cyclohexane with CH_3 and OH)

E. HO (cyclohexane with CH_3)

13. Which of the following is NOT an example of a conjugated system?

A. 1,2-butadiene

B. cyclobutadiene

C. benzene

D. 1,3-cyclohexadiene

E. 2,4-pentadiene

14. Which of the following would show the LEAST regioselectivity for HBr addition?

A. $(CH_3)_2C=C(CH_3)CH_2CH_3$

B. $H_2C=C(CH_3)CH_2CH_3$

C. $CH_2HC=C(CH_3)CH_2CH_3$

D. $(CH_3)_2C=CHCH_2CH_3$

E. $CH_2=CHCH_3$

15. Which statement is true in the oxymercuration-reduction of an alkene?

A. *Anti*-Markovnikov orientation and *anti*-addition occur

B. *Anti*-Markovnikov orientation and *syn*-addition occur

C. Markovnikov orientation and *anti*-addition occur

D. Markovnikov orientation and *syn*-addition occur

E. Zaitsev orientation and *anti*-addition occur

16. Which of the following compounds is/are geometric isomers?

    I. Isobutene

    II. (*E*)-2-butene

    III. *cis*-2-butene

    IV. *trans*-2-butene

A. I and II only

B. II and III only

C. III and IV only

D. II, III and IV only

E. I, II, III and IV

17. Consider the following alcohol A.

The major product resulting from the dehydration of A is:

A.

C.

B.

D.   **E.** None of the above

18. What is the major product of the following reaction?

$+ \, Br_2 / H_2O \rightarrow$?

A.

C.

B.

D.

E.

19. Which of the following reactions does NOT proceed through a bromonium ion intermediate?

   A. $CH_3CH=CH_2 + Br_2 + H_2O \rightarrow CH_3CH_2OHCH_2Br + HBr$
   B. $CH_2=CHCH_2CH_2CH=CH_2 + Br_2 \rightarrow CH_2BrCHBrCH_2CH_2CHBrCH_2Br$
   C. $CH_3CH_2CH=CH_2 + Br_2 \rightarrow CH_3CH_2CHBrCH_2Br$
   D. $CH_3CH_2CH=CH_2 + HBr \rightarrow CH_3CH_2CHBrCH_3$
   E. None of the above

20. When reacted with HBr, *cis*-3-methyl-2-hexene most likely undergoes:

A. *anti*-Markovnikov *syn*- and *anti*-addition
B. *anti*-Markovnikov *syn*-addition
C. Markovnikov *syn*- and *anti*-addition
D. Markovnikov *syn*-addition
E. none of the above

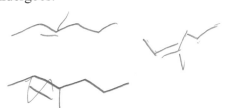

21. All of the following are examples of addition reactions of alkenes, EXCEPT:

A. hydrogenation   C. oxidation
B. hydration   D. bromination   E. ozonolysis

22. Which of the following reactions will NOT occur?

    Reaction 1: butene + NBS → 2-bromobutane
    Reaction 2: 2-methylbutane + 8 O_2 + heat → 5 CO_2 + 6 H_2O
    Reaction 3: 2-methylbutane + Br_2 + *hv* → 2-bromo-2-methylbutane
    Reaction 4: 2-methyl-2-butene + Br_2 + CCl_4 → (*S*)-1,2-dibromo-2-methylbutane
    (+ enantiomer)

A. Reaction 1   C. Reaction 3
B. Reaction 2   D. Reaction 4   E. Reactions 2 and 4

23. Give the possibilities in the structure for a compound with a formula of C_6H_{10}:

A. no rings; no double bonds; no triple bonds
B. one double bond; or one ring
C. two rings; two double bonds; one double bond and one ring; or one triple bond
D. three rings; three double bonds; two double bonds and one ring; one ring and two double bonds; one triple bond and one ring; or one double bond and one ring
E. benzene

24. Which of the following is/are the most stable diene?

A.

C.

B.

D.

E.

25. Products A, B, and C of the following reaction are, respectively:

2-methyl-2-butene + HBr   →   product A

2-methyl-2-butene + HBr / H_2O_2 →   product B

2-methyl-2-butene + H_2O / H^+ / heat   →   product C

Product A	Product B	Product C
A. 2-bromo-2-methylbutane	2-bromo-3-methylbutane	2-methyl-2-butanol
B. 3-methyl-2-bromobutene	3-methyl-2-bromobutane	2-methyl-2-butanol
C. 2-bromo-2-methylbutane	2-bromo-2-methylbutane	3-methyl-2-butanol
D. 1-bromo-2-methyl-2-butene	2-bromo-2-methylbutane	2-methyl-2-butane
E. None of the above		

26. Which of the following is vinyl chloride?

A. $CH_2=CHCl$

B. $CH_2=CHCH_2Cl$

C.

D.

E. CH_3CH_2Cl

27. What reagent(s) is/are needed to accomplish the following transformation?

A. BH_3 / THF

B. ^-OH

C. H_2O / H_2O_2

D. H_2O / H^+

E. 1) BH_3 / THF; 2) ^-OH, H_2O_2, H_2O

28. The reaction below can be classified as a(n):

cis-pent-2-ene → pentane

A. tautomerization

B. elimination

C. oxidation

D. reduction

E. substitution

29. The major product of the following reaction will likely be the result of a(n) [   ] mechanism?

        2-bromobutane + *tert*-butyl alkoxide

A. E₂   **B.** E₁   **C.** S$_N$2   **D.** S$_N$1   **E.** S$_N$1 and E₁

30. What is the major product from the following reaction?

        + HBr → ?

A. [epoxide]—CH₂Br   **C.** HO—CH(CH₃)—CH₂—Br

B. Me—CH(Br)—CH₂—OH   **D.** H₃C—C(=O)—CH₃   **E.** Br—CH₂CH₂CH₂—OH

31. When CH_3–CH=CH₂ is reacted with water in the presence of a catalytic amount of acid, a new compound is formed. What might be the product of this reaction?

A. CH_3–C(=O)–CH_3 **C.** HO—CH₂—CH(CH₃)—OH

B. H₃C—CH(OH)—CH_3 **D.** CH_3–CH–CH₂   **E.** H₃C—CH₂—CHO

32. What is the product of the following reaction?

[cyclobutane]—CH(CH₃)—OH + H₂SO₄/Δ → ?

A. [cyclopentene with CH₃]   **C.** [cyclobutane]—CH=CH₂

B. [cyclopentene with CH₃]   **D.** [cyclobutane]=CHCH₃   **E.** [cyclobutene]—CH₂CH₃

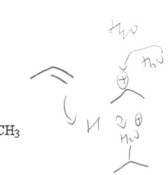

33. Alkenes are more acidic than alkanes. What is the best explanation of this property?

    A. The sp^2 hybridized orbitals in alkenes stabilize the negative charge generated when a proton is abstracted

    B. The sp^2 hybridized orbitals in alkenes destabilize the negative charge generated when a proton is abstracted

    C. The sp^3 hybridized orbitals in alkenes stabilize the negative charge generated when a proton is abstracted

    D. The sp^3 hybridized orbitals in alkenes destabilize the negative charge generated when a proton is abstracted

    E. The alkene is small and less sterically hindered compared to the alkane.

34. What is the major product formed from the reaction of 2-bromo-2-methylpentane with sodium ethoxide?

    A. 2-methylpent-2-ene   **C.** 2-methyl-2-methoxypentane   **E.** 1-methylpentene

    B. 2-methylpent-3-ene   **D.** 2-methylpentene

35. What reagents can best be used to accomplish the following transformation?

    A. 1) $Hg(OAc)_2$, H_2O / THF; 2) $NaBH_4$ **C.** 1) $BH_3 \cdot THF$; 2) HO^-, H_2O_2

    B. 1) $Hg(O_2CCF_3)_2$, CH_3OH; 2) $NaBH_4$ **D.** H^+, H_2O

    E. $NaOH$, H_2O

36. Heating a(n) [   ] results in a Cope elimination.

    A. amine oxide   **B.** imine   **C.** enamine   **D.** oxime   **E.** enol

Chapter 18: Alkynes

1. What is the major organic product that results when 3-heptyne is subjected to excess hydrogen and a platinum catalyst?

A. (*E*)-3-heptene

B. (*Z*)-3-heptene

C. (*Z*)-2-heptene

D. 2-heptyne

E. heptane

2. In the addition of hydrogen bromide to alkynes in the absence of peroxides, which of the following species is thought to be an intermediate?

A. carbene

B. vinyl radical

C. vinyl cation

D. vinyl anion

E. none of the above

3. Which of the following molecular formulas correspond(s) to an acyclic alkyne?

I. C_9H_{20}

II. C_9H_{18}

III. C_9H_{16}

A. I only   B. II only   C. III only   D. I and II only   E. I, II and III

4. What is the term for a family of unsaturated hydrocarbon compounds with a triple bond?

A. alkynes

B. arenes

C. alkanes

D. alkenes

E. none of the above

5. Which of the following molecular formulas correspond(s) to an alkyne?

I. $C_{10}H_{18}$

II. $C_{10}H_{20}$

III. $C_{10}H_{22}$

A. I only   B. II only   C. III only   D. I and II only   E. I, II and III

6. What is the product from the reaction of one mole of acetylene and two moles of hydrogen gas using platinum catalyst?

A. propene

B. propane

C. ethene

D. ethane

E. none of the above

7. Which of the following does NOT properly describe the physical properties of an alkyne?

A. Less dense than water

B. Insoluble in most organic solvents

C. Relatively nonpolar

D. Nearly insoluble in water

E. Boiling point nearly the same as an alkane with a similar carbon skeleton

8. What are the two products from the complete combustion of an alkyne?

    A. CO_2 and H_2O **C.** CO and H_2O

    B. CO_2 and H_2 **D.** CO and H_2

                                E. None of the above

9. The compound propyne consists of how many carbon atoms and how many hydrogen atoms?

    A. 3C,2H   **B.** 3C,6H   **C.** 3C,4H   **D.** 2C,2H   **E.** None of the above

10. Given that 1-butyne has a boiling point of 8.1 °C, what is the phase of propyne at room temperature and 1 atm pressure?

    A. solid   **B.** supercritical fluid   **C.** gas   **D.** liquid   **E.** vapor

11. How many moles of hydrogen are required to convert a mole of pentyne to pentane?

    A. 0   **B.** 1   **C.** 2   **D.** 3   **E.** 4

12. What is the product of the reaction of one mole of acetylene and one mole of bromine vapor?

    A. 1,1,2,2-tetrabromoethane   **C.** 1,2-dibromoethane

    B. 1,1,2,2-tetrabromoethene   **D.** 1,2-dibromoethene   **E.** None of the above

13. What reagents are used to convert 1-hexyne into 2-hexanone?

    A. 1) Si_2BH; 2) H_2O_2, NaOH   **C.** 1) O_3; 2) $(CH_3)_2S$

    B. Hg^{2+}, H_2SO_4, H_2O **D.** 1) CH_3MgBr; 2) CO_2

                                    E. 1) H_2, Ni; 2) $Na_2Cr_2O_7$, H_2SO_4

14. What is the major product of this reaction?

    $H_3C–C≡C–CH_3$ + Na (s), NH_3 (l) → ?

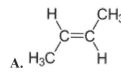

A.

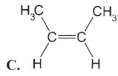

C.

B. (skeletal structure)

D.

E.

15. What is the major product of the following acid/catalyzed hydration reaction?

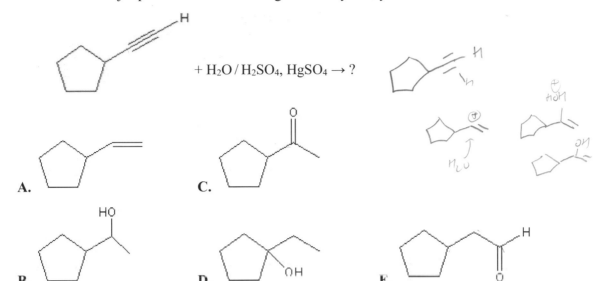

+ H$_2$O / H$_2$SO$_4$, HgSO$_4$ → ?

A.

B.

C.

D.

E.

16. When 2,2-dibromobutane is heated to 200 °C in the presence of molten KOH, what is the major organic product?

A. but-1-yne
B. but-2-yne

C. 1-bromobut-1-yne
D. 1-bromobut-2-yne

E. but-1-ene

17. What class of organic product results when 1-heptyne is treated with a mixture of mercuric acetate [Hg(OAc)$_2$] in aqueous sulfuric acid (H$_2$SO$_4$), followed by sodium borohydride (NaBH$_4$)?

A. diol
B. ketone

C. aldehyde
D. alcohol

E. carboxylic acid

18. Which of the following describes the reaction below?

H$_3$C≡CH$_3$ + H$_2$, Pd, CaCo$_3$, quinolone, hexane →

A. oxidation
B. reduction

C. substitution
D. catalytic hydration

E. elimination

19. What is the general molecular formula for the alkyne class of compounds?

I. C$_n$H$_{2n+2}$ II. C$_n$H$_{2n}$ III. C$_n$H$_{2n-2}$

A. I only
B. II only

C. III only
D. II and III only

E. I, II and III

20. Among the following compounds, which acids are stronger than ammonia?

      I. water   II. ethane   III. butyne   IV. but-2-yne

  A. I and II only   **C.** I and III only
  B. II only   **D.** II and III only   **E.** I, II, III and IV

21. In the reduction of alkynes using sodium in liquid ammonia, which of the species below is NOT an intermediate in the commonly accepted mechanism?

  A. vinyl anion   **C.** anion
  B. vinyl cation   **D.** vinyl radical   **E.** all are intermediates

22. For isomers with the formula $C_{10}H_{16}$, which of the following structural features are NOT possible within this set of molecules?

  A. 2 rings and 1 double bond   **C.** 2 triple bonds
  B. 2 double bonds and 1 ring   **D.** 1 ring and 1 triple bond
                                        E. 3 double bonds

23. What is the product from the reaction of one mole of acetylene and one mole of hydrogen gas using platinum catalyst?

  A. propane   **B.** propene   **C.** ethane   **D.** ethene   **E.** 2-butene

24. Which of the species below is less basic than an acetylide?

      I. CH_3Li II. CH_3MgBr III. CH_3ONa

  A. I only   **B.** II only   **C.** III only   **D.** I and II only   **E.** I, II and III

25. Which is the most stable product for the reaction below:

                + 1) BH₃ / THF; 2) ⁻OH, H_2O_2, H_2O

A. H_3C⌐⌐⌐OH with OH   **C.** H_3C—C(=O)—CH_3

B. $CH_3CH_2CH_2CH=CHOH$ **D.** (aldehyde structure) H, O

                             E. $CH_3CH_2CH_2(OH)C=CH_2$

26. The compound 1-butyne contains:

    A. a ring structure   **C.** a double bond

    B. a triple bond   **D.** all single bonds   **E.** a bromine atom

27. The *pi* bond of an alkyne is [   ] and [   ] than the *pi* bond of an alkene.

    A. longer; stronger   **C.** shorter; stronger

    B. longer; weaker   **D.** shorter; weaker   **E.** none of the above

28. What is the major product of this reaction?

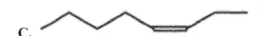

$+ CH_3CH_2MgBr \rightarrow$

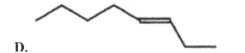

    A.   **C.**

    B.   **D.**

    E.

29. Which of the following is the product for the reaction?

$HC \equiv C$ — CH_3 ...... $+ H_2O + HgSO_4 / H_2SO_4 \rightarrow$

    A. $CH_3CH_2CH_2\underset{\underset{OH}{|}}{C}{=}CH_2$ **C.** H_3C—C(=O)—CH_3

    B. $CH_3CH_2CH_2CH{=}CHOH$ **D.** $CH_3CH_2CH_2CH_2CHO$

                                              E. $CH_3CH_2CH_2CH(OH)CH_2OH$

30. What is the product from the reaction of one mole of acetylene and two moles of bromine vapor?

A. 1,1,2,2-tetrabromoethene

B. 1,1,2,2-tetrabromoethane

C. 1,2-dibromoethene

D. 1,2-dibromoethane

E. none of the above

31. Which of the alkyne addition reactions below involve(s) an enol intermediate?

    I. hydroboration/oxidation

    II. treatment with $HgSO_4$ in dilute H_2SO_4

    III. hydrogenation

A. I only   **B.** II only   **C.** III only   **D.** I and II only   **E.** I and III only

32. Which of the following is the final and major product of this reaction?

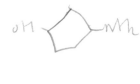

$+ H_2O, H_2SO_4/HgSO_4 \rightarrow$?

A.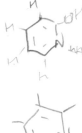

C.

B.

D.

E.

33. If the compound C_5H_7NO contains 1 ring, how many *pi* bonds are there in this compound?

A. 0   **B.** 1   **C.** 2   **D.** 3   **E.** 4

   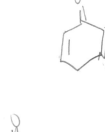

34. Which of the following is the major product of this reaction?

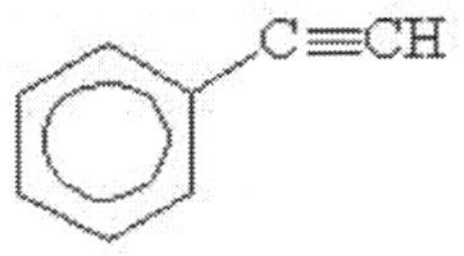

C≡CH

+ 1) BH_3, THF + 2) ⁻OH, H_2O_2, H_2O →

A. 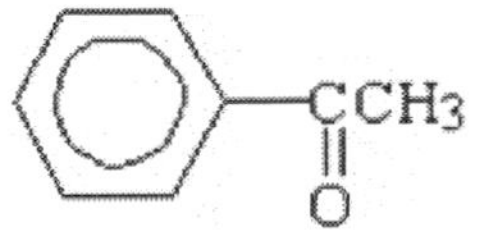 —C 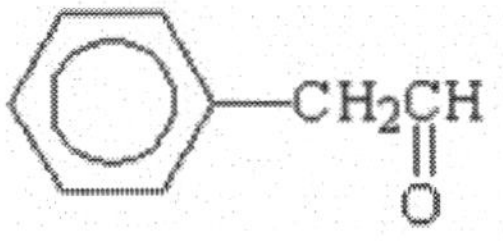 CH3 (with =O)

C. —CH_2CH (with =O)

B. 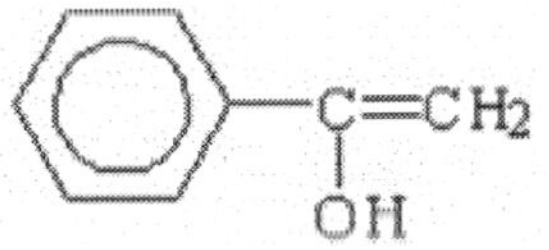 —C=CH₂ / OH

D. 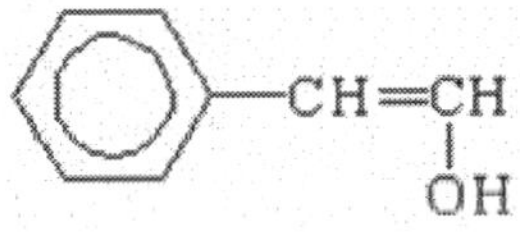 —CH=CH / OH

E. 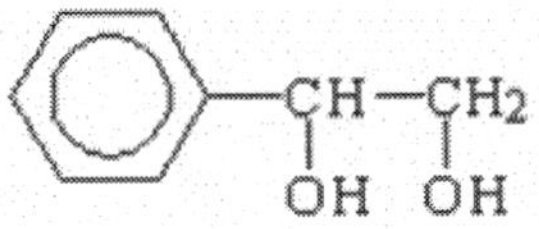 —CH—CH₂ / OH OH

35. Which of the following statements correctly describes the general reactivity of alkynes?

A. Unlike alkenes, alkynes fail to undergo electrophilic addition reactions
B. Alkynes are generally more reactive than alkenes
C. An alkyne is an electron-rich molecule and therefore reacts as a nucleophile
D. The σ bonds of alkynes are higher in energy than the π bonds, and thus are more reactive
E. Alkynes react as electrophiles, whereas alkenes react as nucleophiles

36. What is the major product when C_2H_4 undergoes an addition reaction with 1 mole equivalent of Br_2 in CCl_4?

A. $C_2H_2 + H_2$
B. $C_2H_4Br_2$

C. $C_2HBr + HBr$
D. C_2H_3Br
E. None of the above

| Please, leave your Customer Review on Amazon |

Notes

Chapter 19: Aromatic Compounds

1. What is the major product of this reaction?

$\text{C}_6\text{H}_5\text{-CH}_2\text{-CH}_3$ + C(CH$_3$)$_3$Br + FeBr → ?

A. H_3C-[benzene with Br]

C. H_3C-[4-tert-butyl benzyl]

B. [3,5-di-tert-butyl ethylbenzene]

D. [di-tert-butyl benzene]

E. [structure with H_3C, CH$_3$, Br, and phenyl]

2. All of the following are common reactions of benzene, EXCEPT:

A. nitration   **C.** chlorination

B. hydrogenation   **D.** bromination   **E.** sulfonation

3. How many pairs of degenerate π molecular orbitals are found in benzene?

A. 6   **B.** 5   **C.** 4   **D.** 3   **E.** 2

4. What is the effect of an ammonium substituent on electrophilic aromatic substitution?

A. *ortho/para*-directing with activation   **C.** *meta*-directing with activation

B. *ortho/para*-directing with deactivation   **D.** *meta*-directing with deactivation

     E. neither directing nor activating

5. Which of the following compounds undergoes Friedel-Crafts alkylation with (CH$_3$)$_3$CCl, AlCl$_3$ most rapidly?

A. toluene   **C.** acetophenone

B. iodobenzene   **D.** benzenesulfonic acid   **E.** cyanobenzene

---

6. Which sequence correctly ranks the following aromatic rings in order of increasing rate of reactivity in an electrophilic aromatic substitution reaction?

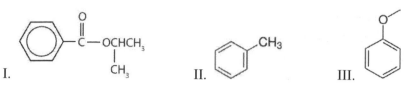

I.   II.   III.

A. II < I < III
B. II < III < I

C. III < I < II
D. I < II < III

E. I < III < II

7. Of the following, which reacts most readily with $Br_2/FeBr_3$ in an electrophilic aromatic substitution?

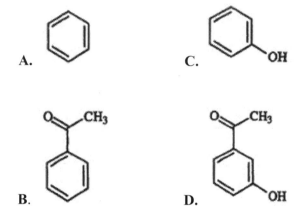

A.   C.

B.   D.

E. All the compounds have the same reactivity

8. In the molecular orbital representation of benzene, how many π molecular orbitals are present?

A. 1   **B.** 2   **C.** 4   **D.** 6   **E.** 8

9. Which of the following structures is aromatic?

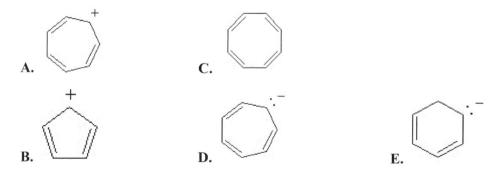

A.   C.

B.   D.   E.

10. In the electrophilic aromatic substitution of phenol, substituents add predominantly in which position(s)?

I. *ortho* to the hydroxyl group
II. *meta* to the hydroxyl group
III. *para* to the hydroxyl group

A. I only
B. II only

C. III only
D. I and III only

E. I, II and III

11. Which of the following is NOT aromatic?

A.

C.

B.

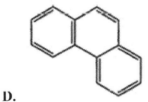

D.

E. All of the above

12. Which of these molecules is aromatic?

A.

C.

B.

D.

E. None of the above

13. What is the most likely regiochemistry of this electrophilic aromatic substitution reaction?

$+ Br_2 / FeBr_3 \rightarrow$?

A.

CH₃

C. Br

CH₃ Br

B. Br

CH₃

D. Br

CH₃ Br

E.

14. A compound is a six-carbon cyclic hydrocarbon. It is inert to bromine in water and bromine in dichloromethane, yet it decolorizes bromine in carbon tetrachloride when a small quantity of $FeBr_3$ is added. Which of the following is the identity of the compound?

A. 1,4-cyclohexadiene   C. benzene

B. 1,3-cyclohexadiene   D. cyclohexane   E. cyclohexyne

15. While electron-withdrawing groups (such as ~NO₂ and ~CO₂R) are *meta*-directing with regard to electrophilic aromatic substitution reactions, they are *ortho-* / *para*-directing in nucleophilic aromatic substitution reactions. This observation would best be explained by using which concept?

A. tautomerism   C. hydrogen bonding

B. aromaticity   D. resonance   E. equilibration

16. Derivatives of the compound shown below are currently being examined for their effectiveness in treating drug addiction and metabolic syndrome. Which sequence ranks the aromatic rings of this compound in order of increasing reactivity (slowest to fastest reacting) in an electrophilic aromatic substitution reaction?

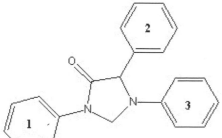

A. 1 < 2 < 3   C. 3 < 2 < 1

B. 2 < 3 < 1   D. 3 < 1 < 2

                     E. 2 < 1 < 3

17. The major aromatic product of the following reaction is:

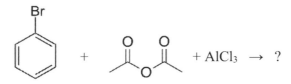 

A. methyl ketone substitutes in the *ortho / para* position
B. methyl ketone substitutes in the *meta* position
C. methyl ketone replacing the bromine
D. formation of phenol
E. formation of benzene

18. In electrophilic aromatic substitution reactions, an extremely reactive electrophile is typically used because the aromatic ring is:

A. a poor electrophile
B. nonpolar
C. reactive
D. a poor nucleophile
E. unstable

19. What is the effect of each of ~Cl substituents on electrophilic aromatic substitution?

A. *meta*-directing with deactivation
B. *meta*-directing with activation
C. *ortho/para*-directing with deactivation
D. *ortho*-directing with activation
E. *para*-directing with activation

20. 1,3-cyclopentadiene reacts with sodium metal at low temperatures according to:

What is the best explanation for this observation?

A. Rehybridization of the saturated carbon atoms provides additional product stability
B. Sodium metal is highly selective for cycloalkenes
C. Aromaticity stabilizes the carbocation
D. The reactant is more unstable at reduced temperatures
E. Aromaticity stabilizes the anion

21. What is the major product of this electrophile aromatic substitution (EAS) reaction?

$+ HNO_3 / H_2SO_4 \rightarrow$?

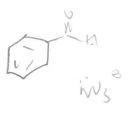

A.

C.

B.

D.

E.

22. Which of the following molecules reacts the slowest in electrophilic nitration?

A. Toluene

C. Anisole (methoxybenzene)

B. Aniline

D. Bromobenzene

E. Phenol

23. In electrophilic aromatic substitution, the aromatic ring acts as a(n):

A. leaving group   B. dienophile   C. nucleophile   D. electrophile   E. spectator

24. What is the effect of ~F substituents on electrophilic aromatic substitution?

A. *meta*-directing with activation
B. *meta*-directing with deactivation

C. *ortho-* / *para*-directing with activation
D. *ortho-* / *para*-directing with deactivation
E. *ortho*-directing with activation

25. Which of the following compounds is least susceptible to electrophilic aromatic substitution?

A. p-H_3CCH_2O–C_6H_4–O–CH_2CH_3

B. p-O_2N–C_6H_4–NH–CH_3

C. p-Cl–C_6H_4–NH_3^+

D. p-CH_3CH_2–C_6H_4–CH_2CH_3

E. benzene

26. Which of the following statements is NOT correct about benzene?

A. The carbon-carbon bond lengths are the same

B. The carbon-hydrogen bond lengths are the same

C. All of the carbon atoms are *sp* hybridized

D. It has delocalized electrons

E. All twelve atoms lie in the same plane

27. Which reaction is NOT characteristic of aromatic compounds?

A. addition

B. halogenation

C. nitration

D. sulfonation

E. acylation

28. The reason why complete hydrogenation of benzene to cyclohexane requires H_2, a rhodium (Rh) catalyst and 1,000 psi pressure at 100 °C is because:

A. the double bonds in benzene have the same reactivity as *pi* bonds of non-aromatic alkenes

B. hydrogenation produces an aromatic compound

C. the double bonds in benzene are more reactive than a typical alkene

D. the double bonds in benzene are less reactive than a typical alkene

E. none of the above

29. Which of the following reactions is NOT an electrophilic aromatic substitution reaction?

A. $CH_3C_6H_5$ + $C_6H_5CH_2CH_2Cl$ / $AlCl_3$

B. $CH_3C_6H_5$ + Br_2 / $FeBr_3$

C. $CH_3C_6H_5$ + $CH_3CH_2CH_2COCl$ / $AlCl_3$

D. $CH_3C_6H_5$ + H_2, Rh / C

E. C_6H_6 + HSO_3 / H_2SO_4

30. Which steps may be used to synthesize 1-chloro-4-nitrobenzene, starting from benzene?

A. 1) Na / NH_3; 2) Cl_2 / $FeCl_3$

B. 1) HNO_3 / H_2SO_4; 2) Cl_2 / $FeCl_3$

C. 1) HCl / H_2O; 2) HNO_3 / H_2SO_4

D. 1) Cl_2 / $FeCl_3$; 2) HNO_3 / H_2SO_4

E. Cl_2 / CCl_4

31. If bromobenzene is treated with sulfur trioxide (SO_3) and concentrated H_2SO_4, what is/are the major product(s)?

A. *ortho*- and *para*-bromobenzenesulfonic acid

B. benzene

C. benzenesulfonic acid

D. *meta*-bromobenzenesulfonic acid

E. toluene

32. Rank the following three molecules in increasing order according to the rate at which they react with $Br_2/FeBr_3$.

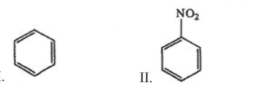

I.

II.

III.

A. II < III < I

B. II < I < III

C. I < II < III

D. I < III < II

E. III < II < I

33. Which of the following is true about the benzene molecule?

A. It is a saturated hydrocarbon

B. The *pi* electrons of the ring move around the ring and have resonance

C. It is a hydrocarbon with the molecular formula of C_nH_{2n+2}

D. It contains heterocyclic oxygen

E. Attachments to the ring can exhibit *cis/trans* isomerism

34. Which of the following statements is supported by the table below?

	Solubility (g/L H_2O)	Melting point (°C)
para-nitrophenol	10	112
meta-nitrophenol	2.7	98
ortho-nitrophenol	0.8	47

A. *Meta*- and *para*-nitrophenol form intramolecular hydrogen bonds

B. *Ortho*-nitrophenol does not form intermolecular hydrogen bonds

C. *Ortho*-nitrophenol has the greatest intramolecular hydrogen bonding

D. *Para*-nitrophenol has the weakest intermolecular hydrogen bonding

E. *Ortho*-nitrophenol has the weakest intramolecular hydrogen bonding

35. Which of the molecules shown below is NOT an *aromatic* compound?

A. Benzimidazoline

C. Quinoline

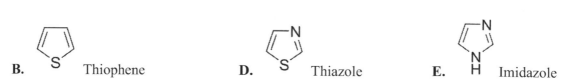

B. Thiophene

D. Thiazole

E. Imidazole

36. What is the degree of unsaturation for benzene?

A. 1   B. 2   C. 3   D. 4   E. 5

Chapter 20: Alcohols

1. Which of the following alcohols has the highest boiling point?

A. 2-methyl-1-propanol   C. ethanol

B. hexanol   D. propanol   E. methanol

2. When phenol acts as an acid, a [   ] ion is produced.

A. phenolic acid   C. phenyl

B. benzol   D. benzyl   E. phenoxide

3. When alcohol reacts with phosphoric acid, the product is referred to as a:

A. pyrophosphate   C. phosphate ester

B. phosphate anion   D. phosphate salt   E. none of the above

4. Which formula is alcohol?

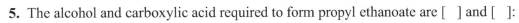

A. R‒C(=O)‒R'   C. R‒C‒O‒H (with =O below C)

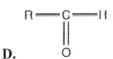

B. R‒C‒O‒R' (with =O below C)   D. R‒C‒H (with =O below C)   E. R‒O‒H

5. The alcohol and carboxylic acid required to form propyl ethanoate are [   ] and [   ]:

A. 1-propanol … ethanoic acid   C. ethanol … propionic acid

B. propanol … propanoic acid   D. methanol … propionic acid

E. 2-propanol … ethanoic acid

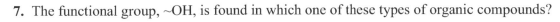

6. Which compound has the highest boiling point?

A. $CH_3CH_2CH_2CH_2OH$ C. $CH_3CH_2CH_2CH_2CH_2OH$

B. $CH_3CH_2CH_2CH_3$ D. $CH_3CH_2CH_2CH_2CH_3$

E. $CH_3CH_2CH_2OH$

7. The functional group, ~OH, is found in which one of these types of organic compounds?

A. amines   B. alcohols   C. alkanes   D. alkenes   E. ethers

8. What is the major product of this reaction?

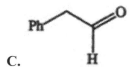 + Na$_2$Cr$_2$O$_7$ / H$_2$SO$_4$ → ?

A.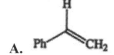

B.

C.

D.

E. None of the above

9. Which of the following reagents is best to convert methyl alcohol to methyl chloride?

A. Cl⁻   **B.** SOCl$_2$ **C.** Cl$_2$/CCl$_4$ **D.** Cl$_2$/hv   **E.** NaCl

10. The compound below has which functional groups?

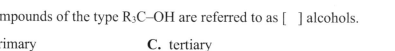

A. ether, alkene and alcohol   **C.** aromatic, alcohol and ether
B. ester, alkene and alcohol   **D.** aromatic, alcohol and ester   **E.** ether and ester

11. Which compound is NOT an unsaturated compound?

A. H$_2$C=CH–Cl   **C.** H$_2$C=CH$_2$
B. CH$_3$–CH$_2$–O–H   **D.** CH$_3$–CH=CH$_2$ **E.** H$_2$C=CH–O–H

12. Compounds of the type R$_3$C–OH are referred to as [   ] alcohols.

A. primary   **C.** tertiary
B. secondary   **D.** quaternary   **E.** none of the above

13. Compounds with the –OH group attached to a saturated alkane-like carbon are known as:

A. ethers   **C.** alcohols
B. hydroxyls   **D.** alkyl halides   **E.** phenols

14. When (S)-2-heptanol is subjected to SOCl$_2$/pyridine, the compound is transformed into:

A. (R/S)-2-chloroheptane   **C.** (S)-2-chloroheptane
B. (R)-2-chloroheptane   **D.** 2-heptone   **E.** heptanoic acid

15. The ester prepared by heating 1-pentanol with acetic acid in the presence of an acidic catalyst is named:

   A. 1-pentyl acetate   **C.** acetic pentanoate   **E.** acetyl pentanol

   B. acetyl 1-pentanoate   **D.** pentanoic acetate

16. Which of the following has the highest boiling point?

   A. ethyl methyl ether   **C.** dimethyl ether

   B. dihexyl ether   **D.** diethyl ether   **E.** dipropyl ether

17. Based on the properties of the attached functional group, which compound interacts most strongly with water, thus making it the most soluble compound?

   A. CH_3–CH_2–S–H   **C.** CH_3–CH_2–F

   B. CH_3–CH_2–I   **D.** CH_3–CH_2–Cl   **E.** CH_3–CH_2–O–H

18. What is the product of the following reaction?

$$CH_3\text{—}\overset{\displaystyle CH_2CH_3}{\underset{\displaystyle H}{|}}\text{—OH} \xrightarrow{\text{TsCl}} \xrightarrow{\text{Cl}^-}$$

A. $TsO\text{—}\overset{\displaystyle CH_2CH_3}{\underset{\displaystyle H}{|}}\text{—}CH_3$

C. $CH_3\text{—}\overset{\displaystyle CH_2CH_3}{\underset{\displaystyle H}{|}}\text{—OTs}$

B. $Cl\text{—}\overset{\displaystyle CH_2CH_3}{\underset{\displaystyle H}{|}}\text{—}CH_3$

D. $CH_3\text{—}\overset{\displaystyle CH_2CH_3}{\underset{\displaystyle H}{|}}\text{—Cl}$

E. $CH_3\text{—}\overset{\displaystyle CH_2CH_3}{\underset{\displaystyle H}{|}}\text{—OCl}$

19. Which of the following alcohols has the lowest boiling point?

   A. hexanol   **C.** propanol

   B. 2-methyl-1-propanol   **D.** ethanol   **E.** benzoic acid

20. The reaction of $(CH_3)_2CHCH_2OH$ with concentrated HBr using controlled heating yields:

   A. $(CH_3)_2CHCH_2OBr$ **C.** $CH_3CH_2CH_2Br$

   B. $(CH_3)_2CHCH_4{}^+Br^-$ **D.** $(CH_3)_2CHCH_2Br$

                               E. $(CH_3)_2CHCH_3$

21. When propanol is subjected to PBr₃, the compounds undergo:

    A. an S_N1 elimination reaction to form propene
    B. oxidation to form an aldehyde
    C. an S_N1 reaction to produce an alkyl halide
    D. addition, elimination and then substitution to form bromopropane
    E. an E_1 reaction to produce propene

22. Which is a product of the oxidation of CH₃–CH₂–CH₂–O–H?

    A. CH₃–CH₂–CH₃

    B. 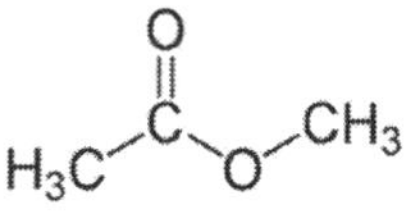 (structure: H₃C–C(=O)–O–CH₃)

    C. (structure: acetone)

    D. 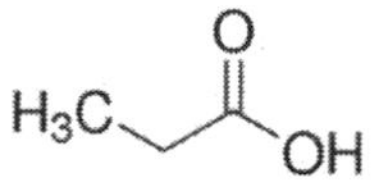 (structure: H₃C–CH₂–C(=O)–OH)

    E. CH₃–CH₂–O–CH₃

23. Which of the following has the highest boiling point?

    A. 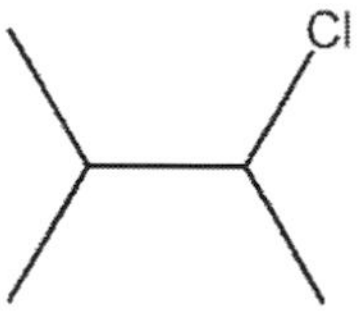 (structure with Cl)

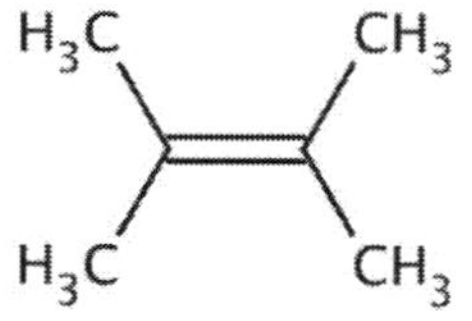

    B. 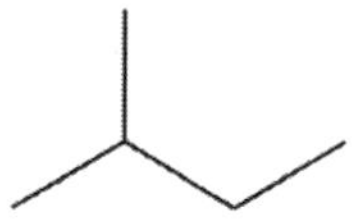 (branched alkane structure)

    C. (tetramethylethylene structure)

    D. 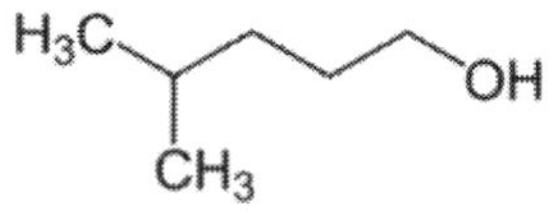 (structure with OH and CH₃)

    E. 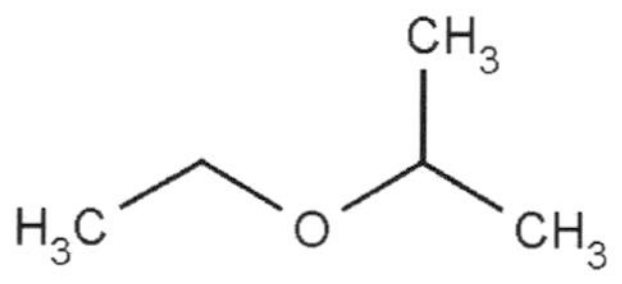 (ether structure with CH₃)

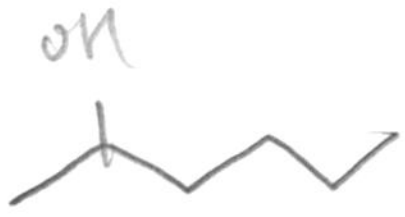

24. What compound is formed by the oxidation of 2-hexanol?

    A. hexanal   **C.** 2-hexanone
    B. hexanoic acid   **D.** 2-hexene   **E.** hexyne

25. Which of the following would have the highest boiling point?

    A. 1-hexyne   **B.** 1-hexene   **C.** hexane   **D.** 1-hexanol   **E.** 1-pentanol

26. The functional group C=O is found in all the species below, EXCEPT:

    A. amides   **C.** aldehydes
    B. ethers   **D.** ketones   **E.** esters

27. Which of the following is an allylic alcohol?

    A. $CH_3CH=CHCH_2OH$

    B. $HOCH=CHCH_2CH_3$

    C. $CH_2=CHCH_2CH_3$

    D. $CH_2=CHCH_2OCH_3$

    E. $CH_2=CHCH_2CH_2OH$

28. Which of the following molecules has the most acidic proton?

    A. 2-pentanol

    B. 3-pentyne

    C. 2-pentene

    D. pentane

    E. *tert*-butanol

29. What is the major product of this reaction?

30. Which of the following alcohols dehydrates with the fastest rate?

31. When (*R*)-2-heptanol is subjected to a two-step mechanism of tosyl chloride followed by Cl⁻, the product is:

    A. (*R*)-2-chloroheptane

    B. heptene

    C. (*R/S*)-2-chloroheptane

    D. (*S*)-2-chloroheptane

    E. (*S*)-3-chloroheptane

32. Phenol exists predominantly:

   A. in the keto form because its keto tautomer is antiaromatic

   B. in the keto form because its keto tautomer is nonaromatic

   C. in the enol form because its keto tautomer is antiaromatic

   D. in the enol form because its keto tautomer is nonaromatic

   E. in the keto form because its keto tautomer is aromatic

33. Treatment of salicylic acid with methanol and nonaqueous acid yields an:

$+ CH_3OH + H_2SO_4 \rightarrow$?

Salicylic acid

   A. acetal   **C.** ester

   B. ether   **D.** hemiacetal   **E.** amide

34. When (*R*)-2-hexanol is subjected to PBr_3, the compound it produces is:

   A. (*R*)-2-bromohexane   **C.** (*R/S*)-2-bromohexane

   B. (*S*)-2-bromohexane   **D.** (*S*)-2-bromopentane   **E.** ketone

35. Which of the following reactions yields an ester?

   A. $C_6H_5OH + CH_3CH_2Br$ **C.** $CH_3COOH + SOCl_2$

   B. $CH_3COOH + C_2H_5OH + H_2SO_4$ **D.** $2CH_3OH + H_2SO_4$

                                         E. $CH_3CH_2Br + CH_3CH_2O^-Na^+$

36. What is the major product of the reaction of 2,2-dimethylcyclohexanol with HBr?

A.   **C.**   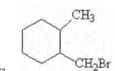

B.   **D.**   **E.**

Chapter 21: Aldehydes & Ketones

1. Oxidation of a ketone produces:

    A. a secondary alcohol   **C.** a carboxylic acid

    B. an aldehyde   **D.** a primary alcohol   **E.** no reaction

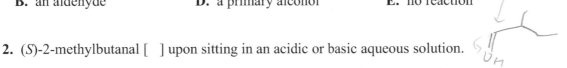

2. (*S*)-2-methylbutanal [   ] upon sitting in an acidic or basic aqueous solution.

    A. racemizes   **C.** inverts completely to the *R* configuration

    B. esterifies   **D.** hydrolyzes

    E. irreversibly forms the hydrate

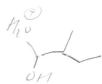

3. What is an ester reduced to with diisobutylaluminum hydride (DIBAL)?

    A. 1° alcohol   **C.** ketone

    B. alkane   **D.** aldehyde   **E.** acetal

4. Which of the following reagents quantitatively converts an enolizable ketone to its enolate salt?

    A. lithium hydroxide   **C.** methyllithium

    B. lithium diisopropylamide   **D.** diethylamine   **E.** pyridine

5. Which type of compound is shown below?

    A. ester   **C.** ketone

    B. carboxylic acid   **D.** aldehyde   **E.** amine

6. Which of the following carbonyl compounds may be synthesized from 1,3-dithiane?

    I. methyl vinyl ketone   III. 3,3-dimethyl-2-butanone

    II. 2-pentanone   IV. 2-phenylethanal

    A. I and IV only   **C.** II and III only

    B. II only   **D.** II and IV only   **E.** I, II and IV only

7. Which of the following organic compounds is most likely NOT a ketone?

A. estradiol (female hormone)

B. progesterone (female hormone)

C. androsterone (male hormone)

D. cortisone (adrenal hormone)

E. testosterone (male hormone)

8. The reagent(s) that convert(s) a carbonyl group of a ketone into a methylene group is:

A. Na, NH$_3$, CH$_3$CH$_2$OH

B. LiAlH$_4$

C. NaBH$_4$, CH$_3$CH$_2$OH

D. Zn(Hg), conc. HCl

E. LiAlH[OC(CH$_3$)$_3$]$_3$

9. The reaction of ethylmagnesium bromide with which of the following compounds yields secondary alcohol after quenching with aqueous acid?

A. (CH$_3$)$_2$CO

B. ethylene oxide

C. H$_2$CO

D. CH$_3$CHO

E. n-butyllithium

10. Which observation denotes a positive Benedict's test?

A. A mirror-like deposit forms from a colorless solution

B. A purple solution yields a brown precipitate

C. A red precipitate forms from a blue solution

D. A red-brown solution becomes clear and colorless

E. A pale-yellow solution with an odor of chlorine changes to a purple color

11. A ylide is a molecule that can be described as a:

A. carbanion bound to a negatively charged heteroatom

B. carbocation bound to a positively charged heteroatom

C. carbocation bound to a carbon radical

D. carbocation bound to a diazonium ion

E. carbanion bound to a positively charged heteroatom

12. Which of the following represents the correct ranking in terms of increasing the boiling point?

A. *n*-butane < 1-butanol < diethyl ether < 2-butanone

B. *n*-butane < 2-butanone < diethyl ether < 1-butanol

C. 2-butanone < *n*-butane < diethyl ether < 1-butanol

D. *n*-butane < diethyl ether < 1-butanol < 2-butanone

E. *n*-butane < diethyl ether < 2-butanone < 1-butanol

13. Which of the following reactions does NOT yield a ketone product?

A. 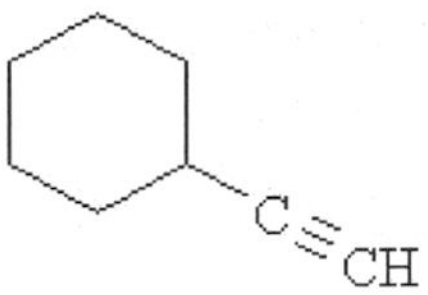 + 1) Sia$_2$BH / THF; 2) H$_2$O$_2$ / ⁻OH →

B. 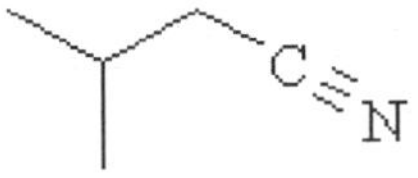 + 1) CH$_3$CH$_2$MgBr; 2) H$_3$O$^+$ →

C. 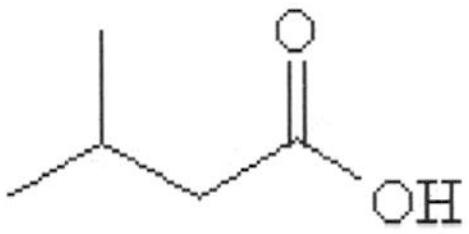 + 1) 2 CH$_3$CH$_2$Li; 2) H$_3$O$^+$ →

D. + AlCl3 →

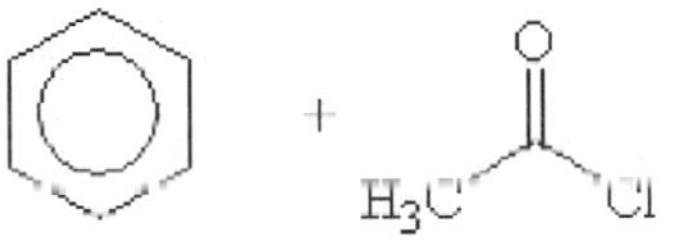

E. 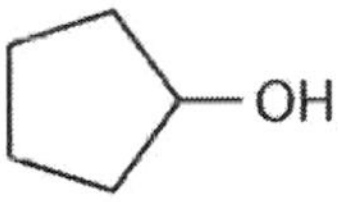 ─OH + PCC →

14. What reagents are needed to complete the following synthesis?

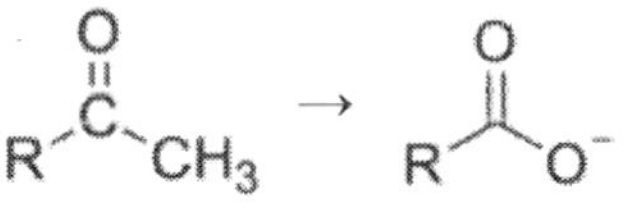

A. 1) NaOH / heat; 2) HCl (*aq*)
B. 1) NaOH / Br$_2$
C. 1) warm conc. KMnO$_4$ / NaOH; 2) HCl (*aq*)
D. 1) Ag(NH$_3$)$_2$OH; 2) HCl (*aq*)
E. None of the above

15. A compound with an ~OH group and an ether-like ~OR group bonded to the same carbon atom is:

A. hemiacetal
B. diol
C. aldol
D. acetal
E. ether

16. Which compound gives a positive indicator with the Tollens' reagent?

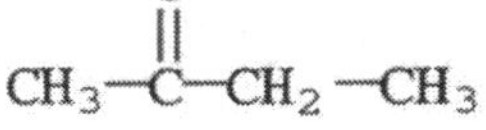

A. 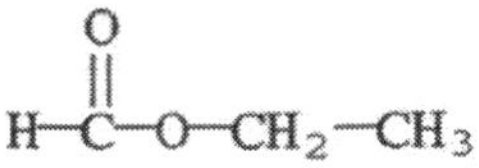
B. 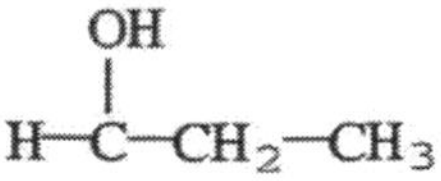
C.
D. 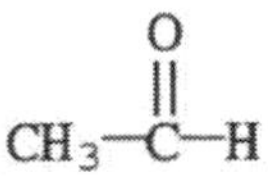
E.

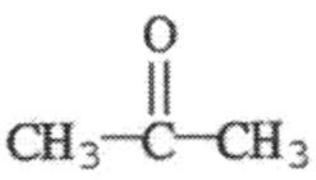

17. Reduction of aldehydes and ketones is a [   ] reaction involving the [   ] ion(s).

    A. two-step; H⁻ and H⁺   **C.** one-step; H⁻

    B. two-step; OH⁻ and H⁺   **D.** one-step; H⁺   **E.** two-step; H⁻ and OH⁻

18. Which of the following is the best Michael acceptor?

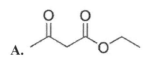 **A.**

C.

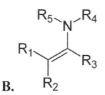 **B.**

D.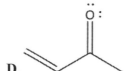

E. None of the above

19. Which of the following pairs have the most similar chemical properties?

    A. alkanes and carboxylic acids   **C.** amines and esters

    B. alkenes and aromatics   **D.** ketones and aldehydes

                                           E. ethers and alcohols

20. Which compound gives a positive Tollens' test?

    A. pentane   **C.** 3-pentanone

    B. pentanoic acid   **D.** 2-pentanone   **E.** pentanal

21. Consider the equilibrium of each of the carbonyl compounds with HCN to produce cyanohydrins. Which is the correct ranking of compounds in order of increasing K_{eq} for this equilibrium?

    A. H_2CO < cyclohexanone < CH_3CHO < 2-methylcyclohexanone

    B. CH_3CHO < 2-methylcyclohexanone < cyclohexanone < H_2CO

    C. cyclohexanone < 2-methylcyclohexanone < H_2CO < CH_3CHO

    D. cyclohexanone < 2-methylcyclohexanone < CH_3CHO < H_2CO

    E. 2-methylcyclohexanone < cyclohexanone < CH_3CHO < H_2CO

22. Which of the following functional groups represents a ketone?

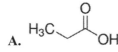 **A.**

C.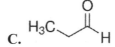

B. H₃C ... CH₃

D.

E.

23. All of the following statements about oxidation of carbonyls are true, EXCEPT:

    A. oxidation of aldehydes produces carboxylic acids
    B. ketones do not react with mild oxidizing agents
    C. Tollens' test involves the oxidation of Ag^+
    D. Benedict's test involves the reduction of Cu^{2+}
    E. all of the statements are true

24. Which of the following classes of compounds has a carbonyl group?

    A. phenol   **C.** amine
    B. ether   **D.** alcohol   **E.** none of the above

25. All of the statements concerning the carbonyl group in aldehydes and ketones are true, EXCEPT:

    A. in condensed form, the aldehyde group can be written as ~CHO
    B. the carbonyl group is planar
    C. the bond angles about the central carbon atom are 120°
    D. the bond is polar with a slight negative charge on the oxygen atom
    E. since the bond is polar, carbonyl groups readily form hydrogen bonds with each other

26. Which of the following compound is the most soluble in water?

    A. acetone   **C.** 2-butanone
    B. cyclohexanone   **D.** 3-butanone   **E.** benzophenone

27. Treatment of a nitrile with a Grignard reagent, followed by hydrolysis, results in:

    A. ester   **C.** aldehyde
    B. ketone   **D.** ether   **E.** alcohol

28. Oxidation of an aldehyde produces a:

    A. tertiary alcohol   **C.** primary alcohol
    B. secondary alcohol   **D.** carboxylic acid   **E.** ketone

29. Which of the following will alkylate a lithium enolate most rapidly?

    A. methyl bromide   **C.** neopentyl bromide
    B. isopropyl bromide   **D.** bromobenzene
                         E. 2-methylbromobenzene

30. In Benedict's test:

      I. an aldehyde is oxidized
      II. a red/brown precipitate is formed
      III. copper (II) ion is reduced

    A. I only   **B.** II only   **C.** III only   **D.** I and II only   **E.** I, II and III

31. Of the following, which is the best solvent for an aldol addition?

    A. acetone   **C.** propanol
    B. methyl acetate   **D.** dimethyl ether   **E.** methanol

32. All of the following statements about oxidation of carbonyls are true, EXCEPT:

    A. Benedict's test involves the reduction of Cu^{2+}
    B. Tollens' test involves the reduction of Ag^+
    C. oxidation of primary alcohols produces secondary alcohols
    D. oxidation of secondary alcohols produces ketones
    E. oxidation of aldehydes produces carboxylic acids

33. The reaction of ethylmagnesium bromide with which of the following compounds yields tertiary alcohol after quenching with aqueous acid?

    A. ethylene oxide   **C.** CH_3CHO
    B. $(CH_3)_2CO$ **D.** H_2CO **E.** *n*-butyllithium

34. Which of the following are enol forms of 2-butanone ($CH_3COCH_2CH_3$)?

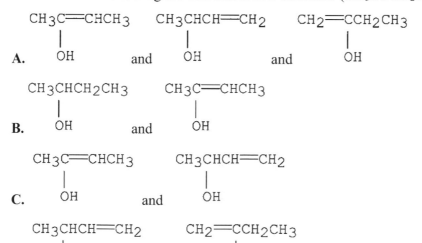

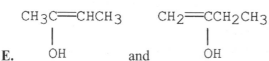

35. Which statement is true regarding the major differences between aldehydes and ketones as compared to other carbonyl compounds?

    A. The carbonyl group carbon atom in aldehydes and ketones is bonded to atoms that do not attract electrons strongly

    B. The polar carbon-oxygen bond in aldehydes and ketones is less reactive than the hydrocarbon portion of the molecule

    C. The carbonyl carbon in aldehydes and ketones has bond angles of 120°, unlike the comparable bond angles in other carbonyl compounds

    D. The molar masses in aldehydes and ketones are much less than in the other types of compounds

    E. The carbonyl carbon in aldehydes and ketones has bond angles of 109.5°, similar to the comparable bond angles in other carbonyl compounds

36. Which series of reactions best facilitates the following conversion?

    A. 1) KMnO$_4$ (*aq*); 2) Hg(OAc)$_2$ (*aq*); 3) NaBH$_4$/$^-$OH

    B. 1) NaBH$_4$; 2) H$_3$PO$_4$/Δ

    C. 1) H$_3$C-MgBr; 2) H$_2$O/H$_3$O$^+$

    D. 1) NaBH$_4$; 2) HBr (*g*); 3) Mg/ether; 4) H$_2$O/H$_3$O$^+$

    E. 1) Raney nickel; 2) H$_3$C-MgBr; 3) H$_2$O/H$_3$O$^+$

Please, leave your Customer Review on Amazon

Notes

Chapter 22: Carboxylic Acids

1. Which of the following functional groups does this organic compound contain?

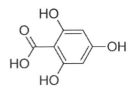

A. amide

C. carboxylic acid

B. amine

D. ester

E. acyl halide

2. What is the major organic product of the reaction shown?

$$CH_3(CH_2)_3COOH + CH_3C(OH)HCH_3 \rightarrow ?$$

A. $CH_3CH_2CH_2COOCH(CH_3)_2$

B. $CH_3CH_2CH_2CH_2C(OH)OCH(CH_3)_2$

C. $CH_3CH_2CH_2CH_2COOCHCH_2CH_3$

D. $CH_3CH_2CH_2CH_2COOCH(CH_3)_2$

E. $CH_3CH_2CH_2CH_2COCH(CH_3)_2$

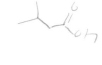

3. What products are formed upon the reaction of benzoic acid with sodium hydroxide, NaOH?

A. Sodium bicarbonate and sodium benzoate

B. Sodium bicarbonate and benzaldehyde

C. Sodium benzoate and water

D. Benzaldehyde and water

E. Toluene and water

4. Which type of compound is shown below?

A. ester   B. carboxylic acid   C. ketone   D. aldehyde   E. amide

5. Which carboxylic acid is used to prepare the ester shown?

$$CH_3-CH_2-O-C-CH_2-CH-CH_3$$

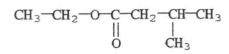

A. $(CH_3)_2CHCH_2COOH$

B. $(CH_3)_2CHCOOH$

C. CH_3COOH

D. CH_3CH_2COOH

E. $CH_3(CH_2)_3COOH$

6. When an amine reacts with a carboxylic acid at high temperature, the major product is a(n):

A. ether   B. thiol   C. amide   D. ester   E. alcohol

7. Which acid is expected to have the highest boiling point?

    A. formic   **B.** oxalic   **C.** acetic   **D.** benzoic   **E.** stearic

8. The reaction of a carboxylic acid with a base-like sodium hydroxide, NaOH, gives:

    A. alcohol   **C.** alkoxide salt

    B. ester   **D.** carboxylate salt   **E.** none of the above

9. What are the products from the reaction of ethanoic acid and methanol with sulfuric acid catalyst?

$$CH_3COOH + CH_3OH + H_2SO_4 \rightarrow ?$$

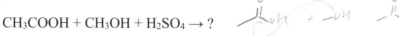

    A. $CH_3CH_2COOH + H_2O$ **C.** $CH_3COCH_3 + H_2O$

    B. $CH_3COOCH_3 + H_2O$ **D.** $CH_3CH_2CHO + H_2O$ **E.** No reaction

10. Which fatty acid is expected to have the highest boiling point?

    A. oxalic, $(CO_2H)_2$ **C.** benzoic, $C_6H_5CO_2H$

    B. formic, HCO_2H **D.** acetic, CH_3CO_2H

                                        E. stearic, $CH_3(CH_2)_{16}CO_2H$

11. Which formula correctly illustrates the form taken by the acetic acid in a basic solution?

    A. $CH_3-\overset{\overset{\displaystyle O}{\|}}{C}-CH_2{}^+$ **C.** (structure with OH)

    B. (structure H_3C, $:O:$, $\overset{..}{O}:{}^-$)   **D.** $CH_3-\overset{\overset{\displaystyle O}{\|}}{C}-OH^+$ **E.** $CH_3-\overset{\overset{\displaystyle O}{\|}}{C}-OH^-$

12. When alcohol reacts with a carboxylic acid, the major product is a(n):

    A. salt   **B.** ester   **C.** amine   **D.** amide   **E.** soap

13. Identify the carboxylic acid and alcohol from which the following ester was made.

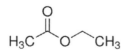

    A. $CH_3CH_2CO_2H$ and CH_3CH_2OH **C.** CH_3CO_2H and CH_3CH_2OH

    B. CH_3CO_2H and CH_3CO_2H **D.** $CH_3CH_2CO_2H$ and $CH_3CH_2CH_2OH$

                                              E. None of the above

14. Which of the following has the highest boiling point?

- **A.** ethyl alcohol, CH_3CH_2OH
- **B.** acetic acid, CH_3COOH
- **C.** ethane, CH_3CH_3
- **D.** dimethyl ketone, CH_3COCH_3
- **E.** formaldehyde, HCHO

15. The ion formed from a carboxylic acid is called the:

- **A.** ester cation
- **B.** ester anion
- **C.** carboxylate cation
- **D.** carboxylate anion
- **E.** amide cation

16. Which of the functional groups below contain(s) a hydroxyl group as a part of its/their structure?

I. anhydride   II. carboxylic acid   III. ester

A. I only   **B.** II only   **C.** III only   **D.** I and II only   **E.** I, II and III

17. Which acid is expected to have the lowest boiling point?

- **A.** formic, HCO_2H
- **B.** oxalic, $(CO_2H)_2$
- **C.** acetic, CH_3CO_2H
- **D.** benzoic, $C_6H_5CO_2H$
- **E.** stearic, $CH_3(CH_2)_{16}CO_2H$

18. Which of the following molecules is acidic?

- **A.** I only
- **B.** II only
- **C.** I and II only
- **D.** I and III only
- **E.** I, II and III

19. Which of the following compounds is the strongest acid?

- **A.** $HOOCCH_2F$
- **B.** $HOOCCH_3$
- **C.** $HOOCCH_2Br$
- **D.** $HOOCCH_2OCH_3$
- **E.** PhOH

20. Explain why caprylic acid $CH_3(CH_2)_6COOH$ dissolves in a 5% aqueous solution of sodium hydroxide, but caprylaldehyde, $CH_3(CH_2)_6CHO$, does not.

- **A.** Caprylic acid reacts to form the water-soluble salt
- **B.** Caprylaldehyde behaves as a reducing agent, which neutralizes the sodium hydroxide
- **C.** Caprylaldehyde can form more hydrogen bonds to water than caprylic acid
- **D.** With two oxygens, caprylic acid is about twice as polar as caprylaldehyde
- **E.** Caprylaldehyde is a gas at room temperature

21. All of the statements about carboxylic acids are true, EXCEPT:

A. they react with bases to form salts which are often more soluble than the original acid
B. they form hydrogen bonds, causing their boiling points to be higher than expected on the basis of molecular weight
C. at low molecular weights, they are liquids with pungent odors
D. they undergo substitution reactions involving the $^-$OH group
E. when they behave as acids, the $^-$OH group is lost, leaving the CO$^-$ ion

22. When a small amount of hexanoic acid [$CH_3(CH_2)_4CO_2H$, p$K_a \approx 4.8$] is added to a separatory funnel which contains the organic solvent diethyl ether and water with a pH of 11.0, it is found mainly in the [ ] phase as [ ]:

A. water; $CH_3(CH_2)_4CO_2H$
B. ether; $CH_3(CH_2)_4CO_2H$
C. water; $CH_3(CH_2)_4CO_2^-$
D. ether; $CH_3(CH_2)_4CO_2^-$
E. none of the above

23. Which of the following compounds acts as an acid?

A. CH_3COCH_3
B. $(CH_3)_2NH$
C. C_2H_5OH
D. C_2H_5COOH
E. $NaNH_2$

24. All of the statements concerning citric acid are true, EXCEPT it:

A. is produced only by plants
B. is used in many consumer products
C. is extremely soluble in water
D. contains three carboxylic acid groups because its carbon skeleton is branched
E. is a weak acid

25. Which of the following molecules would be expected to be the most soluble in water?

A. $CH_3(CH_2)_6CO_2H$
B. $CH_3(CH_2)_{12}CO_2H$
C. CH_3CO_2H
D. $CH_3CH_2CH_2CO_2H$
E. C_6H_{12}

26. Which of the following molecules is the most polar?

A. butane
B. butanoic acid
C. cyclohexane
D. ethanol
E. 1-chlorobutane

27. The most common reactions of carboxylic acid or its derivative involve:

A. replacement of the group bonded to the carbonyl atom
B. oxidation of the R group
C. addition across the double bond between carbon and oxygen
D. replacement of the oxygen atom in the carbonyl group
E. reduction of the R group

28. Which of the following reactions will NOT result in the formation of a carboxylic acid?

A. Oxidation of a secondary alcohol
B. Oxidation of a primary alcohol
C. Hydrolysis of nitriles
D. Grignard reagents reacting with CO_2
E. Oxidation of an aldehyde

29. Which acid would be expected to have the lowest boiling point?

A. oxalic
B. formic
C. benzoic
D. acetic
E. oleic

30. The reaction of butanoic acid with ethanol produces:

A. butyl ethanamide
B. ethyl butanamide
C. butyl ethanoate
D. ethyl butanoate
E. butyl ethyl ester

31. Which of the following are the preferred reagents used in the following synthesis?

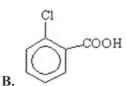

A. 1) $NaBH_4$/THF, 2) H_3O^+
B. 1) Mg/ether; 2) dry CO_2; 3) H_3O^+
C. 1) $LiAlH_4$/THF; 2) H_3O^+
D. 1) Hot $KMnO_4$; 2) H_3O^+
E. 1) $LiAlH(OCH_3)_3$/THF; 2) H_3O^+

32. Which of the following molecules is the strongest acid?

A.

C.

B.

D.

E.

33. The water solubility of compounds containing the carboxylic acid group can be increased by reaction with:

    A. water   **C.** nitric acid

    B. sodium hydroxide   **D.** sulfuric acid   **E.** benzoic acid

34. Which of the following acids is likely to have the weakest conjugate base?

    A. $CH_3Cl_2CCO_2H$ **C.** $(CH_3CH_2)_3CCO_2H$

    B. $CH_3CH_2CH_2CO_2H$ **D.** $CH_3HNCH_2CH_2CH_2CO_2H$

                                         E. $CH_3Cl_2CCH_2CO_2H$

35. The boiling point of acetic acid is 119 °C and that of methyl acetate is 57 °C. What is the reason that acetic acid boils at a much higher temperature than methyl acetate?

acetic acid   methyl acetate

    A. molecular mass   **C.** hydrophobic interactions

    B. presence of an ester linkage   **D.** hydrogen bonding   **E.** London forces

36. The pK_a of acetic acid (CH_3COOH) is 4.8. If the pH of an aqueous solution of CH_3COOH and CH_3COO^- is 4.8, then:

    A. $[CH_3COOH] = [CH_3COO^-]$

    B. $[CH_3COOH] < [CH_3COO^-]$

    C. CH_3COOH is completely ionized

    D. $[CH_3COOH] > [CH_3COO^-]$

    E. CH_3COOH is completely nonionized

Chapter 23: COOH Derivatives

1. The compound below is which type of compound?

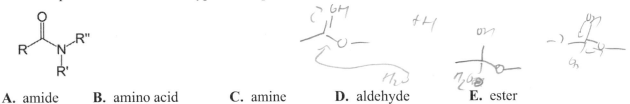

    A. amide   **B.** amino acid   **C.** amine   **D.** aldehyde   **E.** ester

2. The products of acid hydrolysis of an ester are:

    A. alcohol + water   **C.** another ester + water

    B. acid + water   **D.** alcohol + acid   **E.** salt + water

3. Which of the following reactions is favorable, in the direction indicated, under common laboratory conditions?

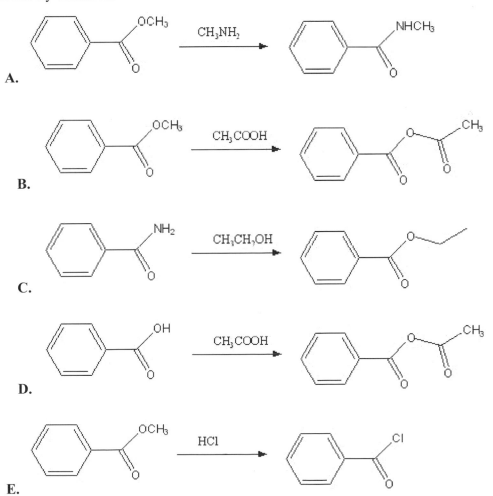

   205

4. Hydrolysis of the ester ethyl acetate produces:

A. butanal and ethanol   **C.** ethanol and acetic acid

B. ethanal and acetic acid   **D.** butanoic acid   **E.** butanol

5. What class of compound has the following general structure?

$$\overset{\displaystyle O}{\overset{\displaystyle \|}{R-C}}-O-R'$$

A. ester   **C.** aldehyde

B. ketone   **D.** anhydride   **E.** carboxylic acid

6. What functional group is NOT present in the following structure for thyroxine (i.e., thyroid hormone)?

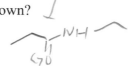

A. organic halide   **C.** carboxylic acid

B. ether   **D.** anhydride   **E.** phenol

7. What are the major organic products of the reaction shown?

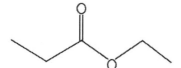

$+ \, H_2O \, / \, H_2SO_4 \rightarrow \, ?$

A. $CH_3COOH + HOCH_2CH_2CH_3$

B. $CH_3CH_2CH_2OH + CH_3CH_2OH$

C. $CH_3CH_2COOH + HOCH_2CH_3$

D. $CH_3CH_2CH_2COO^- + {}^+H_2OCH_2CH_3$

E. $CH_3CH_2COOH + CH_3COOH$

8. What are the products of this reaction?

$$CH_3CH_2CONHCH_2CH_3 + NaOH \rightarrow \, ?$$

A. $CH_3CH_2COO^-Na^+ + CH_3CH_2NH_2$

B. $CH_3CH_2CH_2OH + CH_3CH_2NH_3^-Na^+$

C. $CH_3CH_2COO^-Na^+ + CH_3CH_2NH_3^+Cl^-$

D. $CH_3CH_2COOH + CH_3CH_2NH_2$

E. None of the above

9. Which product is formed during a reaction of acetic acid (CH_3COOH) with methylamine (CH_3NH_2)?

A. ethylammonium hydroxide   **C.** methylacetamine

B. methanol   **D.** methylacetamide   **E.** methylammonium acetate

10. Esters and amides are most easily made by nucleophilic acyl substitution reactions on:

A. alcohols　　　　　　　　　C. carboxylates

B. acid anhydrides　　　　　　D. carboxylic acids　　　　E. acid chlorides

11. The reaction of an amine and a carboxylic acid produces what kind of compound?

A. amine　　　　　　　　　C. anhydride

B. amide　　　　　　　　　D. ketone　　　　　　　E. ester

12. Penicillin can be taken orally if the compound can survive degradation by the low pH of the stomach. The amide bond between the *R* group and 6-APA of dicloxacillin is stable at low pH, because:

A. high hydroxide concentration promotes amide stability

B. amide bonds do not easily undergo hydrolysis

C. hydrogen bonding has stabilization effects

D. aromatic compounds are unaffected by changes in pH

E. none of the above

13. Identify the functional group:

A. anhydride　　　　B. amine　　　C. amide　　　　D. ester　　　　E. nitrile

14. Which of the following is a product of this reaction?

$$CH_3-\overset{O}{\overset{\|}{C}}-OCH_2CH_2CH_3 \; + \; NaOH \rightarrow \; ?$$

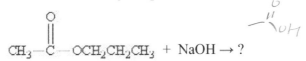

A. CH_3COOH　　　　　　　　　C. CH_3CH_2-OH

B. $CH_3CH_2COO^-\,Na^+$　　　　　D. $CH_3COO^-\,Na^+$　　　　E. none of the above

15. Which sequence correctly ranks each carbonyl group in order of increasing reactivity toward nucleophilic addition?

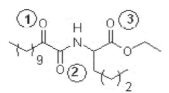

A. $1 < 2 < 3$　　　　　　　C. $3 < 1 < 2$

B. $2 < 3 < 1$　　　　　　　D. $1 < 3 < 2$　　　　E. $3 < 2 < 1$

16. Which functional group(s) below indicate(s) the presence of two atoms connected by a triple bond?

      I. ester   II. nitrile   III. alkyne

   A. I only   **C.** III only

   B. II only   **D.** II and III only   **E.** I, II and III

17. Which of these molecules is an ester?

A.   **C.**

B.   **D.**   **E.** None of the above

18. The products of basic hydrolysis of an ester are:

   A. acid + water   **C.** alcohol + acid

   B. alcohol + water   **D.** another ester + water

                                       E. carboxylate salt + alcohol

19. Which of the following products might be formed if benzoyl chloride was treated with excess CH_3CH_2MgBr?

   A. $C_6H_5CH_2CHO$ **C.** C_6H_5COOH

   B. $C_6H_5C(CH_2CH_3)OHCH_2CH_3$ **D.** $C_6H_5COOCH_2CH_3$

                                       E. none of the above

20. The compound below has which functional groups?

CH₂OH

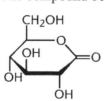

   A. lactone and alcohol   **C.** ester and hemiacetal

   B. ether and alcohol   **D.** ester and acetal

                                   E. ketone and aldehyde

21. Benzoyl chloride, PhC(O)Cl, reacts with water to form benzoic acid, PhCO₂H. In this addition-elimination reaction:

  A. water acts as a nucleophile, benzoyl chloride acts as an electrophile, and chloride acts as a leaving group
  B. water acts as an electrophile, benzoyl chloride acts as a nucleophile, and chloride acts as a leaving group
  C. both water and benzoyl chloride act as electrophiles
  D. there are no nucleophiles or electrophiles
  E. water acts as the electrophile, and benzoyl chloride acts as a nucleophile

22. The reaction of benzoic acid with thionyl chloride followed, by treatment with ammonia, yields which of the following compounds?

  A. *p*-chlorobenzamide
  B. *m*-chlorobenzamide
  C. benzamide
  D. *p*-aminobenzaldehyde
  E. 3-chloro-4-aminobenzaldehyde

23. The compound capsaicin below has which functional groups?

  A. aldehyde and amine
  B. carboxylic acid and amine
  C. nitro and amine
  D. amide and ether
  E. ester and amine

24. What is the name of the product formed by the reaction of propanoic acid with ethanol?

  A. ethyl propanoate
  B. pentanal
  C. pentyl ester
  D. ethylpropylketone
  E. pentanone

25. Which of the following type of bond is depicted below?

  A. amide bond
  B. glycosidic bond
  C. ester bond
  D. ether bond
  E. hydrogen bond

26. The compound below has which functional groups?

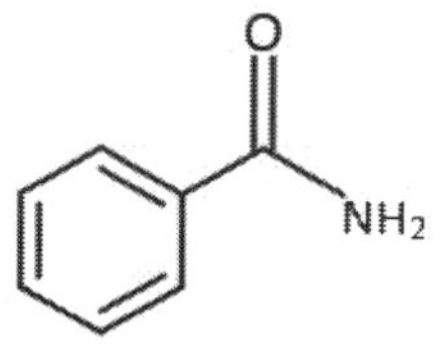

A. aromatic and alcohol

B. aromatic and amine

C. aromatic and amide

D. aromatic and carboxylic acid

E. aromatic and aldehyde

27. What are the products of an acid-catalyzed hydrolysis reaction of amides and water?

A. an alcohol and an alkane

B. an amine and a ketone

C. a carboxylic acid and an amine salt

D. an ester and an ether

E. a carboxylic acid and an alcohol

28. Which of the following compounds is the most susceptible to nucleophilic attack by ⁻OH?

A. propionyl bromide

B. benzyl bromide

C. propanal

D. butanoic acid

E. none of the above

29. What is the major organic product of this reaction?

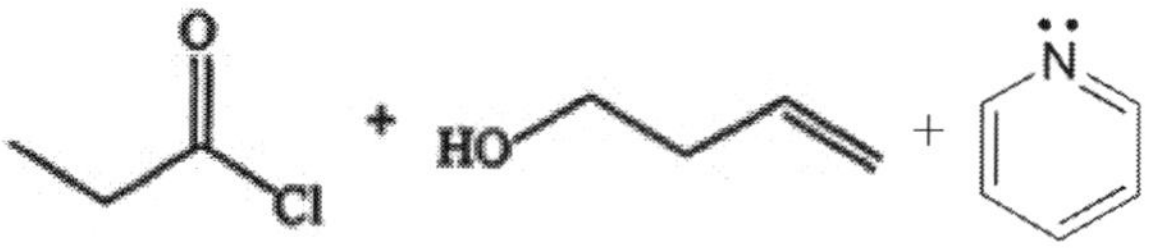

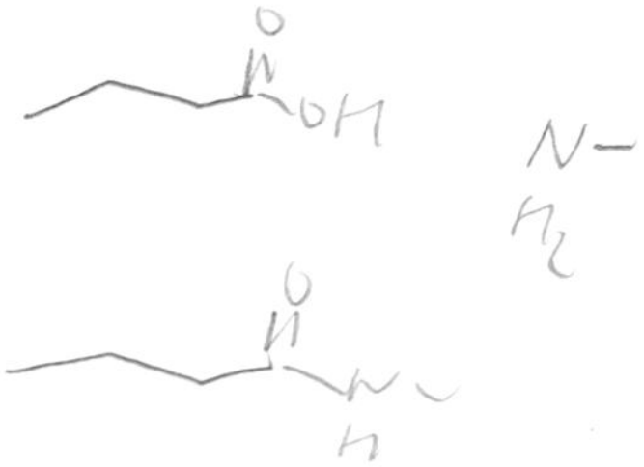

A.

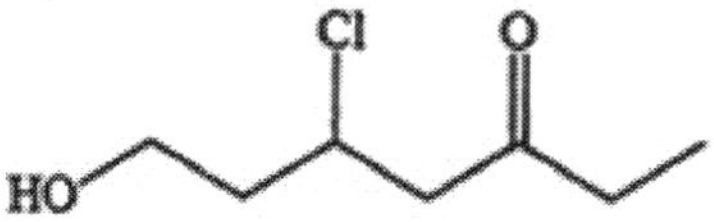

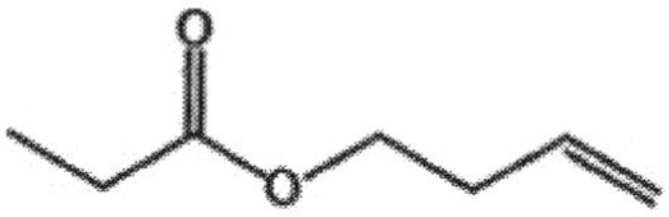

B.

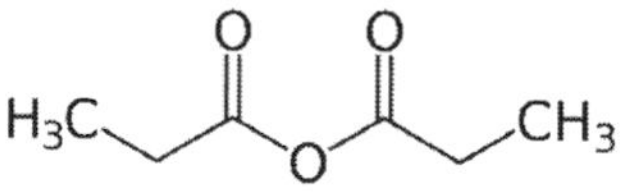

C.

D.

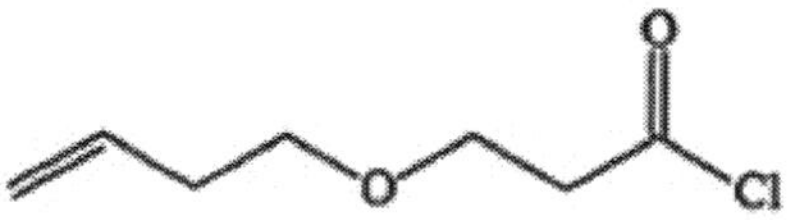

E.

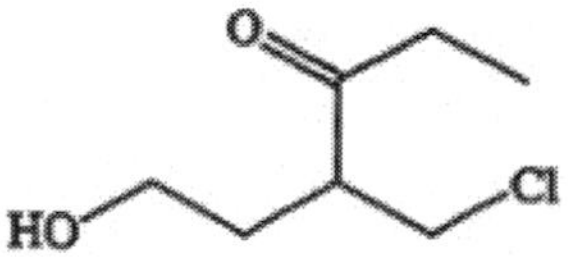

30. What reagent(s) are needed to complete the following reaction?

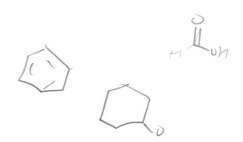

+ ? → HO⟋⟍⟋⟍OH

A. H₂, Pd

B. 1) DIBAL–H; 2) H₃O⁺

C. 1) LiAlH₄; 2) H₃O⁺

D. 1) NaBH₄; 2) H₃O⁺

E. 1) H₂, Pd; 2) H₃O⁺

31. What is the major ring-containing product of this reaction?

+ KOH, H₂O/Δ → H⁺ workup → ?

A.

C.

OH
OH

B.

OH

D.

E.

OEt
OEt

32. What is the name of the product formed by the reaction of butanoic acid with methylamine?

A. *N*-methylbutamide

B. *N*-methylbutanamide

C. pentanone

D. pentylamine

E. *N,N*-methylbutamide

33. Amides are less basic than amines because the:

A. carbonyl group donates electrons by resonance

B. carbonyl group withdraws electrons by resonance

C. nitrogen does not have a lone pair of electrons

D. nitrogen has a full positive charge

E. amides do not contain nitrogen

34. Which of the following products may be formed in the reaction below?

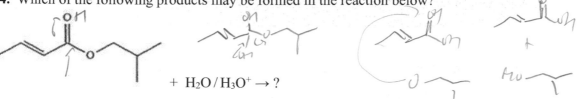

$+ H_2O / H_3O^+ \rightarrow ?$

A. HOCH$_2$CH(CH$_3$)$_2$

B. CH$_3$CH(CH$_3$)$_2$

C. HOOCCH$_2$CH(CH$_3$)$_2$

D. CH$_3$CH=CHCHO

E. HOCH$_2$CH$_2$CH(CH$_3$)$_2$

35. Which is the most reactive of the four derivatives of a carboxylic acid?

A. anhydride

B. acid bromide

C. amide

D. ester

E. thioester

36. What are the products of a hydrolysis reaction of an ester?

A. Alcohol and alkane

B. Carboxylic acid and alcohol

C. Ether and alkene

D. Ketone and aldehyde

E. Alcohol and alkene

Chapter 24: Amines

1. Which compound is a primary amine?

   A. N, N-dimethylethylamine   C. diethylamine
   B. isopropylamine   D. trimethylamine
                                  E. N-ethyl-N-methylpropylamine

2. Which organic functional group is important for its basic properties?

   A. carbonyl   C. amine
   B. hydroxyl   D. aromatic   E. phenol

3. The following is an example of a:

$$H_3C \overset{\overset{\displaystyle H}{|}}{\underset{\underset{\displaystyle H}{|}}{N^+}} H \quad Cl^-$$

   A. primary ammonium salt   C. quaternary amide salt
   B. tertiary ammonium   D. tertiary amine   E. secondary ammonium

4. Which of the following can be synthesized from an arenediazonium salt?

   I. C_6H_5Br II. C_6H_5CN III. C_6H_5OH

   A. I only   B. I and II only   C. I and III only   D. II and III only   E. I, II and III

5. Methyl bromide can generate the corresponding methylamine through alkyl halide ammonolysis. The nitrile reduction pathway generates the corresponding:

   A. ethylmethylamide   C. reduced methylene group
   B. ethylamine   D. dehalogenated methyl group
                            E. none of the above

6. Amines are classified by the:

   A. number of carbons present in the molecule
   B. number of carbons attached to the carbon bonded to the nitrogen
   C. number of hydrogens attached to the nitrogen
   D. number of alkyl groups attached to the nitrogen
   E. none of the above

7. *p*-Toluidine is somewhat soluble in water due to the polarity of:

A. its aromatic ring structure
C. *p*-toludinoic acid
B. its amine group
D. benzene
E. its methyl group

8. Which of the following does NOT contain a polar carbonyl group?

A. an amine
C. an ester
B. a carboxylic acid
D. a ketone
E. none of the above

9. When comparing amine compounds of different classes but similar molar masses, which type most likely has the highest boiling point?

A. primary amines
C. tertiary amines
B. secondary amines
D. quaternary ammonium salts
E. amine oxides

10. Which of the compounds listed is the strongest organic base that functions as a proton acceptor?

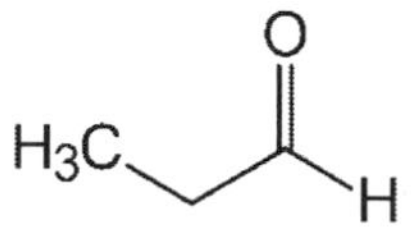

A. 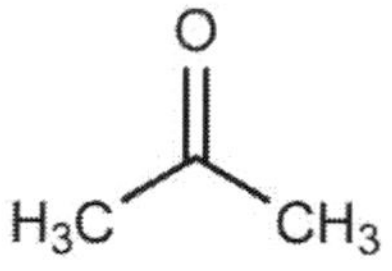 H_3C—C(=O)—CH_3

C. $CH_3CH_2CH_2$—C(=O)—O—CH_3

B. H_3C—CH_2—C(=O)—H

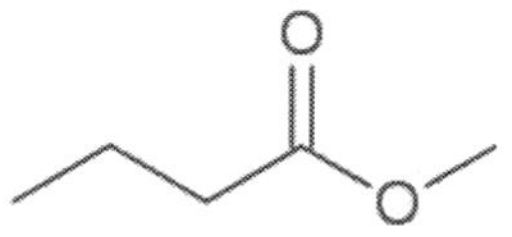

D. 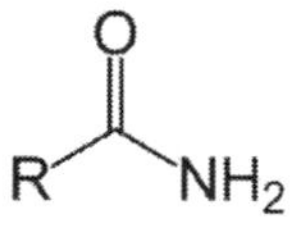 R—C(=O)—NH_2

E. CH_3–CH_2–NH_2

11. Which of the following behaves like a base?

I. $CH_3CONHCH_3$
II. $(CH_3)_2NH$
III. $C_2H_5CONHCH_3$

A. I only
C. III only
B. II only
D. I and II only
E. I, II and III

12. The reaction of an amine with water is best represented by:

A. $R–NH_2 + H_2O \leftrightarrow R–NH_3^+ + OH^-$
B. $R–NH_2 + 2\ H_2O \leftrightarrow R–NH_4^{2+} + 2\ OH^-$
C. $R–NH_2 + 2\ H_2O \leftrightarrow R–N^{2-} + 2\ H_3O^+$
D. $R–NH_2 + H_2O \leftrightarrow R–NH^- + H_3O^+$
E. $R–NH_2 + H_2O \leftrightarrow R–N^{2-} + M^+ + H_3O^+$

13. Which of the following compounds has the lowest boiling point?

    A. dimethylamine   **C.** diethylamine

    B. *sec*-butylamine   **D.** *n*-butylamine   **E.** ethanolamine

14. Which of these molecules is a tertiary amine?

    A. RNH_2 **B.** R_2NH **C.** R_3N **D.** R_3NH^+ **E.** R_4N^+

15. Which formula best represents the form an amine takes in acidic solution?

    A. RNH_2^- **B.** RNH_2^+ **C.** RNH_2 **D.** RNH^- **E.** RNH_3^+

16. The functional group C=O is found in all the species below, EXCEPT:

    A. amines   **C.** carboxylic acids

    B. amides   **D.** aldehydes   **E.** esters

17. A quaternary ammonium salt does NOT carry out substitution reactions with alkyl halides, because the nitrogen atom is not:

    A. an electrophile   **C.** negatively charged

    B. a nucleophile   **D.** saturated   **E.** a radical

18. Amines are most similar in chemical structure and behavior to:

    A. sodium hydroxide   **C.** the hydronium ion

    B. a primary alcohol   **D.** ammonia   **E.** water

19. Why is an amine salt more soluble in water than the corresponding free amine?

    A. The negative charge on the nitrogen atom increases water solubility

    B. It has a higher molecular weight than the corresponding amine

    C. It is ionic and therefore more soluble than covalent compounds with the same structure

    D. All amines are insoluble in water

    E. None of the above

20. Based on the properties of the attached functional group, which compound below interacts most strongly with water, thus making it the most soluble compound?

    A. CH_3-CH_2-I **C.** $CH_3-CH_2-NH_2$

    B. CH_3-O-CH_3 **D.** CH_3-CH_2-H **E.** CH_3-CH_2-S-H

21. Assuming roughly equivalent molecular weights, which of the following has the highest boiling point?

A. alcohol   **C.** tertiary amine

B. ether   **D.** quaternary ammonium salt   **E.** alkyl chloride

22. The compound, trimethylamine is a(n) [ ] and has the formula [ ]:

A. base, $(CH_3)_3N$ **C.** base, $(CH_3)_2NH$

B. acid, $(CH_3)_2NH$ **D.** acid, $(CH_3)_3N$ **E.** base, $(CH_3)NH$

23. Which compound is an example of an amine salt?

A. sulfanilamide   **C.** dimethylammonium bromide

B. thioacetamide   **D.** histamine   **E.** pyridoxine

24. Which statement about the differences between an amine and an amide is NOT correct?

A. Amides act as proton acceptors, while amines do not

B. Amines are basic, and amides are neutral

C. Amines form ammonium salts when treated with acid; amides do not

D. The lone pair of electrons on amides is held more tightly than the lone pair on amines

E. Amine nitrogen atoms are sp^3 hybridized, while amides have sp^2 hybridization

25. What is the conjugate base of CH_3NH_2?

A. NH_2^- **C.** CH_3NH^-

B. NH_4^+ **D.** $CH_3NH_3^+$ **E.** none of the above

26. A functional group containing nitrogen is found in:

A. carboxylic acids   **C.** alcohols

B. amines   **D.** alkenes   **E.** ethers

27. Which of the following is NOT correct about amines?

A. Amines are bases (proton acceptors)

B. Amines are converted to ammonium salts by reaction with HCl

C. Amines are organic derivatives of ammonia

D. Amines are very water soluble

E. Amines are often odorous compounds

28. What is the conjugate acid of CH_3NH_2?

A. NH_4^+ **B.** NH_2^- **C.** $CH_3NH_3^+$ **D.** CH_3NH^- **E.** CH_3^-

29. Which amine has the lowest boiling point?

A. 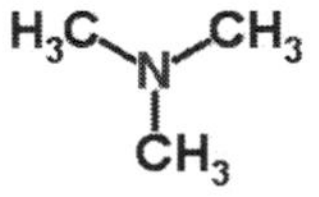 $H_3C-N(CH_3)-CH_3$ (trimethylamine structure)

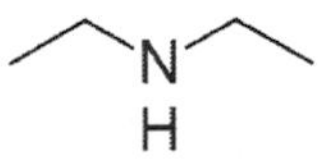

B. 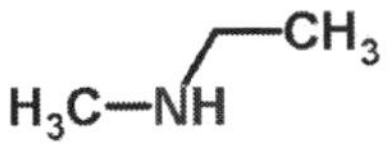 $H_3C-NH-CH_3$

C. $(CH_3CH_2)_2NH$

D. 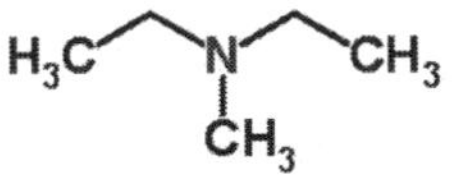 $H_3C-N(CH_2CH_3)(CH_3)$ ethyl methyl structure

E.  $H_3C-CH_2-NH_2$

30. In water, does the molecule lysergic acid diethylamide act as:

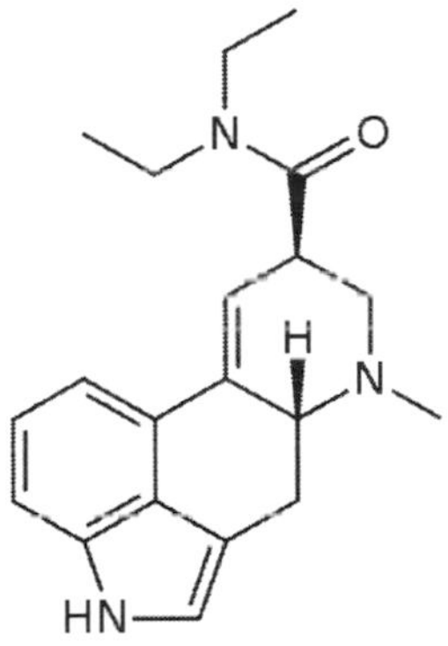

I. acid   II. base   III. neither acid nor base

A. I only
B. II only

C. III only
D. I and II only

E. requires more information

31. Which of the following amines is the most basic in the gas phase?

A. NH_3
B. $(CF_3)_3N$

C. $(CH_3)_3N$
D. H_2NCH_3

E. $HN(CH_3)_2$

32. All of the following are properties of amines, EXCEPT:

A. amines react with acids to form amides at low temperatures
B. amines with low molecular weights are soluble in water
C. amines that form hydrogen bonds have higher boiling points relative to their molecular mass
D. amines frequently have offensive odors
E. amines function as bases in many reactions

33. Which of the compounds shown form hydrogen bonds between a mixture of the molecules?

A. $(CH_3)_3N$
B. $CH_3CH_2OCH_3$

C. $CH_3CH_2CH_2F$
D. $CH_3CH_2CH_2CH_3$

E. $CH_3NHCH_2CH_3$

34. Dodecylamine, $CH_3(CH_2)_{10}CH_2NH_2$, is insoluble in water, but it can be converted to water-soluble form. Which of the species below represents a water-soluble form of this compound?

A. $CH_3(CH_2)_{10}CH_2NHCH_3$

B. $CH_3(CH_2)_{10}CH_2NH_3^+Cl^-$

C. $CH_3(CH_2)_{10}CH_2NH_2-OH$

D. $CH_3(CH_2)_{10}CH_2NH_2-Cl$

E. $CH_3(CH_2)_{10}CH_2NH_2-O-CH_3$

35. Which of the following molecules represents a tertiary amine?

A.
$$CH_3-\underset{\underset{NH_2}{|}}{\overset{\overset{CH_3}{|}}{C}}-CH_3$$

B.
$$CH_3-\underset{\underset{NH-CH_3}{|}}{\overset{\overset{CH_3}{|}}{C}}-CH_3$$

C.
$$CH_3-\underset{\underset{CH_3}{|}}{CH}-CH_2-NH_2$$

D.
$$CH_3-\underset{\underset{CH_3}{|}}{CH}-\underset{\underset{NH_2}{|}}{CH}-CH_3$$

E.
$$CH_3-\underset{\underset{CH_3}{|}}{N}-CH_3$$

36. Which of the following sequences ranks the following isomers in order of increasing boiling points?

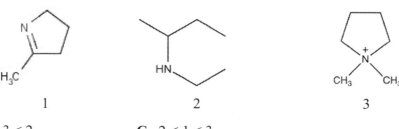

1   2   3

A. $1 < 3 < 2$

B. $3 < 2 < 1$

C. $2 < 1 < 3$

D. $2 < 3 < 1$

E. $1 < 2 < 3$

Chapter 25: Amino Acids, Peptides, Proteins

1. Name the amino acid produced when propanoic acid is subjected to the following sequence of reagents:

   1) PBr_3, Br_2 2) H_2O 3) NH_3, Δ

 A. alanine   **C.** glutamic acid
 B. aspartic acid   **D.** valine   **E.** asparagine

2. What type of molecular attraction is expected to dominate between two threonine amino acids within a folding polypeptide chain?

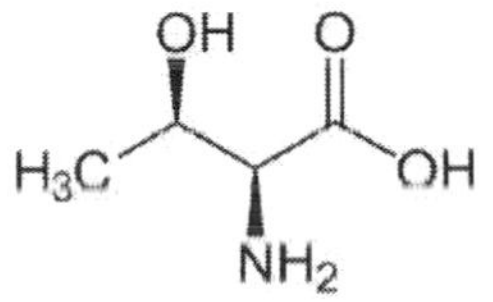

 A. dipole–induced dipole   **C.** ion–dipole
 B. induced dipole–induced dipole   **D.** dipole–dipole   **E.** London forces

3. Which of the standard amino acids is achiral?

 A. lysine   **B.** proline   **C.** valine   **D.** alanine   **E.** glycine

4. Which of the following amino acids does NOT contain an aromatic *R*-group?

 A. tyrosine   **C.** tryptophan
 B. phenylalanine   **D.** histidine   **E.** none of the above

5. The linear sequence of amino acids along a peptide chain determines its:

 A. primary structure   **C.** tertiary structure
 B. secondary structure   **D.** quaternary structure   **E.** none of the above

6. Polar *R* groups, along with acidic and basic *R* groups, are said to be [   ] because they are attracted to water molecules.

 A. unreactive   **C.** hydrophobic
 B. ionized   **D.** hydrophilic   **E.** none of the above

7. An amino acid whose *R* group is predominantly hydrocarbon is classified as:

 A. acidic   **C.** nonpolar
 B. basic   **D.** polar   **E.** isoelectric

8. There are [ ] different types of major biomolecules used by humans.

A. a few dozen **C.** several thousand
B. four **D.** several million **E.** a few hundred

9. Amino acids are linked to one another in a protein by which of the following bonds?

A. amide bonds **C.** ester bonds
B. carboxylate bonds **D.** amine bonds **E.** glycosidic bonds

10. Which of the following amino acids is most likely present in the hydrophobic binding region of a protein?

A. tyrosine **C.** valine
B. glutamine **D.** serine **E.** histidine

11. Identify the functional groups in the following compound.

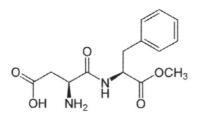

A. alcohol and ketone
B. alcohol, amine and ketone
C. amine and carboxylic acid
D. amine, hydroxide and ketone
E. amine and aldehyde

12. The pH at which the positive and negative charges of an amino acid balance is:

A. isotonic point **C.** isobaric point
B. isobestic point **D.** isoelectric point **E.** isomer point

13. The proton on the nitrogen of saccharin is much more acidic than the proton on the amide nitrogen of aspartame. This is best explained by the fact that:

Aspartame (Asp-Phe)   Saccharin

A. extra resonance stabilization of the resulting anion is provided by the sulfone group
B. the saccharin nitrogen is *sp* hybridized
C. the adjacent sulfone group stabilizes the anion because it is an electron-donating group
D. cyclic amides are more acidic than acyclic amides
E. none of the above

14. 2,4-dinitrofluorobenzene is used in protein analysis to determine the:

A. most reactive amino acid in the protein **C.** amino acid at the *N*-terminus

B. amino acid at the *C*-terminus

D. most frequent amino acid found in the protein

E. none of the above

15. Insulin is an example of a(n):

A. transport protein **C.** structural protein

B. storage protein **D.** enzyme **E.** hormone

16. What type of protein structure corresponds to a spiral alpha helix of amino acids?

A. primary **C.** tertiary

B. secondary **D.** quaternary **E.** none of the above

17. At pH 8, which of the following is true for aspartame shown below?

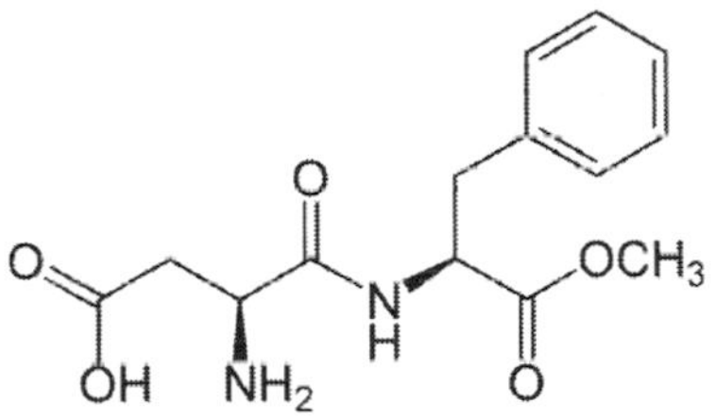

A. Both the acid and amino group are protonated

B. Both the acid and ester group are deprotonated

C. The acid group is deprotonated, and the amino group is protonated

D. The amino group is deprotonated, and the acid group is protonated

E. None of the above

18. Non-polar *R* groups on amino acids are said to be [ ] because they are not attracted to water molecules.

A. ionized **C.** hydrophilic

B. unreactive **D.** hydrophobic **E.** none of the above

19. Which of the following amino acids has its isoelectric point at the lowest pH?

A. arginine **B.** aspartic acid **C.** valine **D.** glycine **E.** methionine

20. In biosynthesis, which amino acid serves as the source of the amino group for other amino acids?

A. D-phenylalanine **C.** racemic phenylalanine

B. L-phenylalanine **D.** L-glutamic acid **E.** D-glutamic acid

21. Proteins are characterized by the fact that they:

    A. always have quaternary structures

    B. retain their conformation above 35-40 °C

    C. have a primary structure formed by covalent linkages

    D. are composed of a single peptide chain

    E. none of the above

22. The reaction mechanism by which 2,4-dinitrofluorobenzene reacts with a protein is:

    A. addition

    B. S_N2

    C. nucleophilic aromatic substitution

    D. electrophilic aromatic substitution

    E. none of the above

23. Members of which class of biomolecules is the building blocks of proteins?

    A. fatty acids

    B. amino acids

    C. glycerols

    D. monosaccharides

    E. nucleic acids

24. If a hair stylist is about to apply a reducing agent to a client with fine hair who wants to have his hair curly, should the reducing agent be regular strength, concentrated, or diluted?

    A. diluted, so as not to cause the hair to fall apart completely

    B. concentrated, in order to add more disulfide cross-linking

    C. concentrated, in order to add more hydrogen bonding

    D. concentrated because in thin hair each strand is made of fewer cysteine amino acids

    E. regular strength

25. All of the bonds below are apparent in the secondary and tertiary structure of a protein, EXCEPT:

    A. electrostatic interactions

    B. peptide bonds

    C. hydrogen bonding

    D. hydrophobic interactions

    E. none of the above

26. Proteins are polymers. They consist of monomer units which are:

    A. keto acids

    B. amide

    C. amino acids

    D. ketones

    E. polyaldehydes

27. Proteins migrate the smallest distance during gel electrophoresis when the protein is at:

    A. high pH

    B. neutral pH

    C. low pH

    D. their isoelectric point

    E. both high and low pH

28. Why might a change in pH cause a protein to denature?

   A. The hydrogen bonds between the hydrophobic portions of the protein collapse due to extra protons

   B. The disulfide bridges open

   C. The functional groups that give the protein its shape become protonated or deprotonated

   D. The water hardens and causes the protein's shape to change

   E. All of the above

29. Which of the following compounds is an amino acid?

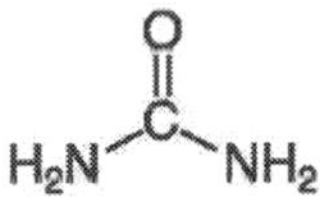

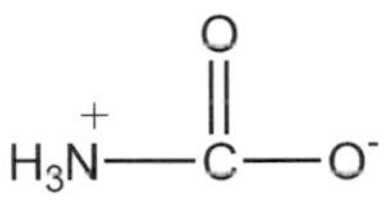

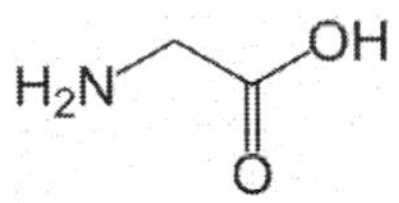

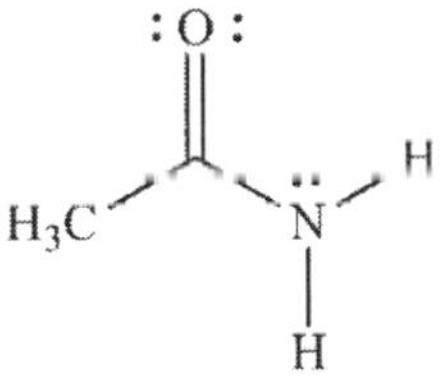

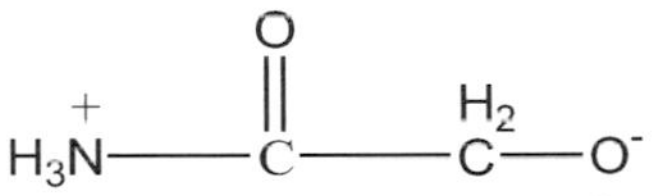

30. The most basic functional group of aspartame is the:

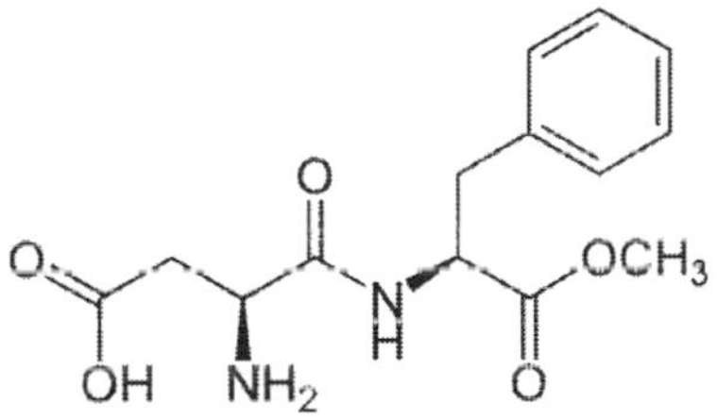

Aspartame (Asp-Phe)

   A. amide nitrogen   **C.** ester carbonyl oxygen

   B. amino group   **D.** aromatic ring   **E.** amide oxygen

31. What is the major product of the following reaction series?

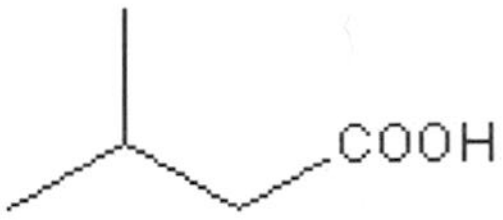

$+ PBr_3 \rightarrow ?$ $+$ excess $NH_3 \rightarrow ?$

   A. Ala   **B.** Gly   **C.** Leu   **D.** Ile   **E.** Val

32. The protein conformation determined mostly from interactions between R groups is:

   A. tertiary structure   **C.** primary structure

   B. quaternary structure   **D.** secondary structure   **E.** none of the above

33. What is the best description of the linkage shown in the following polypeptide?

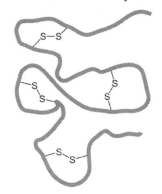

   A. disulfide linkage   **C.** hemiacetal
   B. glucosidic linkage   **D.** acetal
                              E. amide

34. A particular polypeptide can be represented as Gly-Ala-Ala-Phe-Cys-Gly-Ala-Cys-Phe-Cys. How many peptide bonds are there in this polypeptide?

   A. 9   **B.** 10   **C.** 8   **D.** 6   **E.** 11

35. Hydrophobic interactions help to stabilize the [   ] structure(s) of a protein.

   A. primary   **C.** secondary and tertiary
   B. secondary   **D.** tertiary and quaternary
                              E. secondary and quaternary

36. The side chains, or *R* groups, of amino acids can be classified into each of the following categories EXCEPT:

   A. acidic   **C.** non-polar
   B. basic   **D.** polar   **E.** isoelectric

37. Considering the acid/base character of many amino acid side chains, why do changes in pH interfere with the function of proteins?

     I. at high pH, the acidic side chains of amino acids such as glutamic acid and tyrosine become negatively charged as they lose a hydrogen ion
     II. a change in pH can result in a change in the type of molecular attractions that occur among amino acids within a polypeptide
     III. at low pH, the alkaline side chains of amino acids such as lysine and histidine become positively charged as they gain a hydrogen ion

   A. I only   **C.** III only
   B. II only   **D.** I and II only   **E.** I, II and III

38. A particular polypeptide can be represented as Gly-Ala-Phe-Cys-Gly-Ala-Phe-Cys. How many sites with positive or negative charges are in this polypeptide?

    A. 8   **B.** 7   **C.** 4   **D.** 2   **E.** 9

39. Which one of the following amino acids do(es) NOT contain a basic side chain?

    I. arginine   II. lysine   III. threonine

    A. I only   **C.** III only
    B. II only   **D.** I and III only   **E.** II and III only

40. The isoelectric point of an amino acid is the:

    A. pH at which it exists in the zwitterion form
    B. pH equal to its pK_a
    C. pH at which it exists in the basic form
    D. pH at which it exists in the acid form
    E. pH equal to its pK_b

41. Collagen is an example of a(n):

    A. storage protein   **C.** enzyme
    B. transport protein   **D.** structural protein   **E.** hormone

42. The coiling of a chain of amino acids describes a protein's:

    A. primary structure   **C.** tertiary structure
    B. secondary structure   **D.** quaternary structure   **E.** none of the above

43. The laboratory conditions typically used to hydrolyze a protein are:

    A. dilute acid and room temperature   **C.** concentrated acid and heat
    B. dilute base and room temperature   **D.** concentrated base and heat
                               E. exposure to 340 nm light

44. Which of the following is an essential amino acid?

    A. aniline   **B.** valine   **C.** glycine   **D.** serine   **E.** proline

45. What is the name given to the localized bending and folding of a polypeptide backbone of a protein molecule?

    A. primary structure   **C.** tertiary structure
    B. secondary structure   **D.** quaternary structure
                               E. zymogen structure

46. Which of the following macromolecules are composed of polypeptides?

A. amino acids   **C.** carbohydrates

B. proteins   **D.** fats   **E.** steroids

47. Which amino acid can form covalent sulfur-sulfur bonds?

A. proline   **C.** cysteine

B. methionine   **D.** glycine   **E.** phenylalanine

48. Which amino acid is a secondary amine with its nitrogen and alpha carbon joined as part of a ring structure?

A. lysine   **C.** alanine

B. histidine   **D.** aspartic acid   **E.** proline

Notes

Chapter 26: Lipids

1. The molecule shown can be classified as a(n):

$$H_2C-O-\overset{\overset{\displaystyle O}{\|}}{C}-(CH_2)_6-CH_3$$
$$HC-O-\overset{\overset{\displaystyle O}{\|}}{C}-(CH_2)_7-CH=CH-(CH_2)_7-CH_3$$
$$H_2C-O-\overset{\overset{\displaystyle O}{\|}}{C}-O-P-O_3{}^{2-}$$

  A. sphingolipid   **C.** wax

  B. eicosanoid   **D.** glycerophospholipid   **E.** steroid

2. Which molecule is a fatty acid?

  A. CH_3COOH **C.** $(CH_3)_2CH(CH_2)_3COOH$

  B. $CH_2=CHCOOH$ **D.** $CH_3(CH_2)_7CH=CH(CH_2)_7COOH$

                                        E. None of the above

3. What is the purpose of the plasma membrane?

  A. Storing of the genetic material of the cell

  B. Retaining water in the cell to prevent it from dehydrating

  C. Acting as a cell wall to give the cell structure and support

  D. Acting as a boundary, but also letting molecules in and out

  E. None of the above

4. Given a single triglyceride containing three identical and fully saturated fatty acid residues, which of the following terms accurately describes it?

  A. optically inactive   **C.** optically active

  B. *meso*   **D.** chiral   **E.** racemic

5. All of the fatty acids below contain between sixteen and eighteen carbons and range from saturated to three double bonds. Which has the lowest melting point?

  A. palmitic acid (saturated)

  B. oleic acid (one double bond)

  C. linoleic acid (two double bonds)

  D. linolenic acid (three double bonds)

  E. all have approximately the same melting point

6. Which of the following statements correctly describe(s) the relationship between the structure of a fatty acid and its melting point?

    I.   Saturated fatty acids melting points increase gradually with the molecular weights

    II. As the number of double bonds in a fatty acid increases, its melting point decreases

    III. The presence of a *trans* double bond in the fatty acid has a greater effect on its melting point than does the presence of a *cis* double bond

A. I only   **C.** III only

B. II only   **D.** I and II only   **E.** I, II and III

7. The hydrocarbon end of a soap molecule is:

A. hydrophilic and attracted to grease

B. hydrophobic and attracted to grease

C. hydrophilic and attracted to water

D. hydrophobic and attracted to water

E. neither hydrophobic nor hydrophilic

8. It is important to have cholesterol in one's body because:

A. it breaks down extra fat lipids

B. it serves as the starting material for the biosynthesis of most other steroids

C. it is the starting material for the building of glycogen

D. the brain is made almost entirely of cholesterol

E. it mainly serves as an energy reserve

9. Cholesterol belongs to the [   ] group of lipids.

A. prostaglandin   **C.** saccharides

B. triacylglycerol   **D.** steroid   **E.** wax

10. In chemical terms, soaps are best described as:

A. simple esters of fatty acids   **C.** salts of carboxylic acids

B. mixed esters of fatty acids   **D.** long chain acids

                                      E. bases formed from glycerol

11. The function of cholesterol in a cell membrane is to:

A. act as a precursor to steroid hormones

B. take part in the reactions that produce bile acids

C. maintain structure due to its flat rigid characteristics

D. attract hydrophobic molecules to form solid deposits

E. none of the above

12. Which of the following terms best describes the compound below?

$$\begin{array}{l} \text{CH}_2\!-\!\text{O}\!-\!\overset{\displaystyle \overset{O}{\|}}{\text{C}}\!-\!(\text{CH}_2)_{18}\text{CH}_3 \\[4pt] \text{CH}\!-\!\text{O}\!-\!\overset{\displaystyle \overset{O}{\|}}{\text{C}}\!-\!(\text{CH}_2)_{16}\text{CH}_3 \\[4pt] \text{CH}_2\!-\!\text{O}\!-\!\overset{\displaystyle \overset{O}{\|}}{\text{C}}\!-\!(\text{CH}_2)_{18}\text{CH}_3 \end{array}$$

A. unsaturated triglyceride   C. terpene
B. saturated triglyceride   D. prostaglandin   E. lecithin

13. Which fatty acid is a saturated fatty acid?

A. oleic acid   C. arachidonic acid
B. linoleic acid   D. myristic acid   E. none of the above

14. Commercially, liquid vegetable oils are converted to solid fats such as margarine by:

A. oxidation   C. hydrolysis
B. hydration   D. hydrogenation   E. saponification

15. The biochemical roles of lipids are:

A. short-term energy storage, transport of molecules and structural support
B. storage of excess energy, component of cell membranes and chemical messengers
C. catalysis, protection against outside invaders, motion
D. component of cell membranes, catalysis, and structural support
E. neurotransmitters, hormones, transport of molecules

16. Which fatty acid composition yields a triglyceride that is most likely an oil?

A. 3 palmitic acid units   C. 2 linoleic and 1 stearic acid units
B. 2 palmitic and 1 oleic acid units   D. 3 stearic acid units
    E. 2 palmitic and 1 stearic acid units

17. Which of the following molecules is an omega-3 fatty acid?

A. oleic acid   C. linoleic acid
B. linolenic acid   D. palmitic acid   E. none of the above

18. Which of the following is a lipid?

    A. lactose   **B.** aniline   **C.** nicotine   **D.** estradiol   **E.** collagen

19. Which of the following terms best describes the interior of a soap micelle in water?

    A. hard   **C.** hydrophobic
    B. saponified   **D.** hydrophilic   **E.** hydrogenated

20. Which best describes the lipid shown below?

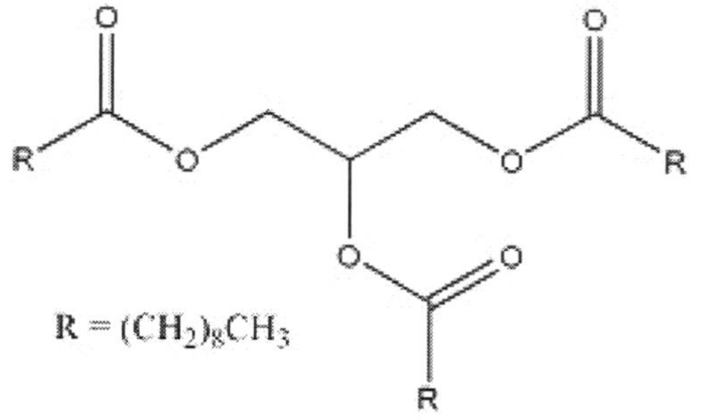

$$R = (CH_2)_8CH_3$$

    A. saturated fatty acid   **C.** wax
    B. unsaturated fatty acid   **D.** triglyceride   **E.** lecithin

21. Lipids are compounds that are soluble in:

    A. glucose solution   **C.** distilled water
    B. organic solvents   **D.** normal saline solution   **E.** oxygen

22. Which statement regarding fatty acids is NOT correct? Fatty acids:

    A. are always liquids   **C.** are usually unbranched chains
    B. are long-chain carboxylic acids   **D.** usually have an even number of carbon atoms
                                        E. none of the above

23. Unsaturated triacylglycerols are usually [   ] because [   ]?

    A. liquids … they have relatively short fatty acid chains
    B. liquids … the kinks in their fatty acid chains prevent their fitting together closely
    C. liquids … they contain impurities from their natural sources
    D. solids … they have relatively long fatty acid chains
    E. solids … the similar zig-zag shape of their fatty acid chains allows them to fit together closely

24. Two families of fatty acids that are significant in nutrition are Ω-6 and Ω-3 fatty acids. Which of the following structures would be classified as a Ω-3 fatty acid?

A.

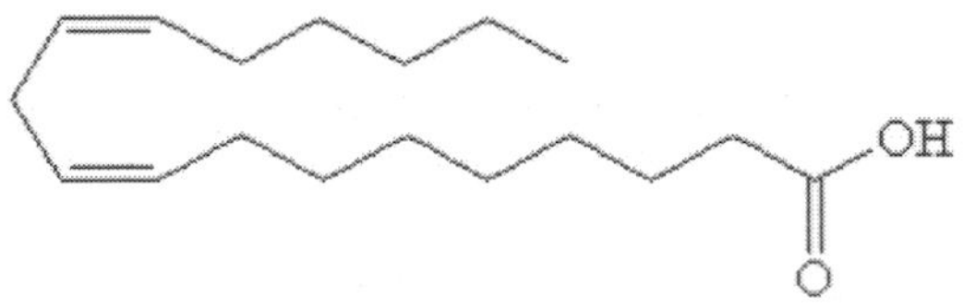

B.

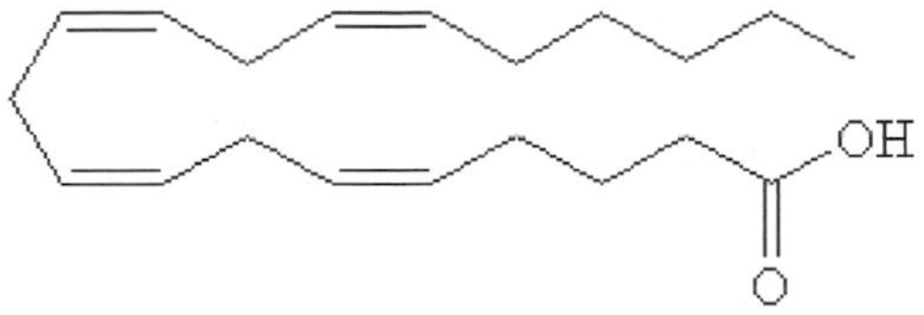

C.

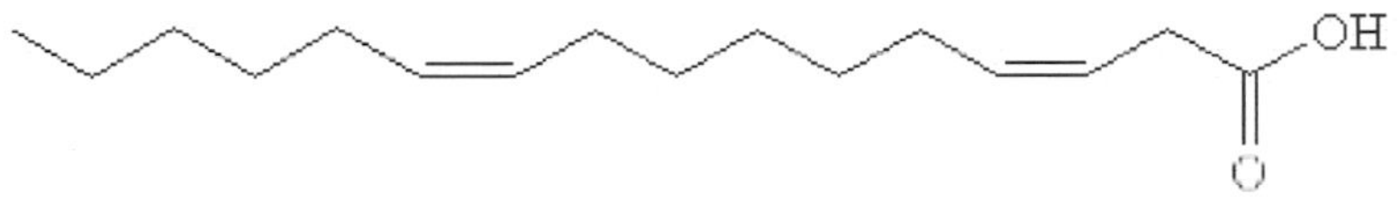

D.

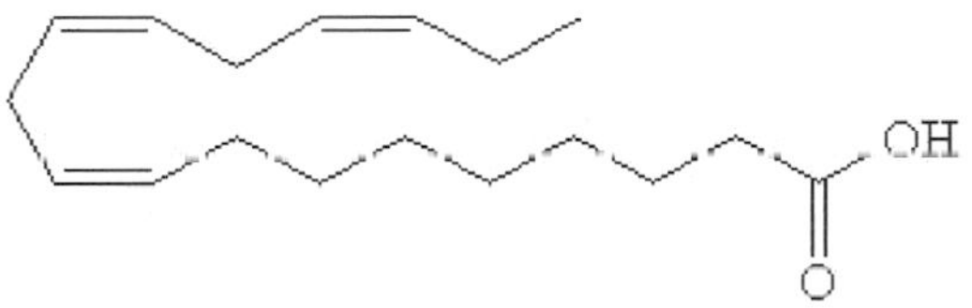

E.

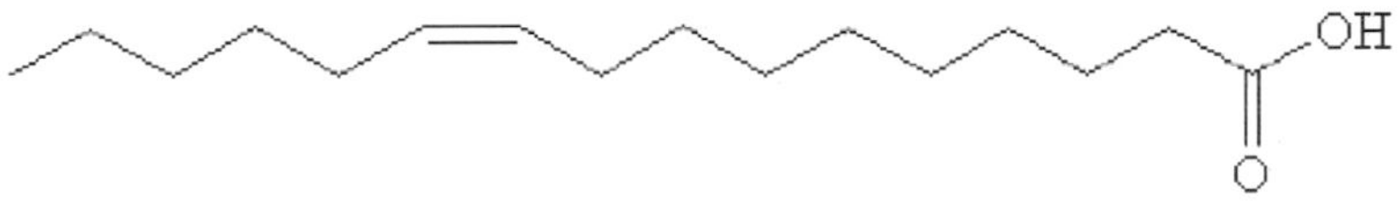

25. Triacylglycerols are compounds which contain combined:

A. cholesterol and other steroids

B. fatty acids and phospholipids

C. fatty acids and glycerol

D. fatty acids and choline

E. lecithin and choline

26. The name of the reaction that occurs when a fat reacts with sodium hydroxide and water is:

A. oxidation

B. hydration

C. reduction

D. hydrogenation

E. saponification

27. Which of the following molecules produce fat from an esterification reaction?

    I. $CH_3(CH_2)_{14}COOH$

    II. $CH_3(CH_2)_7CH=CH(CH_2)_7COCH_2CH_3$

    III. $HOCH_2CHO$

    IV. $HOCH_2CH(OH)CH_2OH$

A. I and IV only

B. II and III only

C. II and IV only

D. I and III only

E. I and II only

28. Oils are generally [   ] at room temperature and are obtained from [   ]:

A. liquids … plants   C. solids … plants

B. liquids … animals   D. solids … animals   E. none of the above

29. Lipids are naturally occurring compounds which all:

A. contain fatty acids as structural units

B. are water-insoluble but soluble in nonpolar solvents

C. contain ester groups

D. contain cholesterol

E. are unsaturated

30. Hydrogenation of vegetable oils converts them into what type of molecule?

A. esters   B. ethers   C. hemiacetals   D. saturated fats   E. polymers

31. A polyunsaturated fatty acid contains more than one:

A. long carbon chain   C. hydroxyl group

B. carbonyl group   D. carboxyl group   E. double bond

32. The molecule shown can be classified as a(an):

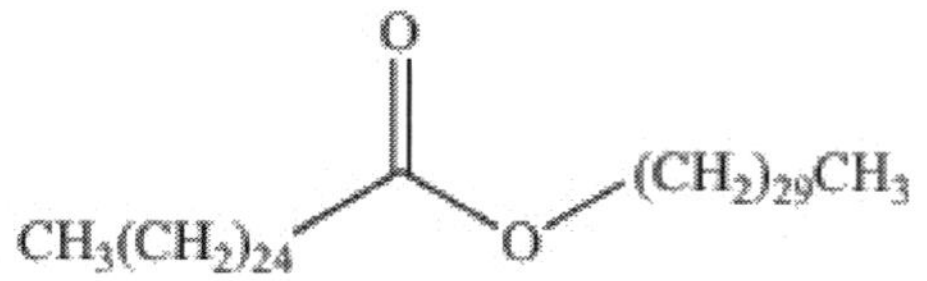

A. steroid   C. wax

B. eicosanoid   D. glycerophospholipid   E. sphingolipid

33. The chemical bond that links glycerol to fatty acid is an example of what type of linkage?

A. ester   C. ether

B. ionic   D. peptide   E. hydrogen bond

34. A molecule that has both hydrophobic and hydrophilic portions is:

A. amphoteric   C. amphiprotic

B. enantiomeric   D. amphipathic   E. allotropic

35. The products of the base-catalyzed breakdown of fat are:

A. salts of fatty acids   C. esters of fatty acids

B. salts of fatty acids and glycerol   D. terpenes

                                                  E. steroids

36. The potassium or sodium salt of a long chain carboxylic acid is called a(n):

A. emollient

B. ester

C. triglyceride

D. soap

E. none of the above

37. A molecule that has both polar and nonpolar parts is:

A. an isomer

B. amphipathic

C. an enantiomer

D. hydrophobic

E. hydrophilic

38. Saturated fats are [ ] at room temperature and are obtained from [ ]?

A. liquids; plants

B. liquids; animals

C. solids; plants

D. solids; animals

E. solids; plants and animals

39. Which of the following is NOT found in a lipid wax?

A. saturated fatty acid

B. long-chain alcohol

C. glycerol

D. ester linkage

E. unsaturated fatty acid

40. How many molecules of fatty acid are needed to produce one molecule of a fat or oil?

A. 1   B. 1.5   C. 2   D. 3   E. 6

41. When dietary triglycerides are hydrolyzed, the products are:

A. glycerol and lipids

B. carbohydrates

C. amino acids

D. alcohols and lipids

E. glycerol and fatty acids

42. Unsaturated fatty acids have lower melting points than saturated fatty acids, because:

A. their molecules fit closely together

B. *cis* double bonds give them an irregular shape

E. *trans* double bonds give them an irregular shape

C. they have fewer hydrogen atoms

D. they have more hydrogen atoms

43. Which of the following is commonly known as glycerol?

A.
$$CH_2-CH-CH-CH_2$$
$$\quad|\quad\ |\quad\ |\quad\ |$$
$$\ OH\ \ OH\ \ OH\ \ OH$$

C.
$$CH_2-CH-CH_2$$
$$\quad|\quad\ |\quad\ |$$
$$\ OH\ \ OH\ \ OH$$

B.
$$CH_2-CH_2-CH_2$$
$$\quad|\qquad\quad\ |$$
$$\ OH\qquad\quad\ OH$$

D.
$$CH_2-CH_2-CH_3$$
$$\quad|$$
$$\ OH$$

E.
$$CH_2-CH-CH_3$$
$$\quad|\quad\ |$$
$$\ OH\ \ OH$$

44. How many fatty acids are in a phospholipid molecule?

A. 0   **B.** 1   **C.** 2   **D.** 3   **E.** variable

45. Which molecule is NOT a fatty acid?

A. $CH_3(CH_2)_{14}COOH$ **C.** $(CH_3)_2CH(CH_2)_3COOH$
B. $CH_3CH_2(CH=CHCH_2)_3(CH_2)_6COOH$ **D.** $CH_3(CH_2)_7CH=CH(CH_2)_7COOH$
                                         E. None of the above

46. The chemical composition of lipids are esters of glycerol with three:

  A. long chain alcohols and fatty acids
  B. identical saturated fatty acids
  C. identical unsaturated fatty acids
  D. predominantly saturated fatty acids
  E. predominantly unsaturated fatty acids

47. Which of the following is NOT a function of lipids within the body?

  A. cushioning to prevent injury   **C.** energy reserve
  B. insulation   **D.** precursor for glucose catabolism
                                                E. precursor for the synthesis of androgens

48. Which of the following lipids is an example of a simple lipid?

  A. oil   **C.** fat
  B. wax   **D.** terpene
                    E. none of the above

Chapter 27: Carbohydrates

1. The conversion of cyclic glucose between the alpha and beta form is called:

   A. dimerization   **C.** mutarotation

   B. cyclization   **D.** polymerization   **E.** hydrolysis

2. Common reducing reactions of monosaccharides are due to:

   A. their cyclic structures

   B. the presence of at least one hydroxyl group

   C. the presence of more than one hydroxyl group

   D. the presence of a carbonyl group, usually on carbon #1

   E. the presence of at least one chiral carbon atom

3. What type of biological compound is characterized by an aldehyde or ketone and alcohol functional groups?

   A. nucleic acid   **C.** sugar

   B. fatty acid   **D.** amino acid   **E.** none of the above

4. Identify the C_3 epimer of the sugar below drawn in its open-chain (acyclic) Fischer projection.

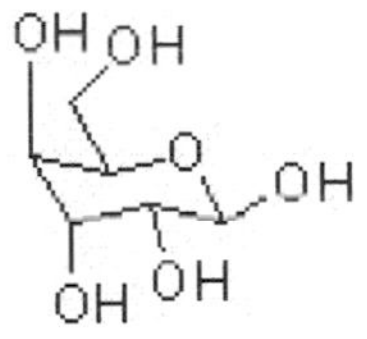

A.

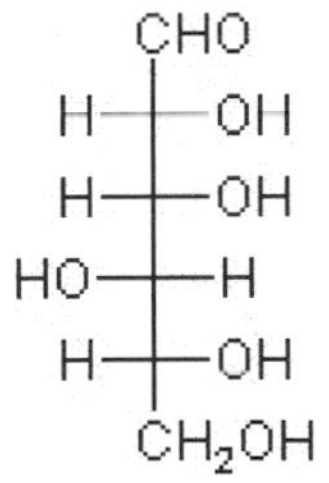

C.

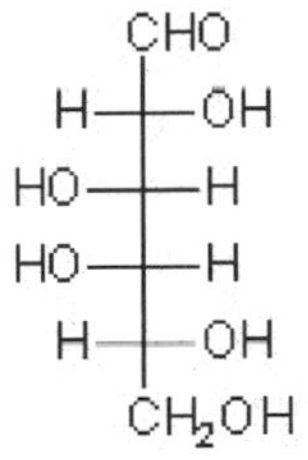

B.

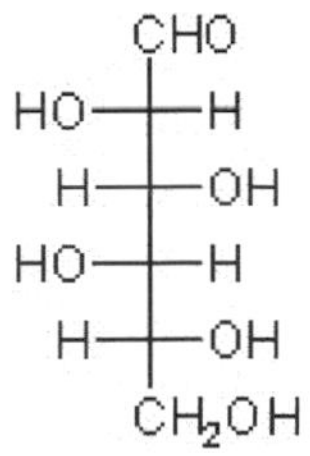

D.

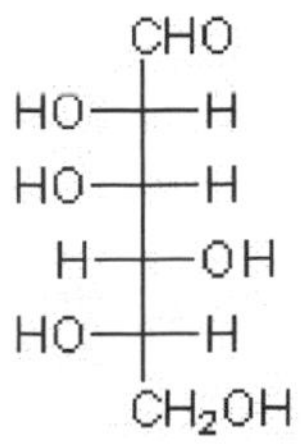

   E. None of the above

---

5. An amylose is a form of starch which has:

A. both $\alpha(1\rightarrow4)$ and $\beta(1\rightarrow4)$ glycosidic linkages between glucose units
B. glycosidic linkages joining glucose units
C. only $\beta(1\rightarrow4)$ glycosidic linkages between glucose units
D. only $\alpha(1\rightarrow4)$ glycosidic linkages between glucose units
E. carbon-carbon glycosidic linkages joining glucose units

6. Fructose can be classified as a(n):

A. aldoketose   **C.** aldohexose
B. aldopentose   **D.** ketopentose   **E.** ketohexose

7. All of the statements concerning monosaccharides are correct, EXCEPT:

A. the number of stereoisomers possible is 2^n, where n is the number of chiral carbon atoms in the molecule
B. monosaccharides with 5 or 6 carbon atoms exist in solution in the cyclic form
C. the two different cyclic forms of a monosaccharide are called tautomers
D. a molecule is classified as a D or L isomer by the position of the hydroxyl group on the chiral center farthest from the carbonyl group
E. monosaccharides have the general formula $C_n(H_2O)_n$, but this only describes the number and kinds of atoms, not their structure

8. Which of the following statements describes most monosaccharides?

A. They are unsaturated compounds
B. They are rarely found as monomers in nature
C. They are composed of carbon, hydrogen, and oxygen with each carbon bound to at least one oxygen
D. They are insoluble
E. None of the above

9. Galactose has the structure shown below. It can be classified as a(n):

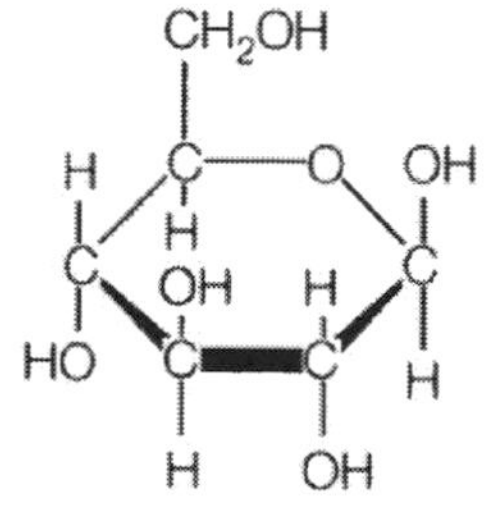

A. monosaccharide   **C.** ketose
B. disaccharide   **D.** ribose   **E.** ketone

10. The three elements found in all carbohydrates are [ ], [ ] and [ ]:

    A. nitrogen, oxygen, hydrogen

    B. carbon, hydrogen, oxygen

    C. carbon, hydrogen, water

    D. nitrogen, oxygen, carbon

    E. carbon, nitrogen, hydrogen

11. When a monosaccharide forms a cyclic hemiacetal, the carbon atom that contained the carbonyl group is identified as the [ ] carbon atom because [ ]:

    A. D ... the carbonyl group is drawn to the right

    B. L ... the carbonyl group is drawn to the left

    C. anomeric ... its substituents can assume an α or β position

    D. acetal ... it forms bonds to an –OR and an –OR'

    E. enantiomeric ... depending on its position, the resulting ring can have a mirror image

12. Which of the following is a non-reducing sugar?

    A. mannose   **B.** sucrose   **C.** lactose   **D.** glucose   **E.** galactose

13. Which of the following is correct regarding the classification of carbohydrate isomers?

    A. Each D-aldohexose has exactly two anomers

    B. There are 16 D-aldohexose stereoisomers

    C. There are 8 aldohexose stereoisomers

    D. Glucose has the same number of stereoisomers as fructose

    E. None of the above

14. Which of the following contains α(1→6) branches?

    A. cellulose   **B.** sucrose   **C.** amylose   **D.** glycogen   **E.** maltose

15. Humans cannot digest cellulose because they:

    A. have intestinal flora which uses up β(1→4) glycosidic bonds

    B. are poisoned by β(1→4) glycosidic bonds

    C. are allergic to β(1→4) glycosidic bonds

    D. lack the necessary enzymes to break β(1→4) glycosidic bonds

    E. cannot digest chlorophyll

16. Mutarotation is a process where:

    A. glucose undergoes reaction to form an equilibrium mixture of anomers

    B. glucose reacts with alcohol forming a cyclic acetal

    C. the aldehyde group present in sugar is converted to a hemiacetal

    D. two glucose molecules react to form a disaccharide

    E. glucose isomerizes to fructose

17. Fructose does not break apart into smaller units because it is a(n):

A. monosaccharide
C. hexose
B. polysaccharide
D. aldose
E. disaccharide

18. Two cyclic isomeric sugars that only differ in the position of the –OH group attached to the hemiacetal carbon are called:

A. enantiomers
C. anomers
B. mutarotation
D. epimers
E. diastereomers

19. Which molecule is a reducing sugar?

A. sucrose
C. starch
B. maltose
D. glycogen
E. amylopectin

20. The glycosidic bond that connects the two monosaccharides in lactose is:

A. $\alpha(1\rightarrow6)$
C. $\alpha(1\rightarrow4)$
B. $\alpha,\beta(1\rightarrow2)$
D. $\beta(1\rightarrow4)$
E. none of the above

21. If one of the carboxylic acids of tartaric acid is reduced to an aldehyde and the other is replaced with a CH_2OH group, which of the following results?

A. aldotetrose
C. ketotriose
B. aldotriose
D. aldopentose
E. none of the above

22. The cyclic structure shown below is classified as a(n):

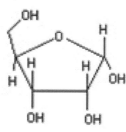

A. ketose   B. aldehyde   C. pentose   D. hexose   E. acetal

23. An acyclic sugar shown by a Fischer projection is classified as a D-isomer if the hydroxyl group on the chiral carbon:

A. nearest to the carbonyl group points to the left
B. nearest to the carbonyl group points to the right
C. farthest from the carbonyl group points to the left
D. farthest from the carbonyl group points to the right
E. α on the carbonyl group points to the left

24. What is the structural difference between deoxyribose and ribose?

    A. methyl group   **C.** carboxyl group

    B. hydroxyl group   **D.** carbonyl group   **E.** none of the above

25. Each of the following yields a positive Benedict's test for reducing sugars, EXCEPT:

    A. α-1,1-glucose-glucose   **C.** glucose

    B. β-1,4-glucose-glucose   **D.** fructose   **E.** maltose

26. How many stereoisomers do carbohydrates have?

    A. 2^n, where n is the number of chiral centers

    B. $2^n - 1$, where n is the number of chiral centers

    C. $2n$, where n is the number of chiral centers

    D. $2n - 1$, where n is the number of chiral centers

    E. $2n - 2$, where n is the number of chiral centers

27. Which of the following molecules is a disaccharide?

    A. fructose   **B.** cellulose   **C.** amylose   **D.** glucose   **E.** lactose

28. Ribose can be classified as a(n):

    A. aldoketose   **C.** aldohexose

    B. aldopentose   **D.** ketopentose   **E.** ketohexose

29. Which functional group is not usually found in carbohydrates?

    A. hydroxyl   **B.** ether   **C.** amide   **D.** aldehyde   **E.** ketone

30. The linkage between Subunits 2 and 3 in acarbose is best described as which of the following?

    A. β-(1→4)   **B.** β-(1→2)   **C.** α-(1→6)   **D.** α-(1→4)   **E.** α-(1→2)

31. A monosaccharide consisting of 5 carbon atoms, one of which is a ketone, is classified as a(n):

A. aldohexose   C. aldotetrose

B. ketotetrose   D. aldopentose   E. ketopentose

32. The monosaccharide shown below is a(n)

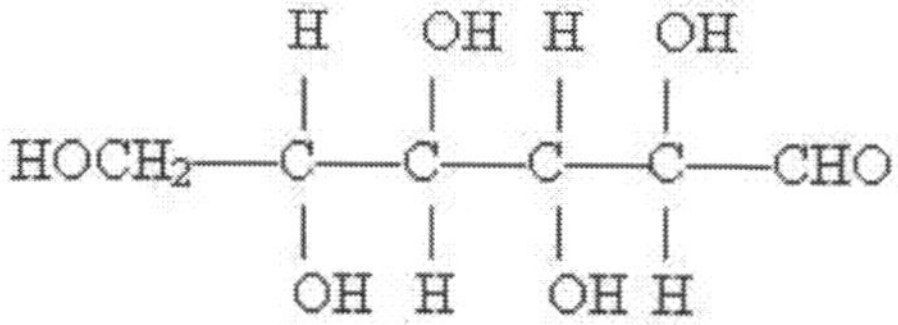

A. aldohexose   C. ketohexose

B. aldopentose   D. ketopentose   E. aldoheptose

33. In the sucrose molecule shown below, which bond joins the disaccharide?

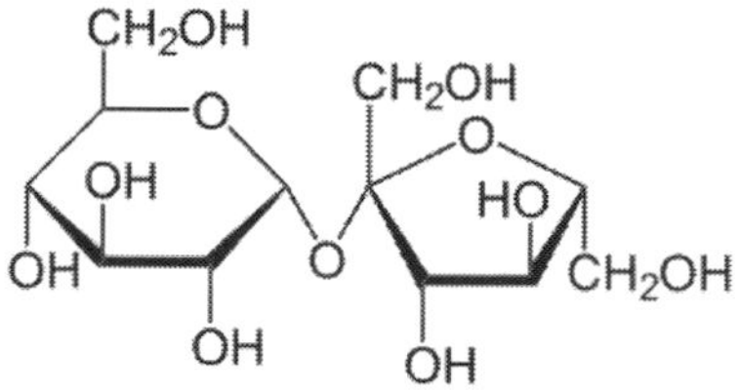

A. α-glucosidic linkage   C. acetal

B. β-glucosidic linkage   D. hemiacetal   E. ester

34. What is the major biological function of the glycogen biomolecule?

A. It is used to synthesize disaccharides

B. It is the building block of proteins

C. It stores glucose in animal cells

D. It is a storage form of sucrose

E. It stores glucose in plant cells

35. What is the minimal number of chiral centers necessary for a *meso* carbohydrate?

A. 0   B. 1   C. 2   D. 3   E. 4

36. A carbohydrate that gives two molecules when it is completely hydrolyzed is known as a:

A. polysaccharide   C. monosaccharide

B. starch   D. disaccharide   E. trisaccharide

37. How many degrees of unsaturation are present in acarbose?

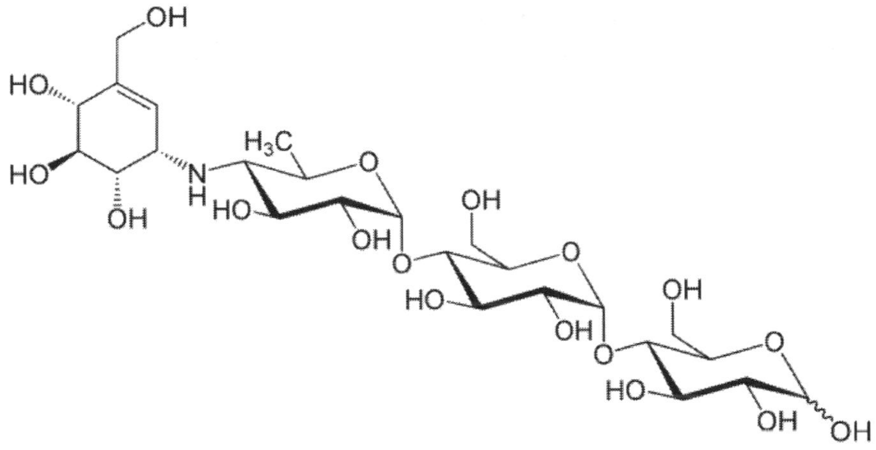

A. 1   **B.** 3   **C.** 4   **D.** 5   **E.** 6

38. Which group of carbohydrates CANNOT be hydrolyzed to give smaller molecules?

A. oligosaccharides

B. trisaccharides

C. disaccharides

D. monosaccharides

E. polysaccharides

39. D-ribulose has the following structural formula. To what carbohydrate class does ribulose belong?

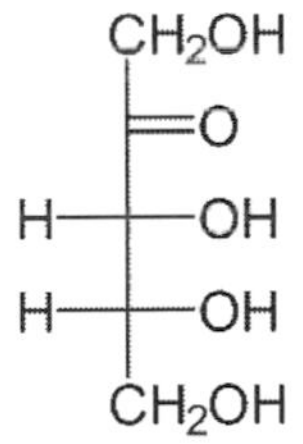

A. ketotetrose

B. ketopentose

C. aldotetrose

D. aldopentose

E. ketohexose

40. Carbohydrate can be defined as a molecule:

A. composed of carbon atoms bonded to water molecules

B. composed of amine groups and carboxylic acid groups bonded to a carbon skeleton

C. composed mostly of hydrocarbons and soluble in non-polar solvents

D. that is an aldehyde or ketone and has more than one hydroxyl group

E. ending in ~*ase*

41. The diagram below shows a step in which of the following processes?

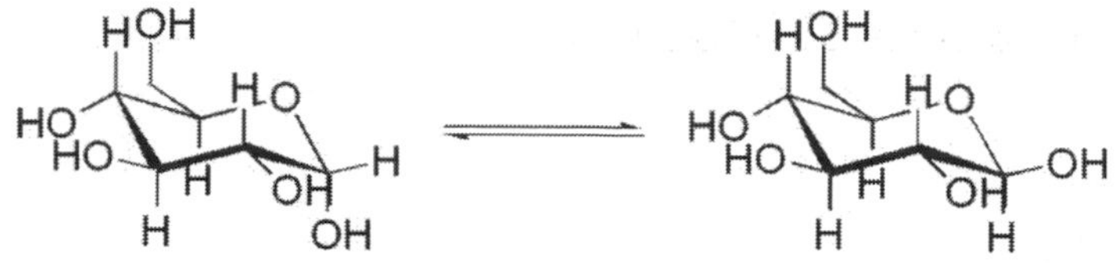

α-D-glucopyranose   β-D-glucopyranose

A. anomerization   **C.** hemiacetal formation

B. mutarotation   **D.** aldehyde formation   **E.** oxidation

42. The compound shown is best described as:

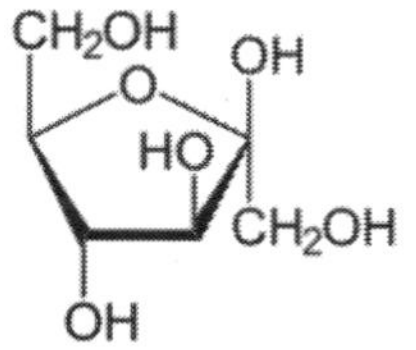

A. furanose form of an aldopentose   **C.** pyranose form of a ketopentose

B. pyranose form of an aldopentose   **D.** furanose form of a ketopentose

                                            E. pyranose form of an aldohexose

43. To what class of compounds does glucose belong?

A. cyclic acetal   **C.** cyclic ketone

B. cyclic hemiacetal   **D.** cyclic aldehyde   **E.** cyclic acid

44. Glucose undergoes an isomerization to yield fructose 1,6-bisphosphate. Which of the following is an isomerization reaction?

A. $CH_3CH_2COCl + H_2O \rightarrow CH_3CH_2COOH + HCl$

B. $CH_2CH_2OHCOOCH_2 + CH_3OH \rightarrow CHCH_2OHCOOCH_3 + CH_3CH_2OH$

C. $CH_2OHCOCH_2CH_2CH_3 \rightarrow CHOCHOHCH_2CH_2CH_3$

D. $CH_3CH_2CH_2CHOHCH_3 \rightarrow CH_3CH_2CHCHCH_3$

E. None of the above

45. Disaccharides are best characterized as:

A. two monosaccharides linked by a nitrogen bond

B. two peptides linked by a hydrogen bond

C. two monosaccharides linked by an oxygen bond

D. two amino acids linked by a peptide bond

E. two glycogens linked by a fatty acid

46. If Benedict's reagent is used to test for reducing sugars, tartaric acid yields:

    A. positive result only in the open-chain configuration

    B. ambiguous result

    C. negative result

    D. positive result

    E. positive result in basic solution

47. Maltose is a:

    A. trisaccharide   **C.** monosaccharide

    B. polysaccharide   **D.** disaccharide

                           E. phosphosaccharide

48. Which molecule shown is a D-isomer?

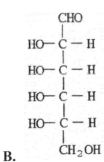

A.
$$CHO$$
$$H-C-OH$$
$$HO-C-H$$
$$H-C-OH$$
$$H-C-OH$$
$$CH_2OH$$

C.
$$CHO$$
$$HO-C-H$$
$$HO-C-H$$
$$H-C-OH$$
$$HO-C-H$$
$$CH_2OH$$

B.
$$CHO$$
$$HO-C-H$$
$$HO-C-H$$
$$HO-C-H$$
$$HO-C-H$$
$$CH_2OH$$

D.
$$CHO$$
$$HO-C-H$$
$$H-C-H$$
$$HO-C-OH$$
$$HO-C-H$$
$$CH_2OH$$

E.
$$CHO$$
$$H-C-OH$$
$$H-C-OH$$
$$H-C-OH$$
$$HO-C-H$$
$$CH_2OH$$

Notes

Chapter 28: Nucleic Acids

1. Which of the following statements describes a cellular activity that happens during both transcription and translation?

- **A.** Protein is formed
- **B.** Transfer RNA is used to link peptides
- **C.** The DNA helix uncoils
- **D.** Nucleotides bind to complementary bases
- **E.** None of the above

2. The two strands of DNA in the double helix are held together by:

- **A.** dipole–dipole attractions
- **B.** metallic bonds
- **C.** ionic bonds
- **D.** covalent bonds
- **E.** none of the above

3. What is the major difference between nucleotides of deoxyribonucleic acid and ribonucleic acid?

- **A.** The ribose nucleic acid is missing a hydroxyl group on the sugar
- **B.** The ribose nucleic acid is missing a hydroxyl group on the nitrogenous base
- **C.** The deoxyribose nucleic acid is missing a hydroxyl group on the sugar
- **D.** The deoxyribose nucleic acid is missing a hydroxyl group on the nitrogenous base
- **E.** Only the nitrogenous bases are different

4. In biochemical reactions, the reduction of carbonyl groups is carried out by:

- **A.** pyruvic acid
- **B.** NADH
- **C.** $LiAlH_4$
- **D.** $NaBH_4$
- **E.** lactic acid

5. What is the complementary DNA sequence to ATATGGTC?

- **A.** CGCGTTGA
- **B.** GCGCAACT
- **C.** TATACCAG
- **D.** TUTUCCAG
- **E.** UAUACCAG

6. What happens to DNA when it is placed into an aqueous solution at physiological pH?

- **A.** Individual DNA molecules repel each other due to the presence of positive charges
- **B.** DNA molecules bind to negatively charged proteins
- **C.** Individual DNA molecules attract each other due to the presence of positive and negative charges
- **D.** Individual DNA molecules repel each other due to the presence of negative charges
- **E.** DNA molecules bind to neutral proteins

---

7. What is the term for the process by which a DNA molecule synthesizes a complementary single strand of RNA?

A. translation
C. replication
B. transcription
D. duplication
E. none of the above

8. Consider the following types of compounds:

I. amino acid
III. phosphate group
II. nitrogen-containing base
IV. five-carbon sugar

From which of the above compounds are the monomers (i.e., nucleotides) of nucleic acids formed?

A. I only
C. II and IV only
B. I and II only
D. II, III and IV only
E. I, II, III and IV

9. The nucleotide sequence, T-A-G, stands for

A. threonine-alanine-glutamine
C. tyrosine-asparagine-glutamic acid
B. thymine-adenine-guanine
D. thymine-adenine-glutamine
E. none of these

10. The two new DNA molecules formed in replication:

A. contain one parent and one daughter strand
B. both contain only the parent DNA strands
C. both contain only two new daughter DNA strands
D. are complementary to the original DNA
E. are identical, with one containing both parent strands and the other containing both daughter strands

11. Which of the following is found in an RNA nucleotide?

I. phosphoric acid
II. nitrogenous base
III. ribose sugar

A. I only
C. III only
B. II only
D. I and II only
E. I, II and III

12. Which of the following descriptions of the nucleoside uridine does NOT apply to the structure of the molecule?

A. The uracil base is directly bonded to the 1' position of ribofuranose in the α position
B. The ribofuranose moiety is only found in the D configuration
C. Nitrogen, at position 1 in the uracil base, is directly bonded to the ribofuranose moiety
D. The 5'~OH group is replaced with phosphate(s) in the nucleotide structure
E. None of the above

13. Which of these nitrogenous base pairs is found in DNA?

A. adenine-guanine   **C.** adenine-cytosine

B. adenine-uracil   **D.** guanine-cytosine   **E.** guanine-thymine

14. If one strand of a DNA double helix has the sequence AGTACTG, what is the sequence of the other strand?

A. GACGTCA   **C.** GTCATGA

B. AGTACTG   **D.** TCATGAC   **E.** AGUACUG

15. The main role of DNA is to provide instructions on how to build:

    I. lipids   II. carbohydrates   III. proteins

A. I only   **B.** II only   **C.** III only   **D.** I and II only   **E.** I, II and III

16. Nucleic acids are polymers of [ ] monomers.

A. monosaccharide   **C.** DNA

B. fatty acid   **D.** nucleotide   **E.** none of the above

17. During DNA transcription, a guanine base on the template strand codes for which base on the growing RNA strand?

A. guanine   **C.** adenine

B. thymine   **D.** cytosine   **E.** uracil

18. Cellular respiration produces the same products as:

A. do nucleic acids   **C.** does catabolism

B. do campfires   **D.** does anabolism   **E.** none of the above

19. What intermolecular force connects strands of DNA in the double helix?

A. hydrogen bonds   **C.** amide bonds

B. ionic bonds   **D.** ester bonds   **E.** none of the above

20. How are codons and anticodons related?

A. Codons are the base pairs on a tRNA that bind to complementary strands of DNA and produce proteins

B. Anticodons are the codons on the mRNA used to bind to DNA

C. Codons start the process of transcription; anticodons end the process

D. Codons and anticodons are complementary base pairs that encode for an amino acid

E. None of the above

21. What type of biological compound is a polymer composed of a sugar, a base, and phosphoric acid?

   A. nucleic acid   **C.** carbohydrate

   B. lipid   **D.** protein   **E.** none of the above

22. What is the term for the process by which a DNA molecule synthesizes an identical molecule of DNA?

   A. transcription   **C.** duplication

   B. translation   **D.** replication   **E.** none of the above

23. The bonds that link the base pairs in the DNA double helix are [   ] bonds?

   A. hydrophobic   **C.** peptide

   B. hydrogen   **D.** ionic   **E.** ester

24. Translation is the process whereby:

   A. protein is synthesized from DNA   **C.** DNA is synthesized from DNA

   B. protein is synthesized from mRNA   **D.** DNA is synthesized from mRNA

                                                  E. mRNA is synthesized from DNA

25. What is the main function of the structural difference of the sugar that makes up RNA, compared to the sugar of DNA?

   A. It stabilizes the RNA outside the nucleus

   B. It acts as an energy source to produce proteins

   C. It allows the RNA to be easily digested by enzymes

   D. It keeps the RNA from binding tightly to DNA

   E. All of the above

26. The double helix of DNA is stabilized mainly by:

   A. ionic bonds   **C.** ion–dipole bonds

   B. covalent bonds   **D.** ester bonds   **E.** hydrogen bonds

27. Which of the following is the correct listing of DNA's constituents in the order of increasing size?

   A. Nucleotide, codon, gene, nucleic acid

   B. Nucleic acid, nucleotide, codon, gene

   C. Nucleotide, codon, nucleic acid, gene

   D. Gene, nucleic acid, nucleotide, codon

   E. Gene, codon, nucleotide, nucleic acid

28. The number of adenines in a DNA molecule is equal to the number of thymines because:

A. adenines are paired opposite of guanine in a DNA molecule
B. of the strong attraction between the nucleotides of adenine and thymine
C. the structure of adenine is similar to uracil
D. adenine is paired to cytosine in a DNA molecule
E. none of the above

29. What is the sugar component in RNA called?

A. fructose
B. galactose
C. glucose
D. ribose
E. deoxyribose

30. What is the process in which the DNA double helix unfolds, and each strand serves as a template for the synthesis of a new strand?

A. translation
B. replication
C. transcription
D. complementation
E. restriction digestion

31. If NADH is the reduced form of the high energy intermediate dinucleotide, which of the following is the oxidized form of this important biomolecule?

A. NAD^{+2}
B. NAD
C. NAD^+
D. $NADH_2$
E. $NADH^+$

32. Which of the following illustrates the direction of flow for protein synthesis?

A. RNA $\rightarrow$ protein $\rightarrow$ DNA
B. DNA $\rightarrow$ protein $\rightarrow$ RNA
C. RNA $\rightarrow$ DNA $\rightarrow$ protein
D. DNA $\rightarrow$ RNA $\rightarrow$ protein
E. protein $\rightarrow$ RNA $\rightarrow$ DNA

33. The attractive force between the cyclic amine bases in DNA is/are:

A. disulfide bridges
B. hydrogen bonding
C. hydrophobic stacking
D. ionic interactions of salt bridges
E. ion-diploe interaction

34. The three-base sequence in mRNA specifying the amino acid is called:

A. rRNA
B. an anticodon
C. a codon
D. tRNA
E. nucleotide

35. Which of the following is an RNA codon for protein synthesis?

I. GUA   II. CGU   III. ACG

A. I only   B. II only   C. III only   D. I and II only   E. I, II and III

36. During DNA replication, an adenine base on the template strand codes for which base on the complementary strand?

A. thymine
B. guanine
C. cytosine
D. adenine
E. uracil

37. Which of the following is NOT part of a nucleotide?

A. cyclic nitrogenous base
B. fatty acid
C. phosphate group
D. cyclic sugar
E. oxygen

38. Which of the following types of linkage is found in a nucleic acid?

A. phosphate linkage
B. ester linkage
C. glycoside linkage
D. peptide linkage
E. amide linkage

39. Which of the following codes for an amino acid during protein synthesis?

A. RNA nucleotide
B. RNA trinucleotide
C. DNA nucleotide
D. DNA trinucleotide
E. none of the above

40. How does RNA differ from DNA?

A. RNA is double-stranded, while DNA is single-stranded
B. RNA is a polymer of amino acids, while DNA is a polymer of nucleotides
C. RNA contains uracil, while DNA contains thymine
D. In RNA G pairs with T, while in DNA G pairs with C
E. DNA has an additional alcohol group compared to RNA

41. The one cyclic amine base that occurs in DNA but not in RNA is:

A. cystine
B. guanine
C. thymine
D. uracil
E. adenine

42. In the synthesis of mRNA, an adenine in the DNA pairs with:

A. guanine
B. thymine
C. uracil
D. adenine
E. cytosine

43. Nucleic acids determine the:

A. quantity and type of prions
B. number of mitochondria in a cell
C. sequence of amino acids
D. pH of the cell nucleus
E. catabolism rate for food

44. What type of biological compound is characterized by alcohol and amine functional groups?

    A. nucleic acid   **C.** carbohydrate

    B. lipid   **D.** protein   **E.** amino acid

45. DNA is a(n):

    A. peptide   **C.** nucleic acid

    B. protein   **D.** enzyme   **E.** steroid

46. Which of the following amine bases is NOT present in DNA?

    A. adenine   **C.** guanine

    B. cytosinc   **D.** uracil   **E.** thymine

47. In transcription:

    A. both strands of the DNA are copied

    B. uracil pairs with thymine

    C. a double helix containing one parent strand and one daughter strand is produced

    D. the mRNA produced is identical to the parent DNA

    E. the mRNA contains the genetic information from DNA

48. The two strands of the double helix of DNA are held together by:

    A. disulfide bridges   **C.** hydrogen bonds

    B. ionic bonds   **D.** covalent bonds

                           E. sugar-phosphate bonds

Please, leave your Customer Review on Amazon

Notes

Chapter 1: Electronic & Atomic Structure; Periodic Table – Answer Key

1: B	11: C	21: A	31: D	41: D	51: A
2: E	12: E	22: C	32: A	42: E	52: B
3: B	13: D	23: C	33: A	43: E	53: A
4: B	14: C	24: A	34: C	44: B	54: E
5: C	15: E	25: A	35: D	45: D	55: C
6: B	16: D	26: E	36: B	46: C	56: E
7: A	17: E	27: D	37: E	47: E	57: B
8: B	18: B	28: A	38: D	48: E	58: B
9: E	19: A	29: E	39: B	49: C	59: E
10: A	20: D	30: D	40: C	50: C	60: A

Chapter 2: Chemical Bonding – Answer Key

1: D	11: B	21: C	31: E	41: C	51: E
2: A	12: E	22: B	32: A	42: A	52: E
3: C	13: A	23: D	33: D	43: A	53: D
4: E	14: D	24: D	34: D	44: D	54: A
5: B	15: C	25: E	35: B	45: B	55: C
6: B	16: C	26: A	36: A	46: D	56: A
7: E	17: A	27: C	37: B	47: C	57: B
8: A	18: D	28: D	38: A	48: D	58: B
9: D	19: C	29: B	39: E	49: A	59: B
10: E	20: D	30: E	40: D	50: C	60: B

Chapter 3: Phases and Phase Equilibria – Answer Key

1: A	11: C	21: D	31: E	41: B	51: B
2: C	12: A	22: D	32: A	42: C	52: D
3: C	13: C	23: A	33: C	43: A	53: E
4: A	14: C	24: B	34: C	44: B	54: A
5: A	15: C	25: E	35: E	45: B	55: C
6: B	16: C	26: A	36: B	46: B	56: A
7: B	17: E	27: B	37: A	47: A	57: B
8: B	18: E	28: D	38: C	48: C	58: E
9: E	19: A	29: C	39: C	49: D	59: B
10: D	20: E	30: B	40: B	50: E	60: C

Chapter 4: Stoichiometry – Answer Key

1: C	11: D	21: B	31: D	41: E	51: B
2: C	12: C	22: C	32: A	42: C	52: C
3: C	13: D	23: C	33: A	43: D	53: D
4: E	14: D	24: E	34: E	44: B	54: B
5: C	15: E	25: E	35: D	45: C	55: C
6: B	16: B	26: A	36: E	46: E	56: D
7: A	17: C	27: E	37: E	47: D	57: A
8: C	18: E	28: A	38: C	48: E	58: E
9: C	19: D	29: A	39: C	49: B	59: C
10: C	20: A	30: C	40: E	50: E	60: D

Chapter 5: Kinetics and Equilibrium – Answer Key

1: A	11: B	21: B	31: C	41: B	51: B
2: B	12: B	22: B	32: E	42: D	52: C
3: A	13: C	23: E	33: C	43: B	53: D
4: A	14: A	24: A	34: B	44: B	54: D
5: C	15: C	25: D	35: C	45: D	55: C
6: B	16: D	26: E	36: D	46: B	56: D
7: D	17: B	27: B	37: E	47: D	57: E
8: D	18: E	28: B	38: E	48: E	58: E
9: B	19: A	29: C	39: C	49: A	59: E
10: D	20: C	30: D	40: E	50: C	60: D

Chapter 6: Solution Chemistry – Answer Key

1: E	11: B	21: B	31: B	41: A	51: C
2: E	12: A	22: B	32: E	42: A	52: E
3: A	13: A	23: D	33: B	43: C	53: D
4: D	14: B	24: A	34: A	44: D	54: A
5: B	15: A	25: D	35: B	45: E	55: E
6: A	16: C	26: B	36: B	46: C	56: E
7: C	17: E	27: B	37: D	47: E	57: B
8: A	18: A	28: A	38: E	48: A	58: E
9: C	19: D	29: D	39: D	49: A	59: E
10: E	20: E	30: A	40: A	50: C	60: D

Chapter 7: Acids and Bases – Answer Key

1: A	11: C	21: E	31: C	41: E	51: D
2: C	12: E	22: C	32: A	42: A	52: C
3: C	13: A	23: B	33: E	43: B	53: D
4: E	14: D	24: E	34: A	44: C	54: C
5: B	15: D	25: D	35: B	45: A	55: D
6: B	16: B	26: E	36: C	46: B	56: C
7: B	17: B	27: C	37: A	47: B	57: D
8: A	18: D	28: A	38: A	48: D	58: E
9: D	19: E	29: D	39: D	49: E	59: A
10: D	20: D	30: B	40: E	50: E	60: E

Chapter 8: Electrochemistry – Answer Key

1: D	11: B	21: C	31: A	41: E	51: B
2: E	12: C	22: E	32: B	42: B	52: D
3: B	13: E	23: A	33: D	43: E	53: B
4: E	14: C	24: B	34: B	44: C	54: B
5: C	15: C	25: C	35: E	45: B	55: C
6: D	16: E	26: A	36: B	46: D	56: D
7: D	17: A	27: B	37: B	47: C	57: A
8: A	18: A	28: B	38: B	48: D	58: B
9: E	19: A	29: D	39: A	49: A	59: B
10: A	20: B	30: A	40: B	50: A	60: E

Chapter 9: Thermochemistry – Answer Key

1: A	11: A	21: A	31: D	41: B	51: C
2: B	12: B	22: B	32: B	42: E	52: D
3: E	13: D	23: C	33: D	43: A	53: E
4: E	14: C	24: C	34: A	44: D	54: C
5: A	15: B	25: A	35: B	45: C	55: D
6: D	16: A	26: D	36: D	46: C	56: E
7: E	17: B	27: A	37: E	47: B	57: C
8: A	18: C	28: E	38: E	48: C	58: C
9: E	19: C	29: B	39: A	49: E	59: B
10: C	20: A	30: C	40: C	50: C	60: B

Chapter 10: Atomic & Nuclear Structure – Answer Key

1: B	11: B	21: B	31: C
2: D	12: C	22: E	32: D
3: E	13: A	23: C	33: B
4: A	14: B	24: E	34: D
5: C	15: D	25: E	35: D
6: C	16: D	26: A	
7: B	17: C	27: B	
8: C	18: A	28: D	
9: C	19: D	29: A	
10: C	20: E	30: C	

Chapter 11: Quantum Chemistry – Answer Key

1: E	11: E	21: A	31: D
2: B	12: D	22: C	32: B
3: C	13: C	23: B	33: B
4: D	14: A	24: C	34: B
5: C	15: D	25: C	
6: B	16: B	26: C	
7: D	17: A	27: C	
8: A	18: A	28: D	
9: D	19: D	29: E	
10: E	20: C	30: C	

Chapter 12: Nomenclature – Answer Key

1: D	11: D	21: A	31: A	41: A
2: C	12: A	22: A	32: B	42: A
3: A	13: D	23: B	33: B	43: C
4: A	14: A	24: A	34: A	44: C
5: B	15: D	25: D	35: C	45: D
6: C	16: B	26: B	36: B	46: B
7: B	17: A	27: D	37: D	
8: D	18: E	28: B	38: A	
9: E	19: B	29: B	39: E	
10: B	20: B	30: C	40: C	

Chapter 13: Covalent Bond – Answer Key

1: D	11: B	21: C	31: C	41: B
2: B	12: E	22: E	32: C	42: E
3: A	13: E	23: C	33: A	43: C
4: D	14: B	24: D	34: D	44: A
5: B	15: B	25: B	35: B	45: B
6: C	16: E	26: D	36: A	46: B
7: D	17: D	27: C	37: C	47: A
8: D	18: C	28: B	38: D	48: C
9: B	19: E	29: B	39: D	
10: B	20: E	30: E	40: B	

Chapter 14: Stereochemistry – Answer Key

1: C	11: B	21: D	31: A	41: D
2: D	12: D	22: B	32: A	42: A
3: D	13: A	23: D	33: C	43: B
4: A	14: D	24: C	34: A	44: B
5: C	15: A	25: A	35: B	45: A
6: C	16: D	26: B	36: A	46: B
7: E	17: D	27: B	37: A	47: D
8: E	18: C	28: E	38: E	
9: B	19: A	29: D	39: C	
10: B	20: C	30: C	40: C	

Chapter 15: Molecular Structure and Spectra – Answer Key

1: D	11: C	21: B	31: B
2: D	12: A	22: C	32: A
3: D	13: C	23: A	33: D
4: A	14: B	24: C	34: B
5: A	15: C	25: A	35: B
6: E	16: B	26: A	36: B
7: D	17: B	27: E	
8: E	18: C	28: A	
9: B	19: A	29: D	
10: C	20: A	30: E	

Chapter 16: Alkanes and Alkyl Halides – Answer Key

1:	C	11:	D	21:	C	31:	D
2:	D	12:	D	22:	D	32:	B
3:	B	13:	D	23:	B	33:	A
4:	D	14:	C	24:	C	34:	B
5:	E	15:	B	25:	C	35:	D
6:	A	16:	D	26:	A	36:	E
7:	B	17:	D	27:	D		
8:	D	18:	B	28:	C		
9:	C	19:	B	29:	A		
10:	B	20:	D	30:	A		

Chapter 17: Alkenes – Answer Key

1:	C	11:	A	21:	E	31:	B
2:	B	12:	C	22:	A	32:	A
3:	D	13:	A	23:	C	33:	A
4:	D	14:	A	24:	C	34:	A
5:	D	15:	C	25:	A	35:	C
6:	A	16:	D	26:	A	36:	A
7:	A	17:	A	27:	E		
8:	D	18:	B	28:	D		
9:	A	19:	D	29:	A		
10:	C	20:	C	30:	B		

Chapter 18: Alkynes – Answer Key

1:	E	11:	C	21:	B	31:	D
2:	C	12:	D	22:	C	32:	A
3:	C	13:	B	23:	D	33:	C
4:	A	14:	A	24:	C	34:	C
5:	A	15:	C	25:	D	35:	C
6:	D	16:	B	26:	B	36:	B
7:	B	17:	D	27:	D		
8:	A	18:	B	28:	A		
9:	C	19:	C	29:	C		
10:	C	20:	C	30:	B		

Chapter 19: Aromatic Compounds – Answer Key

1:	C	11:	C	21:	B	31:	A
2:	B	12:	A	22:	D	32:	A
3:	E	13:	D	23:	C	33:	B
4:	D	14:	C	24:	D	34:	C
5:	A	15:	D	25:	C	35:	A
6:	D	16:	E	26:	C	36:	D
7:	C	17:	A	27:	A		
8:	D	18:	D	28:	D		
9:	A	19:	C	29:	D		
10:	D	20:	E	30:	D		

Chapter 20: Alcohols – Answer Key

1:	B	11:	B	21:	D	31:	D
2:	E	12:	C	22:	D	32:	D
3:	C	13:	C	23:	D	33:	C
4:	E	14:	B	24:	C	34:	B
5:	A	15:	A	25:	D	35:	B
6:	C	16:	B	26:	B	36:	B
7:	B	17:	E	27:	A		
8:	D	18:	B	28:	A		
9:	B	19:	D	29:	A		
10:	A	20:	D	30:	C		

Chapter 21: Aldehydes and Ketones – Answer Key

1:	E	11:	E	21:	E	31:	D
2:	A	12:	E	22:	D	32:	C
3:	D	13:	A	23:	C	33:	B
4:	B	14:	B	24:	E	34:	E
5:	C	15:	A	25:	E	35:	A
6:	D	16:	D	26:	A	36:	B
7:	A	17:	A	27:	B		
8:	D	18:	D	28:	D		
9:	D	19:	D	29:	A		
10:	C	20:	E	30:	E		

Chapter 22: Carboxylic Acids – Answer Key

1: C	11: B	21: E	31: C
2: D	12: B	22: C	32: E
3: C	13: C	23: D	33: B
4: B	14: B	24: A	34: A
5: A	15: D	25: C	35: D
6: C	16: B	26: B	36: A
7: E	17: A	27: A	
8: D	18: D	28: A	
9: B	19: A	29: B	
10: E	20: A	30: D	

Chapter 23: COOH Derivatives – Answer Key

1: A	11: B	21: A	31: B
2: D	12: B	22: C	32: B
3: A	13: C	23: D	33: B
4: C	14: D	24: A	34: A
5: A	15: B	25: A	35: B
6: D	16: D	26: C	36: B
7: C	17: A	27: C	
8: A	18: E	28: A	
9: E	19: B	29: C	
10: E	20: A	30: C	

Chapter 24: Amines – Answer Key

1: B	11: B	21: D	31: C
2: C	12: A	22: A	32: A
3: A	13: A	23: C	33: E
4: E	14: C	24: A	34: B
5: B	15: E	25: C	35: E
6: D	16: A	26: B	36: A
7: B	17: B	27: D	
8: A	18: D	28: C	
9: A	19: C	29: A	
10: E	20: C	30: B	

Chapter 25: Amino Acids, Peptides, Proteins – Answer Key

1: A	11: C	21: C	31: E	41: D
2: D	12: D	22: C	32: A	42: B
3: E	13: A	23: B	33: A	43: C
4: E	14: C	24: A	34: A	44: B
5: A	15: E	25: B	35: D	45: B
6: D	16: B	26: C	36: E	46: B
7: C	17: C	27: D	37: E	47: C
8: B	18: D	28: C	38: D	48: E
9: A	19: B	29: B	39: C	
10: C	20: D	30: B	40: A	

Chapter 26: Lipids – Answer Key

1: D	11: C	21: B	31: E	41: E
2: D	12: B	22: A	32: C	42: B
3: D	13: D	23: B	33: A	43: C
4: A	14: D	24: D	34: D	44: C
5: D	15: B	25: C	35: B	45: C
6: D	16: C	26: E	36: D	46: D
7: B	17: B	27: A	37: B	47: D
8: B	18: D	28: A	38: D	48: D
9: D	19: C	29: B	39: C	
10: C	20: D	30: D	40: D	

Chapter 27: Carbohydrates – Answer Key

1: C	11: C	21: A	31: E	41: B
2: D	12: B	22: C	32: A	42: D
3: C	13: A	23: D	33: A	43: B
4: C	14: D	24: B	34: C	44: C
5: D	15: D	25: A	35: C	45: C
6: E	16: A	26: A	36: D	46: C
7: C	17: A	27: E	37: D	47: D
8: C	18: C	28: B	38: D	48: A
9: A	19: B	29: C	39: B	
10: B	20: D	30: D	40: D	

Chapter 28: Nucleic Acids – Answer Key

1: D	11: E	21: A	31: C	41: C
2: A	12: A	22: D	32: D	42: C
3: C	13: D	23: B	33: B	43: C
4: B	14: D	24: B	34: C	44: A
5: C	15: C	25: C	35: E	45: C
6: D	16: D	26: E	36: A	46: D
7: B	17: D	27: A	37: B	47: E
8: D	18: B	28: B	38: A	48: C
9: B	19: A	29: D	39: B	
10: A	20: D	30: B	40: C	

Chapter 1 Explanations: Electronic and Atomic Structure; Periodic Table

1. B is correct.

Ionization energy (IE) is the amount of energy required to remove the most loosely bound electron of an isolated gaseous atom to form a cation. This is an endothermic process.

Ionization energy is expressed as:

$$X + energy \rightarrow X^+ + e^-$$

where X is an atom (or molecule) capable of being ionized (i.e., having an electron removed), X^+ is that atom or molecule after an electron is removed, and e^- is the removed electron.

The principal quantum number (n) describes the size of the orbital and the energy of an electron and the most probable distance of the electron from the nucleus. It refers to the size of the orbital and the energy level of an electron.

The elements with larger shell sizes (n is large) listed at the bottom of the periodic table have low ionization energies. This is due to the shielding (by the inner shell electrons) from the positive charge of the nucleus.

The greater the distance between the electrons and the nucleus, the less energy is needed to remove the outer valence electrons.

2. E is correct.

Metalloids are semi metallic elements (i.e., between metals and nonmetals). The metalloids are boron (B), silicon (Si), germanium (Ge), arsenic (As), antimony (Sb), and tellurium (Te). Some literature reports polonium (Po) and astatine (At) as metalloids.

Seventeen elements are generally classified as nonmetals. Eleven are gases: hydrogen (H), helium (He), nitrogen (N), oxygen (O), fluorine (F), neon (Ne), chlorine (Cl), argon (Ar), krypton (Kr), xenon (Xe) and radon (Rn). One nonmetal is a liquid – bromine (Br) – and five are solids: carbon (C), phosphorus (P), sulfur (S), selenium (Se) and iodine (I).

3. B is correct.

An element is a pure chemical substance that consists of a single type of atom, distinguished by its atomic number (Z) (i.e., the number of protons that it contains). 118 elements have been identified, of which the first 94 occur naturally on Earth, with the remaining 24 being synthetic elements.

The properties of the elements on the periodic table repeat at regular intervals, creating "groups" or "families" of elements. Each column on the periodic table is a group, and elements within each group have similar physical and chemical characteristics due to the orbital location of their outermost electron.

These groups only exist because the elements of the periodic table are listed by increasing atomic number.

4. B is correct.

Groups IVA, VA, and VIA each contain at least one metal and one nonmetal.

Group IVA has three metals (tin, lead, and flerovium) and one nonmetal (carbon).

Group VA has two metals (bismuth and moscovium) and two nonmetals (nitrogen and phosphorous).

Group VIA has one metal (livermorium) and three nonmetals (oxygen, sulfur, and selenium).

All three groups are part of the *p*-block of the periodic table.

5. C is correct.

Most elements on the periodic table (over 100 elements) are metals.

There are about four times more metals than nonmetals.

Seventeen elements are generally classified as nonmetals. Eleven are gases: hydrogen (H), helium (He), nitrogen (N), oxygen (O), fluorine (F), neon (Ne), chlorine (Cl), argon (Ar), krypton (Kr), xenon (Xe) and radon (Rn). One nonmetal is a liquid – bromine (Br) – and five are solids: carbon (C), phosphorus (P), sulfur (S), selenium (Se) and iodine (I).

6. B is correct.

Isotopes are variants of an element, which differ in the number of neutrons. All isotopes of the element have the same number of protons and occupy the same position on the periodic table.

The number of protons within the atom's nucleus is the atomic number (Z) and is equal to the number of electrons in the neutral (non-ionized) atom. Each atomic number identifies a specific element, but not the isotope; an atom of a given element may have a wide range in its number of neutrons.

The number of both protons and neutrons (i.e., nucleons) in the nucleus is the atom's mass number (A), and each isotope of an element has a different mass number. The atomic mass unit (amu) was designed using ^{12}C isotope as the reference. 1 amu = 1/12 mass of a ^{12}C atom.

Masses of other elements are measured against this standard. If the mass of an atom 55.91 amu, the atom's mass is 55.91 × (1/12 mass of ^{12}C).

7. A is correct. The three coordinates that come from Schrodinger's wave equations are the principal (*n*), angular (*l*) and magnetic (*m*) quantum numbers. These quantum numbers describe the size, shape, and orientation in the space of the orbitals on an atom.

The principal quantum number (*n*) describes the size of the orbital and the energy of an electron and the most probable distance of the electron from the nucleus. It refers to the size of the orbital and the energy level of an electron.

The angular momentum quantum number (*l*) describes the shape of the orbital within the subshells.

The magnetic quantum number (m) determines the number of orbitals and their orientation within a subshell. Consequently, its value depends on the orbital angular momentum quantum number (l). Given a certain l, m is an interval ranging from $-l$ to $+l$ (i.e., it can be zero, a negative integer or a positive integer).

The s is the spin quantum number (e.g., $+\frac{1}{2}$ or $-\frac{1}{2}$).

8. B is correct. Electron shells represent the orbit that electrons allow around an atom's nucleus. Each shell is composed of one or more subshells, which are named using lowercase letters (s, p, d, f).

The first shell has one subshell ($1s$); the second shell has two subshells ($2s, 2p$); the third shell has three subshells ($3s, 3p, 3d$), etc.

An s subshell holds 2 electrons, and each subsequent subshell in the series can hold 4 more (p holds 6, d holds 10, f holds 14).

The shell number (i.e., principal quantum number) before the s (i.e., 4 in this example) does not affect how many electrons can occupy the subshell.

Subshell name	Subshell max electrons	Shell max electrons
1s	2	2
2s	2	2 + 6 = 8
2p	6	
3s	2	2 + 6 + 10 = 18
3p	6	
3d	10	
4s	2	2 + 6 + 10 + 14 = 32
4p	6	
4d	10	
4f	14	

9. E is correct.

The specific, characteristic line spectra for atoms result from photons being emitted when excited electrons drop to lower energy levels.

10. A is correct. In general, the size of neutral atoms increases down a group (i.e., increasing shell size) and decreases from left to right across the periodic table.

Negative ions (anions) are *much larger* than their neutral element, while positive ions (cations) are *much smaller*. All examples are isoelectronic because of the same number of electrons.
Atomic numbers:

$Br = 35$; $K = 19$; $Ar = 18$; $Ca = 20$ and $Cl = 17$

The general trend for the atomic radius is to decrease from left to right and increase from top to bottom in the periodic table. When the ion gains or loses an electron to create a new charged ion, its radius would change slightly, but the general trend of radius still applies.

The ions K^+, Ca^{2+}, Cl^-, and Ar have identical numbers of electrons.

However, Br is located below Cl (larger principal quantum number, n) and its atomic number is almost twice the others. This indicates that Br has more electrons and its radius must be significantly larger than the other atoms.

11. C is correct.

The ground state configuration of sulfur is $[Ne]3s^23p^4$.

According to Hund's rule, the *p* orbitals are filled separately, and then pair the electrons by $+\frac{1}{2}$ or $-\frac{1}{2}$ spin.

The first three *p* electrons fill separate orbitals and then the fourth electron pairs with two remaining unpaired electrons.

12. E is correct.

There are two ways to obtain the proper answer to this problem:

1. Using an atomic number.

Calculate the atomic number by adding all the electrons:

$2 + 2 + 6 + 2 + 6 + 1 = 19$

Find element number 19 in the periodic table.
Check the group where it is located to see other elements that belong to the same group.
Element number 19 is potassium (K), so the elements that belong to the same group (IA) is lithium (Li).

2. Using subshells.

Identify the outermost subshell and use it to identify its group in the periodic table:
In this problem, the outermost subshell is $4s^1$.

Relationship between outermost subshell and group:

s^1 = Group IA

s^2 = Group IIA

p^1 = Group IIIA

p^2 = Group IVA

…

p^6 = Group VIII A

d = transition element

f = lanthanide/actinide element

13. D is correct. The principal quantum number (*n*) describes the size of the orbital and the energy of an electron and the most probable distance of the electron from the nucleus. It refers to the size of the orbital and the energy level of an electron.

The elements with larger shell sizes (*n* is large) listed at the bottom of the periodic table have low ionization energies. This is due to the shielding (by the inner shell electrons) from the positive charge of the nucleus. The greater the distance between the electrons and the nucleus, the less energy is needed to remove the outer valence electrons.

Ionization energy decreases with increasing shell size (i.e., *n* value) and generally increases to the right across a period (i.e., row) in the periodic table.

Moving down a column corresponds to increasing shell size with electrons further from the nucleus and decreasing nuclear attraction.

14. C is correct.

The *f* subshell has 7 orbitals.

Each orbital can hold two electrons. The capacity of an *f* subshell is 7 orbitals × 2 electrons/orbital = 14 electrons.

15. E is correct.

The attraction of the nucleus on the outermost electrons determines the ionization energy, which increases towards the right and increases up on the periodic table.

16. D is correct. An element is a pure chemical substance that consists of a single type of atom, distinguished by its atomic number (Z) (i.e., the number of protons that it contains). 118 elements have been identified, of which the first 94 occur naturally on Earth, with the remaining 24 being synthetic elements.

The properties of the elements on the periodic table repeat at regular intervals, creating "groups" or "families" of elements.

Each column on the periodic table is a group, and elements within each group have similar physical and chemical characteristics due to the orbital location of their outermost electron. These groups only exist because the elements of the periodic table are listed by increasing atomic number.

17. E is correct. A cathode ray particle is a different name for an electron.

Those particles (i.e., electrons) are attracted to the positively charged cathode, which implies that they are negatively charged.

18. B is correct.

The three coordinates that come from Schrodinger's wave equations are the principal (*n*), angular (*l*) and magnetic (*m*) quantum numbers. These quantum numbers describe the size, shape, and orientation in the space of the orbitals on an atom.

The principal quantum number (*n*) describes the size of the orbital, the energy of an electron and the most probable distance of the electron from the nucleus. It refers to the size of the orbital and the energy level of an electron.

The angular momentum quantum number (*l*) describes the shape of the orbital of the subshells.

Carbon has an atomic number of 6 and an electron configuration of $1s^2, 2s^2, 2p^2$.

Therefore, electrons are in the second shell of $n = 2$, and two subshells are in the outermost shell of $l = 1$. The values of *l* are 0 and 1, whereby, only the largest value of *l*, ($l = 1$) is reported.

19. A is correct.

The alkaline earth metals (group IIA), in the ground state, have a filled *s* subshell with 2 electrons.

20. D is correct.

The 3rd shell consists of s, p and d subshells.

Each orbital can hold two electrons.

The s subshell has 1 spherical orbital and can accommodate 2 electrons

The p subshell has 3 dumbbell-shaped orbitals and can accommodate 6 electrons

The d subshell has 5 lobe-shaped orbitals and can accommodate 10 electrons

The $n = 3$ shell can accommodate a total of 18 electrons.

1s
2s 2p
3s 3p 3d
4s 4p 4d 4f
5s 5p 5d 5f ...
6s 6p 6d ... ...

Order of filling orbitals

The element with the electron configuration terminating in 3p^4 is sulfur (i.e., a total of 16 electrons).

21. A is correct.

In general, the size of neutral atoms increases down a group (i.e., increasing shell size) and decreases from left to right across the periodic table.

Positive ions (cations) are *much smaller* than the neutral element (due to greater effective nuclear charge), while negative ions (anions) are *much larger* (due to smaller effective nuclear charge and repulsion of valence electrons).

22. C is correct.

In the ground state, the 3p orbitals fill before the 3d orbitals.

The lowest energy orbital fills before an orbital of a higher energy level.

Aufbau principle to determine the order of energy levels in subshells:

1s
2s 2p
3s 3p 3d
4s 4p 4d 4f
5s 5p 5d 5f
6s 6p 6d
7s 7p

From the table above, the orbitals increase in energy from:
$1s < 2s < 2p < 3s < 3p < 4s < 3d < 4p < 5s < 4d < 5p < 6s < 4f < 5d < 6p < 7s < 5f < 6d < 7p$

23. C is correct.

The atom has 47 protons, 47 electrons, and 60 neutrons.

Because the periodic table is arranged by atomic number (Z), the fastest way to identify an element is to determine its atomic number. The atomic number is equal to the number of protons or electrons, which means that this atom's atomic number is 47. Use this information to locate element #47 in the table, which is Ag (silver).

Check the atomic mass (A), which is equal to the atomic number + number of neutrons.
For this atom, the mass is $60 + 47 = 107$.

The mass of Ag on the periodic table is listed as 107.87, which is the average mass of all Ag isotopes. Usually, all isotopes of an element have similar masses (within 1-3 amu to each other).

24. A is correct.

Congeners are chemical substances related by origin, structure or function. Regarding the periodic table, congeners are the elements of the same group which shares similar properties (e.g., copper, silver, and gold are congeners of Group 11).

Stereoisomers, diastereomers, and epimers are terms commonly used in organic chemistry.

Stereoisomers: are chiral molecules (attached to 4 different substituents and are non-superimposable mirror images. They have the same molecular formula and the same sequence of bonded atoms but are oriented differently in 3-D space (e.g., *R* / *S* enantiomers).

Diastereomers are chiral molecules that are not mirror images. The most common form is a chiral molecule with more than 1 chiral center. Additionally, *cis* / *trans* (*Z* / *E*) geometric isomers are also diastereomers.

Epimers: diastereomers that differ in absolute configuration at only one chiral center.

Anomers: is a type of stereoisomer used in carbohydrate chemistry to describe the orientation of the glycosidic bond of adjacent saccharides (e.g., α and β linkage of sugars). A refers to the hydroxyl group – of the anomeric carbon pointing downward while β points upward.

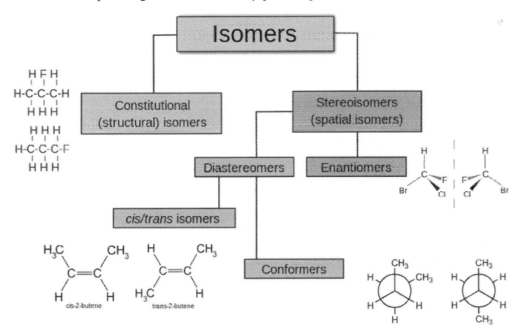

Summary of isomers

25. A is correct.

Metals, except mercury, are solids under normal conditions.

Potassium has the lowest melting point of the solid metals at 146 °F.

The relatively low melting temperature for potassium is due to its fourth shell ($n = 4$), which means its valence electrons are further from the nucleus; therefore, there is less attraction between its electrons and protons.

26. E is correct.

Alkaline earth metals (group IIA) include beryllium (Be), magnesium (Mg), calcium (Ca), strontium (Sr), barium (Ba), and radium (Ra).

Alkaline earth metals lose two electrons to become +2 cations, and the resulting ion has a complete octet of valence electrons.

Transition metals (or transition elements) are defined as elements that have a partially filled *d* or *f* subshell in a common oxidative state.

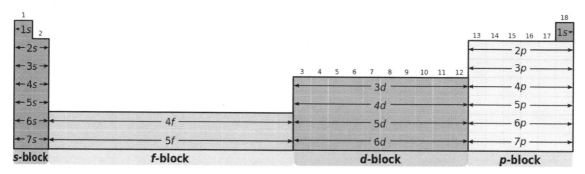

Transition metals occur in groups (vertical columns) 3–12 of the period table. They occur in periods (horizontal rows) 4–7. This group of elements includes silver, iron, and copper.

The *f*-block lanthanides (i.e., rare earth metals) and actinides (i.e., radioactive elements) are also considered transition metals and are known as inner transition metals.

Noble gases (group VIIIA) include helium (He), neon (Ne), argon (Ar), krypton (Kr) xenon (Xe), radon (Rn) and oganesson (Og).

Alkali metals (group IA) include lithium (Li), potassium (K), sodium (Na), rubidium (Rb), cesium (Cs) and francium (Fr). Alkali metals lose one electron to become +1 cations, and the resulting ion has a complete octet of valence electrons.

Halogens (group VIIA) includes fluorine (F), chlorine (Cl), bromine (Br), iodine (I) and astatine (At). Halogens gain one electron to become a –1 anion, and the resulting ion has a complete octet of valence electrons.

27. D is correct.

The metalloids have some properties of metals and some properties of nonmetals. Metalloids are semi metallic elements (i.e., between metals and nonmetals). The metalloids are boron (B), silicon (Si), germanium (Ge), arsenic (As), antimony (Sb), and tellurium (Te). Some literature reports polonium (Po) and astatine (At) as metalloids.

They have properties between metals and nonmetals. They typically have a metallic appearance but are only fair conductors of electricity (as opposed to metals which are excellent conductors), which makes them useable in the semiconductor industry.

Metalloids tend to be brittle, and chemically they behave more like nonmetals. However, the elements in the IIIB group are transition metals, not metalloids.

28. A is correct.

Isotopes are variants of an element which differ in the number of neutrons. All isotopes of the element have the same number of protons and occupy the same position on the periodic table.

The number of protons within the atom's nucleus is the atomic number (Z) and is equal to the number of electrons in the neutral (non-ionized) atom. Each atomic number identifies a specific element, but not the isotope; an atom of a given element may have a wide range in its number of neutrons.

The number of both protons and neutrons (i.e., nucleons) in the nucleus is the atom's mass number (A), and each isotope of an element has a different mass number.

From the periodic table, the atomic mass of a natural sample of Si is 28.1, which is less than the mass of ^{29}Si or ^{30}Si. Therefore, ^{28}Si is the most abundant isotope.

29. E is correct. The initial explanation is that the ray was present in the gas, and the cathode activated it.

The ray was observed even when gas was not present, so the conclusion was that the ray must have been coming from the cathode itself.

30. D is correct.

The three coordinates that come from Schrodinger's wave equations are the principal (n), angular (l), and magnetic (m) quantum numbers. These quantum numbers describe the size, shape, and orientation in the space of the orbitals on an atom.

The principal quantum number (n) describes the size of the orbital and the energy of an electron and the most probable distance of the electron from the nucleus. It refers to the size of the orbital and the energy level of an electron.

The angular momentum quantum number (l) describes the shape of the orbital of the subshells.

The magnetic quantum number (m) determines the number of orbitals and their orientation within a subshell. Consequently, its value depends on the orbital angular momentum quantum number (l). Given a certain l, m is an interval ranging from $-l$ to $+l$ (i.e., it can be zero, a negative integer, or a positive integer).

The fourth quantum number is s, which is the spin quantum number (e.g., $+\frac{1}{2}$ or $-\frac{1}{2}$).

Electrons cannot be precisely located in space at any point in time, and orbitals describe probability regions for finding the electrons.

The values needed to locate an electron are n, m, and l. The spin can be either $+\frac{1}{2}$ or $-\frac{1}{2}$, so four values are needed to describe a single electron.

31. D is correct. Boron's atomic number is 5; therefore, it contains 5 electrons.

Use the Aufbau principle to determine the order of filling orbitals.

Remember that each electron shell (principal quantum number, n) starts with a new s orbital.

32. A is correct. Identify an element using the periodic table is its atomic number.

The atomic number is equal to the number of protons or electrons.

The total number of electrons can be determined by adding all the electrons in the provided electron configuration:

$$2 + 2 + 6 + 2 + 6 + 2 + 10 + 6 + 2 + 10 + 2 = 50.$$

Element #50 in the periodic table is tin (Sn).

33. A is correct.

Electronegativity is defined as the ability of an atom to attract electrons when it bonds with another atom. The most common use of electronegativity pertains to polarity along the *sigma* (single) bond.

The trend for increasing electronegativity within the periodic table is up and toward the right. The most electron negative atom is fluorine (F), while the least electronegative atom is francium (Fr).

The greater the difference in electronegativity between two atoms, the more polar of a bond these atoms form, whereby the atom with the higher electronegativity is the partial (delta) negative end of the dipole.

34. C is correct.

Seventeen elements are generally classified as nonmetals. Eleven are gases: hydrogen (H), helium (He), nitrogen (N), oxygen (O), fluorine (F), neon (Ne), chlorine (Cl), argon (Ar), krypton (Kr), xenon (Xe) and radon (Rn). One nonmetal is a liquid – bromine (Br) – and five are solids: carbon (C), phosphorus (P), sulfur (S), selenium (Se) and iodine (I).

Metals, except mercury, are solids under normal conditions. Potassium has the lowest melting point of the solid metals at 146 °F.

35. D is correct. When an electron absorbs energy, it moves temporarily to a higher energy level. It then drops back to its initial state (also known as the ground state), while emitting the excess energy. This emission can be observed as visible spectrum lines.

The protons do not move between energy levels, so they can't absorb or emit energy.

36. B is correct. The three coordinates that come from Schrodinger's wave equations are the principal (n), angular (l) and magnetic (m) quantum numbers. These quantum numbers describe the size, shape, and orientation in the space of the orbitals on an atom.

The principal quantum number (n) describes the size of the orbital, the energy of an electron and the most probable distance of the electron from the nucleus.

The angular momentum quantum number (l) describes the shape of the orbital of the subshells.

The magnetic quantum number (m) determines the number of orbitals and their orientation within a subshell. Consequently, its value depends on the orbital angular momentum quantum number (l). Given a certain l, m is an interval ranging from $-l$ to $+l$ (i.e., it can be zero, a negative integer, or a positive integer). l must be less than n, while m_l must be less than or equal to l.

37. E is correct.

Alkali metals (group IA) include lithium (Li), potassium (K), sodium (Na), rubidium (Rb), cesium (Cs) and francium (Fr).

Alkaline earth metals (group IIA) include beryllium (Be), magnesium (Mg), calcium (Ca), strontium (Sr), barium (Ba) and radium (Ra).

Halogens (group VIIA) include fluorine (F), chlorine (Cl), bromine (Br), iodine (I) and astatine (At). Halogens gain one electron to become –1 anion and the resulting ion has a complete octet of valence electrons.

Noble gases (group VIIIA) include helium (He), neon (Ne), argon (Ar), krypton (Kr) xenon (Xe), radon (Rn) and oganesson (Og). Except for helium (which has a complete octet with 2 electrons, $1s^2$), the noble gases have complete octets with ns^2 and np^6 orbitals.

Representative elements on the periodic table are groups IA and IIA (on the left) and groups IIIA – VIIIA (on the right).

Polonium (Po) is element 84 is highly radioactive, with no stable isotopes, and is classified as either a metalloid or a metal.

38. D is correct. In general, the size of neutral atoms increases down a group (i.e., increasing shell size) and decreases from left to right across the periodic table.

Positive ions (cations) are *much smaller* than the neutral element (due to greater effective nuclear charge), while negative ions (anions) are *much larger* (due to smaller effective nuclear charge and repulsion of valence electrons).

Sulfur (S, atomic number = 16) is smaller than aluminum (Al, atomic number = 13) due to the increase in the number of protons (effective nuclear charge) from left to right across a period (i.e., horizontal rows). Al^{3+} has the same electronic configuration as Ne ($1s^22s^22p^6$) compared to Al ($1s^22s^22p^63s^23p^1$).

39. B is correct.

The semi metallic elements are arsenic (As), antimony (Sb), bismuth (Bi), and graphite (a crystalline form of carbon).

Arsenic and antimony are also considered metalloids (along with boron, silicon, germanium, and tellurium), but the terms semimetal and metalloid are not synonymous.

Semimetals, in contrast to metalloids, can also be chemical compounds.

40. C is correct.

Noble gases (group VIIIA) include helium (He), neon (Ne), argon (Ar), krypton (Kr) xenon (Xe), radon (Rn) and oganesson (Og). Except for helium (which has a complete octet with 2 electrons, $1s^2$), the noble gases have complete octets with ns^2 and np^6 orbitals.

The metalloids are boron (B), silicon (Si), germanium (Ge), arsenic (As), antimony (Sb), and tellurium (Te). Some literature reports polonium (Po) and astatine (At) as metalloids.

41. D is correct.

Isotopes are variants of an element which differ in the number of neutrons. All isotopes of the element have the same number of protons and occupy the same position on the periodic table.

The experimental results should depend on the mass of the gas molecules.

Deuterium (D or ^{2}H) is known as heavy hydrogen. It is one of two stable isotopes of hydrogen.

The nucleus of deuterium contains one proton and one neutron, compared to H, which has 1 proton and 0 neutrons. The mass of deuterium is 2.0141 daltons, compared to 1.0078 daltons for hydrogen.

Based on the difference of mass between the isotopes, the density, rate of gas effusion, and atomic vibrations would be different.

42. E is correct. Elements are defined by the number of protons (i.e., atomic number).

The isotopes are neutral atoms: # electrons = # protons.

Isotopes are variants of an element which differ in the number of neutrons. All isotopes of the element have the same number of protons and occupy the same position on the periodic table. The superscript on the left denotes the number of protons and neutrons.

Since naturally occurring lithium has a mass of 6.9 g/mol and both protons and neutrons have a mass of approximately 1 g/mol, ^{7}lithium is the predominant isotope.

43. E is correct. Each orbital can hold two electrons.

The f subshell has 7 orbitals and can accommodate 14 electrons.
The d subshell has 5 lobed orbitals and can accommodate 10 electrons.

The $n = 3$ shell contains only s, p and d subshells.

44. B is correct.

Ionization energy (IE) is the amount of energy required to remove the most loosely bound electron of an isolated gaseous atom to form a cation. This is an endothermic process.

Ionization energy is expressed as:

$$X + energy \rightarrow X^+ + e^-$$

where X is an atom (or molecule) capable of being ionized (i.e., having an electron removed), X^+ is that atom or molecule after an electron is removed, and e^- is the removed electron.

The principal quantum number (n) describes the size of the orbital and the energy of an electron and the most probable distance of the electron from the nucleus. It refers to the size of the orbital and the energy level of an electron.

The elements with larger shell sizes (n is large) listed at the bottom of the periodic table have low ionization energies. This is due to the shielding (by the inner shell electrons) from the positive charge of the nucleus. The greater the distance between the electrons and the nucleus, the less energy is needed to remove the outer valence electrons.

Ionization energy decreases with increasing shell size (i.e., n value) and generally increases to the right across a period (i.e., row) in the periodic table.

Chlorine (Cl) has an atomic number of 10 and a shell size of $n = 3$.

Francium (Fr) has an atomic number of 87 and a shell size of $n = 7$.

Gallium (Ga) has an atomic number of 31 and a shell size of $n = 4$.

Iodine (I) has an atomic number of 53 and a shell size of $n = 5$.

Cesium (Cs) has an atomic number of 55 and a shell size of $n = 6$.

45. D is correct. Electrons are electrostatically (i.e., negative and positive charge) attracted to the nucleus and an atom's electrons generally occupy outer shells only if other electrons have completely filled the more inner shells. However, there are exceptions to this rule with some atoms having two or even three incomplete outer shells.

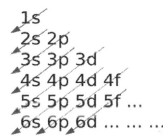

The Aufbau (German for building up) principle is based on the Madelung rule for the order of filling the subshells based on lowest energy levels.

Order of filling electron's orbitals

46. C is correct.

In Bohr's model of the atom, electrons can jump to higher energy levels, gaining energy, or drop to lower energy levels, releasing energy. When an electric current flows through an element in the gas phase, glowing light is produced.

By directing this light through a prism, a pattern of lines known as the atomic spectra can be seen. These lines are produced by excited electrons dropping to lower energy levels. Since the energy levels in each element are different, each element has a unique set of lines it produces, which is why the spectrum is called the "atomic fingerprint" of the element.

47. E is correct.

Obtain the atomic number of Mn from the periodic table.

Mn is a transition metal, and it is in Group VIIB/7; its atomic number is 25.

Use the Aufbau principle to fill up the orbitals of Mn: $1s^2 2s^2 2p^6 3s^2 3p^6 4s^2 3d^5$

The transition metals occur in groups 3–12 (vertical columns) of the period table. They occur in periods 4–7 (horizontal rows).

Transition metals are defined as elements that have a partially filled d or f subshell in a common oxidative state. This group of elements includes silver, iron, and copper.

The transition metals are elements whose atom has an incomplete d sub-shell, or which can give rise to cations with an incomplete d sub-shell. By this definition, all the elements in groups 3–11 (or 12 by some literature) are transition metals.

The transition elements have characteristics that are not found in other elements, which result from the partially filled *d* shell. These include: the formation of compounds whose color is due to *d–d* electronic transitions, the formation of compounds in many oxidation states, due to the relatively low reactivity of unpaired *d* electrons.

The transition elements form many paramagnetic (i.e., attracted to an externally applied magnetic field) compounds due to the presence of unpaired *d* electrons. By exception to their unique traits, a few compounds of main group elements are also paramagnetic (e.g., nitric oxide and oxygen).

48. E is correct. Electronegativity is defined as the ability of an atom to attract electrons when it bonds with another atom.

The most common use of electronegativity pertains to polarity along the *sigma* (single) bond.

The trend for increasing electronegativity within the periodic table is up and toward the right. The most electron negative atom is fluorine (F), while the least electronegative atom is francium (Fr).

49. C is correct. Alkali metals (group IA) include lithium (Li), potassium (K), sodium (Na), rubidium (Rb), cesium (Cs) and francium (Fr). Alkali metals lose one electron to become +1 cations, and the resulting ion has a complete octet of valence electrons.

Alkaline earth metals (group IIA) include beryllium (Be), magnesium (Mg), calcium (Ca), strontium (Sr), barium (Ba), and radium (Ra). Alkaline earth metals lose two electrons to become +2 cations, and the resulting ion has a complete octet of valence electrons.

50. C is correct. The mass number (A) is the sum of protons and neutrons in an atom. The mass number approximates the atomic weight of the element as amu (grams per mole).

The mass number is already provided by the problem: ^{79}Br means the mass number is 79.

The atomic number of ^{79}Br can be obtained from the periodic table. Br is in group VIIA/17, and its atomic number is 35.

51. A is correct. The mass number (A) is the total number of nucleons (i.e., protons and neutrons) in an atom.

The number of protons and neutrons is denoted by the superscript on the left.

The atomic number (Z) is the number of protons in an atom.

The number of neutrons in an atom can be calculated by subtracting the atomic number (Z) from the mass number (A).

52. B is correct. Alkali metals (group IA) include lithium (Li), potassium (K), sodium (Na), rubidium (Rb), cesium (Cs) and francium (Fr).

Alkali metals lose one electron to become +1 cations, and the resulting ion has a complete octet of valence electrons.

The alkali metals have low electronegativity and react violently with water (e.g., the violent reaction of metallic sodium with water).

53. A is correct.

Seventeen elements are generally classified as nonmetals. Eleven are gases: hydrogen (H), helium (He), nitrogen (N), oxygen (O), fluorine (F), neon (Ne), chlorine (Cl), argon (Ar), krypton (Kr), xenon (Xe) and radon (Rn). One nonmetal is a liquid – bromine (Br) – and five are solids: carbon (C), phosphorus (P), sulfur (S), selenium (Se) and iodine (I).

Nonmetals tend to be highly volatile (i.e., easily vaporized), have low elasticity and are good insulators of heat and electricity.

Nonmetals tend to have high ionization energy and electronegativity and share (or gain) an electron when bonding with other elements.

54. E is correct.

Group VIA (16) has three nonmetals: oxygen, sulfur, and selenium.

Metalloids are semi metallic elements (i.e., between metals and nonmetals). The metalloids are boron (B), silicon (Si), germanium (Ge), arsenic (As), antimony (Sb), and tellurium (Te). Some literature reports polonium (Po) and astatine (At) as metalloids.

55. C is correct. Transition metals (or transition elements) are defined as elements that have a partially filled *d* or *f* subshell in a common oxidative state.

Transition metals occur in groups (vertical columns) 3–12 of the period table. They occur in periods (horizontal rows) 4–7. This group of elements includes silver, iron, and copper.

The *f*-block lanthanides (i.e., rare earth metals) and actinides (i.e., radioactive elements) are also considered transition metals and are known as inner transition metals.

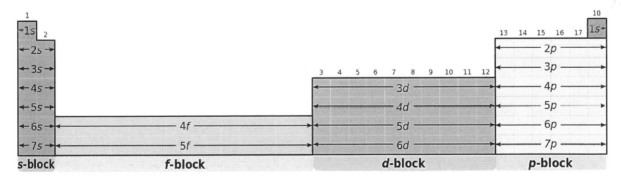

Transition elements have characteristics that are not found in other elements, which result from the partially filled *d* shell. These include: the formation of compounds whose color is due to *d* electronic transitions, the formation of compounds in many oxidation states due to the relatively low reactivity of unpaired *d* electrons. The incomplete *d* sub-shell can give rise to cations with an incomplete *d* sub-shell.

Transition elements form many paramagnetic (i.e., attracted to an externally applied magnetic field) compounds due to the presence of unpaired *d* and *f* electrons. A few compounds of main group elements are also paramagnetic (e.g., nitric oxide and oxygen).

56. E is correct. An element is a pure chemical substance that consists of a single type of atom, distinguished by its atomic number (Z) for the number of protons.

118 elements have been identified, of which the first 94 occur naturally on Earth.

57. B is correct.

Isotopes are variants of an element which differ in the number of neutrons. All isotopes of the element have the same number of protons and occupy the same position on the periodic table.

Alpha decay results in the loss of two protons.

Beta decay is a type of radioactive decay in which a neutron is transformed into a proton, or a proton is transformed into a neutron.

Since isotopes of the same element have the same number of protons (Z), the number of protons lost by α decay must equal the number gained by β decay.

Therefore, twice as many β decays as α decays occurs for a ratio of 1:2 for α to β decay.

58. B is correct.

Elements are defined by the number of protons (i.e., atomic number).

The isotopes are neutral atoms: # electrons = # protons.

Isotopes are variants of an element which differ in the number of neutrons. All isotopes of the element have the same number of protons and occupy the same position on the periodic table.

Cu has an atomic weight of 63.5 grams. Therefore, the other isotope of Cu must be heavier than the more common ^{63}Cu, and the atomic weight is closer to 65.

59. E is correct.

A cathode ray particle is another name for an electron.

Those particles (i.e., electrons) are attracted to the positively charged cathode, which implies that they are negatively charged.

60. A is correct.

The Pauli exclusion principle is the quantum principle that states that two identical electrons cannot have the same four quantum numbers: the principal quantum number (n), the angular momentum quantum number (l), the magnetic quantum number (m_ℓ) and the spin quantum number (m_s). For two electrons in the same orbital, (n, m_ℓ, and l) the spin quantum number (m_s) must be different, and the electrons must have opposite half-integer spins (i.e., + ½ and –½).

Hund's rule describes that the electrons enter each orbital of a given type singly and with identical spins before any pairing of electrons of the opposite spin occurs within those orbitals.

The Heisenberg's uncertainty principle states that it is impossible to accurately determine both the momentum and the position of an electron simultaneously.

Chapter 2 Explanations: Chemical Bonding

1. D is correct.

The valence shell is the outermost shell (i.e., highest principal quantum number, n) of an atom.

Valence electrons are those electrons of the outermost electron shell that can participate in a chemical bond.

The number of valence electrons for an element can be determined by its group (i.e., vertical column) on the periodic table. Except for the transition metals (i.e., groups 3-12), the group number identifies how many valence electrons are associated with an element: all elements of the same group have the same number of valence electrons.

2. A is correct.

Three degenerate p orbitals exist for an atom with an electron configuration in the second shell or higher. The first shell only has access to s orbitals.

The d orbitals become available from n = 3 (third shell).

3. C is correct.

The valence shell is the outermost shell (i.e., highest principal quantum number, n) of an atom.

Valence electrons are those electrons of the outermost electron shell that can participate in a chemical bond.

The number of valence electrons for an element can be determined by its group (i.e., vertical column) on the periodic table. Except for the transition metals (i.e., groups 3-12), the group number identifies how many valence electrons are associated with an element: all elements of the same group have the same number of valence electrons.

To find the total number of valence electrons in a sulfite ion, SO_3^{2-}, start by adding the valence electrons of each atom:

Sulfur = 6; Oxygen = (6 × 3) = 18

Total = 24

This ion has a net charge of –2, which indicates that it has 2 extra electrons. Therefore, the total number of valence electrons would be 24 + 2 = 26 electrons.

4. E is correct.

London dispersion forces result from the momentary flux of valence electrons and are present in all compounds; they are the attractive forces that hold molecules together.

They are the weakest of all the intermolecular forces, and their strength increases with increasing size (i.e., surface area contact) and polarity of the molecules involved.

5. B is correct.

Each hydroxyl group (alcohol or ~OH) has oxygen with 2 lone pairs and one attached hydrogen.

Therefore, each hydroxyl group can participate in 3 hydrogen bonds:

 5 hydroxyl groups × 3 bonds = 15 hydrogen bonds.

The oxygen of the ether group (C–O–C) in the ring has 2 lone pairs for an additional 2 H–bonds.

6. B is correct.

The valence shell is the outermost shell (i.e., highest principal quantum number, n) of an atom.

Valence electrons are those electrons of the outermost electron shell that can participate in a chemical bond.

The number of valence electrons for an element can be determined by its group (i.e., vertical column) on the periodic table.

Except for the transition metals (i.e., groups 3-12), the group number identifies how many valence electrons are associated with an element: all elements of the same group have the same number of valence electrons.

Lewis dot structure for methane

7. E is correct. In covalent bonds, the electrons can be shared either equally or unequally.

Polar covalent bonded atoms are covalently bonded compounds that involve unequal sharing of electrons due to large electronegativity differences (Pauling units of 0.4 to 1.7) between the atoms.

An example of this is water, where there is a polar covalent bond between oxygen and hydrogen. Water is a polar molecule with the oxygen partial negative while the hydrogens are partial positive.

8. A is correct.

Van der Waals forces involve nonpolar (hydrophobic) molecules, such as hydrocarbons. The van der Waals force is the total of attractive or repulsive forces between molecules, and therefore can be either attractive or repulsive. It can include the force between two permanent dipoles, the force between a permanent dipole and a temporary dipole, or the force between two temporary dipoles.

Hydrogens, bonded directly to F, O or N, participate in hydrogen bonds. The hydrogen is partial positive (i.e., delta plus or $\partial+$) due to the bond to these electronegative atoms. The lone pair of electrons on the F, O or N interacts with the $\partial+$ hydrogen to form a hydrogen bond.

Hydrogen bonds are a type of dipole–dipole and are the strongest intermolecular forces (i.e., between molecules), followed by other types of dipole–dipole, dipole–induced dipole and van der Waals forces (i.e., London dispersion).

9. D is correct.

Representative structures include:

$HNCH_2$: one single and one double bond

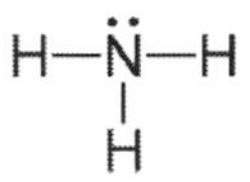

$$H-\overset{\cdot\cdot}{N}-H \\ | \\ H$$

NH_3 : three single bonds

$$H-C\equiv N$$

HCN: one triple bond and one single bond

10. E is correct.

The valence shell is the outermost shell (i.e., highest principal quantum number, n) of an atom.

Valence electrons are those electrons of the outermost electron shell that can participate in a chemical bond.

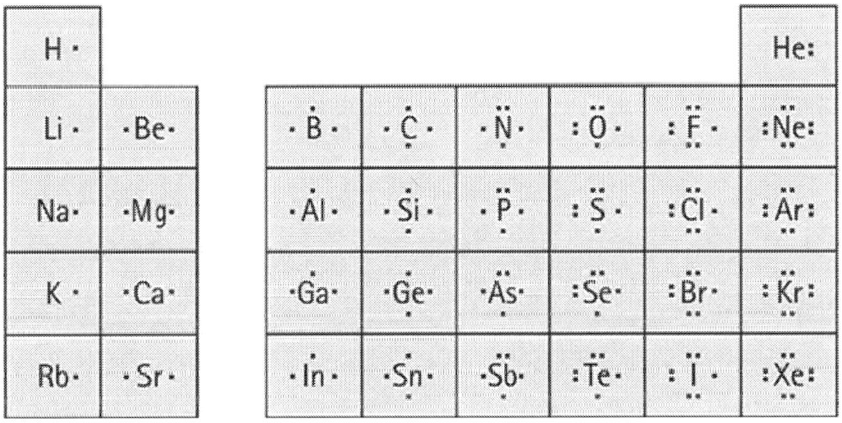

H·							He:
Li·	·Be·	·B·	·Ç·	·N·	:Ö·	:F·	:Ne:
Na·	·Mg·	·Al·	·Si·	·P·	:S·	:Cl·	:Ar:
K·	·Ca·	·Ga·	·Ge·	·As·	:Se·	:Br·	:Kr:
Rb·	·Sr·	·In·	·Sn·	·Sb·	:Te·	:I·	:Xe:

Sample Lewis dot structures for some elements

The number of valence electrons for an element can be determined by its group (i.e., vertical column) on the periodic table.

Except for the transition metals (i.e., groups 3-12), the group number identifies how many valence electrons are associated with an element: all elements of the same group have the same number of valence electrons.

11. B is correct.

The nitrite ion has the chemical formula NO_2^- with the negative charge distributed between the two oxygen atoms.

Two resonance structures of the nitrite ion

12. E is correct. Nitrogen has five valence electrons. In ammonia, nitrogen has three bonds to hydrogen, and a lone pair remains on the central nitrogen atom.

The ammonium ion (NH_4^+) has four hydrogens, and the lone pair of the nitrogen has been used to bond to the H^+ that has added to ammonia.

Formal charge is shown on the ammonium ion

13. A is correct. Electronegativity is a chemical property that describes an atom's tendency to attract electrons to itself.

The most electronegative atom is F, while the least electronegative atom is Fr. The trend for increasing electronegativity within the periodic table is up and toward the right (i.e., fluorine).

14. D is correct. Hydrogen bonds are the strongest intermolecular forces (i.e., between molecules), followed by dipole–dipole, dipole–induced dipole and van der Waals forces (i.e., London dispersion).

London dispersion forces are present in all compounds; they are the attractive forces that hold molecules together. They are the weakest of all the intermolecular forces, and their strength increases with increasing size and polarity of the molecules involved.

15. C is correct. For asymmetrical molecules (e.g., water is bent), use the geometry and difference of electronegativity values between the atoms.

For water, H (2.1 Pauling units) is more electropositive than O (3.5 Pauling units).

For sulfur dioxide, S (2.5 Pauling units) is more electropositive than O (3.5 Pauling units).

The reported dipole moment for water is 1.8 D compared to 1.6 D for sulfur dioxide.

CO_2 does not have any non-bonding electrons on the central carbon atom, and it is symmetrical, so it is non-polar and has zero dipole moment. CCl_4 is symmetrical as a tetrahedron and therefore does not exhibit a net dipole.

CH_4 is symmetrical as a tetrahedron and therefore does not exhibit a net dipole.

16. C is correct. Cohesion is the property of like molecules sticking together. Hydrogen bonds join water molecules.

Adhesion is the attraction between unlike molecules (e.g., the meniscus observed from water molecules adhering to the graduated cylinder).

Polarity is the differences in electronegativity between bonded molecules. Polarity gives rise to the delta plus (on H) and the delta minus (on O), which permits hydrogen bonds to form between water molecules.

17. A is correct. With little or no difference in electronegativity between the elements (i.e., Pauling units < 0.4), it is a nonpolar covalent bond, whereby the electrons are shared between the two bonding atoms.

Among the answer choices, the atoms of H, C and O are closest in magnitude for Pauling units for electronegativity.

18. D is correct.

Positively charged nuclei repel each other while each attracts the bonding electrons. These opposing forces reach equilibrium at the bond length.

19. C is correct.

In a carbonate ion (CO_3^{2-}), the carbon atom is bonded to 3 oxygen atoms. Two of those bonds are single covalent bonds, and the oxygen atoms each have an extra (third) lone pair of electrons, which imparts a negative formal charge.

Three resonance structures for the carbonate ion CO_3^{2-}

The remaining oxygen has a double bond with carbon.

20. D is correct.

A dipole is a separation of full (or partial) positive and negative charges due to differences in electronegativity of atoms.

21. C is correct.

Ionic bonds involve the transfer of an electron from the electropositive element (along the left-hand column/group) to the electronegative atom (along the right-hand column/groups) on the periodic table. Ca is a group II element with 2 electrons in its valence shell.

I is a group VII element with 7 electrons in its valence shell.

Ca becomes Ca^{2+}, and each of the two electrons is joined to I, which becomes I^-.

22. B is correct.

An atom with 4 valence electrons can make a maximum of 4 bonds. 1 double and 1 triple bond equals 5 bonds, which exceeds the maximum allowable bonds.

23. D is correct.
Water molecules stick to each other (i.e., cohesion) due to the collective action of hydrogen bonds between individual water molecules. These hydrogen bonds are constantly breaking and reforming, a large portion of the molecules are held together by these bonds.

Water also sticks to surfaces (i.e., adhesion) because of water's polarity. On an extremely smooth surface (e.g., glass) the water may form a thin film because the molecular forces between glass and water molecules (adhesive forces) are stronger than the cohesive forces between the water molecules.

24. D is correct.

Hydrogen bonds are the strongest intermolecular forces (i.e., between molecules), followed by dipole–dipole, dipole–induced dipole and van der Waals forces (i.e., London dispersion).

When ionic compounds are dissolved, each ion is surrounded by more than one water molecule. The combined force ion–dipole interactions of several water molecules is stronger than a single ionic bond.

25. E is correct.

Hydrogens, bonded directly to F, O or N, participate in hydrogen bonds. The hydrogen is partial positive (i.e., delta plus or ∂+) due to the bond to these electronegative atoms. The lone pair of electrons on the F, O or N interacts with the ∂+ hydrogen to form a hydrogen bond.

The two lone pairs of electrons on the oxygen atom can each participate as a hydrogen bond acceptor. The molecule does not have hydrogen bonded directly to an electronegative atom (F, O or N) and cannot be a hydrogen bond donor.

26. A is correct. Water is a bent molecule with a partial negative charge on the oxygen and a partial positive charge on each hydrogen.

Therefore, the water molecule exists as a dipole. The Na^+ is an ion attracted to the partial negative charge on the oxygen in the water molecule.

27. C is correct.

The molecule H_2CO (formaldehyde) is shown below and has one C=O bond and two C–H bonds.

 The electronegative oxygen pulls electron density away from the carbon atom and creates a net dipole towards the oxygen, resulting in a polar covalent bond. The electronegativity values of carbon and each hydrogen are similar and result in a covalent bond (i.e., about equal sharing of bonded electrons).

28. D is correct.

Group IA elements (e.g., Li, Na, and K) tend to lose 1 electron to achieve a complete octet to be cations with a +1 charge.

Group IIA elements (e.g., Mg and Ca) tend to lose 2 electrons to achieve a complete octet to be cations with a +2 charge.

Group VIIA elements (halogens such as F, CL, Br and I) tend to gain 1 electron to achieve a complete octet to be anions with a –1 charge.

29. B is correct.

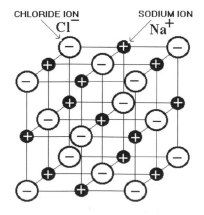

The lattice structure of sodium chloride

30. E is correct. Each positively charged nuclei attracts the bonding electrons.

31. E is correct.

Electronegativity is a measure of how strongly an element attracts electrons within a bond.

Electronegativity is the relative attraction of the nucleus for bonding electrons. It increases from left to right (i.e., periods) and from bottom to top along a group (like the trend for ionization energy). The most electronegative atom is F, while the least electronegative atom is Fr.

The greater the difference in electronegativity between two atoms in a compound, the more polar of a bond these atoms form whereby the atom with the higher electronegativity is the partial (delta) negative end of the dipole.

32. A is correct.

Hydrogen bonds are the strongest intermolecular forces (i.e., between molecules), followed by dipole–dipole, dipole–induced dipole and van der Waals forces (i.e., London dispersion).

Hydrogens, bonded directly to F, O or N, participate in hydrogen bonds. H bonding is a polar interaction involving hydrogen forming bonds to the electronegative atoms such of F, O or N, which accounts for the high boiling points of water. The hydrogen is partial positive (i.e., delta plus or $\partial +$) due to the bond to these electronegative atoms.

The lone pair of electrons on the F, O or N interacts with the $\partial +$ hydrogen to form a hydrogen bond. Polar molecules have high boiling points because of polar interaction.

Molecular geometry of H_2S

H_2S is a polar molecule but does not form hydrogen bonds; it forms dipole–dipole interactions.

33. D is correct.

With a total of 4 electron pairs, the starting shape of this element is tetrahedral.

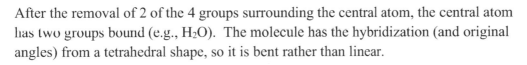

After the removal of 2 of the 4 groups surrounding the central atom, the central atom has two groups bound (e.g., H_2O). The molecule has the hybridization (and original angles) from a tetrahedral shape, so it is bent rather than linear.

34. D is correct.

Salt crystals are held together by ionic bonds. Salts are composed of cations and anions and are electrically neutral. When salts are dissolved in solution, they separate into their constituent ions by breaking of noncovalent interactions.

Water: the hydrogen atoms in the molecule are covalently bonded to the oxygen atom.

Hydrogen peroxide: the molecule has one more oxygen atom than water molecule does, and is also held together by covalent bonds.

Ester (RCOOR'): undergo hydrolysis and breaks covalent bonds to separate into its constituent carboxylic acid (RCOOH) and alcohol (ROH).

35. B is correct. An ionic compound consists of a metal ion and a nonmetal ion.

Ionic bonds are formed between elements with an electronegativity difference greater than 1.7 Pauling units (e.g., a metal atom and a non-metal atom).

(K and I) form ionic bonds because K is a metal and I is a nonmetal.

(C and Cl) and (H and O) only have nonmetals, while (Fe and Mg) has only metals.

(Ga and Si) has a metal (Ga) and a metalloid (Si); they *might* form weak ionic bonds.

36. A is correct. A coordinate bond is a covalent bond (i.e., shared pair of electrons) in which both electrons come from the same atom.

The lone pair of the nitrogen is donated to form the fourth N–H bond

37. B is correct. Dipole moment depends on the overall shape of the molecule, the length of the bond, and whether the electrons are pulled to one side of the bond (or the molecule overall).

For a large dipole moment, one element pulls electrons more strongly (i.e., differences in electronegativity).

Electronegativity is a measure of how strongly an element attracts electrons within a bond.

Electronegativity is the relative attraction of the nucleus for bonding electrons. It increases from left to right (i.e., periods) and from bottom to top along a group (like the trend for ionization energy). The most electronegative atom is F, while the least electronegative atom is Fr.

The greater the difference in electronegativity between two atoms in a compound, the more polar of a bond these atoms form whereby the atom with the higher electronegativity is the partial (delta) negative end of the dipole.

38. A is correct. The valence shell is the outermost shell (i.e., highest principal quantum number, n) of an atom. The noble gas configuration refers to eight electrons in the atom's outermost valence shell, referred to as a complete octet.

Depending on how many electrons it starts with, an atom may have to lose, gain or share an electron to obtain the noble gas configuration.

39. E is correct.

The bond between the oxygens is nonpolar, while the bonds between the oxygens and hydrogens are polar (due to the differences in electronegativity).

Line bond structure of H_2O_2 (hydrogen peroxide) with lone pairs shown

40. D is correct.

HBr experiences dipole–dipole interactions due to the electronegativity difference resulting in a partial negative charge on bromine and a partial positive charge on hydrogen.

41. C is correct.

An ion is an atom (or a molecule) in which the total number of electrons is not equal to the total number of protons. Therefore, the atom (or molecule) has a net positive or negative electrical charge.

If a neutral atom loses one or more electrons, it has a net positive charge (i.e., cation).

If a neutral atom gains one or more electrons, it has a net negative charge (i.e., anion). Aluminum is a group III atom and has proportionally more protons per electron once the cation forms.

All other elements listed are from group I or II.

42. A is correct.

Dipole–dipole (e.g., $CH_3Cl...CH_3Cl$) attraction occurs between neutral molecules, while ion–dipole interaction involves dipole interactions with charged ions (e.g., $CH_3Cl...^-OOCCH_3$).

Hydrogen bonds are the strongest intermolecular forces (i.e., between molecules), followed by dipole dipole, dipole–induced dipole and van der Waals forces (i.e., London dispersion).

43. A is correct.

The phrase "from its elements" in the question stem implies the need to create the formation reaction of the compound from its elements.

Chemical equation:

$$3\ Na^+ + N^{3-} \rightarrow Na_3N$$

Each sodium loses one electron to form Na^+ ions.

Nitrogen gains 3 electrons to form the N^{3-} ion.

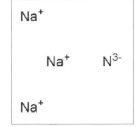

Schematic of an ionic compound

44. D is correct.

The valence shell is the outermost shell (i.e., highest principal quantum number, *n*) of an atom.

Valence electrons are those electrons of the outermost electron shell that can participate in a chemical bond.

The number of valence electrons for a neutral element can be determined by its group (i.e., vertical column) on the periodic table.

Except for the transition metals (i.e., groups 3-12), the group number identifies how many valence electrons are associated with a element: all elements of the same group have the same number of valence electrons.

Lewis dot structures show the valence electrons of an individual atom as dots around the symbol of the element. Non-valence electrons (i.e., inner shell electrons) are not represented in Lewis structures.

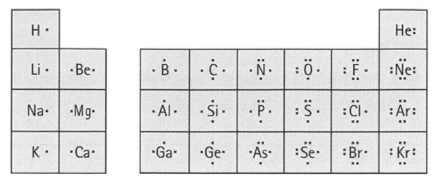

Sample Lewis dot structures for some neutral elements

Mg^{2+} a total of ten electrons, but zero valance (outer shell) electrons. The valence shell (i.e., 3s subshell) has zero electrons, and therefore there are no dots shown in the Lewis dot structure: Mg^{2+}

S^{2-} has eight valence electrons (same electronic configuration as Ar).

Ga^+ has two valence electrons (same electronic configuration as Ca).

Ar^+ has seven valence electrons (same electronic configuration as Cl).

F^- has eight valence electrons (same electronic configuration as Ne). Lewis dot structure for F^- is shown as:

45. B is correct.

The octet rule states that atoms of main-group elements tend to combine in a way that each atom has eight electrons in its valence shell.

46. D is correct.

An ionic compound consists of a metal ion and a nonmetal ion.

Ionic bonds are formed between elements with an electronegativity difference greater than 1.7 Pauling units (e.g., a metal atom and a non-metal atom).

The charge on bicarbonate ion (HCO_3) is −1, while the charge on Mg is +2.

The proper formula is $Mg(HCO_3)_2$

47. C is correct.

Lattice: crystalline structure – consists of unit cells

Unit cell: smallest unit of solid crystalline pattern

Covalent unit and *ionic unit* are not valid terms.

48. D is correct.

The formula to calculate dipole moment:

$\mu = qr$

where μ is dipole moment (coulomb meter or C·m), q is a charge (coulomb or C), and r is radius (meter or m).

Convert the unit of dipole moment from Debye to C·m:

$0.16 \times 3.34 \times 10^{-30} = 5.34 \times 10^{-31}$ C·m

Convert the unit of radius to meter:

$115 \text{ pm} \times 1 \times 10^{-12} \text{ m/pm} = 115 \times 10^{-12} \text{ m}$

Rearrange the dipole moment equation to solve for q:

$q = \mu / r$

$q = (5.34 \times 10^{-31} \text{ C·m}) / (115 \times 10^{-12} \text{ m})$

$q = 4.65 \times 10^{-21} \text{ C}$

Express the charge in terms of electron charge (e).

$(4.65 \times 10^{-21} \text{ C}) / (1.602 \times 10^{-19} \text{ C/e}) = 0.029 \text{ e}$

In this NO molecule, oxygen is the more electronegative atom.

Therefore, the charge experienced by the oxygen atom is negative: $-0.029e$.

49. A is correct.

The greater the difference in electronegativity between two atoms in a compound, the more polar of a bond these atoms form, whereby the atom with the higher electronegativity is the partial (delta) negative end of the dipole.

50. C is correct.

Hydrogen bonds are the strongest intermolecular forces (i.e., between molecules), followed by dipole–dipole, dipole–induced dipole and van der Waals forces (i.e., London dispersion).

Hydrogen is a very electropositive element, and O is a very electronegative element. Therefore, these elements will be attracted to each other, both within the same water molecule and between water molecules.

Ionic or covalent bonding can only form within a molecule and not between adjacent molecules.

51. E is correct.

In a compound, the sum of ionic charges must equal to zero.

For the charges of K^+ and CO_3^{2-} to even out, there must be 2 K^+ ions for every CO_3^{2-} ion.

The formula of this balanced molecule is K_2CO_3.

52. E is correct.

Lewis acids are defined as electron pair acceptors, whereas Lewis bases are electron pair donors.

Boron has an atomic number of five and has a vacant $2p$ orbital to accept electrons.

53. D is correct.

CH_3SH experiences dipole–dipole interactions due to the electronegativity difference resulting in a partial negative charge on sulfur and a partial positive charge on hydrogen.

CH_3CH_2OH experiences dipole–dipole interactions (due to the electronegativity difference resulting in a partial negative charge on oxygen and a partial positive charge on hydrogen.

This example is a type of dipole–dipole known as hydrogen bonding (when hydrogen is bonded directly to fluorine, oxygen or nitrogen).

54. A is correct.

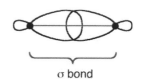

In carbon–carbon double bonds, there is an overlap of sp^2 orbitals and a p orbital on the adjacent carbon atoms. The sp^2 orbitals overlap head-to-head as a *sigma* (σ) bond, whereas the p orbitals overlap sideways as a *pi* (π) bond.

Sigma bond formation showing electron density along the internuclear axis

Bond lengths and strengths (σ or π) depends on the size and shape of the atomic orbitals and the density of these orbitals to overlap effectively.

The σ bonds are stronger than π bonds because head-to-head orbital overlap involves more shared electron density than sideways overlap. The σ bonds formed from two $2s$ orbitals are shorter than those formed from two $2p$ orbitals or two $3s$ orbitals.

Two pi orbitals showing the pi bond formation during sideways overlap – note the absence of electron density (i.e., node) along the internuclear axis.

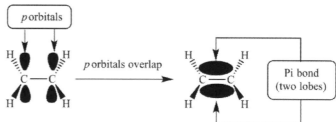

Carbon, oxygen and nitrogen are in the second period ($n = 2$), while sulfur (S), phosphorus (P) and silicon (Si) are in the third period. Therefore, S, P and Si use $3p$ orbitals to form π bonds, while C, N and O use $2p$ orbitals. The $3p$ orbitals are much larger than $2p$ orbitals, and therefore there is a reduced probability for an overlap of the $2p$ orbital of C and the $3p$ orbital of S, P and Si.

B: S, P, and Si can hybridize, but these elements can combine s and p orbitals and (unlike C, O and N) have d orbitals.

C: S, P and Si (in their ground state electron configurations) have partially occupied p orbitals which form bonds.

D: carbon combines with elements below the second row of the periodic table. For example, carbon forms bonds with higher principal quantum number ($n > 2$) halogens (e.g., F, Cl, Br and I).

55. C is correct.

Hydrogen bonds are the strongest intermolecular forces (i.e., between molecules), followed by dipole–dipole, dipole–induced dipole and van der Waals forces (i.e., London dispersion).

Larger atoms have more electrons, which means that they can exert stronger induced dipole forces compared to smaller atoms.

Bromine is located under chlorine on the periodic table, which means it has more electrons and stronger induced dipole forces.

56. A is correct.

Hydrogen bonds are the strongest intermolecular forces (i.e., between molecules), followed by dipole–dipole, dipole–induced dipole and van der Waals forces (i.e., London dispersion).

Hydrogens, bonded directly to F, O or N, participate in hydrogen bonds.

The hydrogen is partially positive (i.e., delta plus: $\partial+$) due to the bond to these electronegative atoms.

The lone pair of electrons on the F, O or N interacts with the partial positive ($\partial+$) hydrogen to form a hydrogen bond.

When –NH or –OH groups are present in a molecule, they form hydrogen bonds with other molecules.

Hydrogen bonding is the strongest intermolecular force, and it is the major intermolecular force in this substance.

57. B is correct.

Potassium oxide (K_2O) contains a metal and nonmetal, which form a salt.

Salts contain ionic bonds and dissociate in aqueous solutions and therefore are strong electrolytes.

A polyatomic (i.e., molecular) ion is a charged chemical species composed of two or more atoms covalently bonded or composed of a metal complex acting as a single unit.

An example of a polyatomic ion is the hydroxide ion (^-OH) consisting of one oxygen atom and one hydrogen atom; hydroxide has a formal charge of -1.

A polyatomic ion does bond with other ions.

A polyatomic ion has various charges.

A polyatomic ion might contain only metals or nonmetals.

A polyatomic ion is not neutral.

oxidation state	-1	$+1$	$+3$	$+5$	$+7$
anion name	chloride	hypochlorite	chlorite	chlorate	perchlorate
formula	Cl^-	ClO^-	ClO_2^-	ClO_3^-	ClO_4^-

58. B is correct.

Nitrogen (NH₃) is neutral with three bonds.

Nitrogen is negative with two bonds (⁻NH₂)

Nitrogen is and positive with four bonds (⁺NH₄)

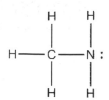

Line bond structure of
methylamine with the lone pair on nitrogen shown

59. B is correct.

Sulfide ion is S^{2-}.

Hydrogen sulfide (i.e., sewer gas) is H_2S.

Hydrosulfide (bisulfide) ion is HS^-.

Sulfite ion is the conjugate base of bisulfite and has the molecular formula of SO_3^{2-}

Sulfur (S) is a chemical element with an atomic number of 16.

Sulfate ion is polyatomic anion (i.e., two or more atoms covalently bonded or metal complex) with the molecular formula of SO_4^{2-}

Sulfur acid (HSO_3^-) results from the combination of sulfur dioxide (SO_2) and H_2O.

60. B is correct.

If the charge of O is −1, the proper formula of its compound with K (+1) should be KO.

Chapter 3 Explanations: Phases and Phase Equilibria

1. A is correct.

Solids, liquids, and gases all have a vapor pressure, which increases from solid to gas.

Vapor pressure is the pressure exerted by a vapor in equilibrium with its condensed phases (i.e., solid or liquid) in a closed system, at a given temperature.

Vapor pressure is a colligative property of a substance and depends only on the number of solutes present, not on their identity.

2. C is correct.

Charles' law (i.e., the law of volumes) explains how, at constant pressure, gases behave when the temperature changes:

$$V \alpha T$$

or

$$V / T = \text{constant}$$

or

$$(V_1 / T_1) = (V_2 / T_2)$$

Volume and temperature are proportional.

Doubling the temperature at constant pressure doubles the volume.

3. C is correct.

Colligative properties include: lowering of vapor pressure, the elevation of boiling point, depression of freezing point, and increased osmotic pressure.

Addition of solute to a pure solvent lowers the vapor pressure of the solvent; therefore, a higher temperature is required to bring the vapor pressure of the solution in an open container up to the atmospheric pressure. This increases the boiling point.

Because adding solute lowers the vapor pressure, the freezing point of the solution decreases (e.g., automobile antifreeze).

4. A is correct.

At a pressure and temperature corresponding to the triple point (point D on the graph) of a substance, all three states (gas, liquid and solid) exist in equilibrium.

The critical point (point E on the graph) is the end point of the phase equilibrium curve where the liquid and its vapor become indistinguishable.

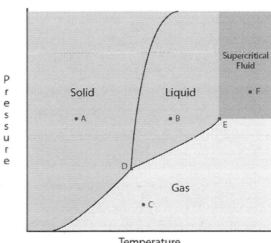

5. A is correct.

In the van der Waals equation, *a* is the negative deviation due to attractive forces and *b* is the positive deviation due to molecular volume.

6. B is correct.

R is the symbol for the ideal gas constant.

R is expressed in (L × atm) / mole × K and the value = 0.0821.

Convert to different units (torr and mL)

0.0821[(L × atm) / (mole × K)] × (760 torr/atm) × (1,000 mL/L)

R = 62,396 (torr × mL) / mole × K

7. B is correct.

Ideal gas law:

PV = nRT

where P is pressure, V is volume, n is the number of molecules, R is the ideal gas constant, and T is the temperature of the gas.

R and n are constant.

From this equation, if both pressure and temperature are halved, there would be no effect on the volume.

8. B is correct.

Kinetic molecular theory of gas molecules states that the average kinetic energy per molecule in a system is proportional to the temperature of the gas.

Since it is given that containers X and Y are both at the same temperature and pressure, then molecules of both gases must possess the same amount of average kinetic energy.

9. E is correct.

A Barometer and manometer are used to measure pressure.

Barometers are designed to measure atmospheric pressure, while a manometer can measure the pressure that is lower than atmospheric pressure.

A manometer has both ends of the tube open to the outside (while some may have one end closed), whereas a barometer is a type of closed-end manometer with one end of the glass tube closed and sealed with a vacuum.

The atmospheric pressure is 760 mmHg, so the barometer should be able to accommodate that.

10. D is correct.

Vapor pressure is the pressure exerted by a vapor in equilibrium with its condensed phases (i.e., solid or liquid) in a closed system, at a given temperature.

Raoult's law states that the partial vapor pressure of each component of an ideal mixture of liquids is equal to the vapor pressure of the pure component multiplied by its mole fraction in the mixture.

In exothermic reactions, the vapor pressure deviates negatively for Raoult's law.

Depending on the ratios of the liquids in a solution, the vapor pressure could be lower than either or just lower than X, because X is a higher boiling point, thus a lower vapor pressure.

The boiling point increases from adding Y to the mixture because the vapor pressure decreases.

11. C is correct.

The molecules of an ideal gas do not occupy a significant amount of space and exert no intermolecular forces, while the molecules of a real gas do occupy space and do exert (weak attractive) intermolecular forces.

However, both an ideal gas and a real gas have pressure, which is created from molecular collisions with the walls of the container.

12. A is correct.

Boyle's law (i.e., pressure-volume law) states that pressure and volume are inversely proportional:

$$(P_1 V_1) = (P_2 V_2)$$

Solve for the final pressure:

$$P_2 = (P_1 V_1) / V_2$$

$$P_2 = [(0.950 \text{ atm}) \times (2.75 \text{ L})] / (0.450 \text{ L})$$

$$P_2 = 5.80 \text{ atm}$$

13. C is correct.

Ideal gas law:

$$PV = nRT$$

where P is pressure, V is volume, n is the number of molecules, R is the ideal gas constant and T is the temperature of the gas.

R and n are constant. If T is constant, the equation becomes $PV = $ constant.

They are inversely proportional: if one of the values is reduced, the other increases.

14. C is correct.

Ideal gas law: $PV = nRT$

from which simpler gas laws such as Boyle's, Charles' and Avogadro's laws are derived.

The value of n and R are constant.

The common format of the combined gas law:

$$(P_1V_1) / T_1 = (P_2V_2) / T_2$$

Try modifying the equations to recreate all the formats of the equation provided by the problem.

$T_2 = T_1 \times P_1 / P_2 \times V_2 / V_1$ should be written as $T_2 = T_1 \times V_1/V_2 \times P_1/P_2$

15. C is correct.

Intermolecular forces act between neighboring molecules. Examples include hydrogen bonding, dipole-dipole, dipole-induced dipole, and van der Waals (i.e., London dispersion) forces.

A dipole-dipole attraction involves asymmetric, polar molecules (based on differences in electronegativity between atoms) that create a dipole moment (i.e., a net vector indicating the force).

Sulfur dioxide with an indicated bond angle

16. C is correct.

Increasing the pressure of the gas above the liquid puts stress on the equilibrium of the system. Gas molecules start to collide with the liquid surface more often, which increases the rate of gas molecules entering the solution, thus increasing the solubility.

17. E is correct.

Avogadro's law states the correlation between volume and moles (n).

Avogadro's law is an experimental gas law relating the volume of a gas to the amount of substance of gas present. A modern statement of Avogadro's law is:

At the same pressure and temperature, equal volumes of all gases have the same number of molecules.

$$V \alpha n$$

or

$$V / n = k$$

where V is the volume of the gas, n is the number of moles of the gas and k is a constant equal to RT/P (where R is the universal gas constant, T is the temperature in Kelvin and P is the pressure).

For comparing the same substance under two sets of conditions, the law is expressed as:

$$V_1 / n_1 = V_2 / n_2$$

18. E is correct.

Colligative properties of solutions depend on the ratio of the number of solute particles to the number of solvent molecules in a solution, and not on the type of chemical species present.

Colligative properties include: lowering of vapor pressure, the elevation of boiling point, depression of freezing point, and increased osmotic pressure.

Boiling point (BP) elevation:

$$\Delta BP = iKm$$

where i = the number of particles produced when the solute dissociates, K = boiling elevation constant and m = molality (moles/kg solvent).

In this problem, acid molality is not known.

19. A is correct.

An ideal gas has no intermolecular forces, indicating that its molecules have no attraction to each other. The molecules of a real gas, however, do have intermolecular forces, although these forces are extremely weak.

Therefore, the molecules of a real gas are slightly attracted to one another, although the attraction is nowhere near as strong as the attraction in liquids and solids.

20. E is correct.

Standard temperature and pressure (STP) has a temperature of 273.15 K (0 °C, 32 °F) and a pressure of 10^5 Pa (100 kPa, 750.06 mmHg, 1 bar, 14.504 psi, 0.98692 atm).

The mm of Hg was defined as the pressure generated by a column of mercury one millimeter high. The pressure of mercury depends on temperature and gravity.

This variation in mmHg and torr is a difference in units of about 0.000015%.

In general,

1 torr = 1 mm of Hg = 0.0013158 atm.

750.06 mmHg = 0.98692 atm.

21. D is correct.

At lower temperatures, the potential energy due to the intermolecular forces are more significant compared to the kinetic energy; this causes the pressure to be reduced because the gas molecules are attracted to each other.

22. D is correct.

Dalton's law (i.e., the law of partial pressures) states that *the pressure exerted by a mixture of gases is equal to the sum of the individual gas pressures*.

The pressure due to N_2 and CO_2:

(320 torr + 240 torr) = 560 torr

The partial pressure of O_2 is:

740 torr – 560 torr = 180 torr

180 torr / 740 torr = 24%

23. A is correct.

Ideal gas law:

$$PV = nRT$$

where P is pressure, V is volume, n is the number of molecules, R is the ideal gas constant, and T is the temperature of the gas.

If the volume is reduced by ½, the number of moles is reduced by ½. The pressure is reduced to 90%, so the number of moles is reduced by 90%. Therefore, the total reduction in moles is (½ × 90%) = 45%.

Mass is proportional to the number of moles for a given gas so that the mass reduction can be calculated directly:

New mass is 45% of 40 grams = (0.45 × 40 g) = 18 grams

24. B is correct.

The molecules of an ideal gas exert no attractive forces.

Therefore, a real gas behaves most nearly like an ideal gas when it is at high temperature and low pressure because under these conditions the molecules are far apart from each other and exert little or no attractive forces on each other.

25. E is correct.

Hydroxyl (~OH) groups greatly increase the boiling point because they form hydrogen bonds with ~OH groups of neighboring molecules.

Hydrocarbons are nonpolar molecules, which means that the dominant intermolecular force is London dispersion. This force gets stronger as the number of atoms in each molecule increases. The stronger force increases the boiling point.

Branching of the hydrocarbon also affects the boiling point. Straight molecules have slightly higher boiling points than branched molecules with the same number of atoms. The reason is that straight molecules can align parallel against each other and all atoms in the molecules are involved in the London dispersion forces.

Another factor is the presence of other heteroatoms (i.e., atoms other than carbon and hydrogen). For example, the electronegative oxygen atom between carbon groups or in an ether (C–O–C) slightly increases the boiling point.

26. A is correct.

Kinetic theory explains the macroscopic properties of gases (e.g., temperature, volume, and pressure) by their molecular composition and motion.

The gas pressure is due to the collisions on the walls of a container from molecules moving at different velocities.

Temperature = $\frac{1}{2}mv^2$

27. B is correct.

Methanol (CH_3OH) is alcohol that participates in hydrogen bonding.

Therefore, this gas experiences the strongest intermolecular forces.

28. D is correct.

Density = mass / volume

Gas molecules have a large amount of space between them; therefore, they can be pushed together, and thus, gases are very compressible. Because there is such a large amount of space between each molecule in a gas, the extent to which the gas molecules can be pushed together is much greater than the extent to which liquid molecules can be pushed together.

Therefore, gases have greater compressibility than liquids.

Gas molecules are further apart than liquid molecules, which is why gases have a smaller density.

29. C is correct.

Vapor pressure is the pressure exerted by a vapor in equilibrium with its condensed phases (i.e., solid or liquid) in a closed system, at a given temperature.

Vapor pressure is inversely correlated with the strength of the intermolecular force.

With stronger intermolecular forces, the molecules are more likely to stick together in the liquid form, and fewer of them participate in the liquid-vapor equilibrium.

The vapor pressure of a liquid decreases when a nonvolatile substance is dissolved into a liquid.

The decrease in the vapor pressure of a substance is proportional to the number of moles of the solute dissolved in a definite weight of the solvent. This is known as Raoult's law.

30. B is correct.

Dalton's law (i.e., the law of partial pressures) states that *the pressure exerted by a mixture of gases is equal to the sum of the individual gas pressures.* It is an empirical law that was observed by English chemist John Dalton and is related to the ideal gas laws.

31. E is correct.

Ideal gas law:

$$PV = nRT$$

where P is pressure, V is volume, n is the number of molecules, R is the ideal gas constant, and T is the temperature of the gas.

At STP (standard conditions for temperature and pressure), it is known that the pressure and temperature for all three flasks are the same. It is also known that the volume is the same in each case – 2.0 L.

Therefore, since R is a constant, the number of molecules "n" must be the same for the ideal gas law to hold.

32. A is correct.

Hydrogens, bonded directly to F, O or N, participate in hydrogen bonds. The hydrogen is partially positive (i.e., delta plus: $\partial+$) due to the bond to these electronegative atoms. The lone pair of electrons on the F, O or N interacts with the partial positive ($\partial+$) hydrogen to form a hydrogen bond.

D: the hydrogen on the methyl carbon and that carbon is not attached to N, O, or F.

Therefore, that hydrogen can't form a hydrogen bond, even though there is available oxygen on the other methanol to form a hydrogen bond.

33. C is correct.

The balanced chemical equation:

$N_2 + 3\ H_2 \rightarrow 2\ NH_3$

Use the balanced coefficients from the written equation, apply dimensional analysis to solve for the volume of H_2 needed to produce 12.5 L NH_3:

$V_{H2} = V_{NH3} \times$ (mol H_2 / mol NH_3)

$V_{H2} = (12.5\ L) \times (3\ mol\ /\ 2\ mol)$

$V_{H2} = 18.8\ L$

34. C is correct.

Dalton's law (i.e., the law of partial pressures) states that *the pressure exerted by a mixture of gases is equal to the sum of the individual gas pressures*.

Convert the masses of the gases into moles:

Moles of O_2:

16 g of O_2 ÷ 32 g/mole = 0.5 mole

Moles of N_2:

14 g of N_2 ÷ 28 g/mole = 0.5 mole

Mole of CO_2:

88 g of CO_2 ÷ 44 g/mole = 2 moles

Total moles:

(0.5 mol + 0.5 mole + 2 mol) = 3 moles

The total pressure of 1 atm (or 760 mmHg) has 38 mmHg (1 torr = 1 mmHg) contributed as H_2O vapor.

The partial pressure of CO_2:

mole fraction × (total pressure of the gas mixture − H_2O vapor)

(2 moles CO_2 / 3 moles total gas)] × (760 mmHg − 38 mmHg)

partial pressure of CO_2 = 481 mmHg

35. E is correct.

Colligative properties are properties of solutions that depend on the ratio of the number of solute particles to the number of solvent molecules in a solution, and not on the type of chemical species present.

Colligative properties include: lowering of vapor pressure, the elevation of boiling point, depression of freezing point, and increased osmotic pressure. Dissolving a solute into a solvent alters the solvent's freezing point, melting point, boiling point, and vapor pressure.

36. B is correct.

Boyle's law (i.e., pressure-volume law) states that pressure and volume are inversely proportional:

$$(P_1V_1) = (P_2V_2)$$

or

$$P \times V = \text{constant}$$

If the volume of a gas increases, its pressure decreases proportionally.

37. A is correct. Standard temperature and pressure (STP) has a temperature of 273.15 K (0 °C, 32 °F) and a pressure of 10^5 Pa (100 kPa, 750.06 mmHg, 1 bar, 14.504 psi, 0.98692 atm).

The mm of Hg was defined as the pressure generated by a column of mercury one millimeter high. The pressure of mercury depends on temperature and gravity.

This variation in mmHg and torr is a difference in units of about 0.000015%.

In general,

$$1 \text{ torr} = 1 \text{ mm of Hg} = 0.0013158 \text{ atm.}$$

$$750.06 \text{ mmHg} = 0.98692 \text{ atm.}$$

38. C is correct. Intermolecular forces act between neighboring molecules. Examples include hydrogen bonding, dipole-dipole, dipole-induced dipole, and van der Waals (i.e., London dispersion) forces.

Stronger force results in a higher boiling point.

CH_3COOH is a carboxylic acid that can form two hydrogen bonds. Therefore, it has the highest boiling point.

Ethanoic acid with the two hydrogen bonds indicated on the structure

39. C is correct.

Ideal gas law: $PV = nRT$

where P is pressure, V is volume, n is the number of molecules, R is the ideal gas constant, and T is the temperature of the gas.

Set the initial and final P, V and T conditions equal:

$$(P_1V_1 / T_1) = (P_2V_2 / T_2)$$

Solve for the final volume of N_2:

$$(P_2V_2 / T_2) = (P_1V_1 / T_1)$$

$$V_2 = (T_2\, P_1V_1) / (P_2T_1)$$

$$V_2 = [(295\ K) \times (750.06\ mmHg) \times (0.190\ L\ N_2)] / [(660\ mmHg) \times (298.15\ K)]$$

$$V_2 = 0.214\ L$$

40. B is correct.

Volatility is the tendency of a substance to vaporize (phase change from liquid to vapor).

Volatility is directly related to a substance's vapor pressure. At a given temperature, a substance with higher vapor pressure vaporizes more readily than a substance with lower vapor pressure.

Molecules with weak intermolecular attraction are able to increase their kinetic energy with the transfer of less heat due to a smaller molecular mass. The increase in kinetic energy is required for individual molecules to move from the liquid to the gaseous phase.

41. B is correct. Barometers and manometers are used to measure pressure.

Barometers are designed to measure atmospheric pressure, while a manometer can measure the pressure that is lower than atmospheric pressure.

A manometer has both ends of the tube open to the outside (while some may have one end closed), whereas a barometer is a type of closed-end manometer with one end of the glass tube closed and sealed with a vacuum. The difference in mercury height on both necks indicates the capacity of a manometer.

$$820\ mm - 160\ mm = 660\ mm$$

Historically, the pressure unit of torr is set to equal 1 mmHg or the rise/dip of 1 mm of mercury in a manometer.

Because the manometer uses mercury, the height difference (660 mm) is equal to its measuring capacity in torr (660 torr).

42. C is correct. The conditions of the ideal gases are the same, so the number of moles (i.e., molecules) is equal.

At STP, the temperature is the same, so the kinetic energy of the molecules is the same.

However, the molar mass of oxygen and nitrogen are different. Therefore, the density is different.

43. A is correct. Vapor pressure is the pressure exerted by a vapor in equilibrium with its condensed phases (i.e., solid or liquid) in a closed system, at a given temperature.

The compound exists as a liquid if the external pressure > compound's vapor pressure.

A substance boils when vapor pressure = external pressure.

44. B is correct. Sublimation is the direct change of state from a solid to a gas, skipping the intermediate liquid phase.

An example of a compound that undergoes sublimation is solid carbon dioxide (i.e., dry ice).

CO_2 changes phases from solid to gas (i.e., bypasses the liquid phase) and is often used as a cooling agent.

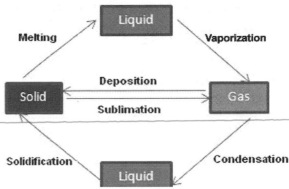

Interconversion of states of matter

45. B is correct. Graham's law of effusion states that the rate of effusion (i.e., escaping through a small hole) of a gas is inversely proportional to the square root of the molar mass of its particles.

Rate 1 / Rate 2 = √(molar mass gas 2 / molar mass gas 1)

The diffusion rate is the inverse root of the molecular weights of the gases.

Therefore, the rate of effusion is:

O_2 / H_2 = √(2 / 32)

rate of diffusion = 1 : 4

46. B is correct. To calculate the number of molecules, calculate moles of gas using the ideal gas law:

PV = nRT

n = PV / RT

Because the gas constant R is in L·atm K^{-1} mol^{-1}, pressure must be converted into atm:

320 mmHg × (1 / 760 atm/mmHg) = 320 mmHg / 760 atm

(Leave it in this fraction form because the answer choices are in this format.)

Convert the temperature to Kelvin:

10 °C + 273 = 283 K

Substitute those values into the ideal gas equation:

n = PV / RT

n = (320 mmHg / 760 atm) × 6 L / (0.0821 L·atm K^{-1} mol^{-1} × 283 K)

This expression represents the number of gas moles present in the container.

Calculate the number of molecules:

number of molecules = moles × Avogadro's number

number of molecules = (320 mmHg / 760 atm) × 6 / (0.0821 × 283) × 6.02 × 10^{23}

number of molecules = (320 / 760)·(6)·(6 × 10^{23}) / (0.0821)·(283)

---

47. A is correct.

At STP (standard conditions for temperature and pressure), the pressure and temperature are the same regardless of the gas.

The ideal gas law:

$$PV = nRT$$

where P is pressure, V is volume, n is the number of molecules, R is the ideal gas constant, and T is the temperature of the gas.

Therefore, one molecule of each gas occupies the same volume at STP. Since CO_2 molecules have the largest mass, CO_2 gas has a greater mass in the same volume, and thus it has the greatest density.

48. C is correct.

Hydrogens, bonded directly to F, O or N, participate in hydrogen bonds. The hydrogen is partially positive (i.e., delta plus: $\partial+$) due to the bond to these electronegative atoms. The lone pair of electrons on the F, O or N interacts with the partial positive ($\partial+$) hydrogen to form a hydrogen bond.

49. D is correct. Calculate the moles of each gas:

moles = mass / molar mass

moles H_2 = 9.50 g / (2 × 1.01 g/mole)

moles H_2 = 4.70 moles

moles Ne = 14.0 g / (20.18 g/mole)

moles Ne = 0.694 moles

Calculate the mole fraction of H_2:

Mole fraction of H_2 = moles of H_2 / total moles in mixture

Mole fraction of H_2 = 4.70 moles / (4.70 moles + 0.694 moles)

Mole fraction of H_2 = 4.70 moles / (5.394 moles)

Mole fraction of H_2 = 0.87 moles

50. E is correct.

Vapor pressure is the pressure exerted by a vapor in equilibrium with its condensed phases (i.e., solid or liquid) in a closed system, at a given temperature.

Boiling occurs when the vapor pressure of a liquid equals atmospheric pressure.

Vapor pressure always increases as the temperature increases.

Liquid A boils at a lower temperature than B because the vapor pressure of Liquid A is closer to the atmospheric pressure.

51. B is correct.

Colligative properties of solutions depend on the ratio of the number of solute particles to the number of solvent molecules in a solution, and not on the type of chemical species present.

Colligative properties include: lowering of vapor pressure, the elevation of boiling point, depression of freezing point, and increased osmotic pressure.

Freezing point (FP) depression:

$\Delta FP = -iKm$

where i = the number of particles produced when the solute dissociates, K = freezing point depression constant and m = molality (moles/kg solvent).

$-iKm = -2 \text{ K}$

$-(1)\cdot(40)\cdot(x) = -2$

$x = -2 / -1(40)$

$x = 0.05 \text{ molal}$

Assume that compound x does not dissociate.

0.05 mole compound (x) / kg camphor = 25 g / kg camphor

Therefore, if 0.05 mole = 25 g

1 mole = 500 g

52. D is correct.

Van der Waals equation describes factors that must be accounted for when the ideal gas law is used to calculate values for nonideal gases. The terms that affect the pressure and volume of the ideal gas law are intermolecular forces and volume of nonideal gas molecules.

53. E is correct.

Ideal gas law:

$PV = nRT$

where P is pressure, V is volume, n is the number of molecules, R is the ideal gas constant and T is the temperature of the gas.

Units of R can be calculated by rearranging the expression:

$R = PV/nT$

$R = atm \cdot L / mol \cdot K$

54. A is correct. Ideal gas law:

$PV = nRT$

where P is pressure, V is volume, n is the number of molecules, R is the ideal gas constant and T is the temperature of the gas.

Set the initial and final P/V/T conditions equal:

$(P_1V_1 / T_1) = (P_2V_2 / T_2)$

STP condition is the temperature of 0 °C (273 K) and pressure of 1 atm.

Solve for the final temperature:

$(P_2V_2 / T_2) = (P_1V_1 / T_1)$

$T_2 = (P_2V_2T_1) / (P_1V_1)$

$T_2 = [(0.80 \text{ atm}) \times (0.155 \text{ L}) \times (273 \text{ K})] / [(1.00 \text{ atm}) \times (0.120 \text{ L})]$

$T_2 = 282.1 \text{ K}$

Then convert temperature units to degrees Celsius:

$T_2 = (282.1 \text{ K} - 273 \text{ K})$

$T_2 = 9.1 \text{ °C}$

55. C is correct.

Atmospheric pressure is the pressure exerted by the weight of air in the atmosphere.

Boiling occurs when the vapor pressure of the liquid is higher than the atmospheric pressure.

At standard atmospheric pressure and 22 °C, the vapor pressure of water is less than the atmospheric pressure, and it does not boil.
However, when a vacuum pump is used, the atmospheric pressure is reduced until it has a lower vapor pressure than water, which allows water to boil at a much lower temperature.

56. A is correct.

Dalton's law (i.e., the law of partial pressures) states that *the pressure exerted by a mixture of gases is equal to the sum of the individual gas pressures*.

The partial pressure of molecules in a mixture is proportional to their molar ratios.

Use the coefficients of the reaction to determine the molar ratio.

Based on that information, calculate the partial pressure of O_2:

(coefficient O_2) / (sum of coefficients in the mixture) × total pressure

$[1 / (2 + 1)] \times 1{,}250$ torr

417 torr = partial pressure of O_2

57. B is correct.

Charles' law (i.e., law of volumes) explains how, at constant pressure, gases behave when temperature changes:

$V \propto T$

or

V / T = constant

or

$(V_1 / T_1) = (V_2 / T_2)$

Volume and temperature are proportional.

Therefore, an increase in one term increases the other.

58. E is correct.

Gay-Lussac's law (i.e., pressure-temperature law) states that pressure is proportional to temperature:

$P \alpha T$

or

$(P_1 / T_1) = (P_2 / T_2)$

or

$(P_1 T_2) = (P_2 T_1)$

or

P / T = constant

If the pressure of a gas increases, the temperature is increased proportionally.

Quadrupling the temperature increases the pressure fourfold.

Boyle's law (i.e., pressure-volume law) states that pressure and volume are inversely proportional:

$(P_1 V_1) = (P_2 V_2)$

or

$P \times V$ = constant

Reducing the volume by half increases pressure twofold.

Therefore, the total increase in pressure would be by a factor of $4 \times 2 = 8$.

59. B is correct.

Graham's law of effusion states that the rate of effusion (i.e., escaping through a small hole) of a gas is inversely proportional to the square root of the molar mass of its particles.

Rate 1 / Rate 2 = $\sqrt{(\text{molar mass gas 2} / \text{molar mass gas 1})}$

Set the rate of effusion of krypton over the rate of effusion of methane:

$\text{Rate}_{Kr} / \text{Rate}_{CH4} = \sqrt{[(M_{Kr}) / (M_{CH4})]}$

Solve for the ratio of effusion rates:

$\text{Rate}_{Kr} / \text{Rate}_{CH4} = \sqrt{[(83.798 \text{ g/mol}) / (16.04 \text{ g/mol})]}$

$\text{Rate}_{Kr} / \text{Rate}_{CH4} = 2.29$

Larger gas molecules must effuse at a slower rate; the effusion rate of Kr gas molecules must be slower than methane molecules:

$\text{Rate}_{Kr} = [\text{Rate}_{CH4} / (2.29)]$

$Rate_{Kr} = [(631 \text{ m/s}) / (2.29)]$

$Rate_{Kr} = 276 \text{ m/s}$

60. C is correct.

Observe information about gas C.

Temperature, pressure, and volume of the gas are indicated.

Substitute these values into the ideal gas law equation to determine the number of moles:

$PV = nRT$

$n = PV / RT$

Convert all units to the units indicated in the gas constant:

volume = 668.5 mL × (1 L / 1,000 mL)

volume = 0. 669 L

pressure = 745.5 torr × (1 atm / 760 torr)

pressure = 0.981 atm

temperature = 32.0 °C + 273.15 K

temperature = 305.2 K

$n = PV / RT$

$n = (0.981 \text{ atm} \times 0.669 \text{ L}) / (0.0821 \text{ L·atm K}^{-1} \text{mol}^{-1} \times 305.2 \text{ K})$

$n = 0.026 \text{ mole}$

Law of mass conservation states that total mass of products = total mass of reactants.

Based on this law, mass of gas C can be determined:

mass product = mass reactant

mass A = mass B + mass C

5.2 g = 3.8 g + mass C

mass C = 1.4 g

Calculate molar mass of C:

molar mass = 1.4 g / 0.026 mole

molar mass = 53.9 g / mole

Chapter 4 Explanations: Stoichiometry

1. C is correct. One mole of an ideal gas occupies 22.71 L at STP.

$$3 \text{ mole} \times 22.71 \text{ L} = 68.13 \text{ L}$$

2. C is correct. Use the mnemonic OIL RIG: <u>O</u>xidation <u>I</u>s <u>L</u>oss, <u>R</u>eduction <u>I</u>s <u>G</u>ain (of electrons).

Oxidation is the loss of electrons, while reduction is the gain of electrons.

An oxidizing agent undergoes reduction, while a reducing agent undergoes oxidation.

Check the oxidation numbers of each atom.

The oxidation number for S is +6 as a reactant and +4 as a product, which means that it is reduced.

If a substance is reduced in a redox reaction, it is the oxidizing agent, because it causes the other reagent (HI) to be oxidized.

3. C is correct.

Balanced equation (combustion): $2 \, C_6H_{14} + 19 \, O_2 \rightarrow 12 \, CO_2 + 14 \, H_2O$

4. E is correct.

An oxidation number is a charge on an atom that is not present in the elemental state when the element is neutral.

Electronegativity refers to the attraction an atom has for additional electrons.

5. C is correct. CH_3COOH has 2 carbons, 4 hydrogens and 2 oxygens: $C_2O_2H_4$

Reduce to the smallest coefficients by dividing by two: COH_2

6. B is correct. Oxidation numbers of Cl in each compound:

$NaClO_2$	+3
$Al(ClO_4)_3$	+7
$Ca(ClO_3)_2$	+5
$LiClO_3$	+5

7. A is correct. Formula mass is a synonym for molecular mass/molecular weight (MW).

Molecular mass = (atomic mass of C) + (2 × atomic mass of O)

Molecular mass = (12.01 g/mole) + (2 × 16.00 g/mole)

Molecular mass = 44.01 g/mole

Note: 1 amu = 1 g/mole

8. C is correct.

Cadmium is in group II, so its oxidation number is +2.

Sulfur tends to form a sulfide ion (oxidation number –2).

The net oxidation number is zero, and therefore, the compound is CdS.

9. C is correct. Use the mnemonic OIL RIG: <u>O</u>xidation <u>I</u>s <u>L</u>oss, <u>R</u>eduction <u>I</u>s <u>G</u>ain (of electrons).

Oxidation is the loss of electrons, while reduction is the gain of electrons.

An oxidizing agent undergoes reduction, while a reducing agent undergoes oxidation.

When there are 2 reactants in a redox reaction, one will be oxidized, and the other will be reduced. The oxidized species is the reducing agent and vice versa.

Determine the oxidation number of all atoms:

I changes its oxidation state from –1 as a reactant to 0 as a product.

I is oxidized, therefore the compound that contains I (NaI) is the reducing agent. Species in their elemental state have an oxidation number of 0.

Since the reaction is spontaneous, NaI is the *strongest* reducing agent in the reaction, because it can reduce another species spontaneously without needing any external energy for the reaction to proceed.

10. C is correct. To determine the remainder of a reactant, calculate how many moles of that reactant is required to produce the specified amount of product.

Use the coefficients to calculate the moles of the reactant:

$$\text{moles } N_2 = (1 / 2) \times 18 \text{ moles} = 9 \text{ moles } N_2$$

Therefore, the remainder is:

$$(14.5 \text{ moles } N_2) - (9 \text{ moles } N_2) = 5.5 \text{ moles } N_2 \text{ remaining}$$

11. D is correct.

$CaCO_3 \rightarrow CaO + CO_2$ is a decomposition reaction because one complex compound is being broken down into two or more parts. However, the redox part is incorrect, because the reactants and products are all compounds (no single elements) and there is no change in oxidation state (i.e., no gain or loss of electrons).

A: $AgNO_3 + NaCl \rightarrow AgCl + NaNO_3$ is correctly classified as a double-replacement reaction (sometimes referred to as double-displacement) because parts of two ionic compounds are exchanged to make two new compounds. It is also a non-redox reaction because the reactants and products are all compounds (no single elements) and there is no change in oxidation state (i.e., no gain or loss of electrons).

B: $Cl_2 + F_2 \rightarrow 2 \text{ ClF}$ is correctly classified as a synthesis reaction because two species are combining to form a more complex chemical compound as the product. It is also a redox reaction because the F atoms in F_2 are reduced (i.e., gain electrons) and the Cl atoms in Cl_2 are oxidized (i.e., lose electrons) forming a covalent compound.

C: $H_2O + SO_2 \rightarrow H_2SO_3$ is correctly classified as a synthesis reaction because two species are combining to form a more complex chemical compound as the product. It is also a non-redox reaction because the reactants and products are all compounds (no single elements) and there is no change in oxidation state (i.e., no gain or loss of electrons).

12. C is correct. Hydrogen is being oxidized (or ignited) to produce water.

The balanced equation that describes the ignition of hydrogen gas in the air to produce water is:

$\frac{1}{2} O_2 + H_2 \rightarrow H_2O$

This equation suggests that for every mole of water that is produced in the reaction, 1 mole of hydrogen and a ½ mole of oxygen gas is needed.

The maximum amount of water that can be produced in the reaction is determined by the amount of limited reactant available. This requires identifying which reactant is the limiting reactant and can be done by comparing the number of moles of oxygen and hydrogen.

From the question, there are 10 grams of oxygen gas and 1 gram of hydrogen gas. This is equivalent to 0.3125 moles of oxygen and 0.5 moles of hydrogen.

Because the reaction requires twice as much hydrogen as oxygen gas, the limiting reactant is hydrogen gas (0.3215 moles of O_2 requires 0.625 moles of hydrogen, but only 0.5 moles of H_2 are available).

Since one equivalent of water is produced for every equivalent of hydrogen that is burned, the amount of water produced is:

(18 grams/mol H_2O) × (0.5 mol H_2O) = 9 grams of H_2O

13. D is correct.

Calculate the moles of Cl^- ion:

Moles of Cl^- ion = number of Cl^- atoms / Avogadro's number

Moles of Cl^- ion = 6.8×10^{22} atoms / 6.02×10^{23} atoms/mole

Moles of Cl^- ion = 0.113 moles

In a solution, $BaCl_2$ dissociates:

$BaCl_2 \rightarrow Ba^{2+} + 2 \, Cl^-$

The moles of from Cl^- previous calculation can be used to calculate the moles of Ba^{2+}:

Moles of Ba^{2+} = (coefficient of Ba^{2+} / coefficient Cl^-) × moles of Cl^-

Moles of Ba^{2+} = (½) × 0.113 moles

Moles of Ba^{2+} = 0.0565 moles

Calculate the mass of Ba^{2+}:

Mass of Ba^{2+} = moles of Ba^{2+} × atomic mass of Ba

Mass of Ba^{2+} = 0.0565 moles × 137.33 g/mole

Mass of Ba^{2+} = 7.76 g

14. D is correct.

Na	Br	O_3
+1	x	(3×-2)
+1	x	-6

The sum of charges in a neutral molecule is zero:

1 + oxidation number of Br:

$1 + x + (-6) = 0$

$-5 + x = 0$

$x = +5$

oxidation number of Br = +5

15. E is correct.

Balanced equation:

$$2\ Al + Fe_2O_3 \rightarrow 2\ Fe + Al_2O_3$$

The sum of the coefficients of the products = 3.

16. B is correct.

$2\ H_2O_2\ (s) \rightarrow 2\ H_2O\ (l) + O_2\ (g)$ is incorrectly classified. The decomposition part of the classification is correct because one complex compound (H_2O_2) is being broken down into two or more parts (H_2O and O_2).

However, it is a redox reaction because oxygen is being lost from H_2O_2, which is one of the three indicators of a redox reaction (i.e., electron loss/gain, hydrogen loss/gain, oxygen loss/gain).

Additionally, one of the products is a single element (O_2), which is also a clue that it is a redox reaction.

$AgNO_3\ (aq) + KOH\ (aq) \rightarrow KNO_3\ (aq) + AgOH\ (s)$ is correctly classified as a non-redox reaction because the reactants and products are all compounds (no single elements) and there is no change in oxidation state (i.e., no gain or loss of electrons). It is also a precipitation reaction because the chemical reaction occurs in aqueous solution and one of the products formed (AgOH) is insoluble, which makes it a precipitate.

$Pb(NO_3)_2\ (aq) + 2\ Na\ (s) \rightarrow Pb\ (s) + 2\ NaNO_3\ (aq)$ is correctly classified as a redox reaction because the nitrate (NO_3^-), which dissociates, is oxidized (loses electrons), the Na^+ is reduced (gains electrons), and the two combine to form the ionic compound $NaNO_3$. It is a single-replacement reaction because one element is substituted for another element in a compound, making a new compound ($2NaNO_3$) and an element (Pb).

$HNO_3\ (aq) + LiOH\ (aq) \rightarrow LiNO_3\ (aq) + H_2O\ (l)$ is correctly classified as a non-redox reaction because the reactants and products are all compounds (no single elements) and there is no change in oxidation state (i.e., no gain or loss of electrons). It is also a double-replacement reaction because parts of two ionic compounds are exchanged to make two new compounds.

17. C is correct. At STP, 1 mole of gas has a volume of 22.4 L.

Calculate moles of O_2:

moles of O_2 = (15.0 L) / (22.4 L/mole)

moles of O_2 = 0.67 mole

Calculate the moles of O_2, using the fact that 1 mole of O_2 has 6.02×10^{23} O_2 molecules:

molecules of O_2 = 0.67 mole × (6.02×10^{23} molecules/mole)

molecules of O_2 = 4.03×10^{23} molecules

18. E is correct.

19. D is correct.

Double replacement reaction:

HCl has a molar mass of 36.5 g/mol:

365 grams HCl = 10 moles HCl

10 moles are 75% of the total yield.

10 moles PCl_3 / 0.75 = 13.5 moles of HCl.

Apply the mole ratios:

Coefficients: 3 HCl = PCl_3

13.5 / 3 = moles of PCl_3

13.5 moles of HCl is produced by 4.5 moles of PCl_3

20. A is correct. All elements in their free state will have an oxidation number of zero.

21. B is correct. Balanced chemical equation:

C_3H_8 + 5 O_2 → 3 CO_2 + 4 H_2O

By using the coefficients from the balanced equation, apply dimensional analysis to solve for the volume of H_2O produced from the 2.6 L C_3H_8 reacted:

V_{H2O} = V_{C3H8} × (mol H_2O / mol C_3H_8)

V_{H2O} = (2.6 L) × (4 mol / 1 mol)

V_{H2O} = 10.4 L

22. C is correct. Use the mnemonic OIL RIG: Oxidation Is Loss, Reduction Is Gain (of electrons).

Oxidation is the loss of electrons, while reduction is the gain of electrons.

An oxidizing agent undergoes reduction, while a reducing agent undergoes oxidation.

The oxidation number of Hg decreases (i.e., reduction) from +2 as a reactant ($HgCl_2$) to +1 as a product (Hg_2Cl_2). This means that Hg gained one electron.

23. C is correct. Balanced equation (synthesis):

$$4 \text{ P } (s) + 5 \text{ O}_2 \text{ } (g) \rightarrow 2 \text{ P}_2\text{O}_5 \text{ } (s)$$

24. E is correct.

Calculate the moles of LiI present. The molecular weight of LiI is 133.85 g/mol.

Moles of LiI:

6.45 g / 133.85 g/mole = 0.0482 moles

Each mole of LiI contains 6.02×10^{23} molecules.

Number of molecules:

$0.0482 \times 6.02 \times 10^{23} = 2.90 \times 10^{22}$ molecules

1 molecule is equal to 1 formula unit.

25. E is correct. A combustion engine creates various nitrogen oxide compounds often referred to as NOx gases because each gas would have a different value of x in their formula.

26. A is correct. Use the mnemonic OIL RIG: Oxidation Is Loss, Reduction Is Gain (of electrons).

Oxidation is the loss of electrons, while reduction is the gain of electrons.

An oxidizing agent undergoes reduction, while a reducing agent undergoes oxidation.

Because the forward reaction is spontaneous, the reverse reaction is not spontaneous.

Sn cannot reduce Mg^{2+}; therefore, Sn is the weakest reducing agent.

27. E is correct. To obtain moles, divide sample mass by the molecular mass.

Because all of the options have the same mass, a comparison of molecular mass provides the answer without performing the actual calculation.

The molecule with the smallest molecular mass has the greatest number of moles.

28. A is correct.

The law of constant composition states that *all samples of a given chemical compound have the same chemical composition by mass*.

This is true for all compounds, including ethyl alcohol.

This law is also referred to as the law of definite proportions or Proust's Law because this observation was first made by the French chemist Joseph Proust.

29. A is correct. The coefficients in balanced reactions refer to moles (or molecules) but not grams.

1 mole of N_2 gas reacts with 3 moles of H_2 gas to produce 2 moles of NH_3 gas.

30. C is correct. Calculate the number of moles of Al_2O_3:

$2\ Al\ /\ 1\ Al_2O_3 = 0.2$ moles $Al\ /\ x$ moles Al_2O_3

x moles $Al_2O_3 = 0.2$ moles $Al \times 1\ Al_2O_3\ /\ 2\ Al$

$x = 0.1$ moles Al_2O_3

Therefore:

$(0.1$ mole $Al_2O_3)\cdot(102$ g/mole $Al_2O_3) = 10.2$ g Al_2O_3

31. D is correct. Because Na is a metal, Na is more electropositive than H.

Therefore, the positive charge is on Na (i.e., +1), which means that charge on H is –1.

32. A is correct.

$PbO + C \rightarrow Pb + CO$ is a single replacement reaction because only one element is being transferred from one reactant to another.

However, it is a redox reaction because the lead (Pb^{2+}), which dissociates, is reduced (gains electrons), the oxygen (O^{2-}) is oxidized (loses electrons). Additionally, one of the products is a single element (Pb), which is also a clue that it is a redox reaction.

C: the reaction is double-replacement and not the combustion because the combustion reactions must always have a hydrocarbon and O_2 as reactants. Double-replacement reactions often result in the formation of a solid, water and gas.

33. A is correct.

To calculate number of molecules, start by calculating the moles of gas using the ideal gas equation:

$PV = nRT$

Rearrange to isolate the number of moles:

$n = PV\ /\ RT$

Because the gas constant R is in $L\cdot atm\ K^{-1}\ mol^{-1}$, the pressure has to be converted into atm:

780 torr $\times (1$ atm $/ 760$ torr$) = 1.026$ atm

Convert the volume to liters:

500 mL $\times 0.001$ L/mL $= 0.5$ L

Substitute into the ideal gas equation:

$n = PV\ /\ RT$

$n = 1.026$ atm $\times 0.5$ L $/ (0.08206\ L\cdot atm\ K^{-1}\ mol^{-1} \times 320$ K$)$

$n = 0.513\ L\cdot atm\ / (26.259\ L\cdot atm\ mol^{-1})$

$n = 0.0195$ mol

34. E is correct.

Balancing a redox equation in acidic solution by the half-reaction method involves each of the steps described.

35. D is correct. Formula mass is a synonym for molecular mass/molecular weight (MW).

MW of $C_6H_{12}O_6$ = (6 × atomic mass C) + (12 × atomic mass H) + (6 × atomic mass O)

MW of $C_6H_{12}O_6$ = (6 × 12.01 g/mole) + (12 × 1.01 g/mole) + (6 × 16.00 g/mole)

MW of $C_6H_{12}O_6$ = (72.06 g/mole) + (12.12 g/mole) + (96.00 g/mole)

MW of $C_6H_{12}O_6$ = 180.18 g/mole

36. E is correct.

The molecular mass of oxygen is 16 g/mole.

The atomic mass unit (amu) or dalton (Da) is the standard unit for indicating mass on an atomic or molecular scale (atomic mass). One amu is approximately the mass of one nucleon (either a single proton or neutron) and is numerically equivalent to 1 g/mol.

37. E is correct. Use the mnemonic OIL RIG: Oxidation Is Loss, Reduction Is Gain (of electrons).

Oxidation is the loss of electrons, while reduction is the gain of electrons.

An oxidizing agent undergoes reduction, while a reducing agent undergoes oxidation.

Evaluate the oxidation number in each atom.

S changes from +6 as a reactant to –2 as a product, so it is reduced because the oxidation number decreases.

38. C is correct. Balanced equation (double replacement): $C_2H_5OH\ (g) + 3\ O_2\ (g) \rightarrow 2\ CO_2\ (g) + 3\ H_2O\ (g)$

39. C is correct.

According to the law of mass conservation, there should be equal amounts of carbon in the product (CO_2) and reactant (the hydrocarbon sample).

Start by calculating the amount of carbon in the product (CO_2).

First, calculate the mass % of carbon in CO_2:

Molecular mass of CO_2 = atomic mass of carbon + (2 × atomic mass of oxygen)

Molecular mass of CO_2 = 12.01 g/mole + (2 × 16.00 g/mole)

Molecular mass of CO_2 = 44.01 g/mole

Mass % of carbon in CO_2 = (mass of carbon / molecular mass of CO_2) × 100%

Mass % of carbon in CO_2 = (12.01 g/mole / 44.01 g/mole) × 100%

Mass % of carbon in CO_2 = 27.3%

Calculate the mass of carbon in the CO_2:

Mass of carbon = mass of CO_2 × mass % of carbon in CO_2

Mass of carbon = 8.98 g × 27.3%

Mass of carbon = 2.45 g

The mass of carbon in the starting reactant (the hydrocarbon sample) should also be 2.45 g.

Mass % carbon in hydrocarbon = (mass carbon in sample / total mass sample) × 100%

Mass % of carbon in hydrocarbon = (2.45 g / 6.84 g) × 100%

Mass % of carbon in hydrocarbon = 35.8%

40. E is correct. The number of each atom on the reactants side must be the same and equal in number to the number of atoms on the product side of the reaction.

41. E is correct. Balanced reaction:

$$4 RuS (s) + 9 O_2 + 4 H_2O \rightarrow 2 Ru_2O_3 (s) + 4 H_2SO_4$$

Calculate the moles of H_2SO_4:

49 g × 1 mol / 98 g = 0.5 mole H_2SO_4

If 0.5 mole H_2SO_4 is produced, set a ratio for O_2 consumed.

9 O_2 / 4 H_2SO_4 = x moles O_2 / 0.5 mole H_2SO_4

x moles O_2 = 9 O_2 / 4 H_2SO_4 × 0.5 mole H_2SO_4

x = 1.125 moles O_2 × 22.4 liters / 1 mole

x = 25.2 liters of O_2

42. C is correct. Identify the limiting reactant:

Al is the limiting reactant because 2 atoms of Al combine with 1 molecule of ferric oxide to produce the products. If the reaction starts with equal numbers of moles of each reactant, Al is depleted.

Use moles of Al and coefficients to calculate moles of other products/reactant.

Coefficient of Al = coefficient of Fe

Moles of iron produced = 0.20 moles.

43. D is correct. Na is in group IA, so its oxidation number is always +1.

Oxygen is usually −2, with some exceptions, such as peroxide (H_2O_2), where it is −1.

Cr is a transition metal and could have more than one possible oxidation number.

To determine Cr's oxidation number, use the known oxidation numbers:

$$2(+1) + Cr + 4(-2) = 0$$
$$2 + Cr - 8 = 0$$
$$Cr = 6$$

44. B is correct.

The net charge of $H_2SO_4 = 0$

Hydrogen has a common oxidation number of +1 whereas each oxygen atom has an oxidation number of –2.

H_2	S	O_4
(2×1)	x	(4×-2)

$$2 + x + -8 = 0$$
$$x = +6$$

In H_2SO_4, the oxidation of sulfur is +6.

45. C is correct. Use the mnemonic OIL RIG: <u>O</u>xidation <u>I</u>s <u>L</u>oss, <u>R</u>eduction <u>I</u>s <u>G</u>ain (of electrons).

Oxidation is the loss of electrons, while reduction is the gain of electrons.

An oxidizing agent undergoes reduction, while a reducing agent undergoes oxidation.

Oxidation number for Sn is +2 as a reactant, and +4 as a product; an increase in oxidation number means that Sn^{2+} is oxidized in this reaction.

46. E is correct.

I: represents the volume of 1 mol of an ideal gas at STP

II: mass of 1 mol of PH_3

III: number of molecules in 1 mol of PH_3

47. D is correct. Calculations:

% mass Cl = (molecular mass Cl) / (molecular mass of compound) × 100%

% mass Cl = 4(35.5 g/mol) / [12 g/mol + 4(35.5 g/mol)] × 100%

% mass Cl = (142 g/mol) / (154 g/mol) × 100%

% mass Cl = 0.922 × 100% = 92%

48. E is correct.

I: total ionic charge of reactants must equal total ionic charge of products, which means that no electrons can "disappear" from the reaction, they can only be transferred from one atom to another.

Therefore, the total charge will always be the same.

II: atoms of each reactant must equal atoms of product, which is true for all chemical reactions because atoms in chemical reactions cannot be created or destroyed.

III: any electrons that are gained by one atom must be lost by another atom.

49. B is correct. Determine the molecular weight of each compound.

Note, unlike % by mass, there is no division.

$$Cl_2C_2H_4 = 2(35.5 \text{ g/mol}) + 2(12 \text{ g/mol}) + 4(1 \text{ g/mol})$$

$$Cl_2C_2H_4 = 71 \text{ g/mol} + 24 \text{ g/mol} + 4 \text{ g/mol}$$

$$Cl_2C_2H_4 = 99 \text{ g/mol}$$

50. E is correct. Formula mass is a synonym for molecular mass/molecular weight (MW).

Start by calculating the mass of the formula unit (CH):

$$CH = (12.01 \text{ g/mol} + 1.01 \text{ g/mol}) = 13.02 \text{ g/mol}$$

Divide the molar mass by the formula unit mass.

$$78 \text{ g/mol} / 13.02 \text{ g/mol} = 5.99$$

Round to the closest whole number: 6

Multiply the formula unit by 6:

$$(CH)_6 = C_6H_6$$

51. B is correct.

Ethanol (C_2H_5OH) undergoes combination with oxygen to produce CO_2 and water.

52. C is correct.

Balanced reaction (combustion):

$$2 \text{ } C_3H_7OH + 9 \text{ } O_2 \rightarrow 6 \text{ } CO_2 + 8 \text{ } H_2O$$

53. D is correct.

H_2 is the limiting reactant.

$$24 \text{ moles of } H_2 \text{ should produce: } 24 \times (2 / 3) = 16 \text{ moles of } NH_3$$

If only 13.5 moles are produced, the yield:

$$13.5 \text{ moles} / 16 \text{ moles} \times 100\% = 84\%$$

54. B is correct.

Balanced reaction:

$$H_2 + \frac{1}{2} O_2 \rightarrow H_2O$$

Multiply all the equations by 2 to remove the fraction:

$$2 \text{ } H_2 + O_2 \rightarrow 2 \text{ } H_2O$$

Find the limiting reactant by calculating the moles of each reactant:

Moles of hydrogen = mass of hydrogen / (2 × atomic mass of hydrogen)

Moles of hydrogen = 25 g / (2 × 1.01 g/mole)

Moles of hydrogen = 12.38 moles

Moles of oxygen = mass of oxygen / (2 × atomic mass of oxygen)

Moles of oxygen = 225 g / (2 × 16.00 g/mole)

Moles of oxygen = 7.03 moles

Divide the number of moles of each reactant by its coefficient.

The reactant with the smaller number of moles is the limiting reactant.

Hydrogen = 12.38 moles / 2

Hydrogen = 6.19 moles

Oxygen = 7.03 moles / 1

Oxygen = 7.03 moles

Because hydrogen has a smaller number of moles after the division, hydrogen is the limiting reactant, and all hydrogen will be depleted in the reaction.

$2 H_2 + O_2 \rightarrow 2 H_2O$

Both hydrogen and water have coefficients of 2; therefore, these have the same number of moles.

There are 12.38 moles of hydrogen, which means there are 12.38 moles of water produced by this reaction.

Molecular mass of H_2O = (2 × molecular mass of hydrogen) + atomic mass of oxygen

Molecular mass of H_2O = (2 × 1.01 g/mole) + 16.00 g/mole

Molecular mass of H_2O = 18.02 g/mole

Mass of H_2O = moles of H_2O × molecular mass of H_2O

Mass of H_2O = 12.38 moles × 18.02 g/mole

Mass of H_2O = 223 g

55. C is correct.

Li   Cl O_2

+1 x (2 × –2)

The sum of charges in a neutral molecule is zero:

$1 + x + (2 × –2) = 0$

$1 + x + (–4) = 0$

$x = –1 + 4$

oxidation number of Cl = +3

56. D is correct. Using half-reactions, the balanced reaction is:

To balance hydrogen   To balance oxygen

↓   ↓

$$4[5 \text{ e}^- + 8 \text{ H}^+ + MnO_4^- \rightarrow Mn^{2+} + 4 \text{ (H}_2O)]$$

$$5[(H_2O) + C_3H_7OH \rightarrow C_2H_5CO_2H + 4 \text{ H}^+ + 4 \text{ e}^-]$$

$$12 \text{ H}^+ + 4 \text{ MnO}_4^- + 5 \text{ C}_3H_7OH \rightarrow 11 \text{ H}_2O + 4 \text{ Mn}^{2+} + 5 \text{ C}_2H_5CO_2H$$

Multiply by a common multiple of 4 and 5:

The sum of the product's coefficients: $11 + 4 + 5 = 20$.

57. A is correct.

$PbO \text{ (s)} + C \text{ (s)} \rightarrow Pb \text{ (s)} + CO \text{ (g)}$ is a single-replacement reaction because only one element (i.e., oxygen) is being transferred from one reactant to another.

58. E is correct.

The reactants in a chemical reaction are always on the left side of the reaction arrow, while the products are on the right side.

In this reaction, the reactants are $C_6H_{12}O_6$, H_2O and O_2.

There is a distinction between the terms *reactant* and *reagent*.

A reactant is a substance consumed in the course of a chemical reaction.

A reagent is a substance (e.g., solvent) added to a system to cause a chemical reaction.

59. C is correct. Determine the number of moles of He:

$4 \text{ g} \div 4.0 \text{ g/mol} = 1 \text{ mole}$

Each mole of He has 2 electrons since He has atomic number 2 (# electrons = # protons for neutral atoms).

Therefore, 1 mole of He × 2 electrons / mole = 2 moles of electrons

60. D is correct.

In this molecule, Br has the oxidation number of -1 because it is a halogen and the gaining of one electron results in a complete octet for bromine.

The sum of charges in a neutral molecule = 0

0 = (oxidation state of Fe) + (3 × oxidation state of Br)

0 = (oxidation state of Fe) + (3 × −1)

0 = oxidation state of Fe − 3

oxidation state of Fe = +3

Notes

Chapter 5 Explanations: Kinetics and Equilibrium

1. A is correct.

General formula for the equilibrium constant of a reaction:

$$a\text{A} + b\text{B} \leftrightarrow c\text{C} + d\text{D}$$

$$K_{eq} = ([\text{C}]^c \times [\text{D}]^d) / ([\text{A}]^a \times [\text{B}]^b)$$

For the reaction above:

$$K_{eq} = [\text{C}] / [\text{A}]^2 \times [\text{B}]^3$$

2. B is correct.

Two gases having the same temperature have the same average molecular kinetic energy.

Therefore,

$$(\tfrac{1}{2})m_A v_A^2 - (\tfrac{1}{2})m_B v_B^2$$

$$m_A v_A^2 = m_B v_B^2$$

$$(m_B / m_A) = (v_A / v_B)^2$$

$$(v_A / v_B) = 2$$

$$(m_B / m_A) = 2^2 = 4$$

The only gases listed with a mass ratio of about 4 to 1 are iron (55.8 g/mol) and nitrogen (14 g/mol).

3. A is correct. The slowest reaction would be the reaction with the highest activation energy and the lowest temperature.

4. A is correct.

The rate law is calculated experimentally by comparing trials and determining how changes in the initial concentrations of the reactants affect the rate of the reaction.

$$\text{rate} = k[\text{A}]^x \cdot [\text{B}]^y$$

where k is the rate constant, and the exponents x and y are the partial reaction orders (i.e., determined experimentally). They are not equal to the stoichiometric coefficients.

To determine the order of reactant A, find two experiments where the concentrations of B are identical, and concentrations of A are different.

Use data from experiments 2 and 3 to calculate order of A:

$$\text{Rate}_3 / \text{Rate}_2 = ([\text{A}]_3 / [\text{A}]_2)^{\text{order of A}}$$

$$0.500 / 0.500 = (0.060 / 0.030)^{\text{order of A}}$$

$$1 = (2)^{\text{order of A}}$$

Order of A = 0

5. C is correct. The balanced equation:

$$C_2H_6O + 3\,O_2 \rightarrow 2\,CO_2 + 3\,H_2O$$

The rate of reaction/consumption is proportional to the coefficients.

The rate of carbon dioxide production is twice the rate of ethanol consumption:

$$2 \times 4.0\ \text{M s}^{-1} = 8.0\ \text{M s}^{-1}$$

6. B is correct. K_{eq} = [products] / [reactants]

If the K_{eq} is less than 1 (e.g., 6.3×10^{-14}), then the numerator (i.e., products) is smaller than the denominator (i.e., reactants) and fewer products have formed relative to the reactants.

If the reaction favors reactants compared to products, the equilibrium lies to the left.

7. D is correct. Every reaction has activation energy: the amount of energy required by the reactant to start reacting. On the graph, activation energy can be estimated by calculating the distance between the initial energy level (i.e., reactant) and the peak (i.e., transition state) on the graph. Activation energy is *not* the difference between energy levels of initial and final state (reactant and product).

A catalyst provides an alternative pathway for the reaction to proceed to product formation. It lowers the energy of activation (i.e., relative energy between reactants and transition state) and therefore speeds the rate of the reaction.

Catalysts do not affect the Gibbs free energy (ΔG: stability of products vs. reactants) or the enthalpy (ΔH: bond breaking in reactants or bond making in products).

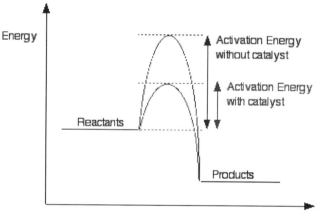

8. D is correct. The activation energy is the energy barrier that must be overcome for the transformation of reactant(s) into product(s).

A reaction with higher activation energy (energy barrier), has a decreased rate (k).

9. B is correct. The activation energy is the energy barrier that must be overcome for the transformation of reactant(s) into product(s).

A reaction with lower activation energy (energy barrier), has an increased rate (k).

10. D is correct. The activation energy is the energy barrier that must be overcome for the transformation of reactant(s) into product(s).

A reaction with higher activation energy (energy barrier), has a decreased rate (k).

If the graphs are on the same scale, the height of the activation energy (R to the highest peak on the graph) is greatest in graph d.

11. B is correct. If the graphs are on the same scale, the height of the activation energy (R to the highest peak on the graph) is the smallest in graph b.

The main function of catalysts is lowering the reaction's activation energy (energy barrier), thus increasing its rate (k).

Although catalysts do decrease the amount of energy required to reach the rate-limiting transition state, they do *not* decrease the relative energy of the products and reactants. Therefore, a catalyst does not affect ΔG.

A catalyst provides an alternative pathway for the reaction to proceed to product formation. It lowers the energy of activation (i.e., relative energy between reactants and transition state) and therefore speeds the rate of the reaction.

Catalysts do not affect the Gibbs free energy (ΔG: stability of products vs. reactants) or the enthalpy (ΔH: bond breaking in reactants or bond making in products).

Catalysts do not affect ΔG (relative levels of R and P). Graph D shows an endergonic reaction with products less stable than reactants. All other graphs show an exergonic reaction with the same relative difference between the more stable products and the less stable reactants; only the energy of activation is different on the graphs.

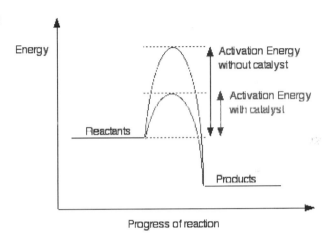

12. B is correct.

A reaction is at equilibrium when the rate of the forward reaction equals the rate of the reverse reaction. Achieving equilibrium is common for reactions.

Catalysts, by definition, are regenerated during a reaction and are not consumed by the reaction.

13. C is correct.

First, calculate the concentration/molarity of each reactant:

H_2 : 0.20 moles / 4.00 L = 0.05 M

X_2 : 0.20 moles / 4.00 L = 0.05 M

HX: 0.800 moles / 4.00L = 0.20 M

Use the concentrations to calculate Q:

$Q = [HX]^2 / [H_2]\cdot[X_2]$

$Q = (0.20)^2 / (0.05 \times 0.05)$

$Q = 16$

Because $Q < K_c$ (i.e., $16 < 24.4$), the reaction shifts to the right. For Q to increase and match K_c, the numerator (i.e., $[HX]^2$) which is the product (right side) of the equation needs to be increased.

14. A is correct. The rate law is calculated by determining how changes in concentrations of the reactants affect the initial rate of the reaction.

$$\text{rate} = k[A]^x \cdot [B]^y$$

where k is the rate constant and the exponents x and y are the partial reaction orders. They are not equal to the stoichiometric coefficients.

Whenever the fast (i.e., second) step follows the slow (i.e., first) step, the fast step is assumed to reach equilibrium, and the equilibrium concentrations are used for the rate law of the slow step.

15. C is correct. The rate law is calculated experimentally by comparing trials and determining how changes in the initial concentrations of the reactants affect the rate of the reaction.

$$\text{rate} = k[A]^x \cdot [B]^y$$

where k is the rate constant and the exponents x and y are the partial reaction orders (i.e., determined experimentally). They are not equal to the stoichiometric coefficients.

Rate laws cannot be determined from the balanced equation (i.e., used to determine equilibrium) unless the reaction occurs in a single step.

From the data, when the concentration doubles, the rate quadrupled.

Since 4 is 2^2, the rate law is second order, therefore the rate $= k[H_2]^2$.

16. D is correct. Lowering temperature shifts the equilibrium to the right because heat is a product (lowering the temperature is similar to removing the product). Increasing the temperature (i.e., heating the system) has the opposite effect and shifts the equilibrium to the left (i.e., toward products).

Removal of H_2 (i.e., reactant) shifts the equilibrium to the left.

Addition of NH_3 (i.e., products) shifts the equilibrium to the left.

A catalyst lowers the energy of activation but does not affect the position of the equilibrium.

17. B is correct. The order of the reaction has to be determined experimentally. It is possible for a reaction's order to be identical with its coefficients. For example, in a single-step reaction or during the slow step of a multi-step reaction, the coefficients correlate to the rate law.

18. E is correct. Two peaks in this reaction indicate two energy-requiring steps with one intermediate (i.e., C) and each peak (i.e., B and D) as an activated complex (i.e., transition states). The activated complex (i.e., transition state) is undergoing bond breaking/bond making events.

19. A is correct. The activation energy for the slow step of a reaction is the distance from the starting material (or an intermediate) to the activated complex (i.e., transition state) with the absolute highest energy (i.e., highest point on the graph).

20. C is correct. The activation energy for the slow step of a reverse reaction is the distance from an intermediate (or product) to the activated complex (i.e., transition state) with the absolute highest energy (i.e., highest point on the graph). The slow step may not have the greatest magnitude for activation energy (e.g., E→ D on the graph).

21. B is correct. The change in energy for this reaction (or ΔH) is the difference between the energy contents of the reactants and the products.

22. B is correct. All chemical reactions eventually reach equilibrium, the state at which the reactants and products are present in concentrations that have no further tendency to change with time. Therefore, the rate of production of each of the products (i.e., forward reaction) equals the rate of their consumption by the reverse reaction.

23. E is correct. Chemical equilibrium refers to a dynamic process whereby the *rate* at which a reactant molecule is being transformed into a product is the same as the *rate* for a product molecule to be transformed into a reactant.

All chemical reactions eventually reach equilibrium, the state at which the reactants and products are present in concentrations that have no further tendency to change with time.

24. A is correct.

Expression for equilibrium constant:

$$K = [H_2O]^2 [Cl_2]^2 / [HCl]^4 \cdot [O_2]$$

Solve for [Cl$_2$]:

$$[Cl_2]^2 = (K \times [HCl]^4 \cdot [O_2]) / [H_2O]^2$$

$$[Cl_2]^2 = [46.0 \times (0.150)^4 \times 0.395] / (0.625)^2$$

$$[Cl_2]^2 = 0.0235$$

$$[Cl_2] = 0.153 \text{ M}$$

25. D is correct. Gases (as opposed to liquids and solids) are most sensitive to changes in pressure. There are three moles of hydrogen gas as a reactant and three moles of water vapor as a product.

Therefore, changes in pressure result in proportionate changes to both the forward and reverse reaction.

26. E is correct. The high levels of CO_2 cause a person to hyperventilate in an attempt to reduce the number of CO_2 (reactant). Hyperventilating has the effect of driving the reaction toward products.

Removing products (i.e., HCO_3^- and H^+) or intermediates (H_2CO_3) drives the reaction toward products.

27. B is correct.

The units of the rate constants:

Zero-order reaction: M sec^{-1}

First-order reaction: sec^{-1}

Second-order reaction: L mole^{-1} sec^{-1}

28. B is correct.

Low activation energy increases the rate because the energy required for the reaction to proceed is lower.

High temperature increases the rate because faster-moving molecules have a greater probability of collision, which facilitates the reaction.

Combined, lower activation energy and a higher temperature results in the highest relative rate for the reaction.

29. C is correct.

The rate law is calculated by comparing trials and determining how changes in the initial concentrations of the reactants affect the rate of the reaction.

$$\text{rate} = k[A]^x \cdot [B]^y$$

where k is the rate constant, and the exponents x and y are the partial reaction orders (i.e., determined experimentally). They are not equal to the stoichiometric coefficients.

Start by identifying two reactions where the concentration of XO is constant, and O_2 is different: experiments 1 and 2. When the concentration of O_2 is doubled, the rate is also doubled. This indicates that the order of the reaction for O_2 is 1.

Now, determine the order for XO.

Find 2 reactions where the concentration of O_2 is constant, and XO is different: experiments 2 and 3.

When the concentration of XO is tripled, the rate is multiplied by a factor of 9. $3^2 = 9$, which means the order of the reaction with respect to XO is 2.

Therefore, the expression of rate law is:

$$\text{rate} = k[XO]^2 \cdot [O_2]$$

30. D is correct.

$$K_{eq} = [\text{products}] / [\text{reactants}]$$

If the numerator (i.e., products) is smaller than the denominator (i.e., reactants), and fewer products have formed relative to the reactants. Therefore, K_{eq} is less than 1.

31. C is correct. The activation energy is the energy barrier for a reaction to proceed. For the forward reaction, it is measured from the reactants to the highest energy level in the reaction.

A reaction mechanism with low energy of activation proceeds faster than a reaction with the high energy of activation.

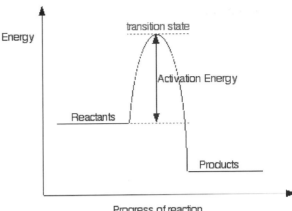

32. E is correct. As the average kinetic energy (i.e., $KE = \frac{1}{2}mv^2$) increases, the particles move faster and collide more frequently per unit time and possess greater energy when they collide. This increases the reaction rate. Hence the reaction rate of most reactions increases with increasing temperature.

For reversible reactions, it is common for the rate law to depend on the concentration of the products. The overall rate is negative (except autocatalytic reactions). As the concentration of products decreases, their collision frequency decreases, and the rate of the reverse reaction decreases. Therefore, the overall rate of the reaction increases.

The main function of catalysts is lowering the reaction's activation energy (energy barrier), thus increasing its rate (k).

33. C is correct. General formula for the equilibrium constant of a reaction:

$$a\text{A} + b\text{B} \leftrightarrow c\text{C} + d\text{D}$$

$$K_{eq} = ([\text{C}]^c \times [\text{D}]^d) / ([\text{A}]^a \times [\text{B}]^b)$$

For the ionization equilibrium (K_i) constant calculation, only include species in aqueous or gas phases (which, in this case, is all):

$$K_i = [\text{H}^+] \cdot [\text{HS}^-] / [\text{H}_2\text{S}]$$

34. B is correct. Reactions are spontaneous when Gibbs free energy (ΔG) is negative, and the reaction is described as exergonic; the products are more stable than the reactants.

Reactions are nonspontaneous when Gibbs free energy (ΔG) is positive, and the reaction is described as endergonic; the products are less stable than the reactants.

35. C is correct. When changing the conditions of a reaction, Le Châtelier's principle states that the position of equilibrium will shift to counteract the change. If the reaction temperature, pressure, or volume is changed, the position of equilibrium will change.

There are 2 moles on each side, so changes in pressure (or volume) do not shift the equilibrium.

36. D is correct.

The enthalpy or heat of reaction (ΔH) is not a function of temperature. Since the reaction is exothermic, Le Châtelier's principle states that increasing the temperature decreases the forward reaction.

37. E is correct. When changing the conditions of a reaction, Le Châtelier's principle states that the position of equilibrium shifts to counteract the change. If the reaction's concentration changes, the position of the equilibrium changes.

According to Le Châtelier's Principle, adding or removing a solid at equilibrium has no effect on the position of equilibrium. However, adding solid $KC_2H_3O_2$ is equivalent to adding K^+ and $C_2H_3O_2^-$ (i.e., product) as it dissociates in aqueous solution. The increased concentration of products shifts the equilibrium toward reactants (i.e., to the left).

Increasing the pH decreases the $[H^+]$ and therefore would shift the reaction to products (i.e., right).

38. E is correct. When changing the conditions of a reaction, Le Châtelier's principle states that the position of equilibrium shifts to counteract the change. If the reaction temperature, pressure or volume is changed, the position of equilibrium will change.

The $K_{eq} = 2.8 \times 10^{-21}$ which indicates a low concentration of products compared to reactants:

$$K_{eq} = [\text{products}] / [\text{reactants}]$$

39. C is correct. All chemical reactions eventually reach equilibrium, the state at which the reactants and products are present in concentrations that have no further tendency to change with time.

Catalysts speed up reactions and therefore increase the rate at which equilibrium is reached, but they never alter the thermodynamics of a reaction and therefore do not change free energy ΔG.

Catalysts do not alter the equilibrium constant.

40. E is correct. To determine the order with respect to W, compare the data for trials 2 and 4.

The concentrations of X and Y do not change when comparing trials 2 and 4, but the concentration of W changes from 0.015 to 0.03, which corresponds to an increase by a factor of 2. However, the rate did not increase (0.08 remains 0.08); therefore the order with respect to W is 0.

The order for X is determined by comparing the data for trials 1 and 3.

The concentrations for W and Z are constant, and the concentration for X increases by a factor of 3 (from 0.05 to 0.15). The rate of the reaction increased by a factor of 9 (0.04 to 0.36). Since $3^2 = 9$, the order of the reaction with respect to X is two.

The order with respect to Y is found by comparing the data from trials 1 and 5. [W] and [X] do not change but [Y] goes up by a factor of 4. The rate from trial 1 to 5 goes up by a factor of 2. Since $4^{1/2} = 2$, the order of the reaction with respect to Y is ½.

The overall order is found by the sum of the orders for X, Y, and Z: $0 + 2 + ½ = 2½$.

41. B is correct. Since the order with respect to W is zero, the rate of formation of Z does not depend on the concentration of W.

42. D is correct.

The rate law is calculated by comparing trials and determining how changes in the initial concentrations of the reactants affect the rate of the reaction.

$$\text{rate} = k[A]^x \cdot [B]^y$$

where k is the rate constant, and the exponents x and y are the partial reaction orders (i.e., determined experimentally). They are not equal to the stoichiometric coefficients.

Use the partial orders determined in question **61** to express the rate law:

$$\text{rate} = k[W]^0[X]^2[Z]^{1/2}$$

Substitute the values for trial #1:

$$0.04 = k\,[0.01]^0[0.05]^2[0.04]^{1/2}$$

$$0.04 = (k) \cdot (1) \cdot (2.5 \times 10^{-3}) \cdot (2 \times 10^{-1})$$

$$k = 80$$

43. B is correct.

The activation energy is the energy barrier that must be overcome for the transformation of reactant(s) into product(s).

The molecules must collide with the proper orientation and energy (i.e., kinetic energy is the average temperature) to overcome the energy of activation barrier.

44. B is correct.

The rate law is calculated experimentally by comparing trials and determining how changes in the initial concentrations of the reactants affect the rate of the reaction.

$$\text{rate} = k[A]^x \cdot [B]^y$$

where k is the rate constant, and the exponents x and y are the partial reaction orders (i.e., determined experimentally). They are not equal to the stoichiometric coefficients.

Comparing Trials 1 and 3, [A] increased by a factor of 3 as did the reaction rate; thus, the reaction is first order with respect to A.

Comparing Trials 1 and 2, [B] increased by a factor of 4, and the reaction rate increased by a factor of $16 = 4^2$. Thus, the reaction is second order with respect to B.

Therefore, the rate $= k[A] \cdot [B]^2$

45. D is correct.

The molecules must collide with enough energy, the frequency of collision, and the proper orientation to overcome the barrier of the activation energy.

46. B is correct.

Increasing $[HC_2H_3O_2]$ and increasing $[H^+]$ will affect the equilibrium because both of the species added are part of the equilibrium equation.

K_{eq} = [products] / [reactants]

K_{eq} = $[C_2H_3O_2^-]$ / $[HC_2H_3O_2]·[H^+]$

Adding solid $NaC_2H_3O_2$: in aqueous solutions, $NaC_2H_3O_2$ dissociates into Na^+ (*aq*) and $C_2H_3O_2^-$ (*aq*).

Therefore, the overall concentration of $C_2H_3O_2^-$ (*aq*) increases and it affects the equilibrium.

Adding solid $NaNO_3$: this is a salt and does not react with any of the reactant or product molecules; therefore, it will not affect the equilibrium.

Adding solid NaOH: the reactant is an acid because it dissociates into hydrogen ions and anions in aqueous solutions. It reacts with bases (e.g., NaOH) to create water and salt.

Thus, NaOH reduces the concentration of the reactant, which will affect the equilibrium.

Increasing $[HC_2H_3O_2]$ and $[H^+]$ increases reactants and drives the reaction toward product formation.

47. D is correct.

Calculate the value of the equilibrium expression: hydrogen iodide concentration decreases for equilibrium to be reached.

K = [products] / [reactants]

K = $[HI]^2$ / $[H_2]·[I_2]$

To determine the state of a reaction, calculate its reaction quotient (Q).

Q has the same method of calculation as equilibrium constant (K); the difference is K must be calculated at the point of equilibrium, whereas Q can be calculated at any time.

If $Q > K$, reaction shifts towards reactants (more reactants, less products)

If $Q = K$, reaction is at equilibrium

If $Q < K$, reaction shifts towards products (more products, less reactants)

Q = $[HI]^2$ / $[H_2]·[I_2]$

Q = $(3)^2$ / 0.4×0.6

Q = 37.5

Because $Q > K$ (i.e., (37.5 > 35), the reaction shifts toward reactants (larger denominator) and the amount of product (HI) decreases.

48. E is correct.

$K = [\text{products}] / [\text{reactants}]$

$K = [CH_3OH] / [H_2O]^2 \cdot [CO]$

None of the stated changes tend to decrease the *magnitude* of the equilibrium constant K.

For exothermic reactions ($\Delta H < 0$), decreasing the temperature increases the magnitude of K.

Changes in volume, pressure, or concentration do not affect the magnitude of K.

49. A is correct.

When two or more reactions are combined to create a new reaction, the K_c of the resulting reaction is a product of K_c values of the individual reactions.

When a reaction is reversed, the new $K_c = 1 / \text{old } K_c$.

Start by analyzing all the reactions provided the problem:

(1) $2 \text{ NO} + Cl_2 \leftrightarrow 2 \text{ NOCl}$ $\qquad\qquad$ $K_c = 3.2 \times 10^3$

(2) $2 \text{ NO}_2 \leftrightarrow 2 \text{ NO} + O_2$ $\qquad\qquad$ $K_c = 15.5$

(3) $\text{NOCl} + \frac{1}{2} O_2 \leftrightarrow \text{NO}_2 + \frac{1}{2} Cl_2$ $\qquad$ $K_c = ?$

Reaction 3 can be created by combining reactions 1 and 2.

For reaction 1, notice that on reaction 3, NOCl is located on the left. To match reaction 3, reverse reaction 1:

$\qquad$ $2 \text{ NOCl} \leftrightarrow 2 \text{ NO} + Cl_2$

The K_c of this reversed reaction is:

$\qquad$ $K_c = 1 / (3.2 \times 10^{-3}) = 312.5$

Reaction 2 also needs to be reversed to match the position of NO in reaction 3:

$\qquad$ $2 \text{ NO} + O_2 \leftrightarrow 2 \text{ NO}_2$

The new K_c will be:

$\qquad$ $K_c = 1 / 15.5 = 0.0645$

Since K of the resulting reaction is the product of K_c from both reactions, add those reactions together:

$\qquad$ $2 \text{ NOCl} \leftrightarrow 2 \text{ NO} + Cl_2$

$\qquad$ $2 \text{ NO} + O_2 \leftrightarrow 2 \text{ NO}_2$

$\qquad$ ─────────────

$\qquad$ $2 \text{ NOCl} + O_2 \leftrightarrow 2 \text{ NO}_2 + Cl_2$

$\qquad$ $K_c = 312.5 \times 0.064 = 20.16$

Divide the equation by 2:

$\qquad$ $\text{NOCl} + \frac{1}{2} O_2 \leftrightarrow \text{NO}_2 + \frac{1}{2} Cl_2$

The new K_c is the square root of the initial K_c:

$\qquad$ $K_c = \sqrt{20.16} = 4.49$

50. C is correct.

Increased pressure or increased concentration of reactants increases the probability that the reactants collide with enough energy and proper orientation to overcome the energy of activation barrier and proceed toward products.

51. B is correct.

The rate law is calculated by comparing trials and determining how changes in the initial concentrations of the reactants affect the rate of the reaction.

$$\text{rate} = k[A]^x \cdot [B]^y$$

where k is the rate constant and the exponents x and y are the partial reaction orders (i.e., determined experimentally). They are not equal to the stoichiometric coefficients.

52. C is correct.

Rates of formation/consumption of all species in a reaction are proportional to their coefficients.

If the rate of a species is known, the rate of other species can be calculated using simple proportions:

coefficient $_{NOBr}$ / coefficient $_{Br2}$ = rate $_{formation\ NOBr}$ / rate $_{consumption\ Br2}$

rate $_{consumption\ Br2}$ = rate $_{formation\ NOBr}$ / (coefficient $_{NOBr}$ / coefficient $_{Br2}$)

rate $_{consumption\ Br2}$ = 4.50×10^{-4} mol L^{-1} s^{-1} / (2 / 1)

rate $_{consumption\ Br2}$ = 2.25×10^{-4} mol L^{-1} s^{-1}

53. D is correct.

When changing the conditions of a reaction, Le Châtelier's principle states that the position of the equilibrium shifts to counteract the change.

If the reaction's concentration of water (i.e., product) is changed, the position of equilibrium changes toward reactants.

54. D is correct. For the general equation:

$$aA + bB \leftrightarrow cC + dD$$

The equilibrium constant is defined as:

$$K_{eq} = ([C]^c \times [D]^d) / ([A]^a \times [B]^b)$$

or

$$K_{eq} = [\text{products}] / [\text{reactants}]$$

If K_{eq} is less than 1 (e.g., 4.3×10^{-17}), then the numerator (i.e., products) is smaller than the denominator (i.e., reactants) and fewer products have formed relative to the reactants.

If the reaction favors reactants compared to products, the equilibrium lies to the left.

55. C is correct.

Use the equilibrium concentrations to calculate K_c:

$$K_c = [N_2] \cdot [H_2]^3 / [NH_3]^2$$

$$K_c = 0.04 \times (0.12)^3 / (0.4)^2$$

$$K_c = 4.3 \times 10^{-4}$$

56. D is correct.

When changing the conditions of a reaction, Le Châtelier's principle states that the position of equilibrium will shift to counteract the change.

If the reaction temperature, pressure, or volume is changed, the position of the equilibrium changes.

Add the molar coefficients in the reaction (i.e., 3 for the reactants and 1 for the product).

In general, decreasing the pressure tends to favor the side of the reaction that has a higher molar coefficient sum (i.e., toward the reactants in this example).

Decreasing the volume favors the side of the reaction that has a smaller molar coefficient sum (i.e., products in this example). Therefore, it would increase the yield of methanol.

Decreasing the temperature of the system favors the production of more heat. It shifts the reaction towards the exothermic side. Because $\Delta H < 0$, the reaction is exothermic in the forward direction (towards product). Therefore, decreasing the temperature increases the yield of methanol.

57. E is correct.

Decreasing the pH: increases the concentration of H^+, which shifts the equilibrium to the left (i.e., increases the chlorine concentration)

Adding HCl: increases the concentration of H^+, which shifts the equilibrium to the left.

Adding HClO: increases the concentration of HClO, which shifts the equilibrium to the left.

Adding NaClO: increases the concentration of ClO^-, which shifts the equilibrium to the left.

58. E is correct.

The main function of catalysts is lowering the reaction's activation energy (energy barrier), thus increasing its rate (k).

Although catalysts do decrease the amount of energy required to reach the rate-limiting transition state, they do *not* decrease the relative energy of the products and reactants.

Therefore, a catalyst does not affect ΔG. Catalysts speed up reactions and therefore increase the rate at which equilibrium is reached, but they never alter the thermodynamics of a reaction and therefore do not change free energy ΔG.

59. E is correct. Balanced reaction:

$3 A + 2 B \rightarrow 4 C$

Moles of A used in the reaction = 1.4 moles – 0.9 moles = 0.5 moles

Moles of C formed = (coefficient C / coefficient A) × moles of A used

Moles of C formed = (4 / 3) × 0.5 moles = 0.67 moles

60. D is correct.

When two or more reactions are combined to create a new reaction, the K_c of the resulting reaction is a product of K_c values of the individual reactions.

When a reaction is reversed:

new K_c = 1 / old K_c

$$PCl_3 + Cl_2 \leftrightarrow PCl_5 \qquad K_c = K_{c1}$$

$$2 NO + Cl_2 \leftrightarrow 2 NOCl \qquad K_c = K_{c2}$$

Reverse the first reaction:

$$PCl_5 \leftrightarrow PCl_3 + Cl_2 \qquad K_c = 1 / K_{c1}$$

Add the two reactions to create a third reaction:

$$PCl_5 \leftrightarrow PCl_3 + Cl_2 \qquad K_c = 1 / K_{c1}$$

$$2 NO + Cl_2 \leftrightarrow 2 NOCl \qquad K_c = K_{c2}$$

_____

$$PCl_5 + 2 NO \leftrightarrow PCl_3 + 2 NOCl$$

$$K = [(1 / K_1) \times K_2]$$

$$K = K_2 / K_1$$

Please, leave your Customer Review on Amazon

Chapter 6 Explanations: Solution Chemistry

1. E is correct.

Solubility is proportional to pressure. Use simple proportions to compare solubility in different pressures:

$P_1 / S_1 = P_2 / S_2$

$S_2 = P_2 / (P_1 / S_1)$

$S_2 = 4.5$ atm $/ (1.00$ atm $/ 1.90$ cc/100 mL$)$

$S_2 = 8.55$ cc $/ 100$ mL

2. E is correct. The correct interpretation of molarity is moles of solute per liter of solvent.

3. A is correct. NaCl is a charged, ionic salt (Na^+ and Cl^-) and therefore is extremely water soluble.

Hexanol can hydrogen bond with water due to the hydroxyl group, but the long hydrocarbon chain reduces its solubility, and the chains interact via hydrophobic interactions forming micelles.

Aluminum hydroxide has poor solubility in water and requires the addition of Brønsted-Lowry acids to dissolve completely.

4. D is correct.

Higher pressure exerts more pressure on the solution, which allows more molecules to dissolve in the solvent.

Lower temperature also increases gas solubility. As the temperature increases, both solvent and solute molecules move faster, and it is more difficult for the solvent molecules to bond with the solute.

5. B is correct. When the compound is dissolved in water, the attached hydrate/water crystals dissociate and become part of the water solvent.

Therefore, the only ions left are 1 Co^{2+} and 2 NO_3^-.

6. A is correct.

An insoluble compound is incapable of being dissolved (especially with reference to water).

Hydroxide salts of Group I elements are soluble, while hydroxide salts of Group II elements (Ca, Sr and Ba) are slightly soluble.

Salts containing nitrate ions (NO_3^-) are generally soluble.

Most sulfate salts are soluble. Important exceptions: $BaSO_4$, $PbSO_4$, Ag_2SO_4 and $SrSO_4$.

Hydroxide salts of transition metals and Al^{3+} are insoluble.

Thus, $Fe(OH)_3$, $Al(OH)_3$ and $Co(OH)_2$ are not soluble.

7. C is correct.

% v/v solution = (volume of acetone / volume of solution) × 100%

% v/v solution = {25 mL / (25 mL + 75 mL)} × 100%

% v/v solution = 25%

8. A is correct.

To find the K_{sp}, take the molarities (or concentrations) of the products (cC and dD) and multiply them.

For K_{sp}, only aqueous species are included in the calculation.

If any of the products have coefficients in front of them, raise the product to that coefficient power and multiply the concentration by that coefficient:

$$K_{sp} = [C]^c \cdot [D]^d$$
$$K_{sp} = [Cu^{2+}]^3 \cdot [PO_4^{3-}]^2$$

The reactant (aA) is solid and is not included in the K_{sp} equation.

Solids are not included when calculating equilibrium constant expressions, because their concentrations do not change the expression.

Any change in their concentrations are insignificant and are thus omitted.

9. C is correct.

In a net ionic equation, substances that do not dissociate in aqueous solutions are written in their molecular form (not broken down into ions).

Gases, liquids, and solids are written in molecular form.

Some solutions do not dissociate into ions in water, or do so in very little amounts (e.g., weak acids such as HF, CH_3COOH).

They are also written in molecular form.

10. E is correct.

Mass % = mass of solute / mass of solution

Rearrange that equation to solve for mass of solution:

mass of solution = mass of solute / mass %

mass of solution = 122 g / 7.50%

mass of solution = 122 g / 0.075

mass of solution = 1,627 g

11. B is correct. Determine moles of NH_3:

Moles of NH_3 = mass of NH_3 / molecular weight of NH_3

Moles of NH_3 = 15.0 g / (14.01 g/mol + 3 × 1.01 g/mol)

Moles of NH_3 = 15.0 g / (17.04 g/mol)

Moles of NH_3 = 0.88 mol

Determine the volume of the solution (solvent + solute):

Volume of solution = mass / density

Volume of solution = (250 g + 15 g) / 0.974 g/mL

Volume of solution = 272.1 mL

Convert volume to liters:

Volume = 272.1 mL × 0.001 L / mL

Volume = 0.2721 L

Divide moles by the volume to calculate molarity:

Molarity = moles / liter of solution

Molarity = 0.88 mol / 0.2721 L

Molarity = 3.23 M

12. A is correct. Solutions with the highest concentration of ions have the highest boiling point.

Calculate the concentration of ions in each solution:

0.2 M $Al(NO_3)_3$ = 0. 2 M × 4 ions = 0.8 M

0. 2 M $MgCl_2$ = 0. 2 M × 3 ions = 0.6 M

0. 2 M glucose = 0. 2 M × 1 ion = 0.2 M (glucose does not dissociate into ions in solution)

0. 2 M Na_2SO_4 = 0. 2 M × 3 ions = 0.6 M

Water = 0 M

13. A is correct.

Calculate the number of ions in each option:

A: $Li_3PO_4 \rightarrow 3\ Li^+ + PO_4^{3-}$ (4 ions)

B: $Ca(NO_3)_2 \rightarrow Ca^{2+} + 2\ NO_3^-$ (3 ions)

C: $MgSO_4 \rightarrow Mg^{2+} + SO_4^{2-}$ (2 ions)

D: $(NH_4)_2SO_4 \rightarrow 2\ NH_4^+ + SO_4^{2-}$ (3 ions)

E: $(NH_4)_4Fe(CN)_6 \rightarrow 4\ NH_4^+ + Fe(CN)_6^{4-}$ (5 ions)

14. B is correct. Note that carbonate salts help remove 'hardness' in water.

Generally, SO_4, NO_3 and Cl salts tend to be soluble in water, while CO_3 salts are less soluble.

15. A is correct. A *spectator ion* is an *ion* that exists in the same form on both the reactant and product sides of a chemical reaction.

Balanced equation:

$$Pb(NO_3)_2 \ (aq) + H_2SO_4 \ (aq) \rightarrow PbSO_4 \ (s) + 2 \ HNO_3 \ (aq)$$

16. C is correct. A polar solute is miscible with a polar solvent.

Ascorbic acid is polar and is therefore miscible in water.

17. E is correct. Apply the formula for the molar concentration of a solution:

$$M_1 V_1 = M_2 V_2$$

Substitute the given volume and molar concentrations of HCl, solve for the final volume of HCl of the resulting dilution:

$$V_2 = [M_1 V_1] / (M_2)$$

$$V_2 = [(2.00 \ M \ HCl) \times (0.125 \ L \ HCl)] / (0.400 \ M \ HCl)$$

$$V_2 = 0.625 \ L \ HCl$$

Solve for the volume of water needed to be added to the initial volume of HCl to obtain the final diluted volume of HCl:

$$V_{H_2O} = V_2 - V_1$$

$$V_{H_2O} = (0.625 \ L \ HCl) - (0.125 \ L \ HCl)$$

$$V_{H_2O} = 0.500 \ L = 500 \ mL$$

18. A is correct. The *–ate* ending indicates the species with more oxygen than species ending in *–ite*.

However, it does not indicate a specific number of oxygen molecules.

19. D is correct. In this case, hydration means dissolving in water rather than reacting with water.

Therefore, the compound dissociates into its ions (without involving water in the actual chemical reaction).

20. E is correct. *Like dissolves like* means that polar substances tend to dissolve in polar solvents and nonpolar substances in nonpolar solvents.

Molecules that can form hydrogen bonds with water are soluble.

Salts are ionic compounds.

The anion and cation bond with the polar molecule of water and are both soluble.

21. B is correct.

Like dissolves like means that polar substances tend to dissolve in polar solvents and nonpolar substances in nonpolar solvents.

Methanol (CH_3OH) is a polar molecule. Therefore, methanol is soluble in water because it can hydrogen bond with the water.

22. B is correct.

Break down the molecules into their constituent ions:

$$CaCO_3 + 2\,H^+ + 2\,NO_3^- \rightarrow Ca^{2+} + 2\,NO_3^- + CO_2 + H_2O$$

Remove all species that appear on both sides of the reaction:

$$CaCO_3 + 2\,H^+ \rightarrow Ca^{2+} + CO_2 + H_2O$$

23. D is correct.

According to the problem, there are 0.950 moles of nitrate ion in a $Fe(NO_3)_3$ solution.

Because there are three nitrate (NO_3) ions for each $Fe(NO_3)_3$ molecule, the moles of $Fe(NO_3)_3$ can be calculated:

$$(1 \text{ mole} / 3 \text{ mole}) \times 0.950 \text{ moles} = 0.317 \text{ moles}$$

Calculate the volume of solution:

Volume of solution = moles of solute / molarity

Volume of solution = 0.317 moles / 0.550 mol/L

Volume of solution = 0.576 L

Convert the volume into milliliters:

$$0.576 \text{ L} \times 1{,}000 \text{ mL/L} = 576 \text{ mL}$$

24. A is correct.

Start by calculating the number of moles:

Moles of LiOH = mass of LiOH / molar mass of LiOH

Moles of LiOH = 36.0 g / (24.0 g/mol)

Moles of LiOH = 1.50 moles

Divide moles by volume to calculate molarity:

Molarity = moles / volume

Molarity = 1.50 moles / (975 mL × 0.001 L/mL)

Molarity = 1.54 M

---

25. D is correct. When AgCl dissociates, equal amounts of Ag^+ and Cl^- are produced.

If the concentration of Cl^- is B, this must also be the concentration of Ag^+.

Therefore, B can be the concentration of Ag.

The concentration of silver ion can also be determined by dividing the K_{sp} by the concentration of chloride ion:

$$K_{sp} = [Ag^+] \cdot [Cl^-].$$

Therefore, the concentration of Ag can be A/B moles/liter.

26. B is correct.

Strong electrolytes dissociate completely (or almost completely) in water. Strong acids and bases both dissociate almost completely, but weak acids and bases dissociate only slightly.

27. B is correct. Since the empirical formula for magnesium iodide is MgI_2, two moles of dissolved I^- result from each mole of dissolved MgI_2.

Therefore, if $[MgI_2] = 0.40$ M, then $[I^-] = 2(0.40$ M$) = 0.80$ M.

28. A is correct. The chlorite ion (chlorine dioxide anion) is ClO_2^-. Chlorite is a compound that contains this group, with chlorine in an oxidation state of $+3$.

Formula	Cl^-	ClO^-	ClO_2^-	ClO_3^-	ClO_4^-
Anion name	chloride	hypochlorite	chlorite	chlorate	perchlorate
Oxidation state	-1	$+1$	$+3$	$+5$	$+7$

29. D is correct. Water softeners cannot remove ions from the water without replacing them. The process replaces the ions that cause scaling (precipitation) with non-reactive ions.

30. A is correct. Hydration involves the interaction of water molecules to the solute. The water molecules exchange bonding relationships with the solute, whereby water-water bonds break and water-solute bonds form.

When an ion is hydrated, it is surrounded and bonded by water molecules. The average number of water molecules bonding to an ion is known as its hydration number.

Hydration numbers can vary but often are either 4 or 6.

31. B is correct. Only aqueous (*aq*) species are broken down into their ions for ionic equations. Solids, liquids, and gases stay the same.

32. E is correct. For K_{sp}, only aqueous species are included in the calculation.

The decomposition of $PbCl_2$:

$$PbCl_2 \rightarrow Pb^{2+} + 2\ Cl^-$$

$$K_{sp} = [Pb^{2+}] \cdot [Cl^-]^2$$

When x moles of $PbCl_2$ fully dissociate, x moles of Pb and $2x$ moles of Cl^- are produced:

$$K_{sp} = (x) \cdot (2x)^2$$

$$K_{sp} = 4x^3$$

33. B is correct. Strong electrolytes dissociate completely (or almost completely) in water.

Strong acids and bases both dissociate nearly completely (i.e., form stable anions), but weak acids and bases dissociate only slightly (i.e., form unstable anions).

34. A is correct. When a solution is diluted, the moles of solute (n) is constant.

However, the molarity and volume will change because n = MV:

$$n_1 = n_2$$

$$M_1V_1 = M_2V_2$$

$$V_2 = (M_1V_1) / M_2$$

$$V_2 = (0.20\ M \times 6.0\ L) / 14\ M$$

$$V_2 = 0.086\ L$$

Convert to milliliters:

$$0.086\ L \times (1,000\ mL / L) = 86\ mL$$

35. B is correct. *Like dissolves like* means that polar substances tend to dissolve in polar solvents, and nonpolar substances in nonpolar solvents. Since benzene is nonpolar, look for a nonpolar substance.

Silver chloride is ionic, while CH_2Cl_2, H_2S, and SO_2 are polar.

36. B is correct. Molarity can vary based on temperature because it involves the volume of solution.

At different temperatures, the volume of water varies slightly, which affects the molarity.

37. D is correct.
Concentration:

solute / volume

For example: 10 g / 1 liter = 10 g/liter

2 g / 1 liter = 2 g/liter

38. E is correct. The NaOH content is 5.0% (w/v). It means that the solute (NaOH) is measured in grams, but the solution volume is measured in milliliters. Therefore, in this problem, the mass and volume of the solution are interchangeable (1 g = 1 mL).

mass of NaOH = % NaOH × volume of solution

mass of NaOH = 5.0% × 75.0 mL

mass of NaOH = 3.75 g

39. D is correct. Adding NaCl increases [Cl⁻] in solution (i.e., common ion effect), which increases the precipitation of $PbCl_2$, because the ion product increases. This increase causes lead chloride to precipitate and the concentration of free chloride in solution to decrease.

40. A is correct. AgCl has a stronger tendency to form than $PbCl_2$ because of its smaller K_{sp}.

Therefore, as AgCl forms, an equivalent amount of $PbCl_2$ dissolves.

41. A is correct.

For the dissolution of $PbCl_2$:

$PbCl_2 \rightarrow Pb^{2+} + 2\ Cl^-$

$K_{sp} = [Pb^{2+}] \cdot [2\ Cl^-]^2 = 10^{-5}$

$K_{sp} = (x) \cdot (2x)^2 = 10^{-5}$

$4x^3 = 10^{-5}$

$x \approx 0.014$

$[Cl^-] = 2(0.014)$

$[Cl^-] = 0.028$

For the dissolution of AgCl:

$AgCl \rightarrow Ag^+ + Cl^-$

$K_{sp} = [Ag^+] \cdot [Cl^-]$

$K_{sp} = (x) \cdot (x)$

$10^{-10} = x^2$

$x = 10^{-5}$

$[Cl^-] = 10^{-5}$

42. A is correct.

The intermolecular bonding (i.e., van der Waals) in all alkanes is similar.

43. C is correct. Ideally, dilute solutions are so dilute that solute molecules do not interact.

Therefore, the mole fraction of the solvent approaches one.

44. D is correct.

Henry's law states that, at a constant temperature, the amount of gas that dissolves in a volume of liquid is directly proportional to the partial pressure of that gas in equilibrium with that liquid.

Tyndall effect is light scattering by particles in a colloid (or particles in a very fine suspension).

A colloidal suspension contains microscopically dispersed insoluble particles (i.e., colloid) suspended throughout the liquid. The colloid particles are larger than those of the solution, but not large enough to precipitate due to gravity.

45. E is correct.

An insoluble compound is incapable of being dissolved (especially with reference to water).

Hydroxide salts of Group I elements are soluble.

Hydroxide salts of Group II elements (Ca, Sr and Ba) are slightly soluble.

Hydroxide salts of transition metals and Al^{3+} are insoluble. Thus, $Fe(OH)_3$, $Al(OH)_3$, $Co(OH)_2$ are not soluble.

Most sulfate salts are soluble. Important exceptions are: $BaSO_4$, $PbSO_4$, Ag_2SO_4 and $SrSO_4$.

Salts containing Cl^-, Br^- and I^- are generally soluble. Exceptions are halide salts of Ag^+, Pb^{2+} and $(Hg_2)^{2+}$. $AgCl$, $PbBr_2$ and Hg_2Cl_2 are all insoluble.

Chromates are frequently insoluble. Examples: $PbCrO_4$, $BaCrO_4$

46. C is correct. The overall reaction is:

$$Zn \ (s) + 2 \ HCl \ (aq) \rightarrow ZnCl_2 \ (aq) + H_2 \ (g)$$

Because HCl and $ZnCl_2$ are ionic, they both dissociate into ions in aqueous solutions:

$$Zn \ (s) + 2 \ H^+ \ (aq) + 2 \ Cl^- \ (aq) \rightarrow Zn^{2+} \ (aq) + 2 \ Cl^- \ (aq) + H_2 \ (g)$$

The common ion (Cl^-) cancels to yield the net ionic reaction:

$$Zn \ (s) + 2 \ H^+ \ (aq) \rightarrow Zn^{2+} \ (aq) + H_2 \ (g)$$

47. E is correct.

To determine the number of equivalents:

(4 moles / liter) × (3 equivalents / mole) × (1/3 liter)

= 4 equivalents

48. A is correct.

An electrolyte is a substance that produces an electrically conducting solution when dissolved in a polar solvent (e.g., water).

The dissolved electrolyte separates into positively charged cations and negatively charged anions.

Electrolytes conduct electricity.

49. A is correct. This is a frequently encountered insoluble salt in chemistry problems.

Most sulfate salts are soluble. Important exceptions are: $BaSO_4$, $PbSO_4$, Ag_2SO_4 and $SrSO_4$.

50. C is correct.

Gas solubility is inversely proportional to temperature, so a low temperature increases solubility.

The high pressure of O_2 above the solution increases both pressure of solution (which improves solubility) and the amount of O_2 available for dissolving.

51. C is correct. Molality is the number of solute moles dissolved in 1,000 grams of solvent.

The total mass of the solution is 1,000 g + mass of solute.

Mass of solute (CH_3OH) = moles CH_3OH × molecular mass of CH_3OH

Mass of solute (CH_3OH) = 8.60 moles × [12.01 g/mol + (4 × 1.01 g/mol) + 16 g/mol]

Mass of solute (CH_3OH) = 8.60 moles × (32.05 g/mol)

Mass of solute (CH_3OH) = 275.63 g

Total mass of solution: 1,000 g + 275.63 g = 1,275.63 g

Volume of solution = mass / density

Volume of solution = 1,275.63 g / 0.94 g/mL

Volume of solution = 1,357.05 mL

Divide moles by volume to calculate molarity:

Molarity = number of moles / volume

Molarity = 8.60 moles / 1,357.05 mL

Molarity = 6.34 M

52. E is correct.

By definition, a 15.0% aqueous solution of KI contains 15% KI and the remainder ($100\% - 15\% = 85\%$) is water.

If there are 100 g of KI solution, it has 15 g of KI and 85 g of water.

The answer choice of 15 g KI / 100 g water is incorrect because 100 g is the mass of the solution; the actual mass of water is 85 g.

53. D is correct.

Mass % of solute = (mass of solute / mass of seawater) × 100%

Mass % of solute = (1.35 g / 25.88 g) × 100%

Mass % of solute = 5.22%

54. A is correct.

Some solutions are colored (e.g., Kool-Aid powder dissolved in water).

The color of chemicals is a physical property of chemicals from (most commonly) the excitation of electrons due to absorption of energy by the chemical. The observer sees not the absorbed color, but the wavelength that is reflected.

Most simple inorganic (e.g., sodium chloride) and organic compounds (e.g., ethanol) are colorless.

Transition metal compounds are often colored because of transitions of electrons between *d*-orbitals of different energy.

Organic compounds tend to be colored when there is extensive conjugation (i.e., alternating double and single bonds), causing the energy gap between the *HOMO* (i.e., highest occupied molecular orbital) and *LUMO* (i.e., lowest unoccupied molecular orbital) to decrease, bringing the absorption band from the UV to the visible region.

Color is also due to the energy absorbed by the compound when an electron transitions from the *HOMO* to the *LUMO*.

A physical change is a change in physical properties, such as melting, the transition to gas, changes to crystal form, color, volume, shape, size, and density.

55. E is correct.

As the name suggests, solubility product constant (K_{sp}) is a product of solubility of each ion in an ionic compound.

Start by writing the dissociation equation of AgCl in a solution:

$$AgCl\ (s) \rightarrow Ag^+\ (aq) + Cl^-\ (aq)$$

The solubility of AgCl is provided in the problem: 1.3×10^{-4} mol/L. This is the maximum amount of AgCl that can be dissolved in water in standard conditions.

There are 1.3×10^{-4} mol AgCl dissolved in one liter of water, which means that there are 1.3×10^{-4} mol of Ag^+ ions and 1.3×10^{-4} mol of Cl^- ions.

K_{sp} is calculated using the same method as the equilibrium constant: concentration of ion to the power of ion coefficient. Only aqueous species are included in the calculation.

For AgCl:

$$K_{sp} = [Ag] \cdot [Cl]$$

$$K_{sp} = (1.3 \times 10^{-4}) \cdot (1.3 \times 10^{-4})$$

$$K_{sp} = 1.7 \times 10^{-8}$$

56. E is correct.

Concentration:

solute / volume

For example: 10 g / 1 liter = 10 g/liter

5 g / 0.5 liter = 10 g/liter

57. B is correct.

The reaction is endothermic because the temperature of the solution drops as the reaction absorbs heat from the environment, and $\Delta H°$ is positive.

The solution is unsaturated at 1 molar so dissolving more salt at standard conditions is spontaneous, and $\Delta G°$ is negative.

58. E is correct.

The heat of a solution is the enthalpy change (or energy absorbed as heat at constant pressure) when a solution forms.

For solution formation, solvent-solvent bonds and solute-solute bonds must be broken, while solute-solvent bonds are formed.

The breaking of bonds absorbs energy, while the formation of bonds releases energy.

If the heat of solution is negative, energy is released.

59. E is correct.

The reaction is endothermic if the bonds formed have lower energy than the bonds broken.

From $\Delta G = \Delta H - T\Delta S$, the entropy of the system increases if the reaction is spontaneous.

60. D is correct. Balanced reaction:

$$BaCl_2 + K_2CrO_4 \rightarrow BaCrO_4 + 2\ KCl$$

In general, most Cl and K compounds are soluble; therefore, KCl is more likely to be soluble than $BaCrO_4$.

Chapter 7 Explanations: Acids and Bases

1. A is correct. An acid dissociates a proton to form the conjugate base, while a conjugate base accepts a proton to form the acid.

2. C is correct. The Brønsted-Lowry acid–base theory focuses on the ability to accept and donate protons (H^+).

A Brønsted-Lowry acid is a term for a substance that donates a proton (H^+) in an acid–base reaction, while a Brønsted-Lowry base is a term for a substance that accepts a proton.

3. C is correct.

A solution's conductivity is correlated to the number of ions present in a solution. The fact that the bulb is shining brightly implies that the solution is an excellent conductor, which means that the solution has a high concentration of ions.

4. E is correct.

To find the pH of strong acid and strong base solutions (where $[H^+] > 10^{-6}$), use the equation:

$$pH = -\log[H_3O^+]$$

Given that $[H^+] < 10^{-6}$, the pH = 4.

Note that this approach only applies to strong acids and strong bases.

5. B is correct.

The self-ionization (autoionization) of water is an ionization reaction in pure water or an aqueous solution, in which a water molecule, H_2O, deprotonates (loses the nucleus of one of its hydrogen atoms) to become a hydroxide ion (^-OH).

6. B is correct.

An electrolyte is a substance that dissociates into cations (i.e., positive ions) and anions (i.e., negative ions) when placed in solution.

NH_3 is a weak acid with a pK_a of 38. Therefore, it does not readily dissociate into H^+ and $^-NH_2$.

HCO_3^- (bicarbonate) has a pK_a of about 10.3 and is considered a weak acid because it does not dissociate completely. Therefore, it does not readily dissociate into H^+ and CO_3^{2-}.

HCN (nitrile) is a weak acid with a pK_a of 9.3. Therefore, it does not readily dissociate into H^+ and ^-CN (i.e., cyanide).

7. B is correct. If the $[H_3O^+] = [^-OH]$, it has a pH of 7 and the solution is neutral.

8. A is correct. pI is the symbol for isoelectric point: the pH where a protein ion has zero net charge.

To calculate pI of amino acids with 2 pK_a values, take the average of the pK_a's:

$$pI = (pK_{a1} + pK_{a2}) / 2$$
$$pI = (2.2 + 4.2) / 2$$
$$pI = 3.2$$

9. D is correct.

Acidic solutions contain hydronium ions (H_3O^+). These ions are in the aqueous form because they are dissolved in water. Although chemists often write H^+ (*aq*), referring to a single hydrogen nucleus (a proton), it exists as the hydronium ion (H_3O^+).

10. D is correct. The ionic product constant of water:

$$K_w = [H_3O^+] \cdot [^-OH]$$
$$[^-OH] = K_w / [H_3O^+]$$
$$[^-OH] = [1 \times 10^{-14}] / [7.5 \times 10^{-9}]$$
$$[^-OH] = 1.3 \times 10^{-6}$$

11. C is correct.

Consider the K_a presented in the question – which species is more acidic or basic than NH_3?

NH_4^+ is correct because it is NH_3 after absorbing one proton. The concentration of H^+ in water is proportional to K_a. NH_4^+ is the conjugate acid of NH_3.

A: H^+ is acidic.

B: NH_2^- is NH_3 with one less proton. If a base loses a proton, it would be an even stronger base with a higher affinity for proton, so this is not a weaker base than NH_3.

D: Water is neutral.

E: $NaNH_2$ is the neutral species of NH_2^-.

12. E is correct. An acid as a reactant produces a conjugate base, while a base as a reactant produces a conjugate acid.

The conjugate base of a chemical species is that species after H^+ has dissociated.

Therefore, the conjugate base of HSO_4^- is SO_4^{2-}.

The conjugate base of H_3O^+ is H_2O.

13. A is correct. Start by calculating the moles of $Ca(OH)_2$:

Moles of $Ca(OH)_2$ = molarity $Ca(OH)_2$ × volume of $Ca(OH)_2$

Moles of $Ca(OH)_2$ = 0.1 M × (30 mL × 0.001 L/mL)

Moles of $Ca(OH)_2$ = 0.003 mol

Use the coefficients from the reaction equation to determine moles of HNO_3:

Moles of HNO_3 = (coefficient of HNO_3) / [coefficient $Ca(OH)_2$ × moles of $Ca(OH)_2$]

Moles of HNO_3 = (2 / 1) × 0.003 mol

Moles of HNO_3 = 0.006 mol

Divide moles by molarity to calculate volume:

Volume of HNO_3 = moles of HNO_3 / molarity of HNO_3

Volume of HNO_3 = 0.006 mol / 0.2 M

Volume of HNO_3 = 0.03 L

Convert volume to milliliters:

0.03 L × 1000 mL / L = 30 mL

14. D is correct.

Acidic solutions have a pH less than 7 due to a higher concentration of H^+ ions relative to ^-OH ions.

Basic solutions have a pH greater than 7 due to a higher concentration of ^-OH ions relative to H^+ ions.

15. D is correct. An amphoteric compound can react both as an acid (i.e., donates protons) as well as a base (i.e., accepts protons).

Examples of amphoteric molecules include amino acids (i.e., an amine and carboxylic acid group), and self-ionizable compounds such as water.

16. B is correct. Balanced reaction:

$H_3PO_4 + 3\ LIOH = Li_3PO_4 + 3\ H_2O$

In neutralization of acids and bases, the result is always salt and water.

Phosphoric acid and lithium hydroxide react; resulting compounds are lithium phosphate and water.

17. B is correct. Base strength is determined by the stability of the compound. If the compound is unstable in its present state, it seeks a bonding partner (e.g., H+ or another atom) by donating its electrons for the new bond formation.

The 8 strong bases are: LiOH (lithium hydroxide), NaOH (sodium hydroxide), KOH (potassium hydroxide), $Ca(OH)_2$ (calcium hydroxide), RbOH (rubidium hydroxide), $Sr(OH)_2$, (strontium hydroxide), CsOH (cesium hydroxide) and $Ba(OH)_2$ (barium hydroxide).

18. D is correct. The formula for pH:

$$pH = -\log[H^+]$$

Rearrange to solve for $[H^+]$:

$$[H^+] = 10^{-pH}$$

$$[H^+] = 10^{-2} \text{ M} = 0.01 \text{ M}$$

19. E is correct. The 7 strong acids are: HCl (hydrochloric acid), HNO_3 (nitric acid), H_2SO_4 (sulfuric acid), HBr (hydrobromic acid), HI (hydroiodic acid), $HClO_3$ (chloric acid) and $HClO_4$ (perchloric acid).

The eight strong bases are: LiOH (lithium hydroxide), NaOH (sodium hydroxide), KOH (potassium hydroxide), $Ca(OH)_2$ (calcium hydroxide), RbOH (rubidium hydroxide), $Sr(OH)_2$, (strontium hydroxide), CsOH (cesium hydroxide) and $Ba(OH)_2$ (barium hydroxide).

20. D is correct. With polyprotic acids (i.e., more than one H^+ present), the pK_a indicates the pH at which the H^+ is deprotonated. If the pH goes above the first pK_a, one proton dissociates, and so on.

In this example, the pH is above both the first and second pK_a, so two acid groups are deprotonated while the third acidic proton is unaffected.

21. E is correct. It is important to identify the acid that is active in the reaction.

The parent acid is defined as the most protonated form of the buffer. The number of dissociating protons an acid can donate depends on the charge of its conjugate base.

$Ba_2P_2O_7$ is given as one of the products in the reaction. Because barium is a group 2B metal, it has a stable oxidation state of $+2$. Because two barium cations are present in the product, the charge of P_2O_7 ion (the conjugate base in the reaction) must be -4.

Therefore, the fully protonated form of this conjugate must be $H_4P_2O_7$, which is a tetraprotic acid because it has 4 protons that can dissociate.

22. C is correct. The greater the concentration of H_3O^+, the more acidic is the solution.

23. B is correct. KCl and NaI are both salts.

Two salts only react if one of the products precipitates.

In this example, the products (KI and NaCl) are both soluble in water, so they do not react.

24. E is correct.

An acid anhydride is a compound that has two acyl groups bonded to the same oxygen atom.

Anhydride means *without water* and is formed via a dehydration (i.e., removal of H_2O) reaction.

25. D is correct. Learn the ions involved in boiler scale formations: CO_3^{2-} and the metal ions.

26. E is correct.

A buffer is an aqueous solution that consists of a weak acid and its conjugate base, or vice versa.

Buffered solutions resist changes in pH and are often used to keep the pH at a nearly constant value in many chemical applications. It does this by readily absorbing or releasing protons (H^+) and ^-OH.

When an acid is added to the solution, the buffer releases ^-OH and accepts H^+ ions from the acid.

To create a buffer solution, there needs to be a pair of a weak acid/base and its conjugate, or a salt that contains an ion from the weak acid/base.

Since the problem indicates that sulfoxylic acid (H_2SO_2), which has a pK_a 7.97, needs to be in the mixture, the other component would be an HSO_2^- ion (bisulfoxylate) of $NaHSO_2$.

27. C is correct.

Acidic salt is a salt that still contains H^+ in its anion. It is formed when a polyprotic acid is partially neutralized, leaving at least 1 H^+.

For example:

$H_3PO_4 + 2\ KOH \rightarrow K_2HPO_4 + 2\ H_2O$: (partial neutralization, K_2HPO_4 is acidic salt)

While:

$H_3PO_4 + 3\ KOH \rightarrow K_3PO_4 + 3\ H_2O$: (complete neutralization, K_3PO_4 is not acidic salt)

28. A is correct. By the Brønsted-Lowry definition, an acid donates protons, while a base accepts protons. On the product side of the reaction, H_2O acts as a base (i.e., the conjugate base of H_3O^+) and HCl acts as an acid (i.e., the conjugate acid of Cl^-).

29. D is correct. The ratio of the conjugate base to the acid must be determined from the pH of the solution and the pK_a of the acidic component in the reaction.

In the reaction, $H_2PO_4^-$ acts as the acid and HPO_4^{2-} acts as the base, so the pK_a of $H_2PO_4^-$ should be used in the equation.

Substitute the given values into the Henderson-Hasselbalch equation:

$pH = pK_a + \log[\text{salt}/\text{acid}]$

$7.35 = 6.87 + \log[\text{salt}/\text{acid}]$

Since $H_2PO_4^-$ is acting as the acid, subtract 6.87 from both sides:

$0.48 = \log[\text{salt}/\text{acid}]$

The log base is 10, so the inverse log will give:

$10^{0.48} = (\text{salt}/\text{acid})$

$(\text{salt}/\text{acid}) = 3.02$

The ratio between the conjugate base or salt and the acid is 3.02 / 1.

30. B is correct. An electrolyte is a substance that dissociates into cations (i.e., positive ions) and anions (i.e., negative ions) when placed in solution. The fact that the light bulb is dimly lit indicates that the solution contains only a low concentration (i.e., partial ionization) of the ions.

An electrolyte produces an electrically conducting solution when dissolved in a polar solvent (e.g., water). The dissolved ions disperse uniformly through the solvent. If an electrical potential (i.e., voltage) is applied to such a solution, the cations of the solution migrate towards the electrode (i.e., an abundance of electrons), while the anions migrate towards the electrode (i.e., a deficit of electrons).

31. C is correct. The Arrhenius acid–base theory states that acids produce H^+ ions (protons) in H_2O solution and bases produce ^-OH ions (hydroxide) in H_2O solution.

The Brønsted-Lowry acid–base theory focuses on the ability to accept and donate protons (H^+).

A Brønsted-Lowry acid is a term for a substance that donates a proton in an acid–base reaction, while a Brønsted-Lowry base is a term for a substance that accepts a proton.

32. A is correct. By the Brønsted-Lowry acid–base theory:

An acid (reactant) dissociates a proton to become the conjugate base (product).

A base (reactant) gains a proton to become the conjugate acid (product).

The definition is expressed in terms of an equilibrium expression:

$$\text{acid} + \text{base} \leftrightarrow \text{conjugate base} + \text{conjugate acid}.$$

33. E is correct. Acidic solutions contain hydronium ions (H_3O^+). These ions are in the aqueous form because they are dissolved in water. Although chemists often write H^+ (*aq*), referring to a single hydrogen nucleus (a proton), it exists as the hydronium ion (H_3O^+).

34. A is correct. With a K_a of 10^{-5}, the pH of a 1 M solution of the carboxylic acid, $CH_3CH_2CH2CO_2H$, would be 5 and is a weak acid.

Only $CH_3CH_2CH_2CO_2H$ can be considered a weak acid because it yields a (relatively) unstable anion.

35. B is correct. The pH of a buffer is calculated using the Henderson-Hasselbalch equation:

$$pH = pK_a + \log([\text{conjugate base}] / [\text{conjugate acid}])$$

When [acid] = [base], the fraction is 1.

Log 1 = 0,

$$pH = pK_a + 0$$

If the K_a of the acid is 4.6×10^{-4}, (between 10^{-4} and 10^{-3}), the pK_a (and therefore the pH) is between 3 and 4.

36. C is correct. K_w is the water ionization constant (also known as water autoproteolysis constant).

It can be determined experimentally and equals 1.011×10^{-14} at 25 °C (1.00×10^{-14} is used).

37. A is correct.

The Brønsted-Lowry acid–base theory focuses on the ability to accept and donate protons (H^+).

A Brønsted-Lowry acid is a term for a substance that donates a proton in an acid–base reaction, while a Brønsted-Lowry base is a term for a substance that accepts a proton.

38. A is correct.

Buffered solutions resist changes in pH and are often used to keep the pH at a nearly constant value in many chemical applications. It does this by readily absorbing or releasing protons (H^+) and ^-OH.

H_2SO_4 is a strong acid. Weak acids and their salts are good buffers.

A buffer is an aqueous solution that consists of a weak acid and its conjugate base, or vice versa.

When an acid is added to the solution, the buffer releases ^-OH and accepts H^+ ions from the acid.

When a base is added, the buffer accepts ^-OH ions from the base and releases protons (H^+).

39. D is correct. Henderson-Hasselbach equation:

$$pH = pK_a + \log(A^- / HA)$$

A buffer is an aqueous solution that consists of a weak acid and its conjugate base, or vice versa.

Buffered solutions resist changes in pH and are often used to keep the pH at a nearly constant value in many chemical applications. It does this by readily absorbing or releasing protons (H^+) and ^-OH.

When an acid is added to the solution, the buffer releases ^-OH and accepts H^+ ions from the acid.

40. E is correct. The balanced reaction.

$$2\ H_3PO_4 + 3\ Ba(OH)_2 \rightarrow Ba_3(PO_4)_2 + 6\ H_2O$$

There are 2 moles of H_3PO_4 in a balanced reaction.

However, acids are categorized by the number of H^+ per mole of acid.

For example:

HCl is monoprotic (has one H^+ to dissociate).

H_2SO_4 is diprotic (has two H^+ to dissociate).

H_3PO_4 is triprotic acid (has three H^+ to dissociate).

41. E is correct. Because Na^+ forms a strong base (NaOH) and S forms a weak acid (H_2S), it undergoes a hydrolysis reaction in water:

$$Na_2S\ (aq) + 2\ H_2O\ (l) \rightarrow 2\ NaOH\ (aq) + H_2S$$

Ionic equation for individual ions:

$$2\,Na^+ + S^{2-} + 2\,H_2O \rightarrow 2\,Na^+ + 2\,OH^- + H_2S$$

Removing Na^+ ions from both sides of the reaction:

$$S^{2-} + 2\,H_2O \rightarrow HS^- + 2\,OH^-$$

42. A is correct. It is important to recognize all the chromate ions:

Dichromate: $Cr_2O_7^{2-}$

Chromium (II): Cr^{2+}

Chromic/Chromate: CrO_4^-

Trichromic acid: does not exist.

43. B is correct.
The acid requires two equivalents of base to be fully titrated and therefore is a diprotic acid.

Using the fully protonated sulfuric acid (H_2SO_4) as an example: At point A, the acid is 50% fully protonated, 50% singly deprotonated: (50% H_2SO_4: 50% HSO_4^-). At point B, the acid exists in the singly deprotonated form only (100% HSO_4^-). At point C, the acid exists as 50% singly deprotonated HSO_4^- and 50% doubly deprotonated SO_4^{2-}. At point D, the acid exists as 100% SO_4^{2-}.

Point A is known as pK_{a1}, and point C is pK_{a2} (i.e., strongest buffering regions). Point B and D are known as equivalence points (i.e., weakest buffering region)

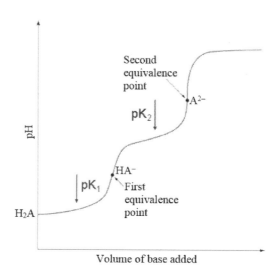

Titration curve: addition of strong base to diprotic acid (H_2A)

44. C is correct. Point C on the graph for the question is pK_{a2}. At this point, the acid exists as 50% singly deprotonated (e.g., HSO_4^-) and 50% doubly deprotonated (e.g., SO_4^{2-}).

The Henderson-Hasselbalch equation:

$$pH = pK_{a2} + \log[salt/acid]$$

$$pH = pK_{a2} + \log[50\%/50\%]$$

$$pH = pK_{a2} + \log[1]$$

$$pH = pK_{a2} + 0$$

$$pH = pK_{a2}$$

45. A is correct.

Point A is pK_{a1}. At this point, the acid exists as 50% fully protonated (e.g., H_2SO_4) and 50% singly deprotonated (e.g., HSO_4^-).

The Henderson-Hasselbalch equation:

$$pH = pK_{a1} + \log[\text{salt} / \text{acid}]$$

$$pH = pK_{a1} + \log[50\% / 50\%]$$

$$pH = pK_{a1} + \log[1]$$

$$pH = pK_{a1} + 0$$

$$pH = pK_{a1}$$

46. B is correct. At point B on the graph (i.e., equivalence point), the acid exists in the singly deprotonated form only (100% HSO_4^- for the example of H_2SO_4).

47. B is correct. The buffer region is the flattest region on the curve (the region that resists pH increases with added base). This diprotic acid has two buffering regions: pK_{a1} (around point A) and pK_{a2} (around point C). A buffer is an aqueous solution that consists of a weak acid and its conjugate base, or vice versa.

Buffered solutions resist changes in pH and are often used to keep the pH at a nearly constant value in many chemical applications. It does this by readily absorbing or releasing protons (H^+) and OH.

When an acid is added to the solution, the buffer releases ^-OH and accepts H^+ ions from the acid. When a base is added, the buffer accepts ^-OH ions from the base and releases protons (H^+).

48. D is correct.

Sodium hydroxide turns into soap (i.e., saponification) from the reaction with the fatty acid esters and oils on the fingertips (i.e., skin).

Fatty acid esters react with NaOH by releasing free fatty acids, which act as soap surrounding grease with their nonpolar (i.e., hydrophobic) ends, while their polar (i.e., hydrophilic) ends orient towards water molecules. This decreases friction and accounts for the slippery feel of NaOH interacting with the skin.

49. E is correct.

I: water is always produced in a neutralization reaction.

II: this reaction is a common example of neutralization, but it is not always the case. For example, weak bases react with strong acids:

$$AH + B \rightleftharpoons A^- + BH^+$$

Or strong bases react with weak acids:

$$AH + H_2O \rightleftharpoons H_3O^+ + A^-$$

III: neutralization occurs when acid donates a proton to the base.

50. E is correct.

Formula to calculate pH of an acidic buffer:

$$[H^+] = ([\text{acid}] / [\text{salt}]) \times K_a$$

Calculate H$^+$ from pH:

$$[H^+] = 10^{-pH}$$

$$[H^+] = 10^{-4}$$

Calculate Ka from pK_a:

$$K_a = 10^{-pKa}$$

$$K_a = 10^{-3}$$

Substitute values into the buffer equation:

$$[H^+] = ([acid] / [salt]) \times K_a$$

$$10^{-4} = ([acid] / [salt]) \times 10^{-3}$$

$$10^{-1} = [acid] / [salt]$$

$$[salt] / [acid] = 10$$

Therefore, the ratio of salt to acid is 10:1.

51. D is correct.

An electrolyte is a substance that dissociates into cations (i.e., positive ions) and anions (i.e., negative ions) when placed in solution. An electrolyte produces an electrically conducting solution when dissolved in a polar solvent (e.g., water). The dissolved ions disperse uniformly through the solvent.

If an electrical potential (i.e., voltage) is applied to such a solution, the cations of the solution migrate towards the electrode (i.e., an abundance of electrons), while the anions migrate towards the electrode (i.e., a deficit of electrons). If a high proportion of the solute dissociates to form free ions, it is a strong electrolyte.

If most of the solute does not dissociate, it is a weak electrolyte. The more free ions present, the better the solution conducts electricity.

52. C is correct.

The more acidic molecule has a lower pK_a.

53. D is correct.

The addition of hydroxide (i.e., NaOH) decreases the solubility of magnesium hydroxide due to the common ion effect. Therefore, the amount of undissociated $Mg(OH)_2$ increases.

54. C is correct.

Strong acids dissociate completely (or almost completely) because they form a stable anion. Hydrogen cyanide (HCN) has a pK_a of 9.3, and hydrogen sulfide (H_2S) has a pK_a of 7.0.

In this example, the strong acids include HI, HBr, HCl, H_3PO_4 and H_2SO_4.

55. D is correct.

Bromothymol blue is a pH indicator often used for solutions with neutral pH near 7 (e.g., managing the pH of pools and fish tanks). Bromothymol blue acts as a weak acid in a solution that can be protonated or deprotonated. It appears yellow when protonated (lower pH), blue when deprotonated (higher pH), and bluish green in neutral solution.

Methyl red has a pK_a of 5.1 and is a pH indicator dye that changes color in acidic solutions: turns red in pH under 4.4, orange in pH between 4.4 and 6.2, and yellow in pH over 6.2.

Phenolphthalein is used as an indicator for acid–base titrations. It is a weak acid, which can dissociate protons (H^+ ions) in solution. The phenolphthalein molecule is colorless, and the phenolphthalein ion is pink. It turns colorless in acidic solutions and pink in basic solutions.

With basic conditions, the phenolphthalein (neutral) $\rightleftharpoons$ ions (pink) equilibrium shifts to the right, leading to more ionization as H^+ ions are removed.

56. C is correct.

The problem is asking for K_a of an acid, which indicates that the acid in question is a weak acid.

In aqueous solutions, a hypothetical weak acid HX will partly dissociate and create this equilibrium:

$$HX \leftrightarrow H^+ + X^-$$

with an acid equilibrium constant, or

$$K_a = [H^+] \cdot [X^-] / [HX]$$

To calculate K_a, the concentration of all species is needed.

From the given pH, the concentration of H^+ ions can be calculated:

$$[H^+] = 10^{-pH}$$

$$[H^+] = 10^{-7} \, M$$

The number of H^+ and X^- ions is equal; concentration of X^- ions is also $10^{-7} \, M$.

Those ions came from the dissociated acid molecules. According to the problem, only 24% of the acid is dissociated. Therefore, the rest of acid molecules (100% – 24% = 76%) did not dissociate. Use the simple proportion of percentages to calculate the concentration of HX:

$$[HX] = (76\% \, / \, 24\%) \times 1 \times 10^{-7} \, M$$

$$[HX] = 3.17 \times 10^{-7} \, M$$

Use the concentration values to calculate K_a:

$$K_a = [H^+] \cdot [X^-] / [HX]$$

$$K_a = [(1 \times 10^{-7}) \times (1 \times 10^{-7})] / (3.17 \times 10^{-7})$$

$$K_a = 3.16 \times 10^{-8}$$

Calculate pK_a:

$$pK_a = -\log K_a$$

$$pK_a = -\log (3.16 \times 10^{-8})$$

$$pK_a = 7.5$$

57. D is correct.

The strongest acid has the largest K_a value (or the lowest pK_a).

58. E is correct.

If the $[H_3O^+]$ is greater than 1×10^{-7}, it is an acidic solution.

If the $[H_3O^+]$ is less than 1×10^{-7}, it is a basic solution.

If the $[H_3O^+]$ equals 1×10^{-7}, it has a pH of 7, and the solution is neutral.

59. A is correct.

An electrolyte is a substance that dissociates into cations (i.e., positive ions) and anions (i.e., negative ions) when placed in solution.

An electrolyte produces an electrically conducting solution when dissolved in a polar solvent (e.g., water).

The dissolved ions disperse uniformly through the solvent.

If an electrical potential (i.e., the voltage generated by the battery) is applied to such a solution, the cations of the solution migrate towards the electrode (i.e., an abundance of electrons), while the anions migrate towards to the electrode (i.e., a deficit of electrons).

60. E is correct.

The Arrhenius acid–base theory states that acids produce H^+ ions in H_2O solution and bases produce OH^- ions in H_2O solution.

The Arrhenius acid–base theory states that neutralization happens when acid–base reactions produce water and salt, and that these reactions must take place in aqueous solution.

There are additional ways to classify acids and bases.

The Brønsted-Lowry acid–base theory focuses on the ability to accept and donate protons.

The Lewis acid–base theory focuses on the ability to accept and donate electrons.

Chapter 8 Explanations: Electrochemistry

1. D is correct. In electrochemical (i.e., galvanic) cells, oxidation always occurs at the anode, and reduction occurs at the cathode.

Br^- is oxidized at the anode, not the cathode.

2. E is correct. Half-reaction:

$H_2S \rightarrow S_8$

Balancing half-reaction in acidic conditions:

Step 1: Balance all atoms except for H and O

$8\ H_2S \rightarrow S_8$

Step 2: To balance oxygen, add H_2O to the side with fewer oxygen atoms

There is no oxygen at all, so skip this step.

Step 3: To balance hydrogen, add H^+:

$8\ H_2S \rightarrow S_8 + 16\ H^+$

Balance charges by adding electrons to the side with higher/more positive total charge.

Total charge on left side: 0

Total charge on right side: $16(+1) = +16$

Add 16 electrons to right side:

$8\ H_2S \rightarrow S_8 + 16\ H^+ + 16\ e$

3. B is correct. An electrolytic cell is a nonspontaneous electrochemical cell that requires the supply of electrical energy (e.g., battery) to initiate the reaction.

The anode is positive, and the cathode is the negative electrode.

For both electrolytic and galvanic cells, oxidation occurs at the anode, while reduction occurs at the cathode.

Therefore, Co metal is produced at the cathode, because it is a reduction product (from an oxidation number of +3 on the left to 0 on the right). Co will not be produced at the anode.

4. E is correct. By convention, the reference standard for potential is always hydrogen reduction.

5. C is correct. Calculate the oxidation numbers of all species involved and look for the oxidized species (increase in oxidation number). Cd's oxidation number increases from 0 on the left side of the reaction to +2 on the right.

6. D is correct. The oxidation number of Fe increases from 0 on the left to +3 on the right.

7. D is correct. Salt bridge contains both cations (positive ions) and anions (negative ions).

Anions flow towards the oxidation half-cell because the oxidation product is positively charged and the anions are required to balance the charges within the cell.

The opposite is true for cations; they will flow towards the reduction half-cell.

8. A is correct. The cell reaction is:

$$Co \ (s) + Cu^{2+} \ (aq) \rightarrow Co^{2+} \ (aq) + Cu \ (s)$$

Separate it into half reactions:

$$Cu^{2+} \ (aq) \rightarrow Cu \ (s)$$

$$Co \ (s) \rightarrow Co^{2+} \ (aq)$$

The potentials provided are written in this format:

$$Cu^{2+} \ (aq) \mid Cu \ (s)$$

$$+0.34 \text{ V}$$

It means that for the reduction reaction:

$$Cu^{2+} \ (aq) \rightarrow Cu \ (s), \text{ the potential is } +0.34 \text{ V}$$

The reverse reaction, or oxidation reaction is:

$$Cu \ (s) \rightarrow Cu^{2+} \ (aq) \text{ has opposing potential value: } -0.34 \text{ V}$$

Obtain the potential values for both half-reactions.

Reverse sign for potential values of oxidation reactions:

$$Cu^{2+} \ (aq) \rightarrow Cu \ (s) = +0.34 \text{ V} \quad \text{(reduction)}$$

$$Co \ (s) \rightarrow Co^{2+} \ (aq) = +0.28 \text{ V} \quad \text{(oxidation)}$$

Determine the standard cell potential:

Standard cell potential = sum of half-reaction potential

Standard cell potential = 0.34 V + 0.28 V

Standard cell potential = 0.62 V

9. E is correct.

The other methods listed involve two or more energy conversions between light and electricity.

It is an electrical device that converts the energy of light directly into electricity by the photovoltaic effect (i.e., chemical and physical processes).

The operation of a photovoltaic (PV) cell has the following 3 requirements:

1) Light is absorbed, which excites electrons.

2) Separation of charge carries opposite types.

3) The separated charges are transferred to an external circuit.

In contrast, solar panels supply heat by absorbing sunlight. A photoelectrolytic / photoelectrochemical cell refers either to a type of photovoltaic cell or to a device that splits water directly into hydrogen and oxygen using only solar illumination.

10. A is correct. Each half-cell contains an electrode; two half-cells are required to complete a reaction.

11. B is correct.

A: electrolysis can be performed on any metal, not only iron.

C: electrolysis will not boil water nor raise the ship.

D: it is probably unlikely that the gases would stay in the compartments.

E: electrolysis will not reduce the weight enough to float the ship.

12. C is correct. Balanced reaction:

$$Zn\ (s) + CuSO_4\ (aq) \rightarrow Cu\ (s) + ZnSO_4\ (aq)$$

Zn is a stronger reducing agent (more likely to be oxidized) than Cu. This can be determined by each element's standard electrode potential ($E°$).

13. E is correct. The positive cell potential indicates that the reaction is spontaneous, which means it favors the formation of products.

Cells that generate electricity spontaneously are considered galvanic cells.

14. C is correct. Electrolysis of aqueous sodium chloride yields hydrogen and chlorine, with aqueous sodium hydroxide remaining in solution.

Sodium hydroxide is a strong base, which means the solution will be basic.

15. C is correct. Balanced equation:

$$Ag^+ + e^- \rightarrow Ag\ (s)$$

Formula to calculate deposit mass:

mass of deposit = (atomic mass × current × time) / 96,500 C

mass of deposit = [107.86 g × 3.50 A × (12 min × 60 s/min)] / 96,500 C

mass of deposit = 2.82 g

16. E is correct. The anode is the electrode where oxidation occurs.

A salt bridge provides electrical contact between the half-cells.

The cathode is the electrode where reduction occurs.

A spontaneous electrochemical cell is called a galvanic cell.

17. A is correct. Ionization energy (IE) is the energy required to release one electron from an element. Higher IE means the element is more stable.

Elements with high IE are usually elements that only need one or two more electrons to achieve stable configuration (e.g., complete valence shell – 8 electrons, such as the noble gases or 2 electrons, as in hydrogen). It is more likely for these elements to gain an electron and reach stability than lose an electron. When an atom gains electrons, its oxidation number goes down, and it is reduced. Therefore, elements with high IE are easily reduced.

In oxidation-reduction reactions, species that undergo reduction are oxidizing agents, because their presence allows the other reactant to be oxidized. Because elements with high IE are easily reduced, they are strong oxidizing agents.

Reducing agents are species that undergo oxidation (i.e., lose electrons).

Elements with high IE do not undergo oxidation readily and therefore are weak reducing agents.

18. A is correct. In electrochemical (i.e., galvanic) cells, oxidation always occurs at the anode and reduction occurs at the cathode.

Therefore, CO_2 is produced at the anode because it is an oxidation product (carbon's oxidation number increases from 0 on the left to +2 on the right).

19. A is correct.

Cu^{2+} is being reduced (i.e., gains electrons), while Sn^{2+} is being oxidized (i.e., loses electrons).

Salt bridge contains both cations (positive ions) and anions (negative ions).

Anions flow towards the oxidation half-cell because the oxidation product is positively charged and the anions are required to balance the charges within the cell.

The opposite is true for cations; they flow towards the reduction half-cell.

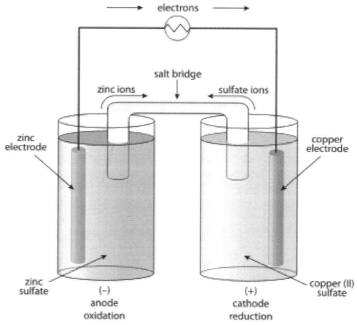

Schematic example of a Zn–Cu galvanic cell

20. B is correct.

In all cells, reduction occurs at the cathode, while oxidation occurs at the anode.

21. C is correct.

ZnO is being reduced; the oxidation number of Zn decreases from +2 on the left to 0 on the right.

22. E is correct. Consider the reactions:

$$Ni\ (s) + Ag^+\ (aq) \rightarrow Ag\ (s) + Ni^{2+}\ (aq)$$

Because it is spontaneous, Ni is more likely to be oxidized than Ag. Ni is oxidized, while Ag is reduced in this reaction.

Now, arrange the reactions in an order such that the metal that was oxidized in a reaction is reduced in the next reaction:

$$Ni\ (s) + Ag^+\ (aq) \rightarrow Ag\ (s) + Ni^{2+}\ (aq)$$

$$Cd\ (s) + Ni^{2+}\ (aq) \rightarrow Ni\ (s) + Cd^{2+}\ (aq)$$

$$Al\ (s) + Cd^{2+}\ (aq) \rightarrow Cd\ (s) + Al^{3+}\ (aq)$$

Lastly, this reaction Ag (s) + H$^+$ (aq) → no reaction should be first in the order, because Ag was not oxidized in this reaction, so it should be before a reaction where Ag is reduced.

$$Ag\ (s) + H^+\ (aq) \rightarrow \text{no reaction}$$

$$Ni\ (s) + Ag^+\ (aq) \rightarrow Ag\ (s) + Ni^{2+}\ (aq)$$

$$Cd\ (s) + Ni^{2+}\ (aq) \rightarrow Ni\ (s) + Cd^{2+}\ (uq)$$

$$Al\ (s) + Cd^{2+}\ (aq) \rightarrow Cd\ (s) + Al^{3+}\ (aq)$$

The metal being oxidized in the last reaction has the highest tendency to be oxidized.

23. A is correct.

The purpose of the salt bridge is to balance the charges between the two chambers/half-cells.

Oxidation creates cations at the anode, while reduction reduces cations at the cathode.

The ions in the bridge travel to those chambers to balance the charges.

24. B is correct.

Since G° = –nFE, when E° is positive, G is negative.

25. C is correct. The electrons travel through the wires that connect the cells, instead of the salt bridge. The function of the salt bridge is to provide ions to balance charges at both the cathode and anode.

26. A is correct. Electrochemistry is the branch of physical chemistry that studies chemical reactions that take place at the interface of an ionic conductor (i.e., the electrolyte) and an electrode.

Electric charges move between the electrolyte and the electrode through a series of redox reactions, and chemical energy is converted to electrical energy.

27. B is correct. Light energy from the sun causes the electron to move towards the silicon wafer. This starts the process of electric generation.

28. B is correct. Oxidation number, also known as oxidation state, indicates the degree of oxidation (i.e., loss of electrons) in an atom.

If an atom is electron-poor, this means that it has lost electrons, and would, therefore, have a positive oxidation number.

If an atom is electron-rich, this means that it has gained electrons, and would, therefore, have a negative oxidation number.

29. D is correct. Batteries run down and need to be recharged while fuel cells do not run down because they can be refueled.

30. A is correct. Disproportionation reaction is a reaction where a species undergoes both oxidation and reduction in the same reaction. The first step in balancing this reaction is to write the substance undergoing disproportionation twice on the reactant side.

31. A is correct. The terms spontaneous electrochemical, galvanic and voltaic are synonymous.

An example of a voltaic cell is an alkaline battery – it generates electricity spontaneously.

Electrons always flow from the anode (oxidation half-cell) to the cathode (reduction half-cell).

32. B is correct. Reaction at the anode:

$$2 H_2O \rightarrow O_2 + 4 H^+ + 4 e^-$$

Oxygen gas is released, and H^+ ions are added to the solution, which causes the solution to become acidic (i.e., lowers the pH).

33. D is correct. Nonspontaneous electrochemical cells are electrolysis cells.

In electrolysis, the metal being reduced is always produced at the cathode.

34. B is correct. Electrolysis is always nonspontaneous because it needs an electric current from an external source to occur.

35. E is correct. MnO_2 is being reduced into Mn_2O_3.

The oxidation number increases from +4 on the left to +3 on the right.

36. B is correct. The anode in galvanic cells attracts anions.

Anions in solution flow toward the anode, while cations flow toward the cathode. Oxidation (i.e. loss of electrons) occurs at the anode. Positive ions are formed, while negative ions are consumed at the anode.

Therefore, negative ions flow toward the anode to equalize the charge.

37. B is correct. In electrochemical (i.e., galvanic) cells, oxidation always occurs at the anode and reduction occurs at the cathode.

Therefore, Al metal is produced at the cathode, because it is a reduction product (from an oxidation number of +3 on the left to 0 on the right).

38. B is correct. Anions in solution flow toward the anode, while cations flow toward the cathode.

Oxidation is the loss of electrons.

Sodium is a group I element and therefore has a single valence electron. During oxidation, the Na becomes Na^+ with a complete octet.

39. A is correct. A salt bridge contains both cations (positive ions) and anions (negative ions).

Anions flow towards the oxidation half-cell because the oxidation product is positively charged and the anions are required to balance the charges within the cell. The opposite is true for cations; they will flow towards the reduction half-cell.

Anions in the salt bridge should flow from Cd to Zn half-cell.

40. B is correct.

This can be determined using the electrochemical series.

For a substance to act as an oxidizing agent for another substance, the oxidizing agent has to be located below the substance being oxidized in the series.

Cu is being oxidized, which means only Ag or Au is capable of oxidizing Cu.

Equilibrium	E°
$Li^+ (aq) + e^- \leftrightarrow Li (s)$	–3.03 volts
$K^+ (aq) + e^- \leftrightarrow K (s)$	–2.92
*$Ca^{2+} (aq) + 2 e^- \leftrightarrow Ca (s)$	–2.87
*$Na^+ (aq) + e^- \leftrightarrow Na (s)$	–2.71
$Mg^{2+} (aq) + 2 e^- \leftrightarrow Mg (s)$	–2.37
$Al^{3+} (aq) + 3 e^- \leftrightarrow Al (s)$	–1.66
$Zn^{2+} (aq) + 2 e^- \leftrightarrow Zn (s)$	–0.76
$Fe^{2+} (aq) + 2 e^- \leftrightarrow Fe (s)$	–0.44
$Pb^{2+} (aq) + 2 e^- \leftrightarrow Pb (s)$	–0.13
$2 H^+ (aq) + 2 e^- \leftrightarrow H_2 (g)$	0.0
$Cu^{2+} (aq) + 2 e \leftrightarrow Cu (s)$	+0.34
$Ag^+ (aq) + e^- \leftrightarrow Ag (s)$	+0.80
$Au^{3+} (aq) + 3 e^- \leftrightarrow Au (s)$	+1.50

41. E is correct. Anions in solution flow toward the anode, while cations flow toward the cathode.

Oxidation (i.e., loss of electrons) occurs at the anode.

Positive ions are formed while negative ions are consumed at the anode.

Therefore, negative ions flow toward the anode to equalize the charge.

42. B is correct.

Electrochemistry is the branch of physical chemistry that studies chemical reactions that take place at the interface of an ionic conductor (i.e., the electrolyte) and an electrode.

Electric charges move between the electrolyte and the electrode through a series of redox reactions, and chemical energy is converted to electrical energy.

43. E is correct.

E° tends to be negative and G positive, because electrolytic cells are nonspontaneous.

Electrons must be forced into the system for the reaction to proceed.

44. C is correct.

To create chlorine gas (Cl_2) from chloride ion (Cl^-), the ion needs to be oxidized.

In electrolysis, the oxidation occurs at the anode, which is the positive electrode.

The positively charged electrode would absorb electrons from the ion and transfer it to the cathode for reduction.

45. B is correct. In electrolytic cells:

The anode is a positively charged electrode where oxidation occurs.

The cathode is a negatively charged electrode where reduction occurs.

46. D is correct.

Dry-cell batteries are the common disposable household batteries. They are based on zinc and manganese dioxide cells.

47. C is correct.

Disproportionation is a type of redox reaction in which a species is simultaneously reduced and oxidized to form two different products.

Unbalanced reaction: $HNO_2 \rightarrow NO + HNO_3$

Balanced reaction: $3\ HNO_2 \rightarrow 2\ NO + HNO_3 + H_2O$

$2\ H_2O \rightarrow 2\ H_2 + O_2$: decomposition

$H_2SO_3 \rightarrow H_2O + SO_2$: decomposition

$Mg + H_2SO_4 \rightarrow MgSO_4 + H_2$: single replacement

48. D is correct. Electrolysis is the same process in reverse for the chemical process inside a battery. Electrolysis is often used to separate elements.

49. A is correct. Fuel cell automobiles are fueled by hydrogen, and the only emission is water (the statement above is reverse of the true statement).

50. A is correct.

Impure copper is oxidized so that it would happen at the anode. Then, pure copper would plate out (i.e., be reduced) on the cathode.

51. B is correct.

Electrolysis is a chemical reaction which results when electrical energy is passed through a liquid electrolyte.

Electrolysis utilizes direct electric current (DC) to drive an otherwise non-spontaneous chemical reaction. The voltage needed for electrolysis is called the decomposition potential

52. D is correct.

Calculate the oxidation numbers of all species involved and identify the oxidized species (increase in oxidation number).

Zn's oxidation number increases from 0 on the left side of reaction I to +2 on the right.

53. B is correct.

Half-reaction: $C_2H_6O \rightarrow HC_2H_3O_2$

Balancing half-reaction in acidic conditions:

Step 1: Balance all atoms except for H and O

$C_2H_6O \rightarrow HC_2H_3O_2$ (C is already balanced)

Step 2: To balance oxygen, add H_2O to the side with fewer oxygen atoms

$C_2H_6O + H_2O \rightarrow HC_2H_3O_2$

Step 3: To balance hydrogen, add H^+ to the opposing side of H_2O added in the previous step

$C_2H_6O + H_2O \rightarrow HC_2H_3O_2 + 4\ H^+$

Step 4: Balance charges by adding electrons to the side with a higher/more positive total charge

Total charge on the left side: 0

Total charge on the right side: $4(+1) = +4$

Add 4 electrons to the right side:

$C_2H_6O + H_2O \rightarrow HC_2H_3O_2 + 4\ H^+ + 4\ e^-$

---

54. B is correct.

In electrochemical (i.e., galvanic) cells, oxidation always occurs at the anode, and reduction occurs at the cathode.

Therefore, CCl_4 will be produced at the anode because it is an oxidation product (carbon's oxidation number increases from 0 on the left to +4 on the right).

55. C is correct.

Battery: spontaneously produces electrical energy.

A dry cell is a type of battery.

Half-cell: does not generate energy by itself

Electrolytic cell: needs electrical energy input

56. D is correct.

Anions in solution flow toward the anode, while cations flow toward the cathode.

Oxidation (i.e., loss of electrons) occurs at the anode.

Positive ions are formed, while negative ions are consumed at the anode.

Therefore, negative ions flow toward the anode to equalize the charge.

57. A is correct.

A reducing agent is a reactant that is oxidized (i.e., loses electrons).

Therefore, the best reducing agent is most easily oxidized.

Reversing each of the half-reactions shows that the oxidation of Cr (*s*) has a potential of +0.75 V, which is greater than the potential (+0.13 V) for the oxidation of Sn^{2+} (*aq*).

Thus, Cr (*s*) is a stronger reducing agent.

58. B is correct.

A salt bridge contains both cations (positive ions) and anions (negative ions).

Anions flow towards the oxidation half-cell because the oxidation product is positively charged and the anions are required to balance the charges within the cell.

The opposite is true for cations; they will flow toward the reduction half-cell.

Anions in the salt bridge should flow from Cd to Zn half-cell.

59. B is correct.

When zinc is added to HCl, the reaction is:

$$Zn + HCl \rightarrow ZnCl_2 + H_2O,$$

which means that Zn is oxidized into Zn^{2+}.

The number provided in the problem is reduction potential, so to obtain the oxidation potential, flip the reaction:

$$Zn \ (s) \rightarrow Zn^{2+} + 2 \ e^-$$

The $E°$ is inverted and becomes +0.76 V.

Because the $E°$ is higher than hydrogen's value (which is set to 0), the reaction occurs.

60. E is correct.

Calculate the mass of metal deposited in cathode:

Step 1: Calculate total charge using current and time

$$Q = current \times time$$

$$Q = 1 \ A \times (10 \ minutes \times 60 \ s/minute)$$

$$Q = 600 \ A{\cdot}s = 600 \ C$$

Step 2: Calculate moles of electron that has the same amount of charge

$$moles \ e^- = Q \ / \ 96{,}500 \ C/mol$$

$$moles \ e^- = 600 \ C \ / \ 96{,}500 \ C/mol$$

$$moles \ e^- = 6.22 \times 10^{-3} \ mol$$

Step 3: Calculate moles of metal deposit

Half-reaction of zinc ion reduction:

$$Zn^{2+} \ (aq) + 2 \ e^- \rightarrow Zn \ (s)$$

$$moles \ of \ Zn = (coefficient \ Zn \ / \ coefficient \ e^-) \times moles \ e^-$$

$$moles \ of \ Zn = (½) \times 6.22 \times 10^{-3} \ mol$$

$$moles \ of \ Zn = 3.11 \times 10^{-3} \ mol$$

Step 4: Calculate mass of metal deposit

$$mass \ Zn = moles \ Zn \times molecular \ mass \ of \ Zn$$

$$mass \ Zn = 3.11 \times 10^{-3} \ mol \times (65 \ g/mol)$$

$$mass \ Zn = 0.20 \ g$$

Notes

Please, leave your Customer Review on Amazon

Chapter 9 Explanations: Thermochemistry

1. A is correct. A reaction's enthalpy is specified by ΔH (not ΔG). ΔH determines whether a reaction is exothermic (releases heat to surroundings) or endothermic (absorbs heat from surroundings).

To predict spontaneity of reaction, use the Gibbs free energy equation:

$$\Delta G = \Delta H° - T\Delta S$$

The reaction is spontaneous (i.e., exergonic) if ΔG is negative.

The reaction is nonspontaneous (i.e., endergonic) if ΔG is positive.

2. B is correct.

Heat is energy, and the energy from the heat is transferred to the gas molecules which increases their movement (i.e., kinetic energy).

Temperature is a measure of the average kinetic energy of the molecules.

3. E is correct.

Heat capacity is the amount of heat required to increase the temperature of *the whole sample* by 1 °C.

Specific heat is the heat required to increase the temperature of *1 gram* of the sample by 1 °C.

Heat = mass × specific heat × change in temperature:

$$q = m \times c \times \Delta T$$

$$q = 21.0 \text{ g} \times 0.382 \text{ J/g·°C} \times (68.5 \text{ °C} - 21.0 \text{ °C})$$

$$q = 21.0 \text{ g} \times 0.382 \text{ J/g·°C} \times (47.5 \text{ °C})$$

$$q = 381 \text{ J}$$

4. E is correct. This is a theory/memorization question.

However, the problem can be solved by comparing the options for the most plausible. Kinetic energy is correlated with temperature, so the formula that involves temperature would be a good choice.

Another approach is to analyze the units. Apply the units to the variables and evaluate them to obtain the answer.

For example, choices A and B have moles, pressure (Pa, bar or atm) and area (m^2), so it is not possible for them to result in energy (J) when multiplied.

Options C and D have molarity (moles/L) and volume (L or m^3); it's also impossible for them to result in energy (J) when multiplied.

Option E is nRT: mol × (J/mol K) × K; all units but J cancel, so this is a plausible formula for kinetic energy.

For questions using formulas, dimensional analysis limits the answer choices on this type of question.

5. A is correct. ΔH refers to enthalpy (or heat).

Endothermic reactions have heat as a reactant.

Exothermic reactions have heat as a product. Exothermic reactions release heat and cause the temperature of the immediate surroundings to rise (i.e., a net loss of energy) while an endothermic process absorbs heat and cools the surroundings (i.e., a net gain of energy).

Endothermic reactions absorb energy to break strong bonds to form a less stable state (i.e., positive enthalpy). Exothermic reaction release energy during the formation of stronger bonds to produce a more stable state (i.e., negative enthalpy).

6. D is correct. Endothermic reactions absorb energy to break strong bonds to form a less stable state (i.e., positive enthalpy). Exothermic reaction release energy during the formation of stronger bonds to produce a more stable state (i.e., negative enthalpy).

The spontaneity of a reaction is determined by the calculation of ΔG using:

$$\Delta G = \Delta H - T\Delta S$$

The reaction is spontaneous when the value of ΔG is negative.

In this problem, the reaction is endothermic, which means that ΔH is positive.

Also, the reaction decreases S, which means that ΔS value is negative.

Substituting these values into the equation:

$$\Delta G = \Delta H - T(-\Delta S)$$

$$\Delta G = \Delta H + T\Delta S, \text{ with } \Delta H \text{ and } \Delta S \text{ both positive values}$$

For this problem, the value of ΔG is always positive.

The reaction does not occur because ΔG needs to be negative for a spontaneous reaction to proceed, the products are more stable than the reactants.

7. E is correct. Chemical energy is potential energy stored in molecular bonds.

Electrical energy is the kinetic energy associated with the motion of electrons (e.g., in wires, circuits, lightning). The potential energy stored in a flashlight battery is also electrical energy.

Heat is the spontaneous transfer of energy from a hot object to a cold one with no displacement or deformation of the objects (i.e., no work done).

8. A is correct. Entropy is higher for less organized states (i.e., more random or disordered).

9. E is correct. This cannot be determined because when the given $\Delta G = \Delta H - T\Delta S$, both terms cancel.

The system is at equilibrium when $\Delta G = 0$, but in this question both sides of the equation cancel:

$$\underbrace{X - RY}_{\Delta G \text{ term}} = \underbrace{X - RY}_{\substack{\Delta H - T\Delta S \\ \text{term}}}, \quad \text{so } 0 = 0$$

10. C is correct. Gibbs free energy: $\Delta G = \Delta H - T\Delta S$

Stable molecules are spontaneous because they have a negative (or relatively low) ΔG.

ΔG is most negative (most stable) when ΔH is the smallest and ΔS is largest.

11. A is correct. ΔH refers to enthalpy (or heat).

Endothermic reactions have heat as a reactant. Exothermic reactions have heat as a product.

The reaction is nonspontaneous (i.e., endergonic) if the products are less stable than the reactants and ΔG is positive.

The reaction is spontaneous (i.e., exergonic) if the products are more stable than the reactants and ΔG is negative.

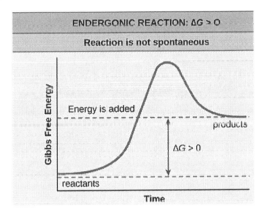 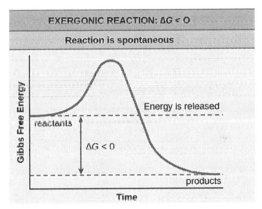

Exothermic reactions release heat and cause the temperature of the immediate surroundings to rise (i.e., a net loss of energy) while an endothermic process absorbs heat and cools the surroundings (i.e., a net gain of energy).

Endothermic reactions absorb energy to break strong bonds to form a less stable state (i.e., positive enthalpy).
Exothermic reaction release energy during the formation of stronger bonds to produce a more stable state (i.e., negative enthalpy).

12. B is correct. Gibbs free energy:

$$\Delta G = \Delta H - T\Delta S$$

Entropy (ΔS) determines the favorability of chemical reactions.

If entropy is large, the reaction is more likely to proceed.

13. D is correct. In a chemical reaction, bonds within reactants are broken down, and new bonds will be formed to create products.

Therefore, in bond dissociation problems,

ΔH reaction = sum of bond energy in reactants – sum of bond energy in products

For $H_2C=CH_2 + H_2 \rightarrow CH_3-CH_3$:

$\Delta H_{\text{reaction}}$ = sum of bond energy in reactants – sum of bond energy in products

$\Delta H_{\text{reaction}}$ = [(C=C) + 4(C–H) + (H–H)] – [(C–C) + 6(C–H)]

$\Delta H_{\text{reaction}}$ = [612 kJ + (4 × 412 kJ) + 436 kJ] – [348 kJ + (6 × 412 kJ)]

$\Delta H_{\text{reaction}}$ = –124 kJ

Remember that this is the opposite of ΔH_f problems, where:

$\Delta H_{\text{reaction}}$ = (sum of ΔH_f products) – (sum of ΔH_f reactants)

14. C is correct. Bond dissociation energy is the energy required to break a bond between two gaseous atoms and is useful in estimating the enthalpy change in a reaction.

15. B is correct. The ΔH value is positive, which means the reaction is endothermic and absorbs energy from the surroundings. ΔH value is always expressed as the energy released/absorbed per mole (for species with a coefficient of 1).

If the coefficient is 2 then it is the energy transferred per 2 moles. For example, for the stated reaction, 2 moles of NO are produced from 1 mole for each reagent. Therefore, 43.2 kcal are produced when 2 moles of NO are produced.

16. A is correct. State functions depend only on the initial and final states of the system and are independent of the paths taken to reach the final state.

Common examples of a state function in thermodynamics include internal energy, enthalpy, entropy, pressure, temperature, and volume. Work and heat relate to the change in energy of a system when it moves from one state to another, which depends on how a system changes between states.

17. B is correct. The temperature (i.e., average kinetic energy) of a substance remains constant during a phase change (e.g., solid to liquid or liquid to gas).

For example, the heat (i.e., energy) breaks bonds between the ice molecules as they change phases into the liquid phase. Since the average kinetic energy of the molecules does not change at the moment of the phase change (i.e., melting), the temperature of the molecules does not change.

18. C is correct. In a chemical reaction, bonds within reactants are broken and new bonds form to create products. Bond dissociation:

$\Delta H_{\text{reaction}}$ = (sum of bond energy in reactants) – (sum of bond energy in products)

O=C=O + 3 H₂ → CH₃–O–H + H–O–H

$\Delta H_{\text{reaction}}$ = (sum of bond energy in reactants) – (sum of bond energy in products)

$\Delta H_{\text{reaction}}$ = [2(C=O) + 3(H–H)] – [3(C–H) + (C–O) + (O–H) + 2(O–H)]

$\Delta H_{\text{reaction}}$ = [(2 × 743 kJ) + (3 × 436 kJ)] – [(3 × 412 kJ) + 360 kJ + 463 kJ + (2 × 463 kJ)]

$\Delta H_{\text{reaction}}$ = –191 kJ

This is the reverse of ΔH_f problems, where:

$\Delta H_{\text{reaction}}$ = (sum of $\Delta H_{f \text{ product}}$) – (sum of $\Delta H_{f \text{ reactant}}$)

19. C is correct.

Entropy indicates how a system is organized; increased entropy means less order. The entropy of the universe is always increasing because a system moves towards more disorder unless energy is added to the system.

The second law of thermodynamics states that entropy of interconnected systems, without the addition of energy, always increases.

20. A is correct. Gibbs free energy: $\Delta G = \Delta H - T\Delta S$

The value that is the largest positive value is the most endothermic, while the value that is the largest negative value is the most exothermic.

ΔH refers to enthalpy (or heat).

Endothermic reactions have heat as a reactant.

Exothermic reactions have heat as a product.

Exothermic reactions release heat and cause the temperature of the immediate surroundings to rise (i.e., a net loss of energy) while an endothermic process absorbs heat and cools the surroundings (i.e., a net gain of energy).

Endothermic reactions absorb energy to break strong bonds to form a less stable state (i.e., positive enthalpy). Exothermic reaction release energy during the formation of stronger bonds to produce a more stable state (i.e., negative enthalpy).

21. A is correct. By convention, the ΔG for an element in its standard state is 0.

22. B is correct. Test strategy: when given a choice among similar explanations, carefully evaluate the most descriptive one. However, always check the statement because sometimes the most descriptive option is not accurate.

Here, the longest option is also accurate, so that would be the best choice among all options.

23. C is correct. ΔG is always negative for spontaneous reactions.

24. C is correct.

Conduction (i.e., transfer of thermal energy through matter) is reduced by an insulator.
Air and vacuum are excellent insulators. Storm windows, which have air wedged between two glass panes, work by utilizing this principle of conduction.

25. A is correct. ΔH refers to enthalpy (or heat).

Endothermic reactions have heat as a reactant. Exothermic reactions have heat as a product.

Exothermic reactions release heat and cause the temperature of the immediate surroundings to rise (i.e., a net loss of energy) while an endothermic process absorbs heat and cools the surroundings (i.e., a net gain of energy).

The reaction is nonspontaneous (i.e., endergonic) if the products are less stable than the reactants and ΔG is positive.

The reaction is spontaneous (i.e., exergonic) if the products are more stable than the reactants and ΔG is negative.

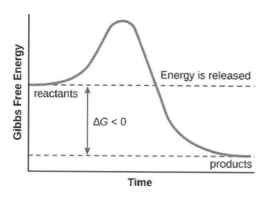 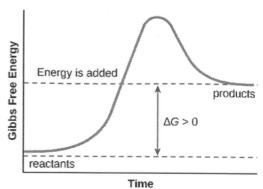

Exergonic reactions (on left above) are spontaneous and have reactants with more energy than the products.

Endergonic reactions (right above) are nonspontaneous and have products with more energy than the reactants.

26. D is correct.

Heat capacity is the amount of heat required to increase the temperature of *the whole sample* by 1 °C.

Specific heat is the heat required to increase the temperature of *1 gram* of sample by 1 °C.

q = mass × heat of condensation

q = 16 g × 1,380 J/g

q = 22,080 J

27. A is correct.

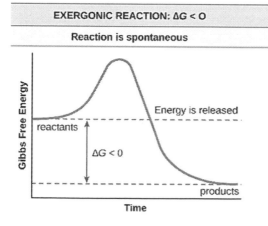 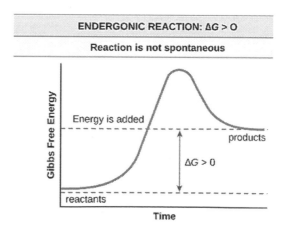

$\Delta G = \Delta H - T\Delta S$ refers to exergonic when ΔG is negative and endergonic when ΔG is positive.

If ΔS is 0 then $\Delta G = \Delta H$ because the $T\Delta S$ term cancels because it equals zero).

ΔH refers to exothermic when ΔH is negative and endothermic when ΔH is positive.

28. E is correct. The heat of formation is defined as the heat required or released upon creation of one mole of the substance from its elements.

If the given reaction is reversed and divided by two, it would be the formation reaction of NH_3:

$$½ N_2 + 3/2 H_2 \rightarrow NH_3$$

ΔH of this reaction would also be reversed (i.e., plus to minus sign) and divided by two:

$$\Delta H = -(92.4 \text{ kJ/mol}) / 2$$

$$\Delta H = -46.2 \text{ kJ/mol}$$

29. B is correct. Gibbs free energy:

$$\Delta G = \Delta H - T\Delta S$$

With a positive ΔH and negative ΔS, ΔG is positive, so the reaction is nonspontaneous.

30. C is correct. Entropy (ΔS) measures the degree of disorder in a system.

When a change causes the components of a system to transform into a higher energy phase (solid $\rightarrow$ liquid, liquid $\rightarrow$ gas), the entropy of the system increases.

31. D is correct. During phase changes, only the mass and heat of specific phase change is required to calculate the energy released or absorbed.

Because water is turning into ice, the specific heat required is the heat of solidification.

32. B is correct. Nuclear energy is considered energy because splitting or combining atoms results in enormous amounts of energy, which is used in atomic bombs and nuclear power plants.

Potential Energy	Kinetic Energy
Stored energy and the energy of position (gravitational)	Energy of motion: motion of waves, electrons, atoms, molecules, and substances.
Nuclear Energy	**Electrical Energy**
Nuclear energy is the energy stored in the nucleus of an atom. It is the energy that holds the nucleus together. The nucleus of the uranium atom is an example of nuclear energy.	Electrical energy is the movement of electrons. Lightning and electricity are examples of electrical energy.

33. D is correct. Entropy is a measurement of disorder.

Gases contain more energy than liquids of the same element and have a higher degree of randomness. Entropy is the unavailable energy which cannot be converted into mechanical work.

34. A is correct.

There are two different methods available to solve this problem. Both methods are based on the definition of ΔH formation as energy consumed/released when one mole of the molecule is produced from its elemental atoms.

Method 1.

Rearrange and add all the equations together to create the formation reaction of C_2H_5OH.

Information provided by the problem:

$$C_2H_5OH + 3\ O_2 \rightarrow 2\ CO_2 + 3\ H_2O \qquad \Delta H = 327\ kcal$$

$$H_2O \rightarrow H_2 + \frac{1}{2}\ O_2 \qquad \Delta H = 68.3\ kcal$$

$$C + O_2 \rightarrow CO_2 \qquad \Delta H = -94.1\ kcal$$

Place C_2H_5OH on the product side. For the other two reactions, arrange them so the elements are on the left and the molecules are on the right (remember that the goal is to create a formation reaction: elements forming a molecule).

When reversing the direction of a reaction, change the positive/negative sign of ΔH.

Multiplying the whole reaction by a coefficient would also multiply ΔH by the same ratio.

$$2\ CO_2 + 3\ H_2O \rightarrow C_2H_5OH + 3\ O_2 \qquad \Delta H = -327\ kcal$$

$$3\ H_2 + 3/2\ O_2 \rightarrow 3\ H_2O \qquad \Delta H = -204.9\ kcal$$

$$\underline{2\ C + 2\ O_2 \rightarrow 2\ CO_2 \qquad\qquad\qquad \Delta H = -188.2\ kcal}$$

$$2\ C + 3\ H_2 + 1/2\ O_2 \rightarrow C_2H_5OH \qquad \Delta H = -720.1\ kcal$$

ΔH formation of C_2H_5OH is -720.1 kcal.

Method 2.

The heat of formation (ΔH_f) data can be used to calculate ΔH of a reaction:

$$\Delta H_{reaction} = \text{sum of } \Delta H_{f\ product} - \text{sum of } \Delta H_{f\ reactant}$$

Apply the formula on the first equation:

$$C_2H_5OH + 3\ O_2 \rightarrow 2\ CO_2 + 3\ H_2O \qquad \Delta H = 327\ kcal$$

$$\Delta H_{reaction} = \text{sum of } \Delta H_{f\ product} - \text{sum of } \Delta H_{f\ reactant}$$

$$327\ kcal = [(\Delta H_f\ CO_2) + 3(\Delta H_f\ H_2O)] - (\Delta H_f\ C_2H_5OH) + 3(\Delta H_f\ O_2)]$$

Oxygen (O_2) is an element, so $\Delta H_f = 0$

For CO_2 and H_2O, ΔH_f information can be obtained from the other 2 reactions:

$$H_2O \rightarrow H_2 + \frac{1}{2}\ O_2 \qquad \Delta H = 68.3\ kcal$$

$$C + O_2 \rightarrow CO_2 \qquad \Delta H = -94.1\ kcal$$

The CO_2 reaction is already a formation reaction – creation of one mole of a molecule from its elements.

Therefore, ΔH_f of $CO_2 = -94.1$ kcal

If the H_2O reaction is reversed, it will also be a formation reaction.

$$H_2 + \frac{1}{2} O_2 \rightarrow H_2O \qquad \Delta H = -68.3 \text{ kcal}$$

Using those values, calculate ΔH_f of C_2H_5OH:

$$327 \text{ kcal} = [2(\Delta H_f \, CO_2) + 3(\Delta H_f \, H_2O)] - [(\Delta H_f \, C_2H_5OH) + 3(\Delta H_f \, O_2)]$$

$$327 \text{ kcal} = [2(-94.1 \text{ kcal}) + 3(-68.3 \text{ kcal})] - [(\Delta H_f \, C_2H_5OH) + 3(0 \text{ kcal})]$$

$$327 \text{ kcal} = [(-188.2 \text{ kcal}) + (-204.9 \text{ kcal})] - (\Delta H_f \, C_2H_5OH)$$

$$327 \text{ kcal} = (-393.1 \text{ kcal}) - (\Delta H_f \, C_2H_5OH)$$

$$\Delta H_f \, C_2H_5OH = -720.1 \text{ kcal}$$

35. B is correct.

$$S + O_2 \rightarrow SO_2 + 69.8 \text{ kcal}$$

The reaction indicates that 69.8 kcal of energy is released (i.e., on the product side).

All species in this reaction have the coefficient of 1, which means that the ΔH value is calculated by reacting 1 mole of each reagent to create 1 mole of product.

The atomic mass of sulfur is 32.1 g, which means that this reaction uses 32.1 g of sulfur.

36. D is correct.

The disorder of the system is decreasing, as more complex and ordered molecules are forming from the reaction of H_2 and O_2 gases.

3 moles of gas are combining to form 2 moles of gas.

Additionally, two molecules are joining to form one molecule.

37. D is correct.

In thermodynamics, an isolated system is a system enclosed by rigid, immovable walls through which neither matter nor energy pass.

Temperature is a measure of energy and is not a form of energy. Therefore, the temperature cannot be exchanged between the system and surroundings.

A closed system can exchange energy (as heat or work) with its surroundings, but not matter.

An isolated system cannot exchange energy (as heat or work) or matter with the surroundings.

An open system can exchange energy and matter with the surroundings.

38. E is correct.

State functions depend only on the initial and final states of the system and is independent of the paths taken to reach the final state.

Common examples of a state function in thermodynamics include internal energy, enthalpy, entropy, pressure, temperature and volume.

39. A is correct. When comparing various fuels in varying forms (e.g., solid, liquid or gas), it's easiest to compare energy released in terms of mass, because matter has mass regardless of its state (as opposed to volume, which is convenient for a liquid or gas, but not for a solid).

Moles are more complicated because they must be converted to mass before a direct comparison can be made between the fuels.

40. C is correct. Convection is heat carried by fluids (i.e., liquids and gases). Heat is prevented from leaving the system through convection when the lid is placed on the cup.

41. B is correct. For a reaction to be spontaneous, the total entropy ($\Delta S_{system} + \Delta S_{surrounding}$) must be positive (i.e., greater than 0).

42. E is correct. Explosion of gases: chemical → heat energy

Heat converting into steam, which in turn moves a turbine: heat → mechanical energy

Generator creates electricity: mechanical → electrical energy

Potential Energy Stored energy and the energy of position (gravitational)	Kinetic Energy Energy of motion: motion of waves, electrons, atoms, molecules, and substances.
Chemical Energy Chemical energy is the energy stored in the bonds of atoms and molecules. Examples of stored chemical energy: biomass, petroleum, natural gas, propane, coal. **Nuclear Energy** Nuclear energy is the energy stored in the nucleus of an atom. It is the energy that holds the nucleus together. The nucleus of the uranium atom is an example of nuclear energy. **Stored Mechanical Energy** Stored mechanical energy is energy stored in objects by the application of a force. Compressed springs and stretched rubber bands are examples of stored mechanical energy. **Gravitational Energy** Gravitational Energy is the energy of place or position. Water in a reservoir behind a hydropower dam is an example of gravitational potential energy. When the water is released to spin the turbines, it becomes kinetic energy.	**Radiant Energy** Radiant energy is electromagnetic energy that travels in transverse waves. Radiant energy includes visible light, x-rays, gamma rays, and radio waves. Solar energy is an example of radiant energy. **Thermal Energy** Thermal energy is internal energy in substances; it is the vibration and movement of atoms and molecules within substances. Geothermal energy is an example of thermal energy. **Motion** The movement of objects or substances from one place to another in motion. Wind and hydropower are examples of motion. **Sound** Sound is the movement of energy through substances in longitudinal (compression/rarefaction) waves. **Electrical Energy** Electrical energy is the movement of electrons. Lightning and electricity are examples of electrical energy.

43. A is correct. The relationship between enthalpy (ΔH) and internal energy (ΔE):

Enthalpy = Internal energy + work (for gases, work = PV)

$$\Delta H = \Delta E + \Delta(PV)$$

Solving for ΔE:

$$\Delta E = \Delta H - \Delta(PV)$$

According to ideal gas law:

$$PV = nRT$$

Substitute ideal gas law to the previous equation:

$$\Delta E = \Delta H - \Delta(nRT)$$

R and T are constant, which leaves Δn as the variable.

The reaction is $C_2H_2 (g) + 2\ H_2 (g) \rightarrow C_2H_6 (g)$

There are three gas molecules on the left and one on the right, which means $\Delta n = 1 - 3 = -2$

In this problem, the temperature is not provided. However, the presence of degree symbols ($\Delta G°$, $\Delta H°$, $\Delta S°$) indicates that those are standard values, which are measured at 25 °C or 298.15 K.

Always double check the units before performing calculations; ΔH is in kilojoules, while the gas constant (R) is 8.314 J/mol K. Convert ΔH to joules before calculating.

Use the Δn and T values to calculate ΔE:

$$\Delta E = \Delta H - \Delta nRT$$

$$\Delta E = -311{,}500 \text{ J/mol} - (-2 \times 8.314 \text{ J/mol K} \times 298.15 \text{ K})$$

$$\Delta E = -306{,}542 \text{ J} \approx -306.5 \text{ kJ}$$

44. D is correct.

A closed system can exchange energy (as heat or work) but not matter, with its surroundings.

An isolated system cannot exchange energy (as heat or work) or matter with the surroundings.

An open system can exchange energy and matter with the surroundings.

45. C is correct.

An increase in entropy indicates an increase in disorder; find a reaction that creates a higher number of molecules on the product side compared to the reactant side.

46. C is correct.

When enthalpy is calculated, work done by gases is not taken into account; however, the energy of the reaction includes the work done by gases.

The largest difference between the energy of the reaction and enthalpy would be for reactions with the largest difference in the number of gas molecules between the product and reactants.

47. B is correct. All thermodynamic functions in $\Delta G = \Delta H - T\Delta S$ refer to the system.

48. C is correct.

To predict spontaneity of reaction, use the Gibbs free energy equation:

$\Delta G = \Delta H° - T\Delta S$

The reaction is spontaneous if ΔG is negative.

Substitute the given values to the equation:

$\Delta G = -113.4$ kJ/mol $- [T \times (-145.7$ J/K mol$)]$

$\Delta G = -113.4$ kJ/mol $+ (T \times 145.7$ J/K mol$)$

Important: note that the units aren't identical, $\Delta H°$ is in kJ and $\Delta S°$ is in J. Convert kJ to J (1 kJ = 1,000 J):

$\Delta G = -113,400$ J/mol $+ (T \times 145.7$ J/K mol$)$

It can be predicted that the value of ΔG would be negative if the value of T is small.

If T goes higher, ΔG approaches a positive value, and the reaction would be nonspontaneous.

49. E is correct. Enthalpy: $U + PV$

50. C is correct.

State functions depend only on the initial and final states of the system and are independent of the paths taken to reach the final state. Common examples of a state function in thermodynamics include internal energy, enthalpy, entropy, pressure, temperature, and volume.

An extensive property is a property that changes when the size of the sample changes. Examples include mass, volume, length, and total charge. Entropy has no absolute zero value, and a substance at zero Kelvin has zero entropy (i.e., no motion).

51. C is correct. In an exothermic reaction, the bonds formed are stronger than the bonds broken.

52. D is correct.

Calculate the value of $\Delta H_f = \Delta H_{f\,product} - \Delta H_{f\,reactant}$

$\Delta H_f = -436.8$ kJ mol^{-1} $- (-391.2$ kJ mol$^{-1})$

$\Delta H_f = -45.6$ kJ mol^{-1}

To determine spontaneity, calculate the Gibbs free energy:

$\Delta G = \Delta H° - T\Delta S$

The reaction is spontaneous if ΔG is negative:

$\Delta G = -45.6$ kJ $- T\Delta S$

Typical ΔS values are around 100–200 J.

If the ΔH value is -45.6 kJ or $-45,600$ J, the value of ΔG would still be negative unless $T\Delta S$ is less than $-45,600$.

Therefore, the reaction would be spontaneous over a broad range of temperatures.

53. E is correct.

Enthalpy is an extensive property: it varies with the quantity of the matter.

Reaction 1 : $P_4 + 6\ Cl_2 \rightarrow 4\ PCl_3$ $\quad \Delta H = -1{,}289$ kJ

Reaction 2 : $3\ P_4 + 18\ Cl_2 \rightarrow 12\ PCl_3$ $\quad \Delta H = ?$

The only difference between reactions 1 and 2 are the coefficients.

In reaction 2, all coefficients are three times reaction 1.

Reaction 2 consumes three times as much reactants as reaction 1, and correspondingly reaction 2 releases three times as much energy as reaction 1.

$\Delta H = 3 \times -1{,}289$ kJ

$\Delta H = -3{,}837$ kJ

54. C is correct.

ΔH refers to enthalpy (or heat).

Endothermic reactions have heat as a reactant.

Exothermic reactions have heat as a product.

Endothermic reactions absorb energy to break strong bonds to form a less stable state (i.e., positive enthalpy). Exothermic reaction release energy during the formation of stronger bonds to produce a more stable state (i.e., negative enthalpy).

The reaction is nonspontaneous (i.e., endergonic) if the products are less stable than the reactants and ΔG is positive. The reaction is spontaneous (i.e., exergonic) if the products are more stable than the reactants and ΔG is negative. Endothermic reactions consume energy, which means that there should be heat on the reactants' side.

55. D is correct.

According to the second law of thermodynamics, the entropy gain of the universe must always be positive (i.e., increased disorder).

The entropy of a system, however, can be negative if the surroundings experience an increase in entropy greater than the negative entropy change experienced by the system.

56. E is correct.

In thermodynamics, an isolated system is a system enclosed by rigid, immovable walls through which neither matter nor energy pass.

Bell jars are designed not to let air or other materials in or out.

Insulated means that heat cannot get in or out.

Evaporation indicates a phase change (vaporization) from liquid to gaseous phase; however, it does not imply that the matter has escaped its system.

A closed system can exchange energy (as heat or work) with its surroundings, but not matter.

An isolated system cannot exchange energy (as heat or work) or matter with the surroundings.

An open system can exchange energy and matter with the surroundings.

57. C is correct.

Temperature is a measure of the average kinetic energy of the molecules.

Kinetic energy is proportional to temperature.

In most thermodynamic equations, temperatures are expressed in Kelvin, so convert the Celsius temperatures to Kelvin:

25 °C + 273.15 = 298.15 K

50 °C + 273.15 = 323.15 K

Calculate the kinetic energy using simple proportions:

KE = (323.15 K / 298.15 K) × 500 J

KE = 540 J

58. C is correct.

The equation relates to the change in entropy (ΔS) at different temperatures.

Entropy increases at higher temperatures (i.e., increased kinetic energy).

59. B is correct.

A change is exothermic when energy is released to the surroundings.

Energy loss occurs when a substance changes to a more rigid phase (e.g., gas → liquid or liquid → solid).

60. B is correct.

At equilibrium, there is no potential and therefore neither direction of the reaction is favored.

Reaction potential (E) indicates the tendency of a reaction to be spontaneous in either direction.

Because the solution is in equilibrium, no further reactions occur in either direction.

Therefore, $E = 0$.

Chapter 10 Explanations: Atomic & Nuclear Structure

1. B is correct.

The Bohr model places electrons around the nucleus of the atom at discrete energy levels. The Balmer series line spectra agreed with the Bohr model because the energy of the observed photons in each spectra matched the transition energy of electrons within these discrete predicted states.

2. D is correct.

This is an example of an electron capture nuclear reaction.

When this happens, the atomic number decreases by one, but the mass number stays the same.

$$^{100}_{44}\text{Ru} + \ ^{0}_{-1}\text{e}^- \rightarrow \ ^{100}_{43}\text{Tc}$$

Ru: 100 = mass number (# protons + # neutrons)

Ru: 44 = atomic number (# protons)

From the periodic table, Tc is the element with 1 less proton than Ru.

3. E is correct.

An alpha particle is composed of two neutrons and two protons and is identical to the nucleus of a ^{4}He atom.

The total mass of two alpha particles:

2 × (2 neutrons + 2 protons) = 8

Mass of a ^{9}Be atom:

5 neutrons + 4 protons = 9

Mass of a ^{9}Be atom > total mass of two alpha particles

The mass of a ^{9}Be atom is greater than the mass of two alpha particles, so its mass is also greater than twice the mass of a ^{4}He atom.

4. A is correct.

The number of neutrons and protons must be equal after the reaction.

Thus the sum of the atomic number before and mass number before should be equal to after the reaction.

Mass number (superscript):

(1 + 235) – (131 + 3) = 102

Atomic number (subscript):

92 – (53) = 39

$^{102}_{39}$Y properly balances the reaction.

5. C is correct.

In β⁻ (beta minus) decay, the atomic number (subscript) increases by 1, but the atomic mass stays constant.

$$^{87}_{37}\text{Rb} \rightarrow {}^{87}_{38}\text{Sr} + {}^{0}_{-1}e + {}^{0}_{0}\nu$$

Sr is the element with 1 more proton (subscript) than Rb.

$^{0}_{0}\nu$ represents an electron antineutrino.

6. C is correct.

The nucleus of an atom is bound together by the strong nuclear force from the nucleons within it. The strong nuclear force must overcome the Coulomb repulsion of the protons (due to their like charges).

Neutrons help stabilize and bind the nucleus together by contributing to the strong nuclear force so that it is greater than the Coulomb repulsion experienced by the protons.

7. B is correct.

The atomic numbers: $^{235}_{92}\text{U} \rightarrow {}^{141}_{56}\text{Ba} + {}^{92}_{36}\text{Kr}$

The subscripts on each side of the expression sum to 92, so adding a proton ($^{1}_{1}\text{H}$) to the right side would not balance.

The superscripts sum to 235 on the left and sum to 233 on the right.

Add two neutrons ($^{1}_{0}\text{n} + {}^{1}_{0}\text{n}$) to the right side to balance both sides of the equation.

8. C is correct. An alpha particle consists of two protons and two neutrons and is identical to a helium nucleus so that it can be written as $^{4}_{2}\text{He}$

For a nuclear reaction to be written correctly, it must be balanced, and the sum of superscripts and subscripts must be equal on both sides of the reaction. The superscripts add to 238, and the subscripts add to 92 on both sides; therefore, it is the only balanced answer.

9. C is correct.

In β⁻ decay a neutron is converted to a proton and an electron and electron antineutrino are emitted. In β⁺ decay a proton is converted to a neutron, and a positron and an electron neutrino are emitted.

$$^{14}_{6}\text{C} \rightarrow {}^{14}_{7}\text{N} + e^{+} + \nu_{e}$$

10. C is correct.

The Balmer series is the name of the emission spectrum of hydrogen when electrons transition from a higher state to the $n = 2$ state.

Within the Balmer series, there are four visible spectral lines with colors ranging from red to violet (i.e., ROY G BIV)

11. B is correct. Larger nuclei (atomic number above 83) tend to decay because the attractive force of the nucleons (strong nuclear force) has a limited range and the nucleus is larger than this range. Therefore, these nuclei tend to emit alpha particles to decrease the size of the nucleus.

Smaller nuclei are not large enough to encounter this problem, but some isotopes have an irregular ratio of neutrons to protons and become unstable. ^{14}Carbon has 8 neutrons and 6 protons, and its neutron to proton ratio is too large; therefore, it is unstable and radioactive.

12. C is correct.

Positron emission occurs during β^+ decay. In β^+ decay a proton converts to a neutron and emits a positron and electron neutrino. The decay can be expressed as:

$$^{44}_{21}\text{Sc} \rightarrow\ ^{44}_{20}\text{Ca} + e^+ + \nu_e$$

13. A is correct. The Pauli Exclusion Principle states that in an atom no two electrons can have the same set of quantum numbers. Thus, every electron in an atom has a unique set of quantum numbers, and a particular set belongs to only one electron.

14. B is correct. Calculate mass defect:

$$m_1 = (2\ \text{protons}) \cdot (1.0072764669\ \text{amu}) + (2\ \text{neutrons}) \cdot (1.0086649156\ \text{amu})$$

$$m_1 = 4.031882765\ \text{amu}$$

$$\Delta m = 4.031882765\ \text{amu} - 4.002602\ \text{amu}$$

$$\Delta m = 0.029280765\ \text{amu}$$

Convert to kg:

$$\Delta m = (0.029280765\ \text{amu} / 1) \cdot (1.6606 \times 10^{27}\ \text{kg} / 1\ \text{amu})$$

$$\Delta m = 4.86236 \times 10^{-29}\ \text{kg}$$

Find binding energy:

$$E = \Delta mc^2$$

$$E = (4.86236 \times 10^{-29}\ \text{kg}) \cdot (3 \times 10^8\ \text{m/s})^2$$

$$E = 4.38 \times 10^{-12}\ \text{J} \approx 4.4 \times 10^{-12}\ \text{J}$$

15. D is correct.

$$A = A_0(\tfrac{1}{2})^{t/h}$$

where A_0 = original amount, t = time elapse and h = half-life

$$0.03 = (1) \cdot (\tfrac{1}{2})^{(t\,/\,20{,}000\ \text{years})}$$

$$\ln(0.03) = (t\,/\,20{,}000\ \text{years}) \cdot \ln(\tfrac{1}{2})$$

$$t = 101{,}179\ \text{years}$$

16. D is correct.

The principal quantum number "n" describes the size of the orbital and large values of n indicates a larger orbital shell size. Consequently, the radial distance between the nucleus and the outer bounds of the orbital shell will increase with increasing values of n.

17. C is correct.

Alpha particles consist of 2 protons and 2 neutrons, hence the +2 charge and mass of 4 amu.

They have a high mass; thus, they have a low speed and a low penetrating power.

18. A is correct.

^{56}Fe has the highest binding energy because its nucleus is "in the middle" in terms of nuclear size.

Thus, the strong nuclear force and the electromagnetic repulsion are most balanced, and the nucleus is at the lowest energy configuration.

Note: all nuclei are most stable at the lowest energy configuration.

19. D is correct. The reactants are $^{15}_{7}N + ^{1}_{1}p$

The superscripts sum to 16 while the subscripts sum to 8.

$^{12}C + ^{4}He$ is the only possible set of products because both the superscript and subscript add to 16 and 8, respectively.

$$^{15}_{7}N + ^{1}_{1}P \rightarrow \ ^{12}_{6}C + ^{4}_{2}He$$

The products $^{14}B + ^{2}Li$ sum to the correct superscript and subscript, but lithium has three protons, so the representation ^{2}Li is not possible.

20. E is correct. The *d* shell has 5 orbitals with two electrons per orbital for a total of 10 electrons.

21. B is correct. All elements with atomic numbers greater than 83 will be radioactive. Bismuth has an atomic number of 83, so all successive elements after bismuth are radioactive.

22. E is correct.

Balmer equation:

$$\lambda = B(n^2 / n^2 - 2^2)$$

The wavelength is shorter when n becomes larger, such that the term in parentheses approaches 1.

Thus, when n = ∞ (the term in parentheses) is minimized (goes to 1) the shortest λ is produced.

$$\lambda = (3.645 \times 10^{-7} \text{ m}) \cdot [\infty^2 / (\infty^2 - 2^2)]$$

$$\lambda = 3.645 \times 10^{-7} \text{ m}$$

23. C is correct.

The reactants are $^{3}_{2}\text{He} + ^{3}_{2}\text{He}$, so the superscripts must sum to 6 while the subscripts must sum to 4.

24. E is correct.

Half-life formula:

$A = A_0(\frac{1}{2})^{t/h}$

where A_0 = original amount, t = time elapse, h = half-life

$A = (10 \text{ g}) \cdot (\frac{1}{2})^{(6 \text{ days} / 2 \text{ days})}$

$A = 1.25 \text{ grams}$

25. E is correct.

Nuclear fusion is the process whereby two lighter elements fuse to form a heavier element. It produces non-radioactive elements, releases a larger amount of energy (as heat), and is the energy source of stars (including the Sun).

26. A is correct.

The Bohr model separates electrons into discrete energy levels with the levels (shells) increasing in the distance away from the nucleus, but the energy difference between the adjacent shells decreases as they get further away from the nucleus.

27. B is correct. Control rods in a nuclear reactor are composed of neutron-absorbing material and serve to regulate the flux of neutrons within the reactor, therefore regulating the fission chain reaction.

28. D is correct. An alpha particle consists of two protons and two neutrons. Missing an alpha particle results in the atomic number decreasing by 2 and the mass number decreases by 4.

29. A is correct.

A neon discharge works by applying a voltage to a tube of neon gas such that the electrons gain energy and are promoted from their ground state to an excited state (higher energy orbital).

As an electron goes back to its ground state, it releases the energy it gained in the form of a photon. This photon has a characteristic wavelength corresponding to the elemental gas within the tube; for neon, this wavelength corresponds to a red color.

30. C is correct.

Similar chemical properties are due to similar valence electron configurations. Elements are grouped in vertical columns to display these similarities; thus, the element below neon has similar chemical properties with the next larger atomic number.

Argon has an atomic number of 18 corresponding to 18 protons and 18 electrons.

31. C is correct.

The energy of transition is the same as the energy of the photon.

$f = c / \lambda$

$E_{ph} = hf$

$E_{ph} = h(c / \lambda)$

$E_{ph} = (6.63 \times 10^{-34} \text{ J·s}) \cdot [(3 \times 10^8 \text{ m/s}) / (1.25 \times 10^{-7} \text{ m})]$

$E_{ph} = 1.6 \times 10^{-18} \text{ J}$

The new energy level differs from the 0 J ground state by 1.6×10^{-18} J.

The ground state represents the lowest energy; the excited state must be positive.

32. D is correct. In nuclear fusion, lighter elements fuse to form heavier elements.

During this process, some of the mass of the three helium nuclei is converted to energy by:

$E = mc^2$

Thus, the net mass of the three helium nuclei is slightly greater than that of the carbon nucleus due to mass conversion into energy.

33. B is correct.

One of the obvious errors of the planetary model is that electrons cannot orbit the nucleus without experiencing acceleration (due to change in direction). As such, the electron would lose its energy as photons (accelerating charges produce electromagnetic radiation) and eventually collapse into the nucleus.

34. D is correct.

Natural line broadening is the extension of a spectral line over a range of frequencies. This occurs due in part to the uncertainty principle, which relates the time in which an atom is excited to the energy of its emitted photon.

$\Delta E \Delta t > \hbar / 2$

where $\hbar$ is reduced Planck's constant

Because energy is related to frequency by:

$E = hf$

where h is Planck's constant

The range of frequencies observed (broadening) is due to the uncertainty in energy outlined by the uncertainty principle.

35. D is correct.

A mass of an element or compound can be measured by its molar mass. The molar mass relates the mass of the element or compound to a discrete number of subunits (atoms for elements, molecules for compounds).

Chapter 11 Explanations: Quantum Chemistry

1. E is correct.

The energy of each incident photon is transferred to an electron, which must then overcome the material's work function to be ejected. Therefore:

hc / λ = Work function

$\lambda = (6.626 \times 10^{-34} \text{ J·s} \cdot 3.00 \times 10^8 \text{ m/s}) / (1.90 \text{ eV} \cdot 1.60 \times 10^{-19} \text{ J/eV})$

$\lambda = 6.53 \times 10^{-7} \text{ m}$

$\lambda = 653 \text{ nm}$

2. B is correct.

The power varies with the number of photons per second and the energy of the photons; therefore, I is incorrect. The energy of the photons varies with the frequency of the light; therefore, III is incorrect.

The intensity of a laser beam depends on the number of photons and the energy of each photon. The energy of the photons varies linearly with the frequency. If the frequency doubles, the energy doubles. Since the number of photons is unchanged, the intensity doubles.

3. C is correct.

The minimum energy of the electron-positron pair is its rest mass ($E = 2m_{electron} c^2$). The photon that creates the pair must have more than the minimum energy. The energy of the photon (hv) must therefore be:

$hv > 2m_{electron} c^2$

$v > 2m_{electron} c^2 / h$

$v > 2 \cdot (9.11 \times 10^{-31} \text{ kg}) \cdot (3.00 \times 10^8 \text{ m/s})^2 / (6.626 \times 10^{-34} \text{ J·s})$

$v > 2.47 \times 10^{20} \text{ Hz}$

4. D is correct.
The energy of each incident photon is transferred to an electron, which must then overcome the material's work function to be ejected. Therefore:

hc / λ > Work function

$\lambda < (6.626 \times 10^{-34} \text{ J·s} \cdot 3.00 \times 10^8 \text{ m/s}) / (2.20 \text{ eV} \cdot 1.60 \times 10^{-19} \text{ J/eV})$

$\lambda < 564 \text{ nm}$

5. C is correct.

$E = hv$

$E = (6.626 \times 10^{-34} \text{ J·s}) \cdot (6.43 \times 10^{14} \text{ Hz}) / (1.60 \times 10^{-19} \text{ J/eV})$

$E = 2.66 \text{ eV}$

6. B is correct. The kinetic energy of the emitted electrons (KE) is the energy of the incident photon minus, at least, the work function of the photocathode surface. Therefore:

$KE = 3.4$ eV $- 2.4$ eV

$KE = (1.0$ eV$)\cdot(1.60 \times 10^{-19}$ J / eV$)$

$KE = 1.60 \times 10^{-19}$ J

7. D is correct. The energy of each incident photon is transferred to an electron, which must then overcome the material's work function to be ejected.

Therefore, to eject an electron:

$hv = hc / \lambda >$ Work function

$\lambda < hc /$ (Work function)

$\lambda < (6.626 \times 10^{-34}$ J·s$)\cdot(3.00 \times 10^8$ m/s$) / (2.9$ eV $\cdot 1.60 \times 10^{-19}$ J/eV$)$

$\lambda < 428 \times 10^{-9}$ m

The illumination range of 400 nm–700 nm that does not satisfy this requirement is:

$\lambda > 428$ nm

8. A is correct. The Balmer formula for Hydrogen is:

$1 / \lambda = (1 / 91.2$ nm$)\cdot(1 / m^2 - 1 / n^2)$

The energy difference of the n = 20 and n = 7 state corresponds to a photon of wavelength:

$1 / \lambda = (1 / 91.2$ nm$)\cdot(1 / 7^2 - 1 / 20^2)$

$\lambda = (91.2$ nm$) / (1 / 7^2 - 1 / 20^2)$

$\lambda = 5092$ nm

The energy of a photon with wavelength λ is:

$E = hc / \lambda$

$E = (6.626 \times 10^{-34}$ J·s$)\cdot(3.00 \times 10^8$ m/s$) / (5092 \times 10^{-9}$ m$)$

$E = (3.93 \times 10^{-20}$ J$) / (1.60 \times 10^{-19}$ J/eV$)$

$E = 0.244$ eV

9. D is correct. The de Broglie wavelength is given by:

$\lambda = h / p$

When the energy ($E = p^2 / 2m$ for a non-relativistic proton) is doubled, the momentum is increased by $\sqrt{2}$, and therefore its de Broglie wavelength decreases by $\sqrt{2}$.

10. E is correct. (Trivially, it is known that the incoming photon must lose energy to the electron in the scattering and therefore its wavelength must increase. There is only one answer with a longer wavelength.)

Using the Compton equation at 120°:

$\Delta\lambda = \lambda_{Compton}\,(1 - \cos\theta)$, where $\lambda_{Compton} = 2.43 \times 10^{-12}\,m$

$\Delta\lambda = .00243\,nm\,(1.5)$

$\Delta\lambda = 0.00365\,nm$

$\lambda = 0.591\,nm + 0.00365\,nm$

$\lambda = 0.595\,nm$

11. E is correct. Wein's displacement law describes the wavelength of maximum emission of radiation of a black body at temperature T. It is:

$\lambda_{max} \cdot T - constant - 0.00290\,m\cdot K$

At T = 5000K:

$\lambda_{max} = 0.00290\,m\cdot K\,/\,5000\,K$

$\lambda_{max} = 580\,nm$

12. D is correct. The uncertainty principle gives energy uncertainty:

$\Delta E \Delta t \geq h\,/\,2\pi$

$\Delta E \geq (6.626 \times 10^{-34}\,J\cdot s\,/\,2\pi)\,/\,(30 \times 10^{-12}\,s)$

$\Delta E \geq (3.5 \times 10^{-24}\,J)$

Converting to eV ($1.6 \times 10^{-19}\,J\,/eV$):

$\Delta E \geq 2.2 \times 10^{-5}\,eV$

13. C is correct.

This is a trick question that has nothing to do with the photocathode or the work function. If the radiation has energy 3.5 eV, then its wavelength is given by:

$E = h\nu = hc\,/\,\lambda = 3.5\,eV$

$\lambda = hc\,/\,(3.5\,eV)$

$\lambda = (6.626 \times 10^{-34}\,J\cdot s)\cdot(3.00 \times 10^{8}\,m/s)\,/\,(3.5\,eV)$

$\lambda = (6.626 \times 10^{-34}\,J\cdot s)\cdot(3.00 \times 10^{8}\,m/s)\,/\,(3.5\,eV)$

$\lambda = (5.679 \times 10^{-26}\,J\cdot m\,/eV)\,/\,(1.6 \times 10^{-19}\,J/eV)$

$\lambda = 355\,nm$

14. A is correct. The energy of a photon is given by:

$E = h\nu = hc / \lambda$

Therefore, if the wavelength is doubled, the energy is halved.

15. D is correct.

The energy of each incident photon is transferred to an electron, which must then overcome the material's work function to be ejected. Therefore:

$h\nu >$ Work function

$\nu > (2.8 \text{ eV} \cdot 1.60 \times 10^{-19} \text{ J/eV}) / (6.626 \times 10^{-34} \text{ J·s})$

$\nu > 6.8 \times 10^{-14} /\text{s}$

16. B is correct.

As the intensity of light increases, the photon flux increases but not the energy of the photons.

The kinetic energy of the ejected electrons depends solely on the energy of the incident photons and the work function of the metal. Since the energy of the incident photons is unchanged, the kinetic energy of the ejected electrons does not change.

On the other hand, the probability of an electron being ejected, and therefore the number of electrons ejected per second, depends on the flux of incident photons. It increases as the intensity of the light increases. The electron is ejected at the same instance as the light is absorbed, independent of the intensity of the light; therefore, the time lag does not change.

Note: the time lag between the illumination of the surface (not the absorption of light) and the ejection of the first electron depends on the probability of ejection, which depends on the intensity of the incident light.

17. A is correct.

The Rydeberg formula for hydrogen for the emission of radiation from the nth level down to the mth (i.e. n > m) is:

$1 / \lambda = (1 / 91.2 \text{ nm}) \cdot (1 / m^2 - 1 / n^2)$

If n = 16 (since the first spectral line is from n = 2) and m = 1, then:

$1 / \lambda = (1 / 91.2 \text{ nm}) \cdot (1 / 1^2 - 1 / 16^2)$

$\lambda = 91.2 \text{ nm} / (1 - 0.004)$

$\lambda = 91.6 \text{ nm}$

18. A is correct.

The energy of each incident photon is transferred to an electron. The electron's energy goes into overcoming the photocathode's 2.5 eV work function.

The remaining energy is then stopped by the stopping potential.

The greatest amount of energy an electron can have comes from a photon with a wavelength of 360 nm.

The remaining energy is then:

remaining energy $= hv - 2.5$ eV

remaining energy $= hc / \lambda - 2.5$ eV

remaining energy $= (6.626 \times 10^{-34}$ J·s$)\cdot(3.00 \times 10^8$ m/s$) / (360 \times 10^{-9}$ m$) - 2.5$eV

remaining energy $= [(5.52 \times 10^{-19}$ J$) / (1.6 \times 10^{-19}$ J/eV$)] - 2.5$ eV

remaining energy $= 3.45$ eV $- 2.5$ eV $= 0.95$ eV

The electron has a charge of e. Therefore, this energy can be stopped by a voltage of 0.95 volts.

19. D is correct.

The de Broglie wavelength is given by:

$\lambda = h / p$

$\lambda = (6.626 \times 10^{-34}$ J·s$) / (1.95 \times 10^{-27}$ kg·m/s$)$

$\lambda = 340$ nm

20. C is correct.

The Balmer formula for Hydrogen for the emission of radiation from the nth level down to the mth (i.e. n > m) is:

$1 / \lambda = (1 / 91.2$ nm$)\cdot(1 / m^2 - 1 / n^2)$

If n = 9 and m = 6, then:

$1 / \lambda = (1 / 91.2$ nm$)\cdot(1 / 6^2 - 1 / 9^2)$

$1 / \lambda = (1 / 91.2$ nm$)\cdot(0.01543)$

Thus:

$v = c / \lambda$

$v = (3.00 \times 10^8$ m/s$)\cdot(1 / 91.2$ nm$)\cdot(0.01543)$

$v = 5.08 \times 10^{13}$ /s

$v = 5.08 \times 10^{13}$ Hz

21. A is correct.

$E = hv$

$E = (6.626 \times 10^{-34}$ J·s$)\cdot(110$ GHz$)$

$E = (6.626 \times 10^{-34}$ J·s$)\cdot(110 \times 10^9$ / s$)$

$E = 7.29 \times 10^{-23}$ J

22. C is correct.

The visible spectrum ranges from 400 nm to 700 nm.

The Balmer formula for Hydrogen for the emission of radiation from the nth level down to the mth (i.e., $n > m$) is:

$$1 / \lambda = (1 / 91.2 \text{ nm}) \cdot (1 / m^2 - 1 / n^2)$$

Consider emission from any level down to the m = 1 level.

The lowest energy is from the n = 2 level, and its wavelength is:

$$91.2 \text{ nm} \cdot (4 / 3) = 121 \text{ nm, which is not visible.}$$

Therefore, no visible lines are radiating down to the m = 1 level.

Consider emission from any level down to the m = 3 level.

The highest energy comes from $n = \infty$ and its wavelength is:

$$91.2 \text{ nm} \cdot 9 = 820 \text{ nm, which is not visible.}$$

Therefore, no visible lines are radiating down to the m = 3 level, nor are there any visible lines radiating down to any m level higher than 3.

Consider radiation from various levels down to the m = 2 level.

From n = 3, the wavelength is:

$$91.2 \text{ nm} / (1 / 4 - 1 / 9) = 91.2 \text{ nm} \cdot 7.2 = 656.6 \text{ nm}$$

From n = 4, the wavelength is:

$$91.2 \text{ nm} / (1 / 4 - 1 / 16) = 91.2 \text{ nm} \cdot 5.333 = 486.4 \text{ nm}$$

From n = 5, the wavelength is:

$$91.2 \text{ nm} / (1 / 4 - 1 / 25) = 91.2 \text{ nm} \cdot 4.762 = 434.3 \text{ nm}$$

From n = 6, the wavelength is:

$$91.2 \text{ nm} / (1 / 4 - 1 / 36) = 91.2 \text{ nm} \cdot 4.5 = 410.4 \text{ nm}$$

From n = 7, the wavelength is:

$$91.2 \text{ nm} / (1 / 4 - 1 / 49) = 91.2 \text{ nm} \cdot 4.355 = 397.2 \text{ nm, which is not visible.}$$

Therefore, there are 4 visible lines:

m = 2 to n = 3   656.6 nm

m = 2 to n = 4   486.4 nm

m = 2 to n = 5   434.3 nm

m = 2 to n = 6   410.4 nm

23. B is correct.

$E = h\nu = hc / \lambda$

$\lambda = hc / E$

$\lambda = (6.626 \times 10^{-34} \text{ J·s})·(3.00 \times 10^8 \text{ m/s}) / (4.20 \text{ eV})$

$\lambda = (4.73 \times 10^{-26} \text{ J·m/eV}) / (1.60 \times 10^{-19} \text{ J/eV})$

$\lambda = 2.96 \times 10^{-7} \text{ m}$

$\lambda = 296 \text{ nm}$

24. C is correct.

The energy of each incident photon is transferred to an electron, which must then overcome the material's work function to be ejected.

Therefore, if a wavelength of light is just able to eject an electron, then:

$h\nu = hc / \lambda = \text{Work function}$

$(6.626 \times 10^{-34} \text{ J·s})·(3.00 \times 10^8 \text{ m/s}) / (500 \times 10^{-9} \text{ m}) = \text{Work function}$

$(3.98 \times 10^{-19} \text{ J}) / (1.6 \times 10^{-19} \text{ J/eV}) = \text{Work function}$

$2.48 \text{ eV} = \text{Work function}$

25. C is correct.

In the Bohr theory, there is a fixed number of de Broglie wavelengths of the electron in orbit.

This number is the principal quantum number:

$n = 2\pi r / \lambda$

The de Broglie wavelength is given by:

$\lambda = h / p$

Therefore:

$n = (2\pi / h)rp$

or:

$n^2 = (2\pi / h)^2 r^2 p^2$

The attractive force of the proton keeps the electron in a circular orbit. The attractive force is proportional to $1 / r^2$, and if that force keeps the electron in orbit, $1 / r^2$ must be proportional to v^2 / r.

Therefore, v^2 (or p^2) is proportional to $1 / r$.

Since $r^2 p^2$ is proportional to n^2, and p^2 is proportional to $1 / r$, then r (i.e. $r^2·1 / r$) is proportional to n^2.

26. C is correct.

The Balmer formula for Hydrogen for the emission of radiation from the nth level down to the mth (i.e., n > m) is:

$$1 / \lambda = (1 / 91.2 \text{ nm}) \cdot (1 / m^2 - 1 / n^2)$$

$$1 / \lambda = (1 / 91.2 \text{ nm}) \cdot (1 / 9^2 - 1 / 11^2)$$

$$\lambda = (91.2 \text{ nm}) / (0.00408)$$

$$\lambda = 22,300 \text{ nm}$$

27. C is correct.

The energy of each incident photon is transferred to an electron, which must then overcome the material's work function to be ejected.

Therefore, if a wavelength of light can eject an electron with energy 2.58 eV, then:

$$h\nu = hc / \lambda = \text{Work function} + 2.58 \text{ eV}$$

$$(6.626 \times 10^{-34} \text{ J·s}) \cdot (3.00 \times 10^8 \text{ m/s}) / (240 \times 10^{-9} \text{ m}) = \text{Work function} + 2.58 \text{ eV}$$

$$\text{Work function} = [(8.28 \times 10^{-19} \text{ J}) / (1.6 \times 10^{-19} \text{ J/eV})] - 2.58 \text{eV}$$

$$\text{Work function} = 2.60 \text{ eV}$$

28. D is correct.

By doubling the frequency of the light, the energy of each photon doubles, but not the number of photons (hence B is wrong).

Although doubling the energy of each photon would cause more electrons to be ejected, it does not, necessarily, double that number, since the number is not linearly proportional to the incident energy (hence A is not always true).

The kinetic energy (*KE*) of the ejected electrons would more than double since the initial kinetic energy is less than the energy of the incident photons - the work function of the surface reduced it (hence C is wrong).

The kinetic energy would increase by at least 2 but not necessarily by 4 (hence D is wrong).

29. E is correct. The Balmer formula for Hydrogen is:

$$1 / \lambda = (1 / 91.2 \text{ nm})(1 / m^2 - 1 / n^2)$$

From the n = 3 level, the transition to the n = 2 level has the lowest energy and therefore the longest wavelength. The Balmer formula for n = 3, m = 2 is:

$$1 / \lambda = (1 / 91.2 \text{ nm})(1 / 2^2 - 1 / 3^2)$$

$$1 / \lambda = (1 / 91.2 \text{ nm})(5 / 36)$$

$$\lambda = 656 \text{ nm}$$

30. C is correct.

Photons are light, and the speed of light is invariant; therefore, I is wrong.

The energy of the photons in a beam of light determines the color of the light. If the color is unchanged, then the average energy of the photons is unchanged, making II wrong.

Changing the brightness of a beam of light increases the number of photons in the beam of light.

31. D is correct.

The uncertainty principle states that the uncertainty in position and momentum must be at least:

$$\Delta x \Delta p \approx h / 2\pi$$

$$\Delta p \approx h / (2\pi \Delta x)$$

If:

$$\Delta x = 5.0 \times 10^{-15} \text{ m}$$

Then:

$$\Delta p \approx 6.626 \times 10^{-34} \text{ J·s} / (2\pi \cdot 5.0 \times 10^{-15} \text{ m})$$

$$\Delta p \approx 2.11 \times 10^{-20} \text{ kg·m/s}$$

The uncertainty in the (non-relativistic) kinetic energy of the proton is then:

$$\Delta KE \approx (\Delta p)^2 / (2m)$$

$$\Delta KE \approx [h / (2\pi \Delta x)]^2 / (2m)$$

$$\Delta KE \approx [(6.626 \times 10^{-34} \text{ J·s}) / (2\pi \cdot 5.0 \times 10^{-15} \text{ m})]^2 / (2 \cdot 1.67 \times 10^{-27} \text{ kg})$$

$$\Delta KE \approx (1.33 \times 10^{-13} \text{ J})$$

Converting to MeV:

$$\Delta KE \approx (1.33 \times 10^{-13} \text{ J}) / (1.6 \times 10^{-13} \text{ J/MeV})$$

$$\Delta KE \approx (0.83 \text{ MeV})$$

32. B is correct.

The electron absorbs the full energy of the photon, losing 2.4 eV as it escapes from the photocathode and an additional 1.1 eV of kinetic energy after it escapes from the photocathode. This allows it to be stopped only with a potential exceeding 1.1 volts.

It therefore absorbs 2.4 eV + 1.1 eV = 3.5 eV from the incident photon.

A photon with energy 3.5 eV has a wavelength given by:

$$h\nu = hc / \lambda = E$$

$$\lambda = hc / E = (6.626 \times 10^{-34} \text{ J·s}) \cdot (3.00 \times 10^{8} \text{ m/s}) / (3.5 \text{ eV} \cdot 1.60 \times 10^{-19} \text{ J /eV})$$

$$\lambda = 355 \text{ nm}$$

33. B is correct.

The Compton effect is a measure of the reduction in wavelength of an x-ray beam as it scatters off a sample.

The reduction in wavelength can be explained if the incident x-ray beam is considered as being made up of individual particles each with momentum and energy, and that electrons scatter those particles in the sample.

Hence, the Compton effect demonstrates the particle nature of electromagnetic radiation.

While the energy content and momenta of the individual x-rays are included in the scattering calculation, they are not directly demonstrated in the Compton effect.

34. B is correct.

The de Broglie wavelength of a matter wave is:

$$\lambda = h / p$$

$$\lambda = h / (m\gamma v)$$

(Since $v / c < 0.1$, this will equal about 1.005 and can be ignored)

$$\lambda = (6.626 \times 10^{-34} \text{ J·s}) / [(9.11 \times 10^{-31} \text{ kg}) \cdot (2.5 \times 10^{7} \text{ m/s})]$$

$$\lambda = 29 \times 10^{-12} \text{ m}$$

$$\lambda = 29 \text{ pm}$$

Please, leave your Customer Review on Amazon

Chapter 12 Explanations: Organic Chemistry Nomenclature

1. D is correct. The longest carbon chain is composed of seven carbon atoms.

There are chlorine, ethyl and methyl substituent for this compound.

2. C is correct.

The longest carbon chain is composed of six carbon atoms and is the cyclohexene substructure.

The molecule contains a methyl group in the fourth position.

3. A is correct. One option is to draw all of the atoms to determine the atom count.

Alternatively, using a subscript of n for the number of carbons, the degrees of unsaturation can be determined from the following formulae:

Alkane: C_nH_{2n+2} = 0 degrees of unsaturation

Alkene: C_nH_{2n} = 1 degree of unsaturation

Alkyne: C_nH_{2n-2} = 2 degrees of unsaturation

Rings = 1 degree of unsaturation

The reference molecule has 2 rings and therefore 2 degrees of unsaturation:

C_nH_{2n-2}

$C_8H_{16-2} = C_8H_{14}$

4. A is correct. The *para* notation means that two of the substituent groups are on opposite sides of the aromatic rings in a C_1–C_4 relationship.

When the bromine atoms are adjacent (C_1–C_2), the isomer is *ortho*.

When the bromine atoms are in a C_1–C_3 relationship, the isomer is *meta*.

5. B is correct.

The longest carbon chain in the molecule has 4 carbon atoms and therefore the root is *but–*.

An alkene is positioned at the second carbon with a suffix of *–ene*.

6. C is correct. The longest carbon chain is composed of five carbon atoms.

The highest priority group is aldehyde.

The substituent groups are the hydroxymethyl group, the ethyl group, the alkene and the alkyne.

7. B is correct.

The cyclohexane is the longest carbon chain, and the alcohol is the highest priority group, making the root name "cyclohexanol."

The chlorine and methyl groups are the substituents.

8. D is correct. The alcohol of this aromatic compound has the highest priority, and the carbon count starts at this position. The root (and suffix) name of the compound is "phenol."

The ethyl group is numbered as three instead of four because the numbering favors the lower position values.

9. E is correct. The longest carbon chain of the molecule is the 3-carbon propane.

There are three substituents in this molecule: two methyl groups are on the nitrogen atom, and one methyl group is at the second position.

10. B is correct. The highest priority groups are *trans* to one another.

The longest carbon chain has seven carbon atoms, and the alkene is in the fourth position (fourth carbon from the alcohol, which is the highest priority group).

11. D is correct. The longest carbon chain contains five carbons.

The highest priority group in the molecule is the alcohol, so the name of the compound has *–ol* as the suffix and *pent–* as the root name.

The methyl substituent is in the second position.

12. A is correct.

Propyl substituents contain a three-carbon chain. If the point of attachment (indicated by the squiggle line) is at the second carbon, the groups is an *iso*propyl group.

B: *tert-* butyl

C: *sec-*butyl

D: isobutyl

E: neopentyl

isopropyl   sec-butyl   isobutyl

tert-butyl   Isopentyl   neopentyl   tert-pentyl
               or isoamyl   or tert-amyl

Common names of alkyl substituents (recognized by IUPAC)

13. D is correct.

A: the molecule is *ortho*-fluorobenzoic acid.

B: the substituents should be given the lowest possible numbering system and alphabetized to give 2-chloro-1,3-dinitrobenzene.

C: the substituents should be alphabetized to give 1-bromo-2-iodobenzene.

14. A is correct.

The longest chain is the cyclohexane; the chlorines are on the same side (*cis*) and are three carbons (1,3) apart.

15. D is correct.

The longest carbon chain has five carbon atoms.

The alcohol is attached to the carbon at the second position, and the methyl group is attached to the carbon in the fourth position.

16. B is correct.

The longest carbon chain is a four-carbon cyclo derivative (i.e., cyclopentane).

There are four substituents located at the first and third positions in the molecule.

17. A is correct.

Drawing the line formula of the carbon chain and proper interpretation of the subscripts.

$$H-\underset{\underset{H}{|}}{\overset{\overset{H}{|}}{C}}-\underset{\underset{H}{|}}{\overset{\overset{H}{|}}{C}}-\underset{\underset{H}{|}}{\overset{\overset{H}{|}}{C}}-\underset{\underset{H}{|}}{\overset{\overset{H}{|}}{C}}-\underset{\underset{H}{|}}{\overset{\overset{H}{|}}{C}}-\underset{\underset{H}{|}}{\overset{\overset{H}{|}}{C}}-\underset{\underset{H}{|}}{\overset{\overset{H}{|}}{C}}-H$$

There are two methyl groups and five methylene (CH_2) in the molecule for a total of seven carbons.

Use the following formula to calculate the degrees of unsaturation:

C_nH_{2n+2}: for an alkane (0 degrees of unsaturation)

18. E is correct.

The longest carbon chain is composed of five carbon atoms.

There are two alkenes, so the root name is "pentadiene."

There is a methyl group in the second position along the carbon chain.

19. B is correct.

Because the group has three carbon atoms, the group is known as a propyl group.

Propyl substituents exist as either the *n*-propyl (i.e., normal or straight chain) or the isopropyl group.

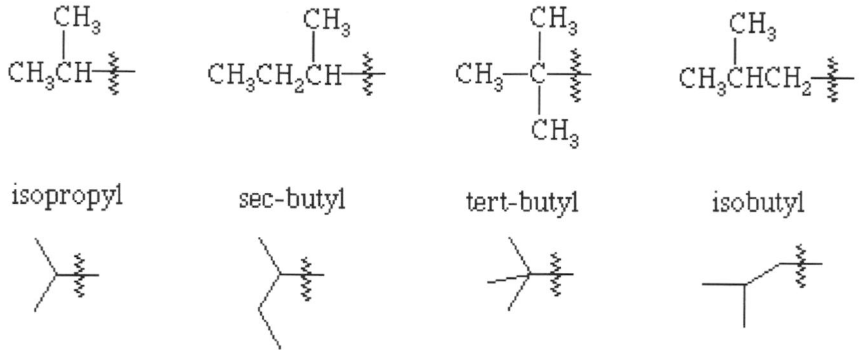

Sample common names for organic substituents used in the nomenclature

20. B is correct.

The longest carbon chain has six carbon atoms.

There are two methyl substituents in the molecule, and there is an isopropoxide substituent at the C4 position.

The stereochemistry of the alkene is *E*.

21. A is correct.

The molecule has four carbon atoms and two alkenes, hence the root name butadiene.

The double bonds of alkenes are in the first and third positions of the carbon chain.

22. A is correct.

The carboxylic acid (*–oic* acid) is considered the 1 position.

The hydroxyl group is in the *ortho* or the two position.

23. B is correct.

The word *acetone* has two important components. The *ace* part is similar to *acetyl* and indicates that the structure includes a methyl group that is bonded to a carbonyl group.

The suffix *–one* indicates that the carbonyl group is a ketone.

24. A is correct.

The name above is the common name for the compound (i.e., toluene is the suffix for a benzene ring with a methyl substituent).

For the IUPAC name, the longest carbon chain in the compound is the six-membered benzene ring.

There are two substituent groups present in the molecule: the ethyl group and the methyl group.

Therefore, the IUPAC name is 1-ethyl-3-methylbenzene.

OH — phenol   CH₃ — toluene   NH₂ — aniline   OMe — anisole

NO₂ — nitrobenzene   CHO — benzaldehyde   COOH — benzoic acid   styrene

SO₃H — benzenesulfonic acid   COMe — acetophenone   Me Me Me — *tert*-butylbenzene

Common names for benzene derivatives

25. D is correct.

Cyclopropane is the only compound listed that contains three carbons.

All other answer choices have four carbons.

Cyclopropane with the stereochemistry of hydrogens indicated

26. B is correct.

The longest carbon chain in the molecule is six carbon atoms long.

The two methyl substituents at the second and fourth positions in the chain.

27. D is correct.

The longest carbon chain that includes the double bond (i.e., alkene functional group) is a five-carbon molecule. The chain is numbered with the alkene given the lowest number.

Ethyl (i.e., 2 carbon) substituent is at the second position in the carbon chain.

28. B is correct.

The longest carbon chain has 5 carbons and is cyclopentane – the root name of the molecule.

It also possesses two substituent groups: the chloride and the methyl group.

Stereochemistry is indicated in the structure; the *cis-* notation is necessary for the compound's name.

29. B is correct. Pentanal:

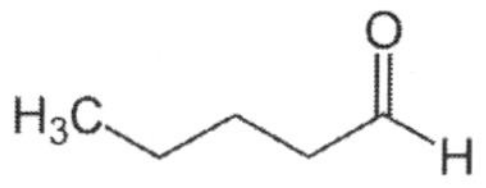

The longest carbon chain in the molecule is five carbon atoms; the molecule contains an aldehyde, so the suffix is *–al*.

The suffix *–one* signifies a ketone and *~oic acid* is for carboxylic acid.

30. C is correct.

The three substituent groups attached to the nitrogen atom include the two methyl groups and the *tert-butyl* group.

31. A is correct.

The longest carbon chain for this molecule is the cyclohexene.

The highest priority group of the molecule is the carboxylic acid, and the carbon atom it is bonded to should be labeled as carbon one.

Therefore, the *oxo~* (i.e., prefix for the ketone) group is positioned at carbon two.

32. B is correct.

The longest carbon chain is composed of seven carbon atoms.

The remaining carbon groups are substituent methyl groups located at the second, fourth and fifth positions along the carbon chain.

33. B is correct.

The longest chain of carbon atom is the cyclohexane ring, hence the root of the molecule's name. There are two methyl substituents located at the first and second positions in the ring. The groups are on the same side of the ring, so they have a *cis* orientation.

34. A is correct.

The longest carbon chain is 8 carbon atoms. The only substituent is the isopropyl group.

35. C is correct.

When numbering the longest carbon chain of a molecule, start on the end that results in the lowest possible numbering for the substituent groups.

Therefore, the correct molecule should have two methyl groups at the second position and one methyl group in the third position.

36. B is correct.

The longest carbon chain in the compound is composed of four carbon atoms.

The highest priority group in the molecule is the amine.

The amine is attached to carbon number 2 (i.e., *sec*-position).

The 5 common names recognized by IUPAC are isopropyl, isobutyl, *sec*-butyl, *tert*-butyl, and neopentyl.

2-butanamine is the IUPAC name for the molecule.

37. D is correct.

Draw the four-carbon chain with the double bond at the second position in the chain.

The second and third position each have a chlorine atom, and these are the highest priority substituents of the alkene.

They must be oriented on the same side of the double bond because the molecule is *cis*.

38. A is correct.

The longest continuous carbon chain in this molecule is six atoms long, making it a substituted hexane chain.

The molecule contains a ketone carbonyl (designated by the suffix –*one*), with the carbon atoms numbered from the end of the chain closest to the carbonyl.

The ethyl substituent is located at carbon 3, while the carbonyl is at carbon 2.

Therefore, the IUPAC name for this molecule 3-ethylhexan-2-one.

39. E is correct.

The longest carbon chain is seven carbon atoms and includes an alkene.

The alkene is the highest priority functional group and is assigned the lowest number (i.e., 1 in this example).

Therefore, the molecule has a chlorine substituent in the fourth position.

40. C is correct.

The longest carbon chain is six carbon atoms.

The two substituents are the chlorine atom and the methyl group.

The highest priority group is chlorine and therefore assumes the lowest number.

41. A is correct.

The suffix ~*oate* signifies an ester functional group as the highest priority group in the molecule.

42. A is correct. The longest carbon chain has seven carbon atoms; it has one chlorine and one methyl substituent.

IUPAC recognizes the following 5 common names in the nomenclature of organic molecules:

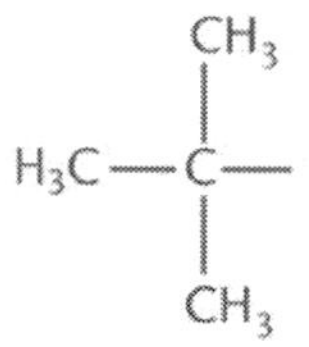

t-butyl 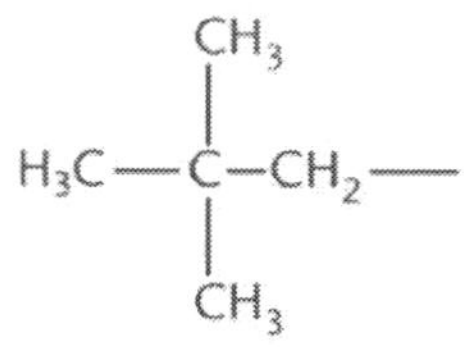   neopentyl 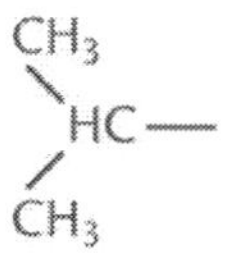   isopropyl

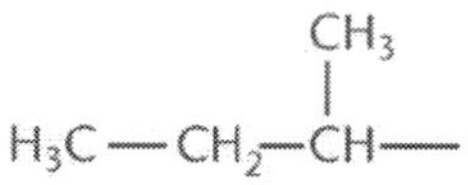

sec-butyl 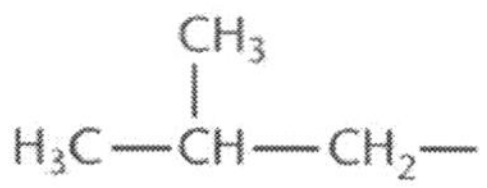   isobutyl

43. C is correct.

The longest carbon chain in the molecule is composed of seven carbon atoms.

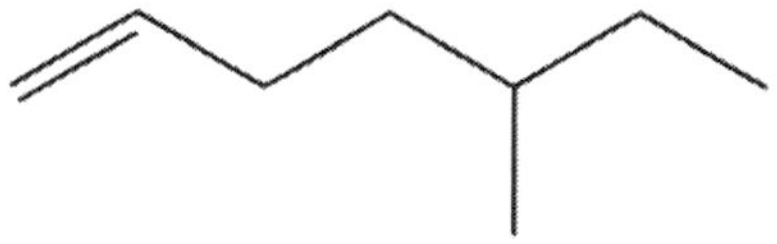

The methyl substituent is at the fifth carbon of the chain.

The alkene *pi* bond is between carbon one and carbon two.

44. C is correct.

Neutral carbon atoms maintain bonds to four other atoms.

Therefore, an acyclic hydrocarbon cannot terminate with a methylene (~CH_2~) group.

Methyl (CH_3) groups are at the ends of alkanes and have a formula of ~CH_3.

Using a subscript of n for the number of carbons, the degrees of unsaturation can be determined from the following formulae:

Alkane: C_nH_{2n+2} = 0 degrees of unsaturation

Alkene: C_nH_{2n} = 1 degree of unsaturation

Alkyne: C_nH_{2n-2} = 2 degrees of unsaturation

$CH_3CH_3CH_3$ has 3 carbons and, according to the formula C_nH_{2n+2}, should have 8 hydrogens.

This molecule has 9 hydrogens; it is impossible because it would require a carbon with 5 bonds.

A: $CH_3CHCH_3CH_2CH_3$ has 5 carbons and, according to the formula C_nH_{2n+2}, should have 12 hydrogens.

B: $CH_3CH_2CH_2CH_2CH_3$ has 5 carbons and, according to the formula C_nH_{2n+2}, should have 12 hydrogens.

D: $CH_3CH_2CH_2CH_3$ has 4 carbons and, according to the formula C_nH_{2n+2}, should have 10 hydrogens.

E: CH_3CH_3 has 2 carbons and, according to the formula C_nH_{2n+2}, should have 6 hydrogens.

45. D is correct.

The number this five-carbon chain beginning at the highest-priority functional group – the alcohol (functional groups with higher oxidation states are higher priority). Thus, alcohol is attached to carbon 1.

The C–C double bond is between carbons 2 and 3, and the C=C triple bond is between carbons 4 and 5.

The stereochemistry about the alkene is '*E*' (highest priority groups are on opposite sides of the alkene). The priority groups are ranked according to the Cahn-Ingold-Prelog rules for prioritization based for the atomic number of atoms attached to the alkene.

Cis–trans relationship cannot be used to describe the molecule because the substituents across the double bond are different.

46. B is correct.

The longest carbon chain in the molecule contains six carbon atoms.

The highest (and sole) functional group is the amide.

Notes

Chapter 13 Explanations: Covalent Bond

1. D is correct.

The benzylic position is one carbon away from benzene or aromatic ring. Without the aromatic ring, the cation is considered an allylic carbocation when it is one carbon away from a double bond.
Vinyl means on the double bond.

2. B is correct. The hydrogen atom bonds by overlapping its 1*s* orbital with the orbital of a bonding partner. The carbon atom is bonded to three atoms and is positively charged, both of which are indications that the carbon atom is sp^2 hybridized.

3. A is correct. Using the formula for calculating the degrees of unsaturation reveals that 2 unsaturation elements (either rings or *pi* bonds) exist.

Structures that contain atoms with satisfied octets are favored.

Molecules with charged carbon atoms tend to be less stable.

4. D is correct.

Wohler's experiment is significant because it demonstrated that organic compounds could be created from inorganic compounds. This result ran counter to the belief that the material that composed life was different from the matter of nonliving things, a theory called vitalism.

5. B is correct.

The allylic cation is a carbocation that is one *sigma* bond away from a double bond (i.e., alkene).

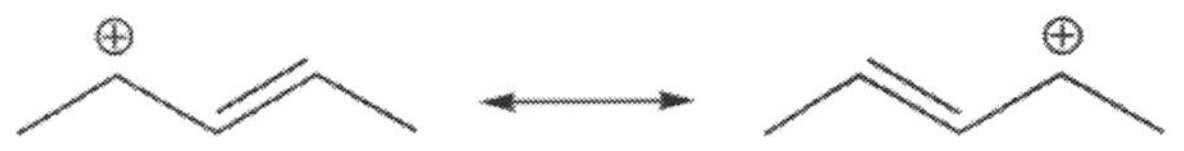

Resonance hybrids of an allylic carbocation

Methylene groups are points of saturation in the molecule that can prevent the conjugation of nearby alkenes.

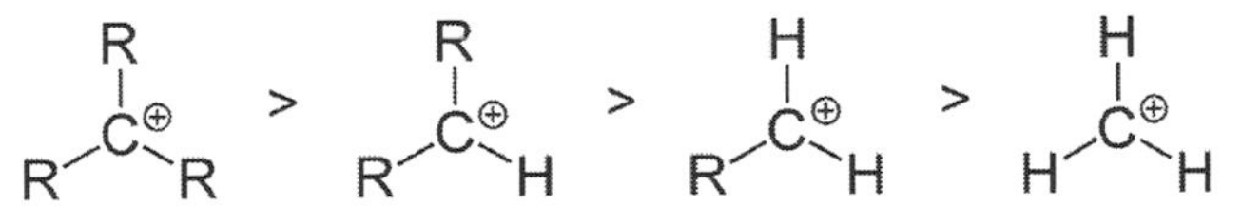

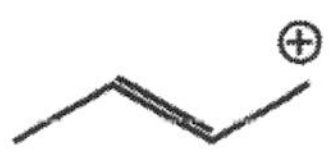 is more stable than 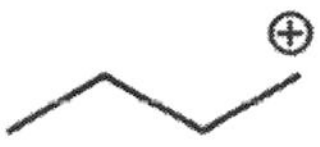

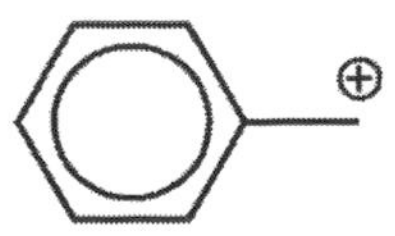 is more stable than 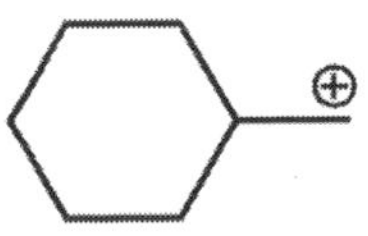

6. C is correct.

Propene is an example of an alkene, which are molecules that have bonding angles of about 120 degrees.

This molecular geometry affords the substituent groups the greatest amount of spatial separation to minimize the intramolecular Van der Waals repulsions among them.

7. D is correct.

The electronegativity difference decides the distribution of electrons between bonded atoms.

This unequal distribution of electrons creates the polarity (∂^+ and ∂^-) of the bond.

8. D is correct.

The molecular formula given above is for an acyclic alkyne.

Acyclic alkynes have a linear geometry (i.e., 180 degrees), and the carbon atoms have an *sp* hybridization.

Cyclic alkynes have two fewer hydrogen atoms because those bonds are replaced with carbon-carbon bonds to form a ring.

9. B is correct.

Tertiary carbocations are more stable than secondary and primary benzylic carbocations, which are more stable than primary or vinylic carbocations.

Methyl cations are the least stable of the carbocations.

10. B is correct.

Nodes only form between the orbitals of atoms if the orbital phases have the opposite sign.

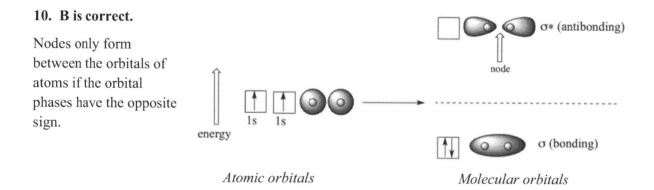

11. B is correct.

As the number of covalent bonds (i.e., triple > double > single) increases between carbon atoms, the bond order and bond strength increases.

Stronger bonds are shorter, so the two carbon atoms that make up the triple bond have the shortest bond.

12. E is correct.

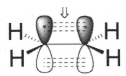

pi bond overlap between the unhybridized orbitals is indicated by the arrow

In organic molecules, the overlap of *pi* bonds is responsible for the formation of carbon-carbon *pi* bonds.

The orbitals of double and triple bonds (alkenes and alkynes, respectively) are unhybridized and are more reactive than the *sigma* bonds of single bonds.

Therefore, the reactions of alkenes typically involve breaking the alkene double bond.

13. E is correct.

Reasonable resonance forms do not allow nuclei to change positions and satisfy the octet rule.

Based on the valence number, hydrogen can only have one bond, and carbon can only have four bonds.

Negative charges should be placed on more electronegative atoms.

14. B is correct.

The nitrogen atom does not contain a formal charge (the formal charge calculation for this atom is 0).

However, the charge is slightly negative because the nitrogen atom withdraws electron density from substituent groups via induction, and the lone pair represents a region of electron density.

15. B is correct.

Compounds that tend to be polar possess electronegative heteroatoms and more carbon-heteroatom bonds. If these groups can ionize to form charges, then they become even more polar.

16. E is correct.

For symmetric compounds like acetylene, no molecular dipole moment exists, because the electron density is evenly distributed on either side of the triple bond.

Asymmetric molecules have molecular dipoles.

17. D is correct.

Except for structure D, the other structures are intermediates for electrophilic aromatic substitution.

These resonance intermediates typically have one cation and no negative charges in the ring.

Resonance hybrids of aniline during electrophilic aromatic substitution

18. C is correct. The bonds between atoms (i.e., intramolecular) are stronger than the bonds between molecules (i.e., intermolecular).

Examples of intermolecular bonds are hydrogen, dipole-dipole, dipole-induced dipole and van der Waals.

Sigma bonds are single bonds and involve overlap along the internuclear axis between the atoms. S*igma* bonds are stronger than the *pi* bond of a double bond.

A: hydrogen bonding is a common intramolecular *bond* in which a *hydrogen* atom of one molecule is attracted to an electronegative atom (nitrogen, oxygen or fluorine).

B: dipole-dipole bonds are attractive forces between the positive end of one polar molecule and the negative end of another polar molecule.

D: ionic bonds result from the complete transfer of valence electron(s) between atoms; it generates two oppositely charged ions. The metal loses electrons to become a positively charged cation, whereas the nonmetal accepts those electrons to become a negatively charged anion. Ionic bonds can be disrupted in water and are much weaker in aqueous solutions than in a dry environment.

19. E is correct.

The nitrogen lone pairs of amines (e.g., pyrrole) are *sp³* hybridized unless there is a *pi* bond between the nitrogen and carbon atom (e.g., pyridine).

Pyrrole has a sp³ hybridized nitrogen (lone pair in the ring)

The nitrogen lone pair of pyridine is in an *sp²* hybridized orbital and is not a part of the aromatic system.

Pyridine has a sp² hybridized nitrogen (lone pair outside the ring)

20. E is correct.

Only the hydrogen atom can bond to other atoms with its unhybridized 1*s* orbital.

The *sigma* bonding of all other elements is described by the hybridization of their atomic orbitals before bonding with other atoms.

Therefore, when a carbon atom forms a *sigma* bond, it does so through the overlap of one of its hybridized orbitals.

However, *pi* bonding involves the indirect overlap of unhybridized *p* orbitals.

21. C is correct. Multiple bonds and rings introduce degrees of unsaturation.

Using a subscript of n for the number of carbons, the degrees of unsaturation can be determined from the following formulae:

Alkane: C_nH_{2n+2} = 0 degrees of unsaturation

Alkene: C_nH_{2n} = 1 degree of unsaturation

Alkyne: C_nH_{2n-2} = 2 degrees of unsaturation

Rings = 1 degree of unsaturation

Double bonds = 1 degree of unsaturation

There is one degree of unsaturation for this compound (the ring).

Therefore, with no other degrees of unsaturation present, there are no alkenes or double bonds present in the molecule.

22. E is correct.

Hydrogen atoms only bond with other atoms using their 1*s* orbital.

The nitrogen atoms hybridize their atomic orbitals to produce *sp³* orbital hybrids for bonding.

sp³ orbitals are used because the nitrogen atom forms bonds of equal length with 4 other atoms.

23. C is correct.

The bond dipole in H–F is the largest because of the large difference in electronegativity between hydrogen and fluorine. The electrostatic attraction pulls the atoms closer together, so the bond is the shortest and the strongest.

The bond dipole in H–I is the smallest because the electronegativity between the atoms is the lowest; therefore, H–I bond is the longest and weakest.

24. D is correct.

Tertiary carbocations are more stable than secondary carbocations, which are more stable than primary carbocations.

Carbocation stability: 3° > 2° > 1° > methyl

The more substituted the cation, the more it benefits from hyperconjugation stabilizing factors.

25. B is correct. Carbocations are stabilized by resonance and by hyperconjugation.

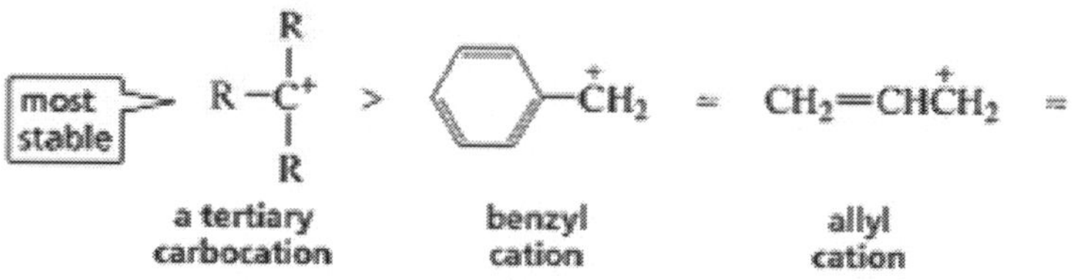

The phenyl ring offers additional stability due to resonance structures with the delocalization of the pi electrons.

The primary non-conjugated carbocation (shown below) will be the least stable (except for vinyl cation).

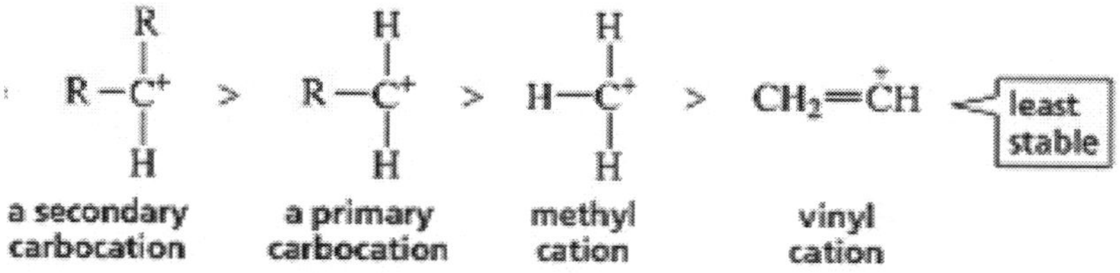

Relative stabilities of carbocations

26. D is correct.

The hybridized orbital is a combination of one *s* and three *p* orbitals.

Therefore, the energy of the hybridized orbital is between the energy of the combined orbitals.

The *s* orbital has lower energy than the *p* orbital.

27. C is correct.

The two allylic cations are resonance forms of each other.

Resonance involves the movement of conjugated *pi* systems, not of the atoms.

A and B are constitutional isomers (i.e., same molecular formula, but different connectivity).

28. B is correct.

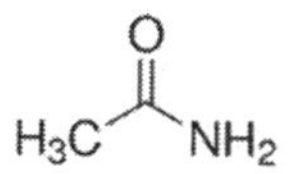

acetamide

The conjugation observed (shown below) for carboxylic acids, and their derivatives (i.e., acetamide) causes the carbonyl to adopt a bond length that is between a C–O single and C=O double bond.

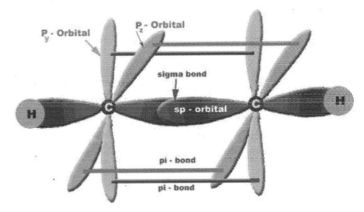

Resonance structures of acetamide

The orbitals involved in resonance are the filled, donating *p* orbital of the nitrogen atom and the adjacent electron-accepting carbonyl *pi** orbital.

29. B is correct.

Acetylene is the common name for ethyne (C_2H_2). Alkynes are linear and contain a bond angle of 180°.

$$H-C\equiv C-H$$

Acetylene has a triple bond and therefore contains sp hybridized carbons.

A carbon of a triple bond is *sp* hybridized (i.e., *sp* + 2 unhybridized *p* orbitals).

The atoms in a triple bond use *sp* hybridized orbitals from the 2*s* orbital merging (i.e., hybridizing) with a 2*p* orbital.

A: 1,3,5–heptatriene contains *sp²* hybridized orbitals (i.e., double bonds) and *sp³* orbitals for single bonds. Bond angles of 120° are trigonal planar and originate from *sp²* orbitals. The molecule also contains single bonds which are *sp³*; therefore, a portion of the molecule is tetrahedral.

C: 2-butyne is an alkyne, but only two carbons are *sp* hybridized, while the remaining carbon is *sp³* hybridized, which results from the combination of the 2*s* and the 2*p* orbitals.

Four *sp³* carbons form and the bond angle is 109.5° with tetrahedral geometry.

Molecular orbital structure for ethyne showing one sigma bond and two pi bonds.

D: dichloromethane has carbon that is *sp³* hybridized because it is attached to two hydrogens and two chlorine atoms.

For the greatest separation between the substituents, the geometry is tetrahedral, and the bond angle is 109.5°.

E: 1,3-hexadiene contains *sp²* hybridized orbitals (i.e., double bonds) and *sp³* orbitals for single bonds.

Bond angles of 120° are trigonal planar and originate from *sp²* orbitals.

The molecule also contains single bonds which are *sp³*; therefore, a portion of the molecule is tetrahedral.

30. E is correct.

There are six *sigma* bonds that connect the carbon atoms in benzene. Furthermore, delocalized *pi* electron density in the ring is described by three *pi* bonds in resonance.

Two resonance Kekule structures of benzene

31. C is correct. Draw each of the bonds in the structure, where the electrons are distributed to satisfy the octets of the carbon and heteroatoms:

$CH_3C\equiv N$

The nitrile has a triple bond composed of a *sigma* bond and two *pi* bonds.

32. C is correct.

ethene

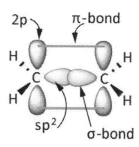

Hybridization and sigma and pi bonds indicated

Hybridization	Bond angle	Geometry
sp^3	109.5°	tetrahedral
$sp^2 + p$ (unhybridized)	120°	trigonal planar (flat)
$sp + p + p$ (two unhybridized)	180°	linear

33. A is correct.

In carbon–carbon double bonds, there is an overlap of sp^2 orbitals and a *p* orbital on the adjacent carbon atoms. The sp^2 orbitals overlap head-to-head as a *sigma* (σ) bond, whereas the *p* orbitals overlap sideways as a *pi* (π) bond.

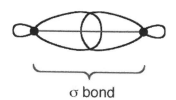

Sigma bond formation showing electron density along the internuclear axis

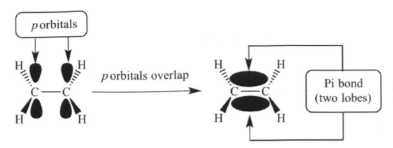

Two pi orbitals showing the pi bond formation during sideways overlap – note the absence of electron density (i.e., node) along the internuclear axis.

Bond lengths and strengths (σ or π) depends on the size and shape of the atomic orbitals and the density of these orbitals to overlap effectively.

The σ bonds are stronger than π bonds because head-to-head orbital overlap involves more shared electron density than sideways overlap.

The σ bonds formed from two $2s$ orbitals are shorter than those formed from two $2p$ orbitals or two $3s$ orbitals.

Carbon, oxygen, and nitrogen are in the second period ($n = 2$), while sulfur (S), phosphorus (P) and silicon (Si) are in the third period.

Therefore, S, P, and Si use $3p$ orbitals to form π bonds, while C, N, and O use $2p$ orbitals. The $3p$ orbitals are much larger than $2p$ orbitals, and therefore there is a reduced probability for an overlap of the $2p$ orbital of C and the $3p$ orbital of S, P, and Si.

B: S, P, and Si can hybridize, but these elements can combine s and p orbitals and (unlike C, O, and N) have d orbitals.

C: S, P and Si (in their ground state electron configurations) have partially occupied p orbitals which form bonds.

D: carbon combines with elements below the second row of the periodic table. For example, carbon commonly forms bonds with higher principal quantum number ($n > 2$) halogens (e.g., F, Cl, Br and I).

34. D is correct.

It is helpful to draw all of the C–H bonds for this compound.

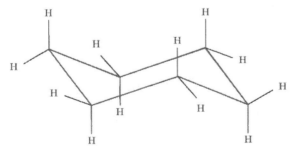

Each carbon atom of the cyclohexane bonds to two hydrogen atoms, because there is one degree of unsaturation (the ring).

Six *sigma* bonds exist in the ring, so the total number of σ bonds is 18.

35. B is correct. There are four regions of electron density around the nitrogen atom (including the lone pair). Therefore, the nitrogen atom is sp^3 hybridized.

The bonding angles of molecules that possess nonbonding lone pairs of electrons is slightly smaller than what is predicted by the hybridization state. The nonbonding electrons exert a greater repulsive force than the bonding electrons between the central atom and the substituent groups. However, the presence of bulky ethyl substituents increases the bond angle from approximately 107° to approximately 109.5°.

Ammonia has a bond angle of approximately 107° due to the electrostatic repulsion of the nitrogen's lone pair on the hydrogen atoms. In amines, as substituents become larger (e.g., $(CH_3CH_2)_3N$), the bond angle between bulky groups increases and the molecular shape approaches a tetrahedral with a bond angle of approximately 109.5°.

36. A is correct. Three degenerate p orbitals exist for an atom with an electron configuration in the second (n = 2) shell or higher. The first (n = 1) shell only has an s orbital. The d orbitals become available from the third shell (n = 3).

37. C is correct. The dipole moment is determined by the magnitudes of the individual bond dipoles and the spatial arrangement of the substituents on the molecule.

The dipole moment is greatest when there is a large difference in electronegativity of the bonded atoms. Therefore, a carbon–carbon bond (i.e., same electronegativity) has no dipole moment, while carbon–halogen bonds have moderately large dipole moments because of the electronegativity difference between carbon and halogen.

$(1R,2S)$-1,2-dichloro-1,2-diphenylethane is effectively *cis* due to restricted rotation.

$(1R,2S)$-1,2-dichloro-1,2-diphenylethane has two phenyl rings attached on one side and two chlorine groups attached on the other side.

The (R/S)–designation indicates that the two highest priority substituents (i.e., chlorine) attached to the same side (priority according to molecular weight, so chlorine has higher priority). The highly electronegative chlorines pull electron density, creating a net dipole.

A: $(1S,2S)$-1,2-dichloro-1,2-diphenylethane contains only single bonds. The (R/S)–designation indicates that the two highest priority substituents (i.e., chlorine) attached on opposite sides (with restricted rotation due to the size of the phenyl substitutes). The highly electronegative chlorines pull electron density in different spatial orientations, canceling a net dipole.

B: 1,2-dichlorobutane has carbon–chlorine bonds that are highly polar, but free rotation about the carbon–carbon single bond cancels any net dipole.

D: (E)-1,2-dichlorobutene differs from the Z configuration (or $1R,2S$ in the correct answer) because the two highest priority substituents are on opposite sides of the double bond. As the chlorine pulls electron density, both dipoles cancel each other for a net dipole of zero.

E: (Z)-1,2-dibromobutene is the Z configuration (or $1R,2S$ in the correct answer) because the two highest priority substituents are on the same side of the double bond. However, bromine is less electronegative than chlorine and therefore has a smaller net dipole.

38. D is correct.

Benzene with sigma and pi bonds shown.

39. D is correct.

Formal charge = group # – nonbonding electrons – ½ bonding electrons

Nitrogen is in group V on the periodic table.

The ammonium cation has four bonds or eight bonding electrons.

The formal charge for the nitrogen atom is $5 - 0 - 8/2 = +1$.

40. B is correct.

Pyrrolidine is not an aromatic compound, so the lone pair of electrons on nitrogen is available for bonding (i.e., function as a base).

The molecule is a secondary alkyl amine, and the nitrogen atom has sp^3 hybridization.

41. B is correct.

The carbonyl carbon is trigonal planar because the double bonded carbon is sp^2 hybridized.

I: each of the two methyl carbons is sp^3 hybridized and tetrahedral.

III: none of the carbons have an unshared pair of electrons (i.e., carbanions) because carbanions are highly reactive and observed in a limited number of examples (e.g., Grignard reagent, Gillman reagent, acetylide anion) and are not present in stable molecules.

42. E is correct.

The allylic cation is able to delocalize the cation at the most substituted position is the most stable molecule.

The other allylic cations are not as stable because the cation is less substituted in the other resonance forms.

43. C is correct.

Resonance structures are derived from the movement of lone pairs and *pi* electrons.

Generated negative charges are placed on the more electronegative atoms and the positive charges on the less electronegative atoms.

44. A is correct.

The oxygen atom contains four regions of electron density (i.e., two lone pairs and two methyl substituents) and adopts a tetrahedral configuration.

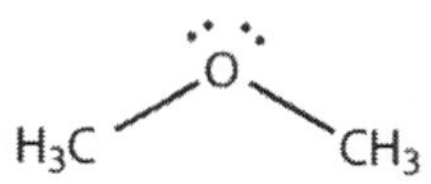

Dimethyl ether has an angle between substituent (i.e., methyl) groups of approximately 109.5 degrees.

45. B is correct. There are four bonding patterns of carbon described by the three hybridization bonding models.

When carbon forms four single (σ) bonds, it is *sp³* hybridized.

When carbon forms one double (π) bond and two single (σ) bonds, it is *sp²* hybridized.

Carbon is *sp* hybridized when it forms one triple (2–π) bond and one single (σ) bond, or it forms two double (π) bonds.

O=CH–CH₂–CH=C=C=CH₂

  sp² sp³ sp² sp sp sp²

46. B is correct. Full arrowheads are used to show the movement of a pair of electrons (compared to single headed – fishhook – arrows for radical reactions).

The only movement of the *pi* (π) electrons is responsible for the stable diene structures to the right.

The *pi* electrons must also be in conjugation.

47. A is correct. There are four regions of electron density around the nitrogen atom (including the lone pair). Therefore, the nitrogen atom is *sp³* hybridized.

Electron geometry describes the geometry of the electron pairs, groups and domains on the central atom, whether they are bonding or non-bonding. Molecular geometry is the name of the shape used to describe the molecule. When atoms bond to a central atom, they do it in a way that maximizes the distance between bonding electrons. This gives the molecule its overall shape. If no lone pairs of electrons are present, the electronic geometry is the same as the molecular shape. When there is a lone pair, it occupies more space than bonding electrons, so the net effect is to bend the shape of the molecule (although the electron geometry still conforms to the predicted shape).

The shape of this molecule is trigonal pyramidal with bonds of approximately 109.5 degrees due to the bulky ethyl substituents. The presence of three substituents (i.e., ethyls) and the lone pair on the nitrogen result in the pyramidal shape consistent with VESPER theory.

48. C is correct. Tertiary carbocations are more stable than secondary or primary carbocation because they experience more hyperconjugation effects from the neighboring C–H bonds.

Resonance stabilization also lowers the energy of the cation.

Chapter 14 Explanations: Stereochemistry

1. C is correct. Draw the different isomers of butene.

This compound can be drawn with the double bond terminal (the carbons are numbered according to IUPAC).

The terminal carbon in the double bond is numbered 1.

There are two geometric isomers of butene (i.e., *cis*-butene and *trans*-butene).

cis-2-butene   trans-2-butene

Geometric isomers are a subset of structural isomers. Geometric requires that the substituents from the double bond can be the same (i.e., *cis* and *trans*) or different (i.e., *E* and *Z*).

1-butene or butene (the position 1 is implied by IUPAC)

Isobutylene (not 2-methyl propene) according to IUPAC

Therefore, there are four structural isomers of butene.

2. D is correct. An asymmetric carbon refers to a chiral carbon: carbon bonded to four different substituents. All the other compounds do not contain asymmetric carbons because at least two of the three atoms or groups bonded to each of their carbon atoms are the same.

3. D is correct. The total number of possible stereoisomers for a given molecule depends on the number of asymmetric carbon atoms (or chiral centers) present in the molecule.

There is a 2^N number of possibilities, where N is the number of chiral centers present.

The molecule has 4 chiral centers: $2^4 = (2 \times 2 \times 2 \times 2) = 16$ stereoisomers.

For some molecules, symmetry elements in the molecule may be redundant structures, which is why the 2^N calculation gives the maximum possible number of stereoisomers and not necessarily the actual number that exists.

4. A is correct. It is important to remember that if an alkene has geminal disubstitution (i.e., two identical moieties bonded to the same alkene carbon), then *cis* and *trans* isomerism is not possible.

5. C is correct. The naming of the compounds reveals that the compounds are the same:

4,7-diethyl-3,6-dimethyldecane

6. C is correct. The bromine substitution changes from vicinal (on adjacent carbons) to geminal (on the same carbon). Because the connectivity changes, the structures are constitutional isomers.

The first molecules cannot be chiral because it has a mirror plane of symmetry.

7. E is correct. The molecules shown above are mirror images of each other.

Assign *R* and *S* at each chiral center to verify the answer to any question asking for the relationship between two chiral molecules.

8. E is correct. In the polarimeter (i.e., plane-polarized light), enantiomers have the same magnitude of specific rotation, but the opposite sign.

9. B is correct. Isomers are compounds that have the same molecular formula but a different structure.

A: "hydrocarbons" refers to organic molecules containing only carbon and hydrogen (i.e., no heteroatoms such as oxygen or nitrogen).

C: homologs are a series of compounds with the same general formula, usually varying by a single parameter (e.g., length of the carbon chain).

D: isotopes have different mass numbers due to differences in the number of neutrons. The number of protons determines the identity of the element.

E: allotropes are each of two or more different physical forms in which an element can exist (e.g., carbon exists as graphite, charcoal, and diamond).

10. B is correct.

(Z)-1-bromo-1-chloropropene   *(E)-1-bromo-1-chloropropene*

These molecules can only adopt one conformation because of the rotational barrier of the alkene.

Configurational isomers involve a double bond. If the molecules have optical activity, they may be enantiomers (non-superimposable mirror images) or diastereomers. If they lack optical activity, they are geometric isomers.

A: constitutional isomers have the same molecular formula but different connectivity. The molecules are not the same, but the connectivity is the same, so they are not constitutional isomers.

C: identical molecules may be drawn with different orientation on the paper but are the same.

D: conformational isomers refer to molecules that are different due to free rotation around single bonds (e.g., Newman projections or chair flips for cyclohexane).

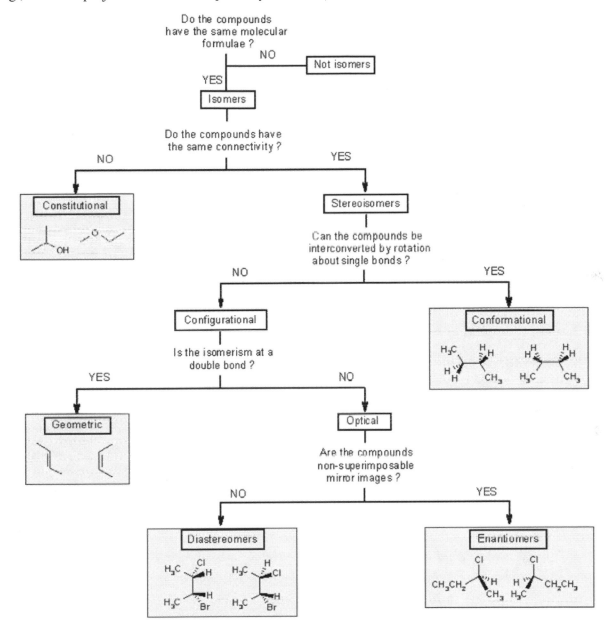

11. B is correct.

Chiral carbons refer to asymmetric carbons that are typically bonded to three other atoms.

Carbon 2 cannot be an asymmetric carbon (or chiral carbon), because carbon atoms with trigonal planar configuration possess a plane of symmetry and are achiral.

12. D is correct.

The number of possible stereoisomers of a molecule depends on the number of chiral centers, which are defined as a carbon bonded to 4 different substituents.

The number of possible stereoisomers is 2^n, where n is the number of chiral centers.

Number all the carbons with the carbonyl carbon as #1.

Carbons 1 and 6 are not chiral centers, because carbon 1 is attached to only three substituents, while carbon 5 has two identical hydrogen substituents.

Carbons 2, 3, 4, and 5 are chiral centers since each is bonded to 4 different groups.

Therefore, the molecule has 4 chiral centers and the number of stereoisomers is $2^4 = 2 \times 2 \times 2 \times 2 = 16$.

13. A is correct.

These molecules are isomers because they have the same number and kinds of atoms, but the bonding is different for each.

B: epimers are two isomers that differ in configuration at only one stereogenic center. All other stereocenters in epimer molecules, if any, are the same.

C: anomers are diastereoisomers for cyclic forms of sugars differing in the configuration at the anomeric carbon (C–1 atom of an aldose or the C–2 atom of a 2-ketose). The cyclic forms of carbohydrates can exist in either α– or β–, based on the position of the substituent at the anomeric center. α–anomers have the hydroxyl pointing down, while β–anomers have the hydroxyl pointing up.

D: allotropes are two or more different physical forms in which an element can exist. Graphite, charcoal, and diamond are all allotropes of carbon.

E: geometric isomers differ from each other in the arrangement of groups with respect to a double bond, ring or other rigid structure.

14. D is correct.

The bromine and hydrogen atom alternate the carbon atoms they are bonded to, so they are constitutional isomers. These molecules cannot be chiral because they have a mirror plane of symmetry.

15. A is correct.

The *anti*-conformer (180° offset) has the lowest energy because it minimizes steric strain (i.e., bulky substituents within van der Waals radii) and torsional strain (i.e., repulsion of bonding electrons when eclipsed). Gauche refers to a dihedral angle of 60°.

anti   gauche   eclipsed

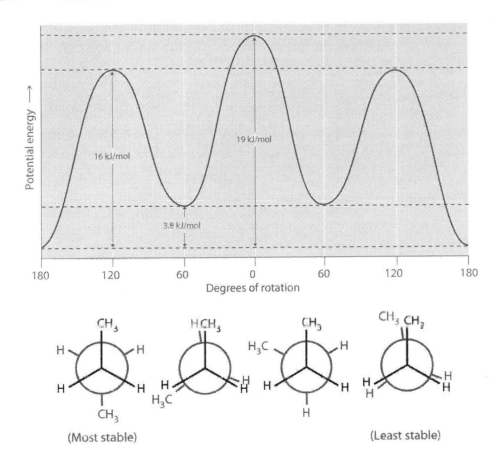

(Most stable)   (Least stable)

16. D is correct. Draw each of the possible isomers and be cognizant of equivalent structures.

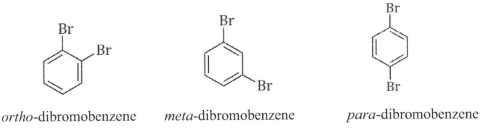

ortho-dibromobenzene   *meta*-dibromobenzene   *para*-dibromobenzene

There are only three possible isomers that can be drawn for the given molecular formula.

17. D is correct.

There are only two possible ways to draw butane, either as the straight chain or the tertiary alkyl constitutional isomer. Note that the term "constitutional isomers" is recognized by IUPAC, while the term "structural isomers" was commonly used historically.

Two constitutional isomers of n-butane (left) and isobutene (right)

18. C is correct. Geometric (configurational) isomers have the same molecular formula, but different connectivity between the atoms due to the orientation of substituents around a carbon-carbon double bond (or ring). In *Z* (*cis* when substituents are the same) isomers, the same substituents are on one side of the double bond or ring, while in *E* (*trans* when substituents are the same) isomers, the same substituents are on opposite sides of the double bond or ring.

19. A is correct. Isomers are molecules with the same molecular formula but different connections (e.g., functional groups) between the atoms. Therefore, the number of carbon atoms, hydrogen atoms and any heteroatoms present must be the same.

20. C is correct.

Cis means that the groups are on the same side of the alkene (or face of a cyclic structure).

Trans means that the groups are on opposite sides.

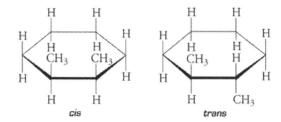

Cis and *trans* isomerism can occur with disubstituted cycloalkanes.

cis-2-butene   trans-2-butene

Cis and *trans* isomerism can occur with alkenes (or for a ring).

21. D is correct. The number of each different kind of atom must be consistent among a pair or group of isomers, meaning that the oxidation state of the carbon atoms of the compound is consistent as well.

A change in the oxidation state of the compound suggests that the hydrogen count is different.

For instance, the isomer of the given alcohol is another alcohol, and not an aldehyde or a ketone.

22. B is correct.

There are two possible stereoisomers for the vicinal disubstituted alkene (1,1-chlorofluoroethene), and there is only one possible isomer of the 1,2 disubstituted alkene (*cis* and *trans*).

23. D is correct. Use the rotation rule (clockwise = *R*, counterclockwise = *S*) to determine the configuration after assigning priorities. When the lowest priority group is on the horizontal bond, the assigned configuration is reversed.

24. C is correct.

Enantiomers are chiral molecules (i.e., attached to four different groups) and are non-superimposable mirror images (i.e., *R* and *S*).

The two molecules are mirror images of each other, so they are enantiomers.

25. A is correct.

There are two possible stereoisomers for the vicinal disubstituted alkene (i.e., *cis* and *trans*).

cis- and *trans*-dichloroethylene

There is only one possible isomer of the geminal (i.e., on the same atom) disubstituted alkene.

1,1-dichloroethene

26. B is correct. To determine the enantiomer of the compound, draw the mirror image of the compound. This requires inverting the two stereocenters, as inverting only one results in a diastereomer.

27. B is correct. All *meso* compounds are molecules with chiral centers and require an inversion center or a plane of symmetry. These elements of symmetry make molecules with asymmetric carbon atoms achiral overall.

28. E is correct. Any molecule that has a nonidentical mirror image is chiral and has an enantiomer.

Draw the structure of the cyclic compound:

cis-1,2-dimethylcyclopentane

Comparison of the molecule reveals an internal plane of symmetry.

A *meso* compound and its enantiomer (i.e., non-superimposable mirror image of a chiral molecule) are the same molecules. Therefore, a *meso* compound does not have an enantiomer.

29. D is correct.

Structural isomers have the same molecular formula, but a different connection of the atoms. With molecular formula $C_4H_8Cl_2$, the carbon skeleton is butane.

Eight structural isomers exist: three isomers have chiral carbons.

From top left and moving to the right: molecules 2, 3 and 6 are chiral (i.e., a carbon attached to four different substituents). Molecule 2 has one chiral carbon; molecule 3 has one chiral carbon.

Structural isomer 6 contains two chiral carbons. One of the stereoisomers of 2,3-dichlorobutane has an internal plane of symmetry, making it the *meso* compound of R/S (or S/R, which is the same molecule) and therefore is achiral and optically inactive.

The other stereoisomer is R/R (or S/S, which is the same molecule) and therefore is chiral and exhibits optical activity.

Therefore, there are three optically active isomers of $C_4H_8Cl_2$.

30. C is correct. Chiral carbon atoms have four different groups bonded to a carbon atom.

The molecule is named with the alcohol as the highest priority group and designated carbon 1.

The carbon atoms with two or more hydrogen atoms (i.e., carbons 1 and 5) are achiral because at least two of the groups are the same.

31. A is correct. Achiral compounds cannot rotate the plane of polarized light.

The solutions of achiral compounds are always optically inactive.

B: there is no relationship between absolute configuration (*R/S*) and the specific rotation (+/–) of light in the polarimeter.

C: *meso* compounds are achiral, but not all achiral molecules are *meso*.

D and E: *meso* compounds are achiral and contain two or more chiral centers and have an internal plane of symmetry.

32. A is correct.

The stereochemistry about the alkene is '*E*' (highest priority groups are on opposite sides of the alkene). The priority groups are ranked according to the Cahn-Ingold-Prelog rules for prioritization based for the atomic number of atoms attached to the alkene.

The chain possessing the heaviest atoms proximal to the alkene generally have higher priority. In this example, the bromomethyl group has a higher priority. The alcohol and methoxy groups contain oxygen atoms, but the methoxy oxygen atom is closer to the double bond.

33. C is correct.

For Fischer projections, horizontal lines represent bonds projecting outward (i.e., wedges), whereas vertical lines represent bonds going back (i.e., dashed lines). A Fischer projection does not include a carbon specified at the cross of the vertical and horizontal lines (i.e., a C is implied but no C is written on the structure).

For assigning *R/S* in Fischer projections, read the ranked (1 → 3) priorities as either clockwise (*R*) or counterclockwise (*S*). If the lowest priority is vertical (i.e., points into the page), then assign *R/S*. If the lowest priority is horizontal (i.e., points out of the page), then reverse (*R* → *S*, *S* → *R*).

Compound I: the order of priority is hydroxyl, carboxyl, methyl, and hydrogen. The order of increasing priority is counterclockwise, and the configuration appears S. However, the lowest priority (group 4 is H) is horizontal (pointing outward), so the absolute configuration is *R*.

Compound II: the order of priority is nitrogen, carboxyl, methyl, and hydrogen. The order of increasing priority is counterclockwise. The lowest priority (group 4 is H) is vertical and therefore points away. The absolute configuration is *S*.

Compound III is achiral because the carbon is not attached to four different groups and therefore the molecule is neither *R* nor *S*.

Compound IV: the order of priority is hydroxyl, carbonyl (aldehyde), methyl (methanol) and hydrogen. The order of increasing priority is counterclockwise. The lowest priority (group 4 is H) is horizontal and therefore points towards the viewer. The absolute configuration is *R*.

Compounds I and IV have the same absolute configuration.

34. A is correct. The root name of the compound is cyclopentane because the ring possesses 5 carbons.

The chlorine substituents are adjacent (i.e., position 1,2) on the ring and must be oriented on opposite sides of the ring.

35. B is correct.

Chiral molecules include carbons that are bonded to four different substituents. This molecule contains no stereogenic centers (i.e., chiral centers), and therefore the molecule cannot be chiral.

---

36. A is correct.

The observed rotation is half the value of the specific rotation for the pure enantiomeric substance. While the effect of the combined opposite enantiomers is canceled, the mixture should have a 50% excess of the pure substance.

Therefore, the mixture must have 75% of the pure enantiomeric substance, where 25% of the rotation cancels the effect of the 25% opposite rotation of its enantiomer.

37. A is correct.

The carbon attached to the leaving group is tertiary (bonded to 3 carbons) and chiral because it is bonded to 4 different substituents, and the molecule is optically active. Tertiary alkyl halides undergo S_N1 reactions (forming a trigonal planar carbocation) but do not undergo S_N2 reactions because of steric hindrance.

In the first step of the S_N1 reaction, the bromine dissociates to form a stable tertiary carbocation, which results in the loss of optical activity. A positively charged carbon is sp^2 hybridized (trigonal planar) and always achiral because it has only three substituents.

In the second step, the HCN nucleophile attacks the trigonal planar (flat) carbocation from either side of the plane (i.e., top or bottom) with approximately equal probability. As a result, the reaction yields approximately equal amounts of two chiral products.

The products are enantiomers (i.e., chiral molecules that are non-superimposable mirror images), and each enantiomer rotates the plane of polarized light to the same extent but in opposite directions.

Therefore, the product is an optically inactive racemic mixture (i.e., both enantiomers in the solution), and there is a loss of optical activity in the solution.

Racemization means loss of optical activity and often involves a carbocation intermediate (S_N1 reaction), whereby the incoming nucleophile attacks from either side of the trigonal planar carbocation.

B: mutarotation occurs in monosaccharides (i.e., sugars) and involves the equilibrium between open-chain forms and cyclic hemiacetal forms (e.g., Haworth projections) in aqueous solutions.

D: inversion of absolute configuration only occurs in S_N2 reactions, whereby a nucleophile attacks the substrate from the side opposite the leaving group (backside) in a one-step reaction.

From the concerted S_N2 reaction, the products have the same absolute configuration (often inverted from the backside attack), and the product is considered chiral.

38. E is correct.

Draw the structure of each of the possibilities and count the total number of isomers.

Two isomers can be formed from the geminal substitution of the chlorine atoms; three isomers result from the (1,2), (1,3) and (1,4) disubstitution.

The last isomer involves a (2,3) dichloro substitution.

The (2,3) disubstitution can exist as a pair of diastereomers.

39. C is correct.

An asymmetric (i.e., chiral) carbon is bonded to four different substituents.

There are three asymmetric carbons in this molecule.

The methylene is symmetrical, the isopropyl group and the geminal dimethyl groups have symmetrical carbons as well.

40. C is correct.

Because one of the stereocenters has a different *R/S* configuration, the molecules are diastereomers.

41. D is correct.

A *meso* compound has chiral centers but is not itself chiral because it has an internal plane of symmetry.

Tartaric acid is a four-carbon polyol with two carboxylic acids and two chiral centers.

There are three stereoisomers: the (+) form, the (–) form, and the *meso* form.

Meso compounds are identical to their mirror images.

Each of the two stereoisomers rotates plane-polarized light as indicated by the notation of (+) or (–), but *meso*-tartaric acid is achiral (i.e., no net rotation of plane-polarized light).

III: racemic mixture refers to a solution that contains enantiomers (i.e., chiral molecules that are mirror images). A *meso* compound is a single molecule that contains two enantiomers joined together.

42. A is correct.

A racemic mixture contains equal quantities of two enantiomers (i.e., isomers that are non-superimposable mirror images).

Compound I is D-fructose in a Fischer projection.

Compound II is D-fructose in a straight chain.

Compound III is D-glucose in a straight chain.

43. B is correct.

The molecule that contains the chiral carbon is the one that has a central carbon with four different groups as substituents. These carbons are also described as asymmetric (i.e., stereogenic center or chiral carbons).

44. B is correct. The chlorine atom occupies the internal (i.e., 2nd) carbon on the first molecule, and the chlorine atom is bonded to a terminal (i.e., 1st) carbon on the second molecule.

Constitutional (i.e., structural or configurational) isomers have the same molecular formula, but different connectivity of the atoms.

A: conformational isomers involve free rotation around a single bond (e.g., Newman projections).

C: diastereomers are chiral molecules (i.e., attached to four different groups) with two or more chiral centers and are non-superimposable non-mirror images (i.e., *R,R* and *S,R*).

D: enantiomers are chiral molecules (i.e., attached to four different groups) and are non-superimposable mirror images (i.e., *R* and *S*).

The exception of the two or more chiral center requirement for diastereomers is geometric isomers that contain double bonds (i.e., *cis* and *trans*).

45. A is correct. For an alkene to experience *cis-trans* isomerization, the *pi* bond of the double bond is broken. The *pi* bond of the alkene makes the double bond rigid. Heating the alkene at high temperatures or exposure to electromagnetic radiation (e.g., UV radiation) may cause the *pi* bond to homolytically cleave to 1,2-diradical and rotate about the *sigma* bond to form the diastereomers.

E / Z and *cis / trans* isomers are geometric isomers and classified as diastereomers.

46. B is correct.

When determining whether an alkene is the *Z / E* (or *cis / trans*) stereoisomer, it is important to identify the higher priority substituent group at each of the two carbon atoms of the alkene.

The priority groups are ranked according to the Cahn-Ingold-Prelog rules for prioritization based for the atomic number of atoms attached to the alkene.

If the higher priority groups are positioned on the same side of the double bond, the molecule is *Z* (*cis* notation can be used if the substituents are the same).

If the higher priority groups are positioned on the opposite sides of the double bond, the molecule is *E* (*trans* notation can be used if the substituents are the same).

The stereochemistry about the alkene is '*Z*.' The highest priority groups – Br and Cl across the double bond – are on the same side of the alkene.

Cis–trans relationship cannot be used to describe the molecule because the substituents across the double bond are different.

47. D is correct.

Determine the molecular formula of the given molecule. 2-methylbutane has 5 carbon atoms and 12 hydrogen atoms.

Only *n*-pentane has the same molecular formula.

The notation *n*– represents normal (or straight chain).

Chapter 15 Explanations: Molecular Structure & Spectra

1. D is correct.

The local magnetic field generated by the circulating current of the benzene ring causes the protons attached to the ring to be further deshielded.

Electron-donating and withdrawing groups attached to the ring may shift the resonances of certain protons up or downfield.

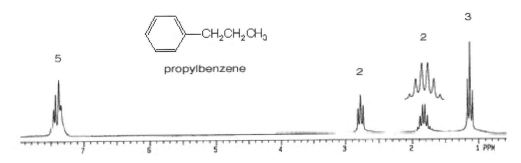

^{1}H NMR spectra with characteristic absorption for the phenyl ring between 6.0-8.0 ppm

2. D is correct.

The shielding effect arises from the electron density associated with the nuclei.

Hydrogen nuclei that have more electron density are more shielded, and their chemical shifts appear more upfield in the spectrum.

3. D is correct.

2-methylpropanoic acid

Carbonyl carbons show an IR absorption between approximately 1630 and 1780 cm^{-1}. The carbonyl of a carboxylic acid is reported to be between 1710 and 1780 cm^{-1}.

Because carboxylic acids contain a hydroxyl group, another signal around 3300 to 3400 cm^{-1} should be expected in the spectrum for this compound.

4. A is correct.

5. A is correct.

The n to *pi** transition for ketones is the electron transition that requires the least amount of energy.

Antibonding orbitals are vacant and serve as the acceptor orbitals for the electron excitation. The orbitals of nonbonding electrons have more energy than the orbitals for *pi* bonds.

Electron transitions from the *sigma* bond are difficult because the electron energy is low and requires high energy to be promoted.

6. E is correct.

The peak area ratios of the spin states correspond to the values derived from Pascal's triangle.

The heights of the peaks may not correspond to the same ratio, but the area does.

n	2^n	multiplet intensities	
0	1	1	Singlet (s)
1	2	1 1	Doublet (d)
2	4	1 2 1	Triplet (t)
3	8	1 3 3 1	Quartet (q)
4	16	1 4 6 4 1	Pentet
5	32	1 5 10 10 5 1	Sextet
6	64	1 6 15 20 15 6 1	Septet
7	128	1 7 21 35 35 21 7 1	Octet
8	256	1 8 28 56 70 56 28 8 1	Nonet

Pascal's triangle

7. D is correct.

The most deshielded protons in the NMR spectrum have the largest δ shift (i.e., downfield).

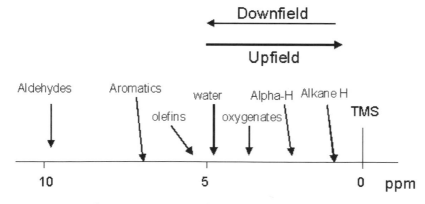

NMR with an approximate δ shift of some functional groups

8. E is correct.

The M–18 peak corresponds to the loss of water. The loss of water in a substrate containing alcohol may suggest that an alkene intermediate is generated during the ionization process.

---

9. B is correct.

The alpha nitrogen atom makes the neighboring C–H bonds less shielded because the nitrogen atom is electronegative and withdraws electron density through an inductive effect.

Terminal or substituted alkyl C–H bonds (away from electronegative atoms) normally resonate between 1 and 2 ppm.

10. C is correct.

3,3-dibromoheptane (below) produces 6 NMR signals.

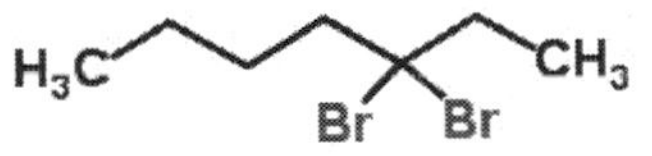

A: 1,1,2-tribromobutane (below) produces 4 NMR signals.

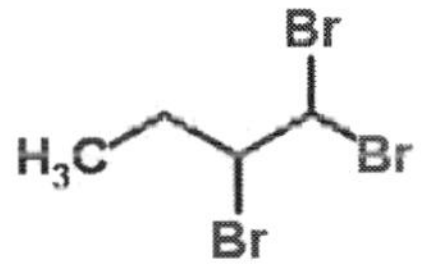

B: bromobutane (below) produces 4 NMR signals.

D: dibutyl ether (below) produces 4 NMR signals.

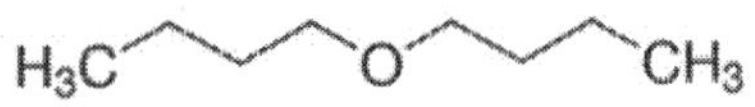

11. C is correct.

Molecules containing the carbonyl functional groups, such as ketones, typically have C=O resonance frequencies at 1710 cm^{-1}.

However, if the carbonyl group is in conjugation with another group (in this case, the alkene), then the stretching frequency is lower.

Resonance contributes to the carbon-oxygen single bond character of the carbonyl, and single bonds are weaker than double bonds.

12. A is correct.

The topicity of the protons can be determined by labeling them as H$_a$ and H$_b$ to produce a "chiral center." If this causes the molecule to have two or more chiral centers, then the protons are diastereotopic.

If the labeling causes the molecule to have only one stereocenter, the labeled protons are enantiotopic.

If labeling the protons as H$_a$ and H$_b$ does not lead to the formation of a chiral center (as in the case of methane), then the protons are homotopic.

---

13. C is correct.

1-chlorobutane (below) has a chiral center and produces 4 NMR peaks.

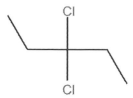

A: 3,3-dichloropentane (below) is a symmetrical molecule that produces 2 NMR proton peaks.

B: 4,4-dichloroheptane (below) is a symmetrical molecule that produces 3 NMR proton peaks.

D: 1,4-dichlorobutane (below) produces 2 NMR proton peaks.

E: dichloromethane (below) produces 1 NMR proton peak.

14. B is correct.

Carboxylic acid protons are some of the most deshielded protons.

These functional groups can partially ionize, causing the hydrogen to develop a high degree of positive (cationic) character.

15. C is correct. The stretching frequency is much higher than a typical carbonyl group.

The chlorine atom is a poor electron donor to the carbonyl through lone pair conjugation, and it tends to withdraw more electron density through induction.

The lone pair of electrons on the oxygen atom can donate to carbon-chlorine *sigma* orbital, thus shortening the bond.

The shorter (or stronger) a bond, the higher is its stretching frequency in the IR spectrum.

If the lone pair conjugation with the carbonyl is the more dominant effect (e.g., amides), then the carbonyl stretching frequency is lower than 1710 cm^{-1}.

If the inductive effect of the heteroatom outweighs the conjugation effect into the carbonyl group, the carbonyl stretching frequency is higher than 1710 cm^{-1}.

16. B is correct.

In the IR spectrum, the various peaks between 900 and 1500 cm^{-1} correspond to the unique fingerprint region.

The prominent peak at 1710 cm^{-1} indicates the carbon-oxygen double bond of a carbonyl group (aldehyde, ketone, acyl halide, anhydride, carboxylic acid, ester or amide).

Note: the presence of a similar (prominent and broad peak) between 3300 and 3500 cm^{-1} is characteristic of alcohol.

The alcohol of a carboxylic acid would show an IR absorption peak around 2800 and 3200 cm^{-1}.

17. B is correct.

Spectroscopy (e.g., NMR) generally is used in the identification of compounds.

Distillation, crystallization, and extraction are commonly used techniques to isolate and purify compounds.

18. C is correct.

For carboxylic acid derivatives, the presence of the heteroatom either increases or decreases the stretching frequency of the carbonyl group.

If the lone pair conjugation with the carbonyl is the more dominant effect (e.g., amides), then the carbonyl stretching frequency is lower than 1710 cm^{-1}.

If the inductive effect of the heteroatom outweighs the conjugation effect into the carbonyl group (e.g., esters and acid chlorides), then the stretching frequency is higher than 1710 cm^{-1}.

19. A is correct.

NMR spectroscopy provides information about the local environment of the proton.

Equivalent hydrogens (i.e., hydrogens in identical locations in relation to other atoms) produce a single NMR signal.

Nonequivalent hydrogens give separate NMR signals on the spectrum.

Since the molecule produces one signal for NMR, all hydrogens are equivalent. In $(CH_3)_3CCCl_2C(CH_3)_3$, the methyl groups are equivalent, and this molecule produces only one signal in NMR.

B: $(CH_3)_2CHCH_2CH_2CH(CH_3)CH_2CH_3$ produces eight signals. Additionally, the splitting produces a complex NMR pattern indicating the number of adjacent Hs.

C: $(CH_3)_2CHCH_2(CH_2)_4CH_3$ produces eight signals. Additionally, the splitting produces a complex NMR pattern indicating the number of adjacent Hs.

D: $CH_3(CH_2)_7CH_3$ produces five signals. For symmetrical molecules, one signal is for the terminal $CH_3(1,9)$, one for the $CH_2(2,8)$, one for the $CH_2(3,7)$, one for the $CH_2(4,6)$ and one for the CH_2 at 5.

20. A is correct.

Note: the displayed masses on the mass spectrum correspond to molecular fragments that have a charge of +1. It is possible to generate dications from the ionization in the mass spectrometer, and therefore an additional calculation may be required to determine the true mass of the fragment.

21. B is correct.

The two nuclear spin states for protons are *alpha* and *beta*.

The *alpha* spin state has less energy than the *beta* spin state because the *alpha* spin state has the same direction as the applied external field.

22. C is correct. IR spectroscopy provides information about functional groups.

A: mass spectrometry (MS) provides information about molecular weight.

B: nuclear magnetic resonance (NMR) spectroscopy provides information about protons.

D: UV spectroscopy provides information about conjugated (i.e., sp^2 hybridization) double bonds.

E: polarity refers to the difference in electron density due to electronegative atoms.

23. A is correct.

The fragmentation pattern of the spectra provides structural information and determination of the molar weight of an unknown compound.

Cleavage occurs at alkyl substituted carbons reflecting the order generally observed in carbocations.

3,3-dimethyl-2-butanone

The base peak for this molecule is the acetyl intermediate. This intermediate results from the ionization of the carbonyl oxygen atom to form an oxygen-centered radical cation.

The carbon-carbon bond between the *tert*-butyl group and the carbonyl can homolytically cleave to give the acylium cation.

For example:

24. C is correct.

Topicity is the stereochemical relationship between substituents.

These groups, depending on the relationship, can be *heterotopic*, *homotopic*, *enantiotopic*, or *diastereotopic*.

The protons are chemically equivalent or homotopic because the groups are equivalent.

If labeling the protons of a methylene group as H_a and H_b does not lead to the formation of "enantiomers," the molecule is homotopic.

25. A is correct.

IR active molecules must have polarized covalent bonds to absorb IR.

When a Cl–Cl bond with atoms of the same electronegativity stretches or bends, no dipole is created and therefore the molecule is IR inactive.

B: CO (C≡O) contains covalent bonds whereby carbon is attached to the electronegative oxygen, which creates a dipole generating an IR signal.

C: $CH_3CH_2CH_2OH$ contains covalent bonds that are also attached to an electronegative oxygen, which creates a dipole generating an IR signal.

D: CH_3Br contains covalent bonds that are also attached to electronegative bromines, which create a dipole generating an IR signal.

E: HCN contains covalent bonds that are attached to the electronegative nitrogen, which create a dipole generating an IR signal.

26. A is correct.

Electromagnetic spectrum:

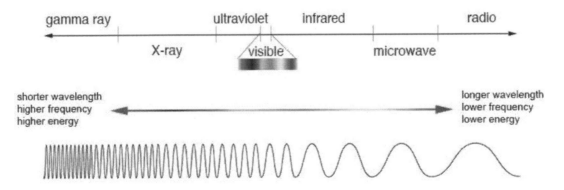

On the electromagnetic spectrum, radio waves have the lowest energy, infrared radiation has more energy than radio waves, and ultraviolet light has more energy than infrared radiation.

27. E is correct.

The type of electromagnetic radiation (EMR) needed to excite an electron in the molecule from the highest energy occupied molecular orbital (*HOMO*) to the lowest energy unoccupied molecular orbital (*LUMO*) corresponds to UV-visible light.

Exciting an electron from the *sigma* bond is more difficult because the *sigma* bond has very low energy and requires higher energy radiation to be promoted to a vacant orbital.

Furthermore, the *sigma** orbital has very high energy, and promoting electrons to this vacant orbital requires stronger radiation as well.

28. A is correct.

UV spectroscopy is useful for identifying compounds that have conjugated double bonds. Neither dimethyl ether nor bromoethane has conjugated double bonds, so UV is not a good analytical technique to distinguish them.

B: mass spectrometry (MS) provides information about the molecular weight, the number, and size of molecular fragments, and a unique fingerprint pattern.

C: infrared (IR) spectroscopy determines if the molecule contains certain functional groups and also gives a unique fingerprint pattern for a molecule.

D: proton nuclear magnetic resonance (NMR) examines the molecular environment of the hydrogens and is related to where the signal is located on the spectrum.

NMR is useful in determining the connectivity of the atoms and identifies the relative numbers of each kind of hydrogen (i.e., integration number given by the area under each signal) and the number of hydrogen atoms on adjacent atoms (i.e., splitting pattern as determined by n + 1, where n = number of adjacent Hs).

29. D is correct.

The compound is an ester. The 3.8 ppm septet corresponds to the single C–H bond near the oxygen atom of the ester.

The singlet at 2.2 ppm suggests that the ~CH₃ group is near the carbonyl group.

The doublet at 1.0 ppm corresponds to the methyl groups of the isopropyl portion of the molecule.

30. E is correct.

Conjugated polyenes absorb light at longer wavelengths than unconjugated alkenes because the additional *p* orbital overlap present in larger *pi* systems decreases the energy difference between the highest occupied molecular orbital (*HOMO*) and the lowest unoccupied molecular orbital (*LUMO*).

The *LUMO* is an antibonding orbital and has more energy than the *HOMO*, which is a bonding orbital.

The longer the conjugated system, the smaller the energy gap between the two molecular orbitals (MO); this requires radiation of less energy (and longer wavelength) for electron transitions.

When a molecule absorbs UV/visible radiation, electrons are promoted from one orbital to a higher energy orbital.

31. B is correct.

For NMR, the position that hydrogen absorbs is determined by the chemical environment.

If the chemical environment of two hydrogens is identical, only one signal is produced.

Therefore, equivalent hydrogens could be replaced by another group to yield the same molecule.

The challenge is in determining whether hydrogens are in identical environments (i.e., symmetric molecules).

1,2-dibromoethane: produces only one absorbance in the NMR spectrum, because a molecule has only one type of hydrogen atom.

A: *tert*-butyl alcohol produces 2 signals.

C: toluene produces 2 signals.

D: methanol produces 2 signals.

E: phenol produces 4 signals.

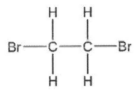

32. A is correct.

IR absorption between 1630 cm^{-1} and 1740 cm^{-1} is characteristic of carbonyls (e.g., aldehydes, ketones, acid anhydrides, anhydrides, carboxylic acids, esters and amides).

An IR absorption of 1735 cm^{-1} is characteristic of an ester.

33. D is correct.

UV light has enough energy to excite electrons to higher energy vacant orbitals to produce photoactivated atoms.

However, this form of radiation generally is not strong enough to eject electrons from atoms of most elements to form ions.

34. B is correct.

Infrared radiation (IR) is useful in the region of 1500 to 3500 cm^{-1} (called wavenumbers). In this range, the molecular vibrations of molecules are active, and the functional groups are identified by their characteristic absorbance frequencies.

Below 1500 cm^{-1} is the fingerprint region and is used for more detailed analysis once the target molecule(s) have been identified.

A: Nuclear magnetic resonance (NMR) spectroscopy involves a sample containing the compound being subjected to a high-intensity magnetic field and scanning through the radio-frequency range of the electromagnetic spectrum for particular absorptions.

NMR relies on the magnetic properties of certain atomic nuclei and determines the physical and chemical properties of atoms within molecules. NMR can be used to deduce the structure (connectivity) of the atoms within the molecule.

C: The UV range (not the IR range) of wavelengths is between 200–400 nm and corresponds to the energy required for electronic transitions between the bonding or nonbonding molecular orbitals and antibonding molecular orbitals.

UV spectroscopy is useful for studying compounds that contain double bonds, especially in conjugated (i.e., alternating double and single bond) molecules.

When molecules containing π-electrons (or non-bonding electrons) absorb UV energy, these electrons are promoted (i.e., excited) to higher antibonding molecular orbitals.

The more easily excited the electrons (i.e., lower energy gap between the *HOMO* and the *LUMO*), the longer the wavelength of UV light it absorbs.

D: MS (mass spectrometry) studies compounds through the fragmentation of molecules, although the unfragmented parent peak also provides useful information.

Note: mass spectrometry destroys (fragments) the sample and is not the preferred method of choice for rare/limited samples.

35. B is correct.

The IR absorbance at 1710 cm^{-1} indicates the presence of the carbonyl group of either a ketone or an aldehyde.

The carbonyl is also present in the derivatives of carboxylic acid: acyl halide, anhydride, carboxylic acid, esters, and amide. NMR can be used to distinguish between an aldehyde (NMR δ 9–10) and a ketone (no characteristic NMR signals).

Aldehydes have additional peaks at 2700–2800 cm^{-1}, while ketones do not.

36. B is correct.

The broad, deep absorption between 3000 cm^{-1} to 3500 cm^{-1} is characteristic for alcohol.

Chapter 16 Explanations: Alkanes & Alkyl Halides

1. C is correct.

A nucleophile donates lone pairs of electrons; therefore, it is a Lewis base.

2. D is correct.

 There are only three tertiary alkyl positions (i.e., carbon bonded to three other carbons) in this molecule.

3. B is correct.

S_N2 is bimolecular; rate = k [substrate] × [nucleophile].

Therefore, if the nucleophile ($^-$OH) concentration is doubled, then the reaction rate also doubles.

Since the alkyl halide is primary, a unimolecular (S_N1) reaction occurs

Water stabilizes the carbocation intermediate and thereby increases the rate of the reaction.

4. D is correct.

Only the concentration of the electrophile controls the rate of the reaction because the rate-determining step is the unimolecular formation of the carbocation.

S_N1 reactions proceed via a carbocation in the first step of the mechanism.

In the second step, the nucleophile forms a new bond by attacking the carbocation.

S_N1 undergoes first-order kinetics, whereby:

$$rate = k[substrate]$$

5. E is correct.

Alkanes are only composed of hydrogen and carbon atoms. Because the electronegativity of these atoms is quite similar, large bond dipoles are not expected.

Hydrogen bonding is a force that acts through highly polarized bonds to form intermolecular bonds to partial positive hydrogen atoms (H attached to F, O or N).

6. A is correct.

The sodium methoxide in this reaction acts as a strong base and abstracts a proton on the carbon atom that neighbors the chloride. The mechanism for this process is E_2.

The reaction is not S_N1, because heat is needed to generate the carbocation, and this is not included in the reaction conditions.

7. B is correct.

The order of stability of carbocations is $3° > 2° > 1°$.

Therefore, more substituted carbocations are more stable.

8. D is correct.

1-bromopropane is a primary halogen and a strong nucleophile, leading to S_N2, which is preferred when there is no steric hindrance.

9. C is correct.

Molecules with double or triple bonds are not able to undergo free rotation because the *pi* bond rigidifies the structure of the compound. To achieve the bond rotation, the *pi* bond(s) must be broken.

Furthermore, for cyclic compounds, the smaller the ring size, the fewer degrees of freedom it has.

Due to strain energy, cyclopropane is unable to rotate freely.

10. B is correct.

The concentrations of both the substrate and nucleophile control the rate of the reaction because the rate-determining step is bimolecular.

S_N2 undergoes second-order kinetics whereby:

$$\text{rate} = k\,[\text{substrate}] \times [\text{nucleophile}]$$

11. D is correct.

The heat of combustion ($\Delta H_c°$) is the energy released (as heat) when a compound undergoes complete combustion with oxygen.

The chemical reaction is typically a hydrocarbon reacting with oxygen to form carbon dioxide, water, and heat. General formula:

$$C_nH_{2n+2} + ((3n+1)/2)O_2 \rightarrow (n+1)H_2O + nCO_2 + \text{energy}$$

The heat of combustion of a compound depends on three main factors: molecular weight, angle strain, and degree of branching.

In most cases, the compound with a higher molecular weight (i.e., more C–C and C–H bonds) has the larger heat of combustion.

For straight-chain alkanes, each addition of methylene groups ($\sim CH_2\sim$) adds approximately -157 kcal/mole to the heat of combustion.

For cycloalkanes, the heat of combustion also increases with increasing angle strain.

Reference: $1\ kJ\cdot mol^{-1}$ is equal to $0.239\ kcal\cdot mol^{-1}$

$\Delta H_c°$ for alkanes increase by about 657 kJ/mol (157 kcal/mol) per $\sim CH_2\sim$ group.

For example, heptane has 4 more $\sim CH_2\sim$ groups than propane:

$$4 \times -157 \text{ kcal per mole} = -628 \text{ kcal/mol}$$

Yields:

$$-530 \text{ (propane)} + -628 = -1,094 \text{ kcal/mol (heptane)}$$

12. D is correct.

Identify the molecules that contain nitrogen or oxygen heteroatoms because these atoms enable molecules to participate in hydrogen bonding and contribute to dipolar interactions.

The cyclopentane is only composed of hydrogen and carbon, so it is the least water soluble.

13. D is correct.

Unimolecular elimination occurs via E_1 and involves the formation of a carbocation in the slow (rate determining) step.

A: a single step (concerted) process describes bimolecular (E_2), not E_1 elimination.

B: homolytic (compared to the more common heterolytic) cleavage of a covalent bond yields free radicals.

C: free radicals occur with peroxides (H_2O_2) or dihalides / UV, and radicals are an intermediate in unimolecular (E_1) elimination.

14. C is correct.

Since an S_N1 reaction proceeds through a planar, sp^2 hybridized carbocation intermediate (which can be attacked from either side), it forms a racemic mixture (i.e., both *R* / *S* stereoisomers are present).

15. B is correct.

S_N1 reactions favor substituted alkyl halides because of the stability of the carbocation intermediates, whereas S_N2 reactions favor unsubstituted reactants due to minimal steric hindrance for the approaching nucleophile.

A: S_N1 reaction rates are greatly affected by electronic factors (degree of substitution and inductive influence of electronegative atoms), while S_N2 reaction rates are greatly affected by steric (hindrance) factors.

C: S_N1 reactions proceed via a carbocation intermediate, but S_N2 reactions (as bimolecular) proceed via a single-step reaction involving a concerted mechanism with a transition state instead of a carbocation.

D: S_N2 reactions are bimolecular reactions that proceed via a single-step reaction with a transition state (i.e., bond making and breaking events) rather than via an intermediate.

E: S_N2 reactions are favored by polar aprotic solvents (i.e., cannot dissociate a proton into the solution), such as THF, DMSO, EtOAc, which do not stabilize the strong (i.e., negatively charged anion) nucleophile, so it remains more reactive to drive the bimolecular reaction of S_N2. S_N1 reactions proceed via polar protic solvents (e.g., H_2O, methanol) which tend to stabilize the carbocation (positive charge) by electrostatic attraction to the resulting anion of the dissociated solvent.

16. D is correct.

Structural isomers have the same molecular formula (C_7H_{16}) but different atomic connections.

Molecular mass would be a consideration if the molecules were not isomers (same molecular formula).

Branching in alkanes lowers the boiling point because branched molecules cannot interact as effectively as unbranched molecules and have less surface area. 2,2,4-trimethylpentane has the lowest boiling point because it is the most highly branched.

Hydrogen bonding is a strong attractive force between molecules (intermolecular force) but requires hydrogen to be attached to an electronegative atom (fluorine, oxygen or nitrogen).

The next most attractive intermolecular force is dipole-dipole interaction.

17. D is correct.

S_N2 reactions are concerted reactions that have a single step and do not involve the formation of charged intermediates.

Carbocation intermediates are a feature of S_N1 and E_1 mechanisms.

18. B is correct.

The twist-boat is located at a local energy minimum (or trough) for the conformers of cyclohexane.

Relative energy diagram for conformers (i.e., chair flips) of cyclohexane

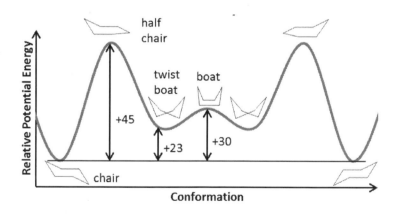

19. B is correct.

To form propyl chloride, any one of six hydrogens (3 on each methyl group) can be substituted. To form isopropyl chloride, the hydrogen extracted has to be one of the two on the middle carbon.

Based on statistical probability, propyl chloride forms in a 3:1 ratio compared to isopropyl chloride.

However, when terminal hydrogen is extracted (to form propyl chloride), a primary radical intermediate is formed.

When an internal hydrogen is extracted (to form isopropyl chloride), a secondary radical intermediate is formed.

Carbon radicals are electron-deficient because they do not have a full octet.

Alkyl groups are electron-donating (via hyperconjugation), so a secondary radical is more stable than a primary radical, and therefore the formation of a secondary radical is more likely.

The reaction proceeding through the secondary radical intermediate is faster. Therefore, the reaction leading to the formation of isopropyl chloride proceeds more readily. This is contrary to strictly statistical considerations, and more isopropyl chloride is formed than the predicted 25%.

Note: it is impossible to predict exactly what percentages form because other factors, such as temperature, are important for the empirical yield determination for each product.

20. D is correct.

S_N1 reactions proceed via a carbocation in the first step of the mechanism.

In the second step, the nucleophile forms a new bond by attacking the carbocation.

S_N1 undergoes first-order kinetics, whereby:

$$\text{rate} \quad k[\text{substrate}]$$

where k is a rate constant determined experimentally.

21. C is correct.

Conformations in which the single bonds are staggered are more stable than those in which they are eclipsed, due to steric repulsion and torsional strain (i.e., bonding electron between adjacent atoms – such as observed in eclipsed Newman projections).

Torsional strain is present in Newman projections when the substituents are eclipsed. It originates from the repulsion of the bonding electrons (i.e., not the steric interactions of the substituents).

Conformations that put the largest substituents in an *anti* (180° offset) arrangement are more stable than those in a *gauche* (60° offset) arrangement.

1,2-dibromoethane shown anti in the Newman projection

22. D is correct.

S_N2 reactions are favored with primary substrates, strong nucleophiles, good leaving groups, and polar aprotic solvents. 1-bromobutane is a primary alkyl halide, ⁻CN is an extremely strong nucleophile, and bromine is a good leaving group.

S_N2 occurs exclusively over elimination E_2 because ⁻CN is a strong, linear nucleophile; ⁻CN is not sterically hindered as a base.

Only when strong bulky bases (e.g., *tert*-butoxide) are used, elimination (e.g., E_2) is favored over substitution (e.g., S_N2).

S_N1 and E_1 reaction mechanisms are not favored with primary alkyl halides because a primary carbocation is unstable.

23. B is correct.

S_N1 proceeds when the substrate forms a carbocation.

Iodide is the best leaving group (i.e., most stable anion) and therefore forms the cation the fastest.

24. C is correct.

Acetate anion

Dimethyl sulfoxide (DMSO) is an organosulfur compound with the formula $(CH_3)_2SO$.

The colorless liquid is an important polar aprotic solvent that dissolves both polar and nonpolar compounds and is miscible with water and a wide range of organic solvents.

25. C is correct.

Strong nucleophiles have a negative formal charge (i.e., lone pairs excess), while weak nucleophiles are neutral species with a lone pair of electrons.

26. A is correct.

E_1 refers to unimolecular elimination that proceeds via a carbocation intermediate in a two-step reaction.

Substitution of the substrate ($3° > 2° > 1° >>$ methyl) increases the rate of E_1 (and S_N1) reactions because highly branched carbon chains (with more substituted carbons) form more stable carbocations.

S_N2 refers to the bimolecular nucleophilic substitution that proceeds via a one-step (concerted mechanisms) displacement of a leaving group by a nucleophile.

S_N2 is favored by unbranched carbon chains because the nucleophilic displacement of a leaving group by a nucleophile is favored due to less steric hindrance.

Secondary carbons could undergo both E_1 and S_N2. The cyanide group is a very poor leaving group because it is an unstable anion and therefore is unlikely to dissociate via E_1 or be displaced via S_N2. Br^- forms a stable anion and can dissociate via E_1 or be displaced by S_N2.

B: $(CH_3CH_2CH_2)_3CBr$ is a tertiary alkyl halide and is not favored.

C: $(CH_3CH_2CH_2)_3CCH_2Cl$ is a primary alkyl halide which lacks β-hydrogens and therefore cannot form a double bond by elimination (E_1 or E_2).

D: $(CH_3CH_2CH_2)_2CHCN$ has the leaving group (cyanide) bonded to a secondary carbon.

E: $CH_3CH_2CH_2CH_2Br$ has the leaving group (bromine) bonded to a primary carbon.

27. D is correct.

Boiling requires the molecules in the liquid phase to overcome the attractive intermolecular forces (e.g., hydrogen bonding, dipole-dipole & London dispersion forces) and move into the gas phase.

The stronger these interactions are, the more energy (i.e., heat) is needed for the molecules to separate from their neighbors and migrate into the gaseous state.

Molecules have lower boiling points when branching increases because branching disrupts the spatial packing of molecules in the solid and liquid phase, and therefore branching reduces intermolecular attractions.

A: *cis*-2-pentene has a slightly higher boiling point because unsaturation establishes a dipole moment that raises their relative boiling point compared to alkanes.

B: 2-pentyne has a slightly higher boiling point because unsaturation establishes a dipole moment that raises their relative boiling point compared with alkanes.

C: pentane is a hydrocarbon and only experiences weak London dispersion forces.

E: 3-pentanol exhibits hydrogen bonding and has a relatively high boiling point compared with molecules of comparable molecular weight that lack hydrogen bonding.

28. C is correct.

A *trans* isomer requires that the substituents point in opposite directions (up and down). Therefore, one substituent is located axial, while the other substituent is equatorial.

In this substituted cyclohexane, the molecule is more stable when the larger substituents are in the equatorial position.

When comparing a methyl and an isopropyl, the isopropyl is larger and therefore is located equatorially.

29. A is correct.

E_1 and S_N1 reactions are strongly favored by highly branched carbon chains and good leaving groups.

E_2 reactions are largely independent of the structure of carbon chains and are favored by good leaving groups which can easily be eliminated by basic conditions.

S_N2 reactions are strongly favored by substrates with unbranched carbon chains.

$(CH_3CH_2CH_2)_3CBr$ is a tertiary alkyl halide.

B: $CH_3CH_2CH_2CH_3$ is a hydrocarbon, where alkanes do not undergo either elimination or nucleophilic substitution. Alkanes are unreactive to most organic chemistry reagents and can either undergo combustion (i.e., burning of propane) or free radical halogenation to introduce a halogen as a leaving group.

C: $(CH_3CH_2)_3COH$ is a highly branched tertiary alcohol carbon chain, so it cannot undergo an S_N2 reaction. Also, ^-OH is a very poor leaving group, so it does not readily undergo substitution. With heat, alcohols undergo elimination via dehydration (i.e., removal of water).

D: $CH_3CH_2CH_2CH_2Br$ is a primary alkyl halide that undergoes S_N2 and E_2, but neither S_N1 nor E_1.

30. A is correct.

In a complete combustion reaction, a compound reacts with an oxidizing element (e.g., oxygen), and the products are compounds of each element in the fuel combined with the oxidizing element.

General formula:

$$C_nH_{2n+2} + [(3n + 1) / 2]O_2 \rightarrow (n + 1)H_2O + nCO_2 + \text{energy}$$

For example, methane yields:

$$CH_4 + 2\,O_2 \rightarrow CO_2 + 2\,H_2O + \text{energy}$$

Nonane:

$$C_9H_{20} + [(3 \times 9 + 1) / 2]O_2 \rightarrow (9 + 1)H_2O + 9\,CO_2 + \text{energy}$$

$$C_9H_{20} + 14\,O_2 \rightarrow 10\,H_2O + 9\,CO_2 + \text{energy}$$

Since nonane has the molecular formula C_9H_{20}, the combustion of 1 mole of neopentane produces 9 moles of CO_2 and 10 moles of H_2O.

31. D is correct.

Free radical halogenation is one of the few reactions (along with combustion) that alkanes undergo, and occurs via a highly reactive halogen radical. A radical is a single, neutrally charged atom which has an unhybridized p orbital with a single unpaired electron that causes it to be reactive.

Steps for free radical halogenation:

> Step I: initiation is the formation of the free radical from a diatomic molecule (X_2) by homolytic bond cleavage. Initiation is shown in the first reaction equation and is usually catalyzed by ultraviolet light ($h\nu$), heat or by an attack by another free radical.

> Step II: propagation involves a radical and a neutral molecule, and the products are a new neutral molecule and new radical. The halogen-free radical attacks the neutral alkane and, via homolytic bond cleavage, produces a new H–X bond and another highly reactive free radical as the alkyl radical.

> The alkyl radical reacts with Br_2 to form the alkyl halide and another halogen radical. This new halogen radical then starts the process again, thus causing a chain reaction (propagation).

> Step III: termination involves the joining of two radicals. For example, an alkyl radical attacks a halogen radical to produce a new neutral molecule.

I: $Br_2 + h\nu \rightarrow 2\,Br\bullet$ is UV light-induced generation of two free radicals and is the chain initiating step.

II: $Br\bullet + RH \rightarrow HBr + R\bullet$ is a chain propagating step because the reaction advances the chain onward by generating a new neutral product plus a new free radical.

III: $R\bullet + Br_2 \rightarrow RBr + Br\bullet$ is a chain propagating step because the reaction advances the chain onward by generating a new neutral product plus a new free radical.

32. B is correct.

As a concerted mechanism, the single step of the S_N2 reaction is a simultaneous substitution occurring with the formation of a new bond while the original bond breaks.

S_N2 undergoes second-order kinetics.

rate = k [substrate] × [nucleophile]

33. A is correct.

Alkanes undergo free radical halogenation to substitute one of the C–H bonds with a C–X bond, where X is a halogen.

Alkenes and alkynes generally undergo addition reactions instead, where an electrophile may add across a carbon-carbon *pi* bond.

34. B is correct.

Bimolecular nucleophilic substitution (S_N2) occurs at the fastest rate when the substrate is the least hindered.

The relative reactivity of the alkyl halides for S_N2 is methyl > primary > secondary >> tertiary.

S_N2 reactions do not occur on sterically hindered tertiary substrates.

A: 1-chloro-2,2-diethylcyclopentane is a secondary alkyl halide.

This substrate does not undergo S_N2 substitution as rapidly as 1-chlorocyclopentane because the presence of branching adjacent to the carbon-containing the leaving group reduces the rate of S_N2 reactions since the approach of the nucleophile is impeded, compared to a straight-chain molecule.

C: 1-chlorocyclopentene does not undergo nucleophilic substitution because it has a halogen attached to a vinylic (i.e., on a double bond) carbon.

D: 1-chloro-1-ethylcyclopentane is a tertiary halide and does not undergo S_N2 nucleophilic substitution.

The mechanism is S_N1 (with a carbocation intermediate).

E: *tert*-butylchloride is a tertiary halide and does not undergo S_N2 nucleophilic substitution.

The mechanism is S_N1 (with a carbocation intermediate).

35. D is correct.

Stable molecules are the best leaving groups.

If all the leaving groups are charged, then the bromide ion is the best leaving group, because the anion is stable (due to atomic size).

The order of the halogens as leaving groups: $I^- > Br^- > Cl^- > F^-$

The order of the halogens as nucleophiles: $I^- > Br^- > Cl^- > F^-$

36. E is correct.

Radical termination steps involve an overall decrease in the number of radicals when comparing the starting materials to the products.

The correct answer involves a decrease in the number of radicals (from two to zero).

A: the number of radicals increases from zero to two, which is an initiation step.

B: the number of radicals (one) does not change, which are propagation steps.

C and D: the number of radicals (one) does not change, which are propagation steps.

E: the number of radicals decreases from two to zero, which is a termination step.

Chapter 17 Explanations: Alkenes

1. C is correct. Although these reactions produce the same products and in the same quantities, what is different is the rate of the borane addition for each alkene.

(*E*)-3-heptene   (*Z*)-3-hexene

The *E* has the highest priority substituents on opposite sides, while the *Z* alkene has both alkyl substituents on the same side.

Therefore, because *Z* alkenes are less thermodynamically stable than *E* alkenes, *Z* alkenes are more reactive.

Furthermore, the approach of the borane to the *Z* alkene is less sterically demanding, because the *Z* alkene is more open to an attack (alkyl groups are on the same side).

2. B is correct.

The addition of deuterium (an isotope of hydrogen) across a C=C double bond is metal-catalyzed and proceeds with *syn* stereoselectivity, adding both deuterium to the same face of the double bond.

3. D is correct.

The trapping of mercury-alkene cations normally opens on the more substituted side, but the *tert*-butyl group sufficiently blocks access to this side.

Therefore, the cation is opened on the more terminal side.

4. D is correct.

Of the given molecules, HI is the strongest acid, so it protonates the fastest (followed by HBr, then HCl).

Also, I^- is the best nucleophile, so it adds to the carbocation most rapidly.

5. D is correct.

In 1,3-butadiene, C–2 and C–3 are both sp^2 hybridized with their unhybridized p orbitals involved in π bonding. The bond between C–2 and C–3 is a result of the overlap of two sp^2 hybridized orbitals.

There cannot be a partial double-bond character due to σ electrons; double bonds result only from π electrons.

6. A is correct. In the first step of the reaction, the H^+ adds to the double bond creating a carbocation. The nucleophilic water attacks the carbocation, and the acid is regenerated in the last step of the reaction.

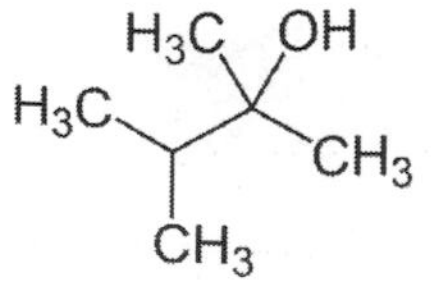

2,3-dimethyl-2-butanol

7. A is correct.

The rate law may not reveal anything about the total number of steps in a reaction mechanism.

Furthermore, the bromination of alkenes proceeds in two steps, not one.

8. D is correct. Draw the structures of the starting material and product to determine which reagent is used.

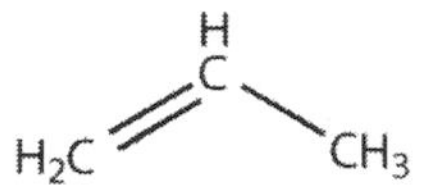

Two halogen atoms are added to the molecule, and an efficient method to achieve this is by exposing the alkene to a diatomic halogen species (e.g., Cl_2 or Br_2).

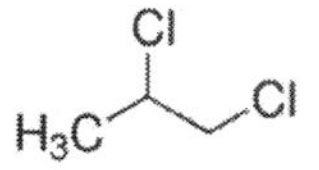

The chlorine atoms add in an *anti*-orientation from the 3-membered ring of the chloronium ion.

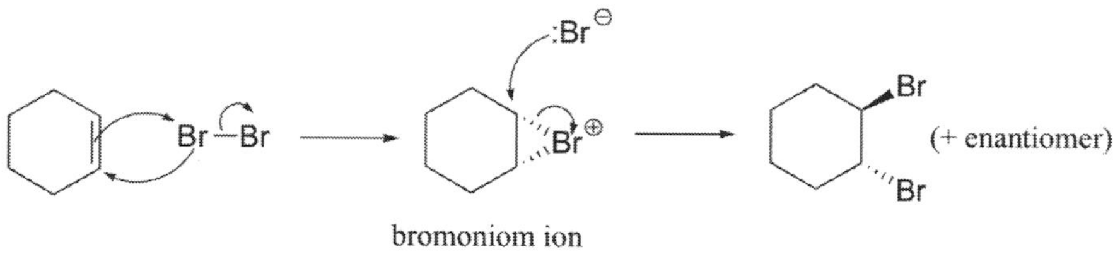

bromoniom ion

Bromonium (like chloronium) ions undergo the same reaction mechanism.

9. A is correct.

The Zaitsev product is one that is the most thermodynamically stable.

Thermodynamically stable alkenes are most substituted ($3° > 2° > 1°$).

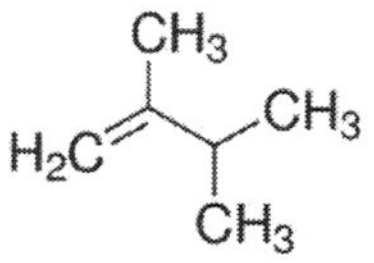

2,3-dimethyl-1-butene has a $1°$ alkene carbon (terminal) and a $3°$ carbon (at position 2).

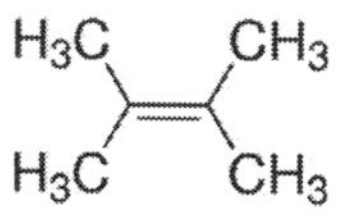

2,3-dimethyl-2-butene has two $3°$ alkene carbons at positions 2 and 3.

The hyperconjugation of the neighboring C–H bonds into the pi^* orbital of the alkene lowers the energy of the alkene.

Furthermore, the sp^3 hybridized alkyl groups help to inductively donate electron density to the more electronegative sp^2 hybridized carbon atoms.

10. C is correct.

Conjugation is the alternation of double and single bonds, which results in delocalization of electrons via resonance through the sp^2 hybridized carbons, resulting in increased stability for the molecule.

1,3,5-heptatriene has three conjugated double (π) bonds.

A: 1,2-hexadiene has two cumulated, rather than conjugated, π bonds.

Cumulated molecules have a sp carbon in the center of the two double bonds – this is unstable and increases the overall energy of the molecule.

B: 1,3-hexadiene has two conjugated double bonds.

D: 1,5-hexadiene has two isolated π bonds.

E: 1,2,3-heptatriene is cumulated. Cumulated molecules have an sp carbon in the center of the two double bonds – this is unstable and increases the overall energy of the molecule.

11. A is correct.

Water, methanol, and acetic acid are poor solvents because they can react as nucleophiles and add to the alkenes.

12. C is correct. The hydration proceeds with Markovnikov addition.

The first step in the reaction is protonation to form the tertiary carbocation; this is trapped by water.

13. A is correct.

A conjugated system contains two or more double or triple bonds separated by a single bond (i.e., sp^2 hybridization at each carbon in the conjugated system).

1,2-butadiene is not conjugated because the double bonds are adjacent to each other (not separated by a single bond). Adjacent double bonds are cumulated and are unstable.

B: cyclobutadiene is conjugated because the molecule has two double bonds separated by single bonds.

C: benzene is conjugated because a single bond separates each double bond.

D: 1,3-cyclohexadiene is conjugated because a single bond separates the double bonds between carbons 1-2 and carbons 3-4.

E: 2,4-pentadiene is conjugated because the molecule has two double bonds separated by a single bond.

14. A is correct.

In $(CH_3)_2C=C(CH_3)CH_2CH_3$, both carbons of the alkene are equally substituted (i.e., tertiary), so the two putative carbocations are approximately equally stable.

The addition of a hydrogen halide across a double bond also has the potential to create two chiral centers, one at each of the former sp^2 carbons. The carbocation forms preferentially at the more substituted carbon.

15. C is correct.

Oxymercuration-reduction of an alkene yields Markovnikov orientation and *anti*-addition as shown in the cycloalkene below.

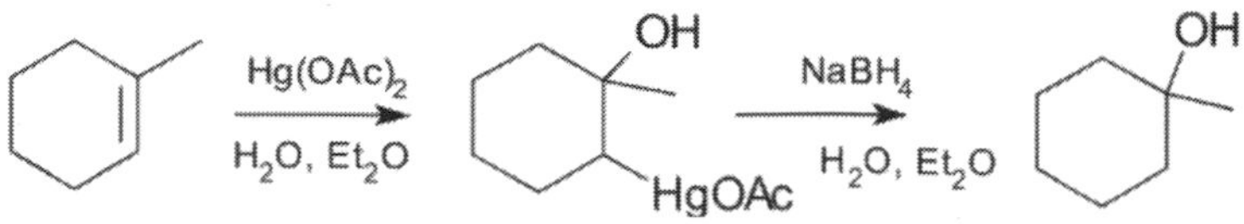

By comparison, hydroboration-oxidation of an alkene is consistent with *anti*-Markovnikov and *syn* addition.

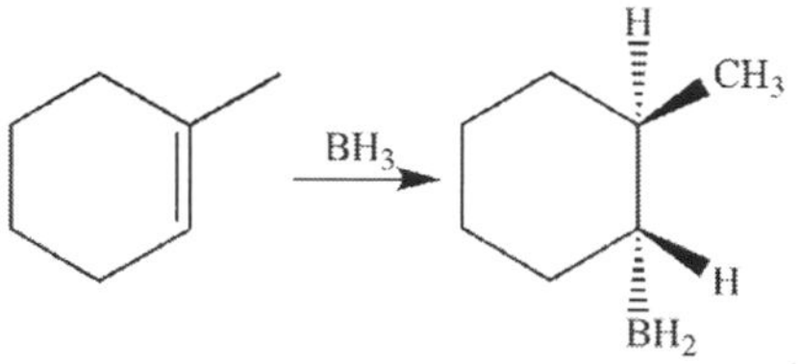

Step one uses BH_3 to add BH_2 and H as *syn* addition across the double bond of the alkene.

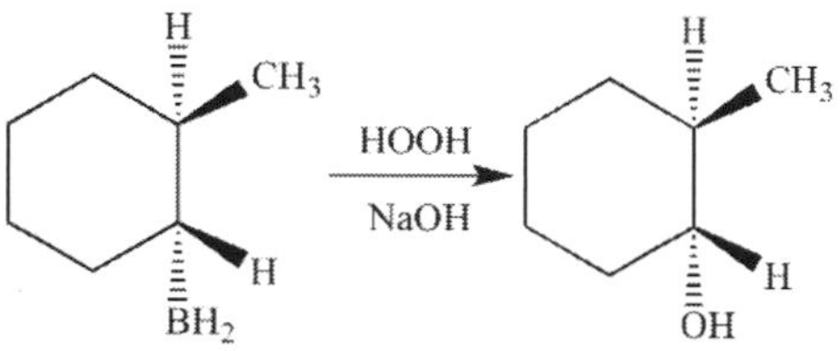

Step two uses peroxides and nucleophilic oxygen for *syn* addition of a hydroxyl. Note other nucleophiles (e.g., methanol) can add with *syn* addition as an ether substituent across the double bond.

16. D is correct.

Geometric isomers have the same molecular formula, but different connectivity between the atoms due to the orientation of substituents around a carbon-carbon double bond (or ring).

In *cis* isomers, the same substituents are on one side of the double bond or ring, while in *trans* isomers, the same substituents are on opposite sides of the double bond or ring.

Isomers (same molecular formula, but different molecules) which have no double bonds cannot be geometric isomers. Isomers include:

Constitutional isomers – different connectivity of the backbone or containing different functional groups;

Enantiomers – mirror images of chiral molecules;

Diastereomers – non-mirror chiral molecules with 2 or more chiral centers or geometric isomers that contain double bonds (i.e., designated as *cis/trans* or *E/Z*).

17. A is correct.

The methyl group adjacent to the carbocation migrates via a methide shift to give a tertiary carbocation, which then loses a proton to form the most substituted alkene (i.e., both carbons of the alkene are tertiary).

18. B is correct.

The reaction conditions are for halohydration of an alkene. The bromonium ion forms first; this is attacked (ring opens) by water as a nucleophile on the more substituted side.

19. D is correct.

A bromonium ion is a cyclic (three-membered ring) structure of a bromine atom attached to two unsaturated carbons (i.e., an alkene).

The bromonium ion is formed when the nucleophilic double bond adds to a bromine atom of Br_2, releasing Br^-.

The resulting bromine anion (or solvent if it is a nucleophile – contains lone pairs of electrons: H_2O, NH_3 or CH_3OH) bonds to the more substituted carbon of the bromonium structure to give the dibrominated product. Cl_2 follows the same reaction mechanism.

An *anti*-product is always formed because the Br^- (or nucleophilic solvent with lone pairs) must approach the three-membered ring of the bromonium ion from the side opposite the bromonium ion.

$CH_3CH_2CH=CH_2 + HBr \rightarrow CH_3CH_2CHBrCH_3$: HBr adds to alkenes via a Markovnikov mechanism. First, the double bond attacks the proton, and hydrogen adds to the carbon of the double bond with fewer alkyl substituents (i.e., less substituted carbon).

As a result, a carbocation intermediate forms on the more substituted carbon.

Second, Br^- adds to the carbocation (more substituted carbon) to form the alkyl halide. The mechanism involves a carbocation and not a bromonium ion.

Unlike a bromonium ion, which always yields the *anti*-stereochemistry, the trigonal planar carbocation undergoes nucleophilic attack from either face (e.g., the top and bottom) and produces enantiomers (a racemic mixture) if the product contains a chiral center on the carbon that was the carbocation.

20. C is correct.

cis-3-methyl-2-hexene undergoes Markovnikov addition because the first step is protonation to give the more stable (more substituted) carbonium ion. It gives *syn*- and *anti*-addition products because in the second step the bromide ion attacks both the top and bottom faces of the carbonium ion.

The addition of a hydrogen halide to an asymmetrical alkene leads to either a halogenated alkene in which the halide is on the more substituted carbon, or to a product in which the halide is on the less substituted carbon.

The former addition follows Markovnikov's rule. The latter is an example of an *anti*-Markovnikov addition. If a mixture of the two products is formed, with a predominance of one product, the reaction is said to be regioselective.

21. E is correct.

Addition reactions require two or more reagents to combine to form a single product.

For the oxidation of an alkene (e.g., epoxidation or dihydroxylation), only the oxygen atoms of a reagent are transferred to the alkene. A reagent byproduct is normally given off in the reaction, such as the carboxylic acid from *m*CPBA oxidation (i.e., peroxyacid) or the reduced metal from potassium permanganate ($KMnO_4$) or osmium tetraoxide (OsO_4) oxidation.

Ozonolysis (O_3 or Cr_2O_7) is a type of oxidation of alkenes that results in splitting the alkene into two separate carbonyl containing products (i.e., cleavage reaction) and is not an addition reaction.

22. A is correct.

Hydrogen bromide will not substitute onto an alkane because alkanes are highly unreactive molecules. Alkanes either undergo substitution only under extreme conditions (e.g., *hv* as UV light) or yield combustion products CO_2 and H_2O.

N-bromosuccinimide (NBS) adds bromine to the allylic position (i.e., one away from a double bond). The product is: butene + NBS → 3-bromobutene

Reaction 2: at high temperatures, alkanes undergo combustion to form CO_2 and H_2O.

Reaction 3: free radical substitution is initiated for highly reactive free radicals (e.g., Br_2 or Cl_2), with Br_2 being more selective, whereby the Br radical adds to the more substituted carbon of the alkene.

Reaction 4: Br_2 in CCl_4 adds bromines to an alkene as a bromonium intermediate, with the second bromide adding to the more substituted carbon of the alkene.

23. C is correct. Use the following formulae to calculate the degrees of unsaturation:

C_nH_{2n+2}: for an alkane (0 degrees of unsaturation)

C_nH_{2n}: for an alkene or a ring (1 degree of unsaturation)

C_nH_{2n-2}: for an alkyne, 2 double bonds, 2 rings or 1 ring and 1 double bond (2 degrees

of unsaturation)

There are two degrees of unsaturation for the compound C_6H_{10}.

24. C is correct.

Conjugated (alternating double and single) bonds are more thermodynamically stable than the unconjugated double bonds.

B: adjacent double bonds of allenes are not conjugated but cumulated because the *pi* bonds are oriented 90 degrees apart. Allenes tend to be less stable, especially when confined to cyclic structures.

The other structures are isolated double bonds with (one or more) intervening sp^3 hybridized carbons between the sp^2 carbons of the double bonds.

25. A is correct. Product A is an example of Markovnikov addition, whereby the hydrogen adds to the least substituted carbon because the most stable carbocation is formed. The bromine then adds to the (most stable) carbocation. In this example, the hydrogen adds to the secondary carbon, and the bromine adds to the tertiary carbon.

Product B involves free radical intermediates because of the presence of hydrogen peroxide (H_2O_2). Hydrogen peroxide causes the reaction to proceed via a radical intermediate (not carbocation) and the regiochemistry (where the substituents add) is *anti*-Markovnikov. The bromine adds to the least substituted carbon, and the H adds to the most substituted carbon radical.

Product C yields 2-methyl-2-butanol, according to Markovnikov addition.

26. A is correct. Vinyl refers to an atom attached to carbon on the double bond.

Allylic refers to an atom attached to a carbon adjacent (β) to the double bond.

The chlorine substituent is directly attached to the alkene carbon atoms in vinyl chloride.

27. E is correct. An *anti*-Markovnikov addition of water across the alkene double bond is needed.

Peroxides (H_2O_2) are a characteristic reagent for *anti*-Markovnikov regiospecificity.

28. D is correct.

Carbon-carbon *pi* bonds are elements of unsaturation, and unsaturated compounds can be reduced to give more reduced molecules (e.g., alkanes).

Alkenes have a higher oxidation state than the alkane and are equivalent to a C–O or C–X bond, where X is a more electronegative atom.

29. A is correct.

An *alkoxide* is the conjugate base of an alcohol and therefore consists of an organic moiety (i.e., group) bonded to a deprotonated (i.e., negatively charged) oxygen atom.

Secondary halides undergo bimolecular elimination (E_2) with strong bases, especially hindered ones like potassium *tert*-butoxide, $KOC(CH_3)_3$.

B: E_1 designates unimolecular elimination, generally observed in protic (i.e., H^+ donating) solvents (e.g., water or alcohols) and not when subjected to a strong alkoxide base.

C: S_N2 designates bimolecular nucleophilic substitution.

D: S_N1 designates unimolecular nucleophilic substitution.

30. B is correct.

The bromine adds to the internal position of the epoxide because the partial positive charge is greater at the more substituted position. The mechanism follows *anti*-addition stereochemistry and would be shown in the final product if both the alcohol and halogen were attached to chiral carbons.

31. B is correct.

Protonation of the alkene results in the formation of the more stabilized carbocation, and this cation forms at the secondary alkyl position. The cation is then trapped by water to form the alcohol.

32. A is correct.

The reaction shown is an acid catalyzed dehydration reaction.

Alcohol in the presence of sulfuric acid and heat is characteristic of the E_1 mechanism to form an alkene.

The generated cation undergoes a ring expansion to give a more stable tertiary carbocation, which is eliminated to form the tertiary (i.e., trisubstituted) alkene.

From the rearranged carbocation, the alpha proton is eliminated by the conjugate base HSO_4^- to regenerate the sulfuric acid.

The ring (i.e., bond angle or Baeyer) strain energy also drives ring expansion.

33. A is correct.

Both alkanes and alkenes have *sigma* bonds.

The *pi* (i.e., double) bond in the alkenes stabilize a negative charge (as an anion) and therefore, are more acidic.

The increased *s* character on the hybridization of a sp^2 orbital of an alkene ($pK_a = 45$) allows the orbital to accommodate the negative charge with more stability than for the sp^3 of an alkane ($pK_a = 50$).

Furthermore, the increased *s* character on the hybridization of a sp orbital of an alkyne ($pK_a = 28$) allows the orbital to accommodate the negative charge with more stability than for the sp^2 of an alkene.

34. A is correct.

Tertiary alkyl halides form alkenes with strong bases, via E_2, such as sodium ethoxide ($NaOCH_2CH_3$).

The most substituted alkene is the major (Zaitsev) product that is internal or more substituted.

The least substituted alkene is the minor (Hofmann) product that is terminal or less substituted.

B: 2-methylpent-3-ene is a molecule whereby the alkene does not connect to carbon that had the bromine or with an adjacent carbon. Rearrangement does not occur in E_2 reactions because rearrangement requires a carbocation (S_N1 or E_1) intermediate.

C: 2-methyl-2-methoxypentane is the product of substitution. Tertiary alkyl halides do not undergo substitution with Lewis bases; elimination is the mechanism for product formation.

D: 2-methylpentene is a less substituted alkene and only occurs with a bulky base (e.g., tert-butyl oxide or LDA).

E: 1-methylpentene is not the product of the reaction because the carbon structure has changed whereby the methyl group has migrated from the second carbon to the first carbon.

Additionally, the molecule would be named 2-hexene according to the longest chain.

35. C is correct.

An *anti*-Markovnikov addition of water is needed across the alkene double bond.

The reagents are borane, followed by hydrogen peroxide and sodium hydroxide.

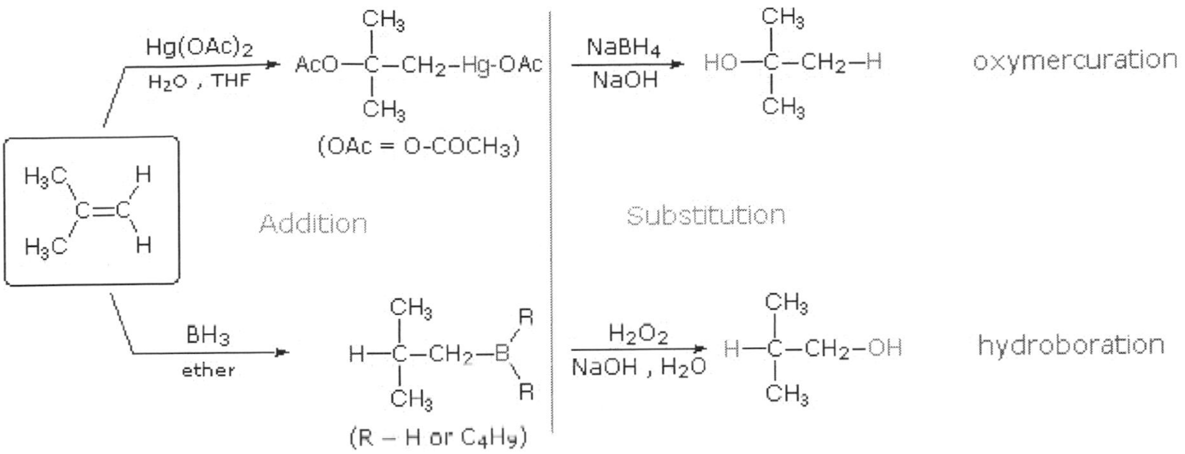

Comparison of Markovnikov vs anti-Markovnikov addition reactions for alkenes.

Each reaction above occurs in separate steps as indicated by the vertical separation line.

A: the product of oxymercuration-demercuration: 1) $Hg(OAc)_2$, H_2O/THF; 2) $NaBH_4$

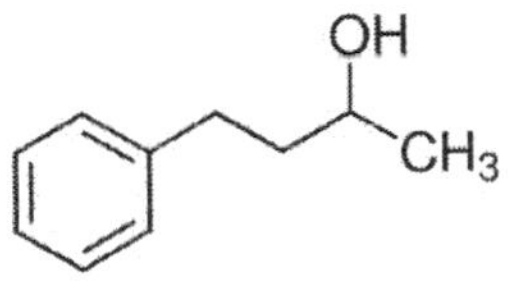

36. A is correct.

The *Cope elimination* is an intramolecular elimination reaction that occurs when the oxygen atom of the oxide of a tertiary amine removes a proton from an adjacent position.

This results in the formation of a *syn* alkene. The reaction requires heat.

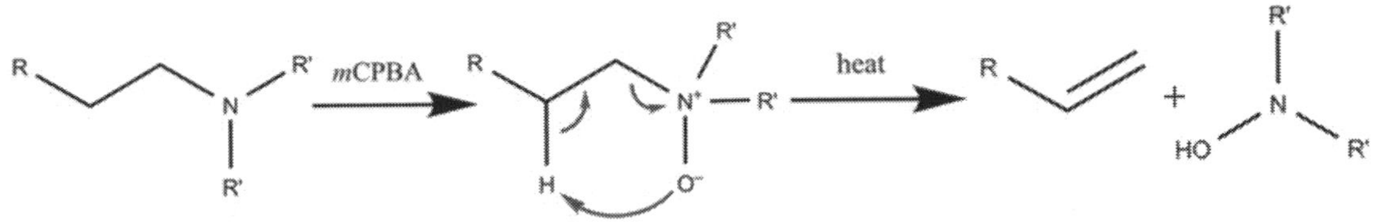

The *Cope elimination* yields the same products as a Hofmann elimination (i.e., exhaustive methylation).

Notes

Chapter 18 Explanations: Alkynes

1. E is correct. In the presence of excess hydrogen gas, the triple bond of 3-heptyne is completely reduced to the alkane.

Platinum and palladium catalysts can be used to reduce alkynes to alkenes or alkanes.

2. C is correct. Protonation of alkynes with acids generates the more substituted carbocation because this cation is the more stable intermediate. Because the cation exists on a vinyl carbon atom, this cation is known as a vinyl cation.

3. C is correct. Use the following formulae to calculate the degrees of unsaturation:

C_nH_{2n+2}: for an alkane (0 degrees of unsaturation)

C_nH_{2n}: for an alkene or a ring (1 degree of unsaturation)

C_nH_{2n-2}: for an alkyne, 2 double bonds, 2 rings or 1 ring and 1 double bond (2 degrees of unsaturation).

The general chemical formula for alkynes is C_nH_{2n-2} because each *pi* bond of the alkyne represents one degree of unsaturation.

Cyclic alkynes have an additional degree of unsaturation because of the cyclic structure.

Therefore, C_9H_{16} is the molecular formula that describes an acyclic alkyne.

4. A is correct. One *sigma* bond and two *pi* bonds are used to make the triple bond of alkynes.

Nitriles are another functional group that contains a triple bond.

5. A is correct. Using a subscript of n for the number of carbons, the degrees of unsaturation can be determined from the following formulae:

Alkane: C_nH_{2n+2} = 0 degrees of unsaturation

Alkene: C_nH_{2n} = 1 degree of unsaturation (1 ring or 1 double bond)

Alkyne: C_nH_{2n-2} = 2 degrees of unsaturation (2 double bonds, 1 double bond and 1 ring or 2 rings)

6. D is correct. Platinum and palladium are used to hydrogenate alkynes to alkenes (or alkanes) or to reduce alkenes to alkanes.

Two moles of hydrogen gas reduces the two pi bonds of the alkyne to an alkane.

7. B is correct. Alkynes are triple bonded molecules made of hydrogen and carbon atoms.

The electronegativity difference between carbon and hydrogen is low, resulting in the molecule being less polar.

Molecules with little polarization may be more soluble in organic solvents as opposed to water.

8. A is correct. Whenever a hydrocarbon is burned (adding O_2), the major byproducts of the reaction are water and carbon dioxide. Ash may also form from the reaction, composed of carbon material that cannot undergo further oxidation.

9. C is correct.

$$H_3C-\!\!\!\equiv\!CH$$

Alkyne: C_nH_{2n-2} = 2 degrees of unsaturation due to the triple bond.

In the name of this molecule, the prefix is *pro–*, which indicates that the molecule is composed of three carbon atoms.

The *–yne* suffix indicates that a carbon-carbon triple bond exists in the molecule.

Therefore, propyne has three carbon atoms and four hydrogen atoms.

10. C is correct. 1-butyne is a gas at room temperature, and 1-propyne has an even lower boiling point, so it is also a gas.

11. C is correct. Two *pi* bonds use one mole of H_2 each, so 2 moles of hydrogen are consumed in the conversion.

12. D is correct. Bromine atoms are added to both sides of the triple bond to produce a vicinal dibrominated alkene.

The addition product has the bromine atoms on opposite sides of the double bond; therefore, this addition proceeds through an *anti*-addition mechanism.

13. B is correct. The substrate contains a carbon-carbon triple bond at the end of the chain. Therefore, to synthesize 2-hexanone from 1-hexyne, oxygen is introduced to the internal carbon atom of the alkene. This reaction requires aqueous acidic conditions so that the addition proceeds as a Markovnikov addition.

$$\text{(alkyne structure)} + Hg^{2+}, H_2SO_4, H_2O \rightarrow \text{(ketone structure)}$$

The protonation of the alkyne results in the formation of a secondary vinyl cation.

This cation is trapped by water to produce an enol that tautomerizes to form the ketone product.

14. A is correct. Radical hydrogenation of a C≡C triple bond in the presence of sodium metal and liquid ammonia adds two hydrogen atoms (i.e., reduction) across the double bond with *anti*-stereoselectivity, producing an *E* alkene.

The mechanism for reducing an alkyne to a trans (E) alkene

Lindlar reagent (i.e., H_2, Pd, $CaCO_3$, quinolone and hexane) reduces the alkyne to the *cis* (*Z*) alkene.

Reaction for reducing an alkyne to a cis (Z) alkene

The Lindlar reagent, unlike the reagents of Na and NH_3, can be used to reduce a terminal alkyne to an alkene. Na and NH_3 is a "poison catalyst" and are unreactive with a terminal alkyne.

15. C is correct.

When terminal alkynes are treated with Lewis acids, such as mercury salts in aqueous conditions, the ketone forms as the major product instead of the aldehyde.

The mercury cation is electron deficient and forms a complex with the alkyne. This coordination increases the electrophilicity of the carbon atoms of the alkyne, and water adds to the internal carbon atom because the partial positive charge is larger at this position. This addition results in the formation of an enol (i.e., hydroxyl attached to a carbon in a double bond) that tautomerizes to the ketone.

A reduction step with sodium borohydride ($NaBH_4$) is not necessary, because the carbon-mercury bond could break (to give Hg^{2+} and the enolate) when the ketone forms.

16. B is correct. Although hydroxide and high temperatures are employed in this reaction, the potassium hydroxide base is not strong enough to catalyze the isomerization of the triple bond, which is why the internal, not terminal, alkyne is recovered from the reaction.

17. D is correct. The oxymercuration-demercuration [$Hg(OAc)_2$] of alkynes occurs with Markovnikov addition to generate a ketone enol. This enol tautomerizes to form a ketone. Sodium borohydride ($NaBH_4$) then reduces the ketone to the secondary alcohol.

18. B is correct.

Hydrogenation (i.e., reduction) involves the addition of hydrogens (H_2) to an unsaturated molecule.

Catalytic hydrogenation (H_2/Pd or Pt) of an alkyne is susceptible to a further reduction to yield an alkane.

Alkynes can be reduced to stereospecific products with special reagents.

An alkyne yields a *cis* alkene which requires the Lindlar catalyst (i.e., H_2, Pd, $CaCo_3$, quinolone, and hexane) and a *trans* alkene with Ni (or Li) metal over NH_3 (*l*).

A: oxidation is an increase in the number of bonds to oxygen. Increasing the number of bonds to oxygen often results from decreasing the number of bonds to hydrogens.

C: adding H_2 (i.e., hydrogenation) is an addition, not a substitution, reaction.

D: a hydration reaction adds water to an unsaturated (i.e., alkene or alkyne) molecule.

E: elimination reaction increases the degree of unsaturation in a molecule. Elimination describes the conversion of an alkane to an alkene (or alkyne) or conversion of an alkene to an alkyne.

19. C is correct. Using a subscript of n for the number of carbons, the degrees of unsaturation can be determined from the following formulae:

Alkane: C_nH_{2n+2} = 0 degrees of unsaturation

Alkene: C_nH_{2n} = 1 degree of unsaturation

Alkyne: C_nH_{2n-2} = 2 degrees of unsaturation

The formula C_nH_{2n-2} is the general formula for acyclic alkynes.

The general molecular formula for cyclic alkynes is C_nH_{2n-4}.

Cyclic alkynes (i.e., bond angle of 180°) are typically larger sized rings with at least 8 carbon atoms in the ring.

20. C is correct.

The higher is the pK_a of a compound, the less acidic is the molecule, and the stronger is the conjugate base.

The pK_a of water is ≈ 15-16.

The pK_a of the terminal alkynes is ≈ 25.

The pK_a of the N-H bonds of neutral amines is ≈ 36-38.

Therefore, water and the terminal alkyne (but-1-yne or butyne) are more acidic.

21. B is correct. When an alkyne is reduced by sodium in liquid ammonia, a single electron is transferred to the alkyne to produce an anion. The intermediate is a vinyl anion because it is on the atom that is in the double bond.

The anion protonates to give the vinyl radical.

The only cations produced during the reaction are the Na^+.

22. C is correct. Use the following formulae to calculate the degrees of unsaturation:

C_nH_{2n+2}: for an alkane (0 degrees of unsaturation)

C_nH_{2n}: for an alkene or a ring (1 degree of unsaturation)

C_nH_{2n-2}: for an alkyne, 2 double bonds, 2 rings or 1 ring and 1 double bond (2 degrees of unsaturation)

A molecular formula of $C_{10}H_{16}$ (C_nH_{2n-6}) has 3 degrees of unsaturation. It is consistent with an acyclic molecule that contains two alkyne functional groups or three alkenes or two alkenes and one ring, etc.

A molecule with two triple bonds has 4 degrees of unsaturation (C_nH_{2n-8}) or $C_{10}H_{14}$.

23. D is correct.

A catalytic system, which may also produce alkenes from alkynes, is Lindlar catalyst (i.e., H_2, Pd, $CaCo_3$, quinolone, and hexane).

An alkyne yields a *cis* alkene when subjected to the Lindlar catalyst.

Hydrogenation reactions catalyzed by platinum or palladium result in the formation of alkane products.

24. C is correct. The acetylide anion has a $pK_a \approx 28$.

Due to the large differences in electronegativity between oxygen and carbon atoms, ions that possess negatively charged oxygen atoms are relatively more stable than carbon anions.

The sodium methoxide is the most stable conjugate base, and therefore the least basic.

The CH_3Li is the Gilman reagent, and CH_3MgBr is the Grignard.

Both are strong bases with a pK_a greater than 40.

25. D is correct.

The hydration of the terminal alkyne with BH_3 proceeds with *anti*-Markovnikov regioselectivity.

Enol is on the left and the keto on the right

The enol intermediate tautomerizes to the keto product, whereby the keto product (more stable) is over 99% of the observed product.

26. B is correct. 1-butyne is a terminal alkyne.

Terminal alkynes have additional chemical properties, such as their ability to form anions when exposed to strong bases (e.g., the acetylide anion that forms with $NaNH_2$).

---

27. D is correct. The bond order for an alkyne is larger than for an alkene. The larger the bond order, the shorter the bond. Therefore, the *pi* bond in an alkyne is shorter.

Furthermore, there is less *p* orbital overlap present in an alkyne than in an alkene.

Because the internuclear overlap is lower, the *pi* bond is weaker.

28. A is correct. The Grignard reagent (CH_3CH_2MgBr), as a carbanion, is a strong base.

In the presence of the terminal alkyne shown, an acid-base reaction occurs by deprotonating the alkyne and producing ethane.

29. C is correct. The hydration of the terminal alkyne proceeds with Markovnikov regioselectivity to produce a ketone.

A: the enol intermediate tautomerizes to the keto product.

B: $CH_3CH_2CH_2CH=CHOH$ is the enol intermediate of the *anti*-Markovnikov reaction (hydroboration with BH_3).

D: $CH_3CH_2CH_2CH_2CHO$ is the aldehyde product of the *anti*-Markovnikov reaction (hydroboration with BH_3).

E: $CH_3CH_2CH_2CH(OH)CH_2OH$ is the germinal diol as would be formed from the treatment of an alkene with OsO_4 (osmium tetroxide to form the *syn*-diol).

30. B is correct. Alkynes can undergo bromination to yield compounds with four bromine atoms incorporated in their structures.

The first halogenation is expected to proceed more quickly than the second halogenation.

Bromine atoms are quite large (about the size of a tertbutyl group), and the first bromination increases the steric bulk of the reactant to form the intermediate alkene.

Furthermore, the bromine atoms are more electronegative than carbon, so the *pi* bond of the alkene intermediate is less electron rich and less nucleophilic than the alkyne *pi* bond.

31. D is correct. Alkynes are oxidized by two common mechanisms to yield either the Markovnikov or *anti*-Markovnikov product.

$$CH_3C{\equiv}CH \xrightarrow[HgSO_4]{H_2O,\ H_2SO_4} \underset{CH_3C=CH_2}{\overset{OH}{|}} \rightleftharpoons \underset{\text{a ketone}}{\overset{O}{\|}}CH_3CCH_3$$

$$CH_3C{\equiv}CH \xrightarrow[\text{2. HO}^-,\ H_2O_2,\ H_2O]{\text{1. disiamylborane}} \underset{CH_3CH=CH}{\overset{OH}{|}} \rightleftharpoons \underset{\text{an aldehyde}}{\overset{O}{\|}}CH_3CH_2CH$$

One of the *pi* bonds of the alkyne undergoes addition to yield an enol intermediate. The enol tautomerizes to generate the Markovnikov ketone or the *anti*-Markovnikov aldehyde.

32. A is correct. The hydration of the alkyne involves the formation of a carbocation and proceeds through a Markovnikov-type mechanism.

The enol intermediate converts (i.e., tautomerizes) to the keto of the methyl phenyl ketone product.

33. C is correct. The compound has five carbons, seven hydrogens, and one nitrogen.

Use the following formulae to calculate the degrees of unsaturation:

C_nH_{2n+2}: for an alkane (0 degrees of unsaturation)

C_nH_{2n}: for an alkene or a ring (1 degree of unsaturation)

C_nH_{2n-2}: for an alkyne, 2 double bonds, 2 rings or 1 ring and 1 double bond (2 degrees of unsaturation)

The molecule has 3 degrees of unsaturation.

Because one of the unsaturation elements is a ring, the molecule contains two *pi* bonds.

34. C is correct. Alkynes can be oxidized to aldehydes or ketones as follows:

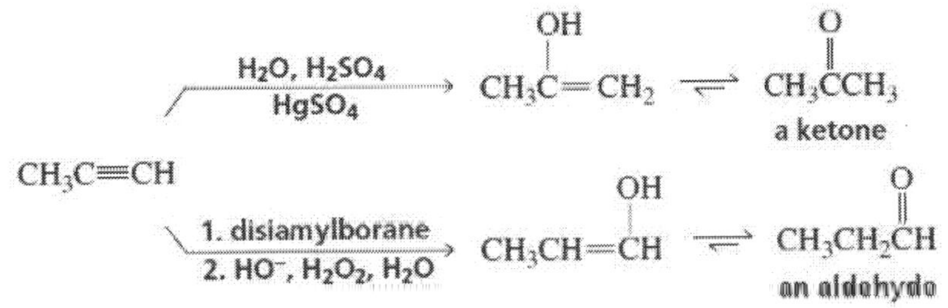

Disiamylborane (BH_3) is used for the hydroboration of alkynes (and alkenes) and involves peroxides in step 2. The hydration of the alkyne (and alkene) proceeds through an *anti*-Markovnikov addition; the preference for the *anti*-Markovnikov addition is due to the minimization of steric interactions.

The peroxide (H_2O_2) and ^-OH converts the RBH_2 bond to an enol (C=C–OH) of the *anti*-Markovnikov product.

The enol (alkene and alcohol attached to the same carbon atom) is less stable and tautomerizes (i.e., migration of a proton) to the aldehyde (aldehyde or ketone are referred to as keto) and is not the final product of the reaction.

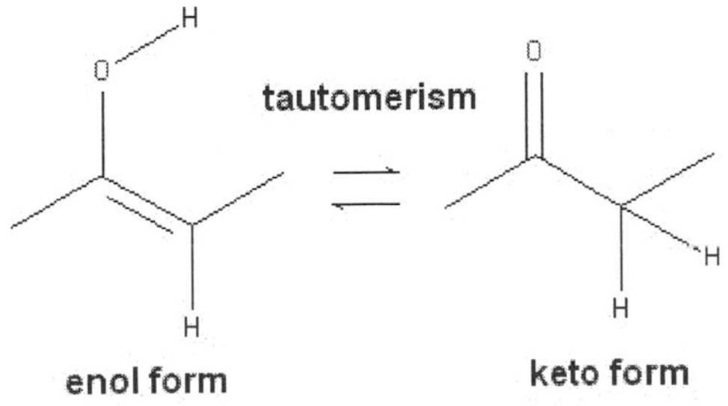

enol form   keto form

The keto and enol form are structural isomers with the keto form more than 99% of the final yield due to stability.

35. C is correct. Like alkenes, alkynes are electron rich functional groups and act as nucleophiles that donate electron density to electron-seeking electrophiles. The reactivity of alkenes and alkynes is similar, and they interact with electrophiles in analogous ways.

36. B is correct. In this reaction, the bromine adds to the alkene group of C_2H_4 and forms 1,2–dibromoethane. The reaction proceeds via *anti*-addition from the 3-membered bridge structure of the bromonium (i.e., halonium) ion.

A: hydrogen gas cannot be generated as a product from this reaction.

Carbon-carbon multibonds do not form from the given reaction conditions, because the reagents do not include any base to eliminate the bromine(s) to form either an alkene or alkyne.

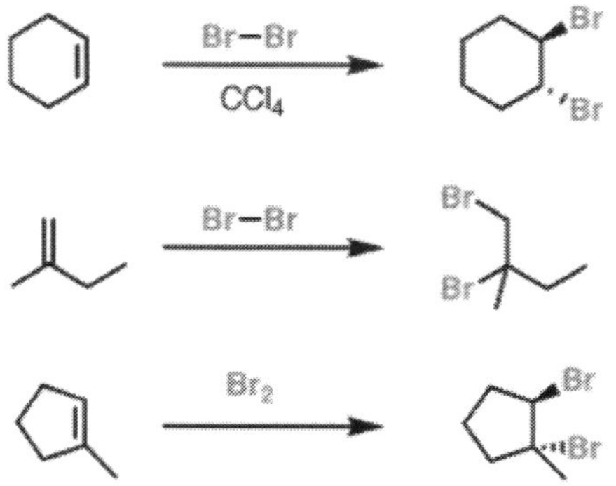

Sample *anti*-stereochemical products from the addition of bromine to an alkene. Each product has an enantiomer that is not shown.

Bromonium ion as an intermediate:

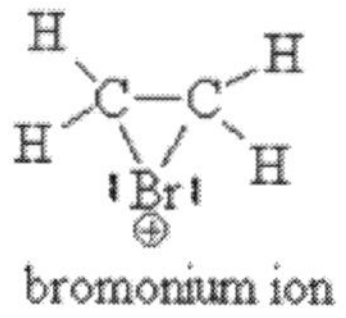

bromonium ion

The reaction is also regioselective (i.e., where) for the addition of the second nucleophile (i.e., Br⁻) to the halonium (i.e., bromonium) structure. The incoming nucleophile attacks the more substituted atom.

Mechanism of Br_2 addition to an alkene:

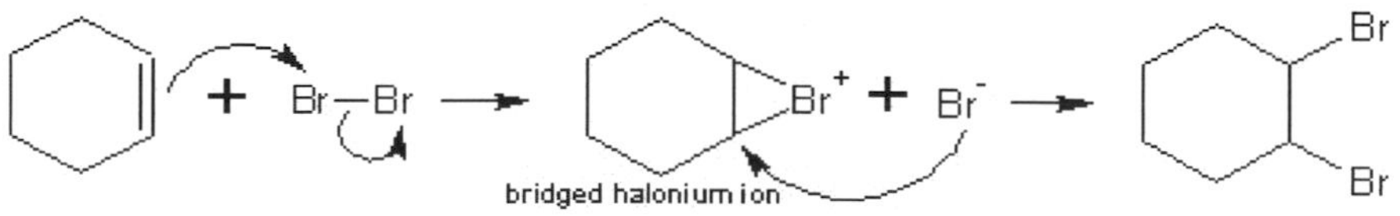

bridged halonium ion

The incoming nucleophile attacks the bromonium bridged-structure ion at the most substituted position. The bromonium ion (i.e., 3-membered bridged-structure) undergoes S_N2 attack for *anti*-addition product formation. The stereochemical (i.e., *trans*) notation would include wedges and dashes.

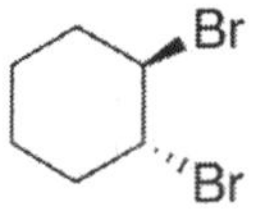

trans-1,2 dibromocyclohexane

Chapter 19 Explanations: Aromatic Compounds

1. C is correct.

$FeBr_3$ acts as a catalyst to activate the alkyl bromide for electrophilic aromatic substitution (EAS) in this Friedel-Crafts alkylation. Since the ethyl substituent on ethylbenzene is slightly electron donating, it functions as an *ortho, para* director for the substitution reaction.

Due to steric hindrance at the *ortho* position, *para* substitution is the major product.

2. B is correct. The aromatic stabilization energy of benzene decreases the reactivity of its *pi* system relative to isolated or conjugated/nonaromatic alkenes. Because of this stabilization, arenes resist metal catalyzed hydrogenation reactions and may require more specialized catalysts to facilitate their reductions.

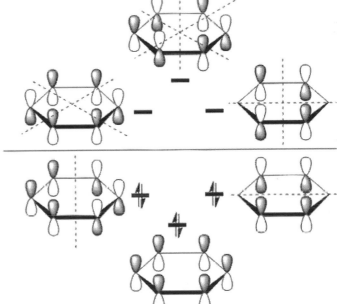

3. E is correct. Degenerate orbitals are orbitals that have the same energy.

Bonding orbitals are below the horizontal plane, while antibonding orbital is above.

In the molecular orbital (MO) diagram for benzene: MOs π2 and π3 are positioned in the second energy level, and π4 and π5 MOs are positioned on the third energy level.

Therefore, there are two pairs of degenerate MOs.

4. D is correct. Because the nitrogen lone pair of the aniline is protonated, the group is unable to donate electron density through the *pi* system of the aromatic ring.

Furthermore, the nitrogen atom has a formal charge of $+1$, and this group can act as a deactivating group because of its inductive effect.

5. A is correct. Methyl substituents on benzene (toluene) is an *ortho- / para*-director and an activator (rate of the electrophilic aromatic substitution is faster than for benzene)

Friedel-Crafts alkylation reactions work best with electron-rich arenes.

Friedel-Crafts alkylation of toluene

6. D is correct.

I: The ester is the least activating moiety shown, because of the electron-withdrawing inductive effect of the electronegative oxygen atom on the carbonyl (ester group) that reduces the electron density in the ring (i.e., deactivation).

II: The methyl group attached to the ring donates electron density via hyperconjugation and activates the ring slightly.

III: The lone pair of electrons on the ether resonates into the ring, which increases the electron density for EAS (i.e., activation).

7. C is correct.

Compared to benzene, electron-donating groups (such as –OH) activate the ring towards EAS reactions.

Electron-withdrawing groups (such as the acetyl group) deactivate the ring, slowing EAS reactions.

Benzene can undergo the bromination reaction as well; however, its rate of bromination is less than the rate for the phenol bromination.

8. D is correct. The *pi* molecular orbitals of benzene are made from the overlap of six *p* orbitals. Because the number of molecular orbitals equals the number of atomic orbitals involved in the overlap, there are six molecular orbitals.

9. A is correct. Four requirements for aromaticity:

   1) molecule is cyclic

   2) molecular is planar (flat)

   3) each atom is sp^2 hybridized (i.e., conjugated)

   4) the number of *pi* electrons satisfies Hückel's rule (4n + 2 *pi* electrons)

Aromatic rings can be positively or negatively charged if the 4 criteria are satisfied.

B, C, and D are antiaromatic with 4n *pi* electrons.

10. D is correct. Phenol (i.e., hydroxybenzene) has an OH group on the benzene ring. The hydroxyl oxygen has two nonbonded pairs of electrons, either of which can be donated (via resonance) to the aromatic ring after addition of an electrophile.

Electron-donating groups stabilize the cations formed upon addition of a substituent to the *ortho* and *para* positions and therefore are *ortho/para*-directing activators.

The OH group is not particularly bulky, and there is a limited steric hindrance that reduces substitution at the *ortho* position.

11. C is correct.

C: contains 4 π electrons and therefore does not satisfy Hückel's rule for aromaticity ($4n + 2$ π electrons).

Additionally, the silicon atom is sp^3 hybridized and would not participate in aromatic conjugation.

12. A is correct. Four requirements for aromaticity:

     1) molecule is cyclic

     2) molecular is planar (flat)

     3) each atom is sp^2 hybridized (i.e., conjugated)

     4) the number of *pi* electrons satisfies Hückel's rule ($4n + 2$ *pi* electrons)

Aromatic rings can be positively or negatively charged if the four criteria are satisfied.

Aromatic compounds have no saturated carbon atoms present in the aromatic ring. The hybridization state of aromatic carbon atoms is sp^2, and the total number of electrons in the aromatic system is consistent with Hückel's rule ($4n + 2$ π electrons).

13. D is correct.

The methyl group is as an electron-donating substituent and therefore is an *ortho* / *para* director.

Due to steric hindrance at the *ortho* position, the formation of the *para* product is the major product.

14. C is correct.

The unknown cyclic hydrocarbon does not react with bromine in dichloromethane, carbon tetrachloride, or water. This means that it cannot contain any non-conjugated double or triple bonds; otherwise, the bromine would have added across the double bonds.

Since the unknown compound reacts when FeBr₃ is added, it must be benzene. The FeBr₃ acts as a Lewis acid and catalyzes aromatic electrophilic addition reactions.

Bromine is not a strong enough electrophile to disrupt the conjugated double bonding in the benzene ring, but the addition of the iron (III) bromide catalyst converts the bromine into a strong enough electrophile that it adds to the benzene ring.

15. D is correct.

The activating, deactivating and directing (*ortho-* / *para-* and *meta*-directing) properties of aromatic substituents in electrophilic aromatic substitutions (EAS) and nucleophilic aromatic substitutions (NAS) are based on resonance stabilization or destabilization.

Through resonance, electron-withdrawing groups introduce a partial positive charge on positions *ortho* and *para*. Resonance forms of nitrobenzene during EAS. The *pi* bonds undergo delocalization for two hybrid structures:

In EAS, the aromatic ring acts as a nucleophile, and the partially positive sites are less nucleophilic, making the electron-withdrawing group *meta*-directing.

In NAS, the aromatic ring acts as an electrophile, and the partially positive sites are more electrophilic, making the electron-withdrawing group an *ortho-* / *para*-director.

16. E is correct. The two arenes activated by nitrogen heteroatoms are more nucleophilic.

The amide does not donate as strongly as the amine, so ring 1 is less nucleophilic than ring 3.

Ring 2 is only activated by the alkyl group and is the least reactive of the three.

17. A is correct. The reaction is a Friedel-Crafts acylation using acetic anhydride, $(CH_3CO)_2O$, as an acylating agent. The product is a methyl ketone.

All halogens are deactivators, but direct *ortho* / *para* because the halogen (like all *ortho* / *para* directors) has lone pairs of electrons (on the atom attached to the ring). The lone pair helps stabilize the positive charge on the ring present in the resonance hybrid intermediates.

In general, deactivators (except for the halogens) are *meta* directors.

18. D is correct. In EAS, the aromatic ring acts as a nucleophile attacking an electrophile.

Due to its aromaticity, however, the aromatic ring is relatively unreactive and is a poor nucleophile.

Extremely reactive electrophiles (and the addition of a Lewis base) are used to overcome this limitation.

19. C is correct. Halides are electron-withdrawing (i.e., deactivating) and are *ortho*/*para*-directing.

Halogens are the exception to the general rule, which states that all electron-withdrawing species are deactivating and *meta*-directing.

The reason that the halogens (despite being electron-withdrawing due to their high electronegativity) are *ortho*/*para*-directing is the lone pair of electrons that localize, via resonance, the electron density at the *o/p* positions.

Resonance hybrids show the anion at both ortho positions.

Note that the resonance structures also include an anion at the *para* position.

Therefore, like all atoms that have lone pairs of electrons attached to the ring, halogens are *ortho-para* directors.

The resonance structure involves forming a double bond between the halide bearing a formal positive charge and the phenyl ring; therefore it is not a significant resonance structure and is unable to overcome the deactivating (due to electronegativity) effect caused by induction (along the *sigma* bond).

20. E is correct. When 1,3-cyclopentadiene reacts with sodium metal, it is converted from nonaromatic to aromatic.

According to Hückel's rule, a planar cyclic compound is aromatic if it is conjugated (adjacent sp^2 hybridized carbon atoms) and has $4n + 2$ *pi* electrons (where n is any whole number).

21. B is correct. Carbonyl compounds are *meta*-directing in EAS reactions.

Since both the nitro and carbonyl groups are deactivating, disubstitution is slow, and single *meta* substitution is the predominant product.

22. D is correct.

Halogens are electron-withdrawing and deactivate a benzene ring toward electrophilic aromatic substitution, so bromobenzene undergoes nitration slower than benzene.

23. C is correct.

In electrophilic aromatic substitution, the aromatic ring acts as a nucleophile, attacking an electrophile that has been treated with a Lewis acid (e.g., $FeBr_3$, $AlCL_3$).

Deprotonation of the aromatic ring at the site of the attack reforms the double bond (an elimination reaction) and restores aromaticity.

The overall reaction substitutes an electrophile (e.g., Br, CH_3, RCO, HSO_3) for hydrogen on the aromatic ring.

24. D is correct.

The halogens are deactivating due to their high electronegativity. However, like all *ortho* / *para*-directors, the halogens have a lone pair of electrons on the atom attached to the ring.

Alkyl chains do not have lone pairs of electrons on the C attached to the ring but are *ortho* / *para* directors due to hyperconjugation.

25. C is correct.

The reactivity of aromatic molecules toward electrophilic aromatic substitution (EAS) depends on the presence of substituents on benzene.

Electron-donating substituents increase the electron density of the benzene ring and therefore activate benzene towards EAS.

Electron-withdrawing substituents deactivate the ring, making it less susceptible to EAS. The benzene ring is deactivated by the electron withdrawing effects of the Cl and NH_3^+ substituents, and the ring is deactivated (compared to benzene) to EAS.

A: p-H_3CCH_2O–C_6H_4–O–CH_2CH_3 contains two electron-donating ethoxy substituents and is highly reactive to EAS.

B: p-O_2N–C_6H_4–NH–CH_3 contains strong electron-withdrawing effects from the nitro (NO_2). The N of the NO_2 group has a formal charge of +, while the single bonded O has a formal charge of –. The NO_2 group offsets the strong electron-donating amino group (lone pair of electrons on N), so the molecule is only slightly reactive to EAS.

D: p-CH_3CH_2–C_6H_4–CH_2CH_3 contains two electron-donating (i.e., activating) ethyl substituents and is more reactive towards EAS.

E: benzene is the reference molecule to determine if particular substituents are activating (relative to benzene) of deactivating (relative to benzene).

26. C is correct.

The carbon atoms of benzene are sp^2 hybridized.

Non-planar molecules cannot be aromatic because the *pi* system must be planar (i.e., flat).

A Kekule structure is a Lewis structure in which bonded electron pairs in covalent bonds are drawn as lines. The Kekule structures illustrate the two most significant resonance contributors of benzene.

Benzene with alternating double and single bonds – hybrid structure as bottom structure.

The alternating single and double drawn for benzene exist as a hybrid resonance structure from the delocalization.

27. A is correct.

Addition reactions are typically not observed for aromatic compounds because the aromaticity is restored during their substitution reactions. When aromatic functional groups react, they may temporarily lose their aromaticity (i.e., high-energy resonance hybrids are the intermediates) and its restoration greatly increases the stability of the molecule.

Electrophilic aromatic substitution (EAS) reactions are favored over nucleophilic aromatic addition (NAS) reactions for aromatic compounds.

28. D is correct.

The double bonds in benzene are less reactive than in a non-aromatic alkene because addition (e.g., hydrogenation) disrupts the aromaticity (i.e., delocalization) of the ring, making it less stable.

The application of heat and high pressure in the presence of the Rh catalyst permits benzene to overcome the energy of activation necessary to transform the highly stable benzene molecule to a non-aromatic product.

29. D is correct.

$CH_3C_6H_5 + H_2$, Rh / C is a reduction reaction with a powerful reducing agent capable of disrupting the stability of the aromatic ring.

The regents reduce the benzene ring catalytically via hydrogenation to form cyclohexane.

Therefore, this is not an electrophilic aromatic substitution.

In general, an aromatic ring is especially susceptible to electrophilic aromatic substitution (EAS) in the presence of a Lewis acid (e.g., $FeBr_3$, $AlCl_3$ or H_2SO_4).

A: $CH_3C_6H_5 + C_6H_5CH_2CH_2Cl$ / $AlCl_3$ is an example of Friedel-Crafts alkylation (EAS), whereby toluene (benzene with a methyl substituent) reacts with an alkyl chloride in the presence of the Lewis acid aluminum trichloride ($AlCl_3$).

The Lewis acid removes chloride from the alkyl halide, forming a carbocation which is then attacked by the benzene ring.

B: $CH_3C_6H_5 + Br_2$ / $FeBr_3$ is an example of electrophilic aromatic substitution (EAS). $FeBr_3$ (similar to $AlCl_3$) is a Lewis acid.

Toluene is activating and the Br substitutes in the *ortho* / *para* position.

C: $CH_3C_6H_5 + CH_3CH_2CH_2COCl$ / $AlCl_3$ is an example of Friedel-Crafts acylation (EAS), whereby toluene reacts with an acyl chloride in the presence of the Lewis acid aluminum trichloride ($AlCl_3$).

The Lewis acid removes chloride from the acyl halide, forming a carbocation which is then attacked by the benzene ring, and then a proton is removed to restore aromaticity of the original ring structure.

E: $C_6H_6 + HSO_3$ / H_2SO_4 is an example of the EAS reaction for sulfonation of a benzene ring.

30. D is correct.

A: of the two substituents, the chloro group is *para*-directing, so it should be substituted first.

Additionally, Na / NH_3 results in the single *trans* hydrogenation of alkenes but does not substitute a nitro group in an EAS reaction.

B: of the two substituents, the chloro group is *para*-directing, so it should be substituted first.

C: while HCl / H_2O adds H and Cl across the double bonds of alkenes, these conditions do not substitute Cl in EAS reactions.

E: Cl_2 / CCl_4 are the conditions to dechlorinate an alkene.

Benzene does not undergo addition reactions due to aromaticity.

31. A is correct.

Benzene is aromatic and undergoes electrophilic aromatic substitution (EAS) with the addition of a Lewis acid (e.g., $AlCl_3$, $FeBr_3$ or H_2SO_4).

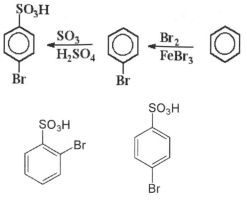

The reagents of SO_3 and concentrated H_2SO_4 are used to sulfonate aromatic compounds, whereby a SO_3H group is substituted onto the benzene ring.

Halogens are *ortho* and *para* directing deactivators.

Therefore, the product is a mixture of *ortho-* and *para-* bromobenzenesulfonic acid.

B: the bromine is not displaced from the aromatic benzene ring and replaced with hydrogen to form benzene.

C: the SO_3H group does not substitute for the bromine of bromobenzene.

D: *meta-* is not formed because halogens are *ortho* and *para* directing deactivators.

E: toluene is benzene with a methyl group attached.

32. A is correct.

Substituents on an aromatic ring affect the rate at which electrophilic aromatic substitution reactions occur.

Since the ring acts as a nucleophile in these reactions, electron-donating substituents increase the rate of reaction, while electron-withdrawing substituents decrease the rate of reaction.

The bromine substituent (III) is slightly deactivating (due to its electronegativity), making it less reactive than benzene (I).

The nitro group is extremely deactivating (due to resonance), making nitrobenzene (II) less reactive than bromobenzene (III).

33. B is correct.

Benzene is a cyclic aromatic hydrocarbon that has 4 degrees of unsaturation.

The *pi* bonds in the molecule are delocalized and impart aromaticity to the molecule.

34. C is correct.

Each molecule has nitro ($\sim NO_2$) and hydroxyl ($\sim OH$) functional groups that can hydrogen-bond.

Proximity is needed for either intramolecular (within the molecule) or intermolecular (between molecules) bonding.

Alignment of the functional groups to permit hydrogen bonding depends on the shape of the individual molecule.

The melting points (transition from packed molecules in a solid to liquid phase), boiling points (transition from associated molecules in a liquid to independent molecules in the gas phase) and water solubility of polar molecules are related to the presence and quantity of intermolecular hydrogen bonding.

The *meta*- and *para*-nitrophenol are more water-soluble and have higher melting points than *ortho*-nitrophenol because *ortho*-nitrophenol tends to form intramolecular hydrogen bonds instead of intermolecular hydrogen bonds.

Intramolecular hydrogen bonds for *ortho*-nitrophenol make the molecule independent so that it takes less energy to disrupt the lattice structure of the molecules (melting).

Likewise, intramolecular hydrogen bonding reduces the molecule's ability to form hydrogen bonds with water, and therefore the molecule is less water-soluble.

A: *meta*- and *para*-nitrophenol form strong intermolecular hydrogen bonds, which leads to a higher melting point.

Additionally, the nitro and hydroxyl groups form hydrogen bonds with water, and the molecules are more water-soluble.

B: *ortho*-nitrophenol forms some intermolecular hydrogen bonds, but less than *meta*- and *para*-nitrophenol.

Meta-nitrophenol forms weak intramolecular bonds due to the large distance between the functional groups.

D: *para*-nitrophenol has the nitro and hydroxyl substituents at opposite ends of the flat molecule and cannot form intramolecular hydrogen bonds.

35. A is correct.

Hückel's rule predicts that for a monocyclic compound to be aromatic, there must be a fully conjugated *pi* (sp^2 hybridization at each atom in the ring) containing $(4n + 2)$ *pi* electrons.

Two *pi* electrons are contributed by each of the double bonds.

The lone pair of electrons on a double bonded N is perpendicular to the *pi* cloud and does not count as the number of *pi* electrons for Hückel's rule.

Note: when N is in a single bond, the unshared electrons are parallel to the *pi* system and count toward aromaticity.

Benzimidazoline is not fully conjugated because there is a ~CH_2~ (sp^3) group in the ring.

Cyclic conjugation is necessary for a molecule to be aromatic.

B: thiophene has a sp^2 hybridized sulfur (like oxygen) and has a lone pair of electrons counted as in the ring. The total number of *pi* electrons is 6.

C: quinoline has 10 *pi* electrons and therefore is aromatic.

The lone pair of electrons on a double bonded N is perpendicular to the *pi* cloud and does not count as the number of *pi* electrons for Hückel's rule.

D: thiazole has 6 *pi* electrons and therefore is aromatic.

The lone pair of electrons on a double bonded N is perpendicular to the *pi* cloud and does not count as *pi* electrons for Hückel's rule.

Sulfur (like oxygen) is *sp²* hybridized and has a lone pair of electrons counted as in the ring.

E: imidazole has 6 *pi* electrons and therefore is aromatic.

The lone pair of electrons on a double bonded N is perpendicular to the *pi* cloud and does not count as *pi* electrons for Hückel's rule.

The lone pair of electrons on a single bonded N is part of the *pi* cloud and does count as *pi* electrons for Hückel's rule.

36. D is correct.

Degrees of unsaturation:

>double bonds = 1 degree of unsaturation

>triple bonds = 2 degrees of unsaturation

>rings = 1 degree of unsaturation

Using the degree of unsaturation calculation:

>benzene (1 ring and 3 double bonds) = 4 degrees of unsaturation

Chapter 20 Explanations: Alcohols

1. B is correct.

Alcohols follow the same trend for boiling points as alkanes with longer chain molecules having higher boiling points. Hexanol is the longest chain and therefore has the highest boiling point.

2. E is correct.

When phenols are deprotonated (i.e., acting as an acid), a phenoxide ion (i.e., phenolate ion) are produced as shown. The pK_a of phenols is much lower than it is for alcohols.

Methanol has a pK_a of 16, while phenols have pK_a values ≈ 9.9.

3. C is correct.

The formation of an inorganic ester by the addition of alcohol and phosphoric acid is an example of dehydration synthesis because an equivalent of water is lost during the process.

4. E is correct.

No carbon-oxygen *pi* bonds exist in alcohols (hydroxyl) functional groups.

Carbonyl groups (i.e., carbon double bonded to oxygen) are indicative of ketones, aldehydes or carboxylic acid derivatives (acyl halide, anhydride, ester, and amide).

5. A is correct.

It is helpful to draw the structure of all known compounds or at least the product of the reaction.

Ethanoate is an ester that has an *n*-propoxy substituent. Therefore, the alcohol that should be used is 1-propanol. The remaining component is ethanoic acid.

6. C is correct.

The five-carbon molecule of *n*-pentanol has the largest alkyl portion (i.e., the greatest number of London forces) and possesses the hydroxyl group, which allows it to hydrogen bond (increases boiling point).

An overall molecular dipole also exists for this molecule that contributes to its high boiling point.

7. B is correct.

The ~OH group is characteristic of both alcohol and carboxylic acids, but the latter also includes a carbonyl group.

---

8. D is correct.

Sodium dichromate ($Na_2Cr_2O_7$) is a strong oxidizing agent which converts primary alcohols to carboxylic acids.

Sodium dichromate converts secondary alcohols to ketones.

9. B is correct.

Thionyl chloride ($SOCl_2$) is a reagent that converts primary and secondary alcohols to alkyl chlorides.

Phosphorous tribromide (PBr_3) is a reagent that converts primary and secondary alcohols to alkyl bromides.

10. A is correct.

The molecule has an alkene on the right side, alcohol near the lower right portion, and a fused ether functional group.

11. B is correct.

Molecules containing rings or multibonds are molecules that have degrees of unsaturation.

A completely saturated compound only consists of single bonds (*sigma* bonds).

12. C is correct.

Primary alcohols have an ~OH group attached to a carbon that is connected to another carbon atom.

Secondary alcohols possess an ~OH group that is bonded to a carbon attached to two other carbon atoms.

Tertiary alcohols have ~OH groups that are bonded to carbon atoms attached to three other carbon atoms.

13. C is correct.

Carboxylic acids are also functional groups that contain an ~OH group bonded to carbonyls (C=O).

Oximes C=N–OH are functional groups that can contain an ~OH group; they are used for reductive amination.

14. B is correct

The reaction between (*S*)-2-heptanol and $SOCl_2$ (thionyl chloride) proceeds via an S_N2 reaction mechanism.

An addition-elimination sequence occurs at the S=O double bond, then substitution by Cl⁻ of the alcohol gives the inverted (*R*)-2-chloroheptane product.

15. A is correct.

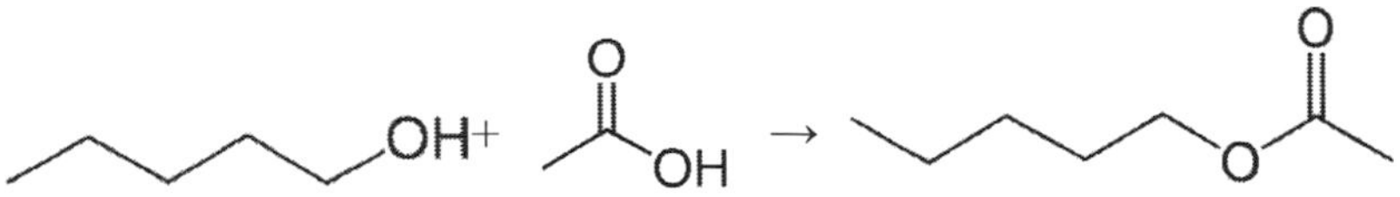

The reaction of 1-pentanol + acetic acid

The alkoxy group has five carbon atoms, and an acyl portion is an acetyl group.

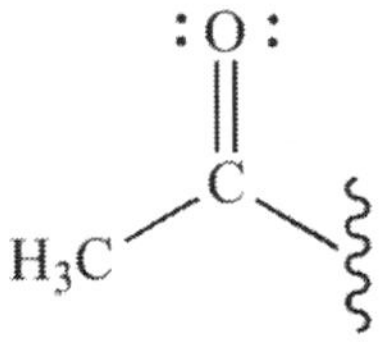

Acetyl group

Acetate is the root for this molecule.

16. B is correct.

Ethers follow the same trend as alkanes, so dihexyl ether has the highest boiling point because it has the greatest molecular weight and has the largest surface area.

17. E is correct.

The most notable intermolecular force for water is hydrogen bonding.

Alcohols donate and receive hydrogen bonds.

Thiols (S–H bonds) have much smaller dipoles compared to O–H bonds, so they do not participate in hydrogen bonding.

18. B is correct.

The tosyl group is added with the retention of stereochemistry because the C–O bond is not broken.

Tosylation of secondary alcohol makes it a better leaving group.

The chloride anion is a good nucleophile, able to displace the tosylate leaving the group to form the secondary alkyl chloride.

D: shows a product that has retained stereospecificity (no inversion).

This retention of stereochemistry occurs when an S_N2 reaction (i.e., inversion) is followed by a second S_N2 reaction.

19. D is correct.

For a given class of compounds, the lower the molecular weight, the lower the boiling point.

Alcohols follow the same trend for the boiling point as alkanes.

Ethanol is a two-carbon chain (i.e., lowest molecular weight) with hydrogen bonding (e.g., alcohols and carboxylic acids). It has the lowest molecular weight of all choices and therefore has the lowest boiling point.

20. D is correct.

HBr is a strong acid that protonates the oxygen atom of the alcohol.

Then, either the bromide displaces the water to give 1-bromo-2-methylpropane, or a hydride shift occurs to form the tertiary carbocation, which can be trapped by the bromide, resulting in 2-bromo-2-methylpropane.

21. D is correct.

The reaction between propanol and PBr_3 (phosphorous tribromide) proceeds via an S_N2 reaction mechanism.

An addition-elimination sequence occurs to the P–Br bond, then substitution by Br¯ of the alcohol gives the inverted (*R/S*) product (i.e., bromopropane).

22. D is correct.

Primary alcohols can be oxidized to the carboxylic acid functional group with an oxidizing agent (e.g., CrO_3 in HCl).

Oxidation:

> primary alcohol → aldehyde → carboxylic acid
> secondary alcohol → ketone
> tertiary alcohol → no reaction

23. D is correct.

Boiling points of compounds are determined by two general factors: molecular weight and intermolecular interactions.

The higher the molecular weight, the harder it is to "push" it into the gas phase, and hence the higher the boiling point.

Similarly, the stronger the intermolecular interactions, the more energy is required to disrupt them and separate the molecules in the gas phase, hence the higher the boiling point.

Alcohols participate in hydrogen bonding due to the hydroxyl group.

The alkane, alkene, ether, and alkyl halide only participate in dipole-dipole interactions and London forces.

24. C is correct.

2-hexanol is secondary alcohol and can be oxidized to a ketone with an oxidizing agent (e.g., CrO_3 in HCl).

The carbon atom of the alcohol is only bonded to one other hydrogen atom; therefore, the highest oxidation state it can acquire is the ketone oxidation state (i.e., +2).

Oxidation: primary alcohol → aldehyde → carboxylic acid

secondary alcohol → ketone

tertiary alcohol → no reaction

25. D is correct.

Alcohols of the same chain length as alkanes, alkenes, and alkynes have higher boiling points due to hydrogen bonding of the –OH group.

Alkanes, alkenes, and alkynes are not able to form hydrogen bonds.

26. B is correct.

Carbonyl groups are indicative of ketones, aldehydes, or carboxylic acid derivatives (acyl halides, anhydrides, esters, and amides).

Ethers are noted as R–O–R and do not contain carbonyl groups.

27. A is correct.

With respect to alkenes, allylic refers to an atom attached to a carbon adjacent (β) to the double bond.

For carbonyl compounds (aldehydes, ketones, acyl halides, anhydrides, carboxylic acids, esters, and amides) the position adjacent to the C of the C=O is the α position.

The hydroxyl group of allylic alcohols is one carbon-carbon *sigma* bond away from the double bond.

Vinyl refers to an atom attached to carbon on the double bond.

28. A is correct.

The electronegativity of the oxygen atom in alcohol helps stabilize the negative charge of the conjugate base (i.e., negative oxygen) of the alcohol.

A more stable conjugate base results in a stronger acid (more readily dissociating its proton).

Secondary alcohols are more acidic than tertiary alcohols.

29. A is correct.

Pyridinium chlorochromate (PCC) is a gentle oxidizing agent which converts primary alcohols to aldehydes.

PCC is also used to convert secondary alcohols to ketones.

B: is a carboxylic acid that would require a more powerful oxidizing agent (e.g., Jones reagent; CrO_3, H_2SO_4 and acetone)

C: is an alkene and would proceed via E_1 when the alcohol is subjected to mineral acid (e.g., H_2SO_4)

D: is a terminal alkyl halide produced in two steps.

First, alcohol becomes an alkene (E_1 when the alcohol is subjected to a mineral acid, H_2SO_4).

Then, the alkene is halogenated in *anti*-Markovnikov regiochemistry when peroxides (H_2O_2) are included in the reaction.

E: is an alkyne which requires an initial alkene, followed by Br_2 (or Cl_2) for the dibromo compound, followed by elimination with two equivalents of base to yield the alkyne.

30. C is correct.

Tertiary alcohol undergoes E_1 reactions at a faster rate (i.e., due to the stability of the carbocation intermediate) than secondary alcohols, which can dehydrate at a faster rate than primary alcohols.

31. D is correct.

A tosyl group (Tos) is $CH_3C_6H_4SO_2$ (derived from $CH_3C_6H_4SO_2Cl$) and forms esters and amides of tosylic acid.

Tosylates are used to increase the efficiency of the original hydroxyl as a leaving group.

Unlike PBr_3 or $SOCl_2$ (both via S_N2), the reaction mechanism preserves the bond between the carbon and the O of the hydroxyl, and therefore no inversion of stereochemistry occurs (during the first step in this example) with the use of a tosylate.

The first step with the tosylate results in retention of the chiral center and the second step (i.e., Cl^- as a nucleophile) produces an inverted product.

32. D is correct.

Aldehydes and ketones undergo tautomerization to exist in equilibrium between the keto and enol forms.

Most molecules (99%) exist predominantly in the keto form because the carbon-oxygen (carbonyl) double bond is more stable than the hydroxyl on the double bond of the enol.

Phenols are one of few aldehydes/ketones that exist predominantly in the enol form in the keto-enol tautomer equilibrium.

The conjugated benzene ring system of phenol provides stability for the enol form.

The keto form of phenol lacks conjugation because the carbon in the ring is sp^3 hybridized.

When the phenol molecule assumes the keto form, aromaticity is lost, and the molecule becomes less stable.

Therefore, the keto form is non-aromatic and thus less stable.

Aromatic molecules are cyclic, planar, have conjugated double bonds (i.e., sp^2 at each atom) and satisfy Hückel's number of *pi* electrons (4n + 2, where n is an integer).

Anti-aromatic compounds are also cyclic, planar, have conjugated double bonds, but have 4n (e.g., 4, 8, 12 and so on) *pi* electrons and therefore are unstable.

Nonaromatic compounds do not meet the four criteria needed for aromatic compounds: cyclic, planar, conjugated double bonds and Hückel's number of *pi* electrons.

33. C is correct.

Treatment of salicylic acid (i.e., aspirin) with methanol and dry acid are conditions for synthesizing an ester in a mechanism known as *Fischer esterification*:

34. B is correct.

The reaction between (*R*)-2-hexanol and PBr_3 (phosphorous tribromide) proceeds via an S_N2 reaction mechanism.

An addition-elimination sequence occurs in the P–Br bond, then substitution by Br^- of the alcohol gives the inverted (*S*)-2-bromohexane product.

35. B is correct.

Esterification occurs when a carboxylic acid reacts with alcohol under catalytic acidic conditions to form an ester + water.

A: C_6H_5OH and CH_3CH_2Br form an ether via Williamson (S_N2) ether synthesis when the alcohol reacts with the alkyl halide.

C: $CH_3COOH + SOCl_2$ is the S_N2 reaction of a carboxylic acid with thionyl chloride and an acyl halide is formed.

D: $2CH_3OH + H_2SO_4$, form dimethyl ether from molecules of methanol and catalytic acid (e.g., sulfuric acid).

E: $CH_3CH_2Br + CH_3CH_2O^-Na^+$ form an ether via Williamson (S_N2) ether synthesis when alcohol reacts with an alkyl halide.

The requirement is that the alkyl halide is less substituted because the reaction proceeds via S_N2.

36. B is correct.

The hydrobromic acid protonates the secondary alcohol that dissociates as water.

The secondary carbocation, formed as an intermediate, is repositioned to the tertiary position through an alkyl (i.e., methide) shift.

After the methide shift, this more stable tertiary carbocation is then attacked by the bromide ion.

Chapter 21 Explanations: Aldehydes & Ketones

1. E is correct.

Ketones are functional groups that can no longer be oxidized by Cr^{VI} reagents.

These groups do not undergo further reactions because there are no C–H bonds to the carbonyl carbon of the ketone.

Aldehydes, however, may have subsequent oxidations to generate carboxylic acids.

2. A is correct.

Aldehydes can convert to the enol form, although the equilibrium constant favors the aldehyde.

Conversion to the enol form destroys the stereocenter because this isomer is achiral.

When the enol form converts back to the ketone, protonation may occur on either face of the group, and this interconverts the configuration (i.e., producing R and S isomers).

The process is catalyzed by the presence of an acid or base.

3. D is correct.

If a stronger reducing agent, such as lithium aluminum hydride ($LiAlH_4$), is used, the aldehyde is reduced to the primary alcohol.

Ester is reduced to an aldehyde with the mild reducing agent of DIBAL

4. B is correct.

For a ketone to be converted to an enolate, a base that is strong enough to completely remove a proton from the alpha position is used.

If hydroxides or alkoxides are used instead of lithium amide bases, an equilibrium exists between both conjugate forms of the ketone.

Methyllithium and diethylamine may add to the ketone instead of deprotonating it. They are too weak to deprotonate the ketone.

5. C is correct.

Ketones are molecules that have alkyl or aryl (i.e., ring) substituents on either side of the carbonyl (C=O) functional group.

The IUPAC name for the molecule is butan-2-one or 2-butanone.

---

6. D is correct.

1,3-dithiane serves as a nucleophilic carbonyl equivalent.

Treatment of 1,3-dithiane with n-BuLi generates a carbanion between both sulfur atoms of the molecule, and this anion can add to electrophiles such as alkyl halides.

Both C–H bonds of the 1,3-dithiane can be substituted with alkyl groups.

The hydrolysis of the dithiane to the carbonyl group requires mercury salts in acidic solution.

7. A is correct.

The compounds ending in ~*one* suggests that the highest priority functional group is the molecule is the ketone.

Compounds that end in ~*ol* may possess alcohol as the highest priority group.

8. D is correct.

These reaction conditions are the Clemmensen reduction reaction conditions.

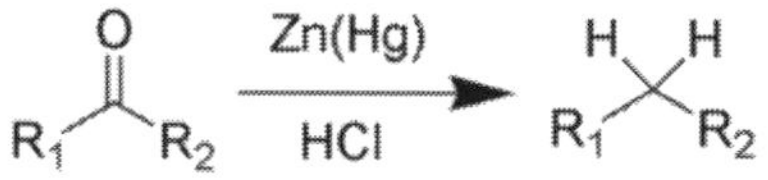

The Clemmensen reduction mechanism involves the protonation of the ketone oxygen atom.

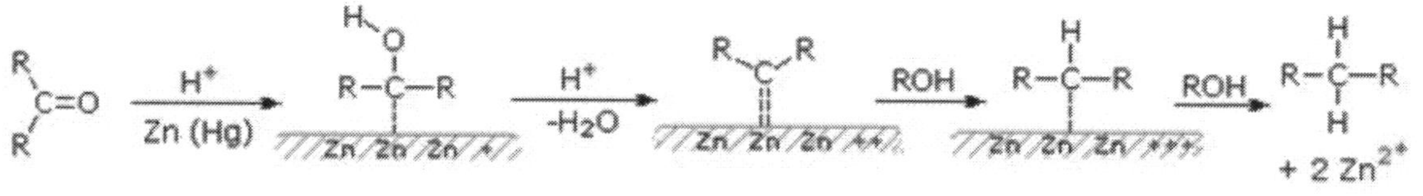

Clemmensen reduction reaction

9. D is correct.

When Grignard (R–MgBr or R–MgCl) or Gilman (R$_2$CuLi) reagents are combined with aldehydes, the product is a secondary alcohol.

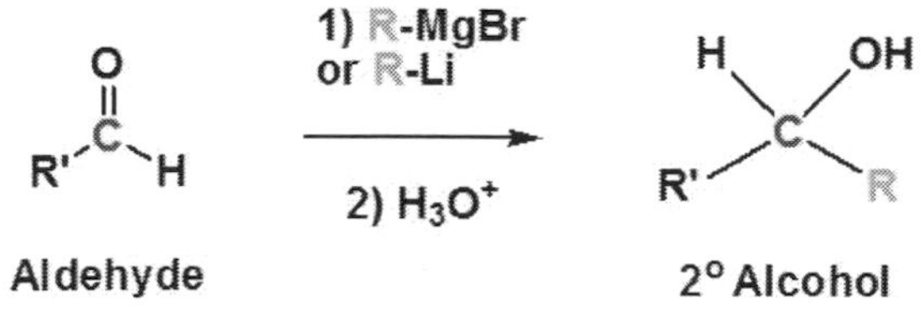

This alcohol may or may not be chiral, depending on which Grignard reagent is used for alkylation.

The alkylation of ketones yields tertiary alcohols (see below).

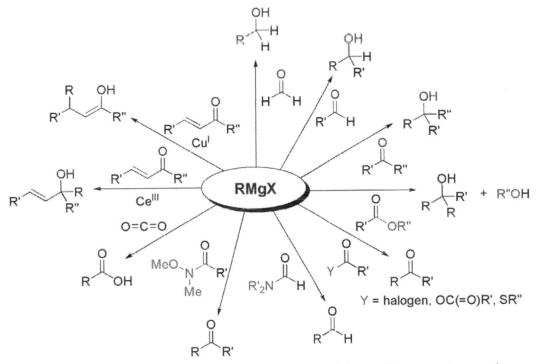

The alkylation of epoxides results in alcohol with an extended carbon chain.

The Grignard reagent (i.e., carbanion in basic conditions) proceeds with the nucleophile (Grignard) attaching the less substituted carbon of the epoxide.

Grignard reaction (RMgX) involving several electrophiles and the resulting products

10. C is correct.

Benedict's test is used to detect reducing sugars.

An oxidized copper reagent is reduced by a sugar's aldehyde, and the aldehyde is oxidized to a carboxylic acid in the process.

All monosaccharides are reducing sugars, while some disaccharides (e.g., lactose and maltose), oligosaccharides and polysaccharides are also reducing sugars.

Reducing sugars (and alpha hydroxyl ketones) give a positive Benedict's test: a red-brown precipitate forms.

Fehling's solution also gives a positive test for reducing sugars by changing from blue to clear and forming a red-brown precipitate.

Tollens' reagent forms silver ions (mirror) as a positive test for reducing sugars.

The Tollens' test for aldehydes involves the reduction of silver cations [Ag^+] to reduced silver; the metal precipitates out of solution and coats the inner surface of the reaction flask.

Benedict's test, like the Tollens' test, involves the oxidation of an aldehyde to form a carboxylic acid.

Sugars able to do this are those that have the aldehyde or hemiacetal functional groups, and these molecules are known as reducing sugars.

11. E is correct.

A common ylide is the phosphonium ylide as a Wittig reagent.

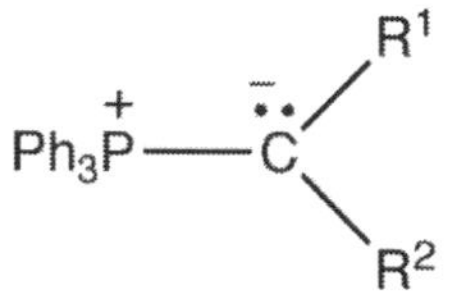

The double-charged (+ and –) resonance structure is the more dominant resonance contributor because the orbitals of phosphorus are larger than the valence orbitals of carbon, thus making the overlap of the carbon and phosphorus *p* orbitals less favorable.

Phosphonium ylide

The minor resonance contributor for this functional group is the charge-neutral pentavalent phosphorus-containing structure formed from the overlap of the carbon and phosphorus *p* orbitals.

12. E is correct.

Hydrocarbons tend to have lower boiling points than molecules containing heteroatoms because hydrocarbons lack large molecular dipoles. These dipoles strengthen the intermolecular forces and raise boiling points.

Furthermore, molecules that can hydrogen bond have the highest boiling points because the hydrogen bond is a strong type of dipole interaction.

13. A is correct.

The treatment of a terminal alkyne with a dialkyl borane results in the formation of a vinyl borane.

The vinyl borane is oxidized to the enol through exposure to hydrogen peroxide and hydroxide base. This group tautomerizes to form an aldehyde.

14. B is correct.

The iodoform reaction (see mechanisms shown below) involves trihalogenating the methyl group to turn it into a good leaving group.

After tribromination of the methyl group has occurred, the group is expelled from the molecule by the addition of hydroxide to the ketone.

Molecule 4 undergoes tribromination before being replaced by the ⁻OH

Acidic conditions only provide the monobrominated compound from the starting ketone; therefore, basic conditions need to be used during the reaction.

15. A is correct.

Hemiacetals are intermediates that can be produced in acetal formation reactions of aldehydes with two equivalents of alcohols.

Hemiacetals are not stable groups and typically cannot be isolated.

The hemiacetal O–H bond collapses to expel an alcohol and regenerates the carbonyl of the aldehyde. This normally occurs because the carbonyl formation increases the entropy of the system (starting from one molecule and converting it to two molecules), and the carbonyl is almost as thermodynamically stable as the hemiacetal form.

16. D is correct.

Benedict's test (or Tollens' reagent) is used to detect reducing sugars. The aldehyde is oxidized to a carboxylic acid in the process. All monosaccharides are reducing sugars, while some disaccharides, oligosaccharides and polysaccharides are also reducing sugars.

Reducing sugars (and alpha hydroxyl ketones) give a positive Benedict's test: a brown precipitate forms (as does for Fehling's solution).

Tollens' reagent forms silver ions (mirror) as a positive test for reducing sugars.

The Tollens' test for aldehydes involves the reduction of silver cations [Ag^+] to reduced silver; the metal precipitates out of solution and coats the inner surface of the reaction flask.

The ethyl formate has a terminal (HC=O) group, but this group does not oxidize in the Tollens' test conditions because the group is an ester and not an aldehyde.

The C–H of the formate ester cannot be oxidized to an O–H bond.

The mechanism for the oxidation of carbonyl C–H bonds typically proceeds through either the hydrate or nucleophilic attack on the carbonyl carbon atom, both of which are not easily done because of the presence of the ester alkoxyl group.

The ester is much less electrophilic than the aldehyde, so it is less reactive.

17. A is correct.

The first step in the reaction is the coordination of the carbonyl oxygen atom with the positively charged counter ion of the reducing reagent and introduction of the hydride to the group.

The second step involves the protonation of the alkoxide (negative oxygen atom) intermediate with a weak acid.

18. D is correct.

A Michael acceptor is an α, β unsaturated carbonyl – the double bond is between the first and second carbons from the carbonyl carbon.

The best Michael acceptor is the electrophile that best stabilizes the resulting negative charge at the alpha position when a nucleophilic attack (i.e., by Michael donor) occurs at the beta position.

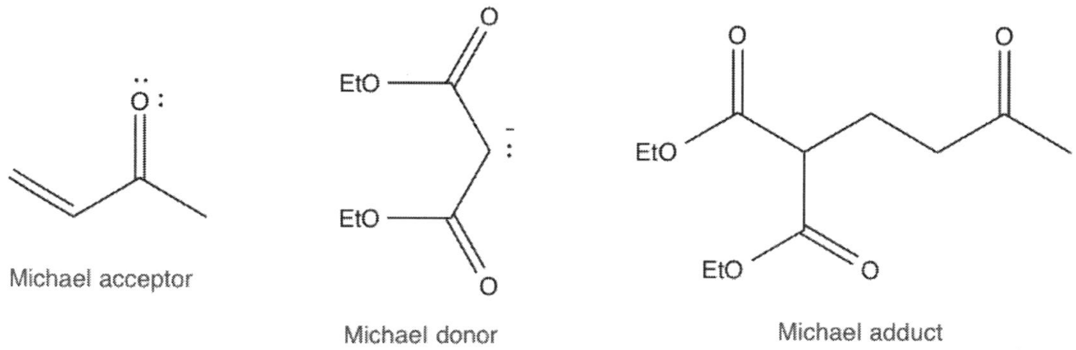

Michael acceptor

Michael donor

Michael adduct

The mechanism for the Michael reaction is shown below:

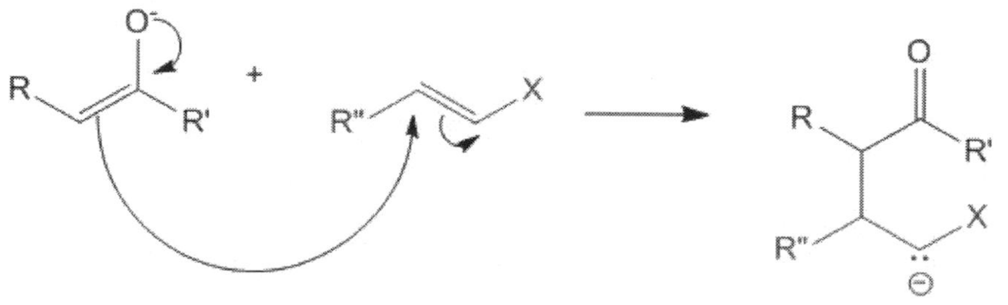

The Michael donor participates in a nucleophilic attack on the Michael acceptor

19. D is correct. Ketones and aldehydes have similar chemical properties because both contain a carbonyl group that is not in conjugation with a heteroatom. They undergo similar reduction and alkylation reactions, although the products of these reactions may be slightly different.

Conversely, aldehydes can undergo an additional oxidation reaction to form carboxylic acids, unlike ketones, which cannot be oxidized further.

20. E is correct. Tollens' reagent or Benedict's test are used to detect reducing sugars (i.e., aldehydes). The aldehyde is oxidized to a carboxylic acid during the reaction. All monosaccharides are reducing sugars, while some disaccharides, oligosaccharides, and polysaccharides are also reducing sugars.

The Tollens' test for aldehydes involves the reduction of silver cations [Ag^+] to reduced silver; the metal precipitates out of solution and coats the inner surface of the reaction flask (i.e., mirror) as a positive test for reducing sugars.

The Tollens' test does not give a positive test with ketones because the ketone is already fully oxidized and lacks a C–H bond to be further oxidized and be converted to C O bonds (e.g., aldehydes to COOH).

21. E is correct. The hydrocyanation (i.e., adding ⁻C≡N) of ketones and aldehydes is essentially an alkylation reaction.

This alkylation reaction is sensitive to the steric environment of the carbonyl electrophile.

Formaldehyde (below) contains two hydrogen substituents and is the most reactive.

Aldehydes (below) are the second most reactive.

Unhindered (below) ketones are the next most reactive.

Hindered (below) ketones are the least reactive.

These alkyl groups block access to the *pi** orbital of the carbonyl, and the more sterically-hindered substrates react more slowly because the nucleophile (⁻C≡N) is impeded in its approach to the delta plus of the carbonyl carbon.

Carbonyl carbon with delta plus carbon (electrophile) indicated

22. D is correct.

The substituents on the carbonyl carbon can be alkyl, alkenyl or aryl groups. The R groups do not need to be the same group (i.e., R and R').

Asymmetric ketones form chiral secondary alcohols if reduced or if alkylated by a carbon nucleophile that is unlike the structure of the ketone alkyl groups.

Asymmetric ketones are known as "prochiral" electrophiles.

A: carboxylic acid functional group.

B: ester functional group.

C: aldehyde functional group.

E: anhydride functional group.

23. C is correct.

A reducing sugar can act as a reducing agent because it has a free aldehyde group or a free ketone group. All monosaccharides are reducing sugars, while some disaccharides, oligosaccharides, and polysaccharides are also reducing sugars.

A reducing sugar becomes oxidized (e.g., aldehyde → carboxylic acid) from reducing another compound.

Benedict's test (or Tollens' reagent) is used to detect reducing sugars. An oxidized copper reagent is reduced by a sugar's aldehyde, and the aldehyde is oxidized to a carboxylic acid in the process.

Reducing sugars (and alpha hydroxyl ketones) give a positive Benedict's test: a red-brown precipitate forms. Fehling's solution also gives a positive test for reducing sugars by changing from blue to clear and forming a red-brown precipitate.

The Tollens' test for aldehydes involves the reduction of silver cations [Ag^+] to reduced silver; the metal precipitates out of solution and coats the inner surface of the reaction flask. Tollens' reagent forms silver ions (mirror) as a positive test for reducing sugars. The aldehyde is oxidized to the carboxylic acid when this occurs.

24. E is correct.

The classes of compounds that contain carbonyl group are ketones, aldehyde, carboxylic acids, and carboxylic acid derivatives (acyl halide, anhydride, ester, and amide).

Other groups may also contain carbonyl groups, such as carbonate, carbamate, urea, etc., and these groups have the same oxidation state as carbon dioxide with four C–X bonds.

25. E is correct.

Carbonyl groups contain lone pairs on the oxygen atom for hydrogen-accepting capabilities.

However, these groups lack a polarized *sigma* bond to hydrogen atoms (assuming the ketone is in the keto tautomer).

Since these molecules cannot donate hydrogen bonds, they cannot form hydrogen bonds with each other.

26. A is correct.

The larger the alkyl portion of an organic molecule, the less likely it can dissolve in water.

When ketones and aldehydes are dissolved in water, they are in equilibrium with their hydrated forms.

The hydrated form enhances the solubility of the compound in water.

27. B is correct. Grignard + nitrile → imine salt + H_3O → ketone

$$RMgX \ + \ R'-C\equiv N \ \longrightarrow \ \underset{\substack{\text{imine} \\ \text{salt}}}{\overset{\overset{\displaystyle NMgX}{\|}}{\underset{R \quad R'}{C}}} \ \xrightarrow[\text{work-up}]{H_3O^+} \ \underset{\text{ketone}}{\overset{\overset{\displaystyle O}{\|}}{\underset{R \quad R'}{C}}}$$

Unlike esters, the nitrile is not subject to over-alkylation, because the negatively charged imine intermediate generated from the alkylation is less electrophilic than the starting nitrile.

28. D is correct. The oxidation of aldehydes to carboxylic acid can be done by exposing aldehydes to chromic acid in water and acetone, or to potassium permanganate.

29. A is correct. Nucleophiles attack sterically hindered alkyl halides at a much slower rate. Smaller or less sterically hindered substrates undergo reactions with nucleophiles at the fastest rate.

Bromobenzene undergoes the addition reaction at a negligible rate because the ring lacks an electron-withdrawing group that can activate the ring towards nucleophilic aromatic substitution.

Furthermore, the bromide of bromobenzene does not undergo S_N2 displacement reactions because the ring blocks access to the carbon-bromine *sigma** orbital.

30. E is correct. Benedict's test (or Tollens' reagent) is used to detect reducing sugars. An oxidized copper reagent is reduced by a sugar's aldehyde; the aldehyde is oxidized to a carboxylic acid in the process.

Reducing sugars (and alpha hydroxyl ketones) give a positive Benedict's test: a red-brown precipitate forms. Fehling's solution also gives a positive test for reducing sugars by changing from blue to clear and forming a red-brown precipitate.

The copper complex is reduced to form a red copper product that is less soluble in aqueous solutions.

The detection of this precipitate means the molecule was oxidized.

31. D is correct. Since the aldol reaction involves deprotonation (abstraction of H^+) by a strong base, the preferred solvents are neither acidic nor electrophilic.

Dimethyl ether, unlike the other solvents listed, does not contain an acidic proton.

32. C is correct. Oxidation of primary alcohols produces aldehydes (by PCC or oxidation in dry conditions). Oxidation of secondary alcohols commonly produces ketones (e.g., by PCC) or carboxylic acids (e.g., Jones oxidation by CrO_3 in H_2SO_4).

A: Benedict's test (or Tollens' reagent) is used to detect reducing sugars. An oxidized copper reagent is reduced by a sugar's aldehyde, and the aldehyde is oxidized to a carboxylic acid in the process.

Reducing sugars (and alpha hydroxyl ketones) gives a positive Benedict's test: a red-brown precipitate forms. Fehling's solution also gives a positive test for reducing sugars by changing from blue to clear and forming a red-brown precipitate.

B: Tollens' reagent forms silver ions (i.e., shiny mirror surface) as a positive test for reducing sugars.

E: aldehydes possess a hydrogen atom that is bonded to the carbonyl carbon, so they can be oxidized to produce carboxylic acids.

33. B is correct. When ketones and aldehydes are alkylated by Grignard nucleophiles, the number of carbon-oxygen bonds decreases by one, and the number of carbon-carbon bonds increases by one.

Oxidation proceeds towards the right, while reduction is shown proceeding to the left.

34. E is correct. The correct tautomer forms of the ketone have the carbon-oxygen bond directly bound to the alkene carbon atom.

35. A is correct. Carboxylic acid derivatives are similar in structure to ketones and aldehydes; however, one of the H or R groups has been replaced with a heteroatom, such as oxygen or nitrogen.

36. B is correct. A ketone is being converted to an alkene. The oxidation state of ketones is larger than the oxidation state of alkenes, and therefore the ketone needs to be reduced.

Reduction of a ketone forms secondary alcohol.

The carbon skeleton rearranges, and this requires the formation of a carbocation. Exposure to phosphoric acid produces the secondary carbocation, and this is followed by an alkyl shift and deprotonation to yield the alkene product.

Chapter 22 Explanations: Carboxylic Acids

1. C is correct. Carboxylic acids are acidic functional groups that have a hydroxyl group directly bonded to the carbonyl group. Carboxylic acids are acidic because the conjugate base is relatively stable due to resonance stabilization of the negative charge on oxygen.

The molecule also contains three hydroxyl groups and an arene.

2. D is correct.

A chemical equilibrium exists for this reaction, and water is given off as a byproduct in the process.

3. C is correct.

benzoic acid
insoluble in water

sodium benzoate
soluble in water

4. B is correct. Carboxylic acids are molecules that contain a terminal carbon atom with three bonds to oxygen. It consists of a hydroxyl (–OH) group and a carbonyl (–C=O) group.

5. A is correct. The carboxylic acid and alcohol starting components for the synthesis of an ester are determined by cleaving the *sigma* bond between the oxygen atom of the alkoxyl (O of the ether) group and the carbonyl (C=O) group.

6. C is correct. The initial reaction between the amine and carboxylic acid is neutralization (i.e., proton transfer).

However, at high temperatures, this proton transfer is reversible, and the reaction has enough energy to promote the nucleophilic attack of the carboxylic acid instead, leading to amide formation.

7. E is correct. All of the acids contain a carboxylic acid functional group, which largely contributes to the boiling points of all of the molecules. The molecule with the largest hydrocarbon region has more intermolecular forces (most of which are London forces) and has the largest boiling point.

The alkyl region of stearic acid consists of 17 saturated carbon atoms.

Stearic acid is a saturated fatty acid and has the highest boiling point.

Among the answer choices, no other acid possesses an alkyl region this large, and this molecule has the largest boiling point.

8. D is correct.

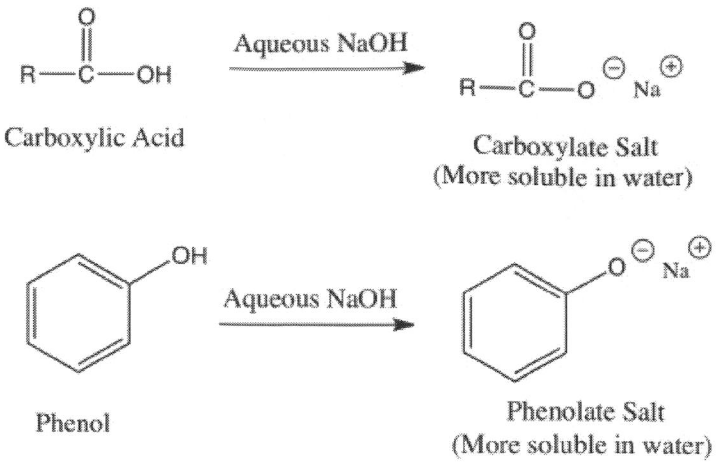

The salt is a sodium carboxylate salt of the carboxylic acid. The byproduct in the reaction is water.

Because carboxylic acids are about 10 or more orders of magnitude more acidic than water, the conversion to the carboxylate form by exposing it to sodium hydroxide is irreversible.

Therefore, no equilibrium is associated with this reaction.

9. B is correct.

When carboxylic acids and alcohols are combined in the presence of acid catalysts (e.g., H_2SO_4), esters form as the product.

Water is also produced as a byproduct in the reaction, and its removal from the reaction drives the reaction forward because an equilibrium exists.

10. E is correct.

The carboxylic acid functional group accounts for at least two sites of hydrogen bonding.

Because all of the answers include carboxylic acids, the hydrocarbon regions of the molecules must be considered. The molecule with the largest hydrocarbon region has more intermolecular forces (most of which are London forces) and has the largest boiling point.

Stearic acid is a saturated fatty acid and has the highest boiling point.

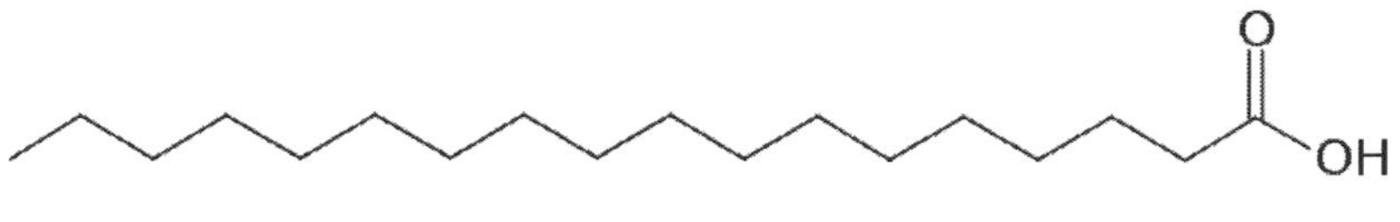

11. B is correct.

Acetic acid is a neutral compound, with all of the atoms in the molecule having no formal charge.

Carboxylic acids are charged when protonated by other acids, as is the case in Fischer esterification reactions or when deprotonated by bases.

12. B is correct.

Ester formations from alcohols and carboxylic acids are condensations, so an equivalent of water is lost as a reaction byproduct as well.

13. C is correct.

The reaction used to combine alcohols and carboxylic acids is the Fischer esterification reaction.

Acid catalysis is needed to activate the carboxylic acid carbonyl group for the nucleophilic attack.

14. B is correct.

Carboxylic acids have some of the highest boiling points due to their ability to hydrogen bond and form dimeric structures.

Alcohols also contain the polar O–H bond and form hydrogen bonds, thus contributing to their high boiling point.

15. D is correct. The negative charge of the carboxylate anion is stabilized by the electronegativity of the oxygen atom and by resonance stabilization. The negative charge delocalizes over the two oxygen atoms of the carboxylate functional group.

Resonance structures of the carboxylate anion

16. B is correct. Molecules that possess the hydroxyl group are alcohols and carboxylic acids.

17. A is correct. In addition to the presence of polar functional groups, the molecular weight of a compound is an important influence on its boiling point. Because carboxylic acids are compared, the one with the highest molecular weight has the highest boiling point.

18. D is correct.

Carboxylic acids are more acidic than phenols. The pK_a of carboxylic acids is ≈ 5, and the pK_a of phenols is ≈ 10.

The aryl (on the C=O) proton of benzaldehyde has a pK_a near the lower 40s, while the ketones (e.g., acetone) have pK_a values of ≈ 20.

19. A is correct.

Acid strength is increased by the inductive effect of electron-withdrawing groups on the neighboring carbon atoms.

Factors that affect the acidity of a molecule:

1) the more electronegative the substituents, the greater the inductive effect;

2) the closer the electronegative group is to the carbonyl carbon, the greater the effect;

3) the greater the number of electronegative substituents, the greater the inductive effect.

Fluoroacetic acid has a $pK_a \approx 2.6$ and is more acidic than others because of the inductive influence of the electronegative fluorine atom.

B: acetic acid (i.e., table vinegar) has a $pK_a \approx 5$ and is the least acidic since it has no electronegative substituents.

C: bromoacetic acid has a $pK_a \approx 3.6$.

D: methoxyacetic acid has a $pK_a \approx 3.6$

E: phenol has a $pK_a \approx 10.0$. The pK_a of phenol is much lower than cyclohexane due to the presence of resonance stabilization of the anion through the *pi* system of electrons in the aromatic ring.

20. A is correct.

When dissolved in the basic solution, the carboxylic acid is deprotonated to form the carboxylate salt.

The salt is charged, and this ion can engage in ion–dipole interactions with the solvent and is therefore soluble.

The aldehyde may also react with the base to form charged species (either the geminal diol or the enolate), but these charged species are formed reversibly.

Therefore, the acid can dissolve, while the aldehyde is not.

21. E is correct. Carboxylic acids exchange protons with bases.

When a neutral compound ionizes through the loss of a proton, the remaining charge of the larger fragment is negatively charged. The proton is positively charged, so the resulting ion is H^+.

The hydroxyl group of a carboxylic acid (or of alcohol) can be replaced (i.e., substitution reaction) with special reagents (e.g., $SOCl_4$ or PBr_3) to form acyl halides (or alkyl halides for alcohol functional groups).

22. C is correct.

The high pH (basic conditions) of the aqueous solution causes the carboxylate to deprotonate and assume its conjugate base form.

This carboxylate form (i.e., the anion of the carboxylic acid) has a higher affinity for the aqueous layer than for the organic layer.

23. D is correct.

The carboxylic acid contains the most acidic functional group among the molecules listed.

Any proton has the potential to protonate a base, given that the base is sufficiently strong to remove the proton from an acid. This requires comparing the pK_a of the acid and base, whereby the base must have a higher pK_a.

Amines can deprotonate carboxylic acids; amide bases can deprotonate alcohols.

Use of strong organometallic bases (e.g., Grignard reagent) may be necessary for the deprotonation of neutral amines and hydrocarbons.

24. A is correct.

Citric acid is a chemical involved in the citric acid (TCA or Krebs) cycle.

Citric acid

The TCA cycle is a metabolic process responsible for ATP production and commonly occurs in most aerobic organisms.

25. C is correct.

All of the molecules contain the carboxylic acid functional group which can hydrogen bond and also ionize to increase its solubility in water.

Besides benzene, the choices differ only in the length of the carbon chain attached to the carboxylic acid.

Saturated carbon chains are hydrophobic, and therefore the shortest-chain carboxylic acid is most water soluble.

26. B is correct.

The most polar molecule is the molecule that possesses the smallest alkyl portion.

Acidic functional groups also enhance the intermolecular forces that exist among molecules, with hydrogen bonding being the largest contributing factor. The more polarized a hydrogen-heteroatom bond is, the more acidic it is and the stronger the intermolecular forces the molecule experiences.

Therefore, the carboxylic acid is the most polar molecule.

27. A is correct.

Nucleophilic acyl substitution (NAS) reactions are the most common type of reactions that carboxylic acid derivatives undergo.

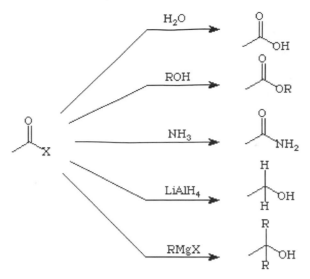

Example reactions involving acyl halides

28. A is correct. Secondary alcohols cannot be oxidized further.

B: primary alcohols undergo oxidation by strong oxidizing agents (e.g., potassium permanganate, O_3 or Jones's reagent) to yield carboxylic acids.

C: acidic or basic hydrolysis of a nitrile yields carboxylic acids.

D: Grignard reagents reacting with CO_2 is a method for preparing carboxylic acids. The carbonation of a Grignard reagent (adding CO_2) forms the magnesium salt of a carboxylic acid. In a subsequent step, the magnesium salt is protonated and converted to a carboxylic acid when treated with mineral acid (e.g., H^+ from HCl).

E: carboxylic acids are formed by the oxidation of aldehydes.

29. B is correct. Acids with smaller alkyl chains have lower boiling points.

Hydrogen bonding also increases the boiling point. Increased molecular mass and hydrogen bonding are the factors which increase the boiling point.

Formic acid (below) has the molecular formula of CH_2O_2: it contains one carboxylic acid functional group and a hydrogen atom for the *R* group.

Formic acid

A: oxalic acid (below) has the molecular formula of CH_2O_4.

Copyright © 2020 Sterling Test Prep. Any duplication (copies, uploads, PDFs) is illegal.

C: benzoic acid (below) has the molecular formula of $C_7H_6O_2$

D: acetic acid (below) has the molecular formula of $C_2H_4O_2$.

E: oleic acid (below) has the molecular formula of $C_{18}H_{34}O_2$.

30. D is correct.

This reaction the Fischer esterification reaction.

Water is given off as the byproduct in this transformation.

To drive the equilibrium of the reaction forward, water should be removed from the reaction or a large excess of one of the two components should be used.

31. C is correct.

Lithium aluminum hydride (LAH or $LiAlH_4$) is a powerful reducing agent and can reduce carboxylic acids and esters to form primary alcohols and reduces nitro groups to amines.

Sodium borohydride ($NaBH_4$) is a weak reducing agent and is only used for the reduction of aldehydes (to primary alcohols) and ketones (to secondary alcohols).

32. E is correct.

The chlorine substitution stabilizes the negative charge of the carboxylate through the inductive withdrawal of electron density through the *sigma* bonds.

The *ortho* substitution also lowers the pK_a of the acid because of its conjugation with the aryl ring decreases (*ortho* effect).

33. B is correct.

Exposing a carboxylic acid to sodium hydroxide produces water and the sodium carboxylate conjugate base. This ionic base has a higher affinity for the aqueous layer due to the negative charge, and this charge forms hydrogen bonds to the hydrogen atoms of water molecules.

34. A is correct. In Brønsted-Lowry theory, an acid is a proton donor, and a base is a proton acceptor.

In solution, a strong acid dissociates its proton and exists predominantly in the deprotonated form as the acid's conjugate base. A strong acid forms a weak conjugate base because the acid's protons dissociated in solution.

The resulting anions of the deprotonated carboxylic acids are stable due to resonance. Resonance is a major contributor to stabilize the anion by delocalizing the negative charge (using *pi* bonds) over several (in this example, two oxygen) atoms.

Acids that contain an electron-withdrawing substituent on the α-carbon (i.e., carbon adjacent to the carbonyl) tend to be stronger acids (donate proton more readily) because induction (via *sigma* bond) pulls the electron density.

Induction has a stabilizing effect on the carboxylate anion (the conjugate base of carboxylic acid).

Conversely, acids with electron-donating α substituents (i.e., methyl chains) tend to be weaker (less likely to dissociate the H^+).

The acid with two electron-withdrawing chlorine substituents forms the most stable carboxylate anion (when H^+ dissociates), and it is, therefore, the strongest acid, meaning that it has the weakest (most stable) conjugate base.

B: $CH_3CH_2CH_2CO_2H$ is a carboxylic acid that has only hydrogens and therefore lacks stability influences from electronegative atoms (F, N, O or Cl).

C: $(CH_3CH_2)_3CCO_2H$ is a carboxylic acid that has a tertiary butyl substituent which is electron-donating via hyperconjugation (i.e., alkyl chains donate electrons).

D: $CH_3HNCH_2CH_2CH_2CO_2H$ is a carboxylic acid that has an amino substituent which is strongly electron-withdrawing via electronegativity of the nitrogen, but the nitrogen is located at a large distance from the COO^- and therefore its influence is minimal.

E: $CH_3Cl_2CCH_2CO_2H$ is a carboxylic acid that contains an electron-withdrawing substituent on the β-carbon that has less effect than at the α-carbon.

35. D is correct.

Hydrogen bonding a strong type of dipole-dipole interaction and raises the boiling point of organic compounds.

Dimer formed from hydrogen bonding of two carboxylic acids.

The carboxylic acid of acetic acid participates in such hydrogen bonding while the ester of methyl acetate does not form similar intermolecular hydrogen bonds.

36. A is correct.

The pK_a is the pH where half of the acid has dissociated to its conjugate base form.

The concentration of the acid and conjugate base is equal when the pK_a of the compound and the pH of the solution are the same.

Henderson-Hasselbalch equation:

$$pH = pK_a + \log[\text{conjugate base}] / [\text{acid}]$$

Chapter 23 Explanations: COOH Derivatives

1. A is correct. Amides are functional groups that possess an amino group bonded to a carbonyl moiety.

The reference molecule is a tertiary amine because it is bonded to three R groups.

2. D is correct. The hydrolysis of an ester is essentially the reverse of Fischer esterification. To drive the reaction forward, excess water and an acid catalyst are used. The ester hydrolyzes to its two simpler components: the corresponding alcohol and carboxylic acid.

The R component of the alcohol product and the alkoxy group of the ester are the same.

3. A is correct. The reaction best suited to occur under "normal conditions," rather than harsh conditions, is the aminolysis of the ester to form an amide. Amides are less electrophilic than esters, and basic conditions are needed to convert the amide back to the ester.

4. C is correct. The hydrolysis of an ester is essentially the reverse of Fischer esterification. To drive the reaction forward, excess water and an acid catalyst are used.

The ester hydrolyzes to its two simpler components: the corresponding alcohol and carboxylic acid.

The R components of the alcohol product and of the alkoxy group of the ester are the same.

5. A is correct. Esters are functional groups that belong to a class of compounds known as carboxylic acid derivatives (along with acyl halides, anhydrides and amides).

Esters have the same oxidation state as carboxylic acids but have different properties compared to carboxylic acid groups, such as enhanced electrophilic properties, decreased polarity and higher pK_a values.

6. D is correct.

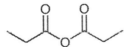

Anhydride functional groups have oxygen between two carbonyl carbons.

The anhydride functional group does not exist in the reference molecule.

7. C is correct. The reaction above is a hydrolysis reaction, and it is the reverse process for the Fischer esterification reaction. In the presence of excess water, the acid catalyst activates the ester carbonyl group to promote nucleophilic attack by water.

This produces the corresponding alcohol and carboxylic acid (in the presence of H^+).

8. A is correct. Sodium hydroxide can act as a base to reversibly deprotonate the N–H of the amide (due to resonance stabilization of the anion). However, the irreversible reaction pathway involves the formation of carboxylate and amine products.

9. E is correct. Summary of some reactions involving carboxylic acids:

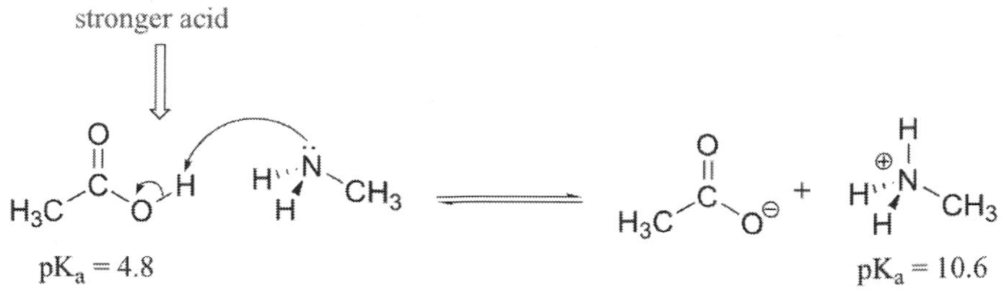

When forming an amide from a carboxylic acid and an amine, higher temperatures are typically needed to drive the reaction forward.

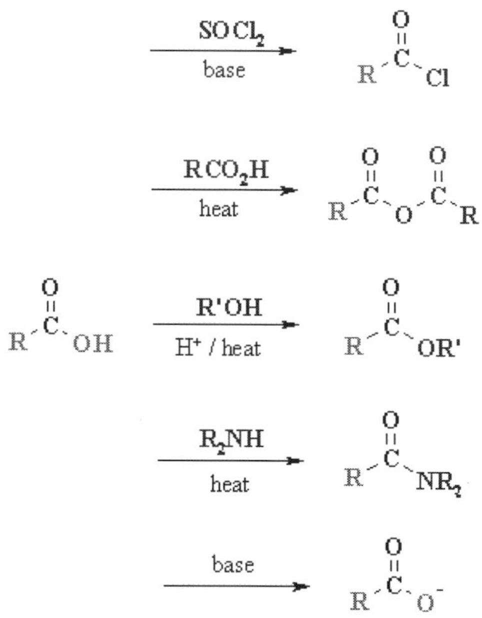

Reactions for a carboxylic acid with specific reagents

The reactivity of the carboxylic acid derivatives is:

acyl chloride > anhydride > carboxylic acid ≈ ester > amide > carboxylate.

An equivalent of water is lost (i.e., dehydration) in the process, so this reaction is a condensation reaction.

10. E is correct. Both acid chlorides and anhydrides combine with alcohols to form esters and with amines to form amides.

Acid chlorides are more reactive than anhydrides, and the chloride is a better leaving group than the carboxylate anion.

These factors contribute to the enhanced reactivity of the acid chloride.

11. B is correct.

The synthesis (below) of amides from carboxylic acids and amines usually requires heating the reaction to high temperatures. This is necessary for the creation of the amide bond and to possibly drive away the water byproduct, so the chemical equilibrium continues to favor the product formation.

$$CH_3-CH_2-\overset{\overset{\text{O}}{\|}}{C}-OH \;+\; H-\overset{\overset{}{|}}{\underset{\underset{H}{|}}{N}}-CH_3 \;\rightarrow\; CH_3-CH_2-\overset{\overset{\text{O}}{\|}}{C}-\overset{\overset{}{|}}{\underset{\underset{H}{|}}{N}}-CH_3 \;+\; H_2O$$

carboxylic acid   amine   amide   water

12. B is correct.

6-APA is the core of penicillins and is the chemical compound (+)-6-aminopenicillanic acid.

Since amides are more stable than carboxylic acids, their hydrolysis is higher in energy.

Penicillin with 2 amide bonds

13. C is correct. An amide is an amine that is directly bonded to a carbonyl group. The carbonyl group accepts the lone pair of electrons on the nitrogen atom through resonance action.

Amides ($pK_a \approx 20$–25) are less electrophilic than esters, and primary and secondary amides have acidic N–H protons ($pK_a \approx 35$).

14. D is correct.

The hydrolysis of esters using basic conditions (e.g., sodium hydroxide) is not a catalytic reaction. It is a base-promoted reaction because the hydroxide is consumed in the reaction and is not regenerated.

On the contrary, acid-catalyzed hydrolysis reactions of esters regenerate the acid catalyst.

15. B is correct. Group 1 is a ketone; 2 is an amide, and 3 is an ester.

Ketones are more electrophilic functional groups than esters. Esters are more electrophilic than amides.

16. D is correct. Nitriles ($-C{\equiv}N$) have the prefix cyano and are similar to alkynes in that both functional groups contain triple bonds, but the nitrile possesses an *sp* hybridized nitrogen atom, giving rise to its alternate chemical reactivity ($pK_a = 25$).

Nitriles are more electron deficient than alkynes and are more susceptible to nucleophilic attack by molecules such as organolithium compounds and Grignard reagents.

Alkynes undergo addition reactions with strong electrophiles, such as bromine.

17. A is correct. Esters are similar in structure to carboxylic acids, but instead of having a hydroxyl group bonded to the carbonyl carbon atom, an alcohol derived group is present.

These groups are less electrophilic than ketones and aldehydes, and they have the same oxidation state as carboxylic acids.

Important esters in the body include triacylglycerides or triglycerides.

18. E is correct. Saponification is the name for the base-promoted hydrolysis of esters. This type of hydrolysis is typically applied to the formation of soap compounds.

For example, triacylglycerol is a lipid that can undergo saponification, which is the breakdown of fatty esters with bases, such as sodium hydroxide or potassium hydroxide.

Base hydrolysis (saponification) of an ester to form a carboxylate salt and an alcohol

19. B is correct.

The reactant benzoyl chloride is an acyl halide that forms a ketone when reacted with an equimolar quantity of a Grignard reagent. Excess Grignard reagent converts the ketone to tertiary alcohol.

Acyl halide + Grignard reagent → ketone + Grignard reagent → tertiary alcohol

Sample addition reactions of carbonyl compounds and excess Grignard:

> Formaldehyde + excess Grignard → primary alcohol
>
> Aldehyde + excess Grignard → secondary alcohol
>
> Ketone + excess Grignard → tertiary alcohol

20. A is correct. There are 4 alcohol functional groups present.

A cyclic ester is also present. A cyclic ester is known as a lactone.

Hemiacetal: alcohol and ether on the same carbon

Acetal: two ethers on the same carbon

21. A is correct. In the addition reaction between water and benzoyl chloride, water donates electrons (acting as a nucleophile) to the electrophilic carbonyl of benzoyl chloride.

The chlorine atom, which is not present in the product, acts as a leaving group during the subsequent elimination step whereby the carbonyl carbon reforms.

22. C is correct.

$+ SOCl_2 \rightarrow$ $+ NH_3 \rightarrow$

The first step in this reaction involves the substitution of the OH group in benzoic acid by the Cl group from thionyl chloride ($SOCl_2$).

The resulting compound is benzoyl chloride – a highly reactive acyl halide which undergoes nucleophilic substitution. Treating this molecule with NH_3 (ammonia) results in the substitution of the Cl group by ~NH_2 group to form an amide (benzamide).

A and B: benzoyl chloride is highly susceptible to nucleophilic substitution, so chlorine is not part of the final product if another nucleophile (NH_3) is present.

D: *p*-aminobenzaldehyde is a benzene ring with an NH_2 substituent *para*- to the aldehyde group which would have replaced the carboxylic acid. The carboxylic acid would not be reduced to the aldehyde. The condition for electrophilic aromatic substitution (EAS) requires an electrophile (e.g., Cl_2) and a Lewis acid (e.g., $FeCl_3$).

E: 3-chloro-4-aminobenzaldehyde is a benzene ring with an aldehyde replacing the carboxylic acid. The carboxylic acid would not be reduced to the aldehyde.

The molecule is named with chlorine in the *meta* position and an amine group at the *para* position.

23. D is correct.

The compound contains an aromatic ring called benzyl.

The amide functional group is denoted by:

where R is an alkyl chain (or H).

An ether functional group is denoted by R–O–R'

Additionally, the molecule contains an aromatic ring, phenol group (i.e., hydroxyl attached directly to a benzene ring) and an alkene (i.e., double bond as a *trans*-alkene).

24. A is correct.

Fischer esterification involves a carboxylic acid and alcohol, with an acid catalyst.

Ethyl propanoate

Esters have the general formula: R–COO–R'

The suffix for an ester is *–oate*. The prefix is the substituent attached to the oxygen adjacent to the carbonyl carbon, and the root is the substituent attached to the carbonyl oxygen.

Excess alcohol is used to drive the chemical equilibrium forward.

Fischer esterification mechanism

25. A is correct. The amide linkage is present between individual amino acids, and these bonds are commonly known as peptide bonds.

The amide bond is formed when the lone pair of electrons on the nitrogen of the amino group makes a nucleophilic attack on the carbonyl of the other amino acid. This process is classified as a condensation (via dehydration) and results in the loss of water as the peptide bond forms.

26. C is correct. The benzene ring (aromatic group) is bonded to the carbonyl of an amide functional group.

27. C is correct. Amides are carboxylic acid derivatives made up of amines, which are carboxylic acid components.

The hydrolysis of carboxylic acid derivatives always results in the formation of the corresponding carboxylic acid and heteroatom-containing component (e.g., an amine or alcohol).

28. A is correct. Consider the susceptibility of different compounds to nucleophilic attack. All of the molecules undergo nucleophilic attack, but the molecule that undergoes attack the easiest is propionyl bromide.

Out of all the carboxylic acid derivatives (acyl halides, anhydrides, esters, carboxylic acids and amides), acyl halides are the most reactive towards nucleophiles due to the electron withdrawing effects of oxygen and the stability of the halide anion as a leaving group.

B: benzyl bromide is susceptible to nucleophilic attack because of the electronegative substituents, but not to the same extent as propionyl bromide. Acid halides are more electrophilic than alkyl halides, aldehydes or ketones.

C: propanal is susceptible to nucleophilic attack since it has a carbonyl carbon, but no electronegative substituents as does propionyl bromide have.

D: butanoic acid has a carbonyl carbon that is slightly susceptible to nucleophilic attack because the double bonded oxygen has an electron-withdrawing effect. However, comparing butanoic acid and its functional derivative propionyl bromide, propionyl bromide has withdrawing effects from the oxygen and the bromide.

29. C is correct. Acyl halides and alcohols form esters.

This addition-elimination reaction begins with the nucleophilic attack of the hydroxyl group to the electrophilic carbonyl of the acid halide in an addition reaction.

This is followed by the elimination of chloride to generate the corresponding ester.

Pyridine is a common basic solvent used in organic chemistry:

HCl is generated as a byproduct in this reaction; therefore a base (e.g., pyridine) is needed

30. C is correct.

This reduction requires two equivalents of lithium aluminum hydride (i.e., powerful reducing agent).

The reactive intermediate involved after the first addition of hydride is a hemiacetal. This hemiacetal may reversibly open to form the aldehyde, and this aldehyde can be subsequently reduced to form the second primary alcohol.

Reduction:

   carboxylic acid / ester → aldehyde → primary alcohol

   ketone → secondary alcohol

Reduction of a carboxylic acid, ester requires LiAlH$_4$.

Reduction of an aldehyde or ketone can proceed with either LiAlH$_4$ or the milder reducing agent NaBH$_4$.

31. B is correct.

Treatment of the ester with potassium hydroxide and heat results in the nucleophilic attack of hydroxide to the carbonyl in an addition-elimination reaction.

The ring product exists as a negatively charged species (cyclohexanol as the alkoxide) because of the presence of a base (KOH), until the second step of the H$^+$ workup. After acidic workup, the alkoxide is protonated to form cyclohexanol.

32. B is correct. The longest continuing chain in the product is four carbon atoms long.

Therefore, the root name is *butan,* and the suffix is *~amide* because it is an amide (i.e., R–CONR$_2$) functional group.

For this example, the nitrogen contains a methyl group.

N-methylbutanamide

33. B is correct. As the acidity of a group increases, its basic properties decrease.

The carbonyl group of the amide withdraws electron density from the nitrogen atom inductively and through conjugation. This causes the N–H bond of the amide to be much less basic (pK_a of an amine ≈ 10 and pK_a of an amide ≈ 35).

34. A is correct. The reaction is the acid hydrolysis of an ester.

When esters are hydrolyzed, they yield carboxylic acids and alcohols.

From the hydrolysis of this ester, 2-butenoic acid and isobutanol are formed.

2-butenoic acid   isobutanol

B: CH$_3$CH(CH$_3$)$_2$ is an alkane, and neither type of compound can be obtained by hydrolyzing an ester.

C: HOOCCH$_2$CH(CH$_3$)2 may look like the carboxylic acid produced from the hydrolysis of the ester, but the carbonyl double bond is absent.

D: CH$_3$CH=CHCHO is an unsaturated aldehyde.

E: HOCH$_2$CH$_2$CH(CH$_3$)$_2$ is alcohol with an additional carbon in the chain.

35. B is correct.

Acid bromides have the best leaving group (i.e., most stable anion), and therefore are the most reactive.

Acyl halides (RCOCl or RCOBr) are so reactive that they are not normally found in nature due to the moisture in the atmosphere, which converts them to carboxylic acids.

The rate of reaction depends on factors such as: the leaving group, the steric environment, and the substituents bonded to the carbonyl carbon. The more stable the leaving group (as an anion), the faster is the reaction. Also, a more electrophilic carbonyl (i.e., induction from neighboring groups) undergoes nucleophile attack more rapidly.

Additionally, steric hindrance (i.e., bulky groups) at the reaction center leads to slower reaction rates.

36. B is correct.

The hydrolysis of an ester is the reverse process of condensation because water is introduced to the ester to produce a carboxylic acid and an alcohol.

A chemical equilibrium exists for the acid-catalyzed process, and the reaction is driven forward with the use of a large excess of water.

A chemical equilibrium does not exist for the base-promoted process, because the alcohol product is unable to add into the carboxylate to reform the ester.

Chapter 24 Explanations: Amines

1. B is correct.

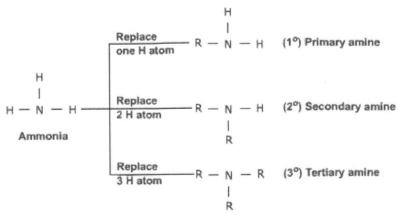

Primary amines are amines that have one alkyl group bonded to the nitrogen atom, secondary amines have two alkyl groups bonded to the nitrogen atom, and tertiary amines contain nitrogen atoms that are bonded to three alkyl groups.

2. C is correct.

Amines possess nitrogen atoms which have lone pairs that are more basic and nucleophilic than oxygen atoms and halogens such as fluorine. This is because the nitrogen atom is a less electronegative heteroatom; therefore, the nonbonding valence electrons of nitrogen have more energy and are more reactive.

3. A is correct.

Nitrogen bonded to an alkyl and two hydrogens is a primary amine.

Nitrogen bonded to an alkyl and three hydrogens results in a positive charge on the nitrogen use the original lone pair on the nitrogen to bond to an H^+. The positive charge on the molecule allows it to be associated with a molecule with an anion (e.g., Cl^-).

Quaternary ammonium salts can be formed from the *N*-alkylation of tertiary amines.

When tertiary amines are converted to ammonium salts, the inductive effects of the nitrogen atom are larger, and the magnitude of the carbon–nitrogen dipoles increases.

4. E is correct.

Arenediazonium salts, which are synthesized from primary aromatic amines, are compounds with an N_2^+ group attached to the aromatic ring. They are useful for synthesizing a wide variety of compounds because they can easily undergo replacement reactions in which molecular nitrogen is released, and a nucleophilic substituent attaches to the aromatic ring in its place.

For example, in the presence of cuprous halides, diazonium salts release molecular nitrogen and form halogen-substituted arenes – the Sandmeyer reaction.

Similarly, in the presence of cuprous cyanide, nitrogen is released and replaced by the cyanide ion, thus forming aromatic nitriles.

In the same way, in cold aqueous solutions, the hydroxyl group replaces the nitrogen to form phenol.

Therefore, compounds I, II, and III can all be obtained by the replacement of nitrogen in arenediazonium salts.

5. B is correct.

Ethylamine is the product since nitrile reduction adds carbon to the alkyl chain.

Cyanide is nucleophilic and can add to methyl bromide, which results in the expulsion of the bromide leaving group. The product of this reaction is cyanomethane.

The nitrile group can be reduced by lithium aluminum hydride ($LiAlH_4$ or LAH) or hydrogenation to form ethylamine.

6. D is correct.

Primary amines have one alkyl group attached to the nitrogen atom; secondary amines have two alkyl groups attached to the nitrogen atom; tertiary amines have three alkyl groups attached to the nitrogen atom.

7. B is correct.

The polar amino group of *p*-toluidine makes it slightly soluble in water:

p-toluidine is soluble in acidic water due to the formation of ammonium salts.

p-toluidine

8. A is correct.

Amines are compounds that are derivatives of ammonia. These compounds contain carbon-nitrogen single bonds and are known to be sufficient bases for strong acids.

Carbonyl-containing compounds are: aldehyde, ketone, acid chloride, anhydride, carboxylic acid, ester, and amide.

9. A is correct.

Although primary and secondary amines can both accept and donate hydrogen bonds, the hydrogen bonding forces are greater for primary amines, because these molecules possess two N–H bonds.

Quaternary ammonium salts cannot form hydrogen bonds because the N has four bonds and no lone pairs of electrons remain on the nitrogen.

10. E is correct. Oxygen and nitrogen atoms can act as proton acceptors if they are not conjugated with electron withdrawing groups.

The amine is the most basic and nucleophilic functional group.

11. B is correct.

Amines are compounds that contain basic nitrogen atoms that can act as nucleophiles as long as steric interactions don't prevent them from doing so.

The nitrogen lone pairs of amides are tied up in conjugation with the carbonyl group and are therefore not basic or nucleophilic.

12. A is correct.

When amines are added to water at neutral pH, the solution becomes basic, and hydroxide ions ($^-$OH) are produced.

Alternatively, carboxylic acids, when added to water at neutral pH generate hydronium ions (H_3O^+).

13. A is correct.

Boiling points of compounds are determined by two general factors: molecular weight and intermolecular interactions. The higher the molecular weight, the harder it is to "push" it into the gas phase, and hence the higher the boiling point.

Similarly, the stronger the intermolecular interactions, the more energy is required to disrupt them and separate the molecules in the gas phase, hence the higher the boiling point.

Dimethylamine (below) has one N–H bond (donor) and one lone pair on the nitrogen (acceptor):

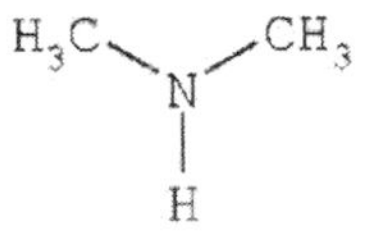

$$H_3C \diagdown \underset{\underset{H}{|}}{N} \diagup CH_3$$

The other answer choices can also accept and donate hydrogen bonds, which increases their boiling points.

E: ethanolamine has the following structure:

$$HO \diagup \diagdown \diagup NH_2$$

Ethanolamine can participate in hydrogen bonding: three with the hydroxyl (two acceptors and one donor) and three with the amino (two donors and one acceptor). Hydrogen bonding increasing the boiling point of molecules.

14. C is correct.

Tertiary amines possess no N–H bonds, while secondary amines have one N–H bond, and primary amines contain two N–H bonds.

15. E is correct.

The nitrogen atom of amines is basic because it possesses a lone pair of electrons that add to the acidic protons of acids, resulting in its protonation.

H
|
H — N⊕ — H
|
H

Ammonium cation

The conjugate acid of amines is the ammonium cation, and the nitrogen atom is covalently bonded to four other atoms. Because the nitrogen atom is bonded to four other atoms, it develops a positive formal charge.

Although the nitrogen atom has a formal charge, this positive charge character is distributed over the less electronegative substituent groups.

16. A is correct.

Carbonyl groups are indicative of aldehydes, ketones, carboxylic acid or the four carboxylic acid derivatives (i.e., acyl halide, anhydride, ester, and amide).

Amines do not contain carbonyl groups.

17. B is correct.

A quaternary ammonium salt has no lone pairs of electrons on the nitrogen atom and therefore cannot function as a nucleophile.

1°, 2° or 3° amines can attack alkyl halides by donating their lone pairs of valence electrons.

Ammonium salts have no available valence electrons and can act as acids (proton donors), but not a nucleophile.

18. D is correct.

Ammonia is a basic compound with a low boiling point and exists as a gas at room temperature.

It is basic, colorless, has a pungent smell and can be toxic if ingested.

19. C is correct.

Amine salts are soluble in water because the nitrogen has a positive charge and can form ion–dipole interactions with water.

A: nitrogen donates its lone pair of electrons when forming a salt; positive charge forms on the nitrogen, not a negative charge.

B: the amine salt has a higher molecular weight than the amine, but it is not the reason why the amine salt is more soluble.

D: some amines are soluble in water. Amines follow a similar solubility pattern to carboxylic acids: up to 6 carbons, they are relatively soluble.

20. C is correct.

The most notable intermolecular force for water is hydrogen bonding.

$CH_3–CH_2–NH_2$ interact with water through hydrogen bonding. Hydrogens, bonded directly to F, O or N, participate in hydrogen bonds. The hydrogen is partial positive (i.e., delta plus or $\partial+$) due to the bond to these electronegative atoms. The lone pair of electrons on the F, O or N interacts with the $\partial+$ hydrogen to form a hydrogen bond.

$CH_3–CH_2–NH_2$ is ethylamine. Amines (i.e., nitrogen) can form hydrogen bonds, but thiols (i.e., sulfur) cannot.

21. D is correct.

Salts form as solids with tightly compact repeating unit structures, thus requiring more heat to boil compared with other substances, typically liquids.

22. A is correct.

Amines are typically bases due to the lone pair of electrons on the nitrogen.

The name suggests that three methyl groups are bonded to the central nitrogen atom.

23. C is correct.

Amine salts are compounds containing a positively charged, tetravalent nitrogen atom and an anionic counter ion.

1°, 2° and 3° amines are neutral species.

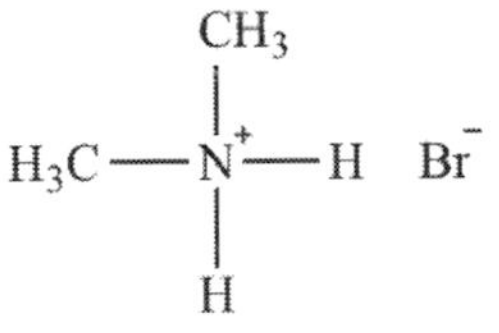

dimethylammonium bromide

A: sulfanilamide (below)

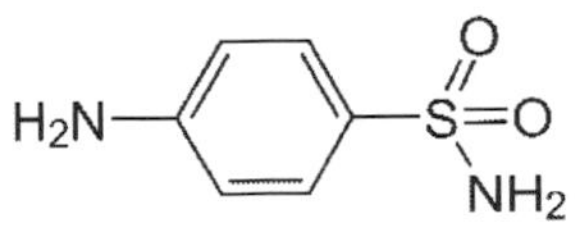

B: thioacetamide (below)

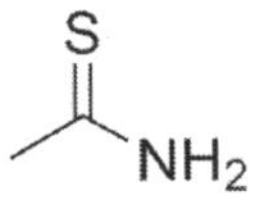

D: histamine (below)

E: pyridoxine (below)

24. A is correct.

Amines tend to be basic and also nucleophilic if they are not sterically bulky.

The attachment of acyl groups to amines causes the nitrogen lone pair to delocalize into the carbonyl π^* orbital, thus greatly reducing the nitrogen's nucleophilic and basic properties.

The amide ($RCONR_2$) group tends to react with electrophiles on the carbonyl oxygen atom because a more stable cationic intermediate is generated.

25. C is correct.

The conjugate base of an acid is essentially the deprotonated form. The most acidic protons of the molecule are the N–H protons, with a pK_a in the mid-30s.

26. B is correct.

Amines are one of several functional groups that contain nitrogen atoms.

The other answer choices only contain carbon, hydrogen, or oxygen atoms.

27. D is correct.

Ammonia groups enhance the water solubility of compounds because of the hydrogen bonding and molecular dipoles that amines possess.

The greater the number of N–H bonds (i.e., primary > secondary > tertiary > quaternary) an amine possesses, the more hydrogen bonds the amine can form and the more soluble it is.

Furthermore, acid can be added to aqueous solutions of amines to enhance the solubility of the molecule.

28. C is correct.

The molecule has a basic site on the nitrogen atom.

The lone pair of electrons on the nitrogen atom can be protonated to form an ammonium cation.

29. A is correct.

Hydrogen bonding increases the boiling point of a molecule.

Amines that have N–H bonds typically have higher boiling points compared to tertiary amines.

Tertiary amines can only accept a hydrogen bond, while primary and secondary amines can donate and accept hydrogen bonds.

30. B is correct.

The most basic site in the molecule is the *N*-methyl tertiary amine because the lone pair of this nitrogen atom is not in conjugation with an electron-withdrawing group or part of an aromatic ring.

31. C is correct.

Amines are Brønsted-Lowry and Lewis bases because the lone pair of electrons on nitrogen can bind to a proton.

It is favorable for the amine to abstract a proton from the acid.

Electron-donating groups attached to the nitrogen in the amine make the amine more basic because by donating electron density, they stabilize the positive ion formed.

Therefore, electron-donating groups (alkyl chains via hyperconjugation) destabilize the lone pair of electrons on the amine and make it more reactive.

Conversely, substituents (e.g., electronegative atoms) are electron-withdrawing, and the amine is less basic.

Alkyl groups, compared to hydrogen atoms, are electron-donating, and therefore basicity decreases in the order trimethylamine > methylamine > ammonia in the gas phase.

The gas phase is specified because, in aqueous solutions, hydrogen bonding also plays a role in stabilizing the salt, and thus may result in a different order.

In addition reactions, electronegative atoms, such as the fluorine of $(CF_3)_3N$, strongly reduce the basicity of the amine because of the inductive electron-withdrawing effect of the electronegative atom.

In this example, it is unfavorable for the nitrogen to acquire a positive charge in forming a salt.

32. A is correct.

Amines can be protonated with Brønsted acids to produce ammonium salts.

Amides can be formed from primary and secondary amines by acylation of the nitrogen of primary and secondary amines.

33. E is correct.

Hydrogens, bonded directly to F, O or N, participate in hydrogen bonds.

The hydrogen is partial positive (i.e., delta plus or $\partial+$) due to the bond to these electronegative atoms.

The lone pair of electrons on the F, O or N interacts with the $\partial+$ hydrogen to form a hydrogen bond.

None of the other molecules can form hydrogen bonds because hydrogen is not attached directly to F, O or N.

34. B is correct.

Exposing bulky amines to an acid such as HCl allows it to become more soluble in water.

The charged ammonium cation allows for stronger dipole interactions with water compared to the neutral amine form.

35. E is correct.

A tertiary amine (R_3N) has three alkyl groups bonded to the nitrogen atom.

A secondary amine (R_2NH) has two alkyl groups bonded to the nitrogen atom.

A primary amine (RNH_2) has one alkyl group bonded to the nitrogen atom.

A, C, and D: are primary amines.

B: is a secondary amine.

36. A is correct.

Structure 1: cyclic secondary enamine

Structure 2: secondary amine

Structure 3: cyclic quaternary amine

The secondary amine (2) contains one N–H bond, and therefore, this amine can form hydrogen bonds.

The cyclic amine (3) and the enamine (1) do not contain N–H bonds, so their boiling points are lower.

Aside from hydrogen bonding considerations, molecules with formal charges (molecule 3) interact via electrostatic forces, which increase their boiling point.

Please, leave your Customer Review on Amazon

Chapter 25 Explanations: Amino Acids, Peptides, Proteins

1. A is correct. In this reaction, an amino acid is prepared from a carboxylic acid.

The first step in this reaction is the conversion of the carboxylic acid to the alphabromo acid bromide intermediate. This intermediate is then hydrolyzed in water to regenerate the carboxylic acid. The alpha bromide is displaced upon exposure to ammonia and heat to form alanine.

Both enantiomers of the compound are expected for this reaction.

2. D is correct. Threonine is an amino acid that contains secondary alcohol as part of the side chain.

The alcohol has a permanent dipole and is capable of hydrogen bonding.

Therefore, the type of intermolecular interactions expected is dipole-dipole interactions (hydrogen bonding is a subset of dipole-dipole interactions).

3. E is correct.

Glycine is an achiral molecule that lacks a substituent at the alpha position. The unsubstituted alpha position is methylene, and a methylene group has a symmetrical center (i.e., bonded to two hydrogens).

4. E is correct. Tyrosine contains a phenol *R* group, phenylalanine has a phenyl group, tryptophan has an indole group, and histidine has an imidazole group.

5. A is correct. The primary structure of a protein is the linear sequence of amino acids.

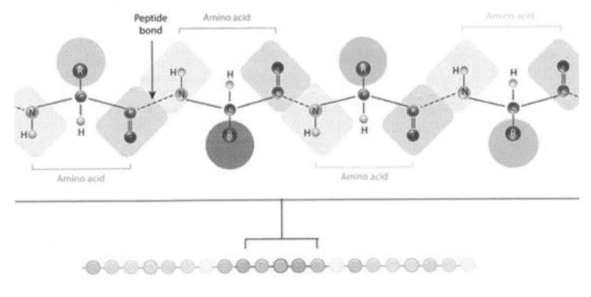

6. D is correct. Hydrophilic amino acids are found near the external regions of proteins and line the walls of protein ion channels because these molecules form more favorable interactions with the aqueous environment than hydrophilic amino acids.

7. C is correct. Nonpolar amino acids are amino acids that have side chains composed of hydrogen and carbon atoms. The incorporation of electronegative heteroatoms, such as oxygen and nitrogen atoms, can make the side groups polar, acidic or basic.

8. B is correct. All of the molecules in the body are divided into four categories. These biomolecular categories are: carbohydrates, lipids, nucleic acids and proteins.

9. A is correct.

Amino acids are linked together in peptides by amide bonds. The peptide forms in a condensation reaction via dehydration (loss of water) when the lone pair on the nitrogen of an amino group of one amino acid makes a nucleophilic attack on the carbonyl carbon of another.

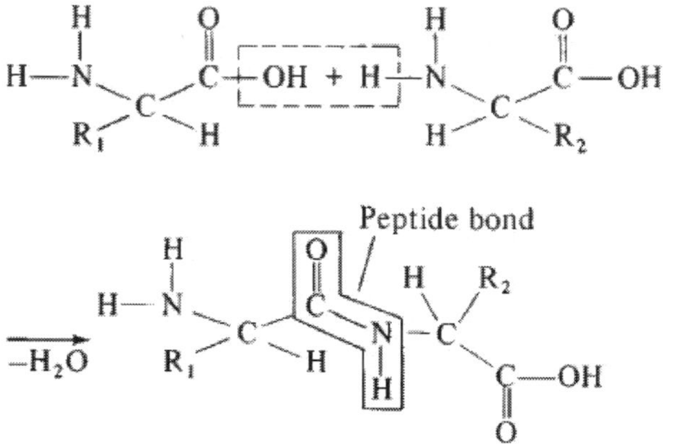

Peptide bond formation from the condensation reaction of 2 amino acids

10. C is correct.

Valine is the only amino acid listed with a hydrophobic (carbon and hydrogen only) side chain.

Group	Characteristics	Name	Example (-Rx)
non-polar	hydrophobic	Ala, Val, Leu, Ile, Pro, Phe Trp, Met	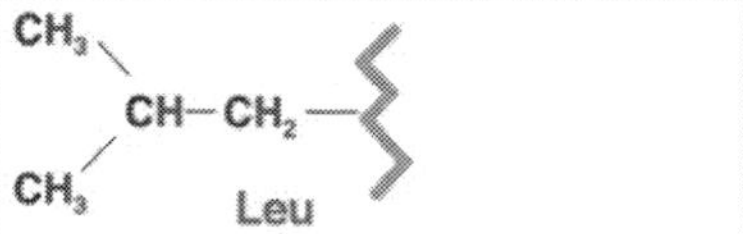 Leu
polar	hydrophilic (non-charged)	Gly, Ser, Thr, Cys, Tyr, Asn Gln	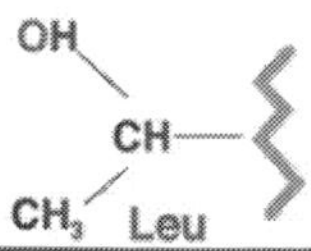 Leu
acidic	negatively charged	Asp, Glu	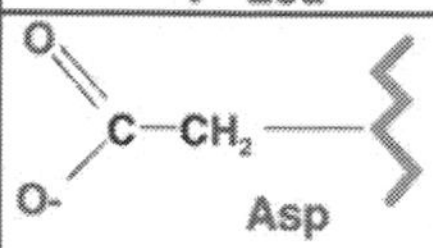 Asp
basic	positively charged	Lys, Arg, His	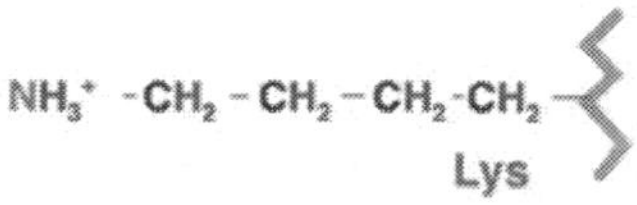 Lys

11. C is correct.

Amino acid – glycine

Amino acid with the amino group, carboxyl group and α-carbon attached to the side chain (R group)

Glycine has no alkyl substituent groups at the *alpha* position (R = hydrogen) and is the smallest known amino acid.

12. D is correct.

The isoelectric point of an amino acid is determined by calculating the average of the pK_a values of the carboxylic acid and the ammonium cation.

When more than one ionizable group is present, the two pK_a that are numerically closer are used for the calculation.

For instance, for acidic amino acids, the isoelectric point can be calculated by averaging the two lower pK_a values.

For basic amino acids, the two highest pK_a values are averaged to determine the isoelectric point.

Amino acid	α-CO₂H pKₐ¹	α-NH₃ pKₐ²	Side chain pKₐ³	pI
Arginine	2.1	9.0	12.5	10.8
Aspartic Acid	2.1	9.8	3.9	3.0
Cysteine	1.7	10.4	8.3	5.0
Glutamic Acid	2.2	9.7	4.3	3.2
Histidine	1.8	9.2	6.0	7.6
Lysine	2.2	9.0	10.5	9.8
Tyrosine	2.2	9.1	10.1	5.7

pK_a values for the 7 amino acids with ionizable side chains

13. A is correct.

The amine N–H bond is acidic because the nitrogen atom is in conjugation with the carbonyl group.

However, the N–H bond of saccharine is much more acidic because the functional group overall is an amide and a sulfonamide.

The sulfone group (~SO_2) also acts as an electron-withdrawing group to stabilize the negative charge that is generated from deprotonation.

The pK_a of saccharin is 1.6.

14. C is correct.

2,4-dinitrofluorobenzene is used to identify the *N*-terminus of a peptide. It reacts with the *N*-terminal amino acid and remains attached even after complete acid hydrolysis, which allows for isolation of the *N*-terminal amino acid from the rest of the polypeptide.

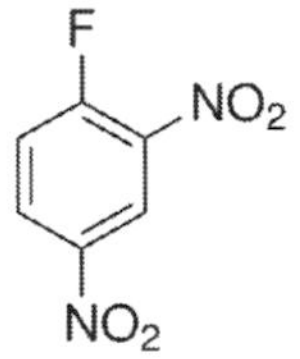

In 1945, Frederick Sanger used 2,4-dinitrofluorobenzene for determining the N-terminal amino acid in polypeptide chains. Dinitrofluorobenzene reacts with the amine group in amino acids to produce dinitrophenyl-amino acids.

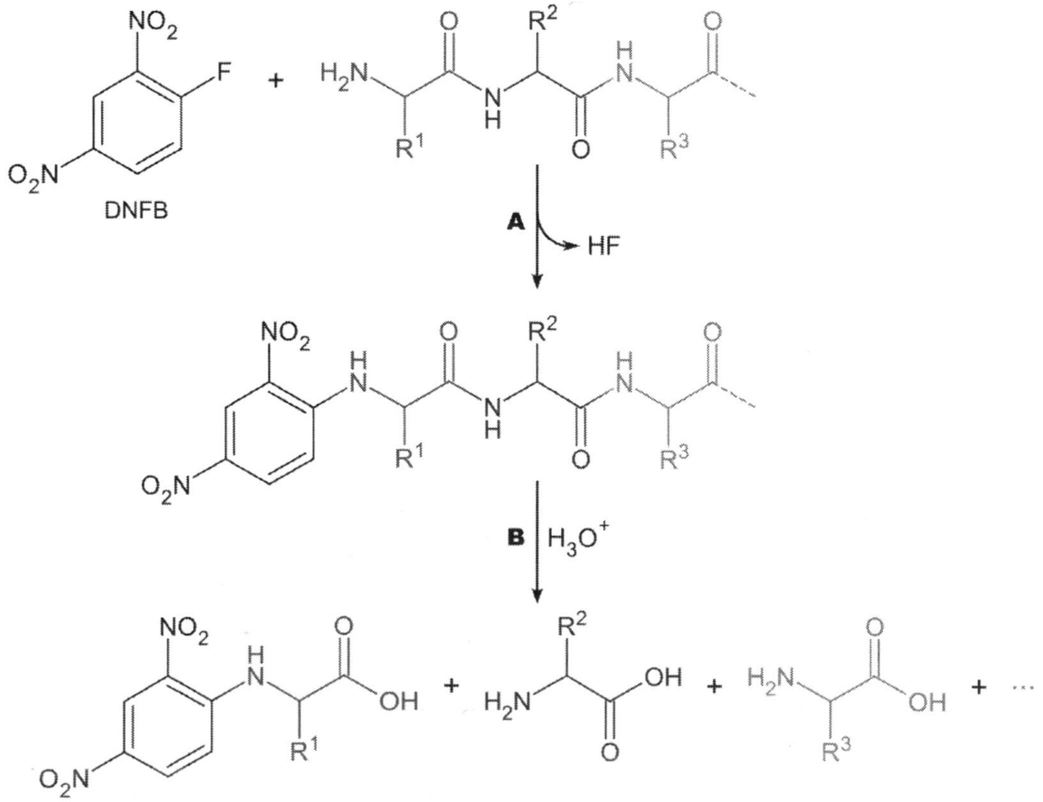

15. E is correct.

Hormones are substances secreted by a gland and released into the blood to affect a target tissue/organ.

Insulin is a hormone composed of amino acids (i.e., peptide hormones) and therefore is a protein molecule. Insulin is composed of two peptide chains (A chain and B chain). The chains are linked together by two disulfide bonds, and an additional disulfide is formed within the A chain. In most species, the A chain consists of 21 amino acids and the B chain – of 30 amino acids.

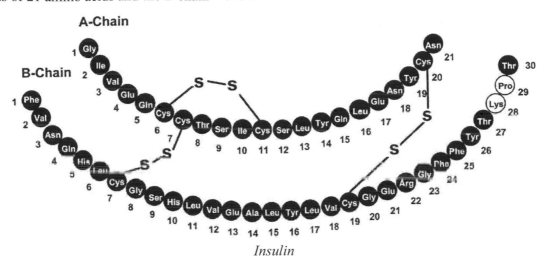

Insulin

Hormones can be lipid molecules, such as steroid derivatives (e.g., testosterone, progesterone, estrogen).

16. B is correct.

The alpha helix structure is one of the two common types of secondary protein structure. The alpha helix is held together by hydrogen bonds between every N–H (amino group) and the oxygen of the C=O (carbonyl) in the next turn of the helix; four amino acids along the chain.

The typical alpha helix is about 11 amino acids long.

The other type of secondary structure is the beta pleated sheet.

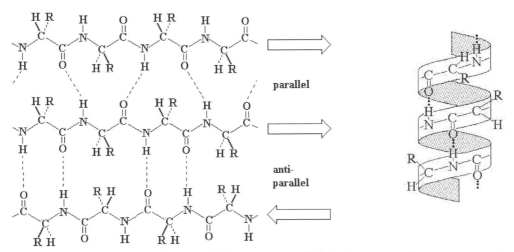

Beta pleated sheets are either parallel or anti-parallel (reference to the amino terminus).

17. C is correct.

A pH of 8 indicates a basic solution whereby the carboxylic acid is deprotonated, and the amino group remains protonated (until the pH reaches the pK_a of the amine at ≈ 9.8).

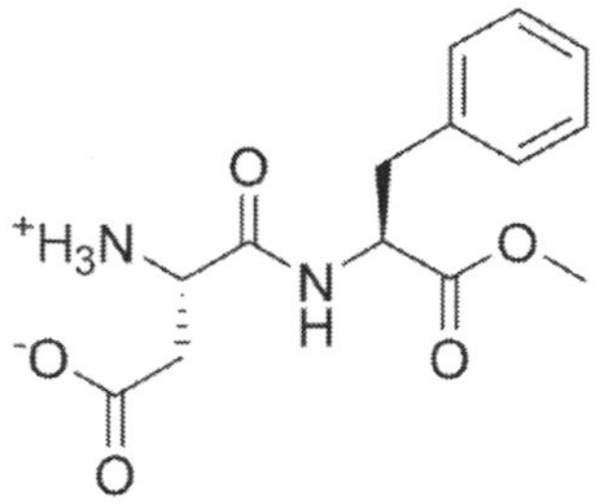

Zwitterion: carboxyl is deprotonated (negative), and the amino is protonated (positive)

18. D is correct.

Amino acids with hydrophobic side chains are not typically found near the external regions of proteins, but rather in the interior regions.

Hydrophobic side group containing amino acids are located along the protein interfaces with lipid layers, such as the external amino acids of proteins embedded in lipid membranes.

19. B is correct.

The isoelectric point is the pH at which the net charge of the amino acid is 0.

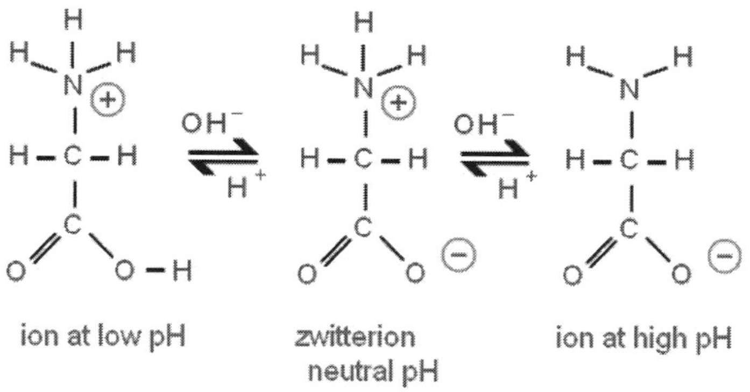

ion at low pH   zwitterion   ion at high pH
                       neutral pH

Aspartic acid is an amino acid that contains an additional carboxylic acid in the side chain.

For this amino acid to maintain an overall neutral polarity, the carboxylic acid must maintain its protonated form, which requires the solution to be acidic.

Therefore, the isoelectric point of aspartic acid is the lowest for the given list of amino acids.

20. D is correct.

In glutamate metabolism, the amino group of glutamic acid is removed through an oxidative deamination reaction with glutamate dehydrogenase.

Ammonia is released during this process and forms urea to be excreted as urine from the body.

21. C is correct.

The primary structure of a protein is the amino acid sequence, which is formed by covalent peptide linkages.

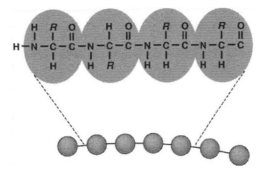

The amino acids (circles) are joined by covalent peptide bonds (lines)

A: only proteins containing more than one peptide subunit have a quaternary structure.

B: proteins are denatured by heating and they lose their conformation above 35-40 °C, not retain it.

D: many proteins contain more than one peptide chain (i.e., have quaternary structure).

22. C is correct.

The reaction mechanism by which 2,4-dinitrofluorobenzene reacts with an amine is known as nucleophilic aromatic substitution.

The nitro groups are electron withdrawing, and therefore, the benzene ring is electrophilic.

23. B is correct.

Amino acids are the building blocks of proteins.

Humans need 20 amino acids, some are made by the body (i.e., nonessential), and others must be obtained from the diet (i.e., essential).

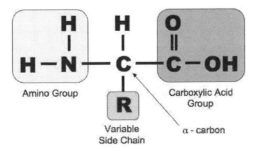

Amino acids contain an amine group, a carboxylic acid, an α-carbon and an R group.

The following table is shown not for memorization but identification of characteristics (e.g., polar, nonpolar) for the side chains.

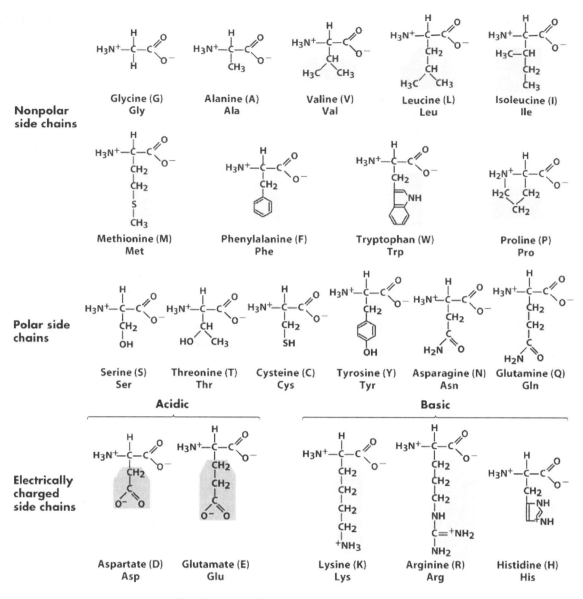

Nonpolar side chains

Glycine (G) Gly   Alanine (A) Ala   Valine (V) Val   Leucine (L) Leu   Isoleucine (I) Ile

Methionine (M) Met   Phenylalanine (F) Phe   Tryptophan (W) Trp   Proline (P) Pro

Polar side chains

Serine (S) Ser   Threonine (T) Thr   Cysteine (C) Cys   Tyrosine (Y) Tyr   Asparagine (N) Asn   Glutamine (Q) Gln

Acidic   **Basic**

Electrically charged side chains

Aspartate (D) Asp   Glutamate (E) Glu   Lysine (K) Lys   Arginine (R) Arg   Histidine (H) His

The 20 naturally occurring amino acids.

24. A is correct. Human hair can be curly without the application of reducing agents due to the cross-linking positions of the disulfide bonds.

$$2 \; \text{Cysteine} \; \underset{[H]}{\overset{[O]}{\rightleftharpoons}} \; \text{Cystine}$$

Cysteine   Cystine

The notation [O] represents oxidation (i.e., from reducing agent such as beta-mercaptoethanol), while [H] represents reduction (i.e., from an oxidation agent such as O_3).

The reducing agents cleave the disulfide bond linkages between peptide strands, enabling the hair to be restructured.

25. B is correct. Peptide bonds link the primary sequence of amino acids in a protein. These bonds form between individual amino acids that then form a peptide chain.

Peptide bonds are never altered when a polypeptide bends or folds to form a secondary structure. Also, when the polypeptide folds into a three-dimensional shape (the tertiary structure of a protein), new peptide bonds do not form.

A: interactions between charged groups (electrostatic interactions) can arise, especially in the tertiary structure of a protein.

C: hydrogen bonds are involved in both the secondary and tertiary structure of a protein. In the secondary structure, the polypeptide chain folds to allow the carbonyl oxygen and amine hydrogen to lie nearby. As a result, hydrogen bonding occurs to form sheets, helices, or turns. Likewise, hydrogen bonding may serve to stabilize the tertiary structure of a protein.

D: hydrophobic interactions also play an important role in the tertiary structure of a protein. For example, in an aqueous environment, the hydrophobic side chains of the amino acids may interact to arrange themselves towards the inside of the protein.

26. C is correct. Amino acids are the basic building blocks for proteins.

Two amino acids (dimer) with peptide bonds indicated by arrows

The peptide bond is rigid due to the resonance hybrids involving the lone pair of electrons on nitrogen forming a double bond to the carbonyl carbon (and oxygen develops a negative formal charge).

27. D is correct.

The isoelectric point is a pH when the amino and carboxyl end of the protein (and/or the side chains) results in a net neutral charge on overall the protein. Only charged species (i.e., anion and cations) migrate under the influence of an electric field in gel electrophoresis.

Ions are molecules that possess a certain charge, either positive (cation) or negative (anion).

The zwitterion ion (containing both a positive and negative region within the same molecule) form is the dominant form at the isoelectric point, and it possesses two charges. However, the charges are opposite and cancel one another, forming an overall electrically neutral compound.

Neutral proteins do not migrate within the electric field during gel electrophoresis.

28. C is correct.

Protonation or deprotonation of an amino acid residue change its ionization state: it may either become positively or negatively charged or neutral. The process may lead to changes in the interactions among amino acid side chains, as some ionic bonds may be compromised from the lack of opposite charge pairing.

Certain hydrogen bonding interactions may also be modulated if Lewis bases are protonated with Brønsted acids, impairing their ability to accept hydrogen bonds from nearby amino acid residues.

29. B is correct.

Amino acids contain an amino (~NH$_2$) and a carboxylic acid (~COOH) functional groups.

The α carbon is between the amino and carboxyl groups and is attached to the R (sidechain) group.

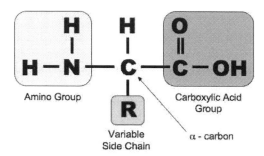

30. B is correct.

The π electron clouds of aromatic rings are not very basic because the aromatic molecule is stable.

Lone pairs on carbonyl oxygen (sp^2 hybridized) are more basic than π electrons but not as basic as the lone pair on nitrogen (sp^3 hybridized).

The nitrogen on an amine is more basic than the nitrogen on the amide because the electrons on the amide participate in resonance.

31. E is correct.

The amino acid *valine*:

Valine has an R group (i.e., side chain) of isopropyl attached to the α carbon of the amino acid backbone.

The first step in the reaction sequence below is the Hell-Volhard-Zelinsky reaction (shown below).

The mechanism for the Hell-Volhard-Zelinsky reaction

The phosphorus tribromide (PBr₃) is electrophilic and can be attacked by the carboxylic acid to generate the acid bromide.

The enol tautomer of this acid bromide can brominate at the alpha position to give the α-bromo acid bromide. The acid bromide can be subjected to water to hydrolyze the group to the carboxylic acid.

Finally, in the presence of excess ammonia, the alpha bromide can be displaced to produce the valine amino acid product.

32. A is correct. The primary structure of proteins consists of the linear sequence of amino acids (i.e., residues) in the polypeptide chain.

The secondary structure of proteins involves the regularly occurring motifs (alpha helix and beta pleated sheets) that are derived from intramolecular localized (within ten amino acids) hydrogen and disulfide bonding.

The tertiary structure involves interactions of amino acid R groups and interactions across different motifs (alpha helix, beta pleated sheets, and loop structures).

The quaternary structure of proteins involves two or more polypeptide chains. The quaternary structure is maintained between the different polypeptide chains (e.g., 4 chains of 2 α and 2 β in hemoglobin) by hydrophobic interactions and by disulfide bridges between cysteines.

Two cysteine residues form a cystine covalent bond.

33. A is correct.

This covalent bond is a disulfide linkage that contributes to the protein's tertiary (3°) and quaternary (4°) structure (for multiple polypeptide chains).

Disulfide linkage of S–S covalent bond between two cysteine residues

34. A is correct.

Peptide bonds are amide bonds that link individual amino acid molecules together.

Two amino acids with the peptide bond indicated by the arrow.

The peptide bond involves 4 atoms: C=O, N and H. The hydrogen must be antiperiplanar (180°) relative to the carbonyl oxygen to permit the lone pair on the nitrogen to participate in a resonance structure and confer rigidity on the peptide bond.

Resonance structure of peptide bond involving the lone pair of electrons on nitrogen.

The number of bonds between each amino acid (i.e., or any monomers) equals n – 1 (where n is the number of monomers).

Therefore, 10 – 1 = 9 peptide bonds.

35. D is correct. The primary structure of proteins refers to the linear sequence of amino acids.

Hydrogen bonding is important for the secondary (alpha helix and beta-pleated sheet) and for tertiary (i.e., overall 3-dimensional shape) structure of proteins.

The hydrophobic interactions involved in tertiary and quaternary (i.e., two or more polypeptide chains) structure arise from the hydrophobic side chains of the amino acid residues.

36. E is correct.

The isoelectric point of an amino acid deals with the average pK_a of the acidic functional groups present in the molecule, and this includes the ammonium and carboxylic acid functional groups as well.

The isoelectric point is a characteristic of the entire protein molecule (not just the side chain) where the net charge is zero.

37. E is correct.

All the described causes of protein denaturation involve inducing changes in the intermolecular forces between the side chains of the residues or amino and carboxylic acid groups.

This denaturation is accomplished through breaking weak bonds or by changing the polarity or charge character of key stabilizing groups.

38. D is correct.

None of the amino acids in the peptide chain contain R groups that have charges in them.

Therefore, the only charges that should exist in the molecule should be the ammonium cation ($^+NH_4$) and the carboxylate anion (COO^-).

39. C is correct. The general structure of an amino acid (where R is the side chain):

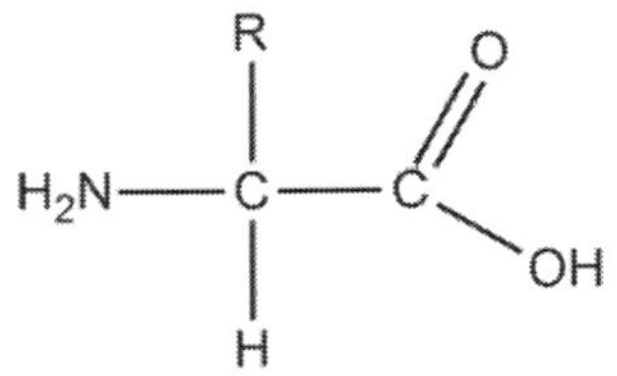

Amino acid – by convention, the amino terminus is drawn on the left.

The three amino acids with basic side chains are lysine (K), arginine (R) and histidine (H).

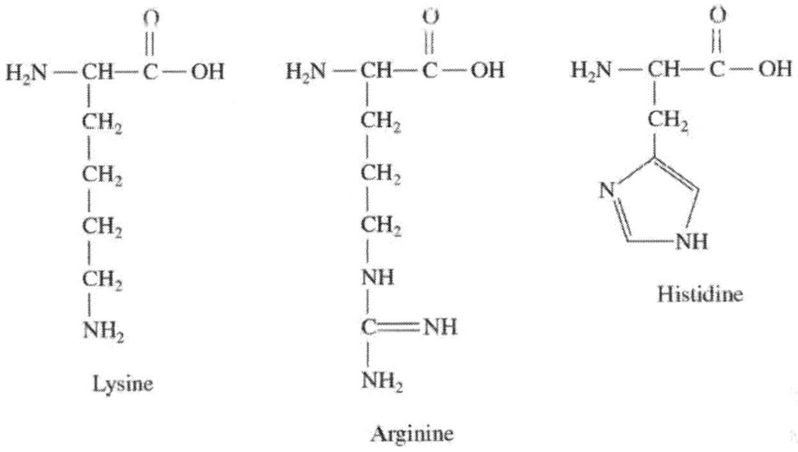

The side chain of threonine contains secondary alcohol.

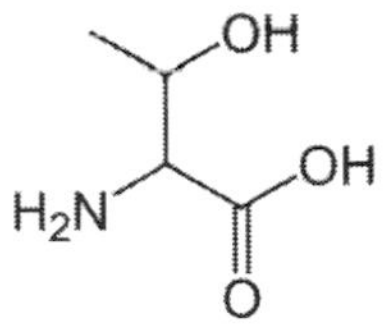

Threonine

Alcohols can be protonated upon exposure to strong acids but are not basic at neutral pH.

40. A is correct.

A zwitterion is a neutral molecule with both a positive and negative charge.

The isoelectric point of an amino acid is the average of the pK_a of the ammonium group and the carboxylic acid.

The isoelectric point is the pH where the carboxylate ion and ammonium cation are dominant in solution.

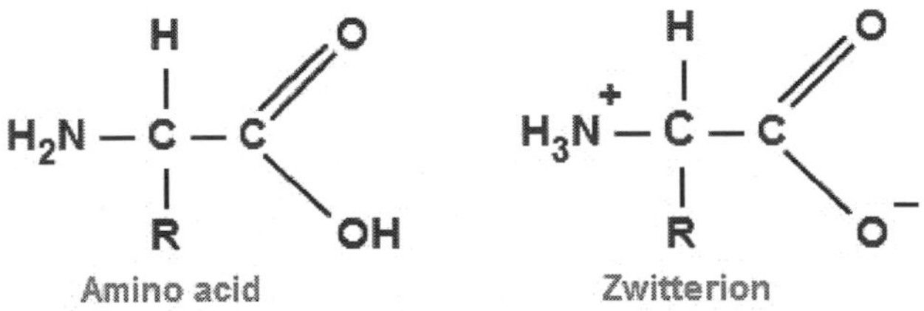

41. D is correct.

Collagen is a protein that supports hair, nails, and skin.

Collagen is composed of a triple helix, and the most abundant amino acids in collagen include glycine, proline, alanine and glutamic acid.

Much of the excess protein that is consumed in an animal's diet is used to synthesize collagen.

42. B is correct.

Secondary structure for proteins involves localized bonding.

The most important intermolecular interaction is hydrogen bonding, which is responsible for maintaining both the alpha helix and beta pleated (parallel and antiparallel) sheet structures.

Alpha helix structure with hydrogen bonding shown as dotted lines

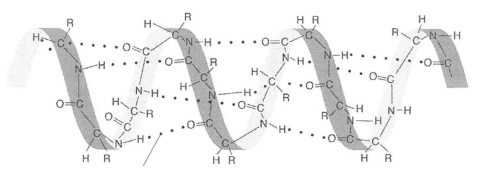

Beta pleated sheets (parallel and antiparallel) with hydrogen bonding shown

43. C is correct.

The standard conditions for breaking the covalent bonds during peptide hydrolysis are concentrated HCl and several hours of reflux.

The reaction time depends on partial or complete hydrolysis of the peptide.

44. B is correct.

Essential amino acids are those that are obtained from the diet.

Nonessential amino acids can be synthesized by the body and do not need to be consumed.

Semi-essential (conditionally essential) amino acids can be synthesized within the body under special physiological conditions (e.g., in premature infants and under severe catabolic distress).

The nine essential amino acids for humans are histidine, isoleucine, leucine, lysine, methionine, phenylalanine, threonine, tryptophan, and valine.

The six conditionally essential amino acids for humans are arginine, cysteine, glycine, glutamine, proline, and tyrosine. The five nonessential amino acids for humans are alanine, aspartic acid, asparagine, glutamic acid, and serine.

45. B is correct.

A polypeptide chain can undergo short range bending and folding to form β sheets or α helices.

These structures arise as the peptide bonds can assume a partial double bond character and so adopt different conformations.

The arrangement of groups around the relatively rigid amide bond can cause *R* groups to alternate from side to side and hence interact with one another.

Also, the carbonyl oxygen in one region of the polypeptide chain could become hydrogen bonded to the amide hydrogen in another region of the polypeptide chain. This interaction often results in the formation of a beta-pleated sheet or an alpha helix.

Localized bending and folding of a polypeptide do not constitute a protein's primary structure.

A: primary structure of a protein is the amino acid sequence; individual amino acids are linked through peptide (i.e., amide) linkages.

C: tertiary structure of a protein is the 3-D shape that arises by further folding of the polypeptide chain. Usually, these nonrandom folds give the protein a particular conformation and associated function.

D: quaternary structure is the spatial arrangement between two or more associated polypeptide chains (often linked by disulfide bridges between cysteine residues).

E: zymogen (proenzyme) structure refers to an inactive enzyme that requires modification (i.e., hydrolysis to reveal the active site or change in configuration) to become an active enzyme.

46. B is correct.

Proteins are biological macromolecules composed of amino acids that are bonded to each other with peptide (amide) bonds.

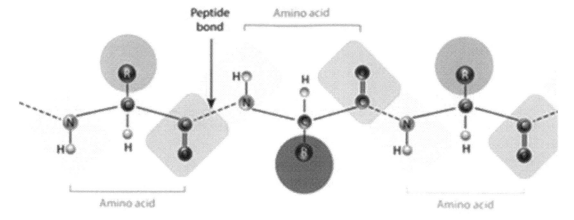

Three amino acids residues of nascent (i.e., growing) polypeptide

47. C is correct.

Sulfur-sulfur bonds are disulfide bonds. The bonds are formed from the dimerization of two cysteine residues.

Cysteine is the only molecule among the common amino acids that possess a thiol (or SH) group.

48. E is correct.

The amino group of all the other common amino acids contains primary amine functional groups.

Proline contains a five-membered ring as part of its structure.

Chapter 26 Explanations: Lipids

1. D is correct.

CH₂——OR

CH——OR'

CH₂——O——P——OR"

Glycerophospholipid

The ceramide lipid shown is a derivative of the triglyceride molecule. It is composed of glycerol, two fatty acid groups, and a phosphate group. The purpose of the phosphate group is to increase the polarity of the molecule so it can be utilized as a part of cell membranes.

Sphingolipids (or glycosylceramides) are a class of lipids containing a backbone of sphingoid bases, a set of aliphatic amino alcohols that includes sphingosine. They are important for signal transmission and cell recognition.

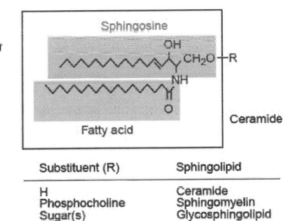

Substituent (R)	Sphingolipid
H	Ceramide
Phosphocholine	Sphingomyelin
Sugar(s)	Glycosphingolipid

Sphingolipid (R group is: H, phosphocholine, sugars, ceramide, sphingomyelin or glycosphingolipid)

Eicosanoids (e.g., prostaglandins and leukotrienes) are signaling molecules made by oxidation of 20-carbon fatty acids. Eicosanoids are derived from either ω-3 or ω-6 fatty acids.

Prostaglandin E1 (with characteristic 5-membered ring)

Waxes are organic compounds that characteristically consist of long alkyl chains.

Wax

2. D is correct. Fatty acids are biological molecules that contain long hydrocarbon groups.

These long hydrophobic chains can have alkene groups, but branching is not typically observed.

3. D is correct.

The plasma membrane is made up of lipids known as phospholipids. These molecules mostly possess nonpolar characteristics due to the long hydrocarbon chains, making the membrane permeable to nonpolar materials and semipermeable to polar or charged molecules.

4. A is correct. Fatty acids and triglycerides do not contain any stereocenters.

The ester and alkene functional groups that exist in some fats possess a plane of symmetry and therefore do not possess asymmetric carbon atoms.

These molecules are achiral and are not optically active.

5. D is correct.

Palmitic acid is a saturated acid, meaning that the molecule does not contain a double bond. Because this molecule lacks a double bond, the molecules are better able to stack together to form solids. Since unsaturated fats are often liquids at room temperature, the fat has a higher melting point.

Linolenic acid is polyunsaturated with three double bonds. Alkenes (i.e., unsaturation) introduce "kinks" in the chain that give the unsaturated fat an overall bent structure. This molecular geometry limits these fats from clustering closely together to form solids.

Therefore, (relative to chain length) polyunsaturated molecules have the lowest melting point.

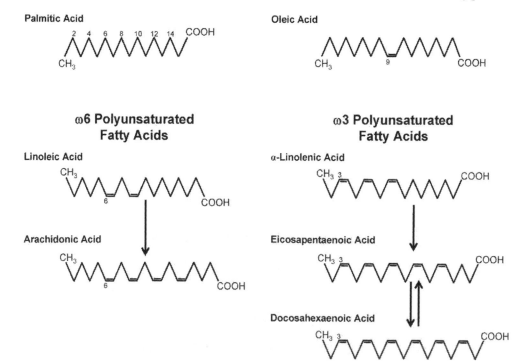

Saturated and unsaturated fatty acids – note the position (omega, ω) of the double bonds.

6. D is correct.

As unsaturated fats become hydrogenated to form saturated fats, the melting point increases.

An equivalent of hydrogen is added across the double bonds of unsaturated fats during hydrogenation, increasing the molecular weight of the compound.

Furthermore, saturation helps to enhance the stacking ability of these compounds in the solid state.

The more saturated the compound is, the higher its melting point.

7. B is correct.

The two ends of a fatty acid compound are the hydrophobic, nonpolar end composed of hydrogen and carbon atoms, and the hydrophilic, polar end of the molecule, which is composed of oxygen atoms and can hydrogen bond with water molecules.

8. B is correct.

Although cholesterol plays a pivotal role in the synthesis of other steroids and the integrity of cell membranes, too much cholesterol in the blood results in the formation of plaque deposits in blood vessels.

9. D is correct.

Steroid molecules are one of the two different kinds of fat molecules, which are composed of fused rings.

Triacylglycerides are composed of long hydrocarbon chains with functionalized head groups.

10. C is correct.

Saponification is the name for the base-promoted hydrolysis of esters. This type of hydrolysis (i.e., saponification) is typically used to form soap compounds.

carboxylate ester   sodium hydroxide   sodium carboxylate   alcohol

Base hydrolysis (saponification) of an ester to form a carboxylate salt and an alcohol

Soap is hard or soft depending on the counter-ion of the carboxylate salt.

If the base used to hydrolyze the fat is sodium hydroxide, a hard soap is produced.

If potassium hydroxide is used for the base hydrolysis reaction, then a soft soap is produced.

Furthermore, other kinds of bases can give rise to these two kinds of soaps.

11. C is correct.

Cholesterol is a lipid molecule also known as a steroid compound.

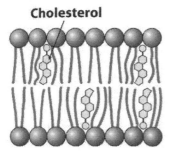

Cholesterol

The fused ring structure of steroid molecules is what makes them rigid and have fewer degrees of motion due to the few conformations that are available for cyclic molecules *vs.* acyclic molecules.

Molecules, such as phospholipids, lack fused-ring structures, and they exist as straight-chained molecules.

Therefore, cholesterol in the cell membrane acts as a bidirectional regulator of membrane fluidity: at high temperatures, it stabilizes the membrane and raises its melting point, whereas, at low temperatures, it intercalates between the phospholipids and prevents them from clustering together and stiffening.

12. B is correct. Triglycerides are one of two common types of lipids that are found in the body. This fat is composed of four components, including one equivalent of glycerol (a triol) and three fatty acid molecules.

These components are combined to form the three ester groups of the triglyceride.

13. D is correct. Saturated fats lack the alkene double bond. Unsaturated fats convert to saturated fats through a process known as hydrogenation.

In this process, hydrogen gas is catalytically added to the alkene groups of the fatty acids to convert them to alkane groups.

14. D is correct.

The hydrogenation of unsaturated fats adds hydrogen across the double bonds of the fat. This causes the fats to be saturated and increases their melting points.

Because of their ability to form solids more easily, the consumption of hydrogenated fats should be limited for health concerns.

15. B is correct. Triglycerides (or triacylglycerides) are used for storage and exist in the adipose tissue of animals.

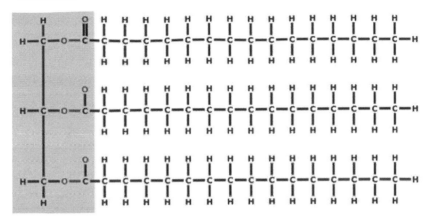

Triglyceride (glycerol and three saturated fatty acid chains)

Phospholipids(below) are the largest component of semi-permeable cell membranes

Phospholipids differ mainly in the composition of the polar head region.

Steroids are lipids used for cell-signaling.

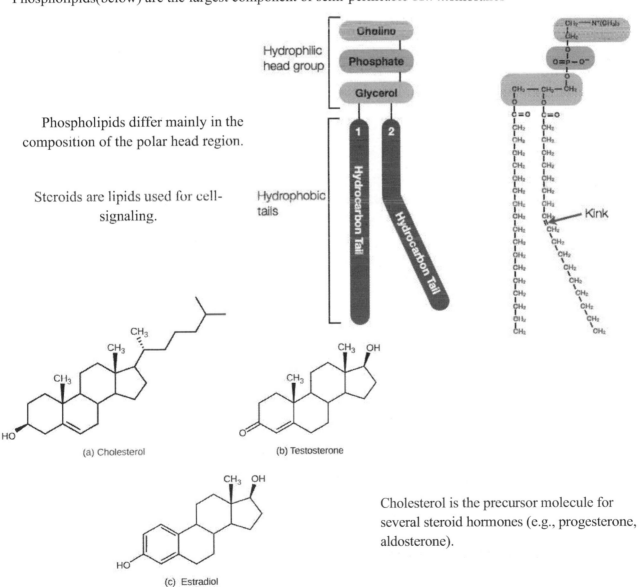

(a) Cholesterol

(b) Testosterone

(c) Estradiol

Cholesterol is the precursor molecule for several steroid hormones (e.g., progesterone, aldosterone).

16. C is correct.

The straight chain fatty acid that possesses the greatest number of alkenes in its structure is the fat that most likely is a liquid at room temperature.

Stearic acid is fully saturated, while linoleic acid has two double bonds.

The triacylglyceride of these fatty acids is a liquid (or oil) at room temperature.

Saturated fat (stearic acid)

Unsaturated fat (linoleic acid)

17. B is correct.

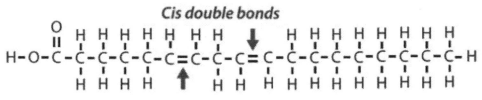

This fatty acid is omega three because a *Z* alkene double bond appears three carbon atoms away from the methyl end of the molecule.

Linolenic is an omega-3 fatty acid while both oleic and linoleic acid are omega-6 fatty acids.

Because these molecules contain one or more double bonds, they are unsaturated fats.

18. D is correct.
Estradiol (shown on the right) is a steroid hormone derived from cholesterol.

Cholesterol (on the left) is a lipid made of four fused rings. Three of the fused rings are six-membered rings, and the fourth ring is a five-membered ring.

Cholesterol is a steroid, which makes up one of two types of lipid molecules.

A triglyceride (i.e., glycerol backbone with three fatty acid chains) is the other type of lipid.

19. C is correct. When micelles form in aqueous environments, the hydrophobic tails cluster together. The polar head regions of these molecules are exposed on the surface of the micelle and exposed to the aqueous environment.

20. D is correct.

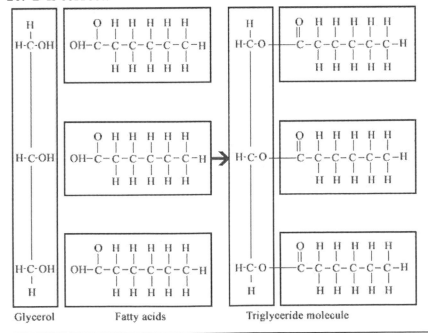

Glycerol   Fatty acids   Triglyceride molecule

Triacylglycerides (also known as triglycerides) are made from one equivalent of glycerol and three equivalents of fatty acids.

The molecule contains a three-carbon chain that is flanked by oxygens. The three fatty acids (–COR chains) are attached via an ester linkage.

A triester is produced when condensation (via dehydration) occurs between the glycerol and three fatty acids.

21. B is correct. Not all lipids are entirely hydrophobic. The ionic and polar heads of soaps and phospholipids, respectively, enable the molecules to interact with aqueous or polar environments.

Nevertheless, the bulk of these molecules are hydrophobic, because they largely consist of hydrocarbon chains or rings.

22. A is correct. For unsaturated fats, the molecules are more likely to exist as oils (i.e., liquids) at room temperature.

Saturated fats tend to be solid at room temperature because the reduced forms of these molecules have better stacking properties, which allow them to form solid states.

23. B is correct. The alkene molecules typically found in fatty acids tend to be *Z* alkenes.

Saturated Fatty Acid

Unsaturated Fatty Acid

The double bond of the alkene (i.e., unsaturated) prevents the fatty acid molecules from stacking closely together. The result is lowering of the melting point for the fat molecule. This may also influence the state of matter of the oil, as unsaturated fats tend to be liquid at room temperature and saturated fats tend to be solids.

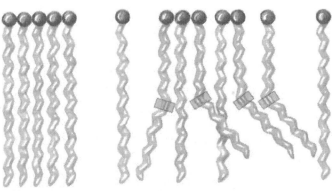

Saturated
fatty acids   Mixture of saturated and
unsaturated fatty acids

24. D is correct.

For omega acids, the number indicates the position of the first double bond from the non-carboxylic acid end (i.e., near the alkyl chain end) of the molecule (hence the "omega" part of the name).

Examples of omega-3 and omega-6 fatty acids.

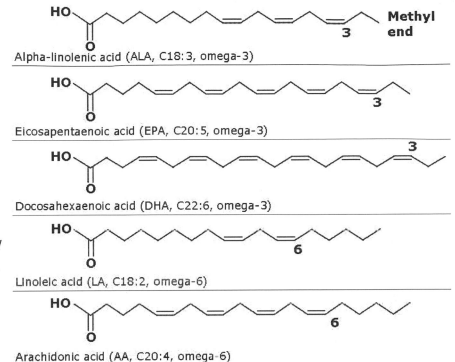

Alpha-linolenic acid (ALA, C18:3, omega-3)

Eicosapentaenoic acid (EPA, C20:5, omega-3)

Docosahexaenoic acid (DHA, C22:6, omega-3)

Linoleic acid (LA, C18:2, omega-6)

Arachidonic acid (AA, C20:4, omega-6)

25. C is correct.

Triacylglycerols are molecules composed of a glycerol substructure and three fatty acids that are condensed to form a triester.

26. E is correct. Triacylglycerol is a lipid that can undergo saponification, which is the breakdown of fatty esters with bases, such as sodium hydroxide or potassium hydroxide.

Saponification reactions are base promoted because sodium hydroxide is consumed in the reaction and not regenerated.

The amount of base needed to saponify 1 gram of fat is known as the saponification number.

27. A is correct.

In esterification reactions, the ester is made from the condensation of carboxylic acids and alcohols.

Fats are formed from the condensation (via dehydration) of fatty acids and glycerol.

For the reaction to take place, an acid catalyst (or enzyme) normally needs to be used. An acid catalyst is needed because carboxylic acids are not electrophilic, and the group needs to be activated by protonation.

Protonation of the carboxylic acid carbonyl oxygen atom causes the carbon-oxygen dipole to increase, allowing alcohol to add to the group.

Protonation of one of the geminal hydroxyl groups and loss of the group as water leads to the formation of the ester.

28. A is correct. Oils are isolated from plant sources and may consist of several different fatty acids. These oils may contain saturated fat, but other fats present in the mixture are unsaturated fat molecules.

The saturated fats that may be present in oil are palmitic and stearic acid and the unsaturated fats found in these oils include oleic, palmitoleic and linoleic acids, as well as others.

29. B is correct.

There are two overall categories of lipids: long chain lipids (e.g., triglycerides) and smaller, polycyclic lipids, such as steroids (e.g., cholesterol and its derivatives, such as estrogen and testosterone).

Lipid molecules are fat soluble, and these molecules are largely soluble in organic/hydrophobic.

30. D is correct.

In hydrogenation reactions, Z and E alkenes are reduced to alkanes, and this process is catalyzed by transitions metals, such as nickel or palladium.

In this reaction, hydrogen (H_2) is added across the double bond of the alkene.

31. E is correct. Many unsaturated fats are known as omega fats because they contain alkene groups.

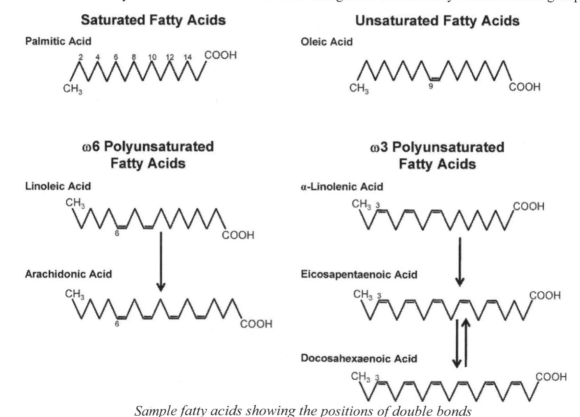

Sample fatty acids showing the positions of double bonds

Omega-3 fats have double bonds that appear three carbon atoms from the methyl end.

Omega-6 fatty acids contain double bonds that are six carbon atoms away from the methyl end. The double bonds tend to have Z (*cis*) geometry.

32. C is correct.

Long alkyl chains present on alkoxy portion and the carboxy backbone of the ester are characteristic features of molecules that are waxes.

Lipid

33. A is correct.

Glycerol can condense with fatty acids to expel water.

The new functional group produced is an ester joined by a glycosidic bond.

Condensation reaction (via dehydration) of glycerol and three fatty acids showing a glycosidic (ester) linkage.

34. D is correct.

Amphipathic refers to molecules that possess both hydrophobic and hydrophilic elements.

Biological molecules, such as fatty acids and some amino acids, have hydrophobic and hydrophilic regions.

A: amphoteric substance can act as either an acid or a base, depending on the medium. Examples include metal oxides or hydroxides, which are amphoteric depending on the oxidation state of the element.

B: enantiomeric compounds are chiral molecules whose molecular structures have a non-superimposable mirror image relationship to each other.

C: amphiprotic molecules can either donate or accept a proton (H^+), depending on the conditions (e.g., amino acids).

E: allotropic is the property of some elements to exist in two or more different forms, in the same physical state because the atoms are bonded together differently (e.g., carbon exists as graphite, diamond, and fullerene).

35. B is correct.

Lipids (i.e., fats) is a term used to describe long chain ester-linked molecules such as triglycerides. The term "lipid" is sometimes used interchangeably with the word "fat," however, lipids also include cyclic biomolecules, such as steroids (e.g., cholesterol and its derivatives such as estrogen and testosterone).

Triacylglycerol is a lipid that can undergo saponification, which is the breakdown of fatty esters with bases, such as sodium hydroxide or potassium hydroxide.

D: terpenes are small alkene-containing hydrocarbon building blocks that can be combined and cyclized to form steroids. Terpenes are simple lipids.

E: steroids do not contain ester groups, so they cannot be hydrolyzed to form soaps.

36. D is correct.

Fatty acids are long molecules containing a hydrophobic chain and a hydrophilic region terminating in a carboxylic acid.

Myristic acid: an unsaturated 14 carbon fatty acid

Soaps are formed from the hydrolysis of fatty acids under basic conditions, in a process known as saponification.

The positively charged counterion (e.g., Na^+, K^+) of the hydroxide base added to the reaction becomes the counter ion of the soap.

A: emollient is a topical agent designed to increase the hydration of the epidermis softer.

B: ester is a functional group in organic chemistry: R–O–R'.

37. B is correct.

Amphipathic refers to molecules that possess both hydrophobic and hydrophilic elements (e.g., detergents, phospholipids of biological membranes).

Lipid molecules are common examples of amphipathic compounds because they possess hydrophobic tails and polar heads. The polar head group is often composed of electronegative heteroatoms, such as oxygen and nitrogen atoms.

38. D is correct.

Saturated fats tend to be solid at room temperature because they lack alkene groups. The presence of alkene groups in fat molecules lowers the melting point for these compounds.

For example, butter is a dairy product made from the fat of cow's milk. It is solid at room temperature and is mostly composed of saturated fat molecules.

39. C is correct.

Although waxes are lipid molecules that contain esters as part of their structure, waxes only contain a single ester functional group.

A monoalcohol is used to form waxes, whereas glycerol is used to form triglycerides and phospholipids.

40. D is correct.

Fatty acids are used to make fat molecules known as triglycerides.

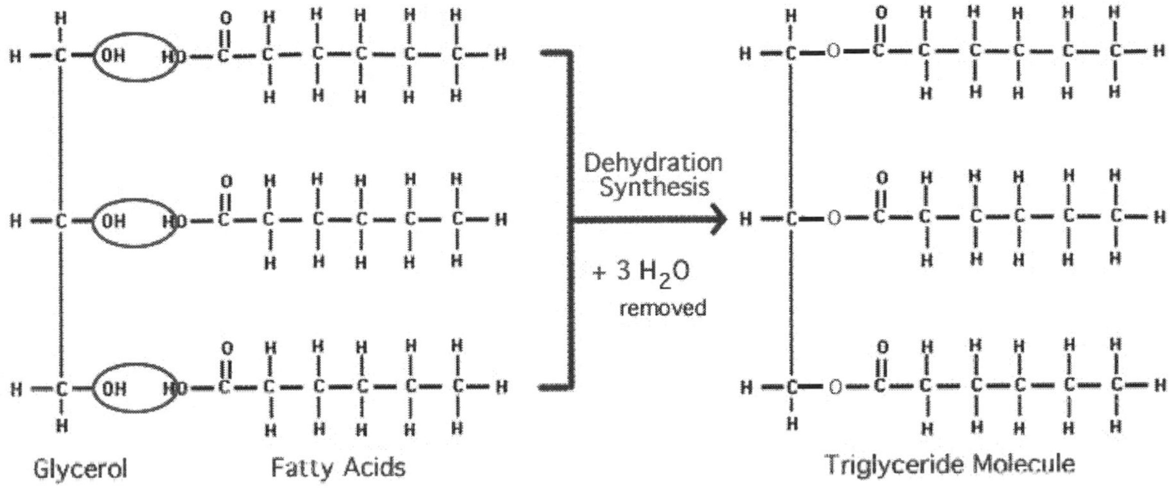

Formation, via dehydration (removal of H₂O), of triglyceride from glycerol and 3 fatty acids.

Fatty acids are made from one equivalent of a triol known as glycerol and three equivalents of acid-containing groups known as fatty acids.

41. E is correct.

Dietary triglycerides are composed of glycerol and three fatty acids.

The hydrolysis of triglycerides yields glycerol and three fatty acid chains.

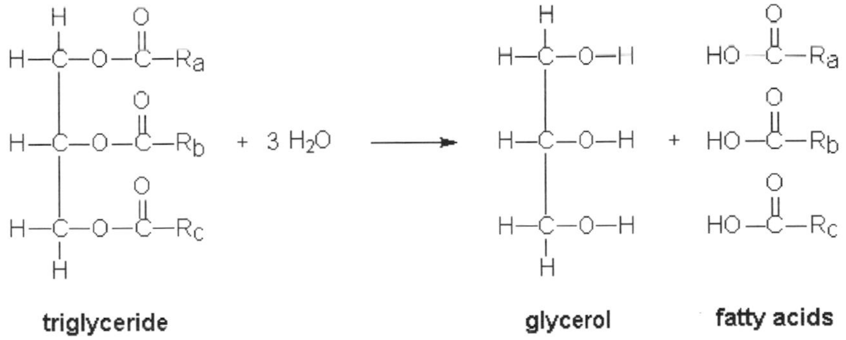

Hydrolysis of a triglyceride

42. B is correct.

The *cis* double bond of unsaturated fatty acids causes these molecules to stack less efficiently and less tightly. The melting point for these compounds is lower than for saturated fats. Therefore, most unsaturated fatty acids are liquids at room temperature.

The presence of double bonds indicates unsaturated fatty acids.

The unsaturated fatty acid contains a *cis* double bond at the 6th position.

Saturated Fatty Acid

Unsaturated Fatty Acid

43. C is correct. Glycerol is an alcohol that possesses three hydroxyl groups; one hydroxyl group is bonded to each of the carbon atoms of glycerol. Glycerol is, therefore, a triol molecule, and this molecule is a key component in the structure of triglyceride molecules.

44. C is correct. Phospholipids are important lipids that make up the bilayer structure of the membranes of cells, organelles, and other enclosed cellular structures.

Phospholipids are composed of two (same or different) fatty acid molecules, a phosphate group and a glycerol backbone.

The phospholipid contains both a hydrophobic (i.e., fatty acid tail) region and hydrophilic (polar head) region. The hydrophobic regions point toward each other in the membrane bilayer while the polar heads point towards the inside (i.e., cytosolic) or outside (i.e., extracellular) sides of the bilayer.

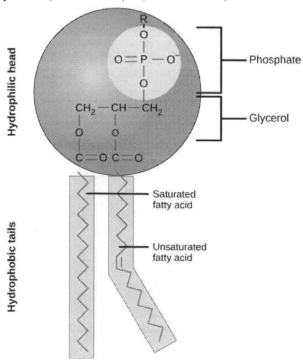

45. C is correct. Fatty acid molecules are composed of long alkyl chains that do not involve branching. This is because each two-carbon segment of the fatty acid straight chain can be enzymatically converted to an acetyl-CoA derivative.

Branching in the alkyl chain may impede the oxidative degradation of these compounds because a beta-ketone must be accessed before cleavage of the chain. Secondary alkyl groups can be oxidized to alcohols but cannot be converted to ketones for this step.

46. D is correct.

Lipids (i.e., fats) is a term used to describe long chain ester-linked molecules such as triglycerides. The term "lipid" is sometimes used interchangeably with the word "fat," however, lipids also include cyclic biomolecules, such as steroids (e.g., cholesterol and its derivatives such as estrogen and testosterone).

Glycerol is a 3-carbon chain with three hydroxyl groups. Each hydroxyl undergoes a condensation reaction with the carboxylic acid end of a fatty acid chain to form a lipid.

Glycerol

Saturated Fatty Acid

Comparison of saturated and unsaturated fatty acids. The unsaturated fatty acid contains one or more double bonds. The unsaturated fatty acid is a cis alkene in the above example.

Unsaturated Fatty Acid

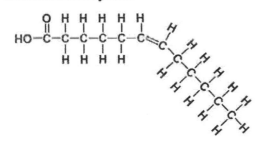

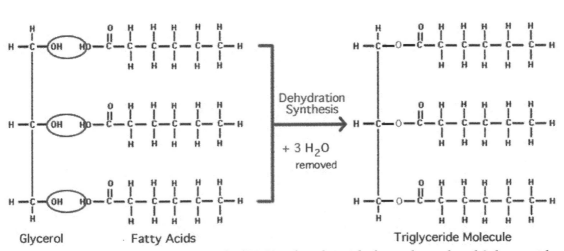

Glycerol   Fatty Acids   Triglyceride Molecule

Formation, via dehydration (removal of H_2O), of triglyceride from glycerol and 3 fatty acids.

47. D is correct.

Fat can be produced from glucose, but glucose is not produced from animal fat.

The excess of glucose consumption in the body can lead to increased levels of fat in the body.

48. D is correct.

There are two overall categories of lipids: long chain lipids (e.g., triglycerides) and smaller, polycyclic lipids, such as steroids (e.g., cholesterol and its derivatives such as estrogen and testosterone).

Terpenes are small alkene-containing hydrocarbon building blocks that can be combined and cyclized to form steroids.

Terpenes are simple lipids.

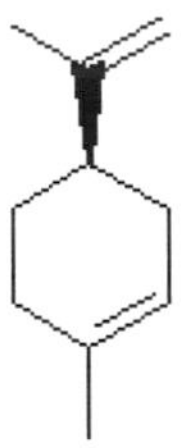

limonene

(found in the skin of citrus fruits)

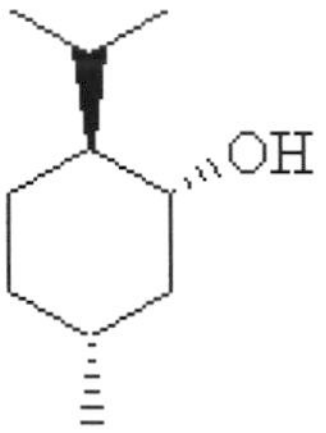

menthol

(peppermint)

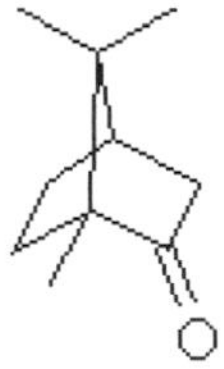

camphor

(camphor tree)

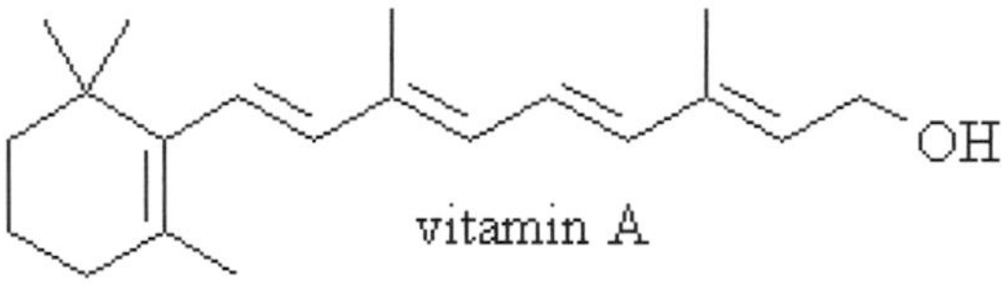

vitamin A

(involved in the chemistry of vision)

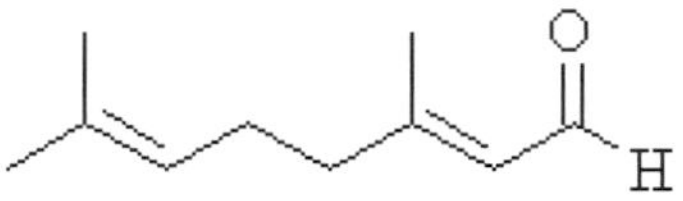

citral

(lemon grass)

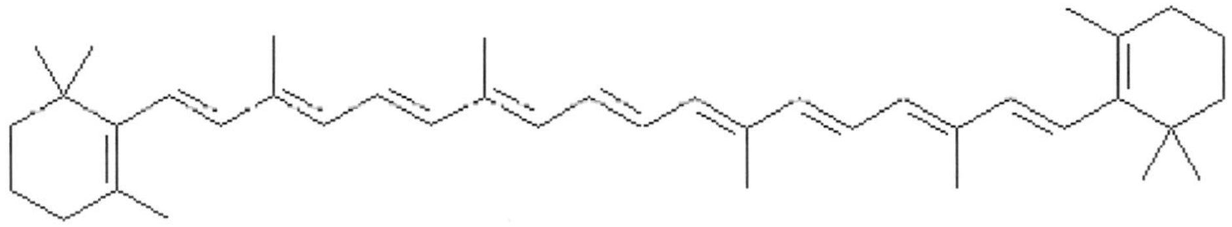

β -carotene

(in carrots and other vegetables, enzymes convert it to vitamin A)

Examples of terpenes

Chapter 27 Explanations: Carbohydrates

1. C is correct.

The conversion of one cyclic glucose stereoisomer to another involves the formation of an acyclic intermediate form. When the molecule cyclizes again, the opposite face of the aldehyde is accessed to generate the other cyclic diastereomer.

2. D is correct.

Glucose is an example of a reducing sugar because it contains an aldehyde that can undergo reduction. The reduction of its aldehyde produces a sugar known as sorbitol. This is a way for the body to reduce blood glucose levels and is typically observed in diabetic patients with high blood sugar levels.

3. C is correct. Sugar molecules typically contain hydrogen, carbon, and oxygen atoms.

Lipids, such as phospholipids, may contain other heteroatom groups (e.g., phosphorus atoms).

Aminosaccharides are sugars that have nitrogen atoms in their structure.

4. C is correct.

It may help to use a molecular model to answer this question. If the hemiacetal is converted to the aldehyde, then the acyclic form of this molecule is represented by the indicated structure.

5. D is correct.

Because amylose is a type of polysaccharide that does not have a β(1→4) glycosidic linkage, this polysaccharide can be digested by humans.

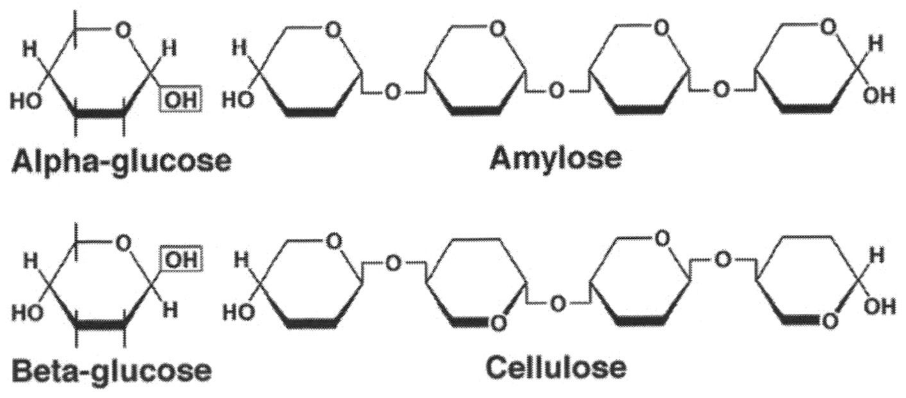

Alpha-glucose   **Amylose**

Beta-glucose   **Cellulose**

Polysaccharides (cellulose) with β(1→4) glycosidic linkages cannot be digested by humans, because they lack the cellulase enzyme to cleave the β(1→4) glycosidic linkages.

---

6. E is correct. Ketohexose, a monosaccharide, is one of the components of sucrose, which is a disaccharide made from fructose and glucose.

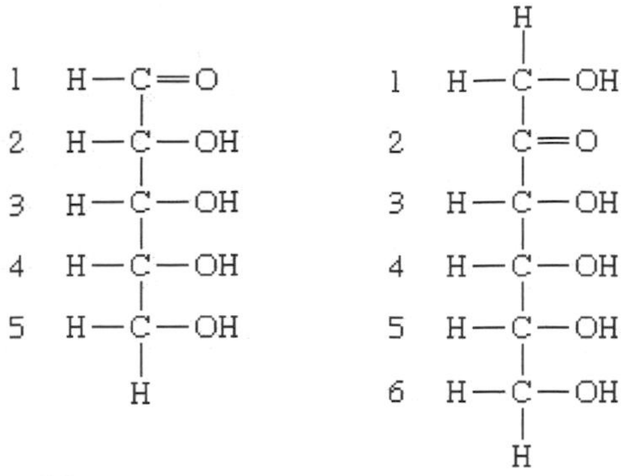

Aldopentose

(5-carbon aldehyde)

Ketohexose

(6-carbon ketone)

Fructose is one of the sweetest tasting natural sugars.

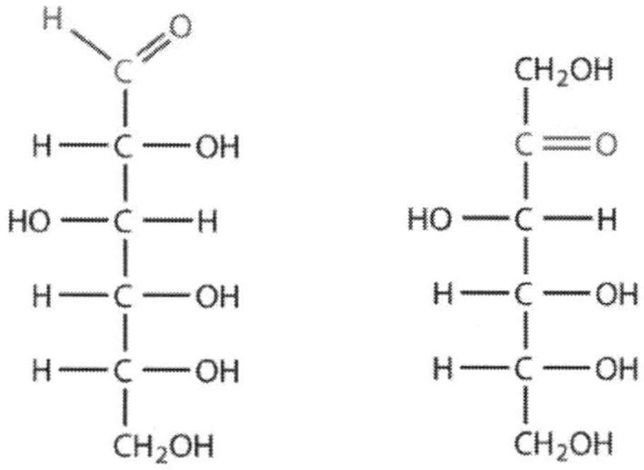

Glucose
(an aldohexose)

Fructose
(a ketohexose)

7. C is correct.

Tautomeric forms of a molecule involve changes in the connectivity of a functional group, and this is typically observed for aldehydes, ketones, and imines.

The two cyclic forms of monosaccharides have the same connectivity, but the configuration of the carbons is different. These forms are, therefore, diastereomers.

8. C is correct.

One exception to the tendency for sugars to have oxygen atoms linked to every carbon atom is in deoxyribose. It is similar in structure to ribose; however, one of the alcohols is replaced with a carbon-hydrogen bond.

9. A is correct. Common monosaccharides are composed of five (pentose) or six (hexose) carbon atoms, hydrogen, and oxygen.

This molecule contains a hemiacetal group, which can open reversibly to form an aldehyde.

The presence of the aldehyde makes this carbohydrate a reducing sugar.

10. B is correct.

The ratio of these atoms that compose sugars is normally 1:2:1 (carbon : hydrogen : oxygen).

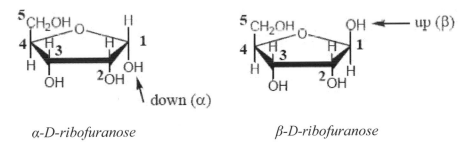

D-ribose: Fisher projections of an example ribose sugar

11. C is correct.

During the formation of disaccharides, the only configuration that can vary is at the anomeric carbon.

α-D-ribofuranose   β-D-ribofuranose

The other alcohols of the carbohydrate are either primary or secondary alcohols that are not adjacent (i.e., allylic) to an oxygen atom (as in the case of anomeric alcohols).

The neighboring oxygen atom in the ring facilitates the ring opening of the anomeric C-1 alcohol, and this may lead to the formation of the other anomer (α ↔ β).

12. B is correct.

Any sugar molecule that lacks the aldehyde or the hemiacetal functional group is a non-reducing sugar. The sugars are not active during chemical tests like the Tollens' test. When reducing sugars react, they are normally oxidized to carboxylic acid molecules.

All monosaccharides are reducing sugars, while some disaccharides (e.g., lactose and maltose), oligosaccharides and polysaccharides are also reducing sugars.

Reducing sugars (and *alpha* hydroxyl ketones) give a positive Benedict's test: a brown precipitate forms (as does for Fehling's solution).

Tollens' reagent forms silver ions (mirror) as a positive test for reducing sugars.

13. A is correct.

When a six-carbon sugar cyclizes (yielding a pyranose), a hemiacetal bond is formed (–linkage between the ~OH at carbon number 5 and the anomeric carbon (C_1)) and the carbonyl of C_1 is converted to alcohol. The resulting C_1 hydroxyl may be in the axial or equatorial positions on the ring with the two possible positions called anomers.

α-D-glucopyranose   β-D-glucopyranose

If the ~OH at carbon number 1 is in the down position (which is axial in the case of D-glucopyranose, or glucose), the ring is referred to as the α anomer.

When the ~OH is in the axial (up) position, it is the β anomer.

A monosaccharide in solution freely converts between the open chain form and the two anomeric forms (mutarotation). It is necessary to specify the anomeric form because the acetal linkage (glycosidic bond) between monosaccharides in di- and polysaccharides prevent mutarotation.

Enzymes accept only one of the two anomers in the formation and hydrolysis of glycosidic linkages.

Hence, all the linkages in starch and glycogen (except at branch points) are α(1→4) glycosidic linkages, whereas all the bonds in cellulose are β(1→4).

Even though all these macromolecules are simple glucose polymers, humans can digest only the former two, since humans lack enzymes for the hydrolysis of β glycosidic linkages (therefore, humans can digest starch but not grass or wood).

14. D is correct.

Glycogen (below) contains α(1→6) glycosidic linkages (below):

Copyright © 2020 Sterling Test Prep. Any duplication (copies, uploads, PDFs) is illegal.

Cellulose (below) contains β(1→4) glycosidic linkages (below):

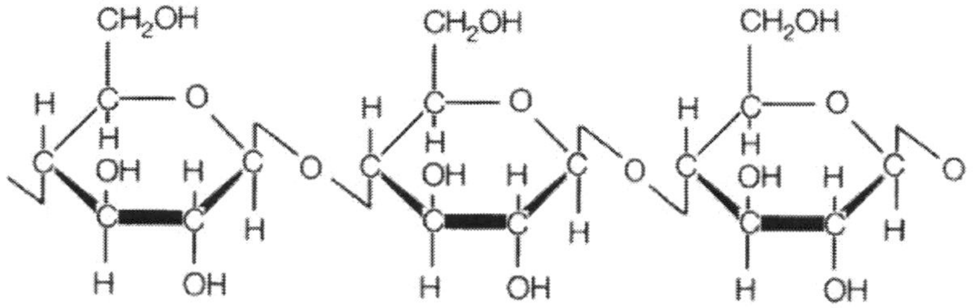

Sucrose (below) contains α (1→2) glycosidic linkages (below):

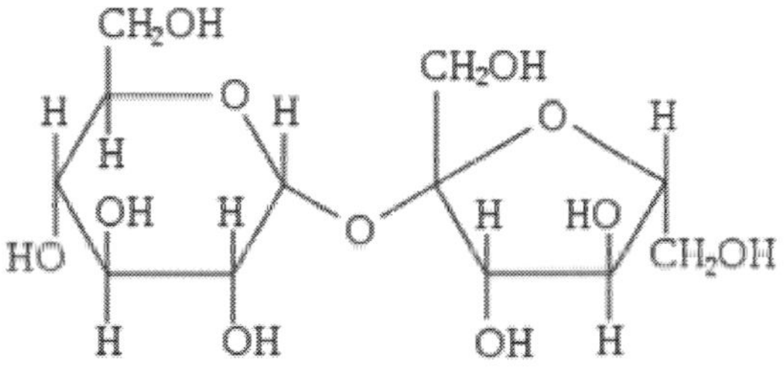

Amylose (below) contains α(1→4) glycosidic linkages (below):

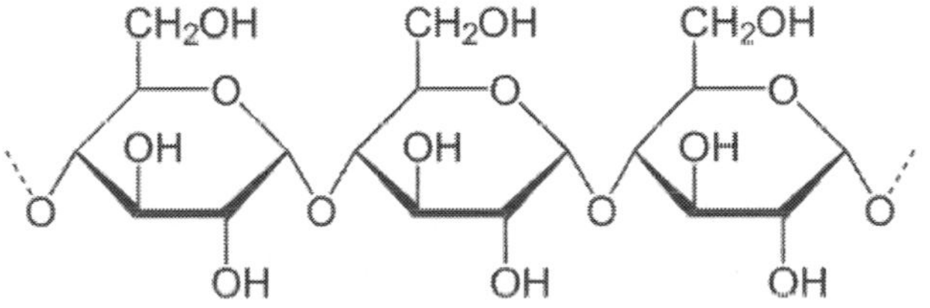

Maltose (below) contains α(1→4) glycosidic linkages (below):

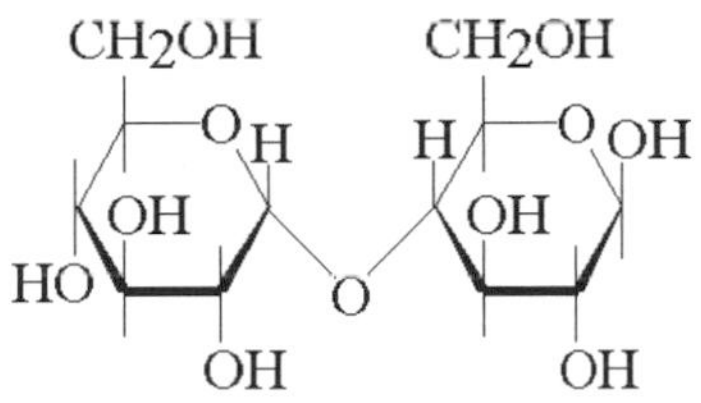

15. D is correct.

Humans are unable to digest cellulose because the appropriate enzymes to breakdown the beta acetal linkages are lacking. The enzyme responsible for cleaving this glycosidic linkage is known as cellulase. Cellulase is produced by plants, bacteria, fungi, and protozoans.

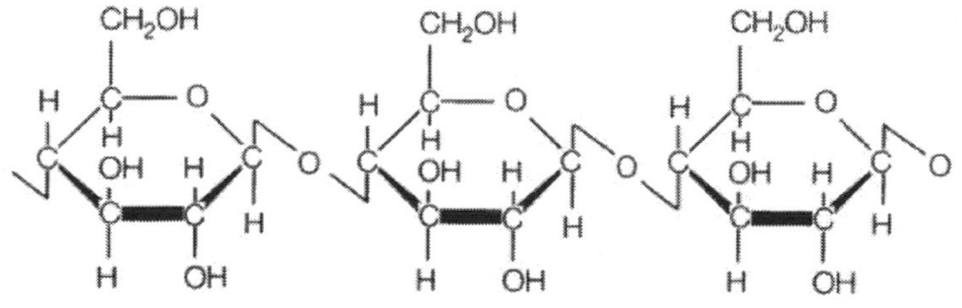

16. A is correct.

Mutarotation is possible because the anomeric carbon is a hemiacetal. When dissolved in water, hemiacetals are known to reversibly open to the acyclic form, allowing the formation of the cyclic diastereomer.

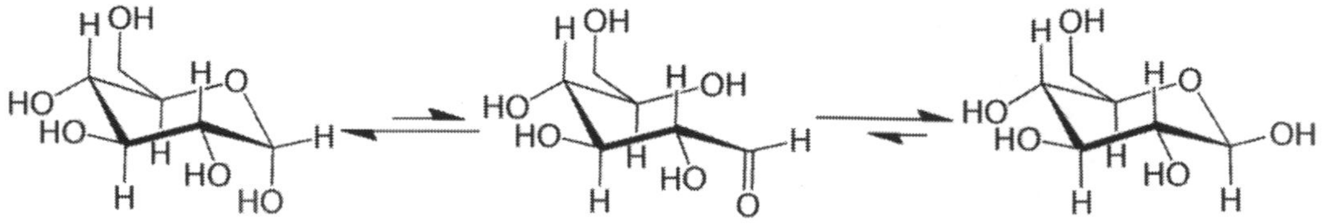

Mutarotation (open chain in the center) with the less stable α-glucose anomer (left) and more stable β-glucose anomer on the right.

The process is accelerated from the addition of acid or base.

17. A is correct. Monosaccharides cannot be broken down into simpler sugar subunits.

However, monosaccharides can undergo oxidative degradation to produce carbon dioxide and carbon monoxide when treated with nitric acid.

18. C is correct.

This is how monosaccharide sugars exist as two different diastereomers.

These diastereomers are classified as α (alpha) and β (beta) diastereomers.

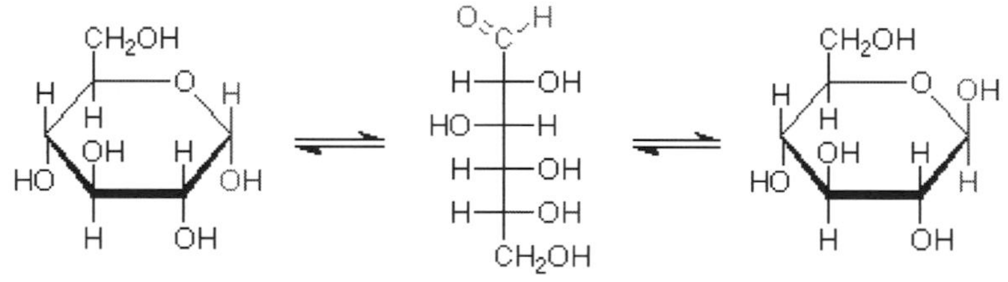

α-D-glucose D-glucose β-D-glucose

Two diastereomers are possible because the alcohol that cyclizes (i.e., mutarotation) to form the ring may add to either face of the aldehyde.

Epimers are isomers that differ at a single chiral center (shown below):

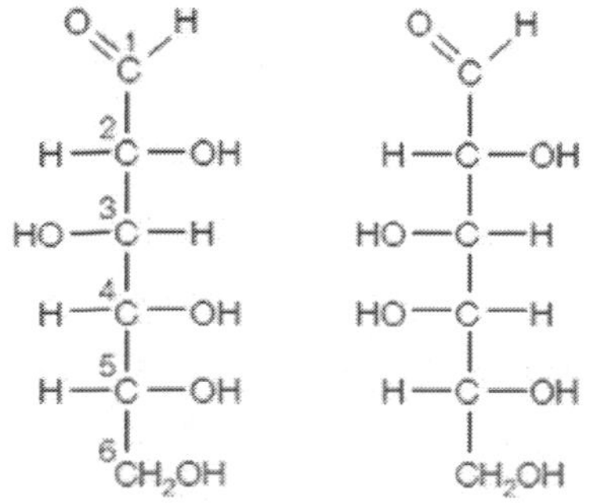

Epimers of D-glucose (left) and D-galactose (right) with inversion at the 4th chiral carbon

19. B is correct. Reducing sugars possess a free aldehyde or a free ketone group. All monosaccharides are reducing sugars, along with some disaccharides, oligosaccharides and polysaccharides.

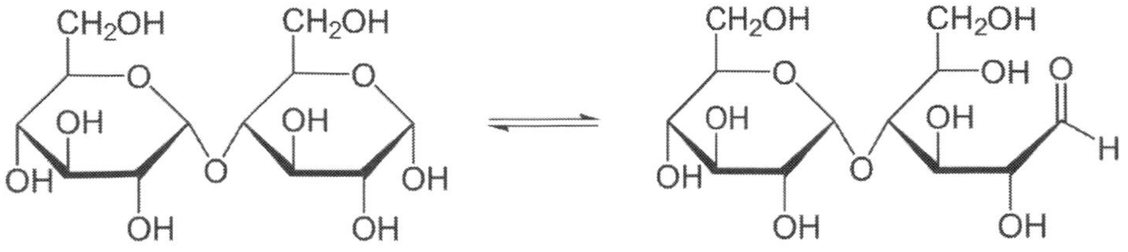

Maltose exists in equilibrium between the closed ring (left) and open form.

Open form (with the aldehyde on the far) is the reducing sugar.

If a cyclic sugar possesses an acetal instead of a hemiacetal at the anomeric carbon, the sugar will not be a reducing sugar.

20. D is correct.

People who cannot produce the lactase enzyme are known to be lactose intolerant. This protein is responsible for the catalytic breakdown of lactose.

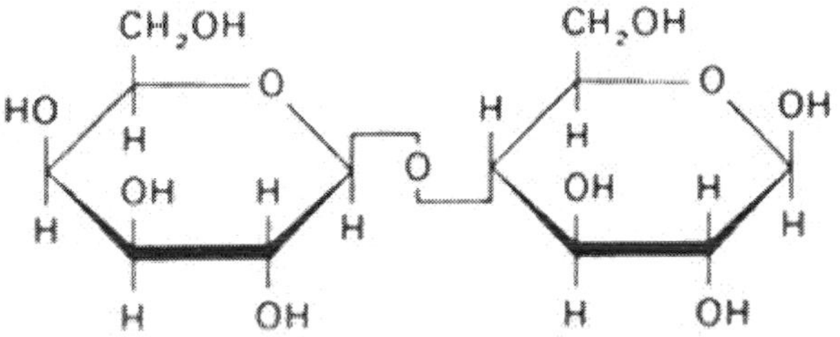

Lactose is a β(1→4) disaccharide comprised of galactose (left) and glucose.

Both lactose and cellulose are two forms of sugar that possess the difficult to digest β(1→4) glycosidic linkage.

21. A is correct. An aldotetrose is a four-carbon carbohydrate with an aldehyde.

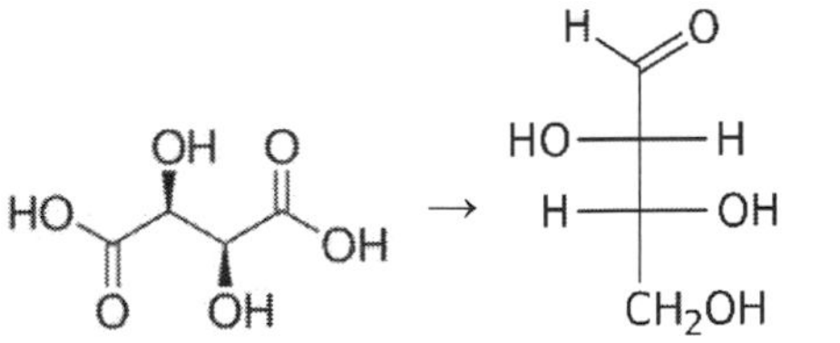

D-(–)-tartaric acid converts to aldotetrose

22. C is correct.

The key to determining a monosaccharide's category involves counting the number of carbon atoms in the structure. There are four carbon atoms in the five-membered ring, and there is a methylene-containing (~CH_2~) substituent bonded to the ring.

Because there are five carbon atoms present, the molecule is a pentose.

---

23. D is correct.

If the chiral carbon farthest from the carbonyl points to the right, then it is a D-sugar.

If the chiral carbon farthest from the carbonyl points to the left, then it is an L-sugar.

The terminal alcohol is not an asymmetric carbon atom, because it is typically bonded to two hydrogen atoms.

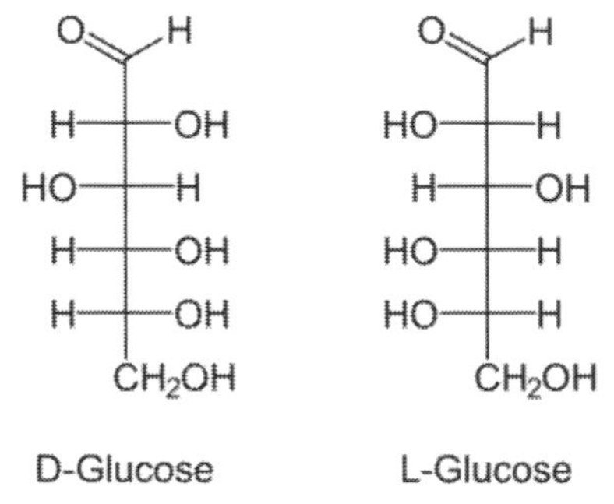

D-glucose and L-glucose are enantiomers (i.e., non-superimposable mirror images)

24. B is correct.

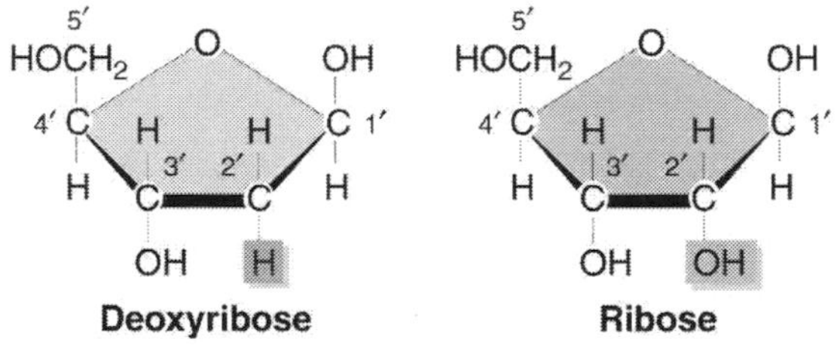

Deoxyribose is the sugar of DNA, while ribose is the sugar of RNA. The difference is the absence of a 2'-hydroxyl (DNA) or the presence of the 2'-hydroxyl (RNA). Both DNA and RNA have a 3'-hydroxyl necessary for chain elongation.

Deoxyribose is a monosaccharide that contains one fewer hydroxyl group than ribose.

Deoxyribose is the sugar in DNA, and ribose is the sugar contained in RNA.

25. A is correct.

In an α-1,1 linkage, both anomeric carbons are in an acetal linkage.

Therefore, mutarotation (i.e., interconversion between the open chain and ring form) is not possible, and no free aldehyde is available to react with Benedict's reagent.

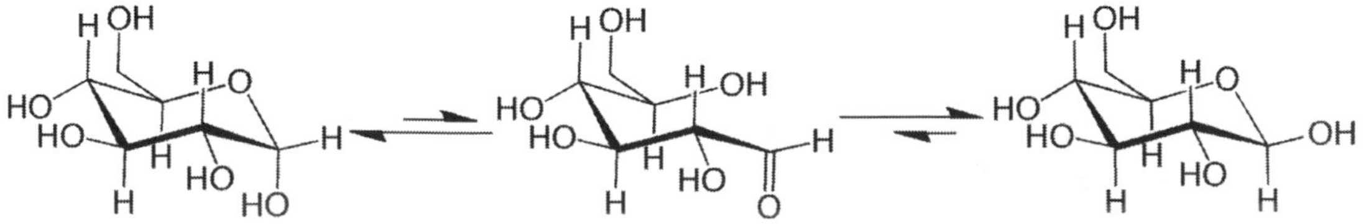

Mutarotation of glucose (α-glucose on the left; β-glucose on the right)

All monosaccharides are reducing sugars, while some disaccharides (e.g., lactose and maltose), oligosaccharides and polysaccharides are also reducing sugars.

B: β-1,4-glucose-glucose is a disaccharide, whereby one glucose unit has its C-1 bound as an acetal and therefore cannot mutarotate, existing only as a ring.

Therefore, the aldehyde is unavailable for reaction with Benedict's reagent. However, the other glucose unit is bonded at its C-4 hydroxyl.

C: glucose has a hemiacetal linkage which allows mutarotation.

Therefore, the aldehyde group is free to react in the test for reducing sugars.

D: fructose has a hemiacetal linkage which allows mutarotation.

Therefore, the aldehyde group is free to react in the test for reducing sugars.

E: maltose is a disaccharide formed from two units of glucose. Through mutarotation, the aldehyde group is free to react in the test for reducing sugars.

26. A is correct.

For a chiral molecule with n chiral centers, the number of stereoisomers is calculated by 2^n, where n is the number of chiral centers. For example, a molecule with 3 chiral centers has 8 ($2 \times 2 \times 2$) stereoisomers. The relationship (relative to the original molecule) is 1 enantiomer and 6 diastereomers.

If there were any *meso* (i.e., internal plane of symmetry) carbohydrates, the number of *meso* forms would be subtracted from the total number of stereoisomers.

27. E is correct.

Lactose is a disaccharide composed of glucose and galactose.

The glycosidic linkage in lactose is a β(1→4) linkage.

28. B is correct.

Ribose is an important monosaccharide that contains an aldehyde and five carbon atoms. This sugar can be found in the structure of mRNA.

The 2'-deoxygenated form of ribose (i.e., deoxyribose), is found in the structure of DNA.

29. C is correct.

Cyclic carbohydrates typically have ether and alcohol functional groups.

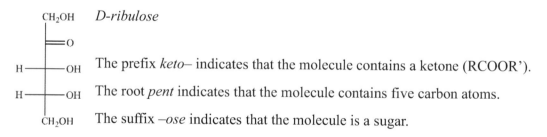

(a) Fischer projection (b) Three-dimensional representantion (c) Cyclic monosaccharide

The hemiacetal and aldehyde forms of these compounds can equilibrate.

30. D is correct.

The numbering of carbohydrates begins at the terminal carbon closest to the most oxidized carbon (i.e., anomeric carbon).

It is an α-linkage because the linking oxygen is pointing down (axial) in the Haworth (i.e., ring) representation.

31. E is correct.

D-ribulose

The prefix *keto–* indicates that the molecule contains a ketone (RCOOR').

The root *pent* indicates that the molecule contains five carbon atoms.

The suffix *–ose* indicates that the molecule is a sugar.

32. A is correct.

D-glucose

The prefix *aldo–* indicates that the molecule contains an aldehyde.

The root *hex* indicates that the molecule contains six carbon atoms.

The suffix *–ose* indicates that the molecule is a sugar.

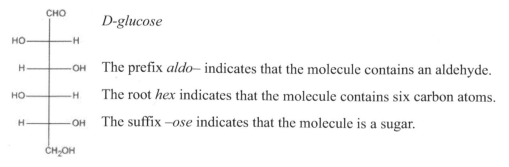

33. A is correct.

Glycosidic bonds join carbohydrates and are formed between the hemiacetal group of a saccharide and the hydroxyl group of some organic compound, such as an alcohol.

α is the designation when the hydroxyl attached to the anomeric carbon points down.

β is the designation when the hydroxyl attached to the anomeric carbon points up.

C: acetal refers to a carbon that is attached to two ethers (RO–C–OR').

D: hemiacetal refers to a carbon that is attached to an ether and a hydroxyl (RO–C–OH).

E: ester refers to oxygen that is attached to two carbon chains (R–O–R).

Formation of a glycosidic bond: glucose and ethanol combine to form ethyl glucoside and water

The reaction often favors the formation of the α-glycosidic bond (as shown), due to the anomeric effect.

The relative size of the equilibrium is indicated by the size of the arrow.

The anomeric effect describes the tendency of an element with lone pairs of electrons adjacent to a heteroatom (e.g., oxygen within a ring) of a cyclohexane ring to prefer the *axial* orientation instead of the less-hindered *equatorial* orientation expected from steric considerations.

The axial orientation permits molecular orbital overlap that increases the overall stability of the molecule.

34. C is correct.

Glycogen is a polymer of glucose that functions as the energy store of carbohydrates in animal cells (plant cells use starch). Glycogen is common in the liver, muscle and red blood cells.

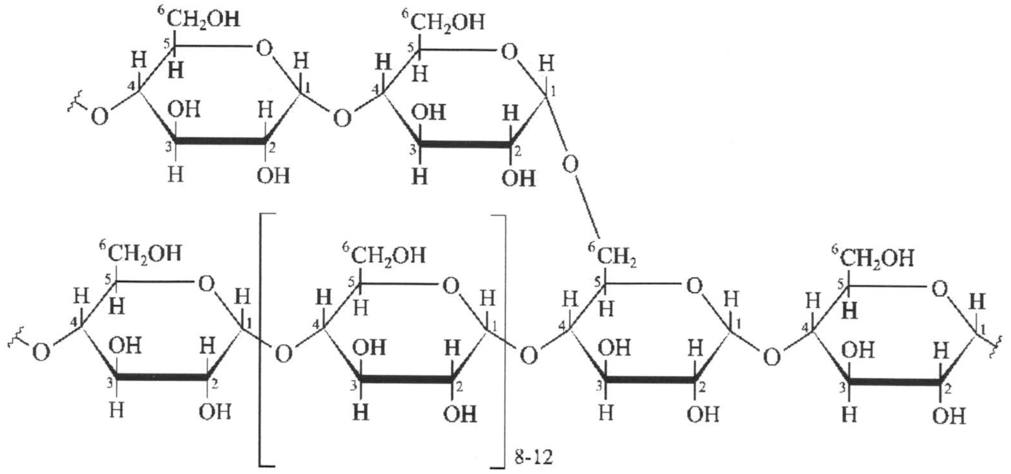

Glycogen is a large biomolecule consisting of repeating glucose subunits.

35. C is correct.

If a compound has only one chiral center, it must be chiral. A *meso* compound has an internal symmetry requiring the presence of at least two chiral centers. This internal symmetry yields an achiral molecule, even though it contains chiral centers.

36. D is correct.

Disaccharides contain a glycosidic linkage that is an ether group. The ether can be protonated with Brønsted acids and hydrolyzed in the presence of water.

All polysaccharides can be hydrolyzed to produce monosaccharides (i.e., individual monomers of the polymer).

37. D is correct.

Multiple bonds and rings introduce degrees of unsaturation.

Using a subscript of n for the number of carbons, the degrees of unsaturation can be determined from the following formulae:

Alkane: C_nH_{2n+2} = 0 degree of unsaturation

Alkene: C_nH_{2n} = 1 degree of unsaturation

Alkyne: C_nH_{2n-2} = 2 degrees of unsaturation

Rings = 1 degree of unsaturation

Double bonds = 1 degree of unsaturation

Acarbose has one double bond and four rings and therefore has a total of five degrees of unsaturation.

38. D is correct.

Monosaccharides are the basic unit of carbohydrates.

Subjecting these compounds to acids or bases will not hydrolyze them any further.

However, they can undergo oxidative decomposition by treating them with periodic acid to form formaldehyde and formic acid.

39. B is correct.

The suffix *ose* is used to denote sugars. The highest priority functional group in the molecule is a ketone.

Therefore, the sugar is a ketose sugar.

The sugar ($C_nH_{2n}O_n$) has a carbon chain of 5, so it is a pentose. If the molecule had an aldehyde instead of a ketone, the molecule would be an aldose sugar.

40. D is correct.

Carbohydrates can be more specifically described as organic compounds that contain carbon, hydrogen, and oxygen. The general molecular formula may vary depending on the type of carbohydrates, but many examples have the formula of $C_nH_{2n}O_n$.

41. B is correct.

Mutarotation occurs when cyclic hemiacetals form from monosaccharides with different configurations around the anomeric carbon (i.e., carbonyl carbon in the straight chain).

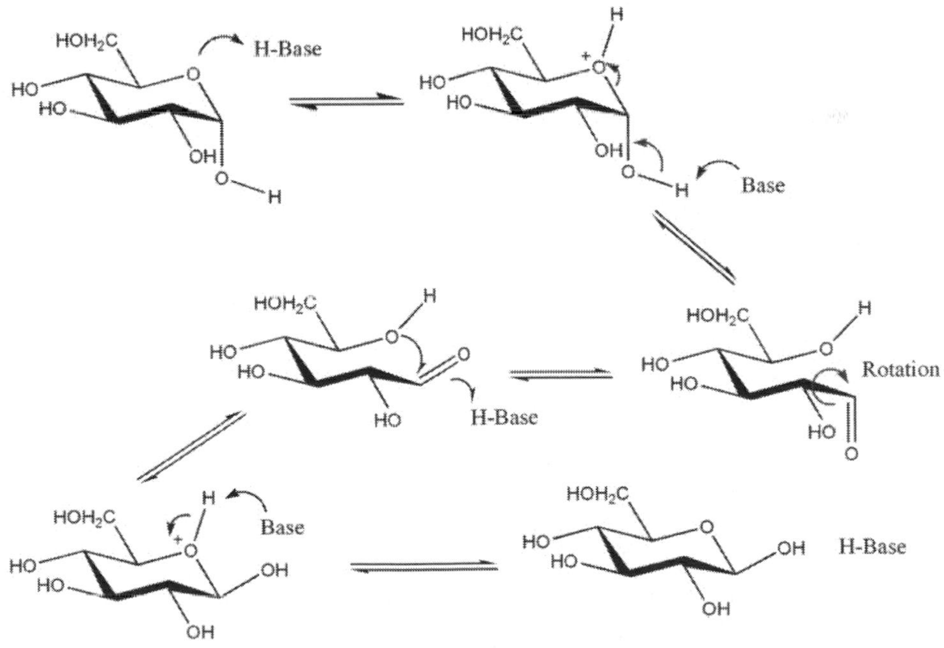

The reaction mechanism for the interconversion of α and β anomers

The bond to the anomeric carbon is easily broken in aqueous solutions, as either α (hydroxyl points downward) or β (hydroxyl points upward) anomer becomes an open chain.

In an aqueous solution, especially if it is slightly acidic, this open chain is easily recyclized, forming a mixture containing both anomers (α or β) in their equilibrium concentrations.

Thus, the initial opening and subsequent closing of the chain results in a mixture of anomers, known as mutarotation.

A: reduction is the decrease in the number of bonds to oxygen (or gain of electrons in inorganic chemistry).

Examples of reduction in organic chemistry include the conversion of an aldehyde to a primary alcohol, a carboxylic acid to either an aldehyde or primary alcohol or a ketone to a secondary alcohol.

C: hemiacetals are formed as a result of the nucleophilic addition of oxygen of a hydroxyl to a carbonyl (aldehyde or ketone).

D: the open chain form has a carbonyl group, and therefore an aldehyde is already formed.

E: oxidation is the increase in the number of bonds to oxygen (or loss of electrons in inorganic chemistry).

Examples of oxidation in organic chemistry include the conversion of a primary alcohol to an aldehyde or a carboxylic acid and the conversion of a secondary alcohol to a ketone.

42. D is correct.

The cyclic hemiacetal forms of sugars exist as either five-membered (furanose) or six-membered (pyranose) rings.   A furanose is a carbohydrate that has a chemical structure with a five-membered ring system consisting of four carbon atoms and one oxygen atom.

Formation of pyranose hemiacetal and representations of β-D-glucopyranose

A ketopentose is an open-chain five-carbon sugar that has a ketone carbonyl group. An aldopentose is an open-chain five-carbon sugar with an aldehyde carbonyl group.

A cyclic hemiacetal is derived from an aldehyde; if the anomeric carbon (i.e., carbon attached to two oxygen) has an H attached – it is an aldose.

A cyclic hemiacetal is derived from an aldehyde if the anomeric carbon lacks an H attached – it is a ketose.

The structure is a furanose form of sugar that has a ketone carbonyl in its open-chain structure.

A: the furanose (five-membered ring) form of an aldopentose is a structure that lacks the H on the anomeric carbon necessary in an aldose.

B: the pyranose (six-membered ring) form of an aldopentose is a structure that lacks the H on the anomeric carbon necessary in an aldose.

D: the pyranose form of a ketopentose is a six-membered ring.

43. B is correct.

The cyclic and acyclic isomers of glucose exist as an equilibrium mixture in aqueous solutions.

Because the cyclization of monosaccharides is reversible, the cyclic isomer also exists as a mixture of diastereomers; α and β isomers.

44. C is correct.

Isomers have identical atoms in different arrangements.

The double bond and hydroxyl groups shift positions, which indicates that one carbon was oxidized, and another was reduced.

In glycolysis, the phosphoglucose isomerase assists in the removal of a hydrogen anion (i.e., hydride ion), which attacks a carbonyl group to form a hydroxyl group.

The carbon where the hydride ion is removed – now a cation – is attacked by a water molecule.

A: $CH_3CH_2COCl + H_2O$ reaction is hydration.

B: the number of carbons in the products is one greater than in the reactants; therefore, this is not an example isomerization reaction which requires the number of all atoms to remain constant.

D: $CH_3CH_2CH_2CHOHCH_3$ reaction is a transesterification reaction.

45. C is correct.

The "di" prefix in the name suggests that there are two smaller subunits.

Monosaccharides are linked together through glycosidic (i.e., oxygen bonded to two ethers) functional groups.

Lactose is a disaccharide formed by a β(1→4) linkage between galactose and glucose.

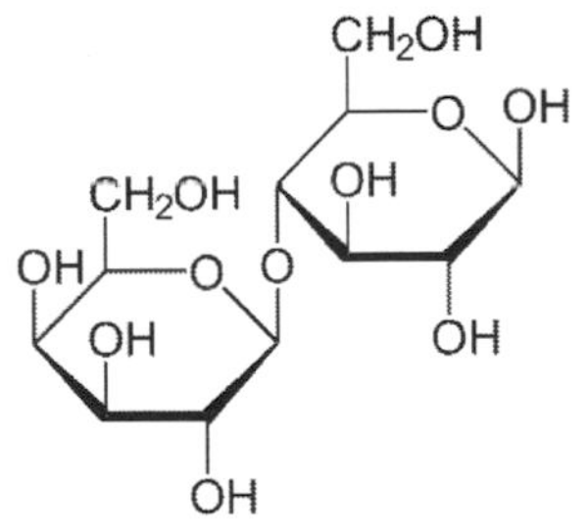

46. C is correct.

Benedict's test (or Tollens' reagent) is used to detect reducing sugars. An oxidized copper reagent is reduced by a sugar's aldehyde, and the aldehyde is oxidized to a carboxylic acid in the process.

Reducing sugars (and alpha hydroxyl ketones) give a positive Benedict's test: a red-brown precipitate forms.

Fehling's solution also gives a positive test for reducing sugars by changing from blue to clear and forming a red-brown precipitate.

Tollens' reagent forms silver ions (mirror) as a positive test for reducing sugars.

Tartaric acid has no aldehyde or ketone to react to because its first and last carbons have carboxylic functional groups.

Therefore, it cannot reduce the reagent and yields a negative result (Tollens' remains clear, while Benedict's and Fehling's remain blue).

47. D is correct.

Maltose is a disaccharide composed of two glucose molecules, and the glycosidic linkage is an α(1→4) linkage.

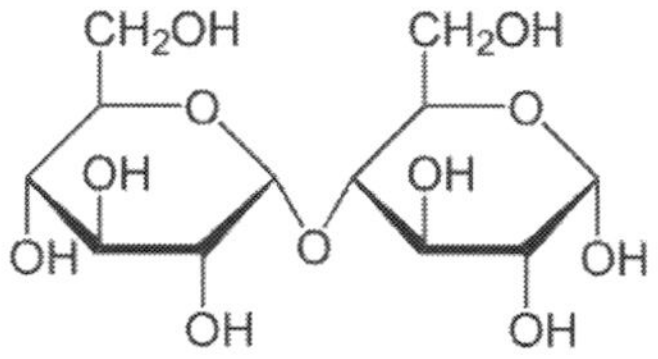

48. A is correct.

For D-sugar monosaccharides, the hydroxyl group of the last asymmetric carbon atom is oriented to the right.

Chapter 28 Explanations: Nucleic Acids

1. D is correct.

A complementary base pair is used for RNA molecules during transcription and translation.

Errors are sometimes introduced to the sequence, and these errors can lead to mutations in the proteins that are assembled from them.

2. A is correct.

The dipole interactions that join the strands of DNA together are more specifically known as hydrogen bonds.

These bonds form from the acid protons between the amides and imide functional groups, and the carbonyl and amide Lewis basic sites of the matched nitrogen base pairs.

3. C is correct.

Deoxyribose sugars are carbohydrates that are utilized in DNA synthesis, while ribose sugars are used to synthesize RNA molecules.

4. B is correct.

NADH is the biochemical equivalent to a hydride (H⁻) reduction reagent for carbonyl groups.

Alternatively, NAD^+ is an oxidizing agent that can accept a hydride equivalent.

5. C is correct.

In double-stranded DNA molecules, adenine nucleotides always pair with thymine and cytosine pairs with guanine nucleotides.

Adenine forms two hydrogen bonds with thymine (A=T).

Cytosine forms three hydrogen bonds with guanine (C≡G).

The strands of DNA are antiparallel with the 5' written on the top left side of the molecule.

5'–ATATGGTC–3'

3'–TATACCAG–5'

6. D is correct.

The DNA molecule has a deoxyribose sugar-phosphate backbone with bases (A, C, G, T) projecting into the center to join the antiparallel strand of DNA (i.e., double helix).

The deoxyribose sugar-phosphate backbone is negatively charged due to the formal charge of the oxygen attached to the phosphate group.

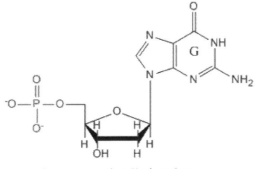

deoxyadenosine 5'-phosphate

deoxythymidine 5'-phosphate

deoxyguanosine 5'-phosphate

deoxycytosine 5'-phosphate

The purines (adenine and guanine) are double-ringed nitrogenous bases, while the pyrimidines (cytosine and thymine) are single-ringed nitrogenous bases.

A nucleotide has a deoxyribose sugar, base and phosphate, while a nucleoside is a deoxyribose sugar and base without the phosphate group.

7. B is correct.

Transcription is a biomolecular event that takes place in the nucleus of the cell. During transcription, RNA molecules are synthesized using complementary base pairs of DNA single strands.

8. D is correct.

Amino acids are the monomers that makeup proteins.

Nucleotides are comprised of a nitrogenous base (i.e., adenosine, cytosine, guanine and thymine or uracil), a phosphate group and a five-carbon sugar (i.e., ribose for RNA or deoxyribose for DNA).

9. B is correct. Four common nucleotides are in DNA molecules:

adenine (A), cytosine (C), guanine (G) and thymine (T)

Four common nucleotides are in RNA molecules:

adenine (A), cytosine (C), guanine (G) and uracil (U)

10. A is correct. When DNA is replicated in the cell, one of the strands of DNA acts as a template for a new strand synthesized as the replication fork opens. This continuously synthesized strand is known as the leading strand and, when combined with one of the old strands of DNA, makes up one new DNA molecule.

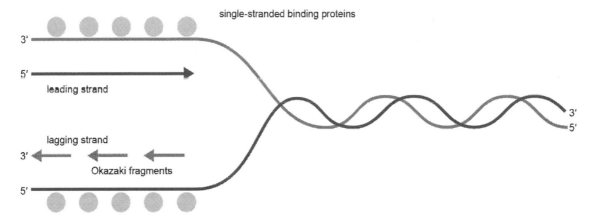

Furthermore, an additional DNA molecule is created in the process, as the other parent strand acts as a template for its complementary strand. This lagging strand is made up of smaller segments called Okazaki fragments (about 150-200 nucleotides long). Okazaki fragments are combined with the enzyme DNA ligase.

11. E is correct.

RNA molecules contain ribose as the carbohydrate component of the backbone.

DNA contains deoxyribose (lacking a 2'-hydroxy) as part of the backbone.

12. A is correct.

A nucleoside is a nitrogenous base linked to a sugar, while a nucleotide is a nucleoside and 1 or more phosphate groups attached to the ribose or deoxyribose sugar.

The uracil base is directly bonded to the 1' position of 2'-ribofuranose (i.e., RNA sugar) moiety, rather than the 2'-deoxyribofuranose (i.e., DNA sugar) ring.

thymidine (DNA)   uridine (RNA)

13. D is correct. The common base pairing that is observed in DNA is adenine-thymine and guanine-cytosine.

Adenine-thymine forms two hydrogen bonds (A=T).

Guanine-cytosine forms three hydrogen bonds (G≡C).

Adenine (A)   Thymine (T)

Guanine (G)   Cytosine (C)

This pairing is consistent with the structure of DNA, and this complementary pairing is what guides the formation of daughter strands of DNA.

14. D is correct.

Because adenine forms two hydrogen bonds with thymine, and cytosine forms three hydrogen bonds with guanine, the complimentary nitrogen base is used by DNA polymerase (in the S phase of interphase) to synthesize the new strand.

15. C is correct.

DNA molecules hold the genetic information of organisms.

RNA molecules are synthesized from the DNA strand to make proteins for the cell.

Genes are the sections of DNA responsible for the synthesis of proteins in cells.

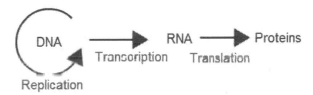

The central dogma of molecular biology (designates information flow)

16. D is correct.

There are five known nucleotides, four of which appear in DNA.

These nucleotides are cytosine, guanine, adenine, and thymine.

In RNA molecules, the thymine is replaced with another pyrimidine nucleotide known as uracil.

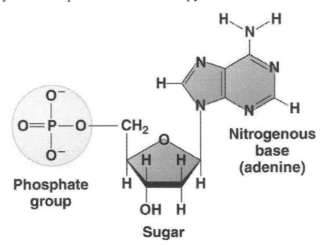

Nucleotides consisting of a phosphate group (note the negative charge on oxygens), deoxyribose sugar (lack a 2'-hydroxyl) and a nitrogenous base (adenine, cytosine, guanine or thymine)

17. D is correct.

DNA	DNA	mRNA	tRNA
A	T	A	U
C	G	C	G
G	C	G	C
T	A	U	A

Complementary base pairing for nucleotides

DNA → DNA (replication); DNA → RNA (transcription); RNA → protein (translation)

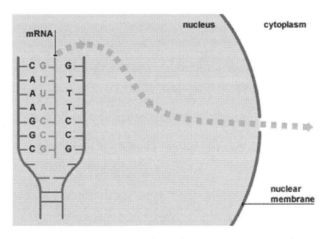

Adenosine (left) and Uracil (replaces thymine in RNA)

A single strand of DNA is the template for RNA synthesis during transcription.
The mRNA (after processing) is translocated to the cytoplasm for translation to proteins.

18. B is correct.

Cellular respiration involves the breakdown of sugar molecules to produce energy. When this occurs, water and carbon dioxide are given off as byproducts.

A campfire (i.e., wood is mainly the sugar of cellulose) gives off the same byproducts of carbon dioxide and water because it is a combustion reaction.

$$\text{wood} + O_2 \rightarrow CO_2 + H_2O$$

19. A is correct.

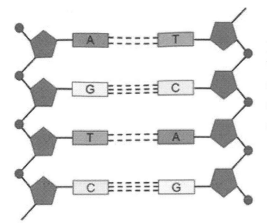

Double-stranded DNA with two hydrogen bonds between A=T and three hydrogen bonds between C≡G. The backbone is comprised of deoxyribose sugar and phosphates (shown as circles between the sugars).

20. D is correct.

Codons are three nucleotide sequences located on the mRNA, while anticodons are three nucleotides sequences on the tRNA. The codon-anticodon sequences hybridize by forming hydrogen bonds to the complementary base pair.

The relationship between codon (on mRNA), anticodon (on tRNA) and the resulting amino acid:

Codon (mRNA):
5'–AUG–CAA–CCC–GAC–UCC–AGC–3'

Anticodon (tRNA):
3'–UAC–GUU–GGG–CUG–AGG–UAG–5'

Amino acids:
Met–Gln–Pro–Asp–Phe–Ser

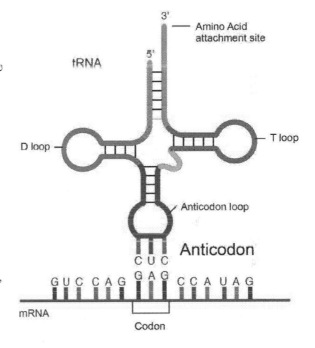

The genetic code is the nucleotide sequence of the codon (mRNA) that complementary base pairs with the nucleotide sequence of the anticodon (tRNA). From the genetic code, the identity of the amino acid encoded by a gene (synthesized during translation into mRNA) can be deduced.

21. A is correct.

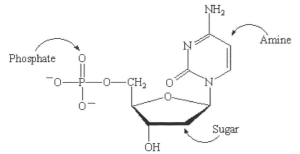

The hexose sugar, nitrogen base, and phosphoric acid group make up nucleotides, and these nucleotides are used to make larger molecules known as nucleic acids.

Nucleotide consisting of sugar, phosphate, and nitrogenous base.

22. D is correct.

Identical copies of DNA are necessary for the division of cells; these cells are also known as daughter cells.

When the daughter strand is synthesized, complimentary nitrogenous base containing nucleotides (A↔T and C↔G) are incorporated into the growing strand.

Replication (i.e., synthesis of DNA) occurs during the S phase (i.e., within interphase) of the cell cycle.

23. B is correct.

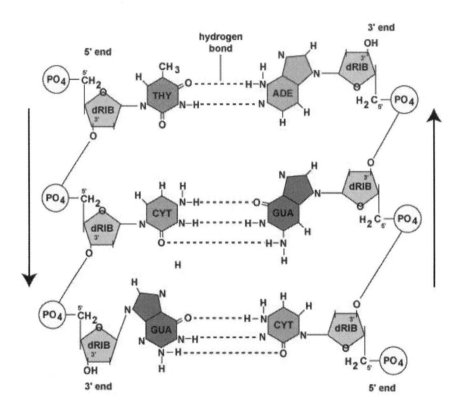

Two antiparallel strands of DNA are shown with the vertical arrows indicate the 3'-hydroxyl of the sugar (i.e., from the point of chain elongation). The nucleotide is the building block of DNA and is comprised of sugar (i.e., deoxyribose), phosphate and base (adenosine, cytosine, guanine, and thymine)

For nucleotide pairs that contain adenine and thymine, there are two hydrogen bonds (A=T) holding the base pairs together.

Cytosine and guanine nitrogen base pairs use three hydrogen bonds (C≡G) to support the nucleic acid structure.

24. B is correct.

The central dogma of molecule biology: DNA → RNA → protein

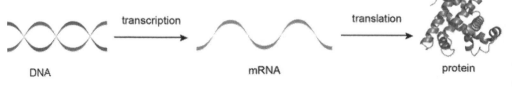

tRNA and ribosomes are used to make peptide chains from mRNA.

Nucleotide triplets known as codons are combined with a complementary tRNA (i.e., containing the anticodon that is complimentary in base pairing with the codon of the mRNA). Each tRNA brings an appropriate (i.e., anticodon ↔ amino acid) to the growing polypeptide during translation.

The amino acid residues are combined in the order of the codon sequence.

25. C is correct. After transcription (DNA → mRNA), the synthesized mRNA is transported out of the nucleus and to the ribosome, so that proteins can be synthesized during translation (mRNA → protein).

RNA contains ribose, a sugar similar to deoxyribose of DNA molecules, except that it has a hydroxyl group (~OH) at the 2' position on the sugar.

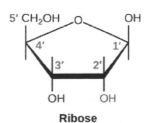 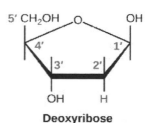

Ribonucleotide (left) and deoxyribonucleotide (right): note the 2' position of the sugars

Nucleic acids (DNA and RNA) bind to each other via hydrogen bonds between bases (A=T/U and C≡G). The sugar and phosphate group form the backbone and do not affect (to any appreciable degree) the hydrogen bonding between bases.

The presence of a hydroxyl group (~OH) in RNA causes the backbone to experience steric and electrostatic repulsion. Therefore, the grooves formed in helixes or hairpin loops between chains are larger. The larger groove permits nucleases (i.e., enzymes that digest DNA or RNA) to more easily bind to the RNA chain and digest the covalent bonds between the alternating sugar-phosphate monomers.

26. E is correct. The nitrogen bases of nucleotides are responsible for the hydrogen bonding that keeps one nucleic acid strand attracted to the other.

The number of hydrogen bonds that exist between the pairs varies between two and three bonds.

Adenine and thymine nitrogenous base pairs bond with two hydrogen bonds (A=T).

Cytosine and guanine nitrogenous base pairs bond with three hydrogen bonds (C≡G).

27. A is correct. Three nucleotides are combined to make a codon or anticodon required for translation.

A larger segment of DNA is called a gene, and sections of different genes make up nucleic acid strands.

Two single strands of DNA are used to make one DNA double helix.

28. B is correct. In any given molecule of DNA, each of the thymine nitrogen bases forms two hydrogen bonds with adenine.

Because each thymine pairs with an adenine residue, there is an equal number of both nitrogen bases in the molecule.

29. D is correct.
Ribose differs from deoxyribose sugars in that ribose lacks one alcohol (i.e., hydroxyl) group.

Both ribose sugar (RNA) and deoxyribose sugar (DNA) are used to synthesize nucleic acid polymers.

30. B is correct.

Replication: DNA → DNA during the S phase of the cell cycle.

A: translation is the process of synthesizing proteins from mRNA.

C: transcription is the process of synthesizing mRNA from DNA.

D: complementation is observed in genetics when two organisms with different homozygous recessive mutations that produce the same mutant phenotype (e.g., thorax differences in *Drosophila* flies), when mated or crossed, produce offspring with the wild-type phenotype.

Complementation only occurs if the mutations are in different genes. Each organism's genome supplies the wild type allele to *complement* the mutated allele of the other. Since the mutations are recessive, the offspring display the wild-type phenotype.

A complementation (i.e., *cis/trans*) test can be used to test whether the mutations are in different genes.

E: restriction digestion is a process used in molecular biology for cleaving (i.e., cutting) DNA for analysis (e.g., restriction fragment analysis) or processing (e.g., PCR amplification).

31. C is correct.
When NADH is oxidized, it loses an equivalent of hydrogen.

Because NADH is a neutral compound, a loss of hydride (H^-) means that the substrate develops a positive charge.

$NAD^+ + H^+ + 2e^- \longrightarrow NADH$

32. D is correct.

The central dogma of molecular biology:

DNA → RNA → protein

DNA → RNA is known as transcription.

RNA → protein is known as translation.

DNA is the nucleic acid biomolecule that can give rise to other nucleic acids and proteins.

DNA strands are synthesized from DNA parental strands during replication.

33. B is correct. The intermolecular forces among the nitrogen base pairs are hydrogen bonds.

Adenine forms 2 hydrogen bonds with thymine (A=T).

Cytosine forms 3 hydrogen bonds with guanine (C≡G).

34. C is correct.

The peptide chain is assembled together depending on the amino acid residue order, dictated by the mRNA sequence.

rRNA is the nucleic acid that comprises the ribosome used during translation (conversion of the codon into a corresponding amino acid in the growing polypeptide chains of the nascent protein).

Each codon of RNA has a corresponding anticodon located on the tRNA.

tRNA molecules have the 3-nucleotide sequence of the anticodon and the appropriate amino acid at its 3' end that corresponds to the anticodon.

The genetic code is the language for the conversion of DNA (i.e., nucleotides) to proteins (i.e., amino acids).

DNA → mRNA → protein

DNA to mRNA is transcription.

mRNA to protein is translation.

There are 20 naturally occurring amino acids. There is one start codon (methionine) and three stop codons (containing releasing factors which dissociate the ribosome).

35. E is correct.

Because RNA utilizes uracil (U) nitrogenous base instead of thymine (T) nitrogenous base, thymine should not appear in the codon.

36. A is correct.

Thymine is a pyrimidine nitrogenous base pair that forms two hydrogen bonds with adenine (purine) in the base-paired structure of DNA.

In RNA molecules, the nitrogenous base thymine is replaced by uracil.

Purines (A, G) are single-ring structures, while pyrimidines (C, T, U) are double-ring structures.

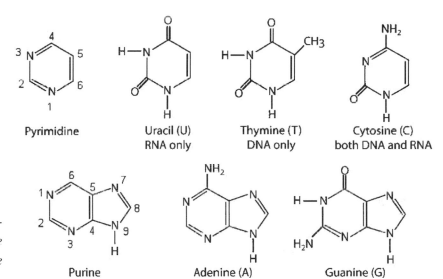

37. B is correct.

There are three general components of nucleotides: a phosphate group, a cyclic five-carbon sugar, and a nitrogenous base.

Fat molecules are biomolecules that make up the structure of phospholipid membranes, storage fat molecules, and other lipid molecules.

38. A is correct.

There are three major components of a nucleotide, the subunit that makes up nucleic acids.

All nucleic acid has a nitrogen base used for hydrogen bonding, a hexose sugar (ribose or deoxyribose) and a phosphate group that contains a phosphate linkage with the sugar.

Ester linkages are found in fats, glycosidic linkages are found in sugars, and peptide linkages are found in proteins.

39. B is correct.

One of the two complementary codes important for the construction of peptide chains is the codon made up of three RNA nucleotides that are complementary to the anticodon of tRNA molecules.

40. C is correct.

Because RNA contains uracil, this nitrogenous base forms hydrogen bonds with adenine. It is important to note that RNA molecules are single-stranded, and DNA molecules are double-stranded.

In DNA:

Adenosine (A) forms two hydrogen bonds with thymine (T).

Cytosine (C) forms three hydrogen bonds with guanine (G).

41. C is correct.

Thymine is a pyrimidine nucleotide base that occurs in DNA but does not occur in RNA. Instead, RNA has uracil.

42. C is correct.

In DNA, thymine hydrogen bonds with adenine.

However, in RNA, the thymine is exchanged for uracil.

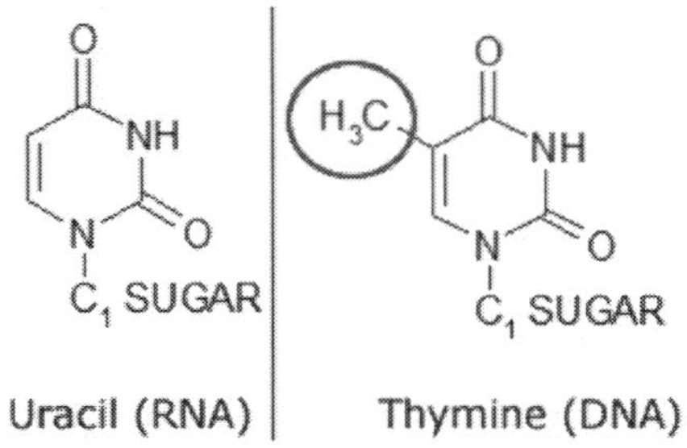

43. C is correct.

Nucleic acids determine the sequences of amino acids because groupings of nucleotides along a sequence corresponding to a particular amino acid.

The information of certain nucleic acids (i.e., mRNA) is translated on ribosomes with the help of tRNA.

Prions are infectious, disease-causing agents of misfolded proteins.

44. A is correct.

The sugar component of nucleic acid, the ribose or deoxyribose sugar, is the portion that contains many alcohol groups.

The nitrogenous base contains a basic nitrogen atom (i.e., amino group) that hydrogen bonds with complementary nitrogen bases.

There are two hydrogen bonds between the nitrogenous bases adenine and thymine (A=T) and three hydrogen bonds between cytosine and guanine (C≡G).

45. C is correct.

DNA (deoxyribonucleic acid) is a long biological molecule composed of smaller units called nucleotides (i.e., sugar, phosphate, and base).

The sugar is deoxyribose (compared to ribose for RNA), and the bases are either adenine, cytosine, guanine, and thymine (with thymine replaced by uracil in RNA).

The strands that these nucleotides make up are called nucleic acids.

46. D is correct.

Ribose is the structural sugar of RNA, while deoxyribose is the sugar for DNA.

Uracil is a nucleotide (i.e., sugar, phosphate, and base) that contains a ribose sugar.

This sugar is similar to deoxyribose; however, one difference is that deoxyribose has one fewer alcohol group (2'~position of the sugar) than ribose.

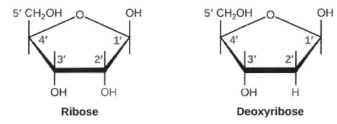

Uracil is a base of RNA and does not appear in DNA strands.

47. E is correct.

During transcription, the two nucleic acid strands of DNA dissociate, and mRNA is synthesized (transcription) by using the nitrogen bases of DNA as a template.

Therefore, the mRNA strand is a complementary strand to the DNA strand.

The mRNA then exits the nucleus to be used as a template for the production of proteins (translation).

48. C is correct.

The bonds that make up every single strand of DNA are covalent bonds, and the bonds linking the antiparallel strands of DNA together are hydrogen bonds.

Two hydrogen bonds form between adenine and thymine (A=T).

Three hydrogen bonds form between cytosine and guanine (C≡G).

We want to hear from you

Your feedback is important to us because we strive to provide the highest quality prep materials. Email us if you have any questions, comments or suggestions, so we can incorporate your feedback into future editions.

Customer Satisfaction Guarantee

If you have any concerns about this book, including printing issues, contact us and we will resolve any issues to your satisfaction.

info@sterling-prep.com

*We reply to all emails – please check your **spam** folder*

Thank you for choosing our products to achieve your educational goals!

Please, leave your Customer Review on Amazon